W9-DCF-765

V&R

Novum Testamentum et Orbis Antiquus / Studien zur Umwelt des Neuen Testaments

Band 71

Vandenhoeck & Ruprecht

David Luckensmeyer

The Eschatology of First Thessalonians

Vandenhoeck & Ruprecht

for Melissa

Bibliografische Information der Deutschen Nationalbibliothek

Die Deutsche Nationalbibliothek verzeichnet diese Publikation in der Deutschen Nationalbibliografie; detaillierte bibliografische Daten sind im Internet über http://dnb.d-nb.de abrufbar.

ISBN 978-3-525-53969-9

Printed in Germany.
Druck und Bindung: ⊕ Hubert & Co., Göttingen.

Gedruckt auf alterungsbeständigem Papier.

Foreword

When I was ten years old, my parents moved from northern California to outback Australia to farm cotton. The nearest town had a population of approximately two-thousand people and supported three churches — Anglican, Catholic and Presbyterian. We went to the Presbyterian church despite the fact that my dad had graduated with a Master of Divinity from Western Conservative Baptist Seminary in the US. At times, while driving home from church on a Sunday morning, dad would "correct" some of the things we heard: "As Baptists, we believe ...".

I grew up in a Baptist home. Consequently, as a teenager, when I developed an interest in theology, I was exposed to systematic theologies representative of literal and dispensational interpretations. I took to reading some of dad's textbooks from the Baptist Seminary, including a book or two on eschatology. Even my parents were surprised by my interest in the subject. They once asked, "Son, why are you reading this stuff?" to which I replied, "Because I find it interesting".

It is sufficient to say that my tertiary studies at the University of Queensland (UQ), Australia, encompassed a significant and challenging period of personal and intellectual growth, due in large part to the teaching expertise of Professor M. Lattke (now Emeritus). When it came to choosing a topic for my PhD dissertation he wisely encouraged me to find an area of personal interest, one which would remain exciting even after years of research. This led me to eschatology – a subject that had long interested me – first to the eschatology of Paul and then more specifically to the eschatology of First Thessalonians. At that time I only had an inkling of an idea that my dispensational heritage of literal interpretations, which included a real "rapture" of the church, would give way to historical-critical investigations, and culminate in an interpretation of the eschatology of First Thessalonians based on epistolary, social, political and rhetorical considerations.

Since the dissertation has been completed, I have had the occasion to expand significantly and rewrite parts of the manuscript for publication. The introduction has been substantially rewritten, and introductions and conclusions to each of the exegetical chapters have been added which hopefully contribute to the readability of the monograph. In addition, a new chapter (on 1 Thess 5:1–11) has been included which means that I now address all pericopes in the letter that relate to the subject matter. I have tried to be as comprehensive as possible in my engagement with the secondary literature. Unfortunately, the article by Stefan Schreiber (2007) appeared too late to be properly incorporated into the discussion. I might have missed a few other important articles which should have been considered.

There are many people who have supported me while I undertook this research project; I wish to thank them publicly here.

My principal supervisor, Emeritus Prof. M. Lattke, deserves the first mention of thanks. He has been very generous with his time and has taught me how to think critically, not only about the world of Paul, but about contemporary issues as well. Thanks go to my other supervisor, Dr R. Strelan, who has also contributed significantly to my scholarly enterprise.

I gratefully acknowledge my principal supervisor's invitation to attend the SNTS 2001 General Meeting in Montreal. In particular, thanks must go to Profs J. A. D. Weima and R. Hoppe for allowing me to participate in the seminar on the Thessalonian Correspondence. At this early stage in my PhD candidature, I found it helpful to meet other Thessalonian specialists and share in scholarly discussion. Also, at the beginning of my candidature, Dr I. Petersson spent many patient hours teaching me German, for which I am very grateful.

In the same year, I travelled to New Haven to undertake a research stint at the Yale Divinity School Library, which, on the advice of Prof. A. J. Malherbe, had every resource available for research on the Thessalonian correspondence. He was correct. I was awarded a Graduate School Research Travel Award from UQ to defray some of the travel expenses. In addition to this, I was also awarded an Australian Postgraduate Award which enabled me to undertake full-time research.

I thank my family for their support. My wife, Melissa, has supported me without reservation, throughout my candidature. I dedicate this monograph to her in acknowledgement of her enduring loyalty and friendship. On numerous occasions my parents, Richard and Drinda, took care of our children, Sarah, Olivia and Ella, so that I could concentrate on writing.

I thank my fellow participants in New Testament *jours fixes* for their support. These seminars were directed by Prof. M. Lattke who encouraged all of us to be more critical of the New Testament and its world. In addition, I wish to thank other significant persons in my life who have been close conversation partners in this project and/or who have given much moral support: Richard and Drinda Luckensmeyer (parents), Jonathan Luckensmeyer (brother), Dr Greta Gaut (sister), and Keith Smith, Stuart Quarterman, John Bowen and Chris Page (friends).

I thank the editors of NTOA for their acceptance of the manuscript, and also Mr Christoph Spill of Vandenhoeck & Ruprecht, for his friendly advice and support throughout the publication process. I also thank Prof. Pauline Allen, Director of the Centre for Early Christian Studies, Brisbane, for giving me time off work to revise the manuscript. The Centre, which supports many research endeavours including early Christianity, Pastristics, China and Islam, has provided a generous subsidy to support the publication of this monograph.

Brisbane, 19 October 2008 David Luckensmeyer

Technical Preface

The author-date referencing system is used throughout this monograph, but not exclusively so. Often, in the introduction (Chapter 1), the full title of secondary literature is provided in the hope that it will aid the usefulness of the chapter as an introduction to First Thessalonians. Only recent publications on First Thessalonians which are considered important for the systematic discussion of the letter are referenced in this way. Otherwise, the author-date referencing system is used.

Multiple references have been ordered in a particular way to serve different purposes. In the introduction, references are ordered chronologically, from oldest to newest. This is done to aid the reader in ascertaining whether the discussion is old or new, and whether it is of increasing or decreasing interest to scholars. In contrast, references in subsequent chapters are ordered alphabetically. This is done to aid the reader in obtaining further bibliographic details for each reference.

The "§" symbol is used to refer to a section or sections of a chapter, not to a paragraph as it might normally be used. References to biblical texts are given in the traditional order. References to the OT Pseudepigrapha and to other ancient sources are given in roughly chronological order. Where a reference is given to the Theodotian text of Daniel, this is indicated by a small "θ" after the reference.

A number of Greek words are used as technical terms (*ekklēsia, kērygma, orgē* and *parousia*). In these cases, the words have been italicised and the Greek "η" has been represented with the English "ē". The problem of the correct representation of παρουσία is especially well-known in German literature, where it is spelled *parusia*. I am aware of this problem but have chosen to use the spelling *parousia*, in keeping with scholarly convention in English literature. Moreover, Greek words and phrases are often supplied in brackets to indicate the basis for a translation, or to inform the reader of the original choice of vocabulary and syntax. Greek verbs are given in the "infinitive" form while nouns are given in the "nominative" form. If it is important to provide a phrase or clause, then the relevant Greek text is reproduced verbatim. The text of NA^{27} is the starting point of the analyses, but all textual critical issues are thoroughly addressed such that the texts for analysis, and particularly the arrangements, are my own.

The abbreviations follow the conventions set out in *The SBL Handbook of Style* edited by P. H. Alexander et al. 1999, and in the *TRE Abkürzungsverzeichnis* compiled by S. M. Schwertner 1994. In addition, the abbreviations for ancient authors and texts appear at each entry in the indices (see §I). *Festschriften* appear under "FS" in the list of abbreviations for the convenience of the reader. These volumes also appear under the editor(s) in the bibliography. This is done to honour the work of the editor(s).

The typesetting of the manuscript was accomplished in Adobe InDesign CS3 for Mac using Garamond Premier Pro from Adobe, LaserGreek in Unicode and LaserHebrew from Linguist's Software, Inc., PO Box 580, Edmonds, WA 98020-0580 USA, ph: (425) 775 1130, www.linguistsoftware.com.

Table of Contents

Chapter 1
Introduction

I. The Thesis

1. Paul, a self-acclaimed apostle, was at the forefront of early Christian mission, not only because he was among the first missionaries to non-Jews but because he continually pushed theological boundaries beyond traditional limits. The earliest missionary proclamation stemmed initially from Jerusalem (the twelve) and then from Antioch, the latter of which was at the centre of the so-called Gentile Christian mission. The letters of Paul provide a first point of reference for investigations of this earliest mission. First Thessalonians is usually considered to be the first extant letter of Paul (and therefore possibly the earliest extant Christian letter), followed by First and Second Corinthians, Galatians, Romans, Philippians and Philemon (Schnelle 2003), although the precise order of Paul's seven authentic letters is debatable. For the purposes of this investigation, it is not important to determine an absolute chronology of Paul. The traditional date of ~50 C.E. for the writing of First Thessalonians is assumed here. The identification and characterisation of an "early" as opposed to a "late" Paul is of secondary importance for a letter which contains a rich mine of information in its own right without having to resort to comparisons with the Pauline *Hauptbriefe*.

In many ways First Thessalonians is representative of Paul's later authentic letters. Paul assumes God as the principal director with Jesus the Lord as principal agent. He also assumes that "Christ" is merely a proper name for Jesus. The proclamation of Jesus as the *Kyrios*, who died and was raised, is a central tenant of Paul's message. Even the significant interpretation that Jesus died "for us" is found in the letter, as is the presumption that Paul's proclamation *is* the word of the Lord or the very gospel of God. Yet First Thessalonians is also different from his subsequent letters. Arguably, there are no explicit quotations from the Old Testament. The epistolary form of the letter, while following many established structures, differs in significant ways raising numerous questions of interpretation (and even of interpolation). There is a strong dependence on Hellenistic philosophical traditions which is not so prevalent in Paul's other letters. Nowhere else does Paul refer so often to the *parousia* of the Lord. Finally, one of the most exciting aspects of First Thessalonians is its apparent closeness to the situation of Paul's founding mission to Thessalonica (perhaps only months). In no other letter does Paul replay so thoroughly the past history between himself and a community (see the extensive *disclosure* of a past-present relationship in 2:1–12). This history is reviewed not only in terms of how Paul conducted himself while with the Thessalonians, but it also reveals Paul's concerns while separated from them.

In First Thessalonians, Paul responds to a community in conflict. The recurrent theme of affliction indicates psychological, social, political and/or physical abuse. Many factors contributed to the Thessalonians' situation including social disruption associated with a conversion experience, Paul's apparent inability to return to the community, the socio-political overtones of Paul's *kērygma*, and probably some other factors which are specific to the city of Thessalonica but more difficult to identify. For example, the peculiar cultic participation of citizens and the political organisation of the city may also play a role. Acts 17 contributes to the picture of conflict although there it appears that the Thessalonians are the orphans, not Paul (cf. Acts 17:1–10 and 1 Thess 2:17).[1]

2. I argue that eschatology is the best hermeneutical key to interpret Paul's pattern of exhortation in First Thessalonians. The modern term "eschatology" is understood as a broad *topos* in Paul which must be situated in terms of its heritage from Jewish eschatology including prophetic and apocalyptic eschatological traditions,[2] and early Christian eschatology formulated out of the *kērygmata* of the earliest Christian movements.[3] The eschatologies of early Jewish and Christian writers are so diverse that it is more accurate to steer clear of generic definitions.[4] Even the vague notion that eschatology refers to assertions that God will act decisively in the future resulting in a different state of affairs is not uniformly expressed in the relevant literature. The relationship between the modern use of the term "eschatology" and its ancient root (ἐσχατ-) further complicates matters since the modern term usually refers to more than just the last or final cosmic occurrences. It also includes implications (a tension) for the present[5] and for the continuity of history itself (see Bultmann 1955). The modern use was first coined in the seventeenth century by Abraham Calov (*Systema locorum theologicorum*, 1655–1677) where "eschatology" referred to "the last things" (τὰ ἔσχατα in Greek; *res novissimae, extremae* in Latin). Consequently, the term "eschatology" does not correlate to specific references in First Thessalonians or in Paul generally. Rather, it is used here as an umbrella term to describe motifs which often but not always refer to the *eschaton*, and which serve a similar function. For example, the *parousia* of the Lord, judgment (including the

[1] Regarding the description of Paul as an orphan, see Burke 2003, 158–160; Aasgaard 2004, 288–289; 2007, 142–143.

[2] See Smend 1982; Uffenheimer 1982; Preuß 1986; Nickelsburg 1992b; Petersen 1992; Haag 1995; H.-P. Müller 1999; Blischke 2007, 7–11.

[3] See Klein 1982; Karrer 1986; Aune 1992; Merklein 1995; Lindemann 1999.

[4] For a general introduction to eschatology, see Schüssler Fiorenza 1976; Wißmann 1982; Fahlbusch 1986; Lona 1986; Cancik 1990; Kreitzer 1993; Söding 1995; Sigel 1998; Filoramo 1999.

[5] For example, with specific reference to missions of the first Christians, see Cullmann 1956a. More generally, see Stuhlmacher 1967.

day of the Lord) and the resurrection of Christians, all point to Paul's vision of the future but also ideologically inform Paul's and the Thessalonians' ethical decisions. When examined systematically, these motifs may be understood on a literary level as part of an "eschatological discourse".[6] However, this does not mean that Paul consciously promoted this discourse or was necessarily even aware of it. It is merely a convenient way for scholars to refer to that particular part of his theology.

By no means do I provides an exhaustive treatment of *paraenesis* in First Thessalonians. By referring to "Paul's pattern of exhortation", there is an explicit acknowledgement of First Thessalonians' strongly paraenetic character. Paul not only exhorts the Thessalonians in the epistolary *letter-paraenesis* (Chapter 2, §VI), but he does so throughout the whole letter. Malherbe is by far the most convincing proponent of this view and his contributions to scholarship have been introduced extensively (but with criticisms; see §III.f below). However, Paul's theology cannot be reduced to *paraenesis* as that category only represents one aspect of his theology, namely, the *imperative* claims of Christian living. But in order to characterise these claims as a function of the eschatological discourse in First Thessalonians, the *indicative* aspect of Paul's theology must first be appropriated. The dialectic between the *indicative* and the *imperative* may be understood as a component of Paul's "rhetorical" or "pastoral" strategy in his letters. It should be noted that the modern phrase "rhetorical strategy" has multiple meanings in the secondary literature, whether as referring to the ancient art of rhetorical theory, or to the persuasive and exhortative character of a text, or to modern literary methods of reading Paul, such that it is difficult to use the phrase unambiguously. Similarly, the phrase "pastoral strategy" has certain anachronistic connotations, despite the widespread use of "pastoral" by Malherbe and his followers. Consequently, both phrases are avoided.

The historical aspect of eschatological statements requires that any characterisations of eschatology in First Thessalonians must be formulated with reference to specific situations and experiences related in the text (see Moule 1964; Carroll 1990), as especially for 1 Thess 4:13–18.[7] All eschatological statements in Paul are over-shadowed by his expectation of an imminent *parousia* of the Lord (cf. even Rom 13:11–13).[8] This recurring emphasis on *parousia* (which need not include

[6] Similarly, Carey formulates a definition of "apocalyptic discourse": "Apocalyptic discourse refers to the constellation of apocalyptic topics as they function in larger early Jewish and Christian literary and social contexts" (1999, 10). Hester builds on this definition by expanding the concept of discourse: "It is possible to think of discourse as the communication of ideas concerning things that are of interest to all members of a community" (2002, 138).

[7] Karrer 1986, 1112; see Klein 1982, 280–282. But I would not push this point so far as to align myself with Bammel (1959), who argues that any expressions of "Naherwartung" are peripheral to Paul's theology.

[8] Cranfield rightly questions whether Paul thought the temporal end of the world was at hand, or whether he was rather expressing a recognition "that history's most significant events have already taken place in the ministry, death, resurrection and ascension of Christ, so that all that remains between his ascension and his parousia can only be a sort of epilogue, during the whole of which, whether the actual

notions of delay) is firmly an eschatological concern of Paul despite his use of apocalyptic imagery throughout. Although it is possible to distinguish between the main concerns of eschatology and apocalyptic (Sauter 1988, 508–509), the eschatology of Paul is essentially apocalyptic and there should be no emphatic antithesis between the terms (Merklein 1995, 868).

3. I argue that Paul's pattern of exhortation provides: (1) a way to understand the Thessalonians' current social disintegration, and (2) a means for integration, not primarily into the social and political realms of Thessalonica, but into an eschatologically identifiable existence. The two aspects of this pattern are comprehensive in application and cannot be separated from each other. That is, Paul's understanding of their social disintegration provides a means for community identity and existence. With eschatology as a hermeneutical key, it is possible to see how Paul is able both to explain why the Thessalonians are experiencing conflict *and* encourage them to a constructive new community identity. On the one hand, the discursive references to opposition of Paul at Philippi (2:2), to the hindrance of his apostolic commission by some Jews (2:14–16) and to Satan as an opposing power (2:18; cf. 3:5), serve to help the Thessalonians understand their own social disintegration. On the other hand, Paul's identification of the Thessalonians as imitators of himself and the Lord, who received the word in much affliction (1:6), the interdependence of Paul's mission and the acceptance of the word of the Lord/God (1:5–8; 2:13) with an associated emphasis on thanksgiving (1:2; 2:13; 3:9), and his acknowledgement that such affliction is a common lot (3:3), serve to develop and reinforce community identity. Similarly, Paul's reference to a report (1:8–10), whether consisting of Jewish mission propaganda or not, emphasises a rupture between the Thessalonians' previous idol-worship and subsequent turning to serve the living and true God (v. 9). But at the same time, the report also contains essential elements of integration, whereby community members corporately await his son from heaven, Jesus who delivers them from *orgē* (v. 10). Paul reinforces integration into an eschatological community by reminding the Thessalonians of their chosen status (1:4), destined for salvation (5:9), already called into God's kingdom and glory (2:12) and participating in the *parousia* of the Lord (2:19; 3:13; 4:15–17; 5:23). The repetition of insider/outsider language throughout the letter serves to strengthen the development of a new community identity. In all, Paul emphasises a cosmic significance. In particular, the eschatological community consists of sons of light and sons of the day (5:5) such that the day of the Lord as manifestation of judgment on the cosmos will not surprise its members (5:4). Ultimately, the fate of the community, living and dead, is to be always with the Lord (4:17).

---

length of time involved is short or long, the end presses upon the life and concerns of the believer as something urgently relevant to the person" (1982a, 504–505). I use the word "imminent" with Cranfield's comments in mind.

4. There are no monographs to date on the eschatology of First Thessalonians.[9] This is an amazing state of affairs given the volume of secondary literature on the Thessalonian correspondence, and specifically on aspects of eschatology and apocalyptic. Thus, while there are numerous studies on virtually every topic associated with First Thessalonians which are contained under the rubric of eschatology (including no less: life and death, resurrection, translation, the day of the Lord, judgment, deliverance and salvation, the kingdom), there are only a handful of articles which attempt to bring the results of these studies into some kind of synthesis. Even many of these fail to engage all the eschatological concerns of the text. Thus, Ware (1979) and Neyrey (1980) over-emphasise the christological and theological aspects of Paul's eschatology, respectively. Koester (1997) and Khiok-Khng (1998) contribute to the systematic discussion, but not in a comprehensive fashion. In my estimation only Selby (1999) provides a thorough examination of the eschatology in First Thessalonians but using a rhetorical approach.[10] Even Malherbe's commentary (2000), from a scholar who has perhaps contributed the most to recent understandings of the letter, does not do justice to the eschatology in it.

5. I propose to fill the current lacuna in Thessalonian scholarship by proceeding with an analysis of 1 Thess 1:9–10, 1 Thess 2:13–16, 1 Thess 4:13–18 and 1 Thess 5:1–11 as fundamental representatives of the eschatological discourse in the letter. This does not mean that other pericopes are irrelevant or ignored. First Thessalonians is shot through with eschatological and apocalyptic themes and images, so much so that a proper characterisation of its eschatological concerns must include, to some extent, consideration of the entire letter as a cohesive act of communication. Consequently, many other references are incorporated in the various discussions of the analysis (e.g. 2:12, 3:11–13 and 5:23, but not limited to these only). Justification for selecting the four fundamental texts and not others arises from the distinctive nature of their contents, from how they are positioned and structured in the letter, and from a history of non-consensus among scholars regarding Paul's purposes and meanings for each. The results of the analysis open the way to a more comprehensive and systematic interpretation of First Thessalonians which makes sense of the motifs represented by the eschatological discourse and therefore makes sense of Paul's purposes in the letter. Such systematic interpretation is carried out in the conclusions of each chapter in a very concise but comprehensive manner.

The question of the epistolary structure of First Thessalonians is important for establishing the purpose and role of each of the fundamental representatives of the eschatological discourse in the letter. Issues of structure, particularly regarding the intensely problematic passage of 1 Thess 2:13–16 as a so-called second *letter-*

[9] The monograph by Nicoll (2004) is the closest anyone comes to filling the lacuna in scholarship, but as discussed below (§V), his synthesis of eschatogy in First Thessalonians is limited by an agenda to find common ground between the situations of First and Second Thessalonians.

[10] These articles are reviewed below.

thanksgiving, are so far removed from receiving any kind of consensus-answer as to require more than an introductory comment (see Chapter 2). My conclusions there, summarised in an outline of the structure of the letter have significant implications for how I interpret each of the selected texts. For example, in Chapter 2, I conclude that the *letter-thanksgiving* is contained in 1 Thess 1:2–10 which gives verses 9–10 a rhetorically important position in the letter. In addition, the epistolary analysis shows that 1 Thess 2:13–16 does not need to be understood as a redactional seam, which prepares for a full-scaled defense of the pericope's authenticity; this makes the motif of judgment in verse 16 more significant for the characterisation of the eschatological discourse of the letter, because its authenticity is no longer questioned. Finally, the conclusion that Paul uses *topoi* to arrange a number of exhortations which are dependent on the Thessalonians' situation is very important for the interpretation of 1 Thess 4:13–18 and 1 Thess 5:1–11, pericopes which bear directly on the pressing issues of death and judgment among community members. The remainder of this investigation consists of four exegetical chapters (Chapters 3–6) and a conclusion (Chapter 7). The conclusion includes systematic observations obtained from the analyses and emphasises the contributions and new insights this study makes to current scholarship.

6. The remainder of this introduction is arranged into three sections. After a short section on the methodology employed (§II), I continue with a topical analysis of First Thessalonians (§III). The results of topical analyses, although eschewed by some as redundant in view of more sophisticated (often rhetorical) approaches, demonstrate awareness of what is (and what is not) contained in First Thessalonians. In addition, the results (see summary in §III.3) provide a useful arrangement for a topical survey of recent secondary literature (§IV). This topical survey focuses on research published in the last twenty-five years or so which approaches the letter as a whole. Each of the subheadings represent various hermeneutical keys which scholars have used to understand First Thessalonians. Many of these "keys" offer, more or less, a basis for understanding the letter. I reconsider these not only as a way to introduce the recent secondary literature of the letter, but also as a comprehensive preparation for the thesis, both in terms of an introductory survey on eschatology as a hermeneutical key (§V below), and in terms of the exegetical chapters to follow. The structure of the letter, the emphases on certain *topoi* typical of eschatological texts and the use of distinctively apocalyptic imagery and themes throughout, serve as an adequate justification of eschatology as a key concept in the letter. Indeed, I argue that eschatology is *the* key for understanding Paul's pattern of exhortation in First Thessalonians.

II. Statement of Method

1. The so-called "historical-critical method" is deliberately chosen since I am primarily interested in questions of history. That is, questions pertaining to the purpose(s) and intention(s) of an author, the occasion and original meaning(s) of a historical text, and the intended readership, are best investigated and answered by this methodology (Barton 1998a, 9). At the least, it attempts to "bridge the gap" between the modern interpreter and a historical circumstance. Since the historical-critical approach is an established methodology used by many scholars in biblical studies, only a brief discussion of aspects I would like to highlight ensue: preliminary issues (§2); preunderstanding (§3); analysis (§4) and interpretation (§5). There is also a short conclusion (§6).

2. The questions asked of a biblical text will shape the interpretation of that text. The methodology adopted in this monograph automatically positions the discussion in a clearly defined framework. The text becomes the boundaries of this framework and is the controlling factor of historical reconstruction(s). The science of textual criticism which seeks to establish the most probable reading is a precursor to subsequent analysis of the text.[11]

Marshall asserts that the aim of historical criticism is two-fold: to determine what actually happened, and, to determine whether the text is historically accurate (1979, 126). This aim implies that it is possible to come to an understanding of the history *behind* the text. Similarly, Brown (1990, 1148) formulates the foundational goal of historical criticism as the identification and reconstruction of the intention(s) of an author and the original meaning(s) of a text; that is, "*The sense which the human author directly intended and which the written words conveyed*" (italics original). In order to accomplish this goal every historical avenue of inquiry suggested by a text must be explored in an attempt to understand the world-view of the author. This approach necessarily involves reconstructions of occurrences and circumstances behind a text, regardless of how tentative or uncertain the evidence is (similarly, Nations 1983, 66). Otherwise, as Dunn puts it, there is only "the door to the anarchy of *eis*egesis" (1984, 24).

I am aware of the controversy surrounding the terminology of "intended" and "original" meaning(s). For some, an attempt to identify such meanings is impossible since there are too many variables in the interpretive process. With reference to Schleiermacher's assertion that all understanding is derived from the acquisition of a particular language at a particular historical time, Prickett and Barnes (1991, 102) conclude:

> It follows that no text has a fixed meaning, intended by the author: all texts (and indeed all human utterances) have a kind of fluid and dynamic existence, which is apprehended somewhat differently each time they are read or heard by a particular individual.

[11] See Aland/Aland 1989; Birdsall 1992; Epp/Fee 1993.

However, there was still a precise meaning in the mind of an author which developed through that author's own grasp of language in his (or her) own time. There is certainly a difference between the intention of the text and authorial intention. But I am not convinced by scholars who propose that a text may be "autonomous".

Even Levenson (a staunch literary critic) asserts: "The question is not whether we make historical judgments; the question can only be whether we do so poorly or well" (1993, 110). Meaning cannot be divorced from history. Even when literary critics claim to do this, I suggest that they are merely substituting one historical reality with another, namely, their own world-view. Thus, there is no independence of meaning here, just appropriations of meaning from new vantage points, i.e. new historical settings (Payne 1994, 79). In so saying, I do not intend to disempower Ricoeur's distinction between the historical processes behind a text and the effects on its readers which occur in front of a text.[12] When I refer to what Paul "intended" I mean to refer to authorial intention as is appropriated from a text, and which is grasped as clearly as possible.

I have chosen historical-critical methodology because it fits with my preunderstanding of the text (see below). I am under no illusion that this method exhausts the meaning(s) of the text. Certainly it does not. But since I am asking primarily historical questions, then historical investigation must enter into the solution (so Brown 1989, 27). Other tools, including rhetorical analysis, structural and reader-response criticism, all have a place within the historical method, as long as the discussion remains focused on answering questions of history. Thus, I prefer to view these other methodologies as diverging paths along the way, each informing my investigation of the text (Stenger 1993, 3–4).[13]

The relationship between epistolary and rhetorical analyses deserves an introduction, especially since both are used to examine the structure of First Thessalonians (Chapter 2). Epistolary analysis (form criticism) remains an indispensable tool for defining the structure of Paul's letters. Perhaps no other approach is better able to characterise the mechanical elements of ancient letters. Indeed, the historical-critical approach retains priority.[14] However, the advances obtained from rhetorical analysis (see the later publications of White) for defining the structure of Paul's letters are substantial. While epistolary analysis allows the exegete to elucidate the individual elements of a letter, rhetorical analysis is more able to show how these elements fit together to form a persuasive act of communication (Donfried 2000a, 38–39). To this end, Jewett (1986, xiii) describes his approach in his monograph on the Thessalonian correspondence:

---

[12] For a discussion of this distinction and other issues of NT interpretation, see Thiselton 1995, 17–20.

[13] Dobbs-Allsopp argues that these tools (which are often thought of as literary tools) should be used to rethink historical cricitism "as a specifically literary method of study and reading" (1999, 238).

[14] Hoppe 2000, 63; Weima 2000, 123–124.

> This study offers a combination of traditional historical-critical research, rhetorical analysis, and a comparative use of social-scientific theorizing in an effort to resolve the dilemma of the Thessalonian correspondence.

Consequently, there has been a move (rightly so in my opinion) to integrate the results of epistolary and rhetorical approaches (Collins 2000, 319; Hughes 2000, 199).[15] But which approach deserves priority? Is it "a marriage of unequal partners" (Wanamaker 2000, 286)? Jewett thinks so. He concludes that "non-rhetorical approaches" suffer from "a methodological confusion between epistolary and topical categories" (1986, 70). Hence, he continues: "There is a need for a more comprehensive analytical method that can incorporate valid exegetical insights from these earlier analyses into a a [*sic*] more convincing view of the letter as a whole" (71). But do rhetorical theorists underemphasise the fundamental importance of epistolary analysis? Thus, to take Jewett as an example again, the charts at the back of his monograph (cf. 216–220) are exceptionally helpful in setting out the epistolary structure of First Thessalonians. It is a pity that his view of epistolary analysis is so negative (68–71). To be fair, Jewett does go on to provide a sophisticated and nuanced rhetorical analysis of the letter (71–78). But I wonder whether epistolary analyses are too quickly rejected since such analyses at least attempt to discover what a letter is mainly about and how a letter has been constructed according to its purpose (Green 2002, 74). Also, the results of rhetorical criticism are not (at this time) forming a consensus either (Wanamaker 2000, 273).

There is agreement among scholars regarding a number of epistolary features in First Thessalonians, despite consistent variations in arrangement (cf. Holmstrand 1997, 38–40). Such agreement is precisely the place to begin defining the structure of First Thessalonians. The fruits of epistolary analyses in the past, including the identification of normative forms in the epistolary process and the establishment of a consensus for the structure of Paul's letters, *are a significant basis* for subsequent rhetorical approaches (Hughes 2000a, 241; Smith 2000, 692). I do not go so far as Weima (1997a) who questions outright the legitimacy of the rhetorical approach, although I share some of his misgivings. In summary of this issue, I acknowledge numerous studies which examine the use of rhetorical approaches for understanding First Thessalonians,[16] In particular, I draw attention to the monograph edited by Donfried and Beutler, *The Thessalonians Debate: Methodological Discord or Methodological Synthesis?* (2000), which examines the debate between epistolary and rhetorical approaches. As the contributions show, the purpose of the monograph

---

[15] For a critical introduction to the problems associated with the application of rhetorical approaches to Paul's letters, as well as a discussion of the differences between rhetoric and epistolography, see Classen's insightful article (1992). See also Malherbe 1977, 4–12; Anderson 1999, 109–127. All references to Collins in this study are to R. F. Collins unless otherwise indicated.

[16] See for example, Hughes 1990; Olbricht 1990; Wuellner 1990; Walton 1995; 2000; Hester 1996; Hoppe 1997; 1998.

is not to elevate one approach over the other (although the different views are put vigorously). Rather, the discussion reveals a complexity of First Thessalonians that can be fruitfully understood from a variety of approaches.

3. All scholars who take the text of the NT seriously must attempt (at least) to identify the assumptions and preunderstandings they bring to a text. Exegesis without presuppositions is an impossibility. The problem then is not the starting point of a particular preunderstanding. It is rather, a failure to criticise one's own preunderstanding in light of his/her findings, or an unwillingness to reformulate or even abandon a cherished *a priori* (Dunn 1984, 25–26). Further, "... there is no innocent reading of the Bible, no reading that is not already ideological" (Aichele et al. 1995, 5). I admit that my interest in eschatology initially stemmed from my background in the conservative Baptist denomination. From an early age I have been taught about the end-time, and particularly about the timing of the so-called "rapture" of the church. In some sense, I seek answers to a contemporary dialogue. Yet, while I am personally interested in the final outcome or conclusion(s) of this study, I am quite prepared to let my preunderstanding be informed and shaped by the text. Bultmann has made clear in his long-famous essay on preunderstanding, however, that the very questions asked and the interpretation which results are always orientated by one's preunderstanding of the text (1984, 72–73). Each instance of interpretation involves working out one's own hermeneutic, alternately educating presuppositions with analysis, and then reformulating those presuppositions (i.e. the "hermeneutical circle"). In my case, Fundamentalist notions of "end-time" and "rapture" (as part of a preunderstanding) have long been left behind. Finally, the success of a methodological procedure does not involve the right choice of methods so much as the acknowledgement that resulting conclusions of any study are not definitive but stand among other and equally valid conclusions (Bultmann 1984, 149–150). A significant goal of this study is to reach an informed understanding of the eschatology of First Thessalonians. I do not presume to identify *the* meaning of the text, since I do not have the final word on the matter. Rather, I seek to present *an* exegesis of the text which is founded on an initial preunderstanding, developed by my methodology, and shaped/reshaped by my analysis of the text (see Hayes/Holladay 1982, 23).

4. The historical-critical approach contains a number of components or tools through which a text may be examined. Each step of the analysis seeks to investigate a text from a different aspect and underscores the fact that "every text speaks in the language of its time and of its historical setting" (Bultmann 1984, 147). The context is an indispensable determination of meaning. This includes, according to Davies (1990, 220), intra-textual meaning (questions of exact wording of a text, literary context and grammatical structure), extra-textual meaning (questions of history, culture, sociology and geography) and inter-textual meaning (questions of the use of one text in another, including oral and written traditional material). Literary criticism forms an important component of the methodology, particularly source,

form and redaction criticism. All three of these are established methodological tools and need no introduction here.

More important for discussion is the relationship between two modes of observation: synchronic and diachronic exegesis. Synchronic investigations examine a text *for what it is at a given point in time*. And this is where semantic theories of meaning, sociological approaches, and reader-response theorists come to the fore. Diachronic investigations, like those of source, form and redaction criticism, seek to move beyond synchronic modes of observation, and discover the history of a text; *how did it come to be what it is*. Ironically however, there has been a progressive development of a kind of thinking among literary critics that assumes that synchronic modes of observation have moved beyond the limited usefulness of diachronic modes (Schneiders 1990, 1160). Yet the sequence of synchronic study and diachronic study is not arbitrary. Synchronic procedures have always stood as preliminary investigations in relation to diachronic procedures. "*Before* the question of *how the text has come to be* (diachronic study) stands the question of *what it is* at a given point in time (synchronic study). ... The latter comes into play when synchronic description cannot sufficiently explain the present state of a text" (Stenger 1993, 26; emphasis original). There is therefore no escape from the historical contingency of biblical texts *even where literary questions are involved*.[17]

The approach taken here views the NT as a window to be looked *through*, rather than as an entity to be looked *at* (or a mirror to look into).[18] And rather than "complete" a text's meaning, for example, by emphasising reader-response methodology, historical criticism emphasises *religionsgeschichtlich* parallels, analogies and origins, in order to inform the meaning of a historical text (Dunn 1984, 22). This part of the analysis of a text pertains both to history and to texts.[19] Knowledge about the history of religions before and during the time of the NT is particularly vital for word studies. Certainly, I wish to avoid reading into a text the entire history of meaning of each of its words. Meaning comes from the relation between words and sentences which form the context of words rather than inherently from the words themselves (Thiselton 1979, 79). However, an investigation of the lines of development (or trajectories) of each word is often a beneficial and enriching part of the analysis of a text (Robinson/Koester 1971). Although word studies do not provide the meaning of a word they can provide its history of meaning and this should be taken into account.

[17] The confusion regarding diachronic and synchronic readings could stem from a failure to distinguish between the literary interests of historical critics (who examine literature in order to answer questions of history) and literary critics (who examine literature as a finished product and have no interest in questions of history); see Barton 1998a, 14.

[18] For a discussion of texts as "windows" and "mirrors", see Reumann 1992.

[19] Historical studies include the fields of Classical Antiquity, Ancient Israel within the Ancient Orient, Judaism within Hellenism and the Roman Empire, Mystery Religions of the Graeco-Roman world, and historiography. Textual studies include the fields of Greek mythology, poetry, philosophy, early Rabbinic traditions, Mandaean texts, Nag Hammadi, Pistis Sophia, Odes of Solomon, NT Apocrypha, and Early Christian Literature.

The translation is really the final output of analysis and stands as a statement of the interpretation. The ideal transference of meaning from one language to another is difficult (if not impossible) to achieve in all its semantic, grammatical and phonological equivalences. The tension between "formal equivalence" (i.e. the imitation of form in word order, syntax, phonology) and "functional equivalence" (i.e. the recreation in the target language of the impact or effect that a text had on its hearers or readers in the original language) remains throughout the translation process. While the translation statement itself seeks to approximate the linguistic form of the original, a goal of all exegesis is to transpose the original meaning of the text into the present (Stenger 1993, 8).

5. While a historical text relates historical events of the past, the meaning of those events can only be expressed in the future of that historical text. Otherwise, it is no longer a "historical" text. Consequently, the historical research of a text must always be carried further, since the preunderstanding of each scholar also has a historical context — which is in the future of that text (Bultmann 1984, 150). I do not propose to embrace Bultmann's existential hermeneutic but merely wish to highlight that the quest for "timeless" or "non-historical" statements cannot be fulfilled (*contra* Paddison 2005). There exists a historical meaning of a text which I hope to find by travelling across the historical gap between First Thessalonians and me; historical criticism attempts to understand the "then" author and the "then" message.

But it *is* possible to transpose a kernel of meaning from a historical text into the present, taking into account the fact that such a transposition will only be partially successful, since the problem of the divergence in world-views between the first and twenty-first centuries is hardly surmountable (Brown 1984, 27; Martin 1979, 223–224). Yet, since the interpreter of a text is himself/herself caught up within the history of meaning of that text, the interpretive process will have to be repeated and conclusions continually modified.

In my interpretation of First Thessalonians, I wish to avoid what seems to be a common pitfall of historical critics. Many scholars attempting historical reconstruction do not acknowledge the lack of information about the world of the first century. In reality, interpretation and the so-called "assured results of modern scholarship" are largely based on hypotheses and probabilities. There is simply not enough information to posit definite statements; the situation may be likened to "swiss cheese" whereby the current knowledge base consists of gaping holes. Yet much of the literature reflects an unfounded confidence, as evidenced by the use of statements like: "It is certain that...", "There is no doubt that...", "it is obvious that..." etc. The problem is that observations built on a number of probabilities may quickly become improbable.[20] There is always an inherent subjectivity to interpretation: each scholar approaches the history of the NT with a different methodology, a different set of questions and a different preunderstanding. Thus I

[20] This point is elegantly made by a non-biblical specialist, so C. S. Lewis (1975, 101).

want to emphasise the impossibility of certainty about the precise meaning of any given text. What is the point then? At least the historical-critical approach

> allows us to attempt to reach commonly accepted truth, at least at some levels, in some areas. The historian displays the basis for an explanation and others can test not only the logic and power of the explanation, but the validity of its factual evidential base (Downing 1990, 285; similarly, Dobbs-Allsopp 1999, 260–261).

6. In conclusion, in the exegetical chapters to follow I offer extensive analysis of four fundamental representatives of the eschatological discourse to be found in First Thessalonians. In keeping with my view that the translation is the final output of the analysis, I have included a detailed arrangement of the text and translation at the beginning of each chapter. As well, I present a number of preliminary issues which I consider important for the analysis; several excursus also appear throughout.

I find there exists a paradoxical tension between developing and sustaining the thesis and analysing a text just for the sake of analysis. Neither do I want to drive the premise forward at the neglect of responsible exegesis nor do I necessarily want to analyse every question arising from a systematic application of the historical-critical approach. In the exegetical chapters I seek a right balance between the two extremes and consequently develop my thesis that eschatology is the best hermeneutical key for understanding Paul's pattern of exhortation *by* offering a thorough analysis of the texts. Implications arising from the analyses are presented throughout each chapter in the form of preliminary syntheses (usually at the end of a verse or group of verses) and in a conclusion at the end of the chapter.

III. Topical Analysis of First Thessalonians

1. There are many topics which are not mentioned (or are hardly mentioned) in First Thessalonians but which are important for Paul's thought in his other letters.[21] Of the anthropological terms in Paul, there are no references to "flesh" (σάρξ) or "mind" (νοῦς), and only one reference to "body" (σῶμα, 5:23), two to "soul" (ψυχή, 2:8; 5:23) and three to "heart" (καρδία, 2:4, 17; 3:13). In contrast, there are five references to "spirit" (πνεῦμα 1:5, 6; 4:8; 5:19, 23), the first three of which are to the "Holy Spirit".[22] There is no mention of "Israel" (Ἰσραήλ), nor of the Adam-typology so prevalent in Romans and First Corinthians. Neither is there any reference to the powers of "sin" (ἁμαρτία) and "death" (θάνατος) although Paul does refer to "the measure of sins" in a different sense (2:16), and to the *topos* of the "dead" (cf. κοιμᾶσθαι) which is of significance in the letter (4:13–18). Paul does allude to the effects of sin in some of his exhortations (4:3–8). There is no mention of the Jewish

[21] I have used the table of contents in Dunn (1998) as a résumé of Paul's thought. Marshall also identifies many of the same theological "absentees" in First Thessalonians (1982, 174–175).

[22] "Power" (δύναμις) occurs in conjunction with the first reference only. 1 Thess 1:5, 6 are anarthrous references while 4:8 has the article (τὸ πνεῦμα τὸ ἅγιον).

"Law" (νόμος).[23] Paul does refer to "the *ethnē*" (τά ἔθνη, 2:16; 4:5) and to "Jews/Judeans" (οἱ Ἰουδαῖοι, 2:14) but not to "Greeks" (Ἕλληνες). The references to "grace" (χάρις) and "peace" (εἰρήνη) are incidental as part of the standard form of a *letter-opening* and *closing* (1:1; 5:23, 28) although the latter term appears once more with an unusual meaning (5:3). Regarding the word group "righteousness/justification" (δίκαιος, δικαιοσύνη, δικαίωμα, δικαίωσις, δικαιοῦν, δικαίως), there is only a single reference to the adverbial form (δικαίως, 2:10). There is no direct reference to "baptism" (βαπτίζειν, βάπτισμα, βαπτισμός), although the motifs of "in Christ" (ἐν Χριστῷ, 2:14; 4:16; 5:18), "in the Lord" (ἐν κυρίῳ, 3:8; 4:1; 5:12) and being "with him" (σὺν αὐτῷ, 4:14; 5:10) are prevalent.

2. There are many more topics to which Paul refers in First Thessalonians, sometimes in passing, and sometimes on numerous occasions. He refers to the "church" (ἐκκλησία) on two occasions (1:1; 2:14), but much more so to those who are "chosen" (ἐκλογή, 1:4) and "called" (καλεῖν, 2:12; 4:7; 5:24) as opposed to those who do not "know" (εἰδέναι, 4:5) God and "disregard" (ἀθετεῖν, 4:8) him;[24] these are "outsiders" (οἱ ἔξω, 4:12), "the rest" (οἱ λοιποί, 4:13, 5:6) and even "the *ethnē*" (τὰ ἔθνη, 4:5).[25] Paul associates "father" (πατήρ) several times with his references to "God" (θεός, 1:1, 3; 3:11, 13) and uses the metaphor of father and children for his own relationship with the Thessalonians (2:11).

In First Thessalonians, Paul's favourite title for Jesus is "Lord" (κύριος) which appears repeatedly throughout the letter.[26] As with his other letters, Paul begins with a note of "thanksgiving" (εὐχαριστεῖν, 1:2; 2:13) which, unlike his other letters is sustained throughout the letter (5:18; see εὐχαριστία in 3:9). He also makes a reference to "prayer" (προσευχή, 1:2). Later he exhorts the Thessalonians to "pray" (προσεύχεσθαι, 5:17) constantly and for himself and his colleages (5:25). The triad (1:3) of "faith" (πίστις), "love" (ἀγάπη) and "hope" (ἐλπίς) introduces three significant themes of First Thessalonians: faith and love appear twice more together (3:6; 5:8). As a single reference, faith (1:8; 3:2, 5, 7, 10) appears more often than love (3:12; 5:13) although there are two references to the verb form (ἀγαπᾶν, 1:4; 4:9). Since hope (2:19; 4:13) is conspicuously absent from the formulations in 3:6 and 5:8 it is possible that hope is the missing ingredient Paul wants to supply (cf. 3:10). The "word" (λόγος, 1:5, 6; 4:18) and "gospel" (εὐαγγέλιον, 1:5; 2:4) as "gospel of God" (εὐαγγέλιον θεοῦ, 2:2, 8, 9), "gospel of Christ" (εὐαγγέλιον Χριστοῦ, 3:2), "word of the Lord" (λόγος κυρίου, 1:8; 4:15) and "word of God" (λόγος θεοῦ, 2:13) and not as "word of flattery" (λόγος κολακείας, 2:5) or "word of men" (λόγος ἀνθρώπων,

[23] However, while there are no explicit references to the Law, von Bendemann characterises numerous phrases and ideas which have an implicit reference (2000, 223–226).

[24] Paul repeatedly uses the "you know" phrase as a rhetorical device in First Thessalonians; cf. the contrasting reference to ignorance (ἀγνοεῖν, 4:13).

[25] The extended polemic in 2:15–16, where Paul is anti-anyone-against-Jesus-as-the-*Kyrios*, serves to emphasise the insider/outsider language in First Thessalonians.

[26] E.g. 1 Thess 1:1, 3, 6; 2:15, 19; 3:11, 12, 13; 4:1, 2, 15, 16, 17; 5:9, 23, 28.

2:13) are recurring themes in the letter.[27] This is more significant because of the exegetical questions surrounding the "word of the Lord" (4:15), and also because one of the most controversial pericopes in First Thessalonians (4:13–18) concludes with the exhortation: "Therefore comfort each other with these words" (v. 18; cf. 5:11).

Paul alludes to the Thessalonians' "imitation" (μιμητής, 1:6) of himself and of the Lord, and also of the churches of God which are in Judea in Christ Jesus (2:14). This imitation made the Thessalonians an "example" (τύπος, 1:7) for others. That is, the Thessalonians "welcomed" (εἴσοδος, 1:9; 2:1) Paul and his colleagues and turned from idols to serve the "living" (ζῆν, 1:9; cf. 3:8; 4:15, 17; 5:10) and "true" God (ἀληθινός, 1:9; cf. ἀληθῶς, 2:13). Furthermore, they awaited the "son" (υἱός, 1:10; cf. 5:5) from "heaven" (οὐρανός, 1:10; 4:16) for, according to Paul, the times and seasons have not come (cf. 5:1). However, Paul warns of the "*orgē* which comes" (ὀργὴ τὴ ἐρχομένη, 1:10) or is going to come (2:16),[28] and of the coming "day of the Lord" (ἡμέρα κυρίου, 5:2; cf. 5:4, 5, 8). Such *orgē* is of God who remains the "avenger" (ἔκδικος, 4:6). The Thessalonians are not "destined" (τιθέναι, 5:9) for *orgē*[29] from which there is no escape (cf. 5:3). Rather, Jesus "delivers" (ῥύεσθαι, 1:10) them to obtain "salvation" (σωτηρία, 5:9; cf. v. 8).[30] There are a number of statements which imply salvation in some aspect including the Pauline sequence that since Jesus "died" (ἀποθνήσκειν, 4:14) and "rose" (ἀνιστάναι, 4:14), or more typically "was raised" (ἐγείρειν, 1:10) from the dead, this makes it possible for "the dead in Christ" (οἱ νεκροὶ ἐν Χριστῷ, 4:16) to be raised. As well, Paul refers to the action of God in bringing (ἄγειν, 4:14) those who have fallen "asleep" (κοιμᾶσθαι, 4:13, 14, 15), and he refers to being "caught up" (ἁρπάζειν, 4:17) to "meet" (ἀπάντησις, 4:17) the Lord and be "with the Lord" (σὺν κυρίῳ, 4:17; cf. σὺν αὐτῷ, 5:10) always.

The notion of conflict is significant in the letter. Both the Thessalonians and the Judean churches "suffered" (πάσχειν, 2:14) the same things. The Thessalonians received the word in much "affliction" (θλῖψις, 1:6) and they were to understand that being "afflicted" (θλίβειν, 3:4) is their lot (3:3), and the lot of Paul as well (3:7; cf. ἀνάγκη). Paul also refers to his own struggles (see ἀγών, 2:2), including "previous suffering" (προπάσχειν, 2:2), "shameful treatment" (ὑβρίζειν, 2:2), "hindrances" by men (κωλύειν, 2:16; cf. ἐκδιώκειν, 2:15) and by Satan (ἐγκόπτειν, 2:18),[31] and to his anxiety at not knowing whether his "labour" (κόπος, 2:9; 3:5; cf. 1:3) would be in "vain" (κένος, 3:5; 2:1). Paul is quite concerned about being separated from the

---

[27] Note the oblique connection to testing (5:21) "prophecy" (προφητεία, 5:20).

[28] The interpretation of 1 Thess 2:16d as refering to a proleptic *orgē* goes against the majority of commentators and its justification is found in the exegesis of that verse (see Chapter 4).

[29] Rather, the worst the Thessalonians might expect is to receive the same treatment as Paul who comments that God "tests" (δοκιμάζειν, 2:4; cf. 5:21) his heart.

[30] Paul is hindered from proclaiming his gospel so that the *ethnē* may be saved (2:16).

[31] Paul alludes to other heavenly powers elsewhere (cf. Rom 8:38–39; 1 Cor 15:24) but besides "Satan" (ὁ σατανᾶς, 2:18), only to "the tempter" (ὁ πειράζων, 3:5), to an "archangel" (ἀρχάγγελος, 4:16) and to "idols" (εἴδωλα, 1:9) in First Thessalonians.

Thessalonians (cf. ἀπορφανίζειν in 2:17) and is not afraid to say so (cf. στέγειν, 3:1, 5; ἐπιποθεῖν, 3:6); he wanted to come to them (2:18).[32] With reference to labour, Paul emphasises "toil" (μόχθος, 2:9) and "working" (cf. ἐργάζεσθαι, 2:9) "night and day" (νυκτὸς καὶ ἡμέρας, 2:9; 3:10); he also exhorts the Thessalonians to work with their own hands (4:11).[33] As well as receiving the word in much affliction, the Thessalonians also received it with "joy" (χαρά, 1:6; cf. 3:9).[34] Joy is linked to a "crown of boasting" (στέφανος καυχήσεως, 2:19) and "glory" (δόξα, 2:20), of which "kingdom" (βασιλεία, 2:12) is also associated as opposed to the glory of men (cf. 2:6).

Another significant aspect of First Thessalonians is the concern exhibited by Paul. He refers several times to the nature of his past conduct: we were "infants" (νήπιοι, 2:7) among you,[35] like a "nurse" (τροφός, 2:7) taking care of her children. He and his colleagues not only shared the gospel, but also of their "own selves" (ἡ ἑαυτῶν ψυχή, 2:8). They did this because they yearned for and took delight in the Thessalonians who had become very dear to them (2:8). Like a father with his children (2:11) they "exhorted" (παρακαλεῖν, 2:12; 3:2; 4:1, 10; 5:14),[36] "encouraged" (παραμυθεῖσθαι, 2:12) and "charged" (μαρτυρεῖν, 2:12; cf. παραγγέλλειν, 4:11) the Thessalonians to lead a life "worthy" (ἀξίως, 2:12) of God. There are many other words and phrases designed to move the Thessalonians towards this worthy living, or to "pleasing" (ἀρέσκειν, 2:4; 4:1; cf. 2:15) God: "establish" (στηρίζειν, 3:2, 13); "beseech" (ἐρωτᾶν, 4:1; 5:12); "instructions we gave you" (παραγγελίας ἐδώκαμεν ὑμῖν, 4:2); "abstain" (ἀπέχειν, 4:3; 5:22); "brotherly love" (φιλαδελφία, 4:9); "aspire" (φιλοτιμεῖσθαι, 4:11); "mind one's own affairs" (πράσσειν τὰ ἴδια, 4:11); "build up" (οἰκοδομεῖν, 5:11); "admonish" (νουθετεῖν, 5:14).

A related theme to worthy living which already finds a connection to the chosen/called terminology identified above is the notion of being set apart. Paul refers to his own conduct as "holy" (ὁσίως, 2:10) and prays that the Thessalonians may be "unblamable in holiness" (ἄμεμπτος ἁγιωσύνῃ, 3:13; cf. οἱ ἅγιοι), "before our God" (ἔμπροσθεν τοῦ θεοῦ, 1:3; 3:9, 13; cf. 2:19). "Sanctification" (ἁγιασμός, 4:3, 4, 7; cf. ἁγιάζειν, 5:23) is presented as the "will of God" (θέλημα τοῦ θεοῦ, 4:3; 5:18; cf. θεοδίδακτος, 4:9) as over against "uncleanness" (ἀκαθαρσία, 4:7; cf. 2:3), against the "transgressing" (ὑπερβαίνειν, 4:6) and "exploiting" (πλεονεκτεῖν, 4:6)

---

[32] Paul even prays that they will be together again (cf. περισσοτέρως ἐσπουδάσαμεν τὸ πρόσωπον ὑμῶν ἰδεῖν, 2:17; ... δεόμενοι εἰς τὸ ἰδεῖν ὑμῶν τὸ πρόσωπον, 3:10; and ... κατευθύναι τὴν ὁδὸν ἡμῶν πρὸς ὑμᾶς, 3:11).

[33] For a complete list of references to the motif of work, see Okorie 1994, 60–61.

[34] See also the injunction to "rejoice always" (πάντοτε χαίρετε, 5:16).

[35] The question of the correct reading of 1 Thess 2:7 (νήπιοι or ἤπιοι) has a long history in the secondary literature and need not be entered into here. I only draw attention to the fact that most scholars today argue for ἤπιοι ("gentle") despite the clear external evidence for νήπιοι. I agree with Weima, "'But We Became Infants Among You': The Case for νήπιοι in 1 Thess 2.7" (2000a), whose contribution to the discussion provides a thoroughly researched consideration of the opposing arguments (550–559) as well as a convincing defence for the function of νήπιοι in 1 Thess 2:5–7b (559–564).

[36] The word group also has connotations of "encouragement" and "comfort" (3:7; 4:18; 5:11).

of a brother, and against "evil" (πονηρός, 5:22; cf. κακός, 5:15). Paul's *paraenesis* in 5:4–8, with its metaphor-pairs of light/dark, day/night, awake/asleep and sober/drunk, is designed to encourage and sustain a set-apart-ness, and is in accordance with his desire for the Thessalonians to "stand fast" (ἱστάναι, 3:8; cf. κατέχειν, 5:21) in the Lord, and to pursue "good" (ἀγαθός, 5:15).

As a fitting conclusion to this topical analysis, attention is drawn to one of the most examined themes in First Thessalonians, namely, the *parousia*. Paul refers to the theme in every major transition of the letter. In 1:10, he indirectly refers to the *parousia* with statements about Jesus as "deliverer" (ῥύεσθαι) and of the "coming" (ἔρχεσθαι) *orgē*. In 2:19, Paul refers to the *parousia* of the Lord Jesus as an opportunity to acknowledge the Thessalonians as his hope or joy or crown of boasting. In 3:13, he refers to the *parousia* of our Lord Jesus with all his saints and he pictures the Thessalonians as unblamable in holiness. Then in 4:15, reference is made to the *parousia* of the Lord with associated apocalyptic details including the Lord's descent (καταβαίνειν, 4:16). Another way of describing this occurrence is the statement that the "day of the Lord" (ἡμέρα κυρίου) is coming (5:2). Finally, Paul begins his *letter-closing* in 5:23 with another reference to the *parousia* of the Lord Jesus Christ.

3. A determination of the *most* important topics in First Thessalonians is difficult because of the subjective nature of the exercise. The number of references to a word or phrase must be an important consideration, but deference should be given to topics with rhetorical emphasis or else which appear to be distinctive to the situation of the Thessalonians. While the secondary literature may be taken as a guide to the major concerns of the letter, some texts and topics are clearly of more interest to scholars than others. The following table outlines the results of a topical analysis of First Thessalonians along with references to representative verses in the letter. The topical survey of recent secondary literature (§IV below) is arranged according to the headings in the table, but also includes a number of other areas of scholarly interest which do not readily fit into any of the categories identified.

- early Christian mission *kērygma* (1:9–10; 4:14)
- chosen and called (1:4; 2:12, 15–16; 4:7, 12, 13; 5:6)
- expectation (hope) of salvation and resurrection (1:10; 4:14, 16, 17; 5:9–10)
- word of the Lord (4:15–17)
- conflict (affliction and suffering; 2:2, 14–16, 18; 3:1–7; 4:13?)
- Paul's concern (exhortation and consolation; 2:7–12; 3:2; 4:1–12, 18; 5:11–22)
- ethics (being set apart; 2:10; 3:13; 4:3, 4, 7, 9)
- *parousia* of the Lord (1:10; 2:19; 3:13; 4:15–16; 5:23)
- judgment (*orgē*, day of the Lord; 1:10; 2:15–16; 5:2, 9)
- being in Christ, with Christ (4:14, 16, 17; 5:10)

IV. Topical Survey of Recent Secondary Literature

1. This topical survey includes recent secondary literature which approaches First Thessalonians as a whole. The focus is therefore systematic and little attempt is made to provide a survey of exegetical issues unless it is unavoidable.[37] The goal of this survey is two-fold. First, I hope to orient the reader to current trends in Thessalonian research by elucidating topical and programmatic concerns in the letter, and by introducing the recent secondary literature. Second, I seek to show how the different topics may be used, more or less, as hermeneutical keys to understand the letter. Certainly, eschatology is by no means the only *topos* relevant for a systematic interpretation of First Thessalonians. Other topics, which may be taken from the topical analysis (see §III above), are not necessarily mutually exclusive and there is some overlap between them.

2. I have arranged the survey according to the results of the topical analysis, and include a consideration of further areas of research: structure of an early Christian letter (§k); priority of Second Thessalonians? (§l); apocalyptic (§m). Under each topic, I introduce the relevant secondary literature and offer a critical evaluation of how well that topic is able to explain the systematic concerns of First Thessalonians. By working through the secondary literature in this way, I am able to better understand what is actually in the letter, and therefore better understand how my chosen hermeneutical key can explain the letter as a cohesive act of communication. Indeed, throughout the survey, I argue that eschatology is the only category in which *all* the systematic concerns of the letter may be incorporated. Therefore, eschatology is *the* key concept in First Thessalonians. Since the commentary by Rigaux (1956) and the survey by Collins (1984) are comprehensive, priority is given to the secondary literature of the last twenty-five years or so.[38]

a. Early Christian Mission *Kērygma*

The consensus that First Thessalonians is the first extant Christian letter[39] is borne out of research on the absolute and relative chronology of Paul.[40] This involves at least a consideration of the data available in the Pauline literature, the problem of method regarding a right interpretation of Acts,[41] and a correlation of these

[37] Contributions to scholarship which focus on one topic (or text) are by no means neglected as they become valuable conversation partners for the exegetical chapters (Chapters 3-6).

[38] Regardless, the reader is directed to the monumental work of Rigaux (1956).

[39] See Koester 1979; Berger/Nord 1999, 40.

[40] See esp. Knox 1950; Suhl 1975; 1995; Jewett 1979; Lüdemann 1980a; Hyldahl 1986; Riesner 1998, 33–227; Schnelle 2003, 29–40.

[41] Regarding Acts 17 and First Thessalonians, issues for discussion include: the movements of Paul and his co-workers; whether there was a synagogue in Thessalonica during the time of Paul (see Nigdelis 1994); the precise length of the founding visit; the nature of the Pauline *kērygma* and whether he proclaimed

considerations with other, external data.[42] Regardless of whether the traditional or revisionist chronology is followed, the Antiochian mission looms in the background of Paul's first missionary *kērygma*.[43] There is considerable discussion concerning whether 1 Thess 1:9–10 contains a summary of Jewish mission propaganda that Paul has inherited, adapted and proclaimed to the Thessalonians.[44] If so, an analysis of this early *kērygma* (esp. of Paul's use of traditional formulae)[45] may provide insight into understanding the letter, particularly if the differences and similarities between the "early" and "late" Paul can be characterised.[46] Hence, a common theme among Pauline scholars is the so-called development of Paul's theology (or christology or eschatology, etc.). I have my reservations.[47] Another, more nuanced key to understanding First Thessalonians is to exploit the differences between the pre-Pauline traditions Paul inherited and the redacted hellenisation of those traditions. In particular, Gundry, "The Hellenization of Dominical Tradition and Christianization of Jewish Tradition in the Eschatology of 1–2 Thessalonians" (1987), systematically examines these differences as a way of understanding the eschatology of the two letters. He finds a hellenising influence to be particularly evident in the *parousia* tradition (including the apocalyptic details of 1 Thess 4:16–17), and a christianising influence on "the day of the Lord" (a thoroughly Jewish tradition taken up in 1 Thess 5:1–11). Much of the discussion is preoccupied with a right interpretation for the apocalyptic detail of "meeting the Lord" (εἰς ἀπάντησιν τοῦ κυρίου, 4:17).[48] But there are certainly other aspects of First Thessalonians for which the key of hellenising/christianising could be applied more systematically. Karrer (2002) notes the influence of Hellenistic thought regarding

---

Jesus as the Christ; the social status of the converts; who persecuted whom; the household of Jason; the politarchs; the decrees of Caesar. As far as the methodological discussion goes, I agree with the consensus that Acts does contain valuable information for a reconstruction of Paul's life, but that information from the authentic letters of Paul takes absolute priority. See esp. Knox 1966; Bruce 1985; Manus 1990; Alexander 1998; Barrett 1999; Mount 2002.

[42] The "Claudius-Edict" and the "Gallio-inscription" are most important in this regard; see Schwank 1971; Slingerland 1991; Murphy-O'Connor 1993.

[43] See Grundmann 1941; Hengel 1982; Becker 1993b; 1997; Löning 1993; Hengel/Schwemer 1997.

[44] See the discussion which substantially began with Wilckens (1961) and is continued by Munck 1963; Friedrich 1965; Langevin 1965; Bussmann 1975; Holtz 1977; Havener 1981. Although the discussion has slowed in recent years, Richard (1995) and Malherbe (2000) provide useful contributions.

[45] See Wengst 1972; Collins 1984c; H. J. de Jonge 1990; Ellis 2000a.

[46] See Donfried 1990; Schulz 1985.

[47] While the concept of development in Paul's life and thought is intuitive, it is difficult, if not impossible, to maintain a wholesale development-theory for Paul; at best, individual topics and texts require careful exegesis and comparison. Even then it is difficult to determine how much is to be attributed to development and how much is to be attributed to the contingency of the texts. On the topic in general see Lowe 1941; Grossouw 1963; Buck/Taylor 1969; Baird 1971; Kuss 1971; Feuillet 1972; Wiefel 1974; Uprichard 1976; Mearns 1981; 1984; Casey 1982; Longenecker 1985; Meyer 1986; Beker 1988; Lindemann 1991; Söding 1991; Lüdemann 1993; Lohse 1996; von Bendemann 2000.

[48] There is a long history of research regarding this phrase, essentially beginning with Peterson 1930 (cf. 1964; Dupont 1952). The discussion has continued into the modern era; see Cosby 1994; Gundry 1996; Plevnik 1999.

the predicate "Jesus, the saviour" in the NT,[49] and Walter finds a similar influence on the resurrection hope in Paul (1998).[50] General studies in this area support the legitimacy of this kind of interpretation.[51] A parallel approach emphasising the Roman imperial culture/ideology is being proposed by a growing number of scholars.[52] Hendrix's pioneering work, *Thessalonicans Honor Romans* (1984), remains essential reading. More specifically, Harrison, "Paul and the Imperial Gospel at Thessaloniki" (2002), and Smith, "'Unmasking the Powers': Toward a Postcolonial Analysis of 1 Thessalonians" (2004), are correct to see Paul's gospel partly as a critique of Roman imperialism.[53] The consideration of hellenising/ christianising and Roman imperial cultural/ideological influences acknowledges the intense social and political atmosphere into which Paul proclaimed his gospel.

b. Chosen and Called

There is a sizeable number of references to election and calling in First Thessalonians (see §III above), which makes this aspect of Paul's theology helpful for understanding the systematic concerns of the letter. Marshall, in "Election and Calling to Salvation in 1 and 2 Thessalonians" (1990), argues that Paul was worried that the Thessalonians might fall away (cf. 1 Thess 3:5); the emphases on election, calling and perseverance, along with Paul's extensive teaching and encouragement, address the insecurity of the Thessalonians (who were fearful for a number of reasons; 260).[54] Thus, Paul explains that their acceptance of the word of God (2:13) is evidence of their response to Paul's *kērygma* such that they are not only an example (1:7) to others but are also destined for salvation (5:9). In addition, Paul refers to the call of God as an invitation which is both eschatologically (2:12; 5:24) and ethically (4:7) oriented (269–270). In a previous article, Becker, "Die Erwählung der Völker durch das Evangelium. Theologiegeschichtliche Erwägungen zum 1 Thess" (1986), articulates *Erwählung* in terms of three themes of Pauline theology in First Thessalonians: the early Gentile mission (1:9–10), the "Auseinandersetzung" with Judaism (2:14–16) and the hope of resurrection (4:13–18).[55] Becker rightly singles out these three aspects (and pericopes) of the letter as important but I argue

[49] See Paul's reference to "Jesus, the deliverer" in 1 Thess 1:10; see also Schneider 1969.

[50] In particular, Walter notes some differences (with regard to a hellenising influence) between the discussions of resurrection in First Thessalonians and First Corinthians, not least of which one is the lack of any reference to "body" (σῶμα) in the former (1998, 110–112).

[51] See the many contributions in the collections edited by Engberg-Pedersen (1995; 2001) as well as the following: Krentz 1988; Perkins 1989; Räisänen 1995.

[52] See Koester 1997; Khiok-Khng 1998; Popkes 2002.

[53] A monograph by Tellbe (2001), which is introduced below (see §IV.e), also contributes to the political character of Paul's gospel.

[54] See also Bammel, "Preparation for the Perils of the Last Days: 1 Thessalonians 3:3" (1981).

[55] In addition, see Collins 1977; Bassler 1989. More generally, see Custer 1975; Reumann 1987; Collins 1991a; Lambrecht 1991.

that the category of eschatology (in which *Erwählung* may be considered a subcategory) provides a more inclusive basis for understanding the data.

c. Expectation (Hope) of Salvation and Resurrection

Explanations of the Thessalonians' problem(s) and Paul's solution(s) inevitably include 1 Thess 4:13–18 where the problem of death and Paul's response is presented.[56] Are there sufficient references to warrant the thesis that an expectation of salvation or a hope of resurrection was at issue? Did not Paul refer to the "christological soteriology"[57] of Jesus' death and resurrection? Or is there some aspect of resurrection that the Thessalonians did not understand? The theories are numerous. For example: the Thessalonians knew about the resurrection of the dead but were influenced by Gnostic agitators;[58] the resurrection of the dead was not part of Paul's founding *kērygma* (even though he was aware of it) because of his strong expectation of the *parousia*;[59] the Thessalonians did not understand the relationship between the resurrection and the *parousia*;[60] in 1 Thess 4:13–18 Paul merely uses motifs and images to express (in a general way) the message of the Christian gospel;[61] the occurrence of deaths in the community precipitated doubts regarding salvation,[62] the *parousia*,[63] or their social status;[64] the Thessalonians thought the living would have an advantage over the dead at the *parousia*;[65] the Thessalonians were under a millenarian (realised eschatological) influence such that deaths before the *parousia* were thought to be permanent.[66] Such reconstructions based on 1 Thess 4:13–18 can only go part way to understanding First Thessalonians as a whole despite the programmatic importance of salvation and resurrection throughout the letter.

---

[56] For a complete survey of the secondary literature on 1 Thess 4:13–18, see Excursus 5.

[57] This phrase is Koperski's, of which she states that it is "a key concept, perhaps *the* key concept, for understanding Paul's theology" (2002, 280).

[58] Schmithals 1965; see also Lütgert 1909; Harnisch 1973.

[59] Marxsen 1969; see also Becker 1976; 1993; Lüdemann 1980a; 1993; Jewett 1986; Schnelle 1986; 2003; Gundry 1987; Wilckens 1988; Nicholl 2004.

[60] The nature of that misunderstanding is of course open to discussion and there are numerous alternative proposals. See, for example, Plevnik 1975a; Giesen 1985; Merklein 1992; Malherbe 2000; Kim 2002a. For individual details, see Excursus 5.

[61] Koester 1979; see Smith (1995) who also does not look for a specific problem behind Paul's discussion.

[62] See Collins 1980a; Otto 1997.

[63] See Hyldahl 1980.

[64] See Donfried 1985; Ascough 2004.

[65] Klijn 1982; see also Magnien 1907; Schweitzer 1953; Cerfaux 1959; Howard 1988; Delobel 1990; Michaels 1994; Harrison 2002.

[66] See Jewett 1986.

d. Word of the Lord

Every discussion of a word of the Lord in First Thessalonians must include the problematic reference in 1 Thess 4:15–17,[67] although Henneken, in *Verkündigung und Prophetie im 1. Thessalonicherbrief. Ein Beitrag zur Theologie des Wortes Gottes* (1969), takes a more systematic approach. He contends that the letter can be understood on the basis of "Verkündigung" and "Prophetie": the proclamation of Paul is the word of God as a received, spiritual word of a new existence; the prophetic language of apostle and community breaks out from the power of the Holy Spirit. To this end, Henneken explains the numerous references to "word" and "word of God" (and similar phrases) in terms of: the self-understanding of Paul and his proclamation (9–42); the reception of the word and its continued proclamation in the community (43–72); and in terms of Paul as prophet and of prophets in the community (73–111). Henneken concludes (112–113):

> Paulus, seine Mitarbeiter und die einzelnen der Gemeinde von Thessalonich sind Propheten. Dabei ist unter prophetischer Rede nicht nur im engeren Sinne die „Weissagung" zu verstehen, sondern die Rede aus der Unmittelbarkeit des Pneuma heraus: eschatologische Existenz!

This original thesis has merit particularly because it provides a clear explanation of an important topic in the letter, and in some respects explains the systematic concerns therein. However, it does not provide a key to understanding many of the distinctive and problematic issues with which Paul is concerned, including for example the polemical and rhetorical statements in 1 Thess 2:13–16 or the detailed and peculiar presentation of resurrection, translation and *parousia* in 1 Thess 4:13–18.

e. Conflict (Affliction and Suffering)

1. Conflict in First Thessalonians is apparent on a number of levels: a reference to violent conflict culminating in the death of Jesus (2:15); conflict arising from Paul's gentile mission (2:2, 15–16); conflict between spiritual powers (1:9; 2:18; 3:5); Paul's anxiety associated with the possibility that his work would be in vain (3:1–7); conflict between the *kērygma* and imperial Rome (4:13–18; 5:3); conflict between community members (5:12–15).[68]

Since Paul did not know what the Thessalonians believed prior to Timothy's return and subsequent report (unless he had heard first-hand about their faith; cf. 1 Thess 1:8–9), the occasion of First Thessalonians must partially be found in the

[67] For a discussion of the phenomenon and possible sources, see Chapter 5, §II.c; for an outline of various proposals regarding 1 Thess 4:15–17, see Excursus 5.

[68] In contrast, Köster observes that there is no challenge against Paul's apostolic authority (1980, 287).

circumstances which led to the sending of Timothy to Thessalonica in the first place. These are outlined in the *apostolic parousia* (2:17–3:13): Paul had been separated from his converts (2:17a) and desires to see them again (2:17b). He wished to come to them more than once but was hindered by Satan (2:18). When Paul could bear the separation no longer (3:1a, 5a) he sent (3:2a, 5b) Timothy with a two-fold purpose: first, to establish the Thessalonians in their faith and to exhort them in the face of afflictions (3:2b); second, that Paul might be reassured about their faith lest his work be in vain (3:5c). Paul strengthens the bond between himself and them by identifying with their afflictions both when he was with them (3:3b, 4) and when he (and Silvanus) received the report from Timothy (3:7). In this way the narrative of the *apostolic parousia* effectively maintains and reaffirms the relationship. An investigation of the theme of affliction provides a basis for a better understanding of the occasion of the letter.

2. To this end, some scholars have understood the references to conflict in terms of the social status of the community. Different emphases are offered, with regard to the disruptive nature of conversion,[69] the maintenance of community well-being,[70] or else a combination of the two.[71] The significance of these references, when it comes to the *Sitz im Leben* of Paul and the Thessalonians, is difficult to determine. At the least, there was some alienation brought about by verbal, social and political harassment.[72] The Thessalonians probably also suffered physical abuse. But whether this led to deaths (martyrdom) or not is more speculative (supported by a minority).[73] Three recent monographs dominate the general discussion: de Vos, *Church and Community Conflicts: The Relationships of the Thessalonian, Corinthian and Philippian Churches with Their Wider Civic Communities* (1999); Still, *Conflict at Thessalonica: A Pauline Church and Its Neighbours* (1999); Tellbe, *Paul between Synagogue and State: Christians, Jews, and Civic Authorities in 1 Thessalonians, Romans, and Philippians* (2001). Thus, de Vos outlines a situation of conflict which arose directly from conversion to Paul's *kērygma*, and probably "centered on the rejection of traditional religious practices and a withdrawal from social/religious activities" (1999, 176). Such "religious practices" and "social/religious activities" may have included worship of typical Greek and Egyptian gods and association with mystery and imperial cults. The conclusions of Still (1999, 287) are similar:

---

[69] See esp. Wanamaker, "'Like a Father Treats His Own Children': Paul and the Conversion of the Thessalonians" (1995); Malherbe, "Conversion to Paul's Gospel" (1998); Ascough, "The Thessalonian Christian Community as a Professional Voluntary Association" (2000); see also Pax 1971; 1972; M. S. Taylor 1995.

[70] See deSilva, "'Worthy of His Kingdom': Honor Discourse and Social Engineering in 1 Thessalonians" (1996); Crook, "Paul's Riposte and Praise of the Thessalonians" (1997).

[71] See Malherbe 1987.

[72] See esp. Barclay, "Conflict in Thessalonica" (1993); Donfried, "The Imperial Cults of Thessalonica and Political Conflict in 1 Thessalonians" (1997); see also Barclay 1992.

[73] See esp. Donfried, "The Theology of 1 Thessalonians as a Reflection of Its Purpose" (1989); see also Donfried 1985; Lindars 1985, 771; Pobee 1985, 113; Collins 1993, 161–162.

> Paul's converts in Thessalonica, I have argued, were verbally, socially and perhaps physically harassed by their fellow Gentiles and were perceived by some of their former associates as exclusive, offensive and even subversive.

But he gives a different emphasis. The resocialisation process of conversion resulted in an insider/outsider clash; Still examines this dynamic through a social-scientific theory of deviance and conflict. Finally, Tellbe examines a "tripartite relation" between Christians, Jews and civic authorities and argues that First Thessalonians provides a "socio-political" rationalisation of a community in conflict. This applies both to Jewish opponents who considered Paul's *kērygma* to be jeopardising the socio-political status of the Jewish community in Thessalonica (2001, 138),[74] and to Gentile opponents who viewed the same *kērygma* as a rejection of imperial ideology (139–140). "The socio-political dimensions of the Thessalonian conflict is indirectly confirmed by the political terminology of 1 Thessalonians, in particular the contrast between Pauline eschatology and imperial propaganda" (139). Many of the subversive political terms in First Thessalonians are eschatologically oriented. This highlights the importance of historical reconstructions which include the social and political climate of the Thessalonian community. Köster's comments, in "Apostel und Gemeinde in den Briefen an die Thessalonicher" (1980), are pertinent (292):

> Paulus schreibt nicht deshalb Briefe, weil er – leider abwesend – nun sein Gewicht durch Briefe geltend machen muß. Vielmehr kommt der Wunsch, die Thessalonicher zu besuchen, unmittelbar aus der Darstellung des Verhältnisses von Liebe und Hingabe ... Und zwar ist dieses Verhältnis wiederum unter eschatologischem Aspekt gesehen.

3. A different approach to understanding the conflict terminology in First Thessalonians involves a reconstruction of various opponents. The monographs of Schmithals, *Paulus und die Gnostiker. Untersuchungen zu den kleinen Paulusbriefen* (1965), and Harnisch, *Eschatologische Existenz. Ein exegetischer Beitrag zum Sachanliegen von 1. Thessalonicher 4,13–5,11* (1973), used to be at the heart of the discussion, but the thesis of a Gnostic influence in Thessalonica has long been rejected on the basis that there is simply insufficient data.[75] Lütgert, in *Die Vollkommenen im Philipperbrief und die Enthusiasten in Thessalonich* (1909), argued that a group within the Thessalonian community radicalised Paul's *kērygma*. These "enthusiasts" proposed an alternative realised eschatology. Among others,[76] Jewett,

---

[74] Tellbe spends considerable space analysing the legal status of Diaspora Judaism under Roman rule (2001, 26–63) and justifying his view that there was a synagogue in first-century Thessalonica despite the meagre evidence (86–90).

[75] Albeit with regard to Paul's christology, Schweizer (1982), upon examination of topics and texts in Paul which have significant contact with Gnosticism, does not refer to First Thessalonians. Despite a general rejection of Harnisch's thesis, his exegetical contributions remain sizeable. In addition, Schmithals' compilation theories regarding First Thessalonians are still a significant part of that discussion (see §IV.k below).

[76] See survey by Jewett 1986, 142–147.

in "Enthusiastic Radicalism and the Thessalonian Correspondence" (1972), first argued for an enthusiastic model of realised eschatology, but later found this model to lack the necessary social theory required especially to explain the apocalyptic components of the letter. Hence, in his book, *The Thessalonian Correspondence: Pauline Rhetoric and Millenarian Piety* (1986), he develops a new model of millenarian radicalism. He uses a combination of standard historical cricism and rhetorical analysis (xiv). In practice, however, Jewett makes significant use of social-scientific models of millenarism (161–178). His thesis breaks new ground for those who include opponents in the historical reconstruction of the community, and who agree with the presuppositions of social theoretical approaches. His reviews are mixed.[77] Equally as original as Jewett is Schlueter, *Filling Up the Measure: Polemical Hyperbole in 1 Thessalonians 2.14–16* (1994), whose thesis focuses solely on the problems posed by Paul's statements in 1 Thess 2:14–16. Her contribution to scholarship regarding the authenticity of the pericope is substantial but I find her emphasis on explaining the text in terms of Paul's situation more interesting. With regard to the rhetorical category of hyperbole, Schlueter hypothesises that, "Paul, a skilled debater, used polemical hyperbole to polarize issues and to move his readers to his side while casting his opponents (in this case, the Jews) completely on the wrong side" (11). My exegesis of the text is often at variance with hers (see Chapter 4), but her theory of hyperbole is innovative and welcome. Schlueter at least provides a way of understanding a developing "in-house" struggle between Paul and "the Jews" (οἱ Ἰουδαῖοι).

4. Finally, reconstructions of the Thessalonian community must acknowledge the extensive conflict language in the letter. There may be "opponents" within the community who have misunderstood or radicalised Paul's *kērygma*, and possibly "opponents" outside the community who preached a different gospel to Paul's. Richards, in "Ministering in a Tough Place: Paul's Pattern in Thessalonica" (1999), systematically develops possible opponents in terms of problems inside and outside the church. The question of whether 1 Thess 2:1–12 is an apology of Paul is a difficult one to answer. The discussions by Weima, "An Apology for the Apologetic Function of 1 Thessalonians 2:1–12" (1997), "The Function of 1 Thessalonians 2:1–12 and the Use of Rhetorical Criticism: A Response to Otto Merk" (2000), and Hoppe, "Verkündiger – Botschaft – Gemeinde. Überlegungen zu 1 Thess 2,1–12.13–16" (2002), provide an excellent introduction to the issues, although for a more extensive analysis see the monograph by Schoon-Janßen, *Umstrittene "Apologien" in den Paulusbriefen. Studien zur rhetorischen Situation des 1. Thessalonicherbriefes, des Galaterbriefes und des Philipperbriefes* (1991).

Consequently, the political and religious history of Thessalonica forms an important background for all such attempts at understanding First Thessalonians. In particular, the history of Macedonia and its fate at the hands of the Romans

---

[77] For example, see Hendrix (1988) and Linss (1992) for a positive and negative review, respectively.

provide insight into first-century Thessalonica.[78] The city obtained status as a free city in approximately 42 B.C.E. It was governed by its own *politarchs*[79] yet Roman benefaction was important.[80] There were numerous cults prevalent, including Egyptian divinities Isis, Serapis and Osiris, mysteries of Samothrace, cults of Dionysus and Cabirus and emperor worship. Donfried, in "The Cults of Thessalonica and the Thessalonian Correspondence" (1985), provides the best introduction to and discussion of the religious climate of the city.[81]

5. I have spent a fair amount of space assessing the secondary literature on the conflict language in First Thessalonians because I think a correct reconstruction of the social and political situations in Thessalonica is essential for understanding the extensive *paraenesis* in the letter. The critical introduction to the discussion here, along with those conversation partners so named, offer an important orientation for determining how Paul uses eschatological motifs to promote his pattern of exhortation, a pattern that addresses disintegration and integration. As well, recognising the extent of the *paraenesis* in First Thessalonians also plays a vital role in the development of my thesis (see §IV.f below).

f. Paul's Concern (Exhortation and Consolation)

1. Much of the discussion regarding the exhortation and consolation of First Thessalonians has as its starting point an investigation of Thessalonica in general and a reconstruction of the Christian community in particular. Enough has been said about both these investigations (see §IV.e above). Therefore, the survey to follow is focused more on the letter itself, with regard to the paraenetic features of the text.

2. Malherbe is one of the most prolific commentators of the Thessalonian correspondence in the modern era. The application of his expert knowledge of philosophic traditions to First Thessalonians in particular provides a new interpretation of Paul's missionary practice — an interpretation that has spanned more than thirty years. In one of his earlier articles, "Gentle as a Nurse': The Cynic Background to I Thess ii" (1970), Malherbe examines numerous parallels between Paul and Dio, and between Paul and Cynicism in general, and concludes that 1 Thess 2:1–12 may not be understood in terms of a personal apology (the traditional view). A few years later, in "Exhortation in First Thessalonians" (1983), Malherbe fills out the thesis that First Thessalonians is paraenetic (239):

---

[78] On Macedonia in general see esp. vom Brocke 2001, 12–101, but see also Edson 1940; 1970; Davies 1963; Hammond 1972; Bruce 1979; 1992; Gill 1994; Koester 1995, 15–20; de Vos 1999, 124–143; Ascough 2000a; Tellbe 2001, 81–86. On Thessalonica in general, see Clemen 1896; Finegan 1962; Vickers 1970; 1972; 1981; Kudlien 1975; Elliger 1978; 2000; Bruce 1980; Jewett 1986, 113–132; Bercovitz 1990; Hendrix 1991; 1992; Koester 1994; Donfried 1996c.

[79] See Koukouli-Chrysanthaki 1981; Horsley 1982; 1994; 1994a.

[80] See esp. Hendrix 1984; 1992a.

[81] See also Edson 1948; Hemberg 1950; Witt 1977; Steimle 2007.

> Paul adopts a manner of exhortation that most likely was familiar to his readers, and he uses popular philosophical traditions with which they can be expected to have been familiar, yet he does so in a way different from the philosophical preachers of his day. ... I draw attention to the Graeco-Roman tradition of moral exhortation.

In this way he compares and contrasts the hortatory tradition of philosophers and Paul's method of exhortation. In "Paul: Hellenistic Philosopher or Christian Pastor?" (1985), Malherbe then develops the notion that Paul was "a type of hellenistic philosopher" and stresses how Paul adopted and adapted philosophical tradition to serve a pastoral function (87). His monograph, *Paul and the Thessalonians: The Philosophic Tradition of Pastoral Care* (1987), continues along the same lines and is at once more general and less technical, and yet more focused on dimensions of Paul's pastoral work. Malherbe explains this practical aspect of Paul's work in terms of "founding", "shaping" and "nurturing" the Thessalonian community.[82] By this stage, and despite his disclaimers,[83] Malherbe pushes the limits of his comparisons between Paul and the philosophic tradition.[84] In his next article, "'Pastoral Care' in the Thessalonian Church" (1990a), Malherbe turns his attention more to the Thessalonians' own strategies of care for each other (cf. 1 Thess 5:14–15), and examines ancient psychagogic traditions of Paul's time. Then, in an ANRW article, "Hellenistic Moralists and the New Testament" (1992), he takes the opportunity to express his views regarding First Thessalonians on a more programmatic scale.[85] He explicitly states that he considers "the character of 1 Thessalonians as a paraenetic letter" (280). He argues that not only is 1 Thess 4–5 to be understood as *paraenesis* (a common conclusion among commentators), but also 1 Thess 1–3 "exhibits the characteristics of a paraenetic letter" (292). On the basis of a presupposition borne from decades of comparisons between Paul and the philosophic traditions,[86] Malherbe presents two articles which provide exegetical

[82] See similarly, Alkier, "Der 1. Thessalonicherbrief als kulturelles Gedächtnis" (1997); Börschel, *Die Konstruktion einer christlichen Identität. Paulus und die Gemeinde von Thessalonich in ihrer hellenistisch-römischen Umwelt* (2001).

[83] For example: "The intention of this book has not been to make Paul a moral philosopher but to illuminate his practice by comparing it to that of his contemporaries who were engaged in a similar, if not identical enterprise" (Malherbe 1987, 108).

[84] In a review of the monograph, Roetzel (1989, 358) comments: "... although Malherbe acknowledges that Paul was no moral philosopher, he believes the Apostle's debt to moral philosophy was direct, conscious, and extensive, and this is where eyebrows will be raised. While few would dispute Paul's use of the Hellenistic idiom and method, many may question the intimacy of the tie Malherbe sees between Paul and the philosophical schools. Given the abundant evidence for Paul's debt to diaspora Judaism, and given the way Hellenism informed that Judaism, how are we to decide if Paul's metaphors, *topoi*, and methods of argumentation were consciously adopted from the philosophical traditions or mediated by the diaspora synagogue out of which Paul came? ... The tension between Malherbe's recognition of Paul's debt to Judaism and his insistence on Paul's conscious, direct, and profound dependence on philosophic language and practice remains to be resolved."

[85] The article goes beyond Malherbe's interest in First Thessalonians, and examines many different sources and topics of Hellenistic moralism.

[86] "We must understand better the ways in which Paul was indebted to the ... philosophers of his day if we are to gain a firmer grasp of how he expressed himself to his Greek readers" (Malherbe 1998, 243).

examinations: "God's New Family in Thessalonica" (1995) and "Conversion to Paul's Gospel" (1998). Both articles, in their particular way, advance the theory that First Thessalonians is paraenetic in intention. It is important to highlight Malherbe's emphasis in the second article, however, on the way Paul is able to use the "same rubrics as the philosophers" and yet invest them with a "radically different content" (1998, 244).[87] His last article to appear, "Anti-Epicurean Rhetoric in 1 Thessalonians" (1999), before his commentary, *The Letters to the Thessalonians: A New Translation with Introduction and Commentary* (2000), finally – but only in part – corrects a long-standing avoidance of the eschatological nature of the letter, although Malherbe cannot resist saying in his introductory paragraphs: "This letter is shot through with moral philosophical traditions" (1999, 136). He disregards (too quickly in my view) the usual political interpretations of παρουσία (1 Thess 4:15) and ἀπάντησις (4:17) and therefore also of εἰρήνη καὶ ἀσφάλεια (5:3) in preference for an anti-Epicurean understanding. Of his commentary there is no need to say anything more than is already said in the *Review of Biblical Literature* (2004)[88] except to draw attention to Malherbe's shortcomings in the areas of theology and eschatology.[89]

3. The pastoral concern of First Thessalonians is exhaustively covered by Malherbe. Consequently, the contributions of others are more or less limited to acceptance or critique of Malherbe's various publications. Chapa, in "Consolatory Patterns? 1 Thes 4,13.18; 5,11" (1990), takes issue with Malherbe's statement that First Thessalonians is a letter of consolation. With regard to 1 Thess 4:13–5:11, Chapa concludes that Paul is dependent on essentially Jewish tradition and that he uses Hellenistic rhetoric to convey his Christian condolence: "Christian consolation springs from a Jewish root, which is approached by a Hellenistic man" (228). In a later article, "Is First Thessalonians a Letter of Consolation?" (1994), Chapa returns to the topic of consolation and this time his conclusion is not so far removed from Malherbe's: "If we should not formally classify 1 Thessalonians as a 'letter of consolation', we may, nevertheless, be justified in calling it a consoling letter without intending to exclude other valid purposes" (160).[90]

4. Malherbe's characterisations of Paul's pastoral concern in First Thessalonians are not satisfactory in my view. For sure, Malherbe's scholarship is of the highest standard and rightly deserves much of the praise received. But he does not provide a reflected description of Paul's theology (he does not even appear to attempt one),

---

[87] In a similar way, Winter, in "The Entries and Ethics of Orators and Paul (1 Thessalonians 2:1–12)" (1993), highlights important differences between Paul and the ethics of first-century orators and sophists, despite his use of some elements of "entry" conventions of his day.

[88] See largely positive reviews by Fitzgerald, Lambrecht, Krentz, Wanamaker, Thom and M. M. Mitchell.

[89] See comments on the general ommision in Krentz (2004, 24–26) and Lambrecht (2004, 20).

[90] See also Merk, "Miteinander. Zur Sorge um den Menschen im Ersten Thessalonicherbrief" (1993); Bickmann, *Kommunikation gegen den Tod. Studien zur paulinischen Briefpragmatik am Beispiel des Ersten Thessalonicherbriefes* (1998); Bridges, "Terms of Endearment: Paul's Words of Comfort in First Thessalonians" (1999).

and his interpretations of the eschatological sections of the letter often ignore the fundamentally Jewish, eschatological and apocalyptic orientations of Paul's theology. Eddy, in "Christian and Hellenistic Moral Exhortation: A Literary Comparison Based on 1 Thessalonians 4" (1993), recognises this shortcoming and subsequently emphasises the Christian motivation and means for living and ethical life (51), but his study on 1 Thess 4 is far too limited to fill the lacunae left by Malherbe. In addition, Smith, in *Comfort one Another: Reconstructing the Rhetoric and Audience of 1 Thessalonians* (1995),[91] also goes beyond Malherbe[92] in that he recognises the pastoral and consolatory elements in the letter but acknowledges that the "principal hermeneutical context reflected in the letter was an apocalyptic one" (59). Smith's approach is an audience-oriented type of literary criticism where a reconstruction of the Thessalonian community may only be undertaken after a thorough investigation of the authorial audience, or of a reconstructed rhetorical audience (22). This approach has its merits in that it does not directly correlate a rhetorical situation with a historical one, but the vagueness of his historical reconstructions demonstrates that he has not properly grappled with the exigencies of First Thessalonians (see Jewett 1996). In conclusion, a significant aspect of my thesis involves describing Paul's pattern of exhortation, but I argue that the *paraenesis* contained in the letter is better understood by applying eschatology as a hermeneutical key, rather than the other way around. Consequently, I take seriously the extensive eschatological discourse of First Thessalonians in a way that goes beyond the work of Malherbe.

g. Ethics (Being Set Apart)

1. Discussions of Pauline ethics must include a consideration of motivating factors,[93] of which it may be argued that eschatology is a, if not *the*, motivating factor.[94] Consequently, as with many of the topics under discussion here, ethics as a significant key to understanding First Thessalonians should not be viewed in competition with my thesis; it merely provides a different and concentrated emphasis.[95] Laub, in *Eschatologische Verkündigung und Lebensgestaltung nach*

---

[91] See also his commentary (Smith 2000).

[92] In his introduction, Smith (1995, 13–14) pays tribute to Jewett (1986) and Malherbe (1987) for their critical interdisciplinary contributions to the study of First Thessalonians.

[93] For example, see Merk 1968.

[94] At the least, Rosner is correct to say: "Paul's moral judgments cannot be understood apart from his theological convictions" (2003, 216). In general, see Owen 1962; Münchow 1981; Duff 1989; Gnilka 1989; see also Kaye, "Eschatology and Ethics in 1 and 2 Thessalonians" (1975).

[95] See Collins, "'This Is the Will of God: Your Sanctification.' (1 Thess 4:3)" (1983a); Carras, "Jewish Ethics and Gentile Converts: Remarks on 1 Thes 4,3–8" (1990); Schnelle, "Die Ethik des 1. Thessalonicherbriefes" (1990). R. M. Evans, *Eschatology and Ethics: A Study of Thessalonica and Paul's Letters to the Thessalonians* (1968), and Hodgson, Jr., "Gospel and Ethics in First Thessalonians" (1988), provide uncritical and therefore disappointing examinations of the theme which is a pity in light of the promising titles.

Paulus. Eine Untersuchung zum Wirken des Apostels beim Aufbau der Gemeinde in Thessalonike (1973), first provides a careful analysis of the Thessalonian situation and of the letter itself;[96] only then does he summarise the ethical implications of Paul's *kērygma* (which is really the "Evangelium Gottes") in his conclusion (202):

> Wer es glaubend annimmt, für den haben sich die Bedingungen des Handelns grundlegend geändert. Die Äonenwende, die sich mit Jesus Christus schon ereignet hat, bestimmt sein Leben nun insofern, als er an dem noch ausstehenden eschatologischen Heil jetzt schon teilhat durch die gottgewirkte Heiligung und den Besitz des Pneumas. In dieser von Gott geschaffenen, neuen Lebenswirklichkeit ist dem Glaubenden ein Handeln möglich, das der Berufung entspricht (2,12) und die Erlangung des endgültigen Heils bei der bevorstehenden Parusie erhoffen läßt (3,13; 5,9.23).

2. Bockmuehl (1998) raises an important methodological issue. Regarding the rationale of Christian ethics, there is little dispute about the influence of Hellenistic traditions of moral exhortation. He goes on to say (345):

> However, just as the use made of such material by Jewish authors is not indiscriminate but ultimately governed by halakhic criteria, so also it will not do to ignore the fundamental rationale behind its appearance in Christian ethical texts. The apostle Paul and others are in fact highly selective and specific in their adoption of Hellenistic moral principles ...

His argument that the NT authors, including Paul, made substantial use of traditional halakhah for Gentiles (with prohibitions of idolatry, sexual immorality and blood offences), indicates that discussions of Christian ethics should give significant weighting to Jewish traditions of torah and halakhah as well as to Hellenistic traditions of moral exhortation. Finally, Sleeper's article, "Christ's Coming and Christian Living" (1999), is an appropriate bridge between an introduction to ethics and the *parousia*, because the latter informs the former. Sleeper concludes that Paul's moral advice includes discouragement of predictions of the day of the Lord, a rationalisation of persecution as part of the eschatological Christian experience, and exhortations to patience and perseverance (133).

h. *Parousia* of the Lord

1. The *parousia* of the Lord is one of the more popular topics for scholarly investigations. Numerous questions are raised about whether the Thessalonians were ignorant of the *parousia*, or misunderstood it, or rejected it, or were perturbed by its delay, or some combination thereof. No other letter of Paul contains references

---

[96] See Rosner 2003, 213. Thus, on the topic of holiness and discipleship, Weima, "'How You Must Walk to Please God': Holiness and Discipleship in 1 Thessalonians" (1996), not only examines the importance of these themes in the overall framework of Paul's teaching (99–103), but also provides a detailed exegesis of relevant pericopes in the letter, including 1 Thess 4:3–8 (103–112) and 4:9–12 (112–118).

to the coming of the Lord with such striking recurrence.[97] Plevnik has been one of the most consistent correspondents in the discussion; his unique interpretation of 1 Thess 4:13–18 has gained a minority following.[98] His extensive earlier article, "The Parousia as Implication of Christ's Resurrection: An Exegesis of 1 Thes 4,13–18" (1975), is followed up with a more systematic treatment of the topic, in *Paul and the Parousia: An Exegetical and Theological Investigation* (1997). In both he proposes that Paul's previous teaching of the *parousia* included an assumption motif. Since persons undergoing assumption had to be alive, then the Thessalonians were concerned that those who had died would not be able to take part in the *parousia*.[99] More generally, Plevnik relates the *parousia* to hope and Christian existence both present and future, to eschatological judgment which is manifested in *orgē* for outsiders and salvation for insiders, to conflict between Christ and hostile powers (e.g. sin, death), to being with Christ in life and death, and to the church as fellowship of all who believe "in Christ" (1997).

2. One of the problematic issues for understanding the *parousia* of the Lord in Paul involves a delineation between the Hellenistic and Jewish connotations of the term. Vena, in *The Parousia and Its Rereadings: The Development of the Eschatological Consciousness in the Writings of the New Testament* (2001), takes up the issue and provides extensive and critical discussions of both Hellenistic and Jewish influences. He concludes that Paul uses a "combination of traditions" and does not force an answer to the problem. "What is so original in Paul is that he uses it [i.e. the term *parousia*] with eschatological connotations in order to refer to the events of the end-time where Jesus Christ acts as the main theophanic revelation of God" (116). Further, for Paul, the *parousia* is imminent and there is no concern for its so-called "delay".[100] More important than "when" is "how". Vena summarises Paul's view of *parousia* in terms of "transformation" (anthropological, sociological and cosmological; 257–258).[101]

3. As I shall show, the eschatological motif of *parousia* is a central part of Paul's pattern of exhortation in First Thessalonians, especially in 1 Thess 4:13–18. But it will not do as a hermeneutical key for understanding the letter, any more than other important topics like salvation, resurrection, judgment, being in Christ

---

[97] The secondary literature is extensive and I draw attention to my introduction of "*Parousia* in Paul" elsewhere (Chapter 5, §II.d).

[98] For references, see Excursus 5.

[99] Plevnik gives a number of supporting arguments for this thesis in an article entitled, "The Taking Up of the Faithful and the Resurrection of the Dead in 1 Thessalonians 4:13–18" (1984).

[100] See Koester 1997, 159; *contra* Arróniz 1983.

[101] The PhD dissertations of Burkeen, "The Parousia of Christ in the Thessalonian Correspondence" (1979), and Ahn, "The Parousia in Paul's Letters to the Thessalonians, the Corinthians, and the Romans, in Relation to Its Old Testament-Judaic Background" (1989), are rarely critical and add little to the discussion. Jurgensen, "Awaiting the Return of Christ: A Re-Examination of 1 Thessalonians 4.13–5.11 from a Pentecostal Perspective" (1994), also does not break new ground and does little more than offer a survey from a pentecostal perspective; see similarly his PhD dissertation, "Saint Paul et la parousie: 1 Thessaloniciens 4.13–5.11 dans l'exégèse moderne et contemporaine" (1992).

and with Christ, for example. This is why I refer to an eschatological discourse in First Thessalonians, such that all these motifs, and others, may be explained systematically.

i. Judgment (*Orgē*, Day of the Lord)

1. Konradt, in *Gericht und Gemeinde. Eine Studie zur Bedeutung und Funktion von Gerichtsaussagen im Rahmen der paulinischen Ekklesiologie und Ethik im 1 Thess und 1 Kor* (2003), fills a lacuna in Pauline scholarship by examining the role of judgment in Paul's theology, not just in terms of its relationship to the important topics of justification or ethics, but in terms of how Paul uses judgment statements in context. To this end he examines at length relevant pericopes in First Thessalonians and First Corinthians.[102] He also provides an overview of "Gerichtsaussagen" in the other Pauline letters.[103] For Konradt and with regard to First Thessalonians, Paul speaks of an "andringenden Strafgericht Gottes" which descends on non-Christians (or Gentiles, or even some Jews), and he uses traditional *orgē* language to do so (187). This negative message remains in harmony with Paul's concerns in the letter such that Konradt claims: "Die angesprochenen Gerichtsaussagen zeigen sich als ein wesentliches Element im Rahmen der paraklestischen Gesamtstrategie des 1 Thess" (191).

2. More specific studies examine the "day of the Lord" motif which is prominent in 1 Thess 5:1–11.[104] My interest does not lie so much with the motif itself, of which any consideration must account for the distinctive phrases, "sons of the day" and "sons of light" (v. 5),[105] the obvious connection between the day of the Lord and *parousia* motifs, and its paraenetic function. Rather, of more relevance are the statements Paul makes in 1 Thess 5:9–10 with the exclusive categories of *orgē* and *sōtēria* (v. 9) and his ambiguous use of sleeping and waking (v. 10).[106] Whether Paul means to use the metaphor of sleeping and waking in terms of being alive or dead (cf. 4:13–18) or in terms of being alert or not (cf. 5:4–8), and how these categories relate to the status of Christians at the *parousia* of the Lord, are questions which must await the analysis of that pericope.[107]

---

[102] These include 1 Thess 1:10; 2:15–16, 19–20; 3:13; 4:1–8; 5:1–11, 23 and 1 Cor 3:5–4:5; 5:1–6:11; 8:1–11:1, 17–34; 16:22.

[103] Texts given such consideration include 2 Cor 5:1–10; Gal 5:13–6:10; Rom 1:18–5:21; 12:1–15:13.

[104] See Fransen 1957; Smitmans 1973; Plevnik 1979; Aejmelaeus 1985; Reicke 1988; Mayhue 1991; März 1992; Gempf 1994; Stanley 2002.

[105] See esp. Focant 1990.

[106] On the distinctive statement that the Lord Jesus Christ died "for us", see generally Hooker 1971; 1978; 1995, 20–46.

[107] See Edgar 1979; Howard 1985; Lautenschlager 1990; Heil 2000; see also Chapter 6.

j. Being in Christ, with Christ

The relationship between the believer (whether while living or dead) and Christ, variously described with the phrases "in Christ" and "with Christ", has been a subject of investigation for some time,[108] although there are no recent monographs.[109] The Thessalonians struggled for a social and theological identity in a context of conflict (see §IV.e above) and this is why Paul's concern is so prevalent in the letter (see §IV.f above). It is possible that Paul's in/with Christ/Lord/him statements provide a basis for understanding the Christians' identity in the early Church such that social and theological interactions are corporately defined — the phrases are ultimate expressions of participation in a new reality brought about by Christ (see Dunn 1998, 400). The crude distinction between "in Christ" as referring to the present life and "with Christ" as referring to the future life is not borne out in Paul's usage; he includes a complex mix of past, present and future references (Harvey 1992). Although the motif of being in Christ (or of participating in Christ) provides an important way into the general discussion of Paul's theology, it does not provide a comprehensive basis for understanding First Thessalonians as an early Christian letter.[110] As such, the *topos* of being in/with Christ is a peripheral but not unimportant aspect of my thesis.

k. Structure of an Early Christian Letter

1. The prominence of the debate regarding the epistolary structure of First Thessalonians is evidenced by a dominating preoccupation in the secondary literature. The discussion is taken up at length elsewhere[111] and this paragraph is intended as a very cursory introduction only. A number of scholars past and present challenge the unity and integrity of First Thessalonians. Their conclusions, which vary considerably, have a significant impact on respective overall interpretations of the letter. At this stage, attention is drawn only to Richard, "Early Pauline Thought: An Analysis of 1 Thessalonians" (1991), who argues that First Thessalonians is a compilation of two letters (2:13–4:2, where 2:14–16 is considered to be an interpolation; and 1:1–2:12 + 4:3–5:28). His subsequent commentary, *1 and 2*

[108] See esp. Schweitzer, *The Mysticism of Paul the Apostle* (1953); see also Büchsel 1949; Dupont 1952; Neugebauer 1958; 1961; Bouttier 1962; Tannehill 1967; Schweizer 1968; Siber 1971.

[109] See Wedderburn's (1985; 1986 = summary of his previous article) now dated comments regarding a perceived gap in Pauline scholarship. More recent articles include: Harvey 1992; Pelser 1998.

[110] The question of the centre of Paul's theology is not pursued here. However, as an aside, I find Schnelle's thesis, "Transformation und Partizipation als Grundgedanken paulinischer Theologie" (2001), compelling. There are some contacts between his thesis (that transformation and participation are categories which form the inner structure of Paul's thinking out of which are formulated concrete applications to different situations) and a more traditional view (that being "in Christ" is a central aspect of Paul's theology).

[111] See Chapters 2 & 4, §II.c, d.

Thessalonians (1995), contains not only a judicious exposition of First Thessalonians, but consistently interprets the letter from his previously developed compilation theory. It is one of the only commentaries to do so. However, against Richard, I argue for the unity and integrity of the letter.

2. Johanson, in *To All the Brethren: A Text-Linguistic and Rhetorical Approach to 1 Thessalonians* (1987), uses various tools of text linguistics, literary theory and both modern and ancient rhetoric to explore and understand First Thessalonians as an act of communication. Holmstrand, in *Markers and Meaning in Paul: An Analysis of 1 Thessalonians, Philippians and Galatians* (1997), examines the use of transition markers in First Thessalonians with the aim of analysing how Paul structures the letter. He uses a combination of epistolary, rhetorical and discourse or text linguistic analyses. Bickmann, in *Kommunikation gegen den Tod. Studien zur paulinischen Briefpragmatik am Beispiel des Ersten Thessalonicherbriefes* (1998), provides a thorough discussion of the epistolary structure of First Thessalonians, which she understands to be a letter of consolation ("Trostbrief"). Weima, in *Neglected Endings: The Significance of the Pauline Letter Closings* (1994), and "The Pauline Letter Closings: Analysis and Hermeneutical Significance" (1995),[112] offers important insights into the structure and function of Paul's *letter-closings*. His thesis, as well as those argued by Johanson, Holmstrand and Bickmann, are presented in the course of discussion on the epistolary form of First Thessalonians (Chapter 2).

1. Priority of Second Thessalonians?

The question of priority between the two Thessalonian letters is a critical one for the interpretation of either letter. A number of scholars have argued that Second Thessalonians was written before First Thessalonians and use this supposition as a key to understanding the Thessalonian correspondence.[113] Important in this regard is Wanamaker's commentary, *The Epistles to the Thessalonians: A Commentary on the Greek Text* (1990), because he systematically writes it with an assumption of priority for Second Thessalonians. Along with Jewett's detailed argument for the priority of First Thessalonians, Wanamaker's discussion of the issues (with argument directed at Jewett) has not been equalled.[114] The epistolary form (i.e. esp. its similarities to First Thessalonians), historical, sociological and theological references, and especially the problematic texts of 2 Thess 2:2, 2:15 and 3:17, are complex enough

[112] See also Weima's review (1999) of M. Müller (1997).

[113] See West 1914; Bristol 1944; Thompson 1945; Manson 1953; Weiss 1959, 286–291; Gregson 1966; Hurd 1968; Buck/Taylor 1969, 146–162; Thurston 1974. In more recent times, see Trudinger (1995) who does not advance the discussion but mainly follows Manson.

[114] See Jewett 1986, 26–30; Wanamaker 1990, 37–45; see also Verhoef 1997; Hughes 1999.

to rule out a superficial decision for or against Pauline authorship.[115] While I have a preliminary opinion regarding the authencity of the letter, there are still many questions to be answered. The extensive conclusions of Nicholl (2004, 183–221) go some way towards establishing the authenticity of Second Thessalonians, although many are not persuaded (including me). There is still work to be done, but not here. In the meantime, I am convinced of the priority of First Thessalonians which makes the contribution of Second Thessalonians of lesser importance for my thesis.

m. Apocalyptic

1. By "apocalyptic" I refer to the adjectival derivative of "apocalypse" which itself refers to a certain genre of literature in antiquity, and "apocalypticism" which refers to social movements associated with such literature.[116] I take the definition of J. J. Collins (1979a, 9) as essential for the ongoing critical discussions:

> "Apocalypse" is a genre of revelatory literature with a narrative framework, in which a revelation is mediated by an otherwordly being to a human recipient, disclosing a transcendent reality which is both temporal, insofar as it envisages eschatological salvation, and spatial insofar as it involves another, supernatural world.

The extention to the definition by A. Yarbro Collins (1986a, 7) should also be noted:

> ... intended to interpret present, earthly circumstances in light of the supernatural world and of the future, and to influence both the understanding and the behavior of the audience by means of divine authority.

In addition, underlying the genre with associated social movements are two broad types of apocalyptic world-views: those which express an otherworldly journey and those which do not. These two broad types may be further broken down into various categories concerning eschatological content, whether historical, cosmic/political or personal (see J. J. Collins 1979a, 13–15). These disinctions are important because only parts of apocalyptic world-views overlap with eschatology and eschatological motifs.[117]

---

[115] See Findlay 1900; Wrede 1903; von Harnack 1910; Graafen 1930; Braun 1953; Trilling 1972; 1981; Lindemann 1977; Bailey 1979; Köster 1980; 1990; Schmidt 1983a; 1990a; Collins 1988a, 209–241; 1990b; Holland 1988; 1990; Giblin 1990; Krentz 1990; Laub 1990; van Aarde 1990; Jewett 1991; Verhoef 1997; Roose 2005.

[116] On the methodological question of how to define the term, including finer distinctions between "apocalyptic", "apocalypse" and "apocalypticism", see Koch 1970; 1986; Hanson 1975; 1976; J. J. Collins 1979a; Glasson 1981; Rowland 1982; Schüssler Fiorenza 1983; Smith 1983; Boomershine 1989; Sturm 1989; Webb 1990; Aune 1993; Hellholm 1998; VanderKam 1998; Bloomquist 1999; Carey 1999; see also Thompson 1996.

[117] See also the general definition of Collins/McGinn/Stein 1998, viii.

2. The debate over whether apocalyptic or eschatology is a better category in which to understand or explain Pauline theology is beyond the scope of this study.[118] Apocalyptic imagery no doubt appears in the letter (see Blake 1925) but even 1 Thess 4:13–18 does not come under the genre of apocalypse (*contra* Hayes 1911),[119] despite the apocalyptic notions of Jesus returning from heaven and of a bodily translation (A. Yarbro Collins 1998, 595). Court picks up on a threefold structure in Mark 13 (evidenced in part by the technical terms ὠδίν, θλῖψις and τέλος) and proposes that Paul's thought may have incorporated this very apocalyptic summary in his letters (1982, 58).[120] It is possible. More important, however, is de Boer's emphasis of the present and future aspects of apocalyptic (2002, 22–23). Elias, in "'Jesus Who Delivers Us from the Wrath to Come' (1 Thess 1:10): Apocalyptic and Peace in the Thessalonian Correspondence" (1992), offers a similar emphasis, but more with a reference to the present struggles of the Thessalonians in the face of afflictions. But de Boer's conclusion, "The whole of God's eschatological saving activity in Jesus Christ, from beginning to end, is apocalyptic" (33), perhaps over-extends the use of the term "apocalyptic" in a similar way that "realised eschatology" is often over-extended as a description of the present component of eschatology proper.[121] Both terms have become so broad as to be more or less useless.

3. Certainly, apocalyptic is a significant hermeneutical key to understanding First Thessalonians primarily because apocalyptic is a conceptual part of the theology of Paul (e.g. see Beker 1982). In addition, such a key provides insight into the imagery prevalent in parts of First Thessalonians,[122] especially with regard to an emphasised near expectation,[123] and perhaps even with regard to Paul's ethical and social concerns. Thus, for example, Snyder, in "Apocalyptic and Didactic Elements in 1 Thessalonians" (1972a), sets out to examine the relationship between apocalyptic motifs and exhortations in the letter. He promotes a structure of the letter based on *disclosure* (1 Thess 1–3; 4:13–5:11) and *petition* (4:1–12; 5:12–22). Unfortunately, Snyder analyses the formal structure of the letter (which is by no means unimportant) rather than the characteristics of apocalyptic motifs and how they explicitly promote an exhortation. His treatment of 4:13–5:11 is particularly perfunctory (see 239) and his conclusions offer nothing new to interpretations of First Thessalonians which consider the apocalyptic elements it contains. Much shar-

---

118 While the literature on this question is extensive, I find the following to be more important representatives: Bultmann 1964c; Käsemann 1969; 1969a; Becker 1970a; Rollins 1971; Beker 1982; Branick 1985; de Boer 1989; Hays 2000. For a recent review of the discussion, see esp. Matlock 1996.

119 Nor is it "a little Apocalypse" (Vielhauer 1975, 86); see A. Yarbro Collins 1988. On the issue of genre, see J. J. Collins 1991; Ego 1996.

120 Cf. ὠδίν (1 Thess 5:3), θλῖψις (1 Thess 1:6; 3:3, 7) and τέλος (1 Thess 2:16).

121 See Sullivan 1988. Vawter observes the false dichotomy between so-called "realised eschatology" and Pauline apocalyptic with its strong expectation of the *parousia* (see 1963, 146–147). For an introduction to the term "realised eschatology", see Aune 1972, 1–8.

122 See for example, Klijn, "1 Thessalonians 4:13–18 and Its Background in Apocalyptic Literature" (1982).

123 See Klein 1973; Schade 1984.

per is the contribution by Wanamaker, in "Apocalypticism at Thessalonica" (1987), who develops a thesis which has certain contacts with my own. He reconstructs the Thessalonians' social context in terms of millenarianism (2–3), and finds clues for the emergence of such a social phenomenon in Paul's references to conversion, external distress and tribulation (3–5). Wanamaker identifies baptism, conversion, dichotomies of light/dark and day/night and election language as significant reinforcements of a sense of separation and new identity. In addition, he observes that the "persecution" motif and the extended *paraenesis* throughout the letter "emphasized the boundary between the old and the new social experience of the Thessalonians" and "established community and supported the new sense of social identity which distinguished the Thessalonians from outsiders" (7), respectively. While I am not convinced by Wanamaker's millenarianistic reconstruction, some of his conclusions fit well with my thesis that Paul uses eschatological motifs to promote a negative and positive pattern of exhortation in First Thessalonians.

In an entirely different vein (and methodology) is the thesis of Hester, "Apocalyptic Discourse in 1 Thessalonians" (2002), who examines the apocalyptic discourse in the letter using the analytical method of Fantasy Theme Analysis (FTA). He refers to Paul's apocalyptic discourse in First Thessalonians as an elaboration of certain fantasy themes.

> In effect he [Paul] has to remind his audience of earlier dramatizing messages and build new ones that will help them chain out new fantasies concerning their ultimate fate and what is expected of them in the meantime. By doing so he would expect to extend the power of his rhetorical vision by making it theirs (143).

Hester finds four major fantasy themes in the letter, including imitation, persecution, vindication and escape from *orgē* (143). He understands Paul's dramatising of these fantasy themes as a way of raising group consciousness not only of earlier messages received and accepted by the community but also of new messages to trigger new chaining (144–145). Further, Hester identifies a number of major sections of apocalyptic discourse: 1 Thess 1:4–10; 2:17–20; 3:12–13; 4:13–17; 5:1–10, 23. Obviously these have significant overlap with my selection of fundamental representatives of an eschatological discourse. Of course, 1 Thess 2:17–20 rather than 2:13–16 is of more significance for an apocalyptic discourse in the letter because of the reference to Satan (v. 18). I do not agree with Hester's wholesale reduction of Paul's theology and christology to "rhetorical vision" as I find it incompatible with the historical-critical approach (see §II above). However, his conclusions regarding the Thessalonians as insiders who share a rhetorical vision of a new social reality and a glorious future, are similar to my own. At one point, Hester (159) asserts:

> The morality and destiny of the insider is defined by the future and enacted in the present as they wait for the Day of the Lord. Eschatology becomes the hermeneutic that allows believers to understand history and be confident of their destiny.

This statement shows how much Hester and I are in agreement despite our different approaches to the letter. I only wish to sharpen it slightly: Paul uses eschatological motifs to provide a way for the Thessalonians not only to understand history, but to understand their own current social disintegration, and more than "be confident of their destiny", such motifs also provide a means for integration into an eschatologically identifiable existence, both in the present and future.

Watson, in "Paul's Appropriation of Apocalyptic Discourse: The Rhetorical Strategy of 1 Thessalonians" (1999), provides a very useful analysis of the apocalyptic discourse of First Thessalonians. It is perhaps more useful than Hester's because he avoids so much jargon which is far removed from Paul's own use of rhetoric. Watson (63) comments at the outset:

> It is my purpose in this chapter to demonstrate how Paul writes from his apocalyptic perspective and uses apocalyptic discourse to create a rhetorically sophisticated letter intended to meet the needs of the Thessalonian congregations in the midst of their persecution.

He sets about fulfilling this purpose by examining how Paul uses traditional beliefs and apocalyptic discourse as part of a rhetorical strategy to address the Thessalonian Christians in their distress (65). To this end, Watson examines the whole letter, which he structures in accordance with modern rhetorical approaches: *exordium* (1:2–10); *narratio* (2:1–3:10); *transition* (3:11–13); *probatio* (4:1–5:22); *peroratio* (5:23–28). Thus, in 1:2–10, Paul emphasises through antithesis – serving idols and serving God – that the Thessalonians no longer share a religious and social reality with their neighbours (66). In 2:1–3:10, Paul reviews his friendship with the Thessalonians and uses this as a basis for exhortations later in the letter (67). Watson emphasises the dualistic apocalyptic understanding of the two ages which is implied in the reference to kingdom (2:12) and also notes how Paul elicits goodwill by portraying both the Thessalonians and himself as fellow sufferers (2:13–16; see 68). Then in 2:17–3:10, Watson discerns an apocalyptic framework whereby "Satan is the chief rival and enemy of God in this age to be overthrown in the coming age" (71). In particular, he looks to Paul's use of apocalyptic references to Satan (2:18), the tempter (3:5) and a general context of eschatological tribulation, to support this framework (see 69–71). The trasition in 3:11–13, with its *parousia* reference becomes an important link between the *narratio* and *probatio*. In 4:1–5:22, Watson argues that Paul employs epideictic rhetoric to affirm and confirm the Thessalonians in their social and ethical identities (72). Thus, he looks to the warning about the Lord being an avenger (4:6) as a clear example of how apocalyptic discourse functions in the exhortations of the letter. As well, Watson notes that consolation is a major function of apocalyptic discourse (4:13–18) while a dualistic world-view provided by numerous apocalyptic antitheses (5:1–11) reinforces Paul's strategies in the letter. I find it surprising that Watson presents 4:13–18 with barely a page of text (see 73–74) while his comments on 5:1–11 are extensive in comparison (see 74–78). With regard to the latter, Watson's conclusions are similar to mine, especially with regard to the function of motifs like labour pangs, the day of the Lord and the insider/outsider boundaries developed through numerous antitheses. His interpretation of γρηγορεῖν and καθεύδειν in 5:10, however, is significantly divergent to mine.[124] Watson (79) concludes:

> ... Paul uses apocalyptic discourse as an integral part of his rhetorical strategy in 1 Thessalonians. The Thessalonians face an uncertain future as they suffer persecution from their neighbors. They await the parousia of Christ but are discouraged by doubts that those who have died will be able to experience it as well ... Paul's rhetorical strategy is to use epideictic rhetoric to confirm the Thessalonians in their newfound faith. He wants to prevent them from returning to the immorality of paganism and to bolster their faith to withstand persecution. He employs apocalyptic discourse to provide ethical warrants for their behavior and to answer their questions about the parousia.

Watson's explanation of how Paul uses apocalyptic discourse is instructive in its similarities and differences to my thesis, but there is one difference that concerns me most here. He understands apocalyptic discourse solely as a means to explain Paul's rhetorical strategy, whereas I place greater emphasis on theological, political and social constructs underlying the rhetoric of the letter. This is illustrated best by our respective analyses of 4:13–18 which are radically different. While Watson glosses over the particulars of the text, I go to great lengths to analyse and interpret the numerous eschatological motifs to be found there.[125] Furthermore, Watson goes beyond the text in his interpretation of Paul's "rhetorical strategy". He comments (63):

> He [Paul] provides them with a new symbolic universe in which the forces arrayed against them are seen in apocalyptic terms of the forces of Satan arrayed against God and God's righteous followers, the members of the Thessalonian congregation.

Yet, Watson bases this construction mainly on oblique references to Satan (2:18) and the tempter (3:5). In contrast, I describe eschatological motifs found throughout the entire letter in terms of an eschatological discourse which directly relates to historical constructions of the *ekklēsia* in Thessalonica. Thus, instead of making too much of a "new symbolic universe" which includes the manufacture of "forces of Satan arrayed against God and God's righteous followers", I prefer to construct my understanding of an eschatological discourse in First Thessalonians based on historical occasions of conversion, imitation, hindrances, conflict, deaths, and the like.

4. In conclusion, if the premise is accepted that all Pauline eschatology is apocalyptic in nature, but not all apocalyptic (or apocalypses or apocalypticism) is eschatological, then it follows that referring to an eschatological discourse rather than to an apocalyptic discourse is more precise when analysing the letters of Paul

[124] See Chapter 6, §III.b.5.
[125] See Chapter 5.

generally, and First Thessalonians specifically. This is precisely the case because there are some aspects of the apocalyptic genre that do not appear in the letter, particularly historical apocalypses, with or without an otherworldly journey. Therefore, while the contributions of Wanamaker, Hester and especially Watson have points of contact with my thesis of eschatology as a hermeneutical key for understanding Paul's pattern of exhortation in First Thessalonians, despite differences in methodological approaches I assert that referring to an eschatological discourse rather than an apocalyptic discourse serves as a more appropriate basis for understanding the contingent pecularities of the letter, particularly with relation to its structure, occasion and purposes.

V. Eschatology as a Hermeneutical Key

1. Eschatology as a hermeneutical key for understanding First Thessalonians has been a concern of several articles but surprisingly hardly any monographs. Since eschatology is the key I propose for understanding the letter, I have taken a little more space to survey the relevant articles and monographs, sometimes including substantial quotations in order to reflect accurately previous contributions. Only articles and monographs which systematically focus on eschatological motifs in First Thessalonians, rather than on 1 Thess 4:13–18, are surveyed here.[126] The discussion below is arranged chronologically.

2. Ware, in "The Coming of the Lord: Eschatology and 1 Thessalonians" (1979), emphasises the christological basis of Paul's eschatology in First Thessalonians (cf. 1:9–10; 4:14 and 5:9–10). Unfortunately he uses the majority of his article to examine 1 Thess 4:13–18 rather than develop a systematic view of Paul's *parousia* of the Lord statements as his title would suggest.[127] However, he does summarise Paul's eschatology in First Thessalonians as follows (120, emphasis omitted):

> Because of the death and resurrection of Jesus, Christians can be assured that those who die in Christ will join him in the Parousia. As they wait for the Parousia, they must live holy lives with the power provided by God himself. They can be conforted [*sic*] at the death of beloved Christian brethren knowing that both the living and the dead in Christ will share in the events of the Parousia and go to be with the Lord always. For Paul the

[126] Thus, important monographs by Harnisch, *Eschatologische Existenz. Ein exegetischer Beitrag zum Sachanliegen von 1. Thessalonicher 4,13–5,11* (1973), Jurgensen, "Saint Paul et la parousie. 1 Thessaloniciens 4.13–5.11 dans l'exégèse moderne et contemporaine" (1992, unpubl.), Mason, *The Resurrection according to Paul* (1993), and Schneider, *Vollendung des Auferstehens. Eine exegetische Untersuchung von 1 Kor 15,51–52 und 1 Thess 4,13–18* (2000), are omitted here because they focus only on one aspect of the text.

[127] Kieffer, in "L'eschatologie en 1 Thessaloniciens dans une perspective rhétorique" (1990), and Still, in "Eschatology in the Thessalonian Letters" (1999a), make the same mistake by examining 1 Thess 4:13–18 and 5:1–11 at the expense of other eschatological references in First Thessalonians. Longenecker, in "The Nature of Paul's Early Eschatology" (1985), agrees with Ware regarding the functional christology underlying Paul's use of eschatological motifs in First Thessalonians, but he seems to think that such motifs only appear in 1 Thess 4:13–18.

Parousia was an imminent hope on the horizon, which offered comfort for those in sorrow and motivation for right living for those in a pagan world.

For my purposes, Ware at least hints at the paraenetic function of the *parousia* motif in First Thessalonians, but there is so much more to be said on the topic of "eschatology and First Thessalonians".

3. In contrast, Neyrey, in "Eschatology in 1 Thessalonians: The Theological Factor in 1:9–10; 2:4–5; 3:11–13; 4:6 and 4:13–18" (1980), argues that an emphasis on christological and apocalyptic aspects of eschatology in First Thessalonians has caused a neglect of other important elements in the letter. In particular, Neyrey argues that 1 Thess 1:9–10, 2:4–5, 3:11–13 and 4:6 contain a strong theological component arising out of traditions of early missionary preaching. Thus, a theological focus needs to be reasserted in order for a proper expression of all the eschatological elements in First Thessalonians. Neyrey concludes that divine judgment is theologically oriented, not christologically so, and that Jesus Christ as recipient of God's saving action is the deliverer from *orgē*. Even in 1 Thess 4:13–18 with its strong christological and apocalyptic focus on the *parousia* of the Lord, the theological elements of Paul's eschatology are clear: God raises the dead; God leads them (226). For Neyrey, Paul's eschatology in First Thessalonians and in general (he gives a brief consideration of Paul's other letters) is theologically oriented and arises from Jewish and Christian missionary preaching, not from statements about the *parousia* of the Lord in Synoptic traditions. He concludes: "... the eschatology of 1 Thess and indeed of all of Paul's letters, contains a strong, even a dominant theological component: God knows, tests hearts, raises the dead, and judges" (229).

Neyrey's thesis offers a corrective regarding the theological component of the eschatology in First Thessalonians, but he does so at the expense of examining many of the eschatological motifs employed by Paul. Clearly, the texts for analysis are chosen on the basis of overt references to God, not because they contain significant eschatological motifs. As a result, Neyrey neglects important texts like 1 Thess 2:13–16 and 5:1–11, and the *parousia* references in 1 Thess 2:19 and 5:23. Alas, a systematic discussion of eschatology in First Thessalonians is not to be found here.

4. Koester, in "Imperial Ideology and Paul's Eschatology in 1 Thessalonians" (1997), makes an important contribution to the discussion because he interprets the letter in terms of one of its most important themes (*parousia*) but in such a way as to de-emphasise exegetical contributions which focus on one text or another. Rather, Koester observes that, "*Parousia* always occurs in contexts in which the preparedness of the entire community is in view" (159), and he uses imperial ideology as a foil, so to speak, for his understanding of Paul's message and aim in the letter. Thus, he interprets ἀπάντησις (4:17) and the slogan εἰρήνη καὶ ἀσφάλεια (5:3) according to political connotations (160) and imperial Roman propaganda (161–162), respectively. In the second half of his article, and on the basis that the day of the Lord is an "event that will shatter the false peace and security of the

Roman establishment" (162), Koester offers an analysis of 1 Thess 5:1–11 which emphasises a unity of the Christian community. He observes (163):

> In faith, love, and hope, the "day" becomes a reality in the life of the community. "The children of the day" or "the children of light," in their "work of faith, labor of love, and patience of hope" (1 Thess. 1:3), are the architects of the new eschatological community in which the future is becoming a present reality.

My conclusions are similar although I place more emphasis on Paul and his role as "architect" of a new eschatological identity for the Jesus-followers in Thessalonica, rather than on the role played by community members. Nevertheless, I am in complete agreement with Koester's conclusion that "Paul envisions a role for the eschatological community that presents a utopian alternative to the prevailing eschatological ideology of Rome" (166).

5. Although Khiok-Khng, in "A Political Reading of Paul's Eschatology in I and II Thessalonians" (1998), uses the evidence of Acts in a non-judicious manner and assumes the authenticity of Second Thessalonians without so much as a hint to the debate, he rightly emphasises the politically loaded nature of Paul's eschatological *kērgyma*. Khiok-Khng argues that the political setting of Thessalonica, which is strongly influenced by Roman benefaction, made Paul's *kērgyma* especially appealing since his statements supported a dissatisfaction with the existing social order (83). The conflict language in First Thessalonians is clearly more than social alienation associated with conversion: "Paul's message of imminent *parousia*, the Lordship of Christ, the grace and benefaction of Jesus posed an obvious challenge and threat to the *pax Romana* and the Benefaction Roma [*sic*]" (79). Paul's employment of politically loaded terms (e.g. παρουσία, ἀπάντησις, κύριος, εὐαγγέλιον) makes it natural "to assume that the Pauline theology and gospel in 1 Thessalonians is intentionally expressed as a critique to the ideology of the imperial cult" (83). Khiok-Khng concludes (86):

> The Pauline apocalyptic ethos is to sustain the constant critique of the social and political injustices on behalf of the powerless, a critique of the complacency and comfort for discovery of greater truth. Ultimately, apocalyptic thought seeks to actualize human existence both by its constant critique by the divine word and by drawing it into openness to the possibilities of the future.

This conclusion is somewhat unsatisfactory because it is not comprehensive enough. There is no mention of many eschatological motifs in the letter, including resurrection, judgment, deliverance/salvation and being "in Christ", to name a few. However, the thesis that Paul consciously formulates these motifs in opposition to imperial ideology is sustained by the text — although Koester's elaboration is far more elegant than Khiok-Khng's. I seek to complement the work of Koester and Khiok-Khng by developing a more comprehensive and systematic statement of Paul's use of eschatological motifs in First Thessalonians which includes the significant political context of the *ekklēsia* in Thessalonica.

6. Selby, in "'Blameless at His Coming': The Discursive Construction of Eschatological Reality in 1 Thessalonians" (1999), provides a detailed systematic rhetorical analysis of Paul's eschatological discourse in First Thessalonians. His article is one of the best contributions to the discussion to date, albeit using a different methodological approach to mine. As a result, it is instructive to examine his investigations and conclusions in detail. His statement of intent is as follows (386–387):

> In this essay I shall explore Paul's eschatological discourse in 1 Thessalonians, focusing on that discourse as a response to the competing demands of a rhetorical situation which called for him to console his readers in the face of their experiences of opposition and loss, while at the same time warning them of the dire consequences of ignoring the ethical requirements of their Christian faith. Specifically I shall argue that Paul employs this language in an effort to encourage his audience to see themselves as the elect of God, living in the end-time and awaiting the sudden and unexpected Parousia of Christ — a self-identification which explains their present misfortune while also demanding that they diligently prepare themselves for the Parousia through holy living. Through this analysis I hope to shed light on the assumptions and processes with which Paul crafted persuasive discourse.
>
> At the same time this essay will explore more broadly the role this visionary language played in the formation of Christianity as a social movement, arguing that it provided much more than simply a commonplace to be exploited for rhetorical embellishment. To the contrary, it formed a central, dramatic narrative which discursively constructed reality for the adherents of the early Christian movement, offering them a structure of meaning which shaped their identity and framed their experience of the world.

Selby then outlines the rhetorical situation of First Thessalonians. He asserts that Timothy's return is the specific event precipitating the writing of the letter, an event which must be understood in terms of the historical clues to violence and opposition. The rhetorical situation includes Paul's reponse, to a community suffering persecution, to the death of some community members, and to a community which felt abandoned by Paul (389–391). Consequently, Selby (392) argues that,

> Paul faces a rhetorical dilemma — how to console, encourage and reassure, while also exhorting and warning. As a critical element in his response to these competing demands Paul draws upon a body of eschatological language and imagery which was current in the early Christian church.

Unlike most examinations of eschatology in First Thessalonians, Selby takes into account many of the eschatological references in the letter. He identifies 1 Thess 1:10, 2:12, 16, 19, 3:13 and 5:23 as six brief passages which appear as deliberate thematic discourse markers with rhetorical significance. These passages appear to remind the audience of what they already know, and Paul does not convey new or unknown material here (396–397). In addition, Paul carefully structures First Thessalonians (398):

> Each major section and sub-section culminates in an eschatological pronouncement so that a strongly eschatological tone pervades the entire epistle. By using visionary language in this way Paul evokes a perspective from which the Thessalonians are invited to see themselves and their circumstances. They are living near the end of time and awaiting the imminent return of Christ, the resurrection of the dead, the judgment before God, and the final reward and punishment which will be meted out at that judgment.

Selby goes on to discuss at some length two major eschatological sections (1 Thess 4:13–18 and 5:1–11). He rightly emphasises the contingent nature of Paul's eschatology and compares 4:13–18 with 1 Cor 15:50–58 to illustrate his point (401–402). Against those who implicitly or explicitly champion 1 Thess 4:13–18 as the primary occasion of the letter, Selby notes that it is situated amongst repeated exhortations to right living including moral purity (4:1–8), brotherly love (4:9–12) and sobriety and watchfulness (5:1–11). He concludes: "By situating his vision of the end in the midst of these exhortations, Paul intended not only to assuage the Thessalonians' grief but, much more, to support and reinforce the imperative of holy living" (403). The primary intent of 1 Thess 5:1–11, then, is to further support Paul's exhortations, and he does this within the parameter of answering questions raised by the Thessalonians (405).

For Selby, Paul's eschatology is a "discursively constructed reality" (387) which has a certain rhetorical effect on his audience. Insights of rhetorical approaches like those gained by Selby are important. However, I suspect that Paul would have accepted a greater correlation between the eschatological discourse of First Thessalonians and the present and future circumstances of the *ekklēsia* in Thessalonica. Selby does give a disclaimer towards the end of his article with regard to Paul's ability to construct a rhetorical discourse: "This in no way implies that Paul did not fully believe the content of his own eschatological discourse. In fact there is every reason to believe that he did ..." (407). But in the same footnote, he goes on to say: "Paul's use of this language in 1 Thessalonians is still strategic, representing a rhetorical choice from among a range of 'available means of persuasion'" (408). Further, in his conclusion he refers to the "world" of eschatological discourse into which the Thessalonians, if they are persuaded, may enter (see 409). Selby's approach emphasises too much the rhetorical situation of the letter and too little the historical, social, theological and philosophical realities of Paul and the Thessalonian community which may be constructed (more or less successfully) out of that rhetorical situation.[128]

[128] Although not on the topic of eschatology, Simpson, in "Shaped by the Stories: Narrative in 1 Thessalonians" (1998), approaches First Thessalonians in a similar way to Selby. Simpson also refers to Paul's "discursive contructions" of reality. But he prefers to analyse Paul's theology in the letter as a "kerygmatic narrative" with a construction and reconstruction of past, present and future realities. Ultimately, Paul shapes the memories of the Thessalonians such that: "The members of the congregation are thus given a home (a metaphor similar in meaning to 'narrative world') so that they will feel no need to wander off looking for some other settling-place or to return to a familiar former residence. Their experiences and those of the missionaries are set within an all-encompassing context and thus made comprehensible and tolerable" (22). Keightley, in "The Church's Memory of Jesus: A Social Science Analysis of 1 Thessalonians" (1987), reaches an analogous conclusion.

However, despite our different methodological approaches, there is much in Selby's explorations with which I agree. Just as he understands Paul's eschatological discourse as a response to conflict and a warning to follow ethical requirements, I understand the same discourse as explaining current social disintegration and offering a means of integration into an eschatological identifiable existence — an existence which includes significant imperative demands. Selby refers to necessary preparations for the coming *parousia* through holy living. I expand this connection extensively in my analysis of *parousia* in First Thessalonians,[129] and even include other eschatological motifs as part of the indicative/imperative paradigm. He refers to a discursively constructed reality which helps shape the Thessalonians' identity, whereas I develop a thesis that Paul's pattern of exhortation reinforces solidarity and eschatological existence. Above all, Selby interprets Paul's use of eschatological language and imagery as a means for consoling, encouraging as well as exhorting and warning. I concur with this interpretation, and seek to buttress its foundation on the basis of extensive exegetical analysis of First Thessalonians.

7. Finally and most recently, Nicholl, in *From Hope to Despair in Thessalonica: Situating 1 and 2 Thessalonians* (2004), attempts to situate both letters according to a plausible course of development with a special interest in the eschatological problems assumed by the letters (3). Nicoll's agenda is clear from the outset; he is most interested in explaining Second Thessalonians as an authentic letter of Paul and he examines First Thessalonians mainly to serve this interest. Thus, the introduction is taken up almost entirely with the problem of Second Thessalonians (see 3–16), as is the conclusion (see 183–221). He also provides a lengthy appendix on 2 Thess 2:6–7 regarding the identity of the restrainer (ὁ κατέχων, τὸ κατέχον). In the first instance, Nicoll (wrongly I think) presupposes that a reconstruction of the eschatological dimension of the situation of First Thessalonians may be obtained by focusing on 1 Thess 4:13–18. His assessment of that pericope contributes nothing new to the discussion. The assertions (48), that the Thessalonians did not know about the resurrection of the dead,[130] that they did not expect deaths in the community,[131] that they thought the deceased would suffer an absolute disadvantage,[132] and that such confusion would have been potentially faith threatening,[133] are all previously well argued (though very much in dispute).[134] In the second instance, Nicoll does examine the remainder of First Thessalonians, looking for specific features which confirm his hypothesis regarding the eschatological situation. To that end, he provides exegetical comments on 1 Thess 1:10, 2:12, 3:6, 10, 5:14 and 5:24, specifically, and more general comments on the rest of the letter (see 85–111). He concludes that First Thessalonians reveals

[129] See Chapter 5, §III.c.3.

[130] See Marxsen 1969, et al.

[131] See Gundry 1987; Holtz 1998, 195–196; Still 1999a.

[132] See Hyldahl 1980; Plevnik 1975a, et al.

[133] See Marxsen 1969; Hyldahl 1980; Jewett 1986; Otto 1997; Ascough 2004.

[134] See Excursus 5.

a neophyte community moving from hope to hopeless grieving and nervous dread. Further, he makes three points (111) which may be summarised as follows: (1) as part of accepting the gospel, the Thessalonians accepted an eschatological hope which focused on the *parousia* and did not include a hope of resurrection; (2) when some members died the Thessalonians became hopeless because they were ignorant of the resurrection of dead saints; (3) the deaths were interpreted as a sign of divine disfavour and the Thessalonians were filled with fear and anxiety. Finally (112):

> We conclude that the unexpected passing away of community members is the primary exigency of 1 Thessalonians, filling the survivors with despair both for their dead and for themselves. We suggest that 1 Thessalonians was written to address Gentile neophytes who, with regard to eschatological expectation, were not joyfully excited or enthusiastic, but, on the contrary, were lacking in hope and indeed anxious, insecure and fearful.

I disagree with Nicoll on numerous exegetical points as will become clear in the chapters to follow.

VI. Conclusion

In this introduction I have sought to formulate a thesis regarding eschatology as a hermeneutical key for understanding First Thessalonians. I have referred to the eschatological discourse of the letter which includes Paul's use of eschatological motifs in a pattern of exhortation. This pattern provides a complimentary way of understanding the Thessalonians' current social disintegration and a means for community identity and existence. I have shown how pervasive are the eschatological motifs throughout and set the groundwork not only for a detailed epistolary analysis of the letter but also for exegetical treatments of various pericopes deemed to be fundamental representatives of the eschatological discourse. In addition, I have introduced the reader to the contents of First Thessalonians and oriented my thesis in relation to the secondary literature. Perhaps most important, I have critically analysed other topics or "keys" used by scholars to interpret the letter, including the theme of apocalyptic. I have no doubt that the themes of apocalyptic and eschatology are the most relevant for an interpretation of First Thessalonians. But neither is their a consensus on Pauline apocalyptic or eschatology, nor is there more than a smattering of articles and isolated monographs in the secondary literature. As such, there remains a need for a more comprehensive approach to the eschatology of First Thessalonians. I attempt to fill this need.

Chapter 2
An Epistolary Analysis of First Thessalonians

In this chapter I offer an epistolary structure of First Thessalonians which results from a combination of epistolary and rhetorical analyses. Cooperation between the approaches not only promotes a consensus for the structure of the letter, but also allows the interpreter more fully to explore the relationship between form and function in letter writing. I propose therefore to examine First Thessalonians as a cohesive act of communication, and show how each pericope is related, and more to the point, how Paul uses eschatological motifs throughout First Thessalonians as an integral part of his pattern of exhortation. The epistolary structure of the letter shows that 1 Thess 1:9–10, 1 Thess 2:13–16, 1 Thess 4:13–18 and 1 Thess 5:1–11 are not isolated texts — indeed, the eschatological motifs employed are misunderstood when interpreted individually. Rather, by emphasising the systematic characteristics of the text, the usefulness of eschatology as a hermeneutical key becomes increasingly evident. Along the way, this chapter also provides an epistolary structure of First Thessalonians which demonstrates the letter's conformity to the norms of letter writing in the first century as well as the freedom Paul exercised in his communication.

I. Setting the Scene

1. The epistolary structure of First Thessalonians remains a *crux* in Pauline scholarship. There are at least two reasons for this. On the one hand, there is little consensus regarding the legitimacy and usefulness of epistolary analysis in view of newer rhetorical approaches. As a result there is some confusion (at a methodological level) over issues of interpretation which are specifically tied to decisions regarding the structure of the letter. On the other hand, some of those issues of interpretation are particularly difficult to resolve and therefore lead to a plethora of viewpoints. For example, the excessive length and form of the *letter-thanksgiving* which have been a focal point in the discussion since Schubert's monograph (1939) are still not adequately explained.[1] Plus, the inability for many scholars to recognise the rhetorical function of the vitriolic and even vituperative statements against

[1] This is illustrated by the fact that scholars are unable to agree on where the *letter-thanksgiving* concludes and the "*letter-body*" begins; see Mullins 1965; Sanders 1962; White 1971, 1972. Specific articles

οἱ Ἰουδαῖοι in 2:13–16 has long contributed to excessive attention paid to an interpolation charge for that pericope, as well as to a charge of Pauline anti-Semitism.[2] Accordingly, there is little agreement on the epistolary structure of 1 Thess 1–3. Another example which illustrates the influence of epistolary structure for interpretation involves the form and function of the *letter-paraenesis*. If parts of 1 Thess 4–5 are identified as examples of the *topos* form then this has significant implications for contingency — i.e. has Paul shaped the *paraenesis* according to the situation in Thessalonica or has he used generic forms independent of that situation?[3] Furthermore, the (in)significance of the περί (δέ) formula (4:9, 13; 5:1; cf. 1 Cor 7:1) has played a role in some attempts to establish the existence of a letter from the Thessalonians to Paul.[4]

2. The unresolved status of such fundamental questions for the interpretation of First Thessalonians serves as an indication of a deeper problem — the problem of how to express the epistolary structure of the letter. There is a need to grapple with the structure of First Thessalonians until some measure of consensus is reached before attempting to resolve those fundamental questions. Otherwise scholarly views on the *letter-thanksgiving*, interpolation theories, Pauline anti-Semitism, contingency, the possible exchange of letters and the like, will continue to multiply *ad infinitum*. But resolving structural difficulties in the letter is only an important by-product of this chapter. The epistolary structure I propose (see §VII below) reveals the rhetorical significance of eschatological motifs *in virtually every epistolary section* of First Thessalonians. This conclusion is of consequence for it offers tangible evidence that my thesis is correct. Therefore, it is worthwhile taking the time to revisit problematic aspects of the text in order to show how Paul develops a pattern of exhortation within the epistolary structure of the letter. For the moment, the authenticity and integrity of the letter are assumed.

---

on the Pauline *letter-thanksgiving* include: Arzt 1994; Lambrecht 1990; O'Brien 1975, 1977, 1980; Palmer 1981; Reed 1996.

[2] There is an astonishing number of articles which focus on interpolation hypotheses and allegations of Pauline anti-Semitism in 2:13–16. On the first issue, for *Forschungsgeschichten*, see Collins 1979a, 67–106; Schlueter 1994, 13–38; for specific articles see Baarda 1985; Bohlen 1987, 1989; Broer 1990; Pearson 1971; Schmidt 1983; Weatherly 1991; see also Johanson 1995; Schippers 1966; Simpson 1988, 1990. On the alleged anti-Semitic (or more correctly, anti-Jewish) nature of 2:13–16, see Broer 1983, 1991; Coppens 1975; Donfried 1984; Geiger 1986; Gilliard 1989, 1994; Holtz 1989; Hurd 1986; Kampling 1993; Michel 1967; Okeke 1981; Stegemann 1990; Verhoef 1995; Wick 1994; Wortham 1995.

[3] For discussion of the form and function of *topoi*, see §VI below.

[4] For a detailed analysis of the περί (δέ) formula in Paul, see Baasland 1988. On the question of whether the Thessalonians wrote to Paul, see Faw 1952; Harris 1898; Malherbe 1990 (discussed in §VI below).

II. Letter-Opening and Closing

1. There is near unanimity regarding the *letter-opening* at 1:1.[5] It contains a superscription (sender), an adscription (recipient/addressee) and a formulaic wish of grace and peace (but no *intitulatio*; Schnider/Stenger 1987, 4–7).[6] Lieu devotes an article to the distinctive Pauline greeting, χάρις ὑμῖν καὶ εἰρήνη, and notes that its form differs from ancient literary conventions of greeting (1986, 178). Although Paul does not present himself as an apostle in the superscription of First Thessalonians, this does not necessarily mean that he did not consider himself an apostle at the time (White 1982, 8).[7] Although with diminished unanimity, the *letter-closing* is defined as 5:23–28[8] or just 5:25–28.[9] Weima (1994, 77–155) provides a definitive analysis of Pauline *letter-closings* and proposes the following typical form: (1) peace benediction (v. 23 with a word of encouragement in v. 24);[10] (2) hortatory section (v. 25); (3) greetings, including a kiss greeting (v. 26; a second-person type; see Mullins 1968, 426) and an autograph (v. 27); (4) grace benediction (v. 28). Jervis (1991, 132–157) and Murphy-O'Connor (1995, 98–113) also provide detailed discussions of Pauline *letter-closings*. Jervis' conclusions are similar to Weima's except she includes verse 27 as part of the hortatory unit (1991, 140–141) and also identifies a fifth element which she calls "a unit that rejoices, using the word χαίρω", common in Pauline *closings* but not present in First Thessalonians (132). With Weima, Murphy-O'Connor finds the same four elements of the *letter-closing*, although he comments that the hortatory section (which Murphy-O'Connor puts first) is amorphous and therefore least susceptible to epistolary analysis (1995, 99).[11]

---

[5] The only apparent exception is Patte who includes v. 2 as well (1983, 128–129).

[6] See Aune 1987, 184–186; Doty 1973, 29–31; Jervis 1991, 69–85; Mullins 1977, 60; Murphy-O'Connor 1995, 45–55; Roetzel 1991, 60–63; Schnider/Stenger 1987, 3–41; White 1984, 1740–1741.

[7] Cf. Rom 1:1; 1 & 2 Cor 1:1; Gal 1:1; cf. also Eph 1:1; Col 1:1; 1 & 2 Tim 1:1; Titus 1:1.

[8] Besides referring to Jewett's charts (1986, 216–220), see Aune 1987, 206; Boers 1976, 142; Collins 2000, 324, 333–334; Doty 1973, 43; Green 2002, 76; Harvey 1998, 261; Havener 1983, 10; Hughes 1990, 116; Lenski 1937, 363; Malherbe 2000, 78–79; P.-G. Müller 2001, 47; Neil 1957, 119; Patte 1983, 128–131; Roetzel 1991, 71; Smith 1995, 67; 2000, 692; Snyder 1972, 235; Thomas 1978, 236; Wuellner 1990, 134–135.

[9] Again, see Jewett 1986, 216–220 (n.b. Bruce [1982, 133–136] is misrepresented — he designates 5:25–28 as the *letter-closing*, not 5:23–28 as indicated by Jewett) and Alford 1958, 282–283; Bickmann 1998, 151–155; Collins 1993, 114–123; Findlay 1891, 38; 1904, lxx–lxxi; Haufe 1999, 7; Hester 1996, 271; Holtz 1998, 32; Johanson 1987, 65–67; Lambrecht 2000, 165; Lee/Lee 1975, 29–30; Légasse 1999, 339; Longenecker 1974, 292; Malbon 1983, 66; M. Müller 1997, 113; Oepke 1970, 159; Olbricht 1990, 235; Reinmuth 1998, 155–156; Ryrie 1959, 17–20; Selby 1999, 394; Staab 1965, 45–46; Vanhoye 1990, 77; von Dobschütz 1909, 27–28; *contra* Schnider/Stenger who conclude that the *Briefschluß* begins at 5:12 (1987, 69–167).

[10] For further discussion on benediction as a NT form, see Champion 1934; Gamble 1977, 67–73; Jewett 1969; Mullins 1977; Wiles 1974. Commenting on a theological level, Bassler expects to find a *petition* to the "God of holiness" (5:23) in view of the significant number of references to holiness and sanctification in the letter. However, she shows that "peace" and "holiness" are not unrelated (1991a, 82–84).

[11] The strong adjuration, though a singular occurrence among Paul's *letter-closings*, comes as no surprise to Collins who emphasises Paul's freedom as a Hellenistic letter writer (1984, 366). For further analysis

2. The peace benediction is interesting because it appears in the disputed 1 Thess 5:23–24 section. Although its form is not as fixed as the grace benediction, Weima shows that it is consistent across the authentic Pauline *letter-closings* except for First Corinthians and Philemon (87, 89).[12] This has already been established by Gamble (1977, 67–68) and followed by Murphy-O'Connor (1995, 109–110). Gamble gives a short but detailed analysis of the constituent parts of the peace benediction and also compares its form with other wish prayers (1977, 68–69).[13] Although the wish prayer (3:11–13) and the peace benediction (5:23–24) have a similar concluding function (Jewett 1969, 24) it does not follow that the peace benediction constitutes the closing of the *main part* of the letter (Weima 1994, 174–175).[14] Rather, the form is part of the *letter-closing*, which becomes an adumbration of the *letter-thanksgiving*: τὴν ἐκλογήν (1:4)/ὁ καλῶν (5:24); πνεῦμα (1:5, 6; 5:23); ἀναμένειν (1:10)/παρουσία (5:23).[15] In addition, Paul uses the peace benediction to replace the customary health wish or word of farewell (Roetzel 1991, 67).

3. The division in scholarship regarding the formal relationship of 1 Thess 5:23–24 within the structure of the letter stems from a failure to distinguish between its (epistolary) form and its (rhetorical) function. In terms of form, the peace benediction belongs to the *letter-closing* (*contra* M. Müller 1997; rightly, Weima 1994).[16] In terms of function, it summarises and concludes the *main part* of the letter as a whole (interestingly, *both* M. Müller and Weima; *contra* McDonald/Porter 2000, 385–386). This is illustrated by the explicit links to themes expressed throughout First Thessalonians including sanctification, *parousia* and a concern about the fate of believers who have died before the Lord comes.[17] The demarcation between the *letter-paraenesis* and the *letter-closing* is established by a strict adherence to epistolary analysis *and* by keeping an eye open to the rhetorical function of various components. Most important, this conclusion draws attention to the eschatological motifs in the *letter-closing*, which highlights the importance of such motifs in the overall rhetoric of First Thessalonians.

---

of *letter-closings* in Hellenistic and Pauline letters, with special emphasis on the problems associated with Rom 16, see Gamble 1977, 57–95.

[12] Cf. Rom 15:33; 16:20; 2 Cor 13:11; Gal 6:16; Phil 4:9; cf. also 2 Thess 3:16; Eph 6:23.

[13] For example, Rom 15:5–6, 13; Phil 4:19; 1 Thess 3:11–13; cf. 2 Thess 2:16–17; 3:5; Heb 13:20–21; 1 Pet 5:10; *Barn.* 21.5.

[14] So also Jervis 1991, 134; *contra* Holmstrand 1997, 68; Jewett 1969, 24; Langevin 1990, 237; M. Müller 1997, 112–124; White 1999, 66–71; Wiles 1974, 63–64.

[15] See Cuming 1976, 110–111; Jervis 1991, 140; Murphy-O'Connor 1995, 109–110; Roetzel 1991, 67; Weima 1999, 349–350. See esp. Weima 1995, where he focuses solely on the peace benediction in 1 Thess 5:23–24 and Gal 6:16; *contra* M. Müller 1997, 112–124; White 1993, 151. White recognises the adumbration even though he does not think the peace benediction is part of the *letter-closing* (1999, 71).

[16] Evidently Weima's monograph is sufficiently convincing to change Collins' mind regarding the end of the letter (cf. Collins 1993, 114–123 and 2000, 324, 333–334).

[17] Collins 2000, 334; Roetzel 1991, 68; Weima 1994, 94–95.

Excursus 1
Multiple Authors in Antiquity

1. The debate about multiple authors in antiquity – and whether and how much Silvanus and Timothy took part in the writing of First Thessalonians – is considerably discordant. The discussion is highly relevant to the exegesis of many pericopes notwithstanding those I have chosen to examine. The problem rises initially from the opening of the letter, Παῦλος καὶ Σιλουανὸς καὶ Τιμόθεος τῇ ἐκκλησίᾳ Θεσσαλονικέων ... (1:1), and secondarily from numerous references to first person plural verb forms and pronouns. It is further complicated by the presence of several instances of the first person singular (2:18; 3:5; 5:27). An examination of Paul's letters reveals that he often uses a scribe when writing (§2). The question is still unresolved whether plural verbs and pronouns in Paul's letters refer to multiple authors or just to Paul. An examination of three instances of the first person singular reveals that First Thessalonians is most likely a co-authored text (§3).

2. Besides the initial reference, and the presence of plural verb forms and pronouns in First Thessalonians, Paul refers explicitly to his co-workers in 1 Thess 2:7 (ὡς Χριστοῦ ἀπόστολοι), 3:2 (καὶ ἐπέμψαμεν Τιμόθεον) and 3:6 (Ἄρτι δὲ ἐλθόντος Τιμοθέου πρὸς ἡμᾶς ἀφ' ὑμῶν).[18] It is, *prima facie*, possible that Silvanus and Timothy were both involved in the writing of First Thessalonians since there is ample evidence to demonstrate not only that secretaries were used in antiquity for letter writing (Bahr 1966; Richards 1991), but also that Paul used them.[19] For example, there is an explicit reference to a secretary in Rom 16:22 (ἀσπάζομαι ὑμᾶς ἐγὼ Τέρτιος ὁ γράψας τὴν ἐπιστολὴν ἐν κυρίῳ).[20] As well, on several occasions Paul draws attention to a change in handwriting (1 Cor 16:21; Gal 6:11; Phlm 19; cf. Col 4:18; 2 Thess 3:17) which indicates the presence of a secretary (Murphy-O'Connor 1995, 7). Regarding First Thessalonians, which contains no "explicit evidence" (Richards 1991, 169), Richards argues that 1 Thess 5:27–28 may be a postscript[21] (i.e. because of the abrupt change to the first person singular), possibly indicating the use of a scribe (179; so also Collins 2000, 329). If Paul did use a scribe, the scribe's identity remains unknown.[22] Likewise, it is difficult if not impossible to determine how Paul's scribe functioned (Richards 1991, 194–198), whether as a recorder, editor or substitute author (Murphy-O'Connor 1995, 8–16). The reticence of some commentators to acknowledge any substantial role in authorship to anyone other than Paul[23] may be explained as an avoidance of the difficulties of interpretation which are inherent in a co-authored text (Ellis 2000a, 311–312). If there is an underlying ideological (or theological) agenda regarding a need to keep Paul as the sole author or at least as the main author of his

[18] For a table with all references in Paul's letters to his co-workers, see Ellis 1993, 184.

[19] For the theory that Silvanus (= Silas) and Timothy wrote First Thessalonians, see already Scott 1909, 215–233. On the question of the identification of Silvanus as Silas, see Schneider 1993.

[20] For discussion of the Tertius reference, see Richards 1991, 169–172.

[21] *Contra* Bahr 1968, 36, who argues that Paul began writing from 1 Thess 4:1.

[22] Murphy-O'Connor suggests that in the early days: "Paul may have had to rely on strangers for the transmission of 1 and 2 Thessalonians" (1995, 40). Binder's comment regarding Silvanus, "Vielleicht war er der Schreiber" (1990, 88), must remain conjecture. The idea that Silvanus was the author of First Thessalonians, on the basis of similarities between the letter and First Peter (and assuming that the reference to Silvanus in 1 Pet 5:12 indicates that he wrote that letter and is the same Silvanus as Paul knows), is rejected (*contra* Selwyn 1947, 365–466) on the grounds that there are other, more plausible reasons for the similarities (Best 1972, 23–25).

[23] So, for example, Best 1972, 28; Brown 1997, 462; Bruce 1980, 329; Simpson 1993, 932.

letters, it is not part of my preunderstanding. Another aspect of the discussion (which is not pursued here) is the use of couriers (see insightful observations by Llewelyn 1994; Murphy-O'Connor 1995, 37–41).

3. It is not my intent to provide a comprehensive discussion of the changes of person and number in verb forms and pronouns in Paul's letters.[24] Rather, it is to explain, as far as is possible, how first person plural verbs and pronouns are used in First Thessalonians. According to Llewelyn, First Thessalonians is distinctive among Paul's letters in that it shows the highest percentage of first person plural pronouns and verb forms (96.7%) when compared to all first person singular and plural pronouns and verbs in the letter (1992, 171; see also Rigaux 1956, 77–78).[25] Like First Thessalonians, Paul's other letters contain more than one person in the opening greeting (Paul and Timothy in Second Corinthians, Philippians and Philemon; Paul and Sosthenes in First Corinthians; "the brothers" in Galatians) except for Romans where only Paul's name is mentioned. Thus, apart from Romans, it must be left open (*contra* BDF 146–147, §280) whether the plural forms refer to Paul and his associates so named in the opening greeting (i.e. a "genuine" plural; so Best 1972, 26–29), whether they refer to Paul (and/or his associates) and his readers (Llewelyn 1992, 170), or whether they refer to just Paul himself (i.e. a "literary" plural; Cranfield 1982, 285).[26] These distinctions cannot be resolved systematically, and the argument for the literary plural in Paul is as difficult to prove as it is to reject (see Dick 1900). Each occurrence, for its determination, must be understood in context.[27] In First Thessalonians this is certainly the case (Collins 1984, 178–180), despite Malherbe's claim that the plural is "characteristic of paraenesis" (2000, 88–89). If nothing more, the plurals "refer to the co-signatories as fellow missionaries in the Thessalonian mission" (Dickson 2003, 91).

Most instructive are the three pericopes where there is an interjection of the first person singular. In 1 Thess 2:17–20 appears the forceful ἐγὼ μὲν Παῦλος (v. 18) in the midst of plural forms which clearly refer to Paul, Silvanus and Timothy. It is not necessary to interpret a literary plural here (*contra* Cranfield 1982, 286; *GGNT* 407), as the highly personal nature of the interjection (n.b. the intrusion of Paul's name) is a satisfactory explanation for the singular formulation (Askwith 1911a, 154–157). Similarly, in 1 Thess 3:1–5, Paul's personal interest interrupts the co-authored text. The reference to being alone (μόνοι, v. 1) suggests that Paul may be using a literary plural to open the pericope (Bruce 1970, 1158). Collins' (1984, 179) suggestion that Paul is referring to being "lonely" is possible but goes against the normal use of the adjective (see BDAG s.v.; Fitzmyer 1991, 440). The argument that anything other than a literary plural is required in 3:2 (καὶ ἐπέμψαμεν Τιμόθεον) is rejected out of common sense, whereby "it is perfectly feasible for a group to dispatch one of its members on a mission, as university faculties and parliaments demonstrate with great regularity" (Murphy-O'Connor 1995, 20). But in 3:4, the first person plural clearly indicates co-authorship because of the reference to the founding mission. Finally, in 1 Thess 5:27 the intrusion of the first person singular, signifying the subscription of a letter scribed by another is further evidence that First Thessalonians has a corporate authorship. But the precise formulation of that co-authorship is

[24] For an introduction, see Askwith 1911a; Cranfield 1982; Lofthouse 1955; Stauffer 1964a; see esp. Byrskog 1996; Murphy-O'Connor 1995, 16–33.

[25] For a table of the frequency of first person verbs and pronouns in Paul's letters, see Llewelyn 1992, 171.

[26] The various nuances of the plural are carefully delineated in *GGBB* 393–394.

[27] *GGBB* 393–399; *GGNT* 406–407; *GNTG*, vol 1, 86–87; Moule 1959, 118–119.

unknown. Green refers to an authorial community including an author/scribe and messenger (2002, 58). It is possible that Paul consulted his companions and gave a dictation (Murphy-O'Connor 1995, 33), or he may well have been more dependent on his co-authors for writing First Thessalonians because of its early date in Paul's mission work (33; so also Haufe 1999, 3). While I refer to Paul as the author of First Thessalonians, this designation is a matter of convenience only and should be understood in terms of this discussion. Likewise, when I refer to "Paul's pattern of exhortation", this is also a matter of convenience. The text of First Thessalonians is generally co-authored.

End of Excursus

III. "Letter-Body" or Main Part?

1. Now that the *letter-opening* and *closing* have been defined it remains to identify and characterise the *main part* of First Thessalonians. For reasons which will be made clear below, the general description of the structure of letters in the ancient world – *letter-opening, main part, letter-closing* – rather than a more specific description of the *main part* as "*letter-body*" with its component parts, is adopted (see Aune 1987, 163; White 1982a, 91). References to "*body*" and "*letter-body*" are unavoidable since this terminology is employed throughout the secondary literature; the inverted commas indicate my disquiet with the terms.

2. According to White (1972), who is a foremost practitioner of epistolary analysis, the structure of the "*letter-body*" may be characterised in terms of a "*body*" opening, a "*body*" middle (plus *eschatological climax* if present) and a "*body*" closing (alternatively named the *apostolic parousia*).[28] White defines 1 Thess 2:1–4 as the "*body*" opening, 2:5–16 as the "*body*" middle and 2:17–3:10 as the "*body*" closing (111–143).[29] He identifies a *disclosure* formula at 2:1 (117), "another formula of major import" at 2:5 (118) and a "formulaic unit" at 2:17 (142) as indications for such a demarcation of the "*letter-body*". However, White's analysis regarding the formal structure of the "*letter-body*" is not compelling. Why are the formulae of 2:5 and 17 of any more importance than those at 2:9, 10–11, 13, 14, usually either with a verb of knowing (οἴδατε) or with direct address (ἀδελφοί)?[30] Why are the paraenetic sections in 4:1–5:22 excluded from the "*letter-body*"? How can White claim on the one hand, that "1 Thessalonians does not have a 'body' of doctrinal or practical information like Paul's letters customarily have" (117) and on the other hand, impose onto First Thessalonians "the formal elements of the body adduced from the study of Galatians and Romans" (117), *which themselves have*

[28] Similarly, McDonald/Porter 2000, 383; Porter 2002, 546–548.

[29] The closing section of the "*letter-body*" is not always an *apostolic parousia* (*contra* Funk 1966, 267, 272; although see Funk 1967, 263–268, esp. 263 n. 1, where he gives a more nuanced discussion of the *apostolic parousia* as a structural element of the Pauline letter). White (1972, 140) does not make this point clear enough but Wanamaker makes the clarification (2000, 262).

[30] Schoon-Janßen appropriately divides the text in keeping with these transitions (1991, 56–62); see the more recent review of the structure of 2:1–12 by Merk (1998, 385–391).

the customary "doctrinal or practical information"? Even if an agreement could be reached regarding the beginning of the "*letter-body*", where does it end? Does it end at 2:16 (so Palmer 1981, 23), or 3:8 (so Roetzel 1991, 71), or 3:13,[31] or 5:22, 24, 25?[32] To be fair, White has moved on from his 1972 dissertation (see particularly his later articles of 1988 & 1993). But these questions still raise doubt over the validity of the term "*letter-body*" as it relates to Paul's letters and to First Thessalonians especially — an issue made all the more pertinent by a lack of consensus regarding the boundaries of this part of Paul's letters.

The elusiveness of the form of the "*letter-body*" defies consistent definition. The epistolary label requires emendation in keeping with Paul's proclivity *not* to follow given structures in the *main part* of his letters (Lambrecht 1990, 201). Paul expresses commands/requests and conveys information, sometimes with recognisable formulae, sometimes without. Doty comments: "My own feeling is that in the body sections of the longer letters, at least, Paul had more inclination to strike out on his own and to be least bound by epistolary structures" (1973, 35). If this holds true for First Thessalonians as well, then to some extent parts of Paul's letters must be analysed on an individual basis. Labels like *letter-thanksgiving* and *letter-paraenesis* are appropriate because they represent recognisably consistent forms across Paul's letters, whereas "*letter-body*" does not represent a consistent form. In parts where Paul "strikes out on his own", it is unhelpful and perhaps misleading to attach a single epistolary label like "*letter-body*" (Donfried 2000a, 38), since these sections (of which 1 Thess 2:1–16 is an example) are heavily shaped by the exigences of the individual letters. As such, "*letter-body*" can become an abstract catch-all term for any section which does not readily fit under another label. To complicate matters, Boers rightly observes that "*body*" implies that the section referred to represents the main purpose(s) of the letter and therefore ought to include the *letter-thanksgiving*, *apostolic parousia* and *letter-paraenesis* (1976, 145; so also White 1988, 97). With regard to 1 Thess 2:1–12, Boers rejects the terminology of "*body*" because it is too restrictive (145). But his alternative label, "central section" for 1 Thess 2:1–12 is little better. At the very least, it does not avoid the implicit localisation of the letter's purpose(s) to that section, one of the reasons why Boers rejected "*body*". It also invites further misunderstanding. Does he mean that 1 Thess 2:1–12 is the centre of the letter (i.e. a "middle" section), that it is central to the letter (i.e. the most "important" part) or something entirely other?[33] Roberts attempts to resolve the form and function of 1 Thess 2:1–12 by identifying "a separate, clearly distinguishable, period of transition" which appears "between thanksgiving/prayer periods and the body opening" (1986, 95). Thus, the *letter-thanksgiving* extends

---

[31] So Doty 1973, 43; Funk 1966, 264; Harvey 1998, 261; Hester 1996, 271; Neumann 1993, 203; White 1984, 1748.

[32] See the discussion of the *letter-closing* (§II above) for further references.

[33] Sandnes also prefers the epistolary label "central section" to "body", although he uses it to refer to 2:1–3:13. His description of the label is no less ambiguous (1991, 191).

from 1:2–10, while 2:1–16 is a "discrete period" of transition (with a second *letter-thanksgiving* in vv. 13–16) to the beginning of the "*letter-body*" at 2:17 (98–99). But Roberts is unable to provide evidence of recognisable epistolary structures in these "transitions". He refers instead, to a number of "transitional techniques" which he identifies in various sections of Paul's letters — if not in previously recognised epistolary structures (*letter-opening*, *letter-thanksgiving*, etc.), then in a newly labelled "discrete period" (96). His article, unfortunately, does not discuss the demarcation between these discrete periods and the *letter-thanksgiving*/"*letter-body*" (the form and position of these junctures are assumed), making it somewhat irrelevant for my purposes. Both Boers and Roberts take issue with the epistolary label "*letter-body*" for 1 Thess 2:1–12, but neither of their respective alternatives is to be preferred. The chief problem is not with their choices of terminology, but with their attempts to label sections which have no structural counterparts in Paul's other letters. It is difficult if not impossible to group such sections under a representative label. This is why I prefer to avoid the term "*letter-body*" altogether.

3. If the terms "*letter-body*", "central section" and "discrete period" are rejected epistolary labels for 1 Thess 2:1–16, how is its form and function to be characterised? The inability for scholars employing epistolary analysis to define this section of the *main part* stems not from a flaw in the approach but from misapplication. It is not necessary to force (known) structural forms onto the whole of a text (Alexander 1989, 90). Nor is it necessary to determine individual sections of a text in the same manner (Holtz 2000, 71).[34] The allowance for variations in the structure of Paul's letters is also relevant for rhetorical approaches. The assumption that Paul felt himself bound by the laws of rhetoric is not valid. Murphy-O'Connor observes:

> Why could Paul not have done as Cicero did? Is it not probable that Paul possessed the "wise adaptability" of Quintilian, and was fully capable of ignoring rhetorical conventions when it suited him? Issues were what mattered, not appearances (1995, 80; see Classen 1992, 341–342).

Accordingly, there are some sections within the *main part* of Paul's letters which require an individualised label. The descriptor "*disclosure* of a past-present relationship" suits 1 Thess 2:1–16 since the pericope begins with a *disclosure*-type formula and proceeds to recount, in narrative form, the relationship Paul has with the Thessalonian Christians. For the purposes of this discussion, there is no need to decide here between an apostolic *apologia* or autobiographical *paraenesis*. It is possible that the pericope functions in both capacities; by the *disclosure* of a past-present relationship Paul is able to review (defend) his actions in the past as well as present a model of exhortation in the present.[35] The problematic 2:13–16 is

[34] Malbon's analysis, although following a different approach (structural exegesis), illustrates this principle (1983, 66–68).

[35] The monograph by Donfried/Beutler (2000) presents a broad range of discussions regarding the issue of whether or not Paul is defending himself in First Thessalonians. See esp. the overview by Donfried 2000, 3–27. Malherbe's article (1970) remains essential reading.

easily incorporated into the *main part* of the letter along with other *eschatological climaxes* (1:9–10; 2:11b–12, 19–20; 3:11–13; 4:13–18; 5:1–11); it is no redundant thanksgiving. If 2:1–12 is a "recollection of the claims which emerged in the preaching of the gospel at Thessalonica" (White 1972, 118) it is not surprising that Paul expresses thanks for the way the Thessalonians appropriated τὸ εὐαγγέλιον τοῦ θεοῦ (2:2, 9; Donfried 1984, 246).

4. In conclusion, the *main part* of the letter, with its general concomitant functions of expressing commands/requests and communication of information (White 1982, 10) *is* the so-called "*letter-body*" on a rhetorical (i.e. functional) level, while the *letter-opening* and *closing* remain solely epistolary labels (Johanson 1987, 64–65). Expanding the designation "*letter-body*" to include the majority of First Thessalonians has significance for each of the pericopes to be analysed as fundamental representatives of the eschatological discourse in the letter. This will become increasingly evident as the discussion proceeds. This redefinition does not rule out the identification of epistolary forms within the *main part* of the letter, namely *letter-thanksgiving, disclosure* and other formulae, *eschatological climaxes, apostolic parousia* and *letter-paraenesis*, some of which receive further treatment below.

IV. Letter-Thanksgiving

1. A perennial problem in the discussion of the structure of First Thessalonians is the delineation of the *letter-thanksgiving*. The thanksgiving formula in 2:13, ἡμεῖς εὐχαριστοῦμεν τῷ θεῷ ἀδιαλείπτως, can be perplexing. Does it mark the beginning of a "second" *letter-thanksgiving*? Is it a continuation or reiteration of a single larger epistolary unit? What about 3:9 where Paul mentions a εὐχαριστίαν ... τῷ θεῷ? The difficulty with the *letter-thanksgiving* of First Thessalonians is not the repetition of εὐχαριστεῖν but with its length and placement within the structure of the letter. Actually, the discussion of where to include 2:13–16 has sometimes led to a not inconsiderable impetus to regard the pericope as an interpolation or else as a prime candidate for a redactional seam.[36]

2. Jervis provides a thorough analysis of the various elements in a typical Pauline *letter-thanksgiving* (1991, 86–109). She identifies these elements to be: (1) the verb εὐχαριστεῖν + indirect object τῷ θεῷ (μου); (2) adverbial and/or participial constructions to indicate the manner of thanksgiving; (3) causal constructions to indicate the reason for thanksgiving, using ἐπί, ὅτι and/or participial clauses; (4) an

[36] For secondary literature on interpolation hypotheses, see fn. 2 above. The principal proponents of compilation theories for 1 (& 2) Thess include: Demke 1973; Eckart 1961; Munro 1983; Murphy-O'Connor 1996; Pesch 1984; Refshauge 1971; Richard 1995; Schenke/Fischer 1978; Schmithals 1964, 1965, 1984; see 1960; Scott 1909. For noteworthy critical analyses of the various theories, see Best (1972, 29–35, 45–50), Jewett (1986, 33–46) and Wanamaker (1990, 29–37) who all conclude the unity of the extant First Thessalonians. A review of recent compilation theories is provided in Chapter 4, §II.d.

explanatory unit which modifies the preceding causal unit and elaborates on the cause for Paul's thanksgiving; it begins with either καθώς or some other consecutive explanatory conjunction such as ὥστε or γάρ; (5) a prayer report often using the verb προσεύχεσθαι with either ἵνα/ὅπως (with the subjunctive) or εἴ πως (with the infinitive; see esp. 86–91).[37] Such an analysis accounts for all of Paul's *letter-thanksgivings*; there is no longer a need to maintain a two-type definition (*contra*, Schubert 1939, 35). Turning specifically to First Thessalonians, the beginning of the *letter-thanksgiving* is identified at 1:2. Accordingly, 1 Thess 1:2a has the verb and indirect object (εὐχαριστοῦμεν τῷ θεῷ), 1:2b has an adverbial phrase of manner (πάντοτε περὶ πάντων ὑμῶν), 1:3, 4, 5 indicate the reason for thanksgiving (μνημονεύοντες, εἰδότες, ὅτι, respectively), and 1:5–10 contains the explanatory unit (καθώς ...). The *letter-thanksgiving* of First Thessalonians does not have the fifth unit identified by Jervis.[38]

3. Where the *letter-thanksgiving* ends is the *crux* of the "thanksgiving problem". Traditionally, three solutions have dominated the discussion:[39] (1) a long *letter-thanksgiving* extending from 1:2 to 3:13;[40] (2) a short *letter-thanksgiving* extending from 1:2 to 1:10;[41] (3) multiple *letter-thanksgivings* beginning at 1:2, 2:13 and 3:9.[42] One approach to resolve this "trilemma" is to define the form of the *letter-thanksgiving* closing.[43] O'Brien has observed a connection between the verb εὐχαριστεῖν and terms like εὐαγγέλιον, μαρτύριον, λόγος, and ὁ λόγος τοῦ θεοῦ (1975, 149). This connection is particularly apparent at 1:2–10 and 2:13 (150). An *eschatological climax* is often associated with the end of a *letter-thanksgiving*, but

[37] Mullins and Lambrecht substantially agree with Jervis' analysis although Mullins is much more general in his presentation (1972, 382) while Lambrecht organises the Pauline *letter-thanksgiving* around a three-fold thematic structure (1990, 187–192).

[38] Cf. Rom 1:10, 13; Phil 1:9–11; Phlm 6; cf. also 2 Thess 1:11–12.

[39] A fourth solution incorporates theories of compilation; see fn. 36 above for references.

[40] See Jewett 1986, 216–220, and Alford 1958, 249; Aune 1987, 206; Bailey 1955, 251; Bultmann (cf. Merk 1985, 192); Collins 1993, 117–119; Ellingworth/Nida 1976, ix; Gorman 2004, 152; Havener 1983, 10; Holtz 1998, 32; Jewett 1969, 24; Koester 1979, 36; Malherbe 1983, 238; 2000, 78–79; Merk 1998, 385; P.-G. Müller 2001, 47; O'Brien 1977, 144; Oepke 1970, 159; Ryrie 1959, 17–20; Schubert 1939, 25–26; Snyder 1972, 235; Staab 1965, 13; Stott 1991, 19–20; Vawter 1960, 34; von Dobschütz 1909, 27–28; Wiles 1974, 51. Malbon identifies 3:11–13 as a blessing so that the *letter-thanksgiving* concludes at 3:10 (1983, 66; so also Jewett 1969, 24). See also overview by Lyons who advocates an "unusually lengthy thanksgiving" (1995, 210–211 n. 93).

[41] See Jewett 1986, 216–220, and Boers 1976, 142; Findlay 1891, 38; 1904, lxx–lxxi; Harvey 1998, 261; Hester 1996, 271; Lenski 1937, 219–220; Moffatt 1910, 5; Neil 1957, 31; Palmer 1981, 23; Reinmuth 1998, 115; Roetzel 1991, 71; Selby 1999, 393; Thomas 1978, 236; Weima 1997, 80; White 1972, 117–118; Wick 1994, 12; Williams 1992, 25; Wuellner 1990, 117–118, 128–129.

[42] Although Collins agrees with Schubert that First Thessalonians has a long *letter-thanksgiving* (i.e. 1:2–3:13) he does emphasise the distinctness of each thanksgiving section (1:2–5; 2:13; 3:9–10) so that he is at least sympathetic to the multiple *letter-thanksgiving* view (1984, 24–25; 358–360; 1990a, 776; 1993, 117–119). Roetzel advocates three *letter-thanksgivings*: 1:2–10, 2:13 and 3:9–10 (1991, 71; so also Funk 1966, 269; Green 2002, 86–87, 138, 171; Lambrecht 1990, 184–194; Schnider/Stenger 1987, 42–49).

[43] Berger comments with regard to the *letter-thanksgiving* section of Hellenistic letters: "Danksagungen ... haben keinen vergleichbaren Inhalt" (1974, 219). But this is not quite true of Pauline *letter-thanksgivings*.

since each of the candidates for a *letter-thanksgiving* has an *eschatological climax* (cf. 1:9–10; 2:16; 3:13), this does not help the decision much. However, the third option of multiple *letter-thanksgivings* is questionable on three counts. First, 3:9–13 contains no recognisable elements of the *letter-thanksgiving* form. Paul atypically uses the noun εὐχαριστία rather than the verb and also incorporates it into a rhetorical question (Sandnes 1991, 190). Second, Jervis contends that the presence of verbs in the optative mood (κατευθύναι in 3:11; πλεονάσαι καὶ περισσεύσαι in 3:12) is highly problematic since there is no other example of a *letter-thanksgiving* concluding in such a way (1991, 92). Third, multiple *letter-thanksgivings* unnecessarily fragment the narrative structure of 2:1–3:10 (Wanamaker 2000, 267–268). Therefore, at least the thanksgiving at 3:9 may be eliminated as part of the *letter-thanksgiving* of First Thessalonians, which puts the viability of option three in doubt.

Another approach to resolve the *crux* is to move away from the form of the *letter-thanksgiving* closing and towards an identification of the form of the "*letter-body*" opening. Although I do not find the terminology "*letter-body*" useful (see §III above), such an approach helps in the attempt to find a boundary between the *letter-thanksgiving* and the next section of the letter. Sanders, on the basis of Schubert's (1939) work to define the *letter-thanksgiving* of Paul's letters, argues that there is a recognisable form of transition to the "*body*" of his letters, which can be of two types (1962, 353). Mullins has analysed both types. The first is a *petition* and has the following elements: (1) background; (2) petition; (3) address; (4) courtesy phrase or as a subset, a divine authority phrase; (5) desired action (1962, 47). The second is a *disclosure* which has a different structure: (1) θέλω; (2) noetic verb in the infinitive; (3) person addressed; (4) information (1965, 46). White identifies a further four formulae (besides the *petition* and *disclosure* formulae) which may introduce the "*letter-body*": (1) joy expression; (2) expression of astonishment; (3) statement of compliance; (4) formulaic use of the verb of hearing or learning (1971, 95–97). But as far as White is concerned the introduction of the "*letter-body*" of First Thessalonians is by means of a *disclosure* formula at 2:1. It has a verb of *disclosure* (αὐτοὶ γὰρ οἴδατε), a vocative of address (ἀδελφοί) and a subject to be disclosed introduced by ὅτι (94; see 1972, 114). Paul commonly uses the *disclosure* formula to introduce the "*letter-body*" (White 1983, 439; 1999, 72).[44] The fact that the form of the *disclosure* is irregular does not seem to be a problem (1972, 117; so also Sanders 1962, 356); but in view of the formula's strict form (regarding content, not sequence) it is probably more accurate to refer to 2:1 as a *disclosure*-type formula. Mullins avoids the conclusion that either a *petition* or *disclosure* form always marks a *letter-thanksgiving* closing since these formulae may appear elsewhere in Paul's letters (1965, 49; so also Sanders 1962, 349).[45] When it comes to distinguishing the end of the *letter-thanksgiving* a more general rule is:

[44] See Rom 1:13; 2 Cor 1:8; Gal 1:11; Phil 1:12.

[45] For example, there are eight instances of the *disclosure* formula at 1:5; 2:1, 2, 5, 11; 3:3–4; 4:2; 5:2.

> [W]hen the Thanksgiving is followed by any recognizable element of another form, the termination of the Thanksgiving is thereby marked. If the Thanksgiving constitutes the *background* of a Petition for example, and is followed by the *petition verb*, that indicates the end of the Thanksgiving form (Mullins 1965, 49).

Option one (above), which is incidentally the traditional position, is hereby ruled out leaving a short *letter-thanksgiving* (option two) as the only solution to the "thanksgiving problem". Incidentally, the conclusions of rhetorical approaches to First Thessalonians also support a shorter *letter-thanksgiving.*[46]

4. The best arrangements of First Thessalonians designate the *letter-thanksgiving* at 1:2–10 with the next section of the letter beginning at 2:1. The presence of two further formulations of thanks, while distinctive, poses no problems. Arzt demonstrates that the formulation of thanks is common in literary sources in a variety of contexts and that it is not confined to a specific section within the arrangement of a letter (1994, 31–38). In a similar vein, Audet (1959, 646–647), in consideration of the dependence of Christian εὐχαριστία upon Jewish εὐχαριστία or ברכה, makes a distinction between the initial "benediction" or "benediction" proper (i.e. which lends its name to the literary genre) and other "benedictions" (e.g. anamnesis, doxology). The significant point, and this has not been properly considered in epistolary discussions of the "thanksgiving problem" of First Thessalonians, is that the appearance of thanksgiving formulae *do not automatically* indicate the introduction of a formal *letter-thanksgiving.*[47] This observation holds true for various formulae in Paul's letters. For example, *disclosure* formulae may appear at the beginning of the "*letter-body*" but they are also found in other parts of his letters. Likewise, 1 Thess 2:13 (and 3:9–10) need not be considered an introduction to a *letter-thanksgiving* despite its form as one such formula (Reed 1996, 89). In conclusion, the epistolary label *letter-thanksgiving* describes that section of Paul's letters which is subsequent to the *letter-opening*, marks the beginning of the *main part* and contains an initial formulation of thanksgiving ending in an *eschatological climax*. Further, the epistolary section (1 Thess 1:2–10) provides an expression of *philophronesis* (Aune 1987, 186; Doty 1973, 11) and functions as a *captatio benevolentiae* (Collins 2000, 333; Hoppe 2002, 327).[48]

5. The identification of the *letter-thanksgiving* in 1 Thess 1:2–10 supports the notion that eschatology is the best hermeneutical key for understanding Paul's pattern of exhortation in two ways. First, such an identification considerably elevates the epistolary (and rhetorical) status of 1 Thess 1:9–10 as one of the fundamental representatives of the eschatological discourse in First Thessalonians. It now stands at the close of the *letter-thanksgiving* rather than appearing in the

[46] Donfried 2000a, 41–44; Hughes 1990, 109–116; Jewett 1986, 72–76; Kennedy 1984, 142; Olbricht 1990, 235; Selby 1999, 393; Smith 1995, 69–75.

[47] See esp. O'Brien 1980, 55–61; see also Berger 1974, 224–225; Friedrich 1976, 225; *contra* Schubert 1939, and followers.

[48] See Berger 1974, 222–224; Johanson 1987, 157–160; Murphy-O'Connor 1995, 62; Smith 1995, 70–75; Wick 1994, 11–14.

middle of a much longer thanksgiving section. In addition, that these verses appear in the *letter-thanksgiving* correlates well with their anticipatory function for the rest of the *main part*.[49] Second, by removing the spectre of a long *letter-thanksgiving*, 1 Thess 2:13–16 is now able to be interpreted in its own right. Thus, rather than being an awkward reiteration of the "real" thanksgiving, these verses are best understood as an *eschatological climax* to 2:1–16. As such, questions of authenticity normally associated with 2:13–16 recede into the background. Furthermore, as with 1:9–10, the importance of 2:13–16 as a second fundamental representative of the eschatological discourse is emphasised. In summary, the epistolary structure of First Thessalonians highlights Paul's ability to exploit eschatological motifs for maximum effect in his pattern of exhortation.

V. Apostolic *Parousia*

1. Another recognisable part of Paul's letters is the *apostolic parousia* first identified by Funk in 1966 and developed in his article of 1967. His structure is based on Rom 15:14–33. He identifies parallel *apostolic parousia* sections in Rom 1:8–13, 1 Cor 4:14–21, Phil 2:19–24, 1 Thess 2:17–3:13 and Phlm 21–22 (1967, 250).[50] Even his summary of its form is too detailed to reproduce here (251–254). Lambrecht provides a condensed version: (1) γράφω ὑμῖν ..., stating Paul's disposition or purpose in writing; (2) basis of Paul's apostolic relation to the recipients; (3) implementation of the *apostolic parousia*; (4) invocation of divine approval and support for the *apostolic parousia*; (5) benefit from the *apostolic parousia* (1990, 196–197). Only some elements of the *apostolic parousia* may be identified in 1 Thess 2:17–3:13 (Funk 1967, 254): desire to see the Thessalonians (2:17b); wish to see them (2:18a); hindrance to his coming (2:18b); dispatch of an emissary (3:2–5); invocation of divine approval through prayer (3:6–11).

2. Some scholars follow Funk in detecting a formal structure to this section of the *main part*.[51] But Mullins (1973) has shown convincingly that Funk has really identified a theme rather than a form.[52] Funk claims to identify a variety of items and a particular order, allegedly part of the *apostolic parousia*. But since there is a confusion of sequence and no persistence in items, there can be no form. In fact, Mullins (1973, 351) notes that only one of the items identified by Funk appears

---

[49] For further details, see §VI.3 below.

[50] Cf. also 1 Cor 16:1–11; 2 Cor 8:16–23; 9:1–5.

[51] Bruce 1982, 53–54, 65–66; Doty 1973, 36–37; Lambrecht 1990, 196–197; Roetzel 1991, 64–65; Schnider/Stenger 1987, 92–107; Schoon-Janßen 1991, 56; Wanamaker 1990, 119–120 (but with criticisms); White 1972, 140–143; 1983, 440.

[52] So also Lyons 1985, 209; McDonald/Porter 2000, 406; see Aune 1987, 190; Wanamaker 2000, 261–262; *contra* Jervis 1991, 110–131; Trebilco 1993, 449. Jervis's attempt to describe the form of the *apostolic parousia* reveals numerous variations across the Pauline letters (1991, 113–114), which appears to support Mullins' critique. Unfortunately, Jervis overlooks Mullins' article (1973) in her discussion.

in all thirteen passages considered (i.e. item 3, implementation of the *apostolic parousia*). However, Mullins does find a recognisable theme of "visit-talk" in non-literary papyri and Paul (352–354). Regardless of the distinction between form/theme, 1 Thess 2:17–3:13 is of crucial importance for the establishment of Paul's apostolic authority in the community. According to Funk, the generation of Paul's apostolic authority is achieved in ascending order by a letter, an apostolic emissary, and his own personal presence (1967, 249). White (1983, 440–441) follows this line adding two further elements of apostolic function: *paraenesis* (4:1–5:22) and a prayer/wish for eschatological peace (5:23–24). However, Mitchell challenges Funk's assumption that Paul's letters are second best – with reference to an emissary or his own presence – when it comes to generating apostolic authority. She asserts (1992, 655) that the *apostolic parousia* is more a

> *retrospective narrative* depicting in detail the full extent of the envoy's mission from Paul's vantage point: the envoy's sending, return, report, and his own response, all described in formulaic terms. The retrospective narrative is comprised of a recital of the relationship, including prehistory and past history and extending into the present time (the moment of the writing of the letter).

It may be argued that the role of the *apostolic parousia* in Paul's letters is even more effective than his own presence in maintaining and reaffirming the relationship between Paul and the Thessalonians (661–662; although cf. 1 Cor 4:17–20).[53]

3. In conclusion, the *apostolic parousia* is not a form but a recognisable theme. The investigations by Funk, Mullins and Mitchell demonstrate how epistolary analysis can be too rigidly applied (so Funk) and corrected (so Mullins). Beyond form alone, the integration of rhetorical considerations into the epistolary theory leads to a better understanding of this section of First Thessalonians. Funk's pioneering examination remains indispensable, but the full import of the *apostolic parousia* is apprehended only by standing back from constituent elements and keeping in mind their rhetorical significance (so Mitchell).

But of more pertinence is the repetitious appearance of the eschatological discourse in First Thessalonians, including references to Satan (2:18), the *parousia* (2:19; 3:13), glory (2:20; see parallel to δόξα in 2:12), affliction (3:3, 4, 7) and to the tempter (ὁ πειράζων, 3:5). Such a high density of references to eschatological motifs does not appear in other Pauline epistolary sections which contain a theme of "visit-talk". In fact, there is only one reference to an eschatological motif in apostolic *parousia* sections outside of First Thessalonians, and that is a reference to the kingdom of God in 1 Cor 4:20. This is quite significant for my purposes because it shows the extent of Paul's weaving eschatological motifs into the discourse of the letter, which in turn demonstrates the applicability of eschatology as a hermeneutical key for understanding First Thessalonians.

[53] Llewelyn (1994, 52–53) comes to a similar conclusion to Mitchell: "One has only to think of the length, detail and personal concern expressed by Paul in his letters ... Why write such long letters if the emissary was the principal agent of his apostolic *parousia*?"

VI. Letter-Paraenesis

1. The *Forschungsbericht* into moral exhortation in the ancient world is too extensive to present here.[54] The word παραίνεσις does not occur in the NT (see non-technical παρῄνει in Acts 27:9 and παραινῶ in v. 22) but as a literary form *paraenesis* is employed throughout, not least by Paul. *Paraenesis* is a technical term for a style of exhortation which is traditional and generally applicable, used to modify the conduct of others.[55] Various forms of *paraenesis*, e.g. antithetic formulations, groups of sayings, *topoi*, household codes or *Haustafeln*, catalogues of virtues and vices, are often arranged (but not necessarily exclusively so) into a *letter-paraenesis* section of Paul's letters (Koester 1982, 66).[56] The focus here is on the epistolary structure of the *letter-paraenesis* rather than on individual paraenetic forms (for a similar distinction see Aune 1987, 191; Roetzel 1991, 66). The importance of this examination lies specifically in the decisions to be made regarding how 1 Thess 4:13–18 and 5:1–11 are to be understood in the context of the *letter-paraenesis*, and more generally in the determination of how the eschatological discourse is weaved into this epistolary section of the letter.

2. The form of the *letter-paraenesis* of First Thessalonians is less controversial than the *letter-thanksgiving*. First Thessalonians 4:1–2 marks a transition to a paraenetic section. Due to the programmatic nature of these verses, most commentators see them as an introduction to the *letter-paraenesis* which stretches from 4:1 to 5:22, not just to the immediate context of verses 3–12 (Malherbe 2000, 217). The section begins with the phrase λοιπὸν οὖν which does not signify the close of a letter in this case (Horsley 1981a, 58) but rather emphasises transition (Alexander 1989, 96–97; Milligan 1908, 46).[57] This is followed by an element of direct address, ἀδελφοί, which marks divisions in the *paraenesis* (cf. 4:1, 10, 13; 5:1, 4, 12, 14; Collins 1984, 301). Paul proceeds with a pair of exhortative verbs, ἐρωτᾶν and παρακαλεῖν. He uses both verbs again, the latter repeatedly, as well as other verbs in the imperative and (hortatory) subjunctive moods (Johanson 1987, 72).[58] The transition between 1:1–3:13 and 4:1–5:28 is impressive when the distribution of verbs in these moods is noted.[59] Malherbe points out several further paraenetic devices used by Paul, namely his repeated references to what he has already told the

---

[54] For a comprehensive introduction, see Malherbe 1992 & 1986; for the specific discussion as it pertains to First Thessalonians, see Laub 1973.

[55] For a more detailed description, see among others: Fiore 1992; Malherbe 1985, 92–93; 1987, 70–71; Stowers 1986, 94–106; Thompson 1993; Wilkins 1997.

[56] It is commonplace to identify Rom 12:1–15:13, 1 Cor 16:13–18, 2 Cor 13:5–11, Gal 5:16–6:10, Phil 4:2–6 and 1 Thess 4:1–5:22 as *letter-paraenesis*.

[57] *Contra* Richard 1995, 179, 181–182; cf. 2 Cor 13:11; Phil 3:1; 4:8; Eph 6:10; 2 Thess 3:1.

[58] For ἐρωτᾶν, see 5:12; for παρακαλεῖν, see 4:10, 18; 5:11, 14. Paul often uses παρακαλεῖν in the *letter-paraenesis* of his letters (Rom 12:1; 1 Cor 16:15; 2 Cor 13:11; Phil 4:2; Bjerkelund 1967, 128).

[59] In the first part of the letter there is only one possible candidate for a verb in the imperative mood (2:9) while there is an abundance of references in the second part (4:18; 5:11*bis*, 13, 14*tetra*, 15*bis*, 16, 17, 18, 19, 20, 21*bis*, 22, 25, 26). Hortatory subjunctives appear at 5:6*ter*, 8.

Thessalonians,[60] his confidence that they are already doing what he is exhorting them to do,[61] and his statements that there is no need to write[62] — all of which echo the paraenetic tradition (1987, 76–77; see 1992, 293). The *disclosure* formula in 4:13, οὐ θέλομεν δὲ ὑμᾶς ἀγνοεῖν, appears in Paul's other letters[63] and gives emphasis to what he is saying regardless of whether the material presented is new or not (Barclay 2000, 3). Another device Paul uses to organise the *letter-paraenesis* of First Thessalonians is περί (δέ) in 4:9, 13 and 5:1 (Collins 2000, 320–321);[64] this is not uncommon in other letters of the first century (Baasland 1988, 70–75; White 1982a, 98). Johanson observes that the *letter-paraenesis* is characterised by a predominantly present-future focus (as opposed to a present-past focus in 1:2–3:13). He also draws attention to Paul's use of ἵνα-clauses (4:1, 12, 13) and infinitival-clauses (4:3, 4, 6, 10, 11; 5:13) to express a change of direction in the future (1987, 78; see von Dobschütz 1909, 174). Lambrecht (2000, 164) makes a distinction between paraenetic material (4:1–12; 5:12–22) and "eschatological" or "didactic" material (4:13–5:11). But such a distinction is misleading since Paul first corrects misunderstandings and on the basis of those corrections urges his readers to correct behaviour (Malherbe 2000, 216; so also Howard 1988, 166–170). While 4:13–5:11 may be both "eschatological" and "didactic", it is clearly also paraenetic (cf. ὥστε, 4:18; ἄρα οὖν, 5:6; διό, 5:11). Besides, sayings of Jesus are sometimes used in *paraenesis* (Koester 1982, 67).[65] Bjerkelund finds two "παρακαλῶ-Sätze" in 4:1–12 and a further two in 5:12–22; between these two groups stand two eschatological "περί-Abschnitte" (1967, 129; followed by Hurd 1998, 72). But in order to maintain such a structure he must ignore the "περί-Abschnitt" in 4:9.[66]

These stylistic devices demarcate the *letter-paraenesis* of First Thessalonians into discrete units (Collins 1993, 135; see also 1998).[67] Paul first gives an introduction (4:1–2) followed by a series of *topoi*: on sanctification (4:3–8); on love of the brothers, living quietly, minding one's own affairs and decorous living (4:9–12); on those who are asleep (4:13–18); on times and seasons (5:1–11). Only then does Paul

---

[60] Paul often uses εἰδέναι (4:2, 4; 5:2; cf. 1:4, 5; 2:1, 2, 5, 11; 3:3, 4; 1 Cor 16:15) and other verbs referring to past teaching: παραλαμβάνειν (4:1), οἴδατε γὰρ τίνας παραγγελίας ἐδώκαμεν ὑμῖν (4:2), προλέγειν (4:6), and παραγγέλλειν (4:11). Further the Thessalonians have been taught by God (ὑμεῖς θεοδίδακτοί ἐστε, 4:9); cf. ἃ προλέγω ὑμῖν, καθὼς προεῖπον (Gal 5:21). See also Davis 1971, 191–192.

[61] See καθὼς καὶ περιπατεῖτε (4:1); καὶ γὰρ ποιεῖτε αὐτὸ ... (4:10); καθὼς καὶ ποιεῖτε (5:11).

[62] See οὐ χρείαν ἔχετε γράφειν ὑμῖν (4:9); οὐ χρείαν ἔχετε ὑμῖν γράφεσθαι (5:1); μὴ χρείαν ἔχειν ἡμᾶς λαλεῖν τι (1:8). Cf. similarly, περὶ μὲν γὰρ τῆς διακονίας τῆς εἰς τοὺς ἁγίους περισσόν μοί ἐστιν τὸ γράφειν ὑμῖν (2 Cor 9:1).

[63] So with minor variations of particles, Rom 1:13; 11:25; 1 Cor 10:1; 12:1; 2 Cor 1:8; cf. also Rom 16:19; 1 Cor 11:3; Col 2:1.

[64] Cf. 1 Cor 7:1, 25; 8:1; 12:1; 16:1, 12.

[65] 1 Thess 4:15–17; so also 1 Cor 7:10–11; cf. 1 Tim 1:15. For a more extended discussion of the collection of Jesus-sayings in exhortations of Paul, see Dibelius 1971, 238–244.

[66] For further criticism of Bjerkelund's thesis, see Johanson 1987, 73–75.

[67] Roetzel presents a summary table which details the structure of the *letter-paraenesis* of Paul's letters (1972, 372).

turn to a group of sayings (5:12–22) arranged under two verbs of exhortation (plus direct address) in verses 12 and 14. The pericope concludes with terse imperatives (vv. 16–22) in a list that might be described as "shotgun paraenesis" (Roetzel 1972, 375).

3. The level of organisation in the epistolary structure of the *letter-paraenesis* indicates that it is a legitimate component of the *main part* and that Paul's pattern of exhortation is also to be found in this section of the letter. This is particularly evident in Paul's preparation for the *letter-paraenesis* in previous parts of the letter. Thus, he uses the summary report of 1 Thess 1:9–10 to organise parts of First Thessalonians (Snyder 1972a, 360–362). The report refers to Paul's founding visit and this is taken up in 2:1. It mentions the Thessalonians' service to God and has a reference to judgment, both of which prepare for the exhortations in 4:3–12. There are striking similarities between 1:10 and 4:14–17, including references to: credal formulae, the name Ἰησοῦς, the resurrection of Jesus, the "dead", an appearance "from heaven". Furthermore, the two passages have a similar sequence — first a confession of Jesus and then of a belief in the expectation of his eschatological coming. Both have a salvific function, where one refers to a rescuing from *orgē* while the other refers to "through him" and "with him" (Collins 1993, 154–155). As well, Paul anticipates at least three of the *topoi* in 1 Thess 4, ἀγάπη (3:12), ἁγιωσύνη (3:13) and παρουσία (3:13). Such organisation indicates that the *letter-paraenesis* is not "tacked" onto the end of the letter (*contra* Longenecker 1985, 88), and demonstrates how carefully Paul uses various motifs to construct his pattern of exhortation.

4. The issue of contingency of the Pauline *paraenesis* is now taken up. It should be noted that the conclusions reached regarding this issue impact directly on the analysis of 1 Thess 4:13–18 and 5:1–11 since these pericopes appear in the *letter-paraenesis* and therefore need to be examined within that epistolary and rhetorical context.

Attention is directed to the question of how (if at all) traditional paraenetic material is relevant to the Thessalonian situation. Since it is clear that First Thessalonians contains various *topoi*, and since the *Forschungsgeschichte* on paraenetic material includes the paraenetic form of the *topos*, then this question has especial significance for the discussion of the letter. Bradley's article (1953), on the form of the *topos* in Paul's *paraenesis*, is as good a place as any to pick up the modern discussion. According to Bradley: "A *topos* may be defined as the treatment in independent form of the topic of a proper thought or action, or of a virtue or a vice, etc." (1953, 240). Further, such *topoi* "are self-contained, unitary teachings which have but a loose, and often even an arbitrary, connection with their context" (243). Bradley identifies two distinctive characteristics: (1) *topoi* are composed of more than one sentence dealing with the same subject; (2) *topoi* often contain a recurring word which may serve as a binding element (243). Thus, for Bradley, a *topos* "can be removed from its context without doing violence to the continuity of the thought of the letter", because the various *topoi* are part of Paul's (and other teachers') "bag of answers to meet recurring problems and questions" (246).[68] Mullins' article (1980), on the same topic, dispenses with Bradley's understanding of the *topos* in preference of a more precise description (542):[69]

> There are three essential elements: an *injunction* urging that a certain course of behavior be followed or avoided; a *reason* for the injunction; and a *discussion* of the logical or practical consequences of the behavior. An optional element is the citing of an *analogous situation* to the one dealt with in the Topos.

Mullins finds no evidence to support Bradley's description of the function of the *topos* as independent of the situation or context. Instead, despite its somewhat stereotyped form, Mullins argues that the *topos* is directly relevant. Often the *topos* form is used repeatedly by an author, on the same subject, but not in the same way (545–546). For example, Mullins points out that Paul uses the *topos* form for the subject of eating meat sacrificed to idols. Paul's position remains the same, but the *topoi* he uses are not pat answers (546).[70] Before going any further in this discussion, it is helpful to note that the question of relevancy (or contingency) of *topoi* is not dependent on its form or definition. The ancient rhetorical sources indicate that the term *topos* came to be used in different ways (Anderson 2000, 117). Quite relevant for the debate between Bradley and Mullins is Anderson's observation (117) that Aristotle distinguishes between set treatments of specific subjects (i.e. τόποι) and abstract argumentative patterns (i.e. κοινοὶ τόποι). Cicero also makes a similar distinction between "extrinsic" and "intrinsic" *loci*; i.e. those directly related to the subject and those not (118).[71] Finally, although Quintilian's treatment is slightly different, there are clear links with Cicero. Quintilian refers to sources of arguments (*sedes argumentorum*) which are related to concrete persons and matters, and *loci communes* which are independent of concrete persons or matters (119). Even without interacting further with Anderson's observations of how the term *topos* is used by ancient rhetoricians, it is clear that a fundamental difficulty of terminology has not been addressed by either Bradley or Mullins. At this juncture, it is helpful to bring Brunt (1985) into the discussion. He emphasises the ambiguity of the term and particularly the schism between ancient and modern definitions (496–498).[72] In addition, Brunt argues that there is no one form termed a *topos*, but a "multiplicity of forms" (499). With regard to the question of contingency, he concludes: "Other criteria, derived from the context of the passage, must be used to determine whether or not a specific situation is being addressed. Appeal to the *topos* form is not helpful" (500).[73] Aune goes one step further when he proposes that a

[68] Bradley is followed closely by Doty 1973, 39.

[69] Mullins is followed closely by Bailey/Vander Broek 1992, 63–65.

[70] Cf. Rom 14:13–15, 16–23; 1 Cor 8:9–13; 10:25–30; cf. also Col 2:16–23.

[71] For primary references, see Anderson 2000, 117–120.

[72] Malherbe also reflects awareness of the ambiguity in the modern use of the term (1992, 320).

[73] Similarly, Funk: "The *topos* is a moral essay in miniature, which may or may not derive from tradition, but which in any case reflects teaching that has become stereotyped in form. Thus, whether or not the *topos* is situational must be determined from context" (1966, 255–256).

topos is not a form at all, but refers to a recurring theme, "consisting of a cluster of constituent stereotypical *motifs* which develop various thematic components" (1987, 173). As such, *topoi* are recognisable because they are found in many different authors, and it is clear that each author adjusts his use of various motifs to suit his rhetorical situation (173; see Roetzel 1991, 79). I prefer the definition of Malherbe because of its clarity: the *topos* refers to "traditional, fairly systematic treatments of moral topics which use clichés, maxims, short definitions, etc." (1992, 320).[74]

It remains, then, to attempt to ascertain whether some or all of 1 Thess 4:1–5:22 is contingent (i.e. dependent on the situation of the Thessalonians). One feature found in *paraenesis*, which has already been noted, is the constant reminder of things previously known: "There is thus an awareness in paraenesis that the hearers or readers already know what is being inculcated, and that repetition of what is already known is to serve as a jog to the memory" (Malherbe 1992, 281). In 1 Thess 4:1, 2, 4, 6, 11 and 5:2 Paul alludes to previous teachings, either using εἰδέναι or other verbs referring to the teaching he presumably gave at the founding visit. I think this in itself gives an indication that Paul's *letter-paraenesis* is contingent.[75] It could be argued, of course, that Paul is not specifically referring to his previous teaching but merely alluding to general paraenetic tradition (so Dibelius 1971, 238–239). That would be true if Paul simply parrots stereotyped material. He does not. Instead, there are numerous instances in 1 Thess 4–5 where Paul adapts stereotypical material, whether in the form of a *topos* or groups of sayings, to make it directly relevant to the Thessalonians' situation. Thus, even though it is often argued that 4:1–8 does not contain any specific reference to the situation of the Thessalonians,[76] it is probable that 4:9–12 contains a more specific application of the preceding exhortations,[77] and may well refer to a concrete situation (Aasgaard 2004, 154). In addition, Paul refers to various social attitudes of the Epicureans (the *topoi* of φιλαδελφία and ἀγάπη are paralleled in the Epicurean *topos* of φιλία),

[74] Some of the older scholarship (*viz.* Dahl 1977, 86; Dibelius 1925, 17–18; Hunter 1961, esp. 52–54; Rigaux 1968, 133), which argued that *paraenesis*, in general, was independent of the situation, may now be dismissed in view of more accurate definitions. Furthermore, in view of Mullins' definition of a *topos* it is not surprising that he considers 4:13–18 not to be an example of a *topos* form. However, according to Malherbe's definition the pericope may easily be described as an example of that form. To such an end, Malherbe is able to give numerous instances where features in 4:13–18 are found in consolatory *topoi*, including: calls for grief to cease; recitations of a teacher's words; complaints that the deceased have been snatched away by death; exhortations to take comfort in the hope that the deceased are now with the gods and virtuous persons of the past; even statements that the deceased will be joined by those living (1983, 255).

[75] Similarly, Collins 1984, 306–307, but see 163.

[76] See Collins 1984, 327; against the trend of research advocated by Collins, see Baumert 1990, 332–333; Lambrecht 1994, 352–353. Laub (1973, 55–56) notes the connection between ἔκδικος κύριος περὶ πάντων τούτων (4:6) and other references to *Zorngericht* (1:10; 3:13; 5:9, 23).

[77] *Contra* Koester 1979, 39; Neil 1957, 79–80; so Howard 1988, 175; Snyder 1972a, 238. In particular, Howard notes that Paul takes up the topic of φιλαδελφία (4:9) which is opposite to transgressing (ὑπερβαίνειν) and taking advantage (πλεονεκτεῖν) of one's brother (4:6).

but in a rather anti-Epicurean fashion,[78] which may add to the concrete nature of Paul's *paraenesis* in 4:9–12.[79] Even more convincing is Witmer's (2006) thesis that Paul draws on Isaiah 54:13 to create a neologism for the purposes of strengthening communal identity and solidarity (240). Witmer relies on translation theory and the fact that distinctive language patterns, including apocalyptic, reinforce a sense of community to support the notion that Paul created and used θεοδίδακτος as part of his "epistolary strategy of strengthening the identity and cohesiveness of the Thessalonian community" (249); υἱοὶ ἡμέρας is used in a similar way. Such a function fits exceedingly well with my own thesis. But there is little doubt that 4:13–18 and 5:1–11 contain numerous references to traditional material which has been heavily redacted by Paul into a contingent *paraenesis*.[80] This makes the *topoi* in 4:13–18 and 5:1–11 very unlikely candidates to be of general concern on which all Christians might need instruction (Hurd 1998, 76). As for 5:12–22, there appear to be a number of exhortations which are peculiar to the Thessalonian situation (*contra* Best 1972, 223). For example, the admonitions about community leaders in verses 12–13 are unusually pointed and the reference to the ἄτακτοι (v. 14) is too singular to be considered general *paraenesis*. Indeed, the articulation of the three groups of community members, ἄτακτοι, ὀλιγόψυχοι and ἀσθενεῖς (v. 14), signal contingency (Laub 1973, 73). In verses 16–18 Roetzel is able to see subtle changes to the paraenetic sayings when compared with parallel sayings in Phil 4:4–6. Specifically, in First Thessalonians Paul emphasises the need for persisting in his imperatives; note πάντοτε (v. 16), ἀδιαλείπτως (v. 17) and ἐν παντί (v. 18). The presence of πάντοτε in verse 15 becomes a catchword for the following group of sayings and thereby gives specificity to the *paraenesis* (1972a, 373–374). As well, the reference to προφητεία (v. 20) seems quite specific (only here in the *paraenesis* of Paul) and perhaps out of place unless there were prophets in the Thessalonian community.[81] It is possible, as Malherbe suggests, that these prophets may have been promoting a divine timetable that Paul refutes in 5:1–11 (1999, 138). Further, Richard is able to discern linguistic and thematic similarities and differences between 5:12–22 and Rom 12:9–18. The similarities reveal general paraenetic concerns; the differences reveal Paul's response to particular Thessalonian issues (1995, 273–274). In conclusion, although every saying cannot, indubitably, be proved to be contingent, there is sufficient evidence to legitimise the contingency of the *letter-paraenesis* of First Thessalonians. Just prior to 1 Thess 4–5 Paul carefully

[78] See Malherbe 1983, 252; esp. 1999, 139–141.

[79] For extensive discussion of contacts between Paul's *paraenesis* in 4:9–12 and Epicurean (and Cynic) philosophies, as well as the implications for contingency on the situation of the Thessalonians, see Malherbe 2000, 242–261. As well, for a specific discussion of the *topoi* περὶ φιλαδελφίας and περὶ ἡσυχίας, as they relate to 4:9–12, see Malherbe 1992, 321–324. For a discussion of the concrete nature of 4:1–12 in general, see Laub 1973, 67–69.

[80] For example, see Collins 1980a; Plevnik 1979; Rigaux 1975.

[81] On the contingent nature of the reference to prophets in First Thessalonians, see Gillespie 1994, 36–50.

describes the occasion of Timothy bringing to Paul good news about the Thessalonians (3:6–9). As well, Paul appears to anticipate at least three of the *topoi* in 1 Thess 4, ἀγάπη (3:12), ἁγιωσύνη (3:13) and παρουσία (3:13), not to mention the summarising function of 1:9–10 (Malherbe 2000, 222). Moreover, the level of sophistication *viz.* the epistolary and rhetorical structure of the *letter-paraenesis* indicates that Paul has the Thessalonians' situation directly in mind (Fiore 1992, 164; Thompson 1993, 923). As a last comment, and in preparation for the possibility that my discussion is unconvincing to some, there remains a mitigating position. A number of scholars choose not to engage in a discursive between contingency and non-contingency but find other categories to explain the stereotypical language in Paul's *letter-paraenesis*. For Johanson, Paul is "selectively reminding his addressees of prior admonitions appropriate to the type of situation they were a part of" (1987, 116). Accordingly, there is no need to choose between alternatives of elaborating a tradition or responding to specific concrete failures (115–116).[82] Similarly, for White, the relevancy of the broader claims of tradition become apparent only within a community context — a context which demotes situational instructions and promotes compliance to a community's general maturation (1993, 152–153; 1983, 441). Accordingly, it is noteworthy that Paul's *paraenesis* is always informed or motivated by his *kērygma*,[83] as ἐν κυρίῳ Ἰησοῦ (4:1), ἵνα ... ὑμᾶς περιπατεῖν καὶ ἀρέσκειν θεῷ (4:1) and διὰ τοῦ κυρίου Ἰησοῦ (4:2) make evident (Eddy 1993, 47–48).

5. Finally, the (in?)significance of the περὶ δέ formula at 4:9 and 5:1 (cf. 4:13) must be dealt with as an important preliminary issue to the analysis. Does the presence of such a formula indicate that the Thessalonians wrote to Paul? If yes, then presumably Paul's *letter-paraenesis* is principally related to the Thessalonians' situation.

Harris (1898) is accredited as the first to suggest that the Thessalonians wrote to Paul.[84] He draws attention to a number of elements in First Thessalonians to support his thesis. In brief, these elements are: the term εὐαγγελίζεσθαι (3:6) refers to such a letter (168); the second καί (2:13), "*we also* give thanks ..." is a reference to the *letter-thanksgiving* of the Thessalonians in their own letter (169); the repetition of εἴσοδος (1:9; 2:1) and κενός (2:1; 3:5) indicates that these elements must have been in the Thessalonian letter (169–170); the "suspicious regularity" of "you know" phrases is regarded as evidence for such a letter (170); the little attested reading, ὑμῶν instead of ἡμῶν (1:9), is preferred by Harris and then understood as a reference to a letter from the Thessalonians to Paul (170–171); finally, Harris argues that the Thessalonians alluded to Paul's "labour and toil"; this is why Paul refers to it in 2:9

[82] Davis argues that just because particular parts of Paul's *letter-paraenesis* may be identified as traditional, or stereotypical, this does not mean that it is any less pertinent to the situation of the Thessalonians (1971, 187); so also Bailey/Vander Broek 1992, 64.

[83] Collins 1984, 324; McNicol 1996, 16–17; Schnelle 1990, 296–297.

[84] Holtz (1998, 31) seems unaware of Harris and begins his discussion of the issue with Faw (1952).

as well as opening his letter with references to "work of faith" and "labour of love" (1:3; 172). Harris then provides a reconstruction of what the "lost Epistle" from the Thessalonians to Paul may have looked like (172–173). He goes even further. On the basis of his recovered letter from the Thessalonians to Paul, Harris reconstructs elements of an initial hypothetical letter from Paul to the Thessalonians, sent via Timothy (173–174). But this enters into the realm of pure speculation.

Despite some acceptance,[85] his thesis is generally rejected as an "ingenious attempt" whereby "the hypothesis is tenable, but the evidence is rather elusive" (Moffatt 1910, 6). Faw (1952) takes up the thesis of Harris but rejects his lines of argumentation.[86] Instead, he argues that there are three converging lines of "really good and objective evidence in First Thessalonians for the existence of a previous letter" (Faw 1952, 220). This alleged evidence may be summarised as follows: (1) The expression περὶ δέ in 4:9, 4:13 (*sic*) and 5:1 (and δέ in 5:12) demonstrates the existence of such a letter since Paul only uses this formula of introduction to reply to a letter previously received (220).[87] Faw also looks to the use of περὶ δέ in Mark 12:26; 13:32; John 16:11 and Acts 21:25 to support the conclusion that it is a formula of reply to various questions or problems (220–221). Unfortunately, he does not refer to Matt 20:6 or 27:46 where περὶ δέ is used in other ways. (2) The abruptness of thought between each new item for discussion is best explained as referring to a previous letter (221). (3) Paul's reluctance to discuss two items (4:9; 5:1) shows that he was requested to write upon these topics (222). Assuming that these arguments are accepted, Faw suggests 5:12 indicates that the letter from the Thessalonians was written by the leaders of the Christian community (222–223), and concomitantly, that 5:12–22 was written specifically for those leaders (224–225). Finally, although it is difficult to distinguish between Paul's responses to oral and written communication from the Thessalonians, Faw argues that 1 Thess 4–5 is a response to the hypothesised letter, and that 1 Thess 1–3 is, logically, a response to Timothy's oral report (223–224; so also Hurd 1998, 77; Kaye 1975, 47). Richard proposes a variation consistent with his thesis of an early and late missive (see his introduction): he views 2:1–12 and 4:3–8 as responses to oral reports and 4:9–5:22 as a response to written questions (1995, 213).[88]

Faw does introduce into the discussion the formula, περὶ δέ, but his argumentation is only convincing to those already won over by the thesis (Jewett 1986, 92). Malherbe (1990) is a modern proponent of the view that the Thessalonians wrote to Paul. First, he acknowledges his predecessors (247–248) and then looks more closely at epistolographic conventions. In particular, there are four which

[85] E.g. Frame 1912, 9; Milligan 1908, xxx, 126.

[86] Indeed, Faw suggests that Harris' line of argument was "intuitive and lacked conclusive objective proof ... [Harris] fastened upon certain suggestive but tenuous evidences and proceeded to draw quite sweeping conclusions from them" (1952, 219).

[87] So 1 Cor 7:1, 25; 8:1; 12:1; 16:1, 12; cf. 1 Cor 7:8; 8:4; 11:2; 15:1.

[88] It should be noted that the *topos* on love of the brothers (4:9) is hardly formulated as a response to a question (Hoppe 2002, 328).

Malherbe believes support (but not prove) the hypothesis that Timothy brought Paul a letter from the Thessalonians (250–252): (1) The expression of longing (3:6), both on the Thessalonians' part and on the part of Paul, describes favourable circumstances for such a letter. (2) Likewise, the reference to "good remembrance" (3:6) is equally appropriate for such a letter (250). (3) Stronger evidence includes the use of περὶ δέ as a way of responding to written inquiry — though the formula is not used exclusively in this way (251; *contra* Faw). (4) Finally, the epistolographic convention of referring to a correspondent's needs (4:9; 5:1) may be indicative of a letter from the Thessalonians (251–252). Even Malherbe admits the evidence is inconclusive (252). But he finds other epistolographic clues in Paul's reception of Timothy's report, two of which include clichéd expressions of joy upon receipt of a letter and thanking of the gods that communication had been affected (3:9; see 1990, 252 for other references). Another clue, which Malherbe considers to be the most important evidence for a Thessalonian letter, is found in 3:10 where Paul expresses that he prays night and day to see the Thessalonians face to face and supply what is lacking in their faith (252). Paul uses well-known epistolographic conventions to indicate that he wants to meet their needs by letter.[89] On the strength of the evidence, Malherbe asserts that 1 Thess 4–5 is written in response to the Thessalonians' needs (253). Even though Paul does not mention a letter from the Thessalonians, Malherbe believes the evidence supports the existence of one. He looks to 1 Cor 16:17 and Phil 2:25–30 as parallel instances where Paul does not refer to a letter from his recipients, even though it is possible one exists (254–255). Malherbe concludes: "... it is quite possible that he had written to them when he first sent Timothy to them, and it is highly probable that they in return wrote him for advice" (255).

The foregoing survey of three articles on whether the Thessalonians wrote to Paul (Harris 1898; Faw 1952; Malherbe 1990) reveals that the formula περὶ δέ is rather insignificant for resolving the contingency issue of the *letter-paraenesis*. The formula is ambiguous: it may be used to introduce a new topic,[90] or to indicate a reply to oral or written requests.[91] None of the uses may be promoted to the exclusion of the others.[92] Furthermore, it is impossible to discern between responses to an oral report and responses to a written letter.[93] The existence of a letter from the Thessalonians is a possibility only, a point which Malherbe implicitly concedes (1990, 253). The argument essentially hangs on whether Paul follows a certain

[89] These include "the preoccupation, night and day, with the inability to see one's correspondent in person, and a view of one's letter as a surrogate for one's physical presence" (1990, 252). Malherbe also gives numerous examples where χρήζειν and ὑστερεῖν are satisfied by a letter (253).

[90] So Collins 2000, 324; Johanson 1987, 51; Lenski 1937, 318.

[91] So Faw 1952, 220–221; Frame 1912, 157, 166, 178; Green 2002, 202; Haufe 1999, 15; Hurd 1976, 900 (see 1998, 75); Richard 1991, 47; Schnelle 1990, 298; Uprichard 1979, 150; White 1993, 156.

[92] See Kloppenborg 1993, 271–272; Marshall 1983, 118–119; Tellbe 2001, 100; Wanamaker 1990, 166–167; *contra* Boers 1976, 157; Manson 1953, 443–446.

[93] Best 1972, 14–15; Bruce 1982, 89; Hurd 1998, 75; Malherbe 2000, 216.

modus operandi, i.e. leaving unmentioned possible letters from his correspondents but rather referring to the bearer of the hypothesised letter (so Malherbe's references to 1 Cor 16:17 and Phil 2:25–30). But is Malherbe building hypothesis on hypotheses?[94] Rather, in the absence of any clear reference to a letter from the Thessalonians (vis-à-vis 1 Cor 7:1), I am convinced that the *letter-paraenesis* of First Thessalonians is contingent only on an oral report from Timothy (3:6–10).[95]

Should this conclusion be accepted, then there is one significant ramification for my thesis, namely, that despite the contingency of the *letter-paraenesis* on an oral report from Timothy, Paul's choices of *topoi* to include in 1 Thess 4:1–5:22 reflect his pattern of exhortation. This observation is especially important for the analyses of 4:13–18 and 5:1–11 where the details and development of didactic and paraenetic material are most pronounced. Thus, it comes as no surprise that eschatological motifs surface repeatedly in these pericopes.

VII. Conclusion

Letter-Opening (1:1)

1:1a superscription
1:1b adscription
1:1c formulaic wish of grace and peace

Main Part (1:2–5:22)

Letter-Thanksgiving (1:2–10)

1:2a principal verb (εὐχαριστεῖν) + indirect object (τῷ θεῷ)
1:2b adverbial phrase of manner (πάντοτε περὶ πάντων ὑμῶν)
1:3–5b indication of reasons for thanksgiving (μνημονεύοντες, εἰδότες, ὅτι)
1:5c–10 explanatory unit (καθώς ..., including *eschatological climax*)

Disclosure of a Past-Present Relationship (2:1–16)

2:1 *disclosure-type* formula (αὐτοὶ γὰρ οἴδατε, ἀδελφοί ...)
2:2–11 εἰδέναι (2:2, 5, 11) and ἀδελφοί (2:9) are organising elements
2:12 eschatological transition
2:13a principal verb (εὐχαριστεῖν) + indirect object (τῷ θεῷ)
2:13b adverbial phrase of manner (ἀδιαλείπτως)
2:13c indication of reason for thanksgiving (ὅτι ...)
2:14–16 explanatory unit (... γάρ ..., including *eschatological climax*)

Apostolic Parousia (2:17–3:13)

2:17 desire to see the Thessalonians
2:18a wish to see them
2:18b hindrance to his coming

[94] This is particularly the case with Philippians. At least 1 Cor 7:1 does refer to such a letter.
[95] So also Holtz 1998, 31; Marxsen 1979, 57; but see Collins 1984, 300 and 1993, 114–116.

2:19–20 eschatological transition
3:1–5 dispatch of an emissary (καὶ ἐπέμψαμεν Τιμόθεον ...)
3:6–10 invocation of divine approval through prayer (αὐτὸς δὲ ὁ θεὸς ...)
3:11–13 (benediction, including *eschatological climax*)

Letter-Paraenesis (4:1–5:22)

4:1–2 introduction
4:3–8 *topos* on sanctification (ἁγιασμός)
4:9–12 *topoi* on love of the brothers (περὶ δὲ τῆς φιλαδελφίας), living quietly (φιλοτιμεῖσθαι), minding one's own affairs (ἡσυχάζειν) and decorous living (ἵνα περιπατῆτε εὐσχημόνως ...)
4:13–18 *topos* on those who are asleep (περὶ τῶν κοιμωμένων)
5:1–11 *topos* on times and seasons (περὶ δὲ τῶν χρόνων καὶ τῶν καιρῶν)
5:12–22 groups of sayings arranged under ἐρωτᾶν (5:12) and παρακαλεῖν (5:14)

Letter-Closing (5:23–28)

5:23–24 peace benediction (with a word of encouragement)
5:25 hortatory section (ἀδελφοί, προσεύχεσθε καὶ περὶ ἡμῶν)
5:26 kiss greeting (second-person type)
5:27 autograph (ἐνορκίζω ὑμᾶς ...)
5:28 grace benediction

1. Parts of the epistolary structure outlined above model the structure found in many of Paul's letters while other parts do not. For example, the *letter-opening*, *letter-thanksgiving*, *letter-paraenesis* and *letter-closing* all follow recognisable epistolary structures. That is, the structure for these sections is more or less the same for all of Paul's letters. Conversely, there are several pericopes in First Thessalonians which find no or little analogy elsewhere in Paul. In particular, 1 Thess 2:1–16 is uniquely tailored to the occasion of First Thessalonians. Moreover, while 2:13–16 and 2:17–3:13 have recognisable structures, they also have a greater fluidity. There is no suggestion whatever that all *eschatological climaxes* follow a thanksgiving formulation. Nor do I mean to give the impression that the *apostolic parousia* has a fixed form. But there is no danger of that if one notes how loosely Funk's proposed structure fits the text of 2:17–3:13.[96] These pericopes evidence Paul's freedom when writing and care must be taken not to force known epistolary structures onto the text.

2. More important is the elimination of the label "*letter-body*" in the epistolary analysis of Paul's letters. The label is not only ambiguous for most letters, but in terms of 1 Thess 2:1–12, it is misleading. Dispensing with the category altogether paves the way for an analysis of the *main part* which is individualised to each letter. Such an approach allows appropriate labelling for generic structures (e.g. *letter-thanksgiving*, *eschatological climax*, *apostolic parousia*, *letter-paraenesis*), and

[96] It does not account for 2:17a and 3:1. Nor does Funk deal particularly well with the benediction of 3:11–13.

at the same time, allows a precise description for non-generic structures. Thus, "*disclosure* of a past-present relationship" is not an alternative label to "*letter-body*", but a description of a distinctive section of First Thessalonians. The expression of commands/requests and the conveyance of information is no longer limited to one section (e.g. "*letter-body*"), but is attributed to the entirety of the *main part*. As a result, the *letter-thanksgiving* does not include 2:1–3:13, either in whole (i.e. a long *letter-thanksgiving* from 1:2–3:13) or in part (i.e. *letter-thanksgiving* reiterations at 2:13 and 3:9). Furthermore, the *letter-paraenesis* is incorporated into the *main part* of the letter. This acknowledges the occasional role it plays in the communication process (i.e. it is not a stereotyped block of *paraenesis* attached to the end of the letter).

3. Throughout, conclusions obtained from advocates of rhetorical analysis have been included in this epistolary analysis of First Thessalonians. Thus, the delineation between the *main part* and the *letter-closing*, with the peace benediction (5:23–24) included in the latter structure, illustrates how the two approaches can work together. Far from demonstrating a methodological confusion (*contra* Jewett 1986, 70), an epistolary approach *is* able to provide a convincing view of the letter's structure, even though rhetorical considerations do give greater nuance to parts of the discussion.

4. The issues discussed in this chapter have significant implications for the thesis that eschatology is the best hermeneutical key to interpret Paul's pattern of exhortation in First Thessalonians. These implications relate to the exegesis of specific pericopes as well as to the systematic concerns of the letter. There is now a firm basis for understanding 1 Thess 1:9–10 as an *eschatological climax* of the *letter-thanksgiving* (vv. 2–10). In a similar way, 2:14–16 serves as an *eschatological climax* of 2:1–16. Both *climaxes* become significant junctures for the structure of the letter and the epistolary arrangement acknowledges the sustained eschatological content of the pericopes. In addition, 2:13–16 now has a clear epistolary and rhetorical starting point for an argument of authenticity. On that issue, there is much more discussion to follow.[97] As well, the occasional nature of Paul's *paraenesis*, in 4:1–5:22 and elsewhere in the letter, supports the notion that Paul uses, systematically, eschatological motifs in First Thessalonians for purposes of exhortation. In virtually every epistolary section of the letter, Paul directly refers to such motifs. For example, besides the *eschatological climax* in 1:9–10, the *letter-thanksgiving* also contains references to the Holy Spirit and affliction (1:5, 6). The *disclosure* of a past-present relationship contains an eschatological transition with a reference to the kingdom and glory (2:12), as well as an *eschatological climax* with a pronouncement of *orgē* (2:14–16). The *apostolic parousia* has a distinctive reference to Satan (2:18), an eschatological transition, with a reference to the *parousia* of the Lord (2:19–20), and an *eschatological climax*, with another reference to the *parousia* of the Lord (3:11–13). The *letter-paraenesis* has a sustained reference to

[97] See Chapter 4, §IV.

sanctification and holiness (4:3–8), and contains numerous eschatological motifs in 4:13–18 and 5:1–11. Finally, the *letter-closing* again explicitly refers to the *parousia* of the Lord (5:23). In conclusion, the epistolary (and rhetorical) analysis of First Thessalonians, as carried out in this chapter, reveals how each section of the *main part* is carefully constructed and integrated, and consistently provides a paraenetic function. This conclusion, coupled with the extensive presence of an eschatological discourse throughout the letter, including eschatological motifs strategically positioned in each epistolary section, highlights the importance of eschatology in First Thessalonians. It remains to be seen just how well eschatology, as a hermeneutical key, may elucidate Paul's pattern of exhortation in the pericopes chosen for analysis.

Chapter 3
First Thessalonians 1:9–10

Among the conclusions of the epistolary analysis of First Thessalonians is the definitive identification of the *letter-thanksgiving* in 1 Thess 1:2–10. There are many *eschatological climaxes* in the letter, but the position of 1:9–10 at the close of the *letter-thanksgiving* indicates a greater rhetorical significance for the eschatological motifs contained in these verses. Thus, conversion, dualism between idols and God, waiting, resurrection, deliverance and *orgē* contribute to a characteristic eschatological discourse in the letter (Paul returns to many of these motifs). I argue that this discourse plays a fundamental role in his purposes for writing.

I. Arranged Text and Translation

9a	αὐτοὶ γὰρ	περὶ ἡμῶν ἀπαγγέλλουσιν		
9b		ὁποίαν εἴσοδον ἔσχομεν		πρὸς ὑμᾶς,
9c	καὶ	πῶς ἐπεστρέψατε		πρὸς τὸν θεὸν ἀπὸ τῶν εἰδώλων
9d		δουλεύειν θεῷ ζῶντι καὶ ἀληθινῷ		
10a	καὶ	ἀναμένειν	τὸν υἱὸν αὐτοῦ	ἐκ τῶν οὐρανῶν,
10b		ὃν ἤγειρεν		ἐκ τῶν νεκρῶν,
10c		Ἰησοῦν	τὸν ῥυόμενον ἡμᾶς	ἐκ τῆς ὀργῆς τῆς ἐρχομένης.

9a	For they themselves report concerning us			
9b		what sort of entrance we had		to you,
9c	and	how you turned		to God from idols
9d		to serve the living and true God		
10a	and	to await	his son	from heaven,
10b		whom he raised		from the dead,
10c		Jesus	who delivers us	from the *orgē* which comes.[1]

[1] My arrangement is very similar to Havener's (1981, 105).

II. Preliminary Issues

a. Arrangement of the Text

The arrangement of the text highlights the function of γάρ (v. 9a),[2] which introduces the reason why Paul need not say anything about the faith of the Thessalonians, and of καί, which is used both in conjunction with πῶς, as an indication of manner (v. 9c)[3] and by itself, as a simple connective (v. 10a), coordinating two indirect interrogative phrases (similarly Bickmann 1998, 160–161). The arrangement also draws attention to the parallel prepositional phrases with πρός (v. 9b, c; cf. v. 8b) and ἐκ (v. 10a, b, c).[4] Other structural features to be noted include the parallel descriptions of Jesus, τὸν υἱὸν αὐτοῦ (v. 10a) and τὸν ῥυόμενον (v. 10c), as well as the pleasing rhythm/rhyme of the phrases effected particularly by the preponderance of words ending in -ω(ν).[5] Perhaps the most provocative proposal for the arrangement of 1 Thess 1:9c–10 is that of Friedrich (1965, 508–510), who argues for a two-strophe hymn-structure (see Excursus 3).

b. The Immediate Context

Vis-à-vis the whole letter, nearly all commentators understand 1:9–10 as part of a thanksgiving section (epistolary analysis) or *exordium* (rhetorical analysis).[6] The pericope is well situated in its context referring both to the foregoing description of Paul's reception among the Thessalonians (1:6–8) and to the subsequent section on his founding activity (2:1–16). Thus, the report (ἀπαγγέλλουσιν, v. 9a) naturally flows from Paul's statement that the word of the Lord (ὁ λόγος τοῦ κυρίου) had sounded forth from them (ἐξήχηται ... ἐξελήλυθεν), so that nothing more need be said (ὥστε μὴ χρείαν ἔχειν ἡμᾶς λαλεῖν τι, v. 8). Further, the recurrence of the word εἴσοδος (v. 9b; 2:1) creates a thematic link with the next section.[7]

---

[2] This is a second γάρ-clause explaining Paul's assertion in v. 7, the first beginning in v. 8 (Holmstrand 1997, 50).

[3] See §III.a.4 below for a defence of πῶς as an indication of manner, not of fact (viz. equal to ὅτι).

[4] Langevin appears to be the only other exegete who notes the striking three-fold repetition of πρός (1965, 267).

[5] So πῶς ... τῶν εἰδώλων (v. 9c), ἀληθινῷ (v. 9d), θεῷ ζῶντι ... τῶν οὐρανῶν (v. 10a), τῶν νεκρῶν (v. 10c; Rigaux 1956, 392).

[6] The only exceptions include: Jewett, who argues that the *exordium* concludes at v. 5, and that 1:6–3:13 forms part of the *narratio* (1986, 76–77); Johanson, who takes a broader view of the "*letter-body*" and includes 1:2–5:24 under that rubric (1987, 59–67), although he admits that 1:2–3:13 is somewhat "*exordium*-like" (160); Morris, who assigns 1:5–2:16 under the title, "reminiscences" (1959, 43); Olbricht, who takes the *exordium* to finish at 1:3, with 1:4–10 being the statement preceding the proof in 2:1–5:11 (1990, 235); Smith, who argues that 1:1–5 sufficiently fulfils the functions of an *exordium* (1995, 69–75; 2000, 687–690).

[7] *Contra* de Jonge who characterises v. 10 as "an excursus in its immediate context" (1979, 133), and a "clearly significant excursus" (1988, 34). Although the two sections are linked (further strengthened

c. The Function of 1:9–10 as a Summary

1. It may be argued that 1:9–10 is a summary (or outline) of First Thessalonians. The report is reminiscent of the triadic motif of faith, love and hope in 1:3.[8] The reference to Paul's founding visit is taken up in 2:1 while the Thessalonians' service to God is expanded in the *paraenesis* of 4:3–12.[9] Finally, the pericope introduces eschatological motifs and prepares for more extensive treatments in 4:13–18 and 5:1–11.[10] Richard rightly concludes: "The report of 1:9–10 then announces the various parts of the body of the letter and from such an analysis one understands Paul's choice of such a handy report" (1995, 75). These observations support the understanding that 1:9–10 is somewhat anticipatory — that which is presented as fact at the beginning of the letter is later developed in detail.[11]

2. The issue of whether 1:9–10 should be regarded as a summary of Paul's missionary proclamation sometimes includes the identification of these verses as Jewish mission propaganda and/or as containing pre-Pauline tradition (see Excursus 3). Regardless of the outcome of that discussion, the function of the report must be described within the epistolary context of First Thessalonians, especially since 1:9–10 constitutes the close of the *letter-thanksgiving*.

III. Analysis

a. Turned to God from Idols (1:9)

1. There are a number of exegetical issues in verse 9 that remain to be resolved. Although there is no pretence here to resolve any of these issues, the development of a comprehensive statement of the eschatology of First Thessalonians will be greatly aided by a careful re-evaluation of the different problems. These will be taken up in the following order: a short discussion on ἀπαγγέλλειν (§III.a.2); the issue of how Paul uses the word εἴσοδος (§III.a.3); the problem of the interrogative pronoun πῶς

by the presence of γάρ in 2:1), there is no doubt that 2:1 begins a new section. Not only is there a shift in perspective, but the direct address (ἀδελφοί) and added emphasis (αὐτοί) serve to reinforce the distinction (Holmstrand 1997, 52–53). The literary unity observed here would seem to discount Pesch's attempt to find two original letters, one written from Athens and the other from Corinth, for which he argues that the double reference to Paul's εἴσοδος is evidence (1984, 44–50).

[8] Thus, "work of faith" is correlated with turning to God from idols, "labour of love" is correlated with serving God, and "patience of hope" is correlated with waiting for the son (Custer 1975, 48).

[9] Watson makes a connection between 1:9–10 and 4:3–12, but in a different way. He asserts that the judgment motif in v. 10 prepares for the exhortations in 4:3–8 against sexual impurity (1999, 67).

[10] Hodges 1982, 68–70; Laub 1976, 22–23; Snyder 1972a, 239. Wuellner adds that 1:9–10 presents a central "theme" of the letter, which is revisited in 3:11–13 and 5:23–24 (1990, 129). Collins comments: "4:14–17 unfolds and makes more precise, by application to the case of those who have died, what Paul has already affirmed in his thanksgiving" (1993, 154–155).

[11] So Munck 1963, 107–108; Snyder 1972, 360–362; Thomas 1978, 248; Vawter 1960, 41.

and how it is to be understood (§III.a.4); a survey of how ἐπιστρέφειν is used in the NT and elsewhere, and a discussion of whether Paul uses it as a *terminus technicus* to describe a "conversion" experience (§III.a.5); a previously underemphasised significance of the πρὸς τὸν θεόν and ἀπὸ τῶν εἰδώλων juxtaposition (§III.a.6); to whom or what Paul is referring in the phrase ἀπὸ τῶν εἰδώλων (§III.a.7); a brief excursus on "conversion" to Christianity (Excursus 2); a discussion of δουλεύειν and its trajectory in the OT and Greek thought (§III.a.8); and finally, the significance of the designation: θεῷ ζῶντι καὶ ἀληθινῷ (§III.a.9). A conclusion which applies the results of the analysis to my thesis appears at the end of the chapter (§IV below).

2. The introductory γάρ, just as in verse 8, confirms the ὥστε-clause in verse 7, that the Thessalonians had become an example to all the believers in Macedonia and Achaia. The verb ἀπαγγέλλειν probably has the weakened sense of "inform", "report", rather than "announce", "declare", since Paul is not so interested in defining the act of reporting, as in what is actually reported;[12] i.e. the faith (πρὸς τὸν θεόν) which has gone forth (v. 8b).[13] Nor does Paul specifically identify who is doing the reporting. The use of αὐτός serves to emphasise that the reports are not his own.[14] Frame suggests that it may refer to the believers in Macedonia and Achaia, although hardly to all of them;[15] more specifically αὐτοί refers to those who made the reports to Paul (1912, 84).[16] The transmission of the reports would seem to be oral rather than written, as suggested by λαλεῖν in verse 8 (for γράφειν, see 4:9; 5:1).

3. The contents of the report consist of two parts, concerning (περί) the entrance (εἴσοδος) of Paul and his co-workers among the Thessalonians (v. 9a, b), and concerning how (πῶς) the Thessalonians turned (ἐπιστρέφειν) to God from idols (v. 9c).[17] The focus of the first part of the report is on the founding mission to

[12] Paul rarely uses the word (only here and in 1 Cor 14:25). In each case it refers to the impression/impact of the word of God (cf. also ὁ λόγος τοῦ κυρίου in 1 Thess 1:8). A similar word, ἀναγγέλλειν, appears in Rom 15:21 where it is found in a quotation of Isa 52:15 (LXX) and seems to be synonymous with εὐαγγελίζεσθαι (Rom 15:20; cf. 1 Pet 1:12), and also in 2 Cor 7:7 where God comforts Paul by a report from Titus (Schniewind 1964, 64–66). The suggestion that ἀπαγγέλλειν is mutually interchangeable with ἀναγγέλλειν (Broer 1990a, 13) may be tentatively accepted.

[13] The translation "your faith in God" (RSV), for ἡ πίστις ὑμῶν ἡ πρὸς τὸν θεόν, is inadequate. Findlay suggests that "your faith, that is turned toward God" better expresses the changed direction and attitude which is apparent in 1:9–10 (1904, 27); similarly, Collins 1984, 216.

[14] It contrasts with ἡμᾶς in v. 8 (BDAG 152, §1.c).

[15] *Contra* Lenski 1937, 232. Bruce suggests that αὐτοί is limited to only those believers in Macedonia and Achaia "who had heard the news", and that, "the faith of the Thessalonians had become a topic of general conversation" (1982, 17). Meeks links the report with the brethren from Macedonia (2 Cor 11:9) who were probably the carriers of money to Paul while he was in Thessalonica (Phil 4:16): "It is likely that they were also the ones who told the story of how things had gone in Thessalonica" (1983, 27).

[16] Malherbe's proposal that Paul may have received the report partly through Timothy is conjectural (2000, 118).

[17] A textual variation (here lies the first of several comments on textual issues; see Fee 1992), where some manuscripts read περὶ ὑμῶν rather than περὶ ἡμῶν, does not significantly affect the exegesis. If the variation did not come about *ex itacismo* (BDF 13, §22), then it is possibly due to the prominent ὑμῶν in v. 8 (Dibelius 1925, 5; Findlay 1904, 14), or for the sake of consistency, since Paul does not focus on himself and his co-workers but on his converts (Best 1972, 81). Thus, ἡμῶν is the *lectio difficilior* as it *does refer* to

Thessalonica, and particularly with "the kind of entrance" (ὁποίαν εἴσοδον) therein; ὁποῖος refers to the kind or quality of entrance Paul and his co-workers had.[18] The word εἴσοδος appears in Paul only here and in 2:1.[19] Taken literally, it would refer either to the *place* or *act* of entering (BDAG 294–295). However, Paul is not referring to a spatial entering, but to a figurative verbal sense of "entrance" or even "access" — a fact recognised by nearly all commentators.[20] This is inferred from the second instance of εἴσοδος (2:1) where the noun must be understood in a verbal way in order to make sense of κενή — Paul refers to his *coming not in vain* (Michaelis 1967, 106).[21] Moreover, the significance of the relatively rare πρός construction following εἴσοδος (both 1:9 and 2:1) is missed by most commentators. Michaelis notes that when πρός (or παρά) is used, εἴσοδος usually emphasises access to persons or things (106).[22] If this is how Paul uses it, then this may accentuate the effectiveness of

---

Paul and his co-workers, *not* to Paul and his converts (Alford 1958, 253). Richard draws attention to a parallel between 1:5–6 and 1:9–10: first there is a focus on Paul and his co-workers ("our gospel came to you", v. 5; "what sort of entrance we had", v. 9b) and then a focus on the converts ("you received the word", v. 6; "you turned to God from idols", v. 9c), providing conclusive internal evidence in favour of ἡμῶν (1995, 51; so also Bickmann 1998, 159; see Johanson 1987, 86).

[18] Paul uses ὁποῖος as a correlative pronoun in Gal 2:6 (cf. Acts 26:29) and as an interrogative pronoun in indirect questions in 1 Cor 3:13 and here (cf. Jas 1:24; Schneider 1991a, 524; *GGNT* 732).

[19] Elsewhere in the NT εἴσοδος appears only in Acts 13:24, Heb 10:19 and 2 Pet 1:11.

[20] A figurative verbal use of εἴσοδος is well attested: e.g. Euripides *Andr.* 930, κακῶν γυναικῶν εἴσοδοί μ᾽ ἀπώλεσαν ("My undoing was bad women coming into the house"); *Andr.* 952, ὑγιὲς γὰρ οὐδὲν αἱ θύραθεν εἴσοδοι δρῶσιν γυναικῶν, ἀλλὰ πολλὰ καὶ κακά ("For visits of women from outside cause nothing good but only trouble aplenty" [Kovacs 1994–2002]); Lysias 1.20, καὶ τὰς εἰσόδους οἷς τρόποις προσίοιτο ("and by what means she procured his entrances" [Lamb 1930]); *Let. Aris.* 120, παρεύρεσιν λαβόντων εἰς τοὺς τόπους εἰσόδου ("they had seized the pretext of moving into the mining areas" [Shutt 1985]); *Cor. Herm.* 1.22, with regard to the guarding of the mind: πυλωρὸς ὢν ἀποκλείσω τὰς εἰσόδους τῶν κακῶν καὶ αἰσχρῶν ἐνεργημάτων ("I will keep guard at the gates, and bar the entrance of the base and evil workings of the senses" [Scott 1968]); Isa 66:11 (LXX), ἵνα θηλάσητε καὶ ἐμπλησθῆτε ἀπὸ μαστοῦ παρακλήσεως αὐτῆς ἵνα ἐκθηλάσαντες τρυφήσητε ἀπὸ εἰσόδου δόξης αὐτῆς ("that you may suck and be satisfied with the breast of her consolation, that sucking the breast, you may indulge with the coming of her glory" [transl. mine]). These examples demonstrate that εἴσοδος even approaches the meaning of εἰσιέναι (Michaelis 1967, 104).

[21] To wit, Frame suggests that εἴσοδος should be equated with παρουσία (1912, 87). Cf. παρουσίας πάλιν πρὸς ὑμᾶς in Phil 1:26; ἐγενόμην πρὸς ὑμᾶς in 1 Cor 2:3; cf. also Gen 30:27; 1 Kgdms 16:4; Mal 3:2; Acts 16:40; 28:30. It has been argued that this verbal (active) sense is only apparent in 2:1 while εἴσοδος in 1:9 has a more passive meaning (i.e. "reception"; "welcome"; so Dibelius 1925, 5; Malherbe 2000, 118; see Henneken 1969, 65). Such a distinction is unlikely since there are no extant references (to my knowledge) of a passive meaning of εἴσοδος (significantly, Malherbe provides some references to the "active" sense, but none for the alleged "passive" sense). The context of 2:1–2 probably indicates that κενή refers to the character of Paul's mission (Donfried 2000a, 47; Malherbe 2000, 136), that is, to Paul's motives for his entrance (Weima 1997, 94; see Lyons 1985, 192–193) rather than emphasising the results of the εἴσοδος (*contra* Still 1999, 127).

[22] So Josephus *Ant.* 18.164, where Agrippa is forbidden access to Caesar (εἴσοδον τὸν πρὸς αὐτόν); Philo *Fug.* 183, which refers to an access to virtue (εἰσόδου τῆς πρὸς ἀρετήν); Marcus Aurelius Antoninus 5.19, where it is said that things cannot take hold of the soul, nor have access to it (οὐδὲ ἔχει εἴσοδον πρὸς ψυχήν); cf. Josephus *B.J.* 4.270. Cf. also Herodotus 3.118, about the laws regarding access to the king: τοῖσι ἐπαναστᾶσι τῷ Μάγῳ ἔσοδον εἶναι παρὰ βασιλέα ἄνευ ἀγγέλου ("that the rebels should come into the king's presence without announcement given" [Godley 1920–1925]); Herm. *Sim.* 9.12.6, ἡ δὲ πύλη ὁ υἱὸς

his (and his co-workers') entrance, i.e. what happened to the Thessalonians as a consequence of his entering (Ellingworth/Nida 1976, 14). Thus, Paul may well be emphasising the power of the gospel, and *its entrance*, rather than merely the entrance of himself and his co-workers (Betz 1998, 252; see Lyons 1995, 195).[23] But Richard is surely right when he says that the translation "welcome", "reception"[24] makes too explicit and overemphasises the successful nature of the entrance, which is developed in 2:1–12 (1995, 51). Perhaps there is a thought of success in the qualitative ὁποῖος (Michaelis 1967, 106), but for Paul, a measure of success is not how many people he is able to get to listen to him, but that they had turned in their spiritual direction (Winter 1993, 65). Consequently, a right interpretation must find a balance between the coming of Paul and his co-workers (foreground) and the accommodation or acceptance of their message (background).[25]

Kim (2005) argues that Paul connects the success of the gospel and/or the faith of the Thessalonians with his εἴσοδος five times (1:5; 1:9–10; 2:1, 13; 3:6), and that his preoccupation for this theme is evidence that 2:1–12 is a sustained *apologia* rather than mere *paraenesis*. While I am not convinced that Kim has successfully critiqued Malherbe's sophisticated interpretation of the latter pericope (see Kim 2005, 524–533), his observation that καθώς (1:5) connects Paul's and his co-workers' conduct with the coming of the gospel strengthens the successful connotations inherent in ὁποῖος (1:9b; 520).

4. The second part of the report is introduced by a head clause, καὶ πῶς ἐπεστρέψατε ... (v. 9c), and continues with two infinitival clauses beginning with δουλεύειν (v. 9d) and ἀναμένειν (v. 10a). The interrogative particle, πῶς, may be understood either as an adverb marking the *manner* of turning, i.e. "how you turned ...", or as a conjunction indicating the *fact* of turning, i.e. "that you turned ..." (= ὅτι). Scholars are evenly divided.[26] Major grammars recognise the encroachment of πῶς on ὅτι, particularly in later Greek, but already apparent in the NT.[27] But there is nothing

τοῦ θεοῦ ἐστιν· αὕτη μία εἴσοδός ἐστι πρὸς τὸν κύριον. ἄλλως οὖν οὐδεὶς εἰσελεύσεται πρὸς αὐτὸν εἰ μὴ διὰ τοῦ υἱοῦ αὐτοῦ ("The gate is the Son of God, that one entrance to the presence of the Lord. No one can enter his presence any other way but by his son" [Osiek 1999]).

[23] Or, along the lines of Fee's observation that the themes of "power" and "spirit" go together, in v. 5 Paul may well be emphasising the entrance of the Holy Spirit into the community (1994, 35–36; Winter 1993, 64–65); at the least he is referring to the fact that his entrance is no mere human achievement but is effected by divine power (v. 6; Oepke 1965a, 660).

[24] Bailey 1955, 264; Balz 1990, 402; Bruce 1982, 17; Eadie 1877, 50–51; Gillman 1990, 62; Wanamaker 1990, 84; BDAG 294, §3; RSV.

[25] So Holtz: "Darin liegen das aktive Moment des Auftretens und das passive der Aufnahme ineinander" (1998, 54); Rigaux: "Mais il n'y a pas de brillante entrée sans accueil triumphal" (1956, 389); see also Haufe 1999, 28; Winter 1993, 67.

[26] Those supporting πῶς as indicating *fact* include: Alford 1958, 253; Frame 1912, 87; Haufe 1999, 28; Holtz 1977, 470; 1998, 54; Milligan 1908, 13; Schenk 1993, 203; so also MM 561. Those supporting πῶς as indicating both *fact* and *manner* include: Auberlen/Riggenbach 1869, 23; Findlay 1891, 58; 1904, 28; Johanson 1987, 86; Jowett 1859, 50; Rigaux 1956, 389; Wanamaker 1990, 85.

[27] So BDF 203–204, §396; *GGNT* 1032; *GNTG* vol. 1, 211; vol. 3, 137.

in the context that demands this limitation.[28] Moreover, the parallel between πῶς and ὁποῖος suggests that Paul uses the particle modally,[29] although this should not be emphasised (Milligan 1908, 13), and probably refers to the affliction (θλῖψις) and joy (χαρά) of verse 6 (Bornemann 1894, 66).[30]

5. The question over Paul's use of πῶς is a small aspect of a much larger discussion centring on whether Paul uses ἐπιστρέφειν as a *terminus technicus* to describe an act of "conversion". It should be noted at the outset that it is impossible to make a definitive decision regarding this issue (*contra* the majority of commentators) because Paul only uses the term on three occasions (1 Thess 1:9; Gal 4:9; 2 Cor 3:16).[31] At first glance, the combination of πῶς ἐπιστρέφετε in Gal 4:9 makes that passage appear to be helpful. However, the context there is not one of turning to God, but rather one which deals with the problem of apostasy (Friedrich 1965, 504; Hübner 1990, 387).[32] The only other instance where Paul uses the word is in 2 Cor 3:16, where it appears in an allusion to Exod 34:34.[33] In the LXX text, the reference is to Moses spatially going in (εἰσεπορεύετο) before the Lord (ἔναντι κυρίου). Paul provides an interpretation of the passage by changing the verb to ἐπιστρέφειν, and by making the subject indefinite (ἡνίκα δὲ ἐὰν ἐπιστρέψῃ) — the application is thereby broadened to include individual "conversions" (Bertram 1971, 728; Furnish 1984, 211).[34] However, neither 2 Cor 3:16 nor Gal 4:9 is a parallel to 1

[28] Schenk lists the following references in support of such equivalence: Mark 2:26 (par.); 12:26, 41; Luke 8:36; 14:7; Acts 11:13; 12:17; 2 Thess 3:7. Best (1972, 82), Burkeen (1979, 85) and Ellingworth/Nida (1976, 15) are less forceful in their reasoning: since there is a lack of compelling evidence for taking the particle as referring to manner, they also assert that it refers only to the fact of turning.

[29] So Auberlen/Riggenbach 1869, 23; Eadie 1877, 51; Malherbe 2000, 118; von Dobschütz 1909, 76; *contra* Légasse 1999, 99. Ironically, Frame also points out the close parallel between ὁποῖος and πῶς, and yet rejects a modal interpretation of the latter (1912, 87).

[30] Even though Best prefers to take πῶς as a conjunction, he comments: "If the element of 'manner' is allowed to enter then it will refer to their conversion in tribulation (v. 6)" (1972, 82). BDAG favours the interpretation of πῶς as a reference to manner, although there is the concession: "... πῶς could have the same meaning as ὅτι *that*, and this equation at the same time suggests how the Hellenic ear grasped the significance of ὅτι" (901, §1.b.α).

[31] Paul does use ἀποστρέφειν (Rom 11:26; cf. 2 Tim 1:15; 4:4; Titus 1:14), ἀναστρέφειν (2 Cor 1:12; cf. Eph 2:3; 1 Tim 3:15; for ἀναστροφή, cf. Gal 1:13; Eph 4:22; 1 Tim 4:12), and μεταστρέφειν (Gal 1:7).

[32] The phrase οὐκ εἰδότες θεόν (Gal 4:8; cf. τὰ ἔθνη τὰ μὴ εἰδότε τὸν θεόν in 1 Thess 4:5) indicates that Paul is exhorting non-Jews not to turn from knowing God, or being known by God (γνωσθέντες ὑπὸ θεοῦ), back to τὰ ἀσθενῆ καὶ πτωχὰ στοιχεῖα (Gal 4:9). The repetition of στοιχεῖα (τοῦ κόσμου, cf. Gal 4:3) suggests that Paul regards the turn to observance of days, months, seasons and years as a *return* to their previous state (note πάλιν, *bis*; Bertram 1971, 726; Betz 1979, 216; Martyn 1997, 411). The concurrence of δουλεύειν is a more important link between Gal 4:9 and 1 Thess 1:9. The Galatians are in danger of turning from being a "slave of God" while the Thessalonians have just become slaves (Byron 2003, 190–192).

[33] Exod 34:34a (LXX) reads: ἡνίκα δ' ἂν εἰσεπορεύετο Μωυσῆς ἔναντι κυρίου λαλεῖν αὐτῷ, περιῃρεῖτο τὸ κάλυμμα ἕως τοῦ ἐκπορεύεσθαι. Differences are obvious, particularly the change of verb: εἰσπορεύεσθαι to ἐπιστρέφειν. Yet, the similarities are sufficient (overall structure; common veil motif), to warrant a literary dependence (for a list of similarities and differences between Exod 34:34a and 2 Cor 3:16, see Belleville 1991, 250–251; Furnish 1984, 211; Thrall 1994, 269).

[34] For discussion on the implied subject of 2 Cor 3:16, see esp. Belleville 1991, 248–250; Hays 1989, 140–149; Thrall 1994, 269–271. Thrall is probably correct in her conclusion: "The subject is Moses, but Moses seen as the type of the Christian convert" (1994, 271). Dunn is in agreement: "Paul deliberately

Thess 1:9, which describes the entrance of non-Jews (i.e. those who worship εἴδωλα) into the Pauline *ekklēsia* (Bussmann 1975, 49).

Turning to other instances of ἐπιστρέφειν outside the Pauline corpus, parallels may be found where the verb describes the "conversion" of non-Jews into the *ekklēsia*, particularly in Acts.[35] Acts 11:21 states that those who believe turned to the Lord (ὁ πιστεύσας ἐπέστρεψεν ἐπὶ τὸν κύριον) as a favourable response to a proclamation of Jesus (εὐαγγελιζόμενοι τὸν κύριον Ἰησοῦν, v. 20). Here Luke implies that the moments of belief and turning coincide (Zumstein 1998, 1232).[36] Other parallels include 14:15, a reference to non-Jews turning to a "living God" (ἐπιστρέφειν ἐπὶ θεὸν ζῶντα)[37] and 15:19, which also refers to non-Jews turning to God (ἐπιστρέφουσιν ἐπὶ τὸν θεόν). Finally, in Acts 26:17–18 the reference is to non-Jews (ἔθνη), whose eyes are opened to turn from darkness to light (ἀπὸ σκότους εἰς φῶς), and from the authority of Satan to God (καὶ τῆς ἐξουσίας τοῦ σατανᾶ ἐπὶ τὸν θεόν), that they may receive forgiveness of sins (τοῦ λαβεῖν αὐτοὺς ἄφεσιν ἁμαρτιῶν).[38] Then in verse 20, ἐπιστρέφειν is coupled with μετανοεῖν,[39] and the action is confirmed by corresponding service (ἔργα πράσσοντας). The process depicted here seems to be three-fold: first repentance, then turning to God, then service (Bertram 1971, 728; Légasse 1991, 40).[40] Paul does not make such a connection between μετανοεῖν and ἐπιστρέφειν (*contra* Walton 2000, 176), nor is the result of turning, for Paul, a forgiveness of sins. In fact, ἐπιστρέφειν is more than a change of thought; it is a change of life (Zumstein 1988, 1232).[41]

---

does not specify the subject of ἐπιστρέψῃ so that its ambiguity might embrace both Moses and the Jews" (1998b, 119). However, regardless of its ambiguity, Paul seems to use ἐπιστρέφειν here for the entrance of *both* Jews and non-Jews (Gaventa 1986, 42).

[35] Various forms of ἐπιστρέφειν appear in Acts 3:19; 9:35, 40; 11:21; 14:15; 15:19, 36; 16:18; 26:18, 20; 28:27. The noun ἐπιστροφή appears in the NT only in Acts 15:3.

[36] Referring to the author of Acts as "Luke" is a matter of convention only.

[37] See §III.a.8 below for further references to the phrase, "living God".

[38] A grouping of similar motifs may be found in Col 1:12–14, including sharing in the light (ἐν τῷ φωτί), being delivered from the authority of darkness (ἐκ τῆς ἐξουσίας τοῦ σκότους), and receiving the forgiveness of sins (τὴν ἄφεσιν τῶν ἁμαρτιῶν). But more important, perhaps, is the strong antithesis expressed in Acts 26:18, which is reminiscent of 1 Thess 1:9; 5:5.

[39] Cf. Acts 3:19; Joel 2:14, where μετανοεῖν and ἐπιστρέφειν are also closely juxtaposed. Haenchen suggests that μετανοεῖν expresses more "the turning away from evil" while ἐπιστρέφειν expresses "the positive new direction, the turning to God" (1971, 208). In Theophilus of Antioch 3.11, there is a significant phrase, ἐπιστρέφειν εἰς μετάνοιαν τοῦ μηκέτι ἁμαρτάνειν ("to convert them to repentance so that they would no longer sin" [Grant 1970]), which seems to underscore Haenchen's suggestion. Although Barrett admits that such a distinction is possible, he concludes: "But the doubling of the verb [in Acts 26:20] ... is probably no more than a means of emphasis" (1994, 202–203).

[40] This distinction may emphasise that the turning itself is an act accomplished by God; cf. for example *T. Zeb.* 9:7, μνησθήσεσθε κυρίου καὶ μετανοήσατε καὶ ἐπιστρέψει ὑμᾶς ("you will remember the Lord and repent, and he will turn you around ..." [Kee 1983]). However, the distinction may be arbitrary, as Behm asserts (concerning *T. 12 Patr.*), "ἐπιστρέφω and μετανοέω stand in synonymous parallelism in the religious and moral sense 'to convert'" (1967, 991); cf. *T. Naph.* 4:3; *T. Ben.* 5:1, 4.

[41] Conzelmann comments: "The combination of μετανοεῖν καὶ ἐπιστρέφειν, 'repent and turn again,' shows that μετανοεῖν, 'repent,' no longer signifies the conversion event as complete and indivisible; it is now divided into a change of mind and a change of conduct" (1987, 29). Indeed, Langevin asserts that

This selected survey of the use of ἐπιστρέφειν in Acts suggests that it is used in a technical sense, for the turning of Jews and non-Jews to the Christian proclamation.[42] Furthermore, there are numerous examples where ἐπιστρέφειν is used to refer to Jews turning or returning to the Lord (both individually and corporately) in the LXX,[43] and in the OT Pseudepigrapha.[44] Likewise, it is used in an opposite sense, of turning away from the Lord.[45] Often, as in 1 Thess 1:9, a contrast is made between God and τὰ εἴδωλα.[46] Moreover, some references specifically indicate that it is non-Jews who are turning to God.[47] Others are more general, but still illustrate the use of ἐπιστρέφειν in a "conversion" context.[48] It should be noted,

---

ἐπιστρέφειν considerably eclipses μετανοεῖν in import: "Il ne s'agit pas de simple *pénitence* ou *regret* de ses fautes" but designates "un *retournement* spirituel capital, décisif, qui engage les valeurs religieuses les plus profondes du *converti*" (1965a, 475).

[42] So Corriveau 1970, 28; Holtz 1998, 59; Laubach 1975, 355; Rigaux 1959, 387.

[43] Deut 30:2, 8, 9, 10 (cf. Philo *Som.* 2.175); 1 Kgdms 7:3–4; 3 Kgdms 8:33; 4 Kgdms 23:25; 1 Par 15:4; 19:4; 30:6, 9; 35:19; Job 33:23; Isa 6:10; Jer 24:7; Hos 5:4; 6:1; 14:2; Zech 1:3; Jdt 5:19; Sir 5:7; 17:25.

[44] *T. Jud.* 23:5; *T. Iss.* 6:3; *T. Dan* 5:9, 11; *T. Naph.* 4:3.

[45] Deut 31:18, 20; 2 Par 36:13; Jer 3:10; Hos 7:10; Amos 4:6, 9; Mal 3:7.

[46] 4 Kgdms 23:25 (cf. v. 24); 2 Par 24:19 (cf. v. 18); 35:19; Tob 14:6; cf. also Deut 4:30; 1 Kgdms 7:3–4; Josephus *Ant.* 10.53. In Philo *Spec.* 2.256, a similar contrast is made: ὄνομα θεῶν ἑτέρων μήτε τῇ ψυχῇ παραδέξῃ εἰς ὑπόμνησιν μήτε φωνῇ διερμηνεύσῃς, ἀλλ' ἑκάτερον, νοῦν καὶ λόγον, μακρὰν τῶν ἄλλων διαζεύξας ἐπίστρεψον πρὸς τὸν πατέρα καὶ ποιητὴν τῶν ὅλων ("Do not admit the name of other gods into thy soul to remember it, nor give expression to it with thy voice. Keep both thy mind and thy speech far apart from these others, and turn to the Father and Maker of all" [Colson/Whitaker 1929–1962]).

[47] Ps 21:28 (22:27 MT); Joel 2:13 (cf. v. 1); Isa 19:22; 55:7; Tob 14:6; *Jos. Asen.* 11:10–11; *T. Ab.* 12:13 (rec. B); *T. Zeb.* 9:8.

[48] E.g. Philo *Post.* 135: ἐὰν οὖν καὶ σὺ μιμησαμένη Λείαν, ὦ ψυχή, <τὰ> θνητὰ ἀποστραφῇς, ἐξ ἀνάγκης ἐπιστρέψει πρὸς τὸν ἄφθαρτον ("Then if thou too, O soul, follow Leah's examples and turn away from mortal things, thou wilt of necessity turn to the Incorruptible One"); Philo *Som.* 2.174: ὁπότε τὸ ἀνθρώπων γένος ἐκτρέποιτο μὲν ἁμαρτήματα, ἐπικλίνοι δὲ καὶ ἐπιστρέφοι πρὸς δικαιοσύνην ("particularly when the human race turns away from its sins and inclines and reverts to righteousness"); Philo *Jos.* 87: ἐπέστρεψε καὶ τοὺς πάνυ δοκοῦντας ἀνιάτως ἔχειν ("he converted even those who seemed to be quite incurable" [Colson/Whitaker 1929–1962]); Epictetus 2.20.22: ἵν' οἱ πολῖται ἡμῶν ἐπιστραφέντες τιμῶσι τὸ θεῖον καὶ παύσωνται ποτε ῥᾳθυμοῦντες περὶ τὰ μέγιστα ("prove it, that our citizens may be converted and may honour the Divine and at last cease to be indifferent about the things that are of supreme importance"). The discourse proceeds, in Epictetus 2.20.23, to outline things which are *not* of supreme importance: ὅτι θεοὶ οὔτ' εἰσίν, εἴ τε καὶ εἰσίν, οὐκ ἐπιμελοῦνται ἀνθρώπων οὐδὲ κοινόν τι ἡμῖν ἐστι πρὸς αὐτούς ("The gods do not exist, and even if they do, they pay no attention to men, nor have we any fellowship with them" [Oldfather 1925–1928]). In another example Lucian uses ἐπιστρέφειν with the idea of "conversion", but with no reference to the gods. Rather, he gives advice to historians who "think they don't even need advice". He goes on to say in *Hist.* 5: οἶδα μὲν οὖν οὐ πάνυ πολλοὺς αὐτῶν ἐπιστρέψων, ("Now I know that I shall not convert very many" [Harmon/Kilburn/MacLeod 1913–1967]). See Theophilus of Antioch 3.11, where ἐπιστρέφειν appears no fewer than six times; cf. also Ps 7:13 (LXX); Jer 3:14; Joel 2:12, 13, 14; Mal 2:6; 3:18; *Jub.* 5:19; Mark 4:12 (par.); Luke 1:17; 17:4; Jas 5:19–20. Finally, I find Luke 22:32 quite significant because ἐπιστρέφειν appears to be used in an allusion to Peter's restoration after his denial of Jesus. The text reads: καὶ σύ ποτε ἐπιστρέψας στήρισον τοὺς ἀδελφούς σου. Is it possible that Luke is referring to the same/similar tradition preserved in John 21:15–19, where Peter is commanded: βόσκε τὰ πρόβατά μου (v. 17)? The reason for such a connection is the occurrence of ἐπιστρέφειν in John 21:20. Consequently, part of Peter's returning to the Lord (after his denial) includes strengthening his brethren and feeding Jesus' sheep. Even if there is no connection between the pericopes, the occurrence of the verb in v. 20 is surely noteworthy, particularly since the verb appears only there in John.

however, that it is not entirely correct to refer to ἐπιστρέφειν as a *terminus technicus* in *all* of its contexts. The instances surveyed above are only a subset of the examples found in antiquity.[49] Often the word is used merely to express a physical change in direction[50] or some other expression (Pax 1971, 230).[51] It could be argued that a subset of references does contain a technical use of ἐπιστρέφειν, but such a division remains to be defined.[52] Consequently, it is not possible to conclusively establish, on the basis of the evidence considered, whether Paul uses the word in a technical sense or not (Corriveau 1970, 27; Légasse 1999, 99–100).[53]

6. The phrase, ἐπιστρέφειν πρὸς τὸν θεόν (v. 9c), is found elsewhere in antiquity. Although the majority of the LXX references are of the form, ἐ. πρὸς κύριον,[54] or ἐ. πρός με,[55] some references contain a combination of κύριον and θεόν,[56] and only one reference each may be found of the form, ἐ. πρὸς θεόν (2 Par 30:6; cf. Philo *Deus* 17) and ἐ. πρὸς τὸν θεόν (Hos 5:4; cf. Philo *Post.* 135). The verb is also followed by ἐπί on numerous occasions.[57] Collins has examined the variations of use in First Thessalonians, between the arthrous and anarthrous construction with θεός, and concludes that there is no reason to distinguish sharply between them (1984, 232).[58] However, a point of singularity which is often underemphasised is the combination of the two prepositional phrases, πρὸς τὸν θεόν and ἀπὸ τῶν εἰδώ-

[49] BDAG (382, §1, 2) lists several "extended definitions" and numerous examples where ἐπιστρέφειν is not associated with turning to God.

[50] 3 Kgdms 13:26; Philo *Conf.* 130–131; *Her.* 46; *Fug.* 124; *Som.* 1.247; *Jos.* 175, 200; *Mos.* 2.247; *Praem.* 95; *Contempl.* 45; *Leg.* 1.272; cf. Matt 12:44; Mark 5:30; 8:33; 13:16 (par.); Luke 2:39; 8:55; 2 Pet 2:22; Rev 1:12.

[51] 2 Esdr 19:28; Ps 77:41 (LXX); Jdt 7:30; Sir 48:10; *Pss. Sol.* 8:27; Plutarch *Alc.* 16.6; *Cat. Min.* 14.1; *Mor.* 21c; Philo *Leg.* 2.8; *Cher.* 37; *Post.* 106; *Agr.* 143; *Conf.* 131; *Migr.* 195; *Mut.* 209; *Som.* 2.144; *Abr.* 176; *Jos.* 230; *Spec.* 2.11, 189; 3.41; *Flacc.* 30, 163.

[52] Langevin agrees that there is a technical sense of the verb in Acts, "pour désigner le mouvement de la *conversion* au Christ", and then asserts that this is an established (and therefore pre-Pauline) use of ἐπιστρέφειν on the basis of its similar use by other authors (1965, 277; cf. Jas 5:20; 1 Peter 2:25). However, this is a far from satisfactory argument because the references in Acts refer to the movement of non-Jews turning (for the first time!) to God, while both Jas 5:20 (cf. also v. 19) and 1 Pet 2:25 refer to a "returning" in the sense of repentance. Laubach seems to acknowledge the existence of a division between a technical and non-technical use of the word when he refers to a "secular meaning" and a "theological meaning" of ἐπιστρέφειν (1975, 355); unfortunately, he does not pursue the issue.

[53] *Contra* Furnish 1984, 211; Dibelius 1925, 6; Holtz 1998, 59; Langevin 1965a, 473–474; Malherbe 1998, 238; 2000, 119; Richard 1995, 52; Stott 1991, 39; Tarazi 1982, 69; Wolter 1980, 442. Pax appears to be on his own when he explicitly denies a technical sense of ἐπιστρέφειν in Paul: "Das Verbum ist kein Terminus technicus, um lediglich den Übertritt vom Heidentum zum Judentum oder Christentum zum Ausdruck zu bringen" (1971, 230). This is a position for which I have sympathy.

[54] 1 Kgdms 7:3; 4 Kgdms 23:25; 2 Par 24:19; 30:9; 35:19; 36:13; Ps 21:28; Isa 19:22; Hos 6:1; 7:10; 14:2; Joel 2:13; Sir 5:7; *T. Jud.* 23:5; *T. Iss.* 6:3; *T. Dan* 5:9, cf. v. 11.

[55] Jer 3:10; Joel 2:12; Amos 4:6, 9; Zech 1:3; Mal 3:7; cf. *Jos. Asen.* 11:11.

[56] Deut 4:30; Hos 6:1; 7:10; 14:2; Joel 2:13; cf. Phil *Fug.* 142.

[57] Deut 30:2, 10; 31:18, 20; 2 Par 15:4; 19:4; Job 33:23; Isa 55:7; Jdt 5:19; Sir 17:25; *T. Naph.* 4:3; cf. Theophilus of Antioch 3.11; Luke 1:16; Acts 9:35; 11:21; 14:15; 15:19; 26:20.

[58] Bornemann suggests that the article indicates a polemic sense such that Paul is contrasting God with false gods (1894, 68–69). Richard suggests that the omission of the article in the subsequent phrase, δουλεύειν θεῷ ζῶντι καὶ ἀληθινῷ, "underscores the text's descriptive character" (1995, 55). While both

λων (see Bussmann 1975, 41). The object from which one turns is rarely identified or expressed.[59] Paul emphasises the turning experience of the Thessalonians by polarising the two choices: God and idols.[60] His use of rhetorical metonymy – using εἰδώλων to describe various gods from which the Thessalonians turned – makes a theological statement: all gods, in contrast to Paul's God, are made to be unreal or spurious, and this is stressed by the repetition of θεός (who is ζῶν and ἀληθινός, v. 9d; BDAG 281, §2). Another point of interest is the order of the two prepositional phrases. Usually, according to von Dobschütz, missionary preaching first proceeds with a polemic against idolatry, before a presentation of the true God (1909, 77).

7. Paul uses εἴδωλον infrequently, and the majority of references is in the Corinthian correspondence.[61] In 1 Cor 8:4–6 Paul takes up the issue of food offered to idols (εἰδωλόθυτον); in verse 4 he states: οἴδαμεν ὅτι οὐδὲν εἴδωλον ἐν κόσμῳ καὶ ὅτι οὐδεὶς θεὸς εἰ μὴ εἷς, thereby seeming to deny the existence of idols. But then in verse 5, Paul continues with the concession that there *are* "so-called gods" (εἴπερ εἰσὶν λεγόμενοι θεοί), indeed, many gods and many lords (ὥσπερ εἰσὶν θεοὶ πολλοὶ καὶ κύριοι πολλοί);[62] yet for Paul there is only one God the Father (ἀλλ' ἡμῖν εἷς θεὸς ὁ πατήρ) and one Lord, Jesus Christ (εἷς κύριος Ἰησοῦς Χριστός, v. 6; Hurtado 1998, 1–2).[63] This assertion stands regardless of what other spiritual (or demonic) beings there might or might not be (Barrett 1971, 192). Thus, when Paul refers to many gods and lords, he is neither denying nor affirming their existence; rather, he is acknowledging others' belief in and worship of those gods and lords (Denaux 1996, 600; Orr/Walther 1976, 233). Paul goes on in 1 Cor 10:14–22 to exhort the Corinthians to flee from idol-worship (εἰδωλολατρία, see v. 14).[64] The point here is that while idols themselves represent no gods (since for Paul there is only one God),[65] the *worship of idols* invokes a spiritual reality — a δαιμόνιον (Conzelmann 1975, 173).[66]

It is in the notion of idol-worship that Paul's use of εἴδωλον in First Corinthians coincides with 1 Thess 1:9. There is probably no reference to demons here, regard-

---

suggestions are possible, according to Collins, it is more likely that Paul is just referring to the only God he knows (1991a, 140; cf. 1 Cor 8:4).

[59] Along with 1 Thess 1:9, the following references are exceptions: 2 Par 6:26; Jer 26:3; 36:3; Ezek 18:21–23; Bar 2:33; Acts 14:15; 26:18; cf. Theophilus of Antioch 3.11.

[60] It is important to distinguish here between God and Jesus. The Thessalonians turned to God, not Jesus. Yet, in the next verse, Jesus is described as the deliverer, not God. The strong polarity here emphasises the distinction between the respective roles ascribed to God and Jesus (Becker 1986, 95–96).

[61] 1 Cor 8:4, 7; 10:19; 12:2; 2 Cor 6:16; cf. Rom 2:22.

[62] Deut 10:17 implies a reality of gods/lords: כִּי יְהוָה אֱלֹהֵיכֶם הוּא אֱלֹהֵי הָאֱלֹהִים וַאֲדֹנֵי הָאֲדֹנִים הָאֵל ("For the Lord your God is God of gods and Lord of lords").

[63] See esp. the monograph by Peterson (1926) on the topic of εἷς θεός.

[64] In v. 19, Paul asks (rhetorically), "Is food offered to idols anything?", and, "Is an idol anything?" (τί οὖν φημι ... ὅτι εἴδωλόν τί ἐστιν;). His own answer, which seems to contradict his earlier statements in 8:4, is found in v. 20: ἀλλ' ὅτι ἃ θύουσιν, δαιμονίοις καὶ οὐ θεῷ [θύουσιν]. The textual difficulties here are of no concern for this discussion.

[65] Cf. Gal 4:8; Josephus *Ant.* 10.50.

[66] Cf. Deut 32:17; Bar 4:7; see Nock 1933, 221–224.

less of the relationship between idol-worship and the invocation of demons (Best 1972, 82). But the relevance of Paul's discussion of idols in First Corinthians is clear: worship of idols is exceedingly close to service of idols (Börschel 2001, 98; Corriveau 1970, 30–31).[67] Such a connection brings insight into just how significant is the action of the Thessalonians' turning to God — it is a social and theological occurrence. Best also points out that if idols do not really represent gods, then a certain ambiguity exists in Paul's argument; the contrast between a "living and true God" and idols is weakened (1972, 82; so also Curtis 1992, 281). Still, allowing for the fact that Paul is writing to converts whose perspective used to be henotheistic or polytheistic (not monotheistic as is Paul's and Best's!), Paul's argument *is* coherent, and his God is distinguished from the gods, even though in reality those gods are lesser beings (BDAG 281, §2).[68]

It is probably best to understand the turning ἀπὸ τῶν εἰδώλων as a turning from one religious domain to another (Richard 1995, 52), rather than attempting to associate Paul's reference with one or other εἴδωλα known to be worshipped in first-century C.E. Thessalonica.[69] Thus, Paul's metonymy describes a joint characteristic of all other gods: they are not ζῶντες or ἀληθινοί. The separation between the two (antithetical) domains is total and all-embracing (Meeks 1983, 95, 165–166; Wanamaker 1990, 86).

Excursus 2
"Conversion" to Christianity

1. Paul usually describes the point of entry of Jews and non-Jews into the *ekklēsia* with terms other than ἐπιστρέφειν, μετανοεῖν, or ἀφιέναι. Yet the English word "conversion" implies (at least at some level) turning, repentance and forgiveness.[70] It is, therefore, misleading to translate ἐπιστρέφειν with "to convert", since the attendant implications are almost entirely

[67] Collins suggests that service is a more radical commitment than worship (1991a, 141). To be sure, 1 Thess 1:9 does not even refer directly to the service of idols — but it is at least implied.

[68] The insistence of turning to the one God supports a monotheistic context. From Paul's perspective, εἴδωλα cannot represent gods (Collins 1991a, 141), and this is consistent with those references where the term εἴδωλα is not only used for the images of gods, but is applied to the gods themselves. Büchsel (1964, 377) supplies numerous references; cf. esp. 1 Chr 16:26; Ps 115:2–8; Isa 44:9–20; Ep Jer 4–72; Wis 13:10; 14:8; Philo *Spec.* 1.25, 28. For further discussion, see Curtis 1992; Mundle 1976a.

[69] It is practically impossible to identify which gods Paul may have had in mind when he refers to τὰ εἴδωλα (vom Brocke 2001, 116). These might include any εἴδωλα of the Egyptian divinities Isis, Serapis, Anubis and Osiris, of the cults of Dionysus, the Cabiri and the goddess Roma, of the mysteries of Samothrace, as well as of other gods including Zeus, Asclepius, Aphrodite, Demeter etc. After an extensive review of each of the various cults (116–142), vom Brocke tentatively suggests that the most likely choice would be either the cult of Cabirus or that of Dionysus (142). See Collins 1993, 53; Donfried 1985; Edson 1948. For a metaphorical use of εἴδωλον, cf. Ezek 14:4; 1QS 2:11.

[70] Hence the word "conversion" appears in inverted commas throughout this discussion.

absent from Paul's letters.[71] For that matter, he hardly ever uses ἐπιστρέφειν either.[72] The reason(s) why he seems to avoid these terms is(are) elusive. One place to start is to consider the impetus which begins the "conversion process". It surely is not the conscious realisation of fear or rewards that awaits a converted person (whether that be spiritual, social, emotional, financial etc.), for such emotions are conjured only after the process has begun.[73] Neither is it feelings of guilt or repentance, since for Paul the theme of "forgiveness of sins" (pl.) is of lesser significance;[74] more important is the theme of release from sin (sing.), and from its power (Bultmann 1952, 287).[75] Instead, for Paul, turning to God is encapsulated in a decision characterised by obedience (317).[76] Although this decision may be thought of as a "turning to God", Paul may have chosen to avoid the word ἐπιστρέφειν because it does not portray a decisive, once-for-all act (Dunn 1998, 326–327).[77] Along a different line, Martyn suggests that Paul rarely uses ἐπιστρέφειν or μετανοεῖν because both terms imply a human act, a mere change of thought: nothing more than attempts to know God. But entry into the *ekklēsia* involves the occurrence of being known by God (1997, 411; so also Gaventa 1986, 44).[78] Thus, the impetus which begins the "conversion process" is more appropriately characterised as a call to faith (Wenk 2000, 71; so Malherbe 1998, 231).[79] Actually, καλεῖν may be viewed as a *terminus technicus* that encompasses the process (Schmidt 1965, 489). This does not mean that God's "call" is not ongoing. To the contrary, in First Thessalonians God is described twice with the present participle, καλῶν (2:12; 5:24) — he continues to "call" (Collins 1993, 62). Indeed, the concept of "call" does not adequately characterise the act of "conversion" unless

[71] The verb μετανοεῖν does appear in Rom 2:4; 2 Cor 7:9–10; 12:21; cf. 2 Tim 2:25. Gaventa observes that, excluding the pastoral reference, Paul uses the word of persons who are already "converted" and therefore it has nothing to do with the initial turning (1986, 43). Note: ἀφιέναι appears only once (Rom 4:7), in a quotation from Ps 32:1; cf. also Col 1:14.

[72] See survey of ἐπιστρέφειν in §III.a.5 above. In First Thessalonians, Paul describes "conversion" otherwise: δεξάμενοι τὸν λόγον (1:6); παραλαβόντες λόγον ... τοῦ θεοῦ ἐδέξασθε (2:13).

[73] *Contra* Bussmann, who opines: "Die Rettung vom Zorn wird dadurch zum Hauptmotiv für die Bekehrung, es zeigt sich noch einmal, daß die Missionspredigt durchaus nicht nur die Predigt vom Kreuz kennt" (1975, 56).

[74] Although cf. Rom 3:25. See esp. Stendahl's discussion on "justification rather than forgiveness" (1976, 23–40).

[75] Rom 6:6, 7, 12, 14, 16–17, 20, 22.

[76] This is particularly evident in 1 Thess 1:9, since the Thessalonians "turned ... to serve the living and true God". For references to δουλεύειν in a context of turning to God, see §III.a.8 below.

[77] See §III.a.5 above for references to the LXX where ἐπιστρέφειν is used repeatedly of Jews returning to God. In contrast, Paul does not use ἐπιστρέφειν to refer to a "Zurückkehren" to God (Bornemann 1894, 66).

[78] This does not mean that μετανοεῖν is not part of the act of turning to the Christian proclamation, but, according to Goetzmann, that Paul uses more specialised terminology (1975, 359). Hence, Behm comments: "... in Paul μετάνοια is comprised in πίστις, the central concept in his doctrine of salvation. He states the idea of conversion as a total refashioning of man's nature and conduct by the grace of God in his own characteristic vocabulary of dying and becoming, i.e., the death of the old man and the rising again of the new man" (1967, 1005); cf. also *1 Clem.* 59.3; *2 Clem.* 17.1; Herm. *Sim.* 9.18.1.

[79] See Klein 1984. Paul refers to his own call (Rom 1:1; 1 Cor 1:1; Gal 1:15; Phil 3:14), as well as to the general call of God (Rom 1:6, 7; 8:28, 30; 9:11, 24; 11:29; 1 Cor 1:2, 9, 24, 26; 7:15, 17, 18, 20, 21, 22, 24; Gal 1:6; 5:8, 13; 1 Thess 2:12; 4:7; 5:24; cf. Eph 1:18; 4:1, 4; Col 3:15; 2 Thess 1:11; 2:14; 1 Tim 6:12; 2 Tim 1:9); cf. also Rom 9:15; 11:5, 7, 28; 1 Thess 1:4. Acceptance of the Christian proclamation is called πίστις (1 Thess 1:3, 8; 3:2, 5, 6, 7, 10; 5:8) or πιστεύειν (1 Thess 1:7; 2:4, 10, 13; 4:14; Bultmann 1952, 89).

the ongoing nature of the "call" is emphasised (Gaventa 1986, 43; Wanamaker 1995, 47).[80] The realm of action is shifted from the anthropological to the theological.[81] Furthermore, the work of the Holy Spirit is an important element of "conversion" (Green 1970, 148). As a result, then, Paul's references to the Holy Spirit in 1 Thess 1:5, 6 are far from insignificant.[82] For Pax, the "conversion" of the Thessalonians was motivated by a decisive encounter with Paul (1972, 30). This may explain the prolepsis between the two references to his entrance (1:9; 2:1), with the "conversion" statement between (1:9c–10).

2. To facilitate a broader discussion of more general aspects of "conversion", Nock's definition formulated in his famous monograph on the subject is a useful point of departure. According to Nock (1933, 7), Christian "conversion" is:

> the reorientation of the soul of an individual, his deliberate turning from indifference or from an earlier form of piety to another, a turning which implies a consciousness that a great change is involved, that the old was wrong and the new is right.

His definition is enduring partly because it does not employ enigmatic terms like "repent", "belief" and "faith" which themselves require definition,[83] and partly because Nock recognises that there is more to "conversion" than a mere change of allegiance, or alignment of thought. The social implications accompanying a turning to God from idols are devastating.[84] Certainly, the previous social status of a convert plays a major factor in such a social adjustment, and since it is generally agreed that 1 Thess 1:9–10 refers to non-Jews turning to the Christian

[80] Although, technically, the focus of this discussion so far has been on the initiation of "conversion", which is itself instantaneous (Malherbe 1998, 237).

[81] "This is consistent with his [Paul's] conviction that it is God who takes the initiative with the world in a new way in the gospel rather than human beings who act to placate or please God" (Gaventa 1992, 1132). On this tack, Wenk notes the significance of Rom 2:4 (ἀγνοῶν ὅτι τὸ χρηστὸν τοῦ θεοῦ εἰς μετάνοιάν σε ἄγει): "Repentance/conversion seems not so much to be the result of Paul's preaching nor something prompted by the conviction of sins, but the result of a positive stimulus, of being enticed by the mercy of God" (2000, 74).

[82] Cf. also 4:8; 5:19. Actually, the role of the Spirit in connection with "conversion" has been largely ignored. Yet in all three texts where Paul uses ἐπιστρέφειν a reference is made to the Spirit. He refers directly to the Spirit in 2 Cor 3:17 (ὁ δὲ κύριος τὸ πνεῦμά ἐστιν), following his reference to a man who "turns to the Lord" (v. 16) and in Gal 4:9, Paul has just referred to the Spirit (τὸ πνεῦμα τοῦ υἱοῦ αὐτοῦ) in v. 6. See Horn's comment on 2 Cor 3:17: "Die Hinwendung zum Kyrios und ihre Folge, von dieser mehrfachen Decke befreit zu werden, muß nach V.17 als Ergebnis eines geistgewirkten Geschehens verstanden werden" (2000, 66). Although this is not the place for an extended discussion of the role of the Spirit in First Thessalonians, the eschatological connection is worth mentioning (Jurgensen 1994, 82; see esp. Vos 1953, 160–171). Fee notes that the Spirit enables the eschatological fulfillment of the promise of inclusion of the Gentiles, an observation quite relevant for this passage. Thus, the references to the Spirit powerfully hint at the eschatological significance of the Thessalonians' turning to God (1994, 812). For further discussion, see Vos 1973, 74–84.

[83] In contrast, MacMullen defines "conversion" as, "that change of belief by which a person accepted the reality and supreme power of God and determined to obey Him" (1984, 5), and as, "that experience by which non-believers first became convinced that the Christian God was almighty, and that they must please Him" (1993, 36). For Green, it is simply, "turning to Christ in repentance and faith" (1970, 152).

[84] Paul's reference to θλῖψις in 1:6 may shed light on these implications. For Malherbe, the term does not refer so much to persecution but "could have a subjective connotation. The Thessalonians experienced social, intellectual, and religious dislocation when they converted, and they must have suffered confusion, bewilderment, dejection, and despair. This was the experience of converts to Judaism as well as philosophy, and the experience was described as θλῖψις, a deep distress" (1998, 235). For further discussion, see Chapter 1, §IV.e.

proclamation (vom Brocke 2001, 114), then it follows that this discussion may rightly be limited to the "conversion" of non-Jews.[85] Stowers' illustration about the renunciation of animal sacrifices highlights some of the implications of turning (1995, 293):

> Imagine a community in the contemporary United States that renounced not only television viewing but also any products, persons, and ideas promoted by television. The group would not vote in elections, drive automobiles, shop in supermarkets, watch athletic contests, or form conventional families. These people would remain citizens of the United States but to a large extent would have abandoned American and Western culture. Understanding what it meant for a Greek, Roman, or Syrian to renounce animal sacrifice requires some such act of comparative imagination.

Social disintegration is followed by a process of socialisation, involving the development and integration of a new community (in this case, the *ekklēsia* of the Thessalonians; N. H. Taylor 1995, 129; Wanamaker 1995, 52–54).[86] Acceptance of Christian proclamation often meant the loss of one's job, since the official worship of the state and of the municipality had to be renounced (Nock 1933, 227). Further, in a culture where polytheism and henotheism is the norm, the only major exception being Jewish monotheism, a renunciation of all gods but one may help explain why Paul's community is particularly outstanding (Ascough 2000, 324; 2003, 186; cf. 1 Thess 1:7–8).

End of Excursus

8. All that remains to be commented upon is the last part of verse 9: δουλεύειν θεῷ ζῶντι καὶ ἀληθινῷ. The two infinitives, δουλεύειν and ἀναμένειν (vv. 9d, 10a respectively), are epexegetical (Lenski 1937, 233; Williams 1992, 33),[87] expressing the goal or result of turning (Malherbe 2000, 120; Marshall 1983, 58).[88] The notion

[85] Perhaps this explains why Paul so strongly emphasises a distinction between God and idols (see §III.a.7 above). The issue of whether it is appropriate to refer to a Jew turning (ἐπιστρέφειν) to God need not be entertained here (for this, see Sanders 1985, 176–177), although it is interesting to consider whether a Pharisee becoming a Sadducee, for example, should be described as undergoing a "conversion" (see discussion by Stendahl 1976, 7–23 on Paul's turning from being a Pharisee to the call of Jesus). Although there is no change in God, as in the case of the non-Jew turning to Christianity, there is still a turning from one set of beliefs (and associated social realities) to another. Of course, if the idea of turning is only one of allegiance, or change of thought, then ἐπιστρέφειν would also be appropriate in such a context (Marshall 1983, 57). See Segal (1992, 296–322) who discusses "conversion" with reference to various religious groups.

[86] Wenk prefers to distinguish between a reorientation of a person's life ("conversion") and the social incorporation of an individual into a new community ("initiation"; 2000, 57–58). Wanamaker follows similar lines in his distinction between different kinds of socialisation: primary (i.e. induction into a new social reality) and secondary (i.e. the emergence of a new social identity based on the alternative social world; 1995, 48–49). While such social theory is well and good, it fails to recognise that once Paul had some converts, these did not have an established group to join. Initially they were all on their own (Börschel 2001, 142). Consequently, the "initiation" (Wenk)/"secondary socialisation" (Wanamaker) component of "conversion" would only have developed after some time.

[87] Further, they introduce parallel phrases which are themselves part of a lengthy adverbial clause (Richard 1995, 52).

[88] Thus, "Die Umkehr zu Gott geschah mit dem doppelten Ziel" (Schneider 1969, 65). Langevin's suggestion that δουλεύειν θεῷ is "la *motivation* de cet acte [of turning]" seems to misunderstand the infinitive (1965, 267), but later he rightly notes the final sense of the infinitives ("un sens final"; 1965a, 475; so Rigaux 1956, 390, 392). Neither do the infinitives express purpose (*contra* Auberlen/Riggenbach 1869, 23; Burkeen 1979, 88; Calvin 1961, 338; Eadie 1877, 51; Frame 1912, 88; Milligan 1908, 14; Thomas

of serving God is almost exclusively defined in terms of OT/Jewish parameters. In the LXX, the δουλ- stem predominately translates the Hebrew עבד (Zimmerli 1967, 673), and is the most common expression for the service of God.[89] The term refers to a total commitment, and always implies an exclusive nature to the relationship (Rengstorf 1964, 267–268): there is no scope for serving both God and gods,[90] particularly in the context of turning to God.[91] Conversely, the concept of service is offensive to Greek thinking, since her or his personal dignity is found in freedom — δουλεύειν means an alien will takes precedence over human autonomy.[92] In the NT, δουλεύειν appears most frequently (by far) in the Pauline letters,[93] and its use is consistent with the LXX (Walton 2000, 175).[94] Rather than demeaning,

---

1978, 247–248), particularly because the second infinitive can hardly be an accurate description of the Thessalonian Christians at the time of turning (Ward 1973, 45).

[89] Cf. Judg 2:7; 10:16B; 1 Kgdms 7:3, 4; 12:10, 14, 20, 23 (not MT), 24; 1 Par 28:9; 2 Par 30:8; 33:16; 34:33; Job 21:15; 36:11; Ps 2:11; 99:2; 101:23; Isa 56:6; 65:8, 13, 14, 15; Ezek 20:40; Dan 4:34; 7:14θ, 27θ; Zeph 3:9; Mal 3:14, 18; Jdt 16:14; Sir 2:1; Tob 4:14; 14:8s; *Pss. Sol.* 17:30; *Jub.* 10:16. There are also numerous passages which describe/deplore the service of other gods (θεοῖς ἑτέροις): Exod 23:33; Deut 28:64; Judg 10:6, 10B, 13B; 1 Kgdms 2:24; 8:8; 26:19; 3 Kgdms 9:6, 9; 16:31; 22:54; 4 Kgdms 10:18; 17:41; 21:3; 2 Par 7:22; 24:18; 33:3, 22; 2 Esd 9:35; Ps 105:36; Jer 2:20; 5:19; 11:10; 13:10; 16:11, 13; 22:9; 25:6; 35:15; *Jub.* 10:6, 10, 13.

[90] In *T. Asher* 3:2, service is to God only, otherwise one is two-faced (οἱ διπρόσωποι), and enslaved to evil desires (ταῖς ἐπιθυμίαις αὐτῶν, cf. 4 Kgdms 21:2–3). The concept of an exclusive service is consonant with Jewish monotheism; first one had to stop serving other gods before being able to serve God (so 1 Kgdms 12:10). Exceptions to this view are few: cf. 4 Kgdms 17:41 where τὰ ἔθνη, who feared the Lord, also served their carved images (τοῖς γλυπτοῖς αὐτῶν ἦσαν δουλεύοντες).

[91] Cf. 1 Kgdms 7:3–4 where turning to the Lord (ἐπιστρέφετε πρὸς κύριον) includes removing the other gods (περιέλετε τοὺς θεοὺς τοὺς ἀλλοτρίους) and serving God only (δουλεύσατε αὐτῷ μόνῳ). In Jer 3:22, the faithless sons are exhorted to return (שׁוּבוּ בָּנִים שׁוֹבָבִים); they respond with the statement, "behold, we come to you" (הִנְנוּ אָתָנוּ לָךְ). The LXX of this passage contains ἐπιστρέφειν (*bis*), and contains a significant change in the latter clause: "behold, we will be slaves to you" (ἰδοὺ δοῦλοι ἡμεῖς ἐσόμεθά σοι). There are many other examples where the concept of turning (either to God or away from him) is connected with the action of service (1 Sam 7:3; 12:20; 1 Kgs 9:6; 2 Chr 34:33; Neh 9:35; Mal 3:18). For exclusivity, cf. Matt 6:24 (par.).

[92] Bussmann 1975, 43; Rengstorf 1964, 261; Sass 1941; 24; Schlier 1964, 487. Cf. Philo *Praem.* 137–139, where Philo describes the evils of slavery: Δουλεία τοῖς ἐλευθέροις ἀφορητότατόν ἐστιν ... ("Slavery to the free is a thing most intolerable ..." [Colson/Whitaker 1929–1962]). Additionally, Philo (with a note of disdain) refers to the glutton being enslaved by the skill of cooks (*Leg.* 3.221), to those enslaved to passion and to the flesh (*Leg.* 3.240; *Abr.* 164), and to those who, being unschooled and untaught, are enslaved to many vices (*Cher.* 71). For an exception, cf. Plato *Apol.* 30. It should be noted, however, that this prevailing view was not necessarily shared by the slaves themselves. Martin points out that the connotations of slave terminology depend on different contexts, particularly with regard to status within society (1990, 46–47).

[93] Rom 6:6; 7:6, 25; 9:12; 12:11; 14:18; 16:18; Gal 4:8, 9, 25; 5:13; Phil 2:22; cf. also Eph 6:7; Col 3:24; 1 Tim 6:2; Tit 3:3. The only other occurrences of the word in the NT include: Matt 6:24; Luke 15:29; 16:13; John 8:33; Acts 7:7; 20:19 (n.b. it is significant that one of only two references of the verb in Acts, i.e. 20:19, is attributed to Paul, in view of the fact that the language of slavery in the NT is predominately a Pauline motif; Walton 2000, 174–175).

[94] Thus, in Rom 7:6, Paul makes a sharp distinction between service under the old written code (παλαιότητι γράμματος) and service in the new life of the spirit (ἐν καινότητι πνεύματος); likewise, in v. 25, note the contrast between serving the law of God (δουλεύω νόμῳ θεοῦ) and serving the law of sin (δουλεύω ... νόμῳ ἁμαρτίας).

the expression of service is an acknowledgement that the δοῦλος (and δούλη) is utterly dependent on God, called by God (Weiser 1990, 350).[95] Turning to God from idols to serve God at least implies that the Thessalonians once served idols.[96] Equally, the designation of God as "living and true" also suggests an opposite designation for idols, as "dead and dumb",[97] although the text does not make this explicit (Börschel 2001, 98). Finally, and paradoxically for Paul, the call to faith and service is a call to freedom — not autonomy, but a new relationship to God (Lattke 1993, 37–38).[98] This new condition of slavery is radically different than before — it *is* freedom.[99]

9. Finally, Paul describes the God whom the Thessalonians serve, as ζῶν and ἀληθινός (v. 9d). He uses ζῶν five times in First Thessalonians (1:9; 3:8; 4:15–17*bis*; 5:10) but it appears only here as a description of God.[100] In contradistinction to idols, a "living God" is one who has a state of being – although *totaliter aliter* – consciously present and the characterisation implies that God is not subject to

---

[95] As opposed to the negative references in Philo (see above), there are also positive ones, which serve as excellent illustrations of the attitude that serving God is an honour rather than a burden: Philo *Cher.* 107, χαίρει δ' ἐπ' οὐδενὶ μᾶλλον ἡ κεκαθαρμένη διάνοια ἢ τῷ δεσπότην ἔχειν τὸν ἡγεμόνα πάντων ὁμολογεῖν· τὸ γὰρ δουλεύειν θεῷ μέγιστον αὔχημα καὶ οὐ μόνον ἐλευθερίας ἀλλὰ καὶ πλούτου καὶ ἀρχῆς καὶ πάντων ὅσα τὸ θνητὸν ἀσπάζεται γένος τιμιώτερον ("The purified mind rejoices in nothing more than in confessing that it has the lord of all for its master. For to be the slave of God is the highest boast of man, a treasure more precious not only than freedom, but than wealth and power and all that mortals most cherish"); Philo *Somn.* 2.100, καὶ γάρ ἐστι τὸ δουλεύειν θεῷ πάντων ἄριστον, ὅσα ἐν γενέσει τετίμηται ("For of all things that are held in honour in this world of creation bondage to God is the best"); Philo *Spec.* 1.57 refers to the Father, ᾧ τὸ δουλεύειν οὐκ ἐλευθερίας μόνον ἀλλὰ καὶ βασιλείας ἄμεινον ("bondage to Whom is better not only than freedom but also than kingship" [Colson/Whitaker 1929–1962]).

[96] Idols are specifically mentioned in contrast to serving God in 2 Chr 24:18; 33:22; Ps 105:36 (LXX); Dan 6:28 (LXX); cf. 1Q22 1:7.

[97] Cf. *Jos. Asen.* 8:5; 11:8; 12:5; 13:11. Hence, for Best, only God *can* be (and ought to be) served. Idols, since they are nothing, cannot be served, except for their connection to demonic beings (1972, 83).

[98] See Gaventa 1986, 43; Rengstorf 1964, 275. Thus, converts were slaves of sin (δοῦλοι ἦτε τῆς ἁμαρτίας, Rom 6:20), set free from sin (ἐλευθερωθέντες δὲ ἀπὸ τῆς ἁμαρτίας, v. 18), and now slaves of righteousness (ἐδουλώθητε τῇ δικαιοσύνῃ, v. 18), slaves of God (δουλωθέντες δὲ τῷ θεῷ, v. 22; cf. 1 Pet 2:16), slaves of Christ (ὁ ἐλεύθερος κληθεὶς δοῦλός ἐστιν Χριστοῦ, 1 Cor 7:22; cf. Rom 12:11; 14:18; 16:18; cf. also Eph 6:7; Col 3:24) and slaves of one another (δουλεύετε ἀλλήλοις, Gal 5:13). It is clear from these references that Richard (1995, 55; cf. Best 1972, 83) is incorrect in his assertion that Paul's use of the δουλ- word group is primarily christological (Wanamaker 1990, 86).

[99] Paul is very aware that his followers could use their freedom incorrectly, to serve someone or something other than God (Schottroff 1991, 107; so Gal 4:9, 5:1; cf. Jer 13:10; *T. Jud.* 18:6). Yet, not only is the service now voluntary rather than forced, but the consequences of slavery to different masters must not be missed (i.e. dead idols; living God). According to Martin, slavery is really a metaphor of deliverance, and this is made explicit in v. 10; from a living master, one can expect life (1990, 62; cf. particularly Rom 6:20–22 for the same idea).

[100] The description of God as "living" may be found in numerous references, particularly in the LXX. Cf. Deut 5:26; Josh 3:10; 1 Sam 17:26 (MT); 1 Kgdms 17:36; 4 Kgdms 19:4, 16; Esth 8:12q; Ps 41:3 (42:2 MT); 83:3 (84:2 MT); Isa 37:4, 17; Dan 6:26–28; Hos 2:1; 4:15; 2 Macc 7:33; 3 Macc 6:28; *Sib. Or.* 3:763; *T. Job.* 37:2; *Hist. Call.* 24:24; Matt 16:16; 26:63; Rom 9:26; 2 Cor 3:3; 6:16; 1 Tim 3:15; 4:10; Heb 3:12; 9:14; 10:31; 12:22; Rev 4:9; 7:2; 10:6; 15:7.

death (van der Watt 1990, 359; BDAG 425, §1.a.ε).[101] The use of the participle as a description of God himself, and never as an adjective for the "image of God", that is a "living image" (cf. 1 Cor 11:7; 2 Cor 4:4), is indicative of the pervasive force of the second commandment against making images of the deity (Llewelyn 2002, 38). Malherbe suggests that Paul's depiction of God as living and also as father[102] may invoke the idea of God as creator (2000, 120).[103] The description of God as "true" is similarly widespread,[104] although Paul does not use it again.[105] It does serve to contrast God from idols,[106] but Paul's use is probably determined by אמת and ἀληθινός signifies more than mere opposition; it portrays "firmness", "solidity", "uprightness" (Bultmann 1964, 249). It also has links to God as creator.[107] Perhaps one of the closest parallels to 1 Thess 1:9 is *Jos. Asen.* 11:8–11, which is part of an address by Aseneth to God. She confesses to God (ἐξομολογήσομαι αὐτῷ) that she has worshipped dead and dumb idols (ἐσεβάσθην εἴδωλα νεκρὰ καὶ κωφά, v. 8). But she has heard: ὅτι ὁ θεὸς τῶν Ἑβραίων θεὸς ἀληθινός ἐστι καὶ θεὸς ζῶν ("that the God of the Hebrews is a true God and a living God", v. 10 [Burchard 1985]). Therefore she turns to him (ἐπιστρέφω πρὸς αὐτόν, v. 11). Thus, similarly to the Thessalonians, Aseneth turns to God from the worship of idols, to a God who is both living and true (Holtz 1998, 57).

b. Jesus – Raised from the Dead (1:10)

1. The infinitive, ἀναμένειν (v. 10a), relates a second aspect of turning to God, the first being to serve (v. 9d). The report becomes identifiably Christian at this point, since the Thessalonians are waiting for "his son from heaven" (τὸν υἱὸν αὐτοῦ ἐκ τῶν οὐρανῶν). The two infinitives, δουλεύειν and ἀναμένειν are descriptive of the

[101] For examples in a context where God is contrasted with idols, cf. Jer 10:10 (MT); Dan 5:23 (LXX); *Jub.* 21:3–4; *Jos. Asen.* 8:5; Acts 14:15; 2 Cor 6:16. The narrative in Bel 5–6θ, is informative: First, the king asks Daniel, "Why do you not worship [προσκυνεῖς] Bel?", to which Daniel replies, ὅτι οὐ σέβομαι εἴδωλα χειροποίητα ἀλλὰ τὸν ζῶντα θεὸν τὸν κτίσαντα τὸν οὐρανὸν καὶ τὴν γῆν καὶ ἔχοντα πάσης σαρκὸς κυριείαν ("Because I do not worship idols made by human hands, but the living God, the one who created heaven and earth and has dominion over all flesh"). Then, the king asks, "Do you not think that Bel is a living god (ζῶν θεός)?". Daniel laughs and points out that Bel is only clay (πηλός) and bronze (χαλκός); cf. also Bel 24–25θ. This text emphasises that only the living God is to be worshipped and this is a strong marker of monotheism — it is inappropriate to offer worship to any other (Hurtado 1993b, 365).

[102] Paul refers to God as father several times in First Thessalonians (1:1, 3; 3:11, 13), but not explicitly in 1:9–10 (n.b. Malherbe's misleading statement in that regard; 1987, 48).

[103] Cf. already, Plato, *Tim.* 28c; 37c; cf. also Sir 18:1; *Sib. Or.* 3:34; *1 En.* 5:1; Philo *Opif.* 19, 24; 45, 46; *Cher.* 44; *Ebr.* 105; *Migr.* 193; *Abr.* 122; *Decal.* 97; *Spec.* 1.41; 2.225; 1 Cor 8:6.

[104] Cf. Exod 34:6; 2 Par 15:3; 1 Esdr 6:18; 8:86; Ps 85:15 (LXX); Isa 65:16; Jer 10:10; 3 Macc 2:11; *Let. Aris.* 140; *Sib. Or.* 5:493, 499; Philo *Legat.* 366; Josephus *Ant.* 8.337–338, 343; 10.263; 11.55; *B.J.* 7.323; John 7:28; 17:3; 1 John 5:20–21; Rev 6:10.

[105] In Rom 3:4 he says: γινέσθω δὲ ὁ θεὸς ἀληθής.

[106] Cf. Tob 14:6; Wis 12:27; Philo *Congr.* 159; *Spec.* 1.332; Josephus *Ant.* 9.256.

[107] Cf. *Apoc. Ab.* 7:11 (mss. A B C K).

Thessalonians' integration into a new eschatologically identifiable existence, as opposed to ἐπιστρέφειν, which is indicative of their current social disintegration. A number of issues require comment in the exegetical discussion of verse 10: the significance of ἀναμένειν (§III.b.2); the trajectory of the term υἱός in antiquity and the implications for Jesus' status and relationship with God (§III.b.3); Paul's understanding of ἐκ τῶν οὐρανῶν (§III.b.4); a critical discussion of Paul's repeated quotation, ὃν ἤγειρεν ἐκ τῶν νεκρῶν (§III.b.5); an exploration of just what is Jesus' role as "deliverer" (§III.b.6); a discussion of the "*orgē* which comes" (§III.b.7); and finally, an excursus investigating whether or not 1:9c–10 may be regarded as a quotation of pre-Pauline traditional formulae (Excursus 3).

2. The verb ἀναμένειν is a *hapax legomenon* in the NT — the textual variant, ὑπομένειν, is to be rejected.[108] Paul usually prefers ἀπεκδέχεσθαι to express eschatological expectation (Grundmann 1964, 56).[109] Thus, Phil 3:20 may be regarded as a parallel to 1 Thess 1:10, *à propos* content, since there are references to heaven (ἐν οὐρανοῖς) and to waiting for Jesus to come from there (ἐξ οὗ καὶ σωτῆρα ἀπεκδεχόμεθα κύριον Ἰησοῦν Χριστόν).[110] Paul probably draws (in both these texts) on a *topos* of waiting found in the LXX, especially from references that indicate an eschatological context (Malherbe 2000, 121). For example, there is an expectation of salvation in Jdt 8:17 (ἀναμένοντες τὴν παρ' αὐτοῦ σωτηρίαν) and of mercy in Sir 2:7 (ἀναμείνατε τὸ ἔλεος αὐτοῦ). In Isa 59:11, there is an expectation of judgment which is equated with salvation (ἀνεμείναμεν κρίσιν ... σωτηρία μακρὰν ἀφέστηκεν ἀφ' ἡμῶν, Bussmann 1975, 45).[111] Perhaps more important is a reference in Job 2:9a (LXX), where ἀναμένειν is in synonymic parallelism with προσδέχεσθαι, a text where the hope of salvation is the object awaited (ἰδοὺ ἀναμένω χρόνον ἔτι μικρὸν προσδεχόμενος τὴν ἐλπίδα τῆς σωτηρίας μου, Langevin 1965a, 481–482). Despite these references, the concept of waiting for an earthly person, albeit an exalted person, is foreign to biblical texts[112] — but Paul keeps a connection with LXX tradition in that the expectation of the son is an expectation of a deliverer (positive) who rescues the faithful from *orgē* (negative; 484).[113] The suggestions, that ἀναμένειν includes the notion of patience and trust (Morris 1959, 64), and

---

[108] 𝔓[46] (*ut videtur*). The variant does not significantly change the meaning of the text and probably reflects the occurrence of ὑπομονή in v. 3 (Hauck 1967, 587). The only other form of the verb in the NT with the stem μεν- is περιμένειν (also a *hapax*) in Acts 1:4 (Hoffmann 1976, 245).

[109] Cf. Rom 8:19, 23, 25; 1 Cor 1:7; Gal 5:5; Phil 3:20. See similar use of προσδέχεσθαι in Titus 2:13.

[110] So Baumgarten 1975, 79; Kim 1981, 152; Lehnert 2002, 20; Wengst 1972, 41.

[111] Then in v. 13, the author explains why there is no justice, nor salvation; it is because they have turned away from following God (καὶ ἀπέστημεν ἀπὸ ὄπισθεν τοῦ θεοῦ ἡμῶν). Cf. 2 Macc 6:14 where the Lord waits patiently (ἀναμένει μακροθυμῶν) to punish the other nations.

[112] Cf. *3 Bar.* 11:2 where the angel Michael is awaited.

[113] The positive aspect of waiting, though not emphasised here, is clear in 1 Thess 2:12 and 5:9 (see Börschel 2001, 104). The negative aspect of this text is significant: if one does not turn to God, then there is no alternative but to suffer *orgē*. See particularly Sir 5:7, which gives the imperative not to delay turning to the Lord (μὴ ἀνάμενε ἐπιστρέψαι πρὸς κύριον), otherwise, suddenly the *orgē* of the Lord will come (ἐξάπινα γὰρ ἐξελεύσεται ὀργὴ κυρίου); cf. *Apoc. Sedr.* 14:7; *T. Ab.* 10:14 (rec. A).

that it implies a sustained expectation (Findlay 1904, 30), are probably over-interpretations.[114] The fact that the Thessalonians are waiting at all may imply a nearness of the person expected (Best 1972, 83; Frame 1912, 88). But in general, only the context implies the manner of waiting (Hoffmann 1976, 245). Finally, the paraenetic force of the infinitive is circuitous but not inconsiderable in view of Paul's further elaborations in the same context of expectation (1 Thess 3:13; 5:23; Marshall 1983, 58).

3. The one expected is described as ὁ υἱὸς αὐτοῦ ἐκ τῶν οὐρανῶν (v. 10a), and he is to be identified as Ἰησοῦς (v. 10c).[115] That τὸν υἱόν appears here is striking[116] because this is the only Pauline occurrence in a *parousia* context. Although this fact has been previously noted,[117] its significance has neither been satisfactorily investigated or discussed. But first, the issue of whether there is a υἱὸς θεοῦ or a υἱὸς ἀνθρώπου tradition (or both?) in this text must be decided.

The traditions underlying the term υἱός are not easily delineated, and it is not necessary here to enter into a protracted attempt to demarcate them. One pertinent aspect of the υἱὸς ἀνθρώπου tradition in the Synoptic Gospels is the association of the term with the *parousia* of Jesus,[118] particularly expressing the function of judge (Hahn 1993, 389).[119] Paul never explicitly refers to the υἱὸς ἀνθρώπου, yet some scholars insist that this figure is presupposed in 1:10 (cf. also 4:15–17).[120] A widespread argument is that Paul draws on a υἱὸς ἀνθρώπου tradition, but changed it to υἱὸς θεοῦ because the former term would have been meaningless to non-Jews.[121] But Hurtado argues, following Nock (1961) and Hengel (1976), that: "... it is difficult to find true Greco-Roman parallels that would account for Paul's view of Jesus as God's 'Son' or render it more intelligible to Paul's Gentile converts" (1993, 900). Consequently, the notion that non-Jews (in general) would understand the designation υἱὸς θεοῦ any better than υἱὸς ἀνθρώπου is rejected (see Smyth 1963, 220–221). For Kim, υἱὸς θεοῦ is more appropriate for Jesus since by his resurrection he was confirmed and exalted as such (1983, 100–101; cf. Rom

---

[114] As a concession, ἀναμένειν does denote "endurance" in Josephus *B.J.* 7.68 (*GGNT* 475), and perhaps gives a sense of longing in Jer 13:16.

[115] The identification of "the son" with the name "Jesus Christ" is linked by the relative clause: "whom he raised from the dead" (Bussmann 1975, 54); cf. Rom 1:3–4; 1 Cor 1:9; 2 Cor 1:19; Acts 9:20.

[116] Paul uses the designation a number of times: Rom 1:3, 9; 5:10; 8:3, 29, 32; 1 Cor 1:9; 15:28; Gal 1:16; 4:4, 6; 1 Thess 1:10; cf. Col 1:13.

[117] Best 1972, 83; Havener 1981, 109; Schweizer 1972, 370.

[118] Matt 24:27–44 (par.); cf. also Matt 10:23; 26:64 (par.); etc.

[119] Matt 25:31–46; Mark 8:38 (par.); Luke 12:8–10.

[120] So Collins 1993, 180; Hoffmann 1979a, 488; Langevin 1965a, 486–487; Pesch 1988, 246; Schweizer 1972, 370, 382; Snyder 1972, 361. Becker reconstructs v. 10a as: "... zu erwarten den Menschensohn aus den Himmeln" (1976, 35; see also 1993b, 140). In this regard, 4Q246 (keeping in mind the horizon of Dan 7) may support the notion that Paul is referring to a υἱὸς ἀνθρώπου tradition, if the document may be understood as a reinterpretation of the term (Labahn/Labahn 2000, 101).

[121] So Cerfaux 1959, 440; Donfried 1990, 48; Fossum 1992, 133–134; Friedrich 1965, 514 (followed by Colpe 1972, 471); Havener 1981, 109; Nickelsburg 1992a, 147; Schweizer 1972, 370; Wengst 1972, 41; also implied by Kim 1983, 101; cf. Vögtle 1994, 169.

1:3–4).[122] Even if a "fusion" of the two traditions is here admitted, where and when it took place is hypothetical, and the answers depend in part on the extent that 1:9–10 is taken to be pre-Pauline.[123]

Approaching the discussion from another angle, it is helpful to examine Paul's use of the υἱὸς θεοῦ designation. To begin with, the older view that Jesus' sonship is a metaphysical description is no longer tenable.[124] According to Hengel such claims have been made without adequate verification (1976, 18; Cullmann 1963, 272). There are very few parallels between the description of Jesus as υἱὸς θεοῦ and Graeco-Roman paganism (Nock 1961).[125] Jewish rather than Hellenistic traditions form a more satisfying explanation of Paul's use of the term (Nock 1928, 96–97), although Hahn is probably correct to identify particular influences on Jewish traditions. For example, Paul focuses the orientation more on the in-breaking of Jesus as the υἱὸς θεοῦ in history, rather than on the usual orientation which emphasises a future/otherworldly aspect (1993, 383).[126]

Against this older view is the assertion that Paul primarily uses υἱὸς θεοῦ to describe a special relationship between Jesus and God.[127] Going further, Paul somehow understands this relationship as vital to his own relationship with God. Thus, in 2 Cor 1:19 Paul refers to Jesus, the υἱὸς θεοῦ, as providing the "yes" required for Paul and his followers to enter into a relationship with God. Gal 2:20 is similar; the life that Paul lives is by faith in the υἱὸς θεοῦ. A titular description is not the primary function of the designation.[128] Instead, υἱός relates Jesus to God the Father

---

[122] Furthermore, Paul's view of the υἱὸς ἀνθρώπου would be quite skewed when compared with Dan 7:13 for example, in that 1 Thess 1:10 has Jesus as a deliverer from *orgē*, not as a judge (Segal 1998, 400–401).

[123] Some scholars argue that a "fusion" occurred during a pre-Pauline stage (Collins 1984, 257; Havener 1981, 109–110), while others are not convinced that Paul did not himself create the link between υἱὸς θεοῦ and υἱὸς ἀνθρώπου in 1:10 (Kim 1981, 133–135; Richard 1995, 56; cf. Schade 1984, 32). This issue is too large to discuss further here. Goulder (2002) provides an excellent introduction to the problems of the υἱὸς ἀνθρώπου debate and in my opinion gives a convincing solution.

[124] Bultmann may be taken as representative of this view. The term supposedly arose from Greek and Hellenistic parallels including: mysteries, dying and rising sons of God, the ruler cult, divine men (θεῖοι ἄνδρες), and the gnostic redeemer myth (1952, 128–133; Milligan 1908, lxvi; cf. Hengel 1976, 21–41). Accordingly, Bultmann asserts, "While the term 'Son of God' secondarily serves to differentiate Christ from the one true God and to indicate Christ's subordinate relation to God, it also serves – and this is the primary thing – to assert his divinity" (1952, 129). Käsemann is even more categorical in his comments on Rom 1:4: "Provisionally one might state that no NT author understood the unique divine sonship of Jesus otherwise than in a metaphysical sense" (1980, 10).

[125] Hurtado suggests that "son of God" as a title was used only by Roman emperors (1993, 901). See Malherbe 1958, 116–117.

[126] For further information on the traditional use of the terms υἱός and υἱὸς θεοῦ, see the large article in *TDNT* (Schweizer 1972); see also Hengel 1976, 41–56; O'Collins 1995, 116–118.

[127] Hengel 1976, 63; 1992, 441; see Cerfaux 1959, 439–460. Wilckens refers to Gal 1:15 and Rom 1:3–4 where Jesus as υἱός is the substance of the revelation (1966, 56).

[128] There does seem to be a titular distinction in Rom 1:3, 4, a text where both υἱός and υἱὸς θεοῦ appear in close juxtaposition (Kramer 1966, 52). In v. 3 Paul qualifies the gospel of God as concerning his son (περὶ τοῦ υἱοῦ αὐτοῦ). Then as part of the contents of that gospel, he states in v. 4 that Jesus was declared son of God (τοῦ ὁρισθέντος υἱοῦ θεοῦ) since his resurrection from the dead (ἐξ ἀναστάσεως

(Schweizer 1972, 382–383),[129] and attributes to Jesus a special standing with God (Hurtado 1993, 903; Plevnik 1989, 261). The son functions as the soteriological and eschatological agent of God[130] which is particularly evident in a *parousia* context (Labahn/Labahn 2000, 119). It is the son's relationship with God, demonstrated by his resurrection, that proves his ability to rescue the Thessalonians from the *orgē* to come (Schade 1984, 32; Wanamaker 1990, 86–87).[131] If this interpretation is correct, then 1:9c–10 identifies the resurrected one with God's son and combines this exaltation christology with the idea of a heavenly deliverer who saves the faithful from God's *orgē* (*contra* Schweizer 1972, 370).[132] Finally, although the emphasis of sonship in 1 Thess 1:9–10 is on the relationship between Jesus and God, this does not preclude Paul envisaging a corresponding relationship between the Thessalonians and God (O'Collins 1995, 115; cf. Rom 8:14–17; Gal 4:5), which is suggested elsewhere in the letter (Börschel 2001, 101).[133]

4. The phrase ἐκ τῶν οὐρανῶν appears in Paul only here,[134] who otherwise prefers ἐξ οὐρανοῦ (1 Cor 15:47; 2 Cor 5:2; Gal 1:8) and to a lesser extent ἀπ' οὐρανοῦ (Rom 1:18; 1 Thess 4:16). The significance of the plural is difficult to ascertain; Paul uses both singular[135] and plural forms (Bussmann 1975, 46).[136] The usual explanation of the plural is either that it is a Hebraism, corresponding to שמים, or that Paul reflects a notion of several heavens.[137] Paul uses ἀπ' οὐρανοῦ in 1 Thess

νεκρῶν). It is the second instance which is significant, because this is the only reference in Paul where he seems to use the designation in a more titular role: "Son of God" (with a capital "S").

[129] 1 Cor 15:28; Phil 2:11; 1 Thess 1:1.

[130] Cf. Rom 5:8–11; 8:2–3, 28, 32; Gal 2:20; 4:4–7; cf. also 1 Cor 15:24–28. This soteriological function – acting as an eschatological agent – becomes a defining characteristic of the relationship between the son and the Father (Kramer 1966, 183–184).

[131] Collins argues that the closeness between Jesus and God is effected by means of the resurrection itself. It is "... a closeness which means that the raised Jesus will henceforth fulfill functions that are properly the functions of God himself, most notably the function of salvation" (1984, 283). But this implies a causal relationship between Jesus' resurrection and his status as υἱὸς θεοῦ, which is grammatically possible in Rom 1:4, but unlikely (Byrne 1996, 45; Käsemann 1980, 12).

[132] Again, as with the υἱὸς ἀνθρώπου discussion above, where and when the designation υἱὸς θεοῦ came to be connected with the *parousia* is unclear. Kramer (probably rightly) suggests that υἱὸς θεοῦ was transferred to the one expected at a very early stage, i.e. a pre-Pauline stage, since no other traces of such a connection remain in Paul (1966, 125–126).

[133] Just as Jesus has been raised (4:14), says Paul, so shall believers be raised (4:16). The resurrection includes being with him (4:17; 5:10). Though Paul does not refer to his converts as children of God, God is called πατὴρ ἡμῶν (1:3; 3:11, 13), and ὁ θεὸς ἡμῶν (2:2; 3:9; cf. 1 Cor 6:11 for the only other occurrence of this phrase in Paul). This leads Collins to conclude: "The relationship between God and the Thessalonian Christians is somehow similar to the relationship that exists between God and Jesus" (1991a, 150). It should be noted that the reference in 2:2 can only refer to Paul and his co-workers, and not to the Thessalonians, since the phrase ἐν τῷ θεῷ ἡμῶν clearly goes with ἐπαρρησιασάμεθα (1993, 222).

[134] For other occurrences of the exact phrase, cf. Mark 1:11 (par.); Ps 148:1 (LXX).

[135] Rom 1:18; 10:6; 1 Cor 8:5; 15:47; 2 Cor 5:2; 12:2; Gal 1:8; 1 Thess 4:16; cf. Eph 1:10; 3:15; 4:10; 6:9; Col 1:5, 16, 20. The plural was almost unknown prior to its appearance in the LXX (see Traub 1967, 498 n. 2 for exceptions).

[136] Phil 3:20; 2 Cor 5:1; 1 Thess 1:10; cf. Col 1:23; 4:1; 2 Thess 1:7.

[137] E.g. 2 Cor 12:2, ἕως τρίτου οὐρανοῦ, Collins 1984, 260; Traub 1967, 510–511; BDF 77–78, §141(1). Lincoln examines every Pauline use of οὐρανός and concludes that the variation between singular and

4:16 in a similar context, and this reference along with 1:10 is as close as Paul gets to an ascension tradition in First Thessalonians.[138] For Paul the exaltation (ὑπερυψοῦν) of Jesus occurs, kerygmatically, at the same time as his resurrection from the dead (ἐκ τῶν νεκρῶν, v. 10b; Kramer 1966, 67),[139] making it unnecessary to refer to any such ascension tradition in order to place Jesus in heaven (Cerfaux 1959, 19; Malherbe 2000, 121).[140] It is not surprising then that Paul directly links the resurrection with an expectation ἐκ τῶν οὐρανῶν (v. 10a; Bussmann 1975, 52; Lohfink 1971, 82).[141] The fact that the Thessalonians' deliverance comes ἐκ τῶν οὐρανῶν confirms the saving action of God and therein οὐρανός is a circumlocution for God. It does not refer to a physical locality but to a dynamic point of departure (Traub 1967, 521) — the *parousia* of the son/Jesus breaks the apocalyptic pattern

plural expressions is simply a stylistic matter, except for the case of Eph 4:10 where the addition of πάντων must be significant (1981, 184). Torm, in his article on the plural οὐρανοί suggests that the use of the plural in the OT is *poetisch* and *feierlich*, and that the progression towards the singular use in the LXX and the NT arises without obvious explanation, although the preference for the singular is surely from Greek language influence (1934, 48–50). It is possible that the original poetic connotation was forgotten from time to time ("konnte die ursprüngliche, poetische Nebenbedeutung mitunter leicht vergessen werden"; 49), but it seems that NT authors were not aware of any inconsistency in the use of both numbers of the noun (e.g. Mark 12:25; 13:32), making it very difficult to determine between an "amplifizierenden Pluralis" and a "Mehrheit von Himmeln" sense (50).

[138] Rom 10:6 does not refer to the ascension as such (cf. Luke 24:50–53; Acts 1:3–11), but merely implies Paul's view that Christ, in some sense, went up to heaven (Whiteley 1974, 152).

[139] Zwiep suggests that the resurrection, in the primitive *kērygma*, is a resurrection to heaven; hence resurrection and exaltation are linked. "This explains e.g. the apparent jump in the train of thought in 1 Thess 1:10, where the expected coming of Christ from heaven is connected with his resurrection from the dead, without an explicit statement on how he came to be in heaven" (1997, 127–128).

[140] See Marshall 1983, 59; Schade 1984, 33, 85; Segal 1980, 1373–1374. Bertram comments: "Exaltation is on the one side the presupposition of His coming again and it thus has eschatological significance" (1972, 612). The verb ὑπερυψοῦν is a *hapax legomenon* in the NT (Phil 2:9), although Paul does refer to the exaltation of Jesus in other ways: he is the Lord of glory (1 Cor 2:8) who was raised from the dead and is at the right hand of God (Rom 8:34; cf. Col 3:1; Eph 1:20; Acts 2:32–33; 5:30–31; 1 Pet 1:21; Bultmann 1952, 82; Evans 1970, 136). Maile argues that there is no disparity between the exaltation of Jesus and the ascension tradition — the ascension stories in Luke-Acts are merely descriptions of Jesus' departure since he was already exalted in his resurrection. Further, Maile suggests that Paul knew of the ascension tradition because he knew the appearances of the risen Lord had come to an end (1993, 277; cf. 1 Cor 15:8). This suggestion is in agreement with Conzelmann's comment on 1 Cor 15:8: "His own vision is apparently meant as the conclusive end of the appearances of the risen Lord" (1975, 259; so also Fee 1987, 732; Marxsen 1970, 81; von Campenhausen 1968, 53–54), although there is some doubt over whether ἔσχατος should be understood other than with a temporal force (cf. 1 Cor 4:9).

[141] Thus Paul transmits the earliest *kērygma*; only later is Jesus' resurrection and exaltation distinguished (cf. Luke 24:36–53; *Barn.* 15.9; Ign. *Smyrn.* 3) concurrently making way for the proclamation of the ascension and making sense of the appearance stories (Hengel 1995, 222). The connection between the resurrection and the *parousia* identifies the son with the earthly Jesus: the one expected is no uncertain and unknown heavenly figure (Holtz 1998, 60; Reinmuth 1998, 121). Haufe comments: "Wahrscheinlich ist hier Auferweckung als Einsetzung Jesu in die eschatologische Sohnes- und Retterfunktion verstanden worden" (1999, 29).

of a "closed heaven" (Schoenborn 1991, 545).[142] Lincoln (1981, 186) explains the significance of verse 10:

> The use of the name Jesus in this context may be meant to underline the identity of the earthly Jesus with the exalted Lord but the perspective of the statement is clearly that the resurrection of Jesus inaugurated the period of salvation in which he is in heaven and that this period will culminate in his coming from heaven.

Paul thus describes the new orientation of his converts: they turned to God and live in a period begun with the resurrection of Jesus, characterised by an expression of waiting, and culminating with the coming of the son (Collins 1984, 261).[143]

5. The confession that God raised Jesus from the dead is one that Paul repeats throughout his letters. It is not entirely fixed in form, but the constituent elements of God as subject, the verb ἐγείρειν (usually Aorist passive) and the prepositional phrase ἐκ (τῶν) νεκρῶν are basic to the confession (Kramer 1966, 21);[144] hence the designation: "resurrection formula" (Vielhauer 1975, 15–16).[145] The exact formulation, ὃν ἤγειρεν ἐκ τῶν νεκρῶν, appears only here and in John 12:9,[146] but relative

---

[142] A closed heaven precludes the possibility of rain (Luke 4:25; Jas 5:17; Rev 11:6), and intimates a concealing of the gracious action of God. Paul obliquely refers to the pattern of concealment in Phil 3:20, in that citizenship is in heaven (πολίτευμα ἐν οὐρανοῖς) and from there the saviour comes (σωτῆρα ... κύριον Ἰησοῦν Χριστόν); it is made explicit in 2 Thess 1:7, where the Lord Jesus is revealed from heaven (ἐν τῇ ἀποκαλύψει τοῦ κυρίου Ἰησοῦ ἀπ' οὐρανοῦ); cf. 1 Cor 1:7.

[143] Langevin sees a link between the phrase "from heaven" with Dan 7:13–14, despite differences, based on the similar themes shared between the texts (which Langevin identifies as waiting, glory, judgment and eschatological arrival of a son). However, any connection here is obtuse, forced on the text by an interpreter who seeks to bolster his evidence for an explicit link to the υἱὸς ἀνθρώπου tradition in Daniel (1965a, 491–492).

[144] In every instance, other than 1 Thess 1:10, Paul excludes the article in the prepositional phrase, ἐκ νεκρῶν (Rom 4:24; 6:4, 9, 13; 7:4; 8:11*bis*; 10:7, 9; 11:15; 1 Cor 15:12, 20; Gal 1:1; cf. Eph 1:20; Col 2:12; 2 Tim 2:8), although Eph 5:14 and Col 1:18 ought to be noted. And since the external evidence for the article's inclusion in 1 Thess 1:10 is as strongly attested (more strongly?) as for its exclusion, then it seems plausible that a scribe would delete the article rather than supply it (Nicholl 2004, 81). With Koester (1985, 223), there is no reason why the article should be placed in square brackets (NA[27]); I regard it as original. However, although Kramer observes that the inclusion of the article is indeed *lectio difficilior*, he is not convinced that it is original. Rather, he suggests that in view of the formidable evidence of Paul's use of the phrase elsewhere, it is more probable that a scribe – "in a period when indiscriminate use of titles had become general" – inserted the article, then that Paul included it himself (1966, 21–22; see Stanley 1961, 83). This view is not convincing primarily because there is no way of knowing when such "indiscriminate use of titles had become general" — making Kramer's argument one from silence. Either way, the meaning is probably not changed (BDAG 668, §B.1; *GNTG* vol. 3, 180; Malherbe 2000, 122), although Nicholl is convinced that its inclusion signifies "the particularity rather than the quality of the substantives" (2004, 81). Zimmer concludes: "Uebrigens ist Zufügung oder Auslassung des Artikels auch sonst beliebt" (1893, 47). I suspect the article is merely prompted by the adjacent ἐκ τῶν οὐρανῶν (so also Wengst 1972, 30).

[145] As opposed to other formulae, e.g. the "dying formula" (Rom 5:6, 8; 14:9; 1 Cor 15:3; 2 Cor 5:15*bis*; Gal 2:21; 1 Thess 5:9–10).

[146] John 12:9 is hardly relevant since it refers to the raising of Lazarus (cf. also John 12:1, 12, 17). However, such references help portray the pervasiveness of this formula in early Christianity. Thus, see Mark 6:14 (par.) where some speculated that Jesus was John the Baptist raised from the dead.

phraseology is found elsewhere.[147] The majority of Pauline references take the form: "he [God] raised him [Jesus] from the dead", either as a finite-verbal[148] or participial construction,[149] and the resurrection formula may also be found throughout the NT with similar structure.[150] Paul rarely repeats the formula without the qualifying ἐκ νεκρῶν,[151] and in every instance, God is the subject or else the implied subject (Hoffmann 1979a, 480).[152] That the resurrection formula appears all over the NT, with a recognisably fixed form, leaves little doubt as to whether the phrase is traditional or not: i.e. it was known and propagated in different trajectories of early Christian writings thereby indicating its antiquity.[153]

The BDAG, EDNT and TDNT entries on ἐγείρειν illustrate the semantic range of the word as well as its use in classical and OT texts, and in early Judaism and the NT.[154] It is sufficient here to note that the notion of resurrection – particularly of individual resurrection – is quite foreign to the OT.[155] It is only by the second century B.C.E. that Jewish eschatology began to include a conception of individual resurrection after death — particularly expressed in apocryphal and pseudepigraphal texts.[156]

---

[147] Acts 3:15; 4:10; 13:37; cf. Ign. *Trall.* 9.2. The relative formulation is considered secondary (Hoffmann 1979a, 480), although the resurrection formula (by itself) is earlier than formulations which combine it with a reference to Jesus' death. Hence, 1 Cor 15:3–8 may not be the earliest representation of the traditions (Marxsen 1990, 53), a view apparently supported by Bovon: "The earliest known Christian sentence is ... an archaic affirmation quoted by Paul in the oldest text of the New Testament: 'God raised him from the dead' (1 Thess 1:10; see also 4:14)" (2001, 374).

[148] Rom 10:9, 1 Cor 6:14, 15:15, Acts 3:15, 4:10, 5:30, 10:40, 13:30, 37 (ἤγειρεν); 1 Cor 15:4, 12, 13, 14, 16, 17, 20 (ἐγήγερται); Rom 6:4 (ἠγέρθη).

[149] Rom 4:24, cf. 1 Pet 1:21 (ἐγείραντα); Rom 8:11a, Gal 1:1, cf. Col 2:12 (ἐγείραντος); Rom 8:11b, 2 Cor 4:14, cf. Eph 1:20; Pol. *Phil.* 2.2 (ἐγείρας); Rom 6:9, 8:34 (ἐγερθείς); Rom 7:4, 2 Cor 5:15 (ἐγερθέντι); cf. 2 Tim 2:8 (ἐγηγερμένον).

[150] Cf. Matt 27:64; Mark 9:9 (par.); John 2:22; 21:14. Besides these examples, there are numerous references about God raising (ἐγείρειν) the dead (in general); so 1 Cor 15:29, 32, 35, 42, 52; Matt 11:5 (par.); 27:52; Mark 12:26 (par.); John 5:21; Acts 26:8; Heb 11:19; cf. Ign. *Magn.* 9.2. It should be noted that there are many references with ἀνάστασις (Rom 1:4; 1 Cor 15:12; Phil 3:11) and ἀνιστάναι (1 Thess 4:14, 16; Eph 5:14; Acts 2:32; 13:33, 34; 17:31), but none with ἔγερσις in Paul (although cf. Matt 27:53).

[151] 1 Cor 6:14, 15:4 and 2 Cor 4:14 are exceptions, although in each of these passages Paul goes on to explain the soteriological implications of Jesus' resurrection (Collins 2002, 427). In 1 Cor 15:14, 15, 16, 17 the context clearly infers the qualification, ἐκ νεκρῶν (cf. v. 20).

[152] None of the references in Paul or elsewhere in the NT indicates primary agency (e.g. ὑπὸ [τοῦ] θεοῦ); thus, scholars refer to the "divine passive" (O'Donnell 1999, 155). The discussion about the grammatical and theological significance of voice for the translation of ἐγείρειν and ἀνιστάναι will be taken up in Chapter 5, §III.d.8.

[153] Holleman 1996, 139–140; Langevin 1965, 275; Lüdemann 1994, 24. Vielhauer notes that it retains its form even when combined with a "Pistisformel" (1975, 15; cf. Rom 4:24; Eph 1:19–20; Col 2:12; 1 Pet 1:21). Thus: "Die Konstanz der Wendung sowie ihre weite Verbreitung gestatten es, sie als selbständige Formel zu beurteilen" (Hoffmann 1979a, 480).

[154] For extensive discussion of the idea of resurrection in antiquity, see Brown 1978; Cavallin 1979; Hoffmann 1979; Nickelsburg 1972; Petterson 2000; Riley 1995.

[155] Or course, see the significant references of Isa 26:19; Dan 12:1–2; Hos 6:1–2.

[156] Cf. esp. 2 Macc; *4 Ezra*; *1 Enoch*; *2 Baruch*.

Paul proclaims that God raised Jesus from the dead: ἐκ τῶν νεκρῶν (v. 10b). His use of ἐκ and not ἀπό is significant even if only because he does not use the latter construction.[157] Yet, it is possible that ἐκ (over ἀπό) simply became associated with the resurrection formula (Hoffmann 1979a, 480). The phrase is by no means redundant since it serves to determine the type of raising effected by God which is important in this context since Paul does not make specific reference to Jesus' death (Collins 1984, 256).[158] According to Kremer, ἐκ τῶν νεκρῶν emphasises Paul's technical use of ἐγείρειν for "the deliverance from death brought about by God, as it was hoped for in the end time" (1990, 375).

The early Christian proclamation of the resurrected son is about a specific historical person. Paul makes this unmistakeably clear by the juxtaposition of the name Ἰησοῦς, directly parallel to τὸν υἱὸν αὐτοῦ, as antecedent to the resurrection formula (Friedrich 1976, 215; Holtz 1977, 482).[159] But it remains that the occurrence of the resurrection was witnessed by no one (von Campenhausen 1968, 47).[160] The resurrection involved a historical person, a particular time and a particular place — all of which can be argued on historical grounds. But the occurrence itself, the unknowable "something" that happened between Jesus' death and the statement of faith by the apostles, is historically unverifiable (Moltmann 1968, 136–137).[161] Consequently, Marxsen is forced to conclude that as a historian, the only possible answer to whether Jesus was raised from the dead must be: "I do not know; I am no longer able to discover" (1970, 119). But this is not the end of the matter. Marxsen goes on to differentiate between the resurrection of Jesus as an occurrence and the subsequent belief in the resurrected one. Since there were no witnesses to the action of God in the resurrection occurrence, then no statement of fact may be found; even this formula in 1:10 is an interpretation of an alleged deed (1990, 42–43). But this does not preclude the absolute occurrence of the event itself. Accordingly, although *historically* unverifiable, the claim of the resurrection (the "something")

[157] Wallace recognises a distinct overlap between the two prepositions (cf. ἐκ τῶν οὐρανῶν in 1:10 and ἀπ' οὐρανοῦ in 2 Thess 1:7; also note the interchange in 1 Thess 2:6). However, he suggests there is a distinction between ἀπὸ τῶν νεκρῶν ("away from the dead") and ἐκ τῶν νεκρῶν ("out from among the dead"); ἐκ is stronger and less ambiguous (*GGBB* 363). Even apart from Paul, ἀπὸ [τῶν] νεκρῶν rarely appears (cf. Matt 14:2; 27:64; 28:7; Luke 16:30; Sir 17:28). Luke 16:30–31 is interesting because it has both constructions: ἀλλ' ἐάν τις ἀπὸ νεκρῶν πορευθῇ πρὸς αὐτοὺς μετανοήσουσιν (v. 30); οὐδ' ἐάν τις ἐκ νεκρῶν ἀναστῇ πεισθήσονται (v. 31). Traub suggests that ἐκ is consonant with a *parousia* theme since it emphasises an idea of origin, of coming from, when compared to the more spatial ἀπό (1967, 523).

[158] See LSJ (s.v.) for numerous examples where ἐγείρειν is used other than in a kerygmatic sense.

[159] The identification of the son as Jesus is strengthened by the further parallel of ἐκ τῶν οὐρανῶν (v. 10a) and ἐκ τῶν νεκρῶν (v. 10b; Haufe 1999, 29).

[160] Marxsen is a little more cautious and simply says that there is no knowledge concerning anyone who witnessed the resurrection (1990, 41).

[161] The issues of interpretation pertaining to the empty tomb and appearances stories will not be taken up here. Such issues lead the discussion into the realm of the nature of Jesus' resurrection body and by implication, of the nature of the believer's resurrection body. Here, it is sufficient to note Fergusson's comment: "The empty tomb and the appearances ... provide the matrix within which the event of the resurrection is grasped and articulated" (1985, 301); see also Lindemann 1998, 63–64.

is capable of *eschatological* verification. The significance and meaning, therefore, is not so much historical as it is eschatological (Moltmann 1968, 137; Krötke 1997, 222). Certainly, this means that God's raising of Jesus was no mere resuscitation of a corpse, but is a theological act comparable with the creation of the world (cf. Rom 4:17, 24).[162] Concomitantly, the death of Jesus may also be understood as more than a historical occurrence (see Schrage 1967). *Yet the eschatological significance of God raising Jesus from the dead does not necessarily preclude (or include) a resuscitation of the body* (G. J. Hughes 1988).[163] Carnley suggests that the historical and eschatological aspects of Jesus' resurrection need not be mutually exclusive but complementary (1987, 144).[164]

The consequences of God raising his son Jesus from the dead are many,[165] but one which is emphasised in 1:10 is a contingent expectation of the *parousia*; there is now one who delivers the Thessalonian believers from the coming *orgē* (Collins 2002, 426–427).[166] This deliverance is positive[167] and is primarily understood as a basis for future hope (Kreitzer 1993a, 806; Langevin 1965a, 498), in which the future comes already into the present (cf. 2 Cor 4:4; Schlier 1971, 142–143). That is, Paul lives between the resurrection of Jesus (1:10) and the resurrection of the dead in Christ (4:15–17) — both *eschatological* occurrences. This is the time of the Holy Spirit and Paul expects it to be of relatively short duration (Collins 1991a, 149).[168]

6. The name Ἰησοῦς appears by itself in those contexts where the historical figure is particularly in view,[169] often in proximity to the subject of Jesus' death and resurrection (Foerster 1965, 289; Schneider 1991, 184),[170] although Kramer argues that when it appears in πίστις-formulations the name has the same meaning as Χριστός (1966, 199–200). In 1:10, it is anarthrous, but Paul easily switches

---

[162] See Evans 1990, 587; O'Collins 1973, 60.

[163] Cf. *quem suscitavit ex mortuis* (1 Thess 1:10 [Vulg.]). Of interest is Porter's (1999a) article on resurrection, where he shows that the notion of a bodily resurrection is not necessarily a Jewish one.

[164] It does seem odd, however, that Paul never once refers to the "empty tomb". Part of the struggle in understanding the significance of the resurrection of Jesus is perhaps bound up in a right balance between the historical and eschatological aspects. Williams suggests that historical critics often fall into the trap of first interpreting the resurrection as if it were a mundane event in history — open to the methods of historical investigation. Rather, he looks beyond the historical aspect and seeks to discover the *kērygma* of the resurrection as a symbolic vehicle of truth (1998, 227).

[165] Most important are the eschatological implications of that event. There is no simple resumption of the old order, but a new era begins (Beasley-Murray 1991, 300).

[166] "Daß Jesus euch vor dem kommenden Zornereignis rettet, ist deshalb so gewiß, weil hinter diesem Jesus Gott steht" (Kegel 1970, 34).

[167] Fascher 1927, 14; Nickelsburg 1992, 688; Söding 1991, 194; cf. 5:9; 1 Cor 1:7–8; Phil 3:19–20.

[168] Cf. 1 Thess 1:6; 4:8; 5:19–20.

[169] Besides numerous references in the Gospels, cf. Rom 3:26; 1 Cor 12:3; 2 Cor 4:5; 11:4; Gal 6:17; Phil 2:10; cf. also Eph 4:21; Heb 2:9; 3:1, 3; 5:7; 6:20; 7:22; 10:19; 12:2, 24; 13:12; 1 John 4:3; Rev 1:9*bis*; 12:17; 14:12; 17:6; 19:10*bis*; 20:1; 22:16.

[170] Cf. Rom 8:11; 2 Cor 4:10*bis*, 11*bis*, 14; 1 Thess 1:10; 4:14*bis*.

between this and the arthrous form (von Dobschütz 1909, 61).[171] The positioning of the name, immediately following the formula in verse 10b, allows it both to specify the object of God's power and to identify the one who will rescue the Thessalonians from the coming *orgē* (*contra* Burchard 2005, 273). There is no need to decide to which phrase it should belong (Collins 1984, 258–259; *contra* Havener 1981, 105–106).[172] Kramer attempts to argue that the name signifies, for Paul, more than a historical personage. He asserts that Ἰησοῦς is to be associated with the resurrection formula, rather than being a Pauline addition.[173] Furthermore, on the basis of 1 Thess 4:14a, where Ἰησοῦς stands as the subject of the sentence and therefore is supposedly equivalent to Χριστός in that context, Kramer proposes that this equivalence is usually inferred in passages containing a similar formula (1966, 199–201). Thus: "*Jesus* means here the person in whom the saving events took place" (201). However, Kramer's line of reasoning is faulty on all fronts. First, there is no certainty about whether Ἰησοῦς was originally associated with the formula (Holtz 1983, 60). Second, his claim that it is equivalent to Χριστός on the basis of 4:14a is strange considering that the name appears only once in that passage, in a prepositional phrase (v. 16), and not as the subject of a sentence. Finally, there is no basis for allowing such an interpretation to be programmatic for Paul's references to the name Ἰησοῦς elsewhere. While Kramer's definition of Ἰησοῦς certainly fits admirably with 1:10, it is likely that Paul does not intend any other meaning than a reference to a historical person.

Jesus, as the deliverer (ὁ ῥυόμενος), is a rather foreign concept to the NT. The word, in an eschatological context, appears only here and in Rom 11:26 in the authentic Paul.[174] However, the notion of deliverance is definitely Pauline (Holtz

---

[171] Cf. 1 Thess 4:14 and 2 Cor 4:11 where both Ἰησοῦς and ὁ Ἰησοῦς appear concurrently. It is unlikely that the arthrous form is due to anaphora (*contra GNTG* vol. 3, 167; cf. 2 Cor 4:10; Eph 4:21; 1 John 4:3) because the letters lack a narrative context (BDF 136, §260[1]).

[172] England makes an interesting case for taking the phrase "whom he raised from the dead" to be an allusion to the cult of Cabirus, and in this context, argues that Paul purposely leaves the name "Jesus" until after the formula in order to heighten the possible reference to Cabirus. In particular, England points to the parallel of the dying and rising god, a motif which is particularly emphasised in the cult: "The hearers are to await the one who will rescue them from the coming anger, but the identification of this saviour is delayed. It could be quite possibly Paul's intention to evoke the image of the god Cabirus in the minds of the Christians, and only then to ensure that the community recognizes that it now worships a new god who has died and is raised, Jesus. Hence the late introduction of Ἰησοῦν which presents an emphatic contrast to the possible allusion to Cabirus" (1995, 58). Ironically, however, this "new god" just happens to be the same "old" God of the Jews, as signified particularly by the epithet that God is "living and true" (Lührmann 1990, 243; cf. Krentz 1987, 28).

[173] Cf. 1 Thess 1:10; 4:14a; 2 Cor 4:14a.

[174] *Contra* Best (1972 85) and Krentz (1987, 27), who overlook Rom 11:26. Paul does use ῥύεσθαι elsewhere, but not often. Cf. Rom 7:24; 15:31; 2 Cor 1:10; cf. also Col 1:13; 2 Thess 3:2; 2 Tim 3:11; 4:17, 18.

1977, 482; see Söding 1991, 187).[175] Usually though, God is the deliverer.[176] The verb σῴζειν appears far more often.[177] The relationship between the two verbs is ambiguous though in some measure overlapping (Kasch 1968, 999).[178] Thus, in Rom 11:26, it appears that ὁ ῥυόμενος mediates the salvation of Israel (πᾶς Ἰσραὴλ σωθήσεται).[179] In this text and 1 Thess 1:10, Paul has Jesus as ὁ ῥυόμενος, and this supports an implied transference of the deliverer function from God to Jesus (Collins 1984, 259–260, 342; Rigaux 1959, 383).[180] This role of divine agent is part of Jesus' exaltation (n.b. 11Q13; Hurtado 1998, 98). If the object from which one is delivered is in view, as in 1 Thess 1:10, then this is denoted either by ἀπό or ἐκ.[181] Lichtenberger suggests that the former focuses on a future deliverance while the latter focuses more on a past or present deliverance (1993, 214). Unfortunately, such a neat solution to the important issue of the present/future/proleptic orientation of the participle is inadequate. That question may only be dealt with after taking into account the final prepositional phrase: ἐκ τῆς ὀργῆς τῆς ἐρχομένης.[182]

---

[175] Cf. Rom 5:9; 7:24; Phil 3:20–21. Kreitzer argues that Gal 1:4 is a text where God and Jesus Christ are co-deliverers, although the word there is not ῥύεσθαι but ἐξαιρεῖν (1987, 126). Similarly, in Philo *Migr.* 15, God is the primary actor of deliverance, mediated through his prophet (ὁ προφήτης αὐτοῦ ῥύεται); cf. also *Jos. Asen.* 15:12.

[176] Rom 15:31; 2 Cor 1:10*ter*; cf. Col 1:13; 2 Thess 3:2; 2 Tim 3:11; 4:17, 18; 2 Pet 2:7, 9; cf. also Matt 6:13; 27:43 (Isa 36:20); Luke 1:74; *Sib. Or.* 3:556, 560–561. The last reference depicts an important difference between Judaism and Christianity in that deliverance is made certain by the resurrected one (see Boring/Berger/Colpe 1995, 491).

[177] Rom 5:9, 10; 8:24; 9:27; 10:9, 13; 11:14, 26; 1 Cor 1:18, 21; 3:15; 5:5; 7:16; 9:22; 10:33; 15:2; 2 Cor 2:15; 1 Thess 2:16.

[178] In Matt 27:40–43 the derisive, σῶσον σεαυτόν, and, ἄλλους ἔσωσεν, ἑαυτὸν οὐ δύναται σῶσαι, are synonymous with the subsequent statement, πέποιθεν ἐπὶ τὸν θεόν, ῥυσάσθω νῦν εἰ θέλει αὐτόν. See 2 Tim 4:18 where both words occur.

[179] *Contra* Kasch (1968, 1003), there is no distinction between the preliminary work of salvation (σῴζειν) and the final preservation of the believer by the deliverer (ῥύεσθαι). Such a distinction is forced; besides, it is problematic to think of the action of the deliverer as future, because of the difficulty in relating this to the action of the cross (Byrne 1996, 355). As far as Rom 11:26 goes, the distinction is not to be made between an alleged time-difference of the two verbs, but between the time of salvation of Israel and the full number of Gentiles (v. 25; Käsemann 1980, 314; Richard 1995, 57–58); cf. Wis 18:20–25.

[180] Stendahl (1995) and Getty (1988) interpret Rom 11:25–27 as a theological text: "all Israel" will be saved by God apart from Jesus Christ. However, the evidence for a christological interpretation, where ὁ ῥυόμενος is understood to be a reference to Jesus Christ, is conclusive (see Davies 1978, 27–28, and any commentary on Romans).

[181] Paul uses ῥύεσθαι with ἐκ twice more (Rom 7:24; 2 Cor 1:10; cf. Col. 1:13; 2 Tim 3:11; 4:17; cf. also Luke 1:74; 2 Pet 2:9) — with ἀπό, only once (Rom 15:31; although cf. 2 Thess 3:2: 2 Tim 4:18; cf. also Matt 6:13). For discussion of the textual variation in 1 Thess 1:10, see the following footnote. Deliverance is required from all sorts of things: from evil (Gen 48:15–16 [LXX]; Philo *Det.* 93; *Fug.* 67; *Leg.* 3.177; Matt 6:13; 2 Thess 3:2; 2 Tim 4:18; *T. Reub.* 4:10; *T. Jos.* 10:3); from darkness (Col 1:13; *Jos. Asen.* 15:12); from persecution (2 Tim 3:11; 2 Pet 2:9; Philo *Mos.* 1.47, 173; *Jos. Asen.* 12:7, 11, 12); from death (Rom 7:24; 2 Cor 1:10; 2 Tim 4:17; Josephus *Ant.* 11.229; *Jos. Asen.* 27:10); from eternal punishment (*2 Clem.* 6.7).

[182] Whether the original reading should be ἐκ or ἀπό is a textual issue rarely raised by commentators. The external evidence favours ἐκ although the evidence is scanty. NA[27] lists א A B P 0278. 33. 81. 1505. 1739. 1881. 2464 *pc*, in support of ἐκ, and C D F G Ψ 𝔐 latt, in support of ἀπό. In an article-length examination, Wallace has shown that the Latin witnesses (*ab ira* [Vulg.]) marginally support ἀπό (1990, 472; *contra* NA[26], but corrected in NA[27]). The Syriac *men* (which is equivalent to the Hebrew מן)

7. While embracing the idea of *orgē* as completely impersonal[183] may be overstepping the mark,[184] the tendency unconsciously to associate the English word "wrath" with an emotional feeling – like "anger" (θυμός) – is incorrect. Paul uses *orgē* fifteen times;[185] only rarely does he include a qualifying (τοῦ) θεοῦ.[186] It is part of the proclamation of the gospel and therefore stands inclusive rather than exclusive of God's love and mercy (Roetzel 1972, 80–81; Stählin 1967, 422). Consequently, *orgē* is all-encompassing because everyone is under sin and death (Rom 3:23; 6:23).[187] The inclusive nature of *orgē* stands dialectically with the Pauline notion

is ambivalent because it allows both readings (*ThesSyr* s.v.; see Molitor 1971, 169; Rigaux 1956, 393–394). The 𝔐 witnesses on the side of ἀπό are meaningless in view of the fact that the list of consistently cited witnesses of the first order (containing 1 Thess 1:10) which 𝔐 represents includes, 𝔓[46.65] ℵ A F I Ψ 0278. 33. 1739. 1881, and yet no small number of these witnesses (i.e. ℵ A 0278. 33. 1739. 1881) are listed on the side of ἐκ! In all, the external evidence points to ἐκ, particularly in view of the weighty support of major uncial manuscripts.

Wallace goes on to devote most of his article to a discussion of internal evidence allegedly in favour of ἀπό. His arguments may be summarised as follows: (1) There is a possibility of an ἀπό to ἐκ change due to dittography, particularly since there are two other (undisputed) occurrences of ἐκ in 1:10 (475–476). (2) For literary purposes, or stylistic consistency, it is most likely that ἀπό was changed to ἐκ in order to read: ἐκ τῶν οὐρανῶν ... ἐκ τῶν νεκρῶν ... ἐκ τῆς ὀργῆς (476). (3) An original reading of ἀπό (giving an ἐκ ... ἐκ ... ἀπό construction) would correspond to Paul's variation of use elsewhere (476–477; cf. 1 Thess 2:6). (4) Paul may have had a "doctrinal" reason for using ἀπό, analogous to his consistent use of ἐκ νεκρῶν rather than ἀπὸ νεκρῶν (477). Wallace concludes his discussion by giving ἀπό an A rating on internal probability and a B/B- rating overall (478). In response to Wallace's arguments, the case for dittography is weakened by the different definite articles: ἐκ τῶν (v. 10a, b) versus ἐκ τῆς (v. 10c). The arguments of style are even more ambiguous. True, an original reading of ἀπό would correspond to Paul's variation of use elsewhere, but this does not strengthen Wallace's case. Either eventuality (i.e. ἀπό to ἐκ/ἐκ to ἀπό) is possible depending on the preference of particular scribes; there is no way to decide between whether a scribe preferred a consistent ἐκ ... ἐκ ... ἐκ reading (and therefore changed ἀπό to ἐκ) or whether a scribe was confronted with the consistent reading and changed ἐκ to ἀπό for stylistic variation. Finally, Wallace may be correct about Paul's supposed "doctrinal" reason for choosing ἀπό (Zimmer 1893, 47), but again, the evidence is circumspect and unconvincing, particularly since Wallace himself notes that there is no established use of one preposition over the other in conjunction with ῥύεσθαι (476). Ironically, Wallace could have strengthened his case for ἀπό by noting a possible chiastic structure in vv. 9–10:

a ἀπὸ τῶν εἰδώλων
  b ἐκ τῶν οὐρανῶν
  b' ἐκ τῶν νεκρῶν
a' ἀπὸ τῆς ὀργῆς τῆς ἐρχομένης

In summary, none of the internal evidence given so far is conclusive. But there is a case to be made for an original reading of ἐκ, based on Rom 11:26. There, Paul gives a quotation of Isa 59:20 (LXX), but changes the preposition from ἕνεκεν to ἐκ (which may come from Ps 13:7 [LXX]). This then, is the only conclusive evidence for a specific Pauline preference of one preposition over another, and since the external evidence supports an original reading of ἐκ, I am inclined to support the text of NA[27] (sincere thanks must go to E. J. Epp for his correspondence on this issue).

[183] So Dodd 1959; Hanson 1957, 69–71; MacGregor 1961.

[184] Best 1972, 84–85; Borchert 1993, 991; Bruce 1982, 20; Collins 1984, 259; Stählin 1967, 424–425.

[185] Rom 1:18; 2:5*bis*, 8 (with θυμός, cf. also Zeph 2:2, 3); 3:5; 4:15; 5:9; 9:22*bis*; 12:19; 13:4, 5; 1 Thess 1:10; 2:16; 5:9; cf. also Eph 2:3; 4:31; 5:6; Col 3:6, 8; 1 Tim 2:8.

[186] Rom 1:18; cf. Eph 5:6; Col 3:6. This simply serves to emphasise how strongly Paul is aware of God in all things, rather than to show that the concept of *orgē* is autonomous (Stählin 1967, 424).

[187] It is the expression of divine retribution (BDAG 720, §2.b). Thus, *orgē* must be understood as applicable to insiders as well as outsiders (Schlueter 1994, 184).

of his followers *not* being destined for *orgē* (1 Thess 5:9; Rom 9:22–23), and this is indicative of the problem of how to express a primarily eschatological *orgē* in the present (Bultmann 1952, 288–289); the issue of whether Jesus' action of delivering is in the present or future is part of the same dilemma.[188] First Thessalonians 1:10 presents an escape clause, a major "however", for those who have turned to God (Collins 1984, 249; Lehnert 2002, 22); apart from this deliverance there is only *orgē* (Pesch 1991, 530).[189] There is no thought of the individual here; the Thessalonians are delivered as a community. The emphatic ἡμᾶς (v. 10c) is inclusive. Deliverance from *orgē* has more to do with membership in the *ekklēsia* rather than with individual acts of each member (Bormann 2002, 56).

The significance of the qualifying participle, τῆς ἐρχομένης, should not be overlooked because it specifically characterises this *orgē* as a future judgment that will occur at the time of the *parousia* (Börschel 2001, 103; Hester 2002, 153).[190] The phrase ἐκ τῆς ὀργῆς τῆς ἐρχομένης does not appear elsewhere, although there is a possible parallel in the statement: τίς ὑπέδειξεν ὑμῖν φυγεῖν ἀπὸ τῆς μελλούσης ὀργῆς; (Matt 3:7 = Luke 3:7; Wengst 1972 37). Thomas suggests that τῆς ἐρχομένης shows a greater degree of imminence than does τῆς μελλούσης (1978, 249). For Frame, the emphasis of Paul is more on the nearness of the judgment, rather than its certainty (1912, 89; but cf. 1 Thess 5:3). This orientation is somewhat different to Paul's references to *orgē* in Romans, which have much more present connotations.[191]

In summary, and keeping in mind that the *orgē* of 1 Thess 1:10 predominantly lies in the future, it is time to move back to the discussion of the present/future/proleptic orientation of the participle, ὁ ῥυόμενος. Some scholars argue that the substantive function of the present participle indicates a durative aspect.[192] Others argue that the aspect of the participle is timeless, and therefore cannot be

[188] Donfried appeals to the "already, not yet" motif in Paul's thinking to understand the dilemma. "Already now, in the present, God acts decisively in the revelation, death and resurrection of his Son, but the imminent consummation, the approaching deliverance of 'the wrath to come' and the fulfillment of the promise of salvation is yet to occur" (1996c, 398–399).

[189] The word "escape" is used hesitantly, because it may shift the emphasis away from the delivering function of Jesus, and imply a notion of escaping or avoiding *orgē* altogether. But the inclusive nature of *orgē* underscores the fact that Jesus delivers Paul's followers ἐκ τῆς ὀργῆς (Bussmann 1975, 56).

[190] So in BDAG, the participle is taken as future: "the wrath which will be revealed (at the judgment)" (394, §4.a.β); likewise, in BDF, attention is drawn to the futuristic use of the present, particularly with ἔρχομαι (168, §323). But this does not mean that *orgē* cannot impinge upon the present (so Rom 1:18–3:20; 1 Thess 2:16?). Thus, the coming *orgē* makes *imperative* a certain holiness/sanctification (ἁγιασμός; 1 Thess 4:3, 6–7) in the present, so that one remains blameless (ἄμεμπτος) at the *parousia* of Jesus (3:13; 5:23; Collins 1984, 248–249); see Elias 1992, 123–124; Lattke 1987, 357. The dual themes of *parousia* and judgment also appear together in 1 Thess 5:1–11; 1 Cor 1:7–8; 4:5 (Siber 1971, 20).

[191] Cf. esp. Rom 1:18; 3:5; 4:15; 9:22*bis*; 12:19; 13:4, 5.

[192] Alford 1958, 253; Auberlen/Riggenbach 1869, 24; Bruce 1982, 19–20; Denney 1892, 60; Eadie 1877, 53; Elias 1992, 124; Findlay 1891, 60; 1904, 31; Friedrich 1976, 215; Ward 1973, 47; Williams 1992, 33. It is the tense of the participle, not the context, which lends credence to this argument. Thus, Heb 7:25 may not be invoked as a parallel passage, in support of the notion that Jesus is the continually delivering one (*GGBB* 620; see Bailey 1955, 265).

made to support a present or future deliverance.[193] Still others solve the problem by acknowledging the future orientation of *orgē* and therefore future aspect of deliverance, but asserting that this deliverance has already started in the present (and simply awaits completion) — as such, it is a proleptic deliverance.[194] For Rigaux, the present participle indicates "la fonction permanente qui aura son application dans le futur" (1956, 395; followed by Malherbe 2000, 122), and this is probably closest to Paul's statement. There is no opposition between a present and future work of the deliverer (Collins 1984, 259). Thus, Paul is able to express an "already, not yet" tension without contradiction, even in the same verse (Rom 5:9). There, the "already" of σωτηρία is expressed in δικαιωθῆναι. Justification is positive and present (Donfried 1976, 100–101).[195] The "not yet" is expressed by the statement: σωθησόμεθα δι' αὐτοῦ ἀπὸ τῆς ὀργῆς, and this is a direct parallel to 1 Thess 1:10. Both pericopes refer to a future deliverance from *orgē*.[196] Essentially, although σωτηρία is begun in the death and resurrection of Jesus, its conclusion remains predominantly future and therefore incomplete (Lövestam 1963, 54; O'Collins 1992, 912);[197] indeed, the future aspect of 1 Thess 1:10 is emphatic.[198]

Excursus 3
Pre-Pauline Traditional Formulae and 1:9c–10

1. The identification and characterisation of a traditional formula is not a straight-forward matter.[199] A problem arises over whether all, part, or only verse 10b of 1:9c–10 should be

---

[193] Bornemann 1894, 69–70; Morris 1959, 64; Stanley 1961, 85. Milligan suggests that the deliverance is so certain as to be already completed (1908, 15).

[194] Ahn 1989, 191; Best 1972, 84; Burkeen 1979, 91; Laub 1973, 165; Légasse 1999, 105; Richard 1995, 76; Stott 1991, 42. Although Wanamaker espouses this view, he suggests that the present aspect of the participle should not be pushed (1990, 88).

[195] As a consequence of the inclusive nature of *orgē*, ῥύεσθαι may imply a justification of the godless; this would make sense of Jesus' role as deliverer, by his death "for us" (cf. 1 Thess 5:9; Hengel/Schwemer 1997, 306).

[196] Foerster 1971, 993; Holtz 1977, 480; Käsemann 1980, 138.; cf. 1Q14 1:5–7; 1QpHab 12:14.

[197] Cf. esp. Rom 11:26; 13:11; Phil 1:19; 3:20–21.

[198] Börschel 2001, 104; Havener 1981, 109–110; Langevin 1965a, 506–507; Merk 1991, 100–101.

[199] Vielhauer provides a useful list of clues for which to look when attempting to establish pre-formed traditions in a given text (1975, 12). Summarised briefly, these are: (1) clear citation formulae; (2) stereotyped or poetic style such as rhythmic structure, strophic construction, etc.; (3) unusual terminology; (4) theological ideas which deviate from the author's; (5) repetition or modification of set phrases; (6) thought which goes beyond the context or which is particularly well formulated; (7) grammatical incorrectness and stylistic difficulties. See Vielhauer for details and examples.

It should be noted at the outset of this discussion that Wanamaker challenges the very notion of "pre-Pauline", asserting that it is a misnomer to use that term: "Paul's missionary activity went back to the very earliest days of the Christian faith ..., and we know of no organized mission to the Gentiles in the earliest period except for the one carried out by Paul" (1990, 85. It is strange that he specifically refers to Holtz's article (1977) to support this view, when Holtz says nothing to corroborate such a thesis. Furthermore, since Wanamaker makes these assertions without discussion, it will here be presupposed that the mainline

regarded as a quotation of traditional material(s). A purely lexical approach to the problem is inconclusive. Certainly, it is possible to point to some words or phrases which may be characterised as unusual in Paul.[200] But such evidence does not categorically rule out the possibility that 1:9c–10 is primarily Pauline redaction of traditional material.[201] A separate but related issue, assuming dependency on tradition material, is whether strands of tradition influencing the text may be identified.

2. J. Munck (1963) may be taken as a point of departure for the specific discussion of 1 Thess 1:9c–10 and its possible dependence on pre-Pauline traditional material.[202] Whereas the traditional view contends that 1:9c–10 reproduces a summary of first-century missionary preaching – put forward as the best explanation for the large number of lexical anomaly in the verses (100–103)[203] – Munck takes an entirely different route. Rather than isolate or dissociate the tradition(s) from First Thessalonians, Munck strongly argues that the verses must be understood within the historical context of the letter (105). He observes that, rather than a summary *per se*, verses 9c–10 are anticipatory of later pericopes in the letter, namely, 1 Thess 4:13–18 and 5:9–10 (107–108). Perhaps his most important contribution to the discussion is his conclusion: "... the apostle in his introductory words states the essential message of the letter. What is expressed as a fact at the beginning of the letter may thus express something which should be a fact, and which Paul later in the letter urges the church to make into a reality" (108). Consequently, the pericope is not a summary of first-century missionary preaching, but, at best, an incomplete report describing that to which the Thessalonians converted (104–105). Snyder (1972) essentially repeats Munck's thesis, restated in an epistolary analysis of *petition* and *disclosure*.

3. G. Friedrich, in a stimulating article (1965), looks to stylistic observations to decide not only that 1:9c–10 is pre-Pauline, but an early Christian hymn coming from a *Taufsituation* and *Taufverkündigung* (516). He posits the hypothesis that the pericope is a quotation of traditional material, arranged in a two-strophe structure each comprised of three parts.[204]

---

view, which differentiates between the earliest Hellenistic-Christian communities and Paul, is correct (Bultmann 1952, 63–183; Merk 1991, 101; Porter 1999, 320–321).

[200] So for example ἐπιστρέφειν is a near *hapax legomenon* in Paul (cf. Gal 4:9; 2 Cor 3:16); εἴδωλον is associated with Jewish mission propaganda literature (see particularly, Bussmann 1975); ζῆν is rarely used by Paul to describe God (cf. Rom 9:26 [n.b. Hos 2:1]; 2 Cor 3:3; 6:16); ἀληθινός is a *hapax legomenon* in Paul while ἀναμένειν is a *hapax* in the NT; υἱός is only here in such an eschatological connection and ἐκ τῶν οὐρανῶν occurs only here in Paul who usually omits the article (Becker 1976, 35); Paul prefers the singular form, οὐρανός, over the plural form, οὐρανοί (Havener 1981, 106; Richard 1995, 57; although cf. Eph 1:10; 3:15; 4:10; 6:9; Col 1:5, 16, 20); ῥύεσθαι is usually predicative of God, not Jesus (Rom 7:24; 11:26; 15:31; 2 Cor 1:9–10); besides, Paul usually uses σῴζειν when referring to an eschatological deliverer (cf. Rom 10:9; 1 Cor 3:15; 5:5; Friedrich 1965, 506). Finally, ἐκ τῆς ὀργῆς τῆς ἐρχομένης is an unusual formulation. Although Paul refers to *orgē* (of God) elsewhere, it is only here that he qualifies it as a "coming *orgē*" (Neyrey 1980, 221).

[201] Thus for example, Havener argues that the ἐπιστρέφειν phrase is not un-Pauline at all (1981, 106–108); similarly, εἴδωλον could be Pauline redaction, and Hengel has shown that ὁ υἱός is a vital element of his gospel and is not out of place in an eschatological context (cf. 1 Cor 15:28; 1976, 9–10).

[202] Although this discussion persists from its roots in nineteenth-century German scholarship, Munck's article makes a distinctive contribution to the modern discussion and therefore offers itself as a likely juncture to begin afresh.

[203] Munck lists commentaries by Dewailly, Lueken, Masson, Morris, Neil, Oepke and Rigaux as supporting this explanation; he notes dissent by Frame, Milligan, Plummer and Wohlenberg (1963, 101).

[204] Friedrich also reiterates the arguments in his commentary (1976, 215). This structure is closely followed by de Jonge (1988, 34) and Murphy-O'Connor (1996, 122) although neither acknowledge Friedrich.

9b ἐπεστρέψατε πρὸς τὸν θεὸν ἀπὸ τῶν εἰδώλων
δουλεύειν θεῷ ζῶντι καὶ ἀληθινῷ,
10a καὶ ἀναμένειν τὸν υἱὸν αὐτοῦ ἐκ τῶν οὐρανῶν,
10b ὃν ἤγειρεν ἐκ τῶν νεκρῶν,
Ἰησοῦν τὸν ῥυόμενον ἡμᾶς
ἐκ τῆς ὀργῆς τῆς ἐρχομένης.

In the first strophe, each line begins with a verb: ἐπεστρέψατε, δουλεύειν, (καὶ) ἀναμένειν, and although these are not strictly past, present and future, Friedrich argues that the sense of the strophe would indicate this time distinction.[205] The second strophe is linked to the first by the close proximity of the phrases ἐκ τῶν οὐρανῶν and ἐκ τῶν νεκρῶν, the first of which presupposes the second. The focus shifts from God to Jesus, whom God has raised from the dead (past), and Jesus rescues the Thessalonians (present) from the coming *orgē* (future).[206] Again, Friedrich notes that the third part of the second strophe is not strictly future, but argues that the present participle ἐρχομένης makes a confident assertion about the future (508–510).[207] Leaving aside for the moment the contentious issue of the origin(s) of the traditional material, Friedrich *has* identified specific stylistic elements in 1:9c–10 which suggest Paul's dependency on traditional material, although Rigaux had already recognised many of them.[208]

4. P.-E. Langevin (1965), independent of Friedrich, takes up (again) the view that 1 Thess 1:9c–10 is a summary of general missionary preaching which Paul has passed on. He approaches the issue by first establishing ground rules for identifying a pre-Pauline text (268–274) and then applying these rules to the verses (274–282). In a subsequent addition to his first article, Langevin proceeds with a detailed exegesis (473–512). However, Collins criticises Langevin for his reliance on Rigaux (1956; 1959); and it seems that his article merely reinforces the pre-Pauline character of 1 Thess 1:9c–10. The question of Pauline redaction versus direct quotation of traditional material has yet to be answered.

5. The monograph by C. Bussmann (1971; ²1975) stands as perhaps the most influential work regarding the impact of late-Jewish and Hellenistic mission literature on Paul's proclamation. In particular, he identifies many parallels between 1:9c–10 and *Missionspredigt* (39–47; see Schnelle 2003, 180–182). But most important for this discussion is his rejection of

[205] Thus, Paul's converts, in the past, turned to God from idols. In the present, they are serving a living and true God. Finally, the notion of waiting indicates a future orientation.

[206] Friedrich echoes a longstanding interpretation when he says that the pericope shifts from a proclamation of monotheism to one which "bringt das spezifisch Christliche" (509; see already Bornemann 1894, 66). Kraft notes that such a distinction is somewhat artificial and arbitrary. Although he does not deny that the resurrection formula in v. 10b *is* specifically Christian, it would be misleading to suggest that the earlier clauses, which Friedrich characterises as comprising the first strophe, are specifically *not* Christian. Just because a text lacks "clues" for identifying what is "Christian", does not mean that such texts may be excluded from the category of being specifically Christian (1975, 180).

[207] Regardless of whether one is convinced of his thesis or not, Friedrich's past-present-future schema may be retained (*contra* Havener 1981, 108). In this sense, the pericope may be regarded as a summary of Christian history. For Paul, the Christ-event defines more than the beginning of the Christian faith. It is a vindication of present service and waiting as well as of the future hope of Jesus' coming (Richard 1995, 75–76).

[208] "Quand Paul se laisse aller à son lyrisme naturel, sa pensée se fait plus pleine et les expressions de sa prédication reviennent drues de sens sous sa dictée. On remarquera même que sans pouvoir parler de stiques et de poésie, la forme rejoint la formulation prophétique par petites phrases ou membres de phrases qui forment un tout et ne manquent pas de rythme" (1956, 392).

what many scholars would conclude from these parallels: that these verses are a quotation of traditional material. Bussmann questions whether the arguments put thus far – lexical, stylistic, ideological, theological (etc.) – are adequate. Just because there are traditional elements in 1:9c–10, this is not sufficient, "die ganze Stelle 1 Thess 1,9f als Formel zu erweisen" (1975, 47). In particular, Bussmann takes Wilckens (1961) to task for his questionable presupposition; he is too eager to find "eine geprägte christlich-missionarische Tradition" (49). Bussmann seeks to demonstrate that 1 Thess 1:9c–10 *is* a quotation of tradition material on other grounds; the significance of the resurrection formula (v. 10b) is determinative (50). He asserts that the formula became associated with the traditional material in verses 9–10 at a pre-Pauline stage (see Bornemann 1894, 68) for the following reasons: (1) The resurrection formula makes possible the coming of Jesus as deliverer. This causal connection is not present in 4:14–17, nor elsewhere in First Thessalonians, making it unlikely to be due to Pauline redaction. (2) The clause identifies the function of the son of God with Jesus. The link between 1:9c–10 and *hellenistisch-jüdischer Literatur*, along with an association of the resurrection formula with that literature provides evidence that the insertion of the clause is not by Paul.[209] (3) The correlation between the resurrection of Jesus and the eschatological deliverance gives certainty to that latter deliverance (so Hahn 1966, 290), although Bussmann comments that this reason is not much more than a reformulation of point one.[210] (4) The clause serves to explain more fully ("dient als Auffüllung") the language of the coming deliverer; in such a well constructed text it is improbable that Paul would have inserted the clause himself.[211] (5) Presupposing the second reason, the resurrection formula helps explain why the deliverer is coming (51–55). Consequently, Bussmann forms two conclusions based on the assertions that the resurrection formula (v. 10b) is pre-Pauline, and that the formula is completely integrated into the context of the verses: first, the formulation of 1 Thess 1:9c–10 is not due to Pauline redaction; and second, the tradition probably stems from "der hellenistisch-jüdischen Missionstradition" (56).

6. T. Holtz (1977) does not begin his article on the form and content of 1 Thess 1:9–10 with the presupposition that the pericope contains pre-Pauline material that was part of an early missionary proclamation. Rather, he focuses on the christological elements contained in the verses and downplays the possibility of a specific Hellenistic-Jewish quotation, although he does admit that the call to God is part of the *Missionspredigt*, which can be demonstrated from parallel passages including Heb 6:1; Acts 14; 17 (460–461).[212] However, *contra* Wilckens, those parallel passages cannot be made to prove that all of 1 Thess 1:9c–10 is a quotation of *Missionspredigt*, because the dual theme of serving and waiting is not consistently found in those texts (462). Further, Holtz proposes that the *Christus-Botschaft* had a christo-

[209] "Die Zusammenordnung von Götzenablehnung, Zorn Gottes und Rettung aus dem Zorn ist auffallend genug, um für dieselbe Zusammenordnung 1 Thess 1,9f hellenistisch-jüdische Herkunft anzunehmen. Die Feststellung, daß die Auferweckung Jesu in diesem Zusammenhang nicht nur bei Paulus, sondern auch Apg 17,31 aufgenommen wurde, deutet darauf hin, daß der Einschub nicht auf Paulus zurückzuführen ist" (53).

[210] Besides, "Es bedarf meines Erachtens keiner Vergewisserung der eschatologischen Geschehnisse, diese Erwartung steht fest" (53).

[211] "Wenn man zudem annimmt, daß Paulus eine Formel zitiert, ist eine nur beiläufige Einstreuung noch unwahrscheinlicher" (54).

[212] Holtz is certainly not the first to find parallels between 1 Thess 1:9–10 and Heb 5:11–6:2. Wilckens (1961, 83–84) asserts that the two pericopes reflect a common tradition, despite their different *Sitz im Leben*.

logical grounding, and "in keiner Weise ... mit der Verkündigung des einen Gottes begann" (463). He finds it difficult to maintain that there is a hymn preserved here (*contra* Friedrich). Friedrich's argument for a two-strophic structure is not convincing; rather, the alleged second strophe is nothing more than an enlargement or elaboration on the theme of turning to God. Holtz also rejects a baptismal situation by noting that the resurrection from the dead and the coming *orgē* have nothing to do with a *Taufsituation* or *Taufverkündigung* (463–465). Far more important is the curious link between serving God and waiting for the son from heaven (464). For much of the remainder of his article, Holtz examines the context of 1 Thess 1:9–10 within the letter as a whole (467–472), as well as the unmistakeable identification of some elements of the text with *hellenistisch-jüdischer Missionsliteratur* (472–482). In conclusion, he emphasises an observation first made by Munck, and which is often neglected in this discussion: namely, that Paul is delivering a report of what he had heard (v. 9a). In this way, Holtz gives a satisfactory explanation of the un-Pauline vocabulary and turns of phrase (470):

> Dem steht die allgemeine Formulierung αὐτοὶ γὰρ ... ἀπαγγέλλουσιν entgegen, die alle Christen so wie im Folgenden angegeben berichten läßt und mithin kein Einzelwort im Auge haben kann. Paulus selbst faßt zusammen, wie andernorts über die Thessalonicher gesprochen wird; aber seine Zusammenfassung will das wiedergeben, was andere sagen. Wir haben also von der Art unseres Satzes her damit zu rechnen, daß geprägtes, und nicht auf den spezifischen Sprachgebrauch des Paulus zurückgehendes Sprach- und Vorstellungsmaterial in ihm enthalten ist.

His conclusion, that 1:9c–10, as a whole, is a Pauline formulation which draws upon traditional language, but does not make an explicit quotation (483), is a superior thesis to previous contributions because it properly balances two identified aspects of the text: (1) it explains the traditional elements found by all scholars; (2) it accounts for the way these verses so admirably prepare for what is to follow. His predecessors considered above (Munck, Friedrich, Langevin and Bussmann), manage to overemphasise one aspect or the other.

7. I. Havener's contribution (1981) to the discussion primarily focuses on the identification of pre-Pauline christological credal formulae. First he establishes beyond doubt that verse 10b is a fixed (resurrection) formula (105–106).[213] He then takes up the specific question of whether Paul is drawing upon or giving a quotation of pre-Pauline material in 1:9c–10. Havener is not convinced that the ἐπιστρέφειν clause is pre-Pauline; he finds the parallels between it and Gal 4:9, 2 Cor 3:16 should not be dismissed easily (107). Furthermore, he observes that verse 9b stands at the head of two infinitive clauses (vv. 9d, 10a), not parallel with them. This is best accounted for, according to Havener, by Pauline redaction (108). Convinced that verse 9b, at least, is not a quotation of traditional material, Havener consequently rejects Friedrich's two-strophe hymn-structure. He finds Friedrich's past-present-future schema to be "highly questionable" since "basic grammatical structural considerations have been largely ignored" (108). In particular, why should the prepositional phrase, ἐκ τῆς ὀργῆς τῆς ἐρχομένης, be singled out in a separate line, except to bolster the evidence for an alleged hymnic structure? Along similar lines, Wanamaker remarks that the careful construction and balance normally expected of a pre-Pauline traditional quotation are lacking.[214] Havener concludes that 1:9c–10 is not poetic, but prose which is conducive to memory — probably used for catechesis

[213] See §III.b.5 above for further discussion.

[214] In particular, Wanamaker notes the change in person between ἐπεστρέψατε (v. 9c) and ἡμᾶς (v. 10c) as grammatically disruptive; the repetition of θεός (vv. 9c, d) is clumsy; and the resurrection formula (v. 10b) interrupts the flow of thought in v. 10 (1990, 85; so also Richard 1995, 57). Havener also notes

(108–109). Unlike Bussmann, he regards the resurrection formula as a later addition to the text (though still at a pre-Pauline stage), and concludes that the earliest discernable level of the tradition history of these verses looked like this (109):

... δουλεύειν θεῷ ζῶντι καὶ ἀληθινῷ
καὶ ἀναμένειν τὸν υἱὸν αὐτοῦ ἐκ τῶν οὐρανῶν
τὸν ῥυόμενον ἡμᾶς ἐκ τῆς ὀργῆς
τῆς ἐρχομένης

Thus, for Havener, Paul utilises a catechetical formula, which does not rule out the possibility "that it [i.e. the formula] also contains a summary of the *topoi* of the Hellenistic Jewish-Christian mission to the Gentiles", and which displays several levels of tradition history. The resurrection credal formula (v. 10b) is not part of the original catechetical tradition (110).

8. Despite this extended discussion about pre-Pauline traditional formulae in 1:9c–10, the evidence falls short from conclusively showing that all of 1:9c–10 is a direct quotation. Munck contributes the important observation that 1:9c–10 is foreshadowed by the context of the report (v. 9a), but his emphasis on an anticipatory function obscures any conclusions which may be had regarding the possible quotation of pre-Pauline formula(e). Friedrich's thesis that Paul is reproducing a *Tauflied* is not convincing,[215] although many of his observations regarding the structure of the passage are compelling. Best (1972, 86), Bruce (1982, 10–11), Burkeen (1979, 85–86), Collins (1984, 129–130), de Jonge (1988, 34), Neyrey (1980, 220) and Richard (1995, 75–76) agree with Friedrich that there are substantial pointers to an exceptional if not poetic structure. More important for this discussion is the fact that Friedrich side-tracked (rightly in my opinion) the discussion away from a preoccupation with the idea that Paul is presenting an early summary of missionary preaching; so again, Langevin, who despite detailed exegesis, fails to resolve the question of whether Paul has given a quotation of tradition material. Bussmann's contribution breaks new ground by showing that the resurrection formula (v. 10b) is not due to Pauline redaction, but is firmly a part of the pre-Pauline tradition history. Bussmann seeks to demonstrate that 1:9c–10 may not be divided into the components of traditional and (Pauline) redacted material. Instead, since the resurrection formula is inextricably embedded in the pericope, and since the resurrection formula itself has been inserted at a pre-Pauline stage, then, according to Bussmann, the entire pericope must consist of a quotation of traditional material. His argumentation has not found general acceptance among scholars — the main stream view prefers to distinguish the fixed resurrection formula from its context. Thus, Havener highlights various levels of tradition history of the text. He rejects Friedrich's structure and proposes that an original catechetical tradition might best explain the exceptional characteristics of 1:9c–10. In this sense it is pre-Pauline, but not a direct reproduction or quotation.

Holtz provides the key perspective required to satisfactorily conclude this discussion. Paul most likely is not reproducing a summary-quotation of early missionary preaching because

---

the disruption of the thought flow but unlike Wanamaker concludes that the formula was simply a later addition to the quotation (1981, 109).

[215] Collins' assessment may be considered representative: "Friedrich's hypothesis goes far beyond the available evidence and, so far as I know, it has not yet won the approval of a single expositor of 1 Thess" (1984, 152). Becker appears to be an exception, and comments on v. 10: "Diese Formulierung erinnert so auffällig an die Täuferpredigt, daß man hier wohl doch mit einem traditionsgeschichtlichen Zusammenhang, vermittelt über die Jesuspredigt, rechnen muß. ... Das hebt *Friedrich*, Tauflied 514f, mit Recht hervor" (1976, 36).

he explicitly states that he is only giving a report of what others are saying about his converts in Thessalonica. The inference, that this is precisely why there are so many unusual words and typically un-Pauline expressions and not because Paul is using a quotation of traditional material, is missed by everyone (except Malherbe and Richard).[216] Malherbe admits that some of the language used by Paul is indeed traditional, but the emphasis should remain on the fact that Paul is formulating statements, not about what he proclaimed, but more precisely about that to which the Thessalonians turned (2000, 132; cf. 1998, 237).[217] Richard points out that Paul, in verbalising what he and his colleagues had heard, perhaps uses traditional material stemming from Jewish mission propaganda (1995, 74; so also Bruce 1982, 19).[218] Further, Dibelius remarks that Paul's "dependence" is not limited just to his own proclamation (*Predigt*) in Thessalonica, nor to particular common Christian missionary catechism, but must be understood in terms of the overall *Missionsbetrieb*, which (1925, 6; so also Laub 1976, 21–22):

> ... hat dagegen zweifellos zahlreiche prägnante Wendungen produziert und auf unliterarischem Wege fixiert, die einander ähnelten, ohne voneinander abhängig zu sein[,] s. die christologischen Aussagen der Acta-Reden.

Rigaux comments along the same lines: "Le climat de son expression est juif et vétéro-testamentaire. Ici il n'y a plus citation mais utilisation naturelle et même inconsciente. C'est l'humus qui a produit la plante" (1956, 95).[219] As long as the significance of verse 9a (i.e. that Paul is writing within the boundaries of a report) is emphasised, there is probably nothing wrong with the suggestion that 1:9c–10 is a summary of *Missionsverkündigung* or *Missionspredigt*,[220]

[216] The conclusions of Nicholl (2004, 81) are similar.

[217] It is this point that effectively vetoes any suggestion that because of theological issues vv. 9c–10 must be a quotation of pre-Pauline tradition. The argument follows, that if Paul was not relating such a quotation, then he would scarcely have missed the opportunity to emphasise the cross as a central element of his proclamation (Best 1972, 85–86; Bruce 1982, 18; Friedrich 1965, 507; see von Dobschütz 1909, 79); cf. 1 Cor 1:18, 23; 2:2; Gal 3:1; 6:14. But Munck has already shown, quite apart from the issue of the context of the report, that the staurology of First Corinthians and Galatians is emphasised in a historical and polemical context, one not shared in First Thessalonians: "... missionary preaching is sketched in a summary in which the essence is not the whole" (1963, 105–108). That Paul does not mention the death of Jesus here is unproblematic in view of Paul's use of the formulation in 4:14: Ἰησοῦς ἀπέθανεν καὶ ἀνέστη (cf. Rom 14:9; 1 Cor 15:3–4; esp. 2 Cor 5:15). Kremer comments: "Beide Formulierungen hat Paulus bereits vorgefunden und als gleichbedeutend erachtet" (1993, 1178).

[218] Frame goes too far in his suggestion that vv. 9c–10 are entirely Pauline (1912, 28). Although he appeals to the fact that Paul's vocabulary is not exhausted in any or all of his genuine letters, there are too many indications which suggest at least some dependency on one or more traditions (Collins 1984, 254). Haufe questions whether Paul is dependent on Jewish mission propaganda, esp. because such propaganda is highly polemic, while 1:9c–10 is not. Although he admits that the assertion of a monotheistic God as "living and true" is indirectly reminiscent of polemic, Haufe argues that Paul's first priority was to convert the Gentiles to undivided service to this God (see Best 1972, 86). Thus, he raises the question of whether the traditional material behind these verses might simply be early Christian mission language (1999, 28–29).

[219] Thus, "Bei seiner Heilsverkündigung greift Paulus auf Vorliegendes zurück; er schafft seinen Wortschatz nicht, sondern er findet ihn in der Christengemeinde vor und entlehnt ihn von ihr" (Rigaux 1972, 9); cf. Hoffmann 1979a, 488; Holtz 1998, 57.

[220] Bussmann characterises these verses "als die Inhalte der christlichen Botschaft" (1975, 47). They express, "the mission-preaching to pagans in a nutshell" (von Harnack 1904, 108). Thus, Milligan understands 1:9–10: "as a convenient summary of the earliest Pauline teaching with its two *foci* of Monotheism, the belief in the one living and true God, as distinguished from the vain idols of heathenism, and the

although it is telling that many elements of that proclamation (including *Kaufpreis*, *Passaopfer* and *Versöhnung*) are not present (Schade 1984, 119; see Lenski 1937, 235; Krentz 1987, 28). For that matter, so too the descriptors for monotheism, εἷς or μόνος, are lacking (Schrage 2001a, 195).

End of Excursus

IV. Conclusion

1. Both elements of Paul's pattern of exhortation, pertaining to disintegration and subsequent integration, are clearly articulated in 1 Thess 1:9–10. The dual observations that this pericope forms the climax of the *letter-thanksgiving*, and the way these verses act as a summary or outline of the letter, are corroborated by the appearance of the eschatological motifs of resurrection, deliverance and *orgē*, which are programmatically part of the eschatological discourse of First Thessalonians. Thus, the motif of resurrection figures importantly in 4:13–18, both in terms of Jesus' death and resurrection and in terms of the extrapolation that Jesus-followers will also be raised (vv. 14, 16). Similarly, the motifs of deliverance and *orgē* are also sustained. The negative association of *orgē* is especially developed in 2:13–16 as part of Paul's insider/outsider rhetoric, and in 5:1–11 where the emphasis is similar to here, such that the Thessalonians are expected to be delivered from it (v. 9).

2. There are other features of the text which are also part of the eschatological discourse of First Thessalonians, but which are not so programmatic: the entrance of Paul into the community, the conversion of the Thessalonians, dualism between idols and God and waiting for his son from heaven. These features are more subtle contributions to the eschatological discourse because as individual motifs the first two are not usually considered to be eschatologically oriented, and all four are not repeated in First Thessalonians. Yet, with eschatology as a hermeneutical key, these motifs contribute significantly to Paul's pattern of exhortation.

The εἴσοδος of Paul coincides with the εἴσοδος of the gospel. References to the Holy Spirit (1:5, 6), an eschatological power, allude to the eschatological overtones of Paul's founding visit. As I showed in the analysis (§III.a.3 above), Paul is not just referring to the fact of his entrance, but also to the Thessalonians' acceptance of his gospel, which is recalled in 2:1–16. It is this acceptance which makes the report about the Thessalonians so extraordinary — Paul's entrance into the community is not in vain (2:1), but rather marks the beginning of an extensive relationship between the newly formed community and its founders. On the basis of this relationship, and contingent on a context of affliction, Paul feels compelled to offer guidance in the form of *paraenesis*. In relation to the question of whether and to

---

Judgment, as heralded by the Parousia of God's Son from heaven" (1908, xlii–xliii). Stuhlmacher develops the idea of Milligan, that these verses are a *summary of Paul*, not necessary the contents of a mission proclamation, by highlighting the significance of the phrase τὸ εὐαγγέλιον τοῦ θεοῦ (1968, 259; 2:2; cf. 1:5); see Bailey 1955, 264; Cerfaux 1959, 439; Neyrey 1980, 221; Sanders 1991, 21.

what extent there is pre-Pauline traditional material in these verses, it is significant to note that 1:9–10 contains extensive Pauline redactions (see Excursus 3). Thus, Paul employs a local report and formulates that report using traditional material in order to introduce a pattern of exhortation which is sustained in the eschatological discourse of First Thessalonians.

But accepting Paul's *kērygma* leads to catastrophic social consequences in the present. Paul's unusual reference to ἐπιστρέφειν, and the apocalyptic dualism between idols and the living and true God, serve to emphasise disintegration. The singularity of the terminology leads to the discussion on "conversion" (Excursus 2) where I found the phenomenon of conversion to be well described by social disintegration and reintegration. Paradigmatically, however, Paul proposes a new identity defined by service (δουλεύειν) and waiting (ἀναμένειν). More than that, these two infinitives characterise a pattern of exhortation by which the Thessalonians are to understand the emergence of a new community (*ekklēsia*). The reference to Jesus as "son" highlights the relationship between Jesus and God, and also between the Thessalonians and God. The importance of this relationship gains eschatological significance in that the resurrection of Jesus becomes a basis for a positive existence, one in which Jesus as divine agent, delivers the Thessalonians from *orgē*. This implicit association of the death, resurrection and *parousia* of Jesus, which is made more explicit in 4:13–18, ultimately expresses the means for integration into an eschatologically identifiable existence. That is, the Thessalonians' current social disintegration, which is characteristic of *orgē*, does not end in death. Rather, the new *ekklēsia* is defined as an eschatological existence, one which is destined for deliverance.

3. But before Paul describes the Thessalonians' new existence in fuller detail, he goes on to illustrate the extent of disintegration which accompanies the proclamation and acceptance of his gospel (i.e. 1 Thess 2:13–16). I now turn to the analysis of that pericope.

Chapter 4
First Thessalonians 2:13–16

1. First Thessalonians 2:13–16 is an infamous pericope of Paul! At least, in terms of scholarly discussion, it is the most thoroughly examined section of the letter. Of course, largely controversial and problematic to the discussion are the vitriolic and even vituperative statements against "the Jews" (οἱ Ἰουδαῖοι) in verses 15–16. Nowhere else does Paul make such thoroughly penchant assertions ostensibly dismissing his own people.[1] Actually, it is the alleged distasteful nature of 2:13–16 which drives a significant portion of scholars to question its authenticity. This preliminary hurdle would normally need surmounting before any attempt is made at analysis of the text. However in recent years the joint discussion of authenticity and various interpolation hypotheses has reached an impasse. A way forward involves a substantial discussion and appraisal of the literature that (re) incorporates a comprehensive analysis of the text. Consequently, a discussion of authenticity is postponed until after the analysis (§IV below). One component may not be satisfactorily postponed because it significantly impacts the analysis. Some scholars tend to solve the problem of 2:13–16 by identifying its function in terms of compilation theories (§II.d). Discussion of these theories forms a final conclusion to the question of the epistolary structure of First Thessalonians (Chapter 2) and is a requisite preamble to the analysis and ensuing discussion of authenticity. The presupposition of my thesis is that 2:13–16 *is* authentic although the worth of any supporting argument for such a conclusion remains to be seen. It is precisely the controverted nature of 2:13–16 that leads me to include the whole pericope in the analysis even though my chief interest is in verse 16d. Thus the exegetical discussion includes all four verses although I am selective in the depth of presentation of the various discussions.

2. The emphases on thanksgiving, conflict and judgment reinforce Paul's pattern of exhortation in First Thessalonians. In particular, the theological clash between those who have accepted Jesus as the *Kyrios* and those who have not are interpreted in the context of Paul's mission and ultimately in dualistic terms of

---

[1] Consequently, 1 Thess 2:13–16 generally tops the list in discussions of alleged Pauline anti-Semitism. For a discussion of this sensitive issue in NT scholarship, see Excursus 4. It should be noted that the ostensible aspect of Paul's statement must be stressed. Paul is certainly not referring to all Jews, as if they can be grouped together. Nor should it be assumed that he identifies with those Jews of whom he is referring. The problems surrounding the phrase οἱ Ἰουδαῖοι are discussed at length below (§III.c.2).

salvation and judgment. On the one hand, the Thessalonians have accepted the word of God which is working in them (v. 13f). On the other hand, there are those whose actions are so reprehensible to Paul that he can confidently assert that *orgē* is going to come on them finally (v. 16d). In 1 Thess 2:13–16 Paul provides a way to understand the Thessalonians' current social disintegration with negative references, to the word of men as opposed to the word of God (vv. 13d, e), to suffering (v. 14d) and to a catalogue of deeds which separate those who are under *orgē* from those who are delivered from it (1:10; 5:9).[2] At the same time, he also emphasises the Thessalonians' new identity as part of the *ekklēsia*, with positive references, to their receiving the word of God (v. 13c) and to their imitation of the *ekklēsiai* of God (vv. 14a, b). Thus, the eschatological discourse here continues to sustain the Thessalonians in the midst of conflict.

3. With regard to the second fundamental representative of the eschatological discourse in First Thessalonians, I am most interested in understanding how Paul uses eschatological motifs to promote his pattern of exhortation. By admitting that 1 Thess 2:16d is my "chief interest" in the analysis this does not mean that verses 14–16c are irrelevant for the thesis. Rather, the results of the analysis on these verses show that Paul uses several motifs, of thanksgiving, of reception and acceptance of the word of God, of imitation, which contribute to the positive aspect of his pattern of exhortation. It is readily acknowledged, however, that the negative aspect, delineated in the accusations against "the Jews" (οἱ Ἰουδαῖοι), and the reference to *orgē*, are more characteristic of the eschatological discourse found elsewhere in the letter.

4. In the course of this chapter no apology is made for the lengthy analysis of compilation and interpolation hypotheses. While the question of authenticity has already been broached via the epistolary analysis of First Thessalonians, the balance of scholarly opinion on the matter is sufficiently even as to make the inclusion at all of 2:13–16 a most controversial decision. Consequently, integral to contributing to the thesis that eschatology is a hermeneutical key for understanding First Thessalonians is a full-scale defence of the pericope's authenticity.

[2] Konradt provides an extensive discussion of "Gerichtsthematik" in terms of a consolidation of the community. On 1 Thess 2:15–16, see esp. 2003, 73–93.

I. Arranged Text and Translation

13a καὶ διὰ τοῦτο
13b καὶ ἡμεῖς εὐχαριστοῦμεν τῷ θεῷ ἀδιαλείπτως,
13c ὅτι παραλαβόντες λόγον ἀκοῆς παρ᾽ ἡμῶν τοῦ θεοῦ
13d ἐδέξασθε οὐ λόγον ἀνθρώπων
13e ἀλλὰ καθώς ἐστιν ἀληθῶς λόγον θεοῦ,
13f ὃς καὶ ἐνεργεῖται ἐν ὑμῖν τοῖς πιστεύουσιν.
14a ὑμεῖς γὰρ μιμηταὶ ἐγενήθητε, ἀδελφοί,
14b τῶν ἐκκλησιῶν τοῦ θεοῦ
14c τῶν οὐσῶν ἐν τῇ Ἰουδαίᾳ ἐν Χριστῷ Ἰησοῦ,
14d ὅτι τὰ αὐτὰ ἐπάθετε καὶ ὑμεῖς ὑπὸ τῶν ἰδίων συμφυλετῶν
14e καθὼς καὶ αὐτοὶ ὑπὸ τῶν Ἰουδαίων
15a τῶν καὶ τὸν κύριον ἀποκτεινάντων Ἰησοῦν
15b καὶ τοὺς προφήτας
15c καὶ ἡμᾶς ἐκδιωξάντων
15d καὶ θεῷ μὴ ἀρεσκόντων
15e καὶ πᾶσιν ἀνθρώποις ἐναντίων,
16a κωλυόντων ἡμᾶς τοῖς ἔθνεσιν λαλῆσαι
16b ἵνα σωθῶσιν,
16c εἰς τὸ ἀναπληρῶσαι αὐτῶν τὰς ἁμαρτίας πάντοτε.
16d ἔφθασεν δὲ ἐπ᾽ αὐτοὺς ἡ ὀργὴ εἰς τέλος.

13a and therefore
13b we also thank God constantly,
13c because having received the word of God which you heard from us
13d you accepted it not as the word of men
13e but as what it really is, the word of God,
13f which also is working in you believers.
14a For you became imitators, brothers,
14b of the *ekklēsiai* of God
14c which are in Judea in Christ Jesus,
14d because you also suffered the same things at the hands of your own countrymen
14e as also they did at the hands of the Jews
15a who killed both the Lord Jesus
15b and the prophets
15c and drove us out
15d and do not please God
15e and oppose all men,
16a by hindering us to speak to the *ethnē*
16b in order that they may be saved,
16c so that always to complete the full measure of their sins.
16d But *orgē* is going to come on them finally.

II. Preliminary Issues

a. Arrangement of the Text

1. First it is helpful to highlight various features in the arrangement of the text. There is little doubt that καὶ διὰ τοῦτο (v. 13a) marks a formal transition in First Thessalonians,[3] although whether its reference is to the preceding or following text is disputed. Verse 13 may be set out in a number of ways: the arrangement highlights the prominence of the two conjunctions, ὅτι (causal; v. 13c) and ἀλλά (contrastive; v. 13e), and presents in parallel the two complementary verbs, παραλαμβάνειν (v. 13c) and δέχεσθαι (v. 13d). Quite arresting is the three-fold repetition of λόγος (vv. 13c, d, e), of which there is a relative clause dependent on the third recurrence (v. 13f).[4] In contrast, Richard picks up on the parallel verbs, and proposes a chiastic structure (1995, 118):

a having *received* the word of God
  b as heard from us
  b' you *accepted* it not as the word of mortals
a' but ... God's word

This structure must be rejected because it fails to do justice to the word order of verse 13c; the somewhat problematic – ἀκοῆς παρ' ἡμῶν – phrase may not be so easily removed onto a separate line as does Richard.[5]

2. Verse 14 begins, as in the previous verse, with a clearly recognisable transition: it opens with an explicative γάρ, has an element of direct address (ἀδελφοί) and incorporates the Pauline *mimēsis* motif (v. 14a), whose object, τῶν ἐκκλησιῶν τοῦ θεοῦ (v. 14b), is qualified by an adjectival participle (of εἶναι) and a pair of prepositional phrases with ἐν (v. 14c). Paul's reasoning about how the Thessalonians were imitators naturally forms the second half of the verse, beginning with another ὅτι (v. 14d) and concluding with parallel prepositional phrases with ὑπό (vv. 14d, e). The final phrase of the verse, ὑπὸ τῶν Ἰουδαίων, stands syntactically as the head of the majority of what follows (i.e. vv. 15a–16c), and for this reason the arrangement fails to assign that phrase an appropriate syntactical priority (i.e. by moving it fully up against the left margin). However, its parallelism with the ὑπό phrase in verse 14d would seem to justify its current position.

3. Verses 15–16 are arranged as a unit, with οἱ Ἰουδαῖοι as head (v. 14e). There are five staccato-like charges against οἱ Ἰουδαῖοι (vv. 15a–e), with a possible sixth charge (vv. 16a–c) which defines the fifth (and perhaps also the fourth; Schlueter 1994, 66).[6] Further, Schlueter detects a rhetorical symmetry whereby the repetition

---

[3] So Hübner 1993c, 43: "1Thess 2,13 hat Übergangscharakter".

[4] See Ellingworth/Nida for a similar arrangement (1976, 39).

[5] The problems of translation and interpretation of this awkward phrase need not be examined further.

[6] Richardson prefers to arrange the text into five indictments against the Jews — the first four are in

of καί (vv. 15a–e) at the beginning of each phrase and the continuity of sound at the end (except for v. 15b) tends to encourage a persuasive assent to the building climax of the passage in verse 16c (114). The statement, that the charges against οἱ Ἰουδαῖοι may be divided into two groups, the first with three aorist participles and the second with three present participles, is not supported by the text (*contra* Schlueter 1994, 66; 112–113). In reality, there are only two of each (see vv. 15a, c, d, 16a).[7] However, despite this observation there does appear to be a triadic pattern with events of the past grouped into one unit and events of the present into a second unit (ARRANGEMENT A, below). Rather than organise verses 15–16 into past and present events, Richardson suggests that the charges against οἱ Ἰουδαῖοι should be arranged into actual incidents and attitudes behind those events (1969, 104). Consequently, there is a progression of ideas between the distinct parts (ARRANGEMENT B, below).

ARRANGEMENT A	ARRANGEMENT B
the Jews who	persecution of
1. killed both the Lord even Jesus	1. the Lord Jesus
2. and the prophets	2. the prophets
3. and persecuted us	3. us
and	contrary to
1. do not please God	1. God
2. and oppose all men,	2. all men
3. by hindering us to speak to the *ethnē*[8]	3. us

Although there is a progression of thought from God/Jesus to the anthropological level (Schlueter 1994, 119), Richardson's distinction is not helpful on two fronts: (1) it fails to properly express verse 15a (τῶν καὶ τὸν κύριον ἀποκτεινάντων Ἰησοῦν) which is more than persecution, and; (2) in verses 16a, b, Paul does not merely relate the attitude behind the event(s) of persecution (v. 15c) but actually describes the mode of that persecution (v. 16a, b) and the results thereof (v. 16c). Verses 16c, d may be arranged in parallel (Frame 1912, 114; followed by Schlueter 1994, 21):

ἀναπληρῶσαι	αὐτῶν	τὰς ἁμαρτίας	πάντοτε
ἔφθασεν δὲ	ἐπ᾽ αὐτοὺς	ἡ ὀργὴ	εἰς τέλος

Finally, a primary concern in this pericope is the proclamation and reception of the gospel, since verses 13 and 16 form an *inclusio* on that theme (Malherbe 2000, 164); the λόγος θεοῦ (v. 13e) has a soteriological orientation (v. 16b; Becker 1986, 92).

---

close parallelism while the last one has a different introduction, length, form and separate subordinate clause (1969, 103).

[7] Auberlen/Riggenbach 1869, 41; Frame 1912, 111.

[8] So Schlueter 1994, 118, following Marrow 1986, 59–70.

b. A Parallel between 2:13–16 and 1:2–10

1. A striking similarity has often been observed between 2:13–16 and 1:2–10, with three verbal parallels: a thanksgiving formula, εὐχαριστοῦμεν τῷ θεῷ... ἀδιαλείπτως (1:2; 2:13); a *mimēsis* motif, ὑμεῖς ... μιμηταὶ ... ἐγενήθητε (1:6; 2:14);[9] a reference to *orgē* (1:10; 2:16).[10] Besides these, there are numerous other parallels including: a similar contrast between λόγος/δύναμις (1:5) and λόγος ἀνθρώπων/λόγος θεοῦ (2:13; Bruce 1982, 45); a common motif of a reception of the word (δεξάμενοι τὸν λόγον, 1:6; ἐδέξασθε ... λόγον, 2:13),[11] and this reception is in a similar context — θλῖψις (1:6) and πάσχειν (2:14);[12] parallel themes of deliverance (ῥύεσθαι, 1:10) and salvation (σῴζειν, 2:16; Rigaux 1956, 450). Hence, de Boer observes that the sequence of thought, "runs from thanksgiving, to Paul's preaching, to divine working in the hearers, to imitation and suffering" (1962, 108).[13]

2. The parallels are so extensive that some scholars have sought to identify a more formal structure based on these observations. Thus, Hurd sets out the sequence of 1:2–10 and 2:13–16 in columns and proposes an ABA "sonata form" structure (1986, 28–30; reiterated in 1998, 69–70). Thus, 1:2–2:16 consists of a triptych (1:2–10, 2:1–12 and 2:13–16) where each member opens with a formal structural signal and closes with an *eschatological climax*.[14] Donfried suggests that Paul purposely uses the thanksgiving theme to reintroduce and further specify various ideas. In 2:13–16 Paul reiterates the themes of imitation and affliction, the latter of which is picked up in chapter three (cf. 3:4, 7) and provides further reason for thanksgiving (3:9) in chapters three and four with regard to the problem of

[9] In 1:6 imitation is evidence of the Thessalonians' election and demonstration of the fullness of the gospel; in 2:14 the imitation is paralleled — it is evidence of their true acceptance of the word and of God having worked in them (de Boer 1962, 123; see Wanamaker 1990, 112). Although the objects of imitation differ (μιμηταὶ ἡμῶν ... καὶ τοῦ κυρίου in 1:6a; μιμηταὶ ... τῶν ἐκκλησιῶν τοῦ θεοῦ in 2:14a–b), Holmstrand observes the proximity of the *mimēsis* motif to references to τὸν κύριον ... ἡμᾶς (2:15a, c), which further strengthens the parallel (1997, 54–55; cf. 84–87). As well, the references are comparable in that the Thessalonians are an example (τύπος) to believers in Macedonia and Achaia (1:7) just as the Judean *ekklēsiai* are a model for imitation by the Thessalonians (2:14; Lyons 1985, 203; von Dobschütz 1909, 108).

[10] So Johanson 1987, 99. Harvey also notes the recurrence of the adverb πάντοτε at 1:2 and 2:16 (1998, 262), but this recurrence is not in the same order as are the other verbal parallels highlighted.

[11] de Boer 1962, 98; see Rigaux 1956, 90; Sandnes 1991, 221–222.

[12] Both fit "in den größeren Rahmen urchristlicher Leidensgeschichte" (Haufe 1999, 42).

[13] Such qualifications of 2:13–16 as, "further explanation" (Auberlen/Riggenbach 1869, 39), "concise restatement" (de Boer 1962, 108), "intensification and expansion" (Donfried 1984, 246), "points of contact" (Ellingworth/Nida 1976, 37), "repetition" (Hurd 1986, 33; Malherbe 2000, 164), "reiteration" (Johanson 1987, 99), "a striking parallel" (Lyons 1995, 191), "precise description" (Rigaux 1956, 88) and "strong terminological relationship" (Sandnes 1991, 190), with relation to 1:2–10, are commonplace.

[14] This arrangement is closely followed by Harvey (1998, 261–263), Still (1999, 30–31) and White (1993, 153–157; 1999, 74–75); see Tellbe 2001, 97, 106. Sumney (1990) adapts Hurd's observations in order to defend the unity of Second Thessalonians. He finds a similar ABA structure: 2 Thess 1:3–12 is recapitulated in 2:13–3:5, with a middle member between (2:1–12).

hope (1984, 245–247; cf. 1:3).[15] Schlueter (1994, 32–36) essentially follows Hurd and Donfried. Johanson prefers to characterise 1:2–2:16 as a "strategy of ring-composition" with the same triptych structure. As Hurd and Donfried have noted, this structure is supported by recurring expressions and motifs. However, Johanson also discerns, on a rhetorical level, a ring-structure of a *pathos* appeal (1:2–10; 2:13–16), with an *ethos* appeal in the middle (2:1–12).[16] He finds that the thanksgiving in 2:13–16 develops (rhetorically) differently from 1:2–10 whereby the *vituperatio* in 2:15–16 balances the *laudatio* in 1:7–9a (1987, 99).[17] Moreover, Johanson (149) and Lee/Lee (1975, 37) have detected a chiastic pattern in the overall structure of First Thessalonians.[18] For Lee/Lee, the grouping of second person verbs and pronouns in 1:2–10 and 2:13–16 and first person verbs and pronouns in 2:1–12 is significant (36; so also Holmstrand 1997, 54). Johanson is more detailed, and delineates between a chiastic and alternating pattern (1987, 149):[19]

	CHIASTIC PATTERN			ALTERNATING PATTERN
1:2	A εὐχαριστοῦμεν τῷ θεῷ		1:3	A μνημονεύοντες ... κόπου
1:6	μιμηταὶ ... ἐγενήθητε			
1:6	δεξάμενοι ... λόγον			
1:10	ὀργῆς			
2:2	B ὑμᾶς τὸ εὐαγγέλιον τοῦ θεοῦ		2:4	B οὐχ ... ἀνθρώποις
2:3	παράκλησις			ἀρέσκοντες ... θεῷ
2:5	θεὸς μάρτυς			
2:7	ὡς ... ἑαυτῆς τέκνα			
2:9	B' ὑμᾶς τὸ εὐαγγέλιον τοῦ θεοῦ		2:9	A' μνημονεύετε ... κόπον
2:10	μάρτυρες ... θεός			
2:11	ὡς ... τέκνα ἑαυτοῦ			
2:12	παρακαλοῦντες			

[15] Holmstrand argues that the καί in 2:13 leads the argument from one part of the *letter-thanksgiving* to the next; cf. the opening καί in 1:6 and 1:9. "The consequence-describing διὰ τοῦτο in 2:13 and the recurrences of material from 1:2, 6 in 2:13 ff. suggest to the listener that the section beginning at 2:13 rounds off the one that began in 1:2" (1997, 55; cf. Lee/Lee 1975, 32). For further discussion of v. 13a, see §III.a.2 below.

[16] Similarly, Smith 1995, 77–80.

[17] See Tellbe 2001, 106. The reception of the gospel in 1:6 brought joy but in 2:13 it brought suffering (Schlueter 1994, 33).

[18] White (1986, 30; 1993, 155–157) agrees with Hurd's observation that the whole letter may be understood in terms of a chiastic structure. So Hurd (regarding 1:2–3:13): "On the basis of internal parallels we have seen that the first three chapters fall into two sections (1:2–2:16; 2:17–3:13) each with three panels. The pattern is A B A' C D C'. Each major section is chiastic, in a loose sense of the term, in that the third panel repeats the first. It is probably evidence of the same tendency toward symmetrical structures that the last panel of all (3:9–10, at least) is cast in the form of a *letter-thanksgiving*, which is the form of the first panel of all (1:2–10). Again Paul ends as he began" (1998, 71).

[19] Porter/Reed (1998, 213) sound an important note of caution regarding the delineation of "macro-chiasms" (i.e. "chiasms of larger units such as several chapters"). It appears that chiasm does not figure in ancient rhetorical theory, or if it does, it is only "a vague idea of inverted parallelism" (217). Accordingly, the chiastic structure proposed by Johanson must remain a modern literary construction (217–218). For critical discussion along these lines, see Murphy-O'Connor 1995, 86–95.

2:13	A' εὐχαριστοῦμεν τῷ θεῷ	2:15	B' θεῷ μὴ ἀρεσκόντων ...
2:13	ἐδέξασθε ... λόγον		ἀνθρώποις
2:14	μιμηταὶ ἐγενήθητε		
2:16	ὀργή		

In addition, 2:1–16 appears to be a cohesive unit bound together by the aorist passive form of γίνεσθαι (Schubert 1939, 19–20; see Marxsen 1979, 47).[20] If one or more of these structural observations have merit then this possibly could be evidence against an interpolation at 2:13–16.[21] Ironically, the similarity between 1:2–10 and 2:13–16 is one of the arguments *for* an interpolation at 2:13–16!

c. Paul's Letter Structure and 2:13–16

1. In Chapter 2 the structure of First Thessalonians is established as consisting of three parts: *letter-opening* (1:1); *main part* (1:2–5:22); *letter-closing* (5:23–28). The identification of 2:13–16 as a component of the *main part* rather than of the *letter-thanksgiving* is crucial for the exegesis of the pericope since such identification provides "legitimate parameters for the kinds of exegetical conclusions that can be drawn" (Porter 2002a, 549). Further, the *main part* (or redefined "*letter-body*" in a less technical sense) of First Thessalonians consists of a *letter-thanksgiving* (1:2–10), *disclosure* of a past-present relationship (2:1–16), *apostolic parousia* (2:17–3:13) and *letter-paraenesis* (4:1–5:22). As well as 2:13–16, there are other *eschatological climaxes* and *transitions* within the letter (1:9–10; 2:12, 19–20; 3:11–13; 4:13–18; 5:1–11). The extensive parallels between 2:13–16 and 1:2–10 demonstrate how carefully Paul (or a redactor!) incorporates those sections into the rhetoric of First Thessalonians.

2. Since 1 Thess 2:13–16 is grouped together with 1 Thess 2:1–12, it would be pertinent to examine whether the latter pericope is apologetic/defensive. But this would require no little interaction with the enormous volume of literature devoted to it. Unfortunately, taking the discussion down that path, although worthwhile, is beyond the current study.[22] That the emphasis of the *disclosure* of a past-present relationship is on thanksgiving and building up the Thessalonians is suggested by a total lack of admonition here (Wick 1994, 19). Rather, Paul links the situation of

[20] The verb occurs eleven times in First Thessalonians. The aorist passive form appears in 2:5, 7, 8, 10, 14 (cf. 1:5, 6); the only other occurrence of γίνεσθαι in 2:1–16 is a perfect active form in 2:1 (cf. also 1:7; 3:4, 5; White 1972, 126). On the relationship between 2:1–12 and 2:13–16, see Merk 1998, 385–387.

[21] Again, with regard to the chiastic structure set out above, the identification of such a structure has little impact (positively or negatively) for the unity of First Thessalonians. See particularly the section entitled "Significance for the Integrity Debate" in Porter/Reed's article (1998, 228–231) where, with reference to the discussion of the unity of Philippians, Porter/Reed demonstrate that the identification of a macro-chiastic writing strategy would *not* prove the unity of that letter. Still, the observation that 2:13–16 is no mere slavish imitation of 1:2–10 is of vital importance for the discussion of authenticity (White 1993, 155).

[22] For a recent introduction to the discussion, see Hoppe 2002.

suffering with thanksgiving for their faith. Thus, the reference to judgment becomes subordinate to a comforting purpose (20).[23] Beyond that, further qualification must await the analysis proper (§III.a–d below).

d. Compilation Theories

1. The question of the unity of First Thessalonians has occasionally entered the discussion resulting, with regard to the structure of the letter, in an assortment of compilation theories. Since 2:13–16 figures decisively in all of these theories they are relevant to this discussion of preliminary issues of the analysis. The principal proponents of compilation theories for First (and Second) Thessalonians are Eckart (1961), Schmithals (1964, 1965, 1984; see 1960), Refshauge (1971), Demke (1973), Schenke/Fischer (1978), Munro (1983), Pesch (1984), Richard (1995) and Murphy-O'Connor (1996).[24] All but the most recent compilation theories have previously been critically examined and there is no need to rehash the arguments here. Although Eckart (1961) is the first to seriously posit a compilation theory his hypothesis has been soundly crushed by Kümmel (1962) and Thieme (1963). Schmithals admires Eckart's pioneering work but rejects many of his conclusions; Schmithals develops his own compilation theories (1964, 1965). The fact that his argumentation is much more enduring than Eckart's may be some indication that his theories have more merit.[25] Both Refshauge (1971) and Demke (1973) elaborate a thesis involving multiple interpolation and redactional elements — though each has a quite different methodology and entirely different conclusion. Yet, the observation remains that the resultant fragmented letters make little rhetorical or epistolary sense (Hurd 1998, 52–54; Jewett 1986, 43–44). Schenke/Fischer (1978, 65–76) are also preoccupied with developing a similar compilation theory but do not add significantly to the discussion. Clearly, there *are* structural peculiarities in First Thessalonians to be explained but partitioning the letter into several is not the only, or even best, solution. Bjerkelund (1967, 125–140) examines Schmithals' thesis at length.[26] More general are noteworthy critical analyses offered by Best (1972, 29–35, 45–50), Jewett (1986, 33–46) and Wanamaker (1990, 29–37) who all conclude the unity of the extant First Thessalonians (see also Porter 1999, 315–316).

---

[23] Getty 1990, 281–282; Simpson 1990, 51–52; *contra* Koester 1979, 38. This point is entirely missed by Beck (1994, 77).

[24] The compilation theory of Scott (1909, 215–233) – that Timothy wrote 1 Thess 1–3 and Silvanus wrote 1 Thess 4–5 – was an anomaly at the time, and stands as one of the earliest theories for the compilation of First Thessalonians.

25 Schmithals' revision of his original thesis in subsequent publications (see esp. 1984, 111–124) makes plain the plurality of his theories.

[26] See also Gamble 1975; Suhl 1975, 96–102; Trilling 1987, 3381–3385.

Collins provides an extensive review of the integrity of First Thessalonians by carefully sifting through interpolation and compilation theories (1979a, 67–106). He concludes his article with an attack against presuppositions shared by many theorists which, at the risk of missing much pertinent material, may be summarised into one key statement: the assumptions, that (1) Paul is consistent in his articulation of thought and that (2) his epistolary composition has a normative form, are unfounded (97–98).[27] Furthermore, in an excursus on the unity of First Thessalonians, Riesner raises two "basic considerations" which argue against interpolation and compilation theories. First, there are absolutely no parallels in antiquity for the piecing together of letters (other than by the original author), and second, in view of the fact that Paul's letters were exchanged between *ekklēsiai*, the compiler, after finishing his work, would have had to destroy the originals (1998, 404–406; see Ellis 1999, 430).

2. It is necessary, then, only to comment on more recent compilation theories by Munro, Pesch, Richard and Murphy-O'Connor. Munro (1983) contends that there is extensive interpolation and redaction of the Pauline letter corpus and First Peter whereby an identifiable pastoral stratum has been incorporated into earlier texts (1–26).[28] On the basis of ideological, stylistic and contextual observations, she concludes that 1 Thess 1:5b, 6a, 7, 2:1–16, 4:1–12, 5:12–15, 21b, 22 belong to a later stratum (86–93). But one of her main preoccupations – the identification of frequent antithetical parallelism as a decisive style marker of a later stratum (87–89) – amounts to a circular argument. Munro makes, without defense, an assumption that such a style is *a priori* post-Pauline; her failure to engage with Malherbe's publications is particularly telling. Malherbe has conclusively shown that not only is antithetical style an integral part of the rhetorical tradition and of the moral philosophy of the first century but that Paul certainly appropriated this style for himself.[29] Thus, Jewett (1986, 44–45) and Wanamaker (1990, 36–37), who both critically engage with and ultimately reject her thesis, are to be followed.

3. Along entirely different lines, Pesch (1984) argues for a compilation theory which seeks to make sense of an alleged "Wiederholungen und Dopplungen" form (see 39–57).[30] He asserts, on the basis of structural observations and on supposed different life situations ("Absenderangabe"; 20), that First Thessalonians is a re-

---

[27] So also Riesner 1998, 406–407; Still 1999, 29–30. Thus, regarding the "thanksgiving problem", Smith comments (2000, 692): "... we need not think that Paul was straitjacketed by the theoretical epistolary patterns of his day. In fact, the presence of several thanksgiving notices should signal the greater importance for Paul of continuously giving thanks, just as he later directly exhorts the church to do (5:18)".

[28] Her ideology appears to be similar to Demke's but strangely Munro does not refer to his thesis.

[29] See esp. Malherbe's discussion of Paul's παρρησία in 1970, 208–217; see also Holtz 2000, 72–76; Hoppe 1997, 236; Malherbe 1986, 24, 125, 136–139; 1992, 290, 296–298; Rigaux 1968, 127.

[30] Pesch is followed by Bohlen (1987, 1989). It is understandable that the major commentaries of Malherbe (2000), P.-G. Müller (2001), Richard (1995) and Wanamaker (1990) do not refer to Pesch's booklet because it was published as a pocket book. In contrast, see Haufe (1999), Holtz (1998) and Légasse (1999). Collins also considers Pesch's thesis but ultimately rejects it (1993, 147).

dactor's combination of two original letters — one written from Athens and the other from Corinth (20–22). Pesch concludes that 2:13–16, 2:1–12, 2:17–3:5, 4:1–8 and 3:11–13 form the structure of the earlier letter (the "Präskript" must be supplied); the second letter originally consisted of 1:1–10, 3:6–10, 4:9–5:28 (see 69–111 for a detailed commentary defending this reconstruction). Pesch's arguments are not well-founded. Again, besides the fact that the resulting letters make little rhetorical sense there is no persuasive evidence why the two hypothetical letters could not have the same provenance (*contra* Bohlen 1989, 133–134). Consequently "this makes it unnecessary to consider the rather complex redactional process for which Pesch does not offer any convincing justification" (Murphy-O'Connor 1985, 457).

4. Richard (1991) suggests that the discussion has focused too much on Schmithals' theories rather than dealing with the text's inherent difficulties. He identifies these "difficulties" to be: (1) the probable interpolation of 2:14–16; (2) the presence of a double *letter-thanksgiving* (1:2–10; 2:13–16); (3) the conclusion-like character of 3:11–4:2; (3) the temporal tension between 1 Thess 1, 4–5 (which allegedly presumes a lapse of time between the founding mission and Paul's writing) over against 2:17–3:13 (which allegedly presumes only a short interval; 41). He adds to this the difference in tone between 2:13–4:2, where Paul fears that he had laboured in vain but then found that he had not, and 1:2–2:1, 4:3 onwards, where Paul knows that he did not labour in vain and deals with problems and issues of a maturing community (1995, 11). Richard thus proposes a compilation theory of his own in which 2:13–4:2 is identified as an earlier missive written in Athens (early forties) and inserted into a later Thessalonian letter (1:1–2:12 + 4:3–5:28) written in Corinth (later forties).[31] It is a pity that he does not refer to Pesch's considerably earlier booklet particularly since his own hypothesis resembles Pesch's. Quite apart from this, Richard's thesis is not persuasive on a number of fronts: (1) There is no argument whatsoever that would preclude the "later missive" being written at the same time as the alleged earlier one. First Thessalonians 1:7–8 need not require more than a few months between Paul's leaving of the Thessalonians and the writing of his letter;[32] further, the statement that 2:1–12 must refer to later oral reports from the Thessalonians and that the περὶ δέ formulation (4:9, 13, 5:1)

[31] Richard appears to have first proposed his compilation theory in 1988 (see 248–252). There he comments: "... we are led, in agreement with other scholars, to defend the composite character of 1 Thessalonians" (249). When he refers to "other scholars", he only mentions Murphy-O'Connor, who briefly posits the same theory in an article of 1982. Murphy-O'Connor does not defend the theory except to comment that the partition of First Thessalonians is "convincingly argued by W. Schmithals" (82).

[32] A determination of the time between the writing of First Thessalonians and the founding visit is part of a much larger discussion of the dating of First Thessalonians. Besides the frequent arguments based on 1:7–9, the situation presupposed by 2:14–16 (regardless of whether it is authentic or not), Paul's repeated attempts to return to the Thessalonians (2:18), the fact that some of the community had already died (4:13–18), and that 5:12 indicates a quite developed ecclesial structure, are often put forward as indications of a later date of First Thessalonians. See any good commentary, but esp. Best (1972, 7–13), Kümmel (1975, 259–260) and Malherbe (2000, 71–74) for critical discussions. Certainly, the unusual wording of 2:17

is an indication of Paul responding to a letter which he may have received[33] is not sufficient evidence to conclude that those sections must be part of a latter missive (Collins 1997, 787). (2) Richard's compilation theory creates more problems than it solves. First Thessalonians 2:17, supposedly the opening of the "*letter-body*" of the earlier missive does not contain any of the formulae consistent with such an opening. Similarly, Richard's claim that 3:11–13 marks a "*body*" closing of the same letter fails to recognise the function of that benediction, namely, to prepare for themes later in the letter (precisely those themes which are part of Richard's second missive).[34] As well, 4:1–2 is an unlikely candidate for a closing exhortation (early missive) because it forms "a quite obvious inclusio with 4:11–12" (Weima 1997b, 762; so also Bjerkelund 1967, 129). (3) Finally, Collins, who agrees with Richard's assessment of Second Thessalonians as pseudonymous, observes that such a thesis speaks against the composite character of First Thessalonians since it requires an early date for the completion of any redactional process for First Thessalonians (i.e. prior to the composition of Second Thessalonians). Yet what indeed could be the *Sitz im Leben* of such a compilation — certainly not the formation of the Pauline corpus to which Second Thessalonians belongs (1997, 786)? These criticisms of Richard's compilation theory would seem to be sufficient defence of the unity of First Thessalonians.

5. Murphy-O'Connor indicates his distaste for the traditional presupposition of unity in a review of Jewett's monograph (1986), where he concludes: "There are sufficient indications to justifying treating 1 Thess 2:13–4:2 as a separate letter" chief among which must be the "absurdity of a thanksgiving running from 1:2 to 3:13" (1988, 311).[35] But it is not only the problematic *letter-thanksgiving* that gives impetus to Murphy-O'Connor's theory. Like Richard before him (see Schmithals), Murphy-O'Connor also argues that 3:11–4:2 is evocative of a Pauline *letter-closing*. Consequently he concludes a similar compilation theory to Richard, namely, that an earlier letter from Athens (2:13–4:2) has been inserted into a later one from Corinth (1:1–2:12 + 4:3–5:28).[36] The position of the insertion is dictated, according to Murphy-O'Connor, by the similarity between 2:11–12 and 4:1–2, which means that 4:3–12 still flows smoothly from the insertion, and by the match between 2:12 and 2:13, because the "call" of God (v. 12) is taken up in the "word of God" (v.

(πρὸς καιρόν and πρὸς ὥρας) as well as the fact that Paul had only visited the Thessalonians once (2:1, 18; cf. 2 Thess 2:5; 3:10) indicate an earlier date (Jewett 1986, 52; see Fatum 1994, 252; Haufe 1999, 15).

[33] See the discussion of περί (δέ) in Chapter 2, §VI.5.

[34] Wiles 1974, 52–63; see Weima (1994, 77–155), where Paul's *closing* conventions are carefully and convincingly delineated. In particular, see 101–104 where Weima describes the specific differences between such *closing* structures and what he calls "other benedictions", of which 1 Thess 3:11–13 is one example.

[35] Murphy-O'Connor's presuppositions differ from Lambrecht's: "One remains somewhat baffled at the ease with which certain scholars use the three thanksgivings as an argument for their hypothetical conflation of two letters or a so-called interpolation of 2,13–16" (Lambrecht 1990, 192).

[36] This partition is supported in a review of Murphy-O'Connor's monograph by Richardson (1997, 594).

13). "At both ends, therefore, the harmonization was too neat not to be capitalized upon" (1996, 106; see 105–106). Such observations – "similarity"/"integrate perfectly" – are not evidence that 2:13–4:2 is an insertion between 2:12 and 4:3. Murphy-O'Connor proceeds on an (as yet) unproven supposition. Perhaps the most significant reinforcement of Murphy-O'Connor's compilation theory are his observations of an alleged different tone between the two letters (so Pesch). Specifically, he argues that 2:13–4:2 is exactly what is expected of Paul to write in reaction to Timothy's good news. The extant form of First Thessalonians is unlikely, for Paul would have hardly restrained his emotional response for two whole chapters (106–107). Further, Murphy-O'Connor claims that the hypothesised second letter makes no allusion to persecution, is didactic without the "effervescent warmth" of the first letter, contains few compliments, and makes no hint of Paul's desire to see the Thessalonians again. He concludes: "The emotional distance between *Letter A* and *Letter B* implies that some considerable time separates them" (110). Once again however, he proceeds with an assumption of disunity rather than proving this to be the case. It is a real oversight that Murphy-O'Connor does not interact with Weima especially when he criticises scholars (who reject a compilation theory) for "forgetting" that First Thessalonians has two conclusions (Murphy-O'Connor 1996, 105 n. 19). Since he is insistent on maintaining a compilation theory, Murphy-O'Connor's thesis would have been greatly strengthened by a measured response to Weima's crucial (and devastating to Murphy-O'Connor's compilation theory) monograph on Pauline *letter-closings* (1994; see 1997b). Further, must Paul make sure to pepper his whole letter with allusions to persecution, with an "effervescent warmth", with compliments and a desire to see the Thessalonians again, in order to stave off such an inconsistent-in-tone charge as presented by Murphy-O'Connor? Indeed he does not. It has already been shown that Paul wrote his letter within the boundaries of first-century epistolary and rhetorical forms (see Chapter 2). Surely more certain evidence is required to topple the text of First Thessalonians from its position of *jus possessionis*.[37] In fact, until Murphy-O'Connor and other scholars promoting compilation theories provide a more extensive critique of the burgeoning epistolary and rhetorical analyses of First Thessalonians which are increasingly found to be adequate explanations of the letter's extant form, rather than re-working various compilation theories, such theories cannot be regarded as convincing.

[37] Collins 1984, 125; see Broer 1983, 65–66; 1990, 139–142; 1991, 328; Walker 1987; *contra* Bohlen 1989, 134. In a second article Walker (1988) attempts to provide criteria to "objectively" identify interpolations but he is not convincing (see Tellbe 2001, 105).

III. Analysis

a. Thanksgiving for the Word of God (2:13)

1. The repetition of the λόγον θεοῦ/ἀνθρώπων (vv. 13c, d, e)[38] and παραλαμβάνειν/δέχεσθαι parallel (vv. 13c, d) and the associated motif of receiving/accepting traditional material is worth further investigation.[39] However, the analysis below examines the opening καὶ διὰ τοῦτο (v. 13a) because its interpretation contributes, in considerable measure, to the discussion of whether 2:13–16 is an interpolation or not (§III.a.2).

2. It has already been shown that 2:13 does not mark the beginning of a second *letter-thanksgiving* even though it is of the proper form (Chapter 2). Due to the alleged abrupt nature of the connection between 2:12 and 2:13 compilation theorists and advocates of an interpolation hypothesis commonly refer to the phrase in their arguments.[40] Thus for example, Schmithals proposes that καὶ διὰ τοῦτο is "eine redaktionelle Floskel" and "mehr formal als sinnvoll" (1964, 305). He also takes issue with the formulation καὶ ἡμεῖς (v. 13b) and specifically questions why Paul would emphasise that he *too* gives thanks (1965, 96–97; see Bornemann 1894, 97–99). Alternatively, although Boers agrees with Schmithals' observations regarding the grammatical difficulties in 2:13 he is not satisfied with the compilation theory solution. Rather, he explains the phrase according to Pearson's interpolation theory. The reference of καὶ διὰ τοῦτο is to the ὅτι clause (v. 13c), with the initial καί acting as a copulative particle, while καὶ ὑμεῖς highlights the shift of focus from the Thessalonians to Paul (1976, 151–152). The confusion regarding the reference of καὶ διὰ τοῦτο (forward, backward or both) is a predominant part of the discussion (see already, Eadie 1877, 75–76). Consequently, one place for fruitful inquiry is the investigation of the phrase in Paul and elsewhere.

The phrase καὶ διὰ τοῦτο occurs seven times in the NT.[41] It occurs only four times in the LXX;[42] but the shortened phrase διὰ τοῦτο occurs over three hundred fifty times. Paul himself uses the latter fifteen times[43] and it appears a further forty

[38] See Walton, who notes a connection between 2:13 and Acts 20:32 in the phrase λόγον θεοῦ (2000, 179). He points to a context of power in both texts. Wenham makes an interesting observation that 1:6 and 2:13 may be possible echoes to the parable of the sower (Mark 4:1–20 [par.]). Common themes include: (1) the word of God at work in people; (2) an emphasis on hearing (cf. Rom 10:14–17); (3) the idea of "receiving" the word; (4) an association of hearing the word with both "joy" and "tribulation" (1995, 87). He notes a word of caution, however, that agricultural imagery is commonplace in the ancient world (87–88).

[39] See esp. Henneken 1969, 47–55; see also Orchard 1938; Schippers 1966; Ware 1992, 130.

[40] Eckart 1961, 33; Refshauge 1971, 5; Richard 1995, 111–112; Schenke/Fischer 1978, 70; Schmidt 1983, 273. That Pearson (1971) does not refer to the phrase at all is significant considering that he is one of the earlier and most thorough interpolation hypothesisers.

[41] Mark 6:14 (par. Matt 14:2); Luke 14:20; John 5:16; 1 Thess 2:13; 2 Thess 2:11; Heb 9:15.

[42] Isa 30:18; Sus 21θ; 4 Macc 16:19; Wis 14:14.

[43] Rom 1:26; 4:16; 5:12; 13:6; 15:9; 1 Cor 4:17; 11:10, 30; 2 Cor 4:1; 7:13; 13:10; 1 Thess 2:13; 3:5, 7; Phlm 15; cf. also Eph 1:15; 5:17; 6:13; Col 1:9; 2 Thess 2:11; 1 Tim 1:16; 2 Tim 2:10.

two times in the NT.[44] It could be argued that all seven NT occurrences of καὶ διὰ τοῦτο have an antecedent reference, but, with the possible exception of John 5:16, such argument is irrelevant because of the governing importance of the ὅτι construction in 1 Thess 2:13.[45] John 5:16 is quite interesting because the καὶ διὰ τοῦτο phrase refers to the preceding pericope (5:1–15) and yet has a ὅτι construction immediately following: καὶ διὰ τοῦτο ἐδίωκον οἱ Ἰουδαῖοι τὸν Ἰησοῦν, ὅτι ταῦτα ἐποίει ἐν σαββάτῳ. Actually, a search through the LXX and NT for διὰ τοῦτο + ὅτι constructions identifies a more relevant subset from the pool of four hundred plus references with διὰ τοῦτο.[46] Of this subset, it is interesting to see that the majority of the ὅτι constructions are causal.[47] More important is the observation that in attempting to define whether the διὰ τοῦτο phrase has an antecedent reference or not it does not matter whether ὅτι expresses cause or content.[48] This is a startling observation in view of the frequent argument that since the ὅτι of 1 Thess 2:13c is causal then the initial phrase καὶ διὰ τοῦτο must have a forward reference.[49] Similarly, but from the opposite side, Weatherly argues that the ὅτι of verse 13c is *not* causal and that demonstration of this fact indicates an antecedent reference (1991, 81–82; see Bornemann 1894, 96–97). Such argumentation is groundless. Both 1 Thess 3:7–8 and Matt 13:13, which contain a διὰ τοῦτο + causal ὅτι construction, may be singled out as examples.[50] In the first text (διὰ τοῦτο παρεκλήθημεν ... ὅτι νῦν ζῶμεν ...) it is clear that Paul is referring to Timothy's "good news" in verse 6, if not to the whole of 3:1–6. In the second text (διὰ τοῦτο ἐν παραβολαῖς αὐτοῖς λαλῶ, ὅτι βλέποντες οὐ βλέπουσιν ...) there is an abrupt change between the aphorisms of verses 11–12 and the explanation of verse 13. These two examples, both with a

---

[44] Cf. also *Barn.* 8.7; Ign. *Magn.* 9.2; Herm. *Sim.* 7.2; 9.19.1.

[45] Nicholl too quickly asserts an anaphoric reference for διὰ τοῦτο without considering the ὅτι construction (2004, 93).

[46] Examples include (this list is fairly complete but not intended to be exhaustive): Gen 11:9; 21:31; Num 20:12; 2 Esd 6:6; Esth 9:26; Ps 118:104 (LXX); Eccl 8:11; Isa 9:16; 24:6; 30:12–13; 52:6; 57:10; Jer 10:21; Amos 4:12; 5:13; Jonah 4:2; Hab 1:4; Sir 2:13; 10:13; Wis 5:16; 14:11; Matt 13:13; 21:43; 24:44; John 5:16, 18; 6:65; 7:22; 8:47; 9:23; 10:17; 12:18, 39; 13:11; 15:19; 16:15; 1 Thess 3:7–8; 1 John 3:1; Rev 12:12; 18:8.

[47] Exceptions include: Ps 118:104 (LXX); Isa 52:6; Matt 21:43; John 6:65; 7:22; 9:23; 13:11; 16:15. The ὅτι in 1 Thess 2:13 is causal (so Holtz 1998, 97; Malherbe 2000, 166; Wanamaker 1990, 110; 2000, 265; *contra* Thomas 1978, 256–257).

[48] Thus, instances of διὰ τοῦτο + causal ὅτι construction with an antecedent reference include: Gen 11:9; 21:31; Esth 9:26; Ps 118:104 (LXX); Isa 9:16; 24:6; 30:12–13; 57:10; Jer 10:21; Amos 4:12; 5:13; Jonah 4:2; Hab 1:4; Sir 2:13; 10:13; Wis 5:16; 14:11; Matt 24:44; John 5:18; 8:47; 10:17; 12:18, 39; 15:19; 1 Thess 3:7–8; Rev 12:12; 18:8. But there are also instances of διὰ τοῦτο + causal ὅτι construction without an antecedent reference (albeit fewer in number): Num 20:12; 2 Esd 6:6; Eccl 8:11; Matt 13:13; 1 John 3:1. Likewise, there are instances of διὰ τοῦτο + non-causal ὅτι construction with an antecedent reference (Matt 21:43; John 7:22; 9:23; 13:11; 16:15) and without (Isa 52:6; John 6:65); see *GGBB* 333.

[49] Bruce 1982, 44; Richard 1995, 112; Wanamaker 1990, 110; see Boers 1976, 151; Cranfield 1979, 225.

[50] Space prevents me from giving further examples. These two texts have been selected because the one is found adjacent to 1 Thess 2:13 and the other is a particularly clear example of διὰ τοῦτο without an antecedent reference.

causal ὅτι – one with an antecedent and one with a postcedent reference – serve to illustrate a non-correlation between a causal ὅτι and a forward reference for καὶ διὰ τοῦτο. Consequently, scholars who continue to pursue an interpolation hypothesis will have to mount a new argument for an exclusively forward reference for καὶ διὰ τοῦτο if they wish to use this avenue as evidence for interpolation. It is possible then, that there may be an antecedent reference. But it remains unclear whether Paul means to refer to just 1 Thess 2:12, or 2:1–4, or even to the whole of 2:1–12.[51] Johanson, after noting that this ambiguity is precisely one of the reasons for various interpolation theories, observes that an anaphoric reference of 2:13–16 does not rest solely on καὶ διὰ τοῦτο alone (1987, 95). The point of Paul's thanksgiving that the Thessalonians received God's word as such picks up on the preceding references to the role the Thessalonians played in the missionaries' visit to them (Konradt 2003, 75).[52] As well, Johanson suggests that there are further parallels between the antithetical formulations in 2:1–12 and that of verses 13d (οὐ λόγον ἀνθρώπων) and 13e (ἀλλὰ ... λόγον θεοῦ), and also between the phrase λόγον ἀνθρώπων and the negative connotations invoked under the rubric κενή in 2:1–12 (see Smith 2000, 703). Johanson concludes, especially in view of the coherence of 2:1–12 and its link with the Thessalonians' acceptance of the gospel as a reason for thanksgiving, that καὶ διὰ τοῦτο is best understood as referring to 2:1–12 (95–96). These observations indicate that an antecedent reference cannot be ruled out — the best solution embraces an ante- and postcedent reference for καὶ διὰ τοῦτο.[53] Thus, since an antecedent reference is possible, the results of the above analysis of καὶ διὰ τοῦτο suggest that 2:13, at least, is not an interpolation.

b. Imitation and Suffering (2:14)

1. The two clauses, ὑμεῖς γὰρ μιμηταὶ ἐγενήθητε (v. 14a) and ὅτι τὰ αὐτὰ ἐπάθετε καὶ ὑμεῖς (v. 14d) dominate this verse. Interpolation theorists often raise a number of questions with regard to the historical accuracy of these statements — these questions must be addressed in defense of the claim for authenticity. Of importance for the discussion is the charge that the *mimēsis* motif is used in an un-Pauline way. Would Paul have used the *ekklēsiai* in Judea as an example to be imitated? If

[51] See Findlay 1904, 50–51; Frame 1912, 106; Haufe 1999, 43; Holmstrand 1997, 55; Holtz 1998, 94; Lambrecht 1990, 200–201; Malherbe 2000, 165; P.-G. Müller 2001, 141; O'Brien 1977, 154; Rigaux 1956, 437; Weatherly 1991, 81–82; *contra* Wanamaker 1990, 109–110.

[52] Furthermore, it would appear that Paul's expression of thanks is not out of place considering that he just made reference to God's kingdom (βασιλεία) and glory (δόξα) in the previous verse. Green comments: "Kings were the supreme human benefactors, and so the previous note about the Thessalonians' calling to God's kingdom would naturally give rise to thanksgiving" (2002, 139).

[53] Frame 1912, 106–107; Holtz 1998, 94–97; Jowett 1859, 59; Kim 2005, 522; Marshall 1983, 77; O'Brien 1977, 154; Rigaux 1956, 437; *contra GGBB* 333; Alford 1958, 258–259. *Barn.* 8.7 is particularly interesting because the author uses the phrase καὶ διὰ τοῦτο οὕτως with a double reference to ὅτι, ante- (8.6) and postcedent (8.7)!

so, why and how does Paul consider the Thessalonians to be imitators (§III.b.2)? Is the inference of suffering among those *ekklēsiai* at that time even historically accurate (§III.b.3)? More to the point, what is meant by the phrase ὑπὸ τῶν ἰδίων συμφυλετῶν (v. 14d) and what are the circumstances of the Thessalonians' own suffering (§III.b.4)? Vital to the discussion is an informed understanding of the reference to οἱ Ἰουδαῖοι (v. 14e), but since it is of highest syntactical importance for the analysis of verses 15–16, that discussion will be taken up later (see §III.c.2 below).At this juncture, a preliminary synthesis is offered to draw together some of the results of the analysis for my thesis (III.b.5).

2. Paul does not use μιμητής often but it remains a powerful motif in his letters. On two occasions he gives the striking command, μιμηταί μου γίνεσθε (1 Cor 4:16; 11:1), and it appears in 1 Thess 1:6 as an explanation of Paul's thanksgiving where he also includes ὁ κύριος as an object of imitation. The only other place where it is used by Paul is here in 1 Thess 2:14 where the object of imitation is: τῶν ἐκκλησιῶν τοῦ θεοῦ (v. 14b).[54] The fact that it appears only five times in the Pauline corpus (including the Ephesian reference) leads to one conclusion straight away: there is very little evidence on which to base Paul's normative use of the motif.[55] Consequently, the fact that three out of four instances (in the authentic Paul) have Paul as the object of the imitation is hardly enough evidence to make the categorical statement that μιμητής in 1 Thess 2:14 is used in an un-Pauline way.[56]

In view of Paul's recollection of his proclamation of the gospel (2:1–12) it makes sense that he would now express thanks for the way the Thessalonians had accepted the gospel of God (cf. 2:2, 8, 9). The explanation of imitation is a confirmation of this (de Boer 1962, 98). Paul is accustomed to using other *ekklēsiai* as examples to support his exhortations and so there is no difficulty with accepting such reasoning as authentic.[57] But what remains enigmatic is why Paul chooses specifically to refer to the Judean *ekklēsiai* — this is his only mention of them (Bammel 1959, 306). Would not any *ekklēsia* which was or had been undergoing similar suffering suffice for comparison? For that matter, why does he not refer to his own suffering as in 2:2 (Setzer 1994, 20)? Best provides a number of possibilities why Paul went out of his way to compare the *ekklēsiai* but concludes that it is impossible to know (1972, 112–113). Stanley attempts to build a connection between the *ekklēsiai* by asserting that the persecution history of the Jerusalem *ekklēsia* and subsequently

---

[54] Cf. also Eph 5:1 and Heb 6:12 for the only other references to μιμητής in the NT.

[55] The word group occurs only rarely outside of Paul (for example, cf. μιμεῖσθαι in 4 Macc 9:23; 13:9; Wis 4:2; 15:9; 2 Thess 3:7, 9; Heb 13:7; 3 John 11; μίμημα in Wis 9:8; συμμιμητής in Phil 3:17), and not much may be gained in how Paul uses the word. Stanley (1959, 859) and Clarke (1998, 330) are understandably reticent to explain μιμητής in terms of μαθητής or ἀκολουθεῖν.

[56] Schade 1984, 123; see Michaelis 1967a, 667; *contra* Beck 1994, 77; Pearson 1971, 87–88; Richard 1995, 119. Simpson (1988, 115; 1990, 52) notes that the occurrences of the *mimēsis* motif in First Thessalonians are distinctive from those in First Corinthians because they are both in the past tense (ἐγενήθητε).

[57] Jewett 1986, 39; Malherbe 2000, 167; *contra* Baur 1875, 87; cf. Rom 15:26–27; 1 Cor 16:1; 2 Cor 8:1–6; 9:2.

of the Antiochian *ekklēsia* was part of Paul's *kērygma* (1959, 868–869).[58] But this suggestion has little to commend itself and relies too heavily on the evidence of Acts.[59] Perhaps there is no other reason than just that the Judean *ekklēsiai* were the first and best known.[60] Or perhaps as Hengel suggests, Paul is being ironic in the fact that he himself persecuted those *ekklēsiai* and so thinks of them when he himself is persecuted (1991, 73),[61] although Gal 1:22 goes against this idea (Wanamaker 1990, 113). More recently, Smith argues that comparison between the two *ekklēsiai* is one of survival in the face of a forced separation from their leaders (2000, 704–705).[62] The precise reason is lost to me.[63] However, it is clear that Paul goes out of his way to refer to the Judean *ekklēsiai*.[64]

Before moving onto a discussion of whether such reference to suffering at that time is even historically accurate (see §III.b.3 below) it is possible to glean from the context several further observations. First, despite some debate over whether Paul envisages an active or passive imitation, the construction with ὅτι and the prepositional phrase with ὑπό (v. 14d) suggest the latter.[65] Thus, Michaelis paraphrases (1967a, 667):

> What is meant is that (through nothing that you have done) the same fate has overtaken you; you have to suffer the same things as they did before. What Paul is saying is that you are not the first on whom this fate has fallen. It is no exception, but the rule, as the example of the first Christian churches can teach you.

The example of the Judean *ekklēsiai* becomes a point of comparison (see καθῶς in v. 14e) regarding suffering (πάσχειν) rather than the Thessalonians actively imitating

[58] Similarly, Marshall suggests that Paul referred to the Judean *ekklēsiai* because he wanted to relate the suffering of the Thessalonians to an attitude which stemmed from persecutors in Palestine (1983, 78).

[59] Stanley adopts a too undifferentiated understanding of the persecution carried out by "the Jews". In a later publication he argues that Paul would have mentioned – as part of his proclamation – the role played by "the Jews" in the death of Jesus, how Jesus' death was prefigured in the martyred prophets, and how "the Jews" persecuted and hindered his mission (1984, 136). But characterising Paul as "apostle of the pagans" does not mean that he is insensitive to the plight of his own people. "The Jews" are not to be whitewashed as an amorphous people who are all opposed to the "Christian traditions", as Stanley would have it.

[60] Green 2002, 141–142; Milligan 1908, 29; Nicholl 2004, 94; Stott 1991, 55; Ward 1973, 72; see Oepke 1970, 164–165.

[61] See Baumbach 1983, 70; Malherbe 2000, 173.

[62] "What is often missed when considering this passage is that 'the churches of God in Judea' (v. 14) evidently have survived. Even with the loss of their leaders—whether through death, as in the case of Christian prophets (e.g. Stephen and James the brother of John), or through separation, as with other Christian leaders like Paul, these churches did not disintegrate. Similarly, the church of Thessalonica, despite the absence of its leaders (as Paul will soon explicitly note, 3:6), still survives ..." (Smith 2000, 704).

[63] So also Frame 1912, 109; P.-G. Müller 2001, 143.

[64] Donaldson 1997, 227. Findlay even suggests that it is primarily the input of Silvanus (because of his relation with the Jerusalem *ekklēsia*) that explains the link to the Judean *ekklēsiai* (1904, 52).

[65] Haufe 1999, 45; Michaelis 1967a, 667; Wanamaker 1990, 112; *contra* Milligan 1908, 29.

their fellow Jewish Christians in Judea.[66] This interpretation avoids the difficulty of attempting to explain how the Thessalonians knew about the Judean Christians so that they could imitate them.[67] Second, and quite apart from that difficulty, the context of verse 14 in juxtaposition to verse 13 (and therefore to 1:6) indicates that imitation is closely linked to the affliction/suffering motif (θλῖψις, 1:6; πάσχειν, 2:14) which is associated with the proclamation of the word of God and therefore with Paul and the Lord.[68] If there is any active element whatsoever then it is an active acceptance of this word from Paul and an imitation of Paul's attitude in the face of opposition (see 2:2).[69]

3. In advocating an interpolation at 2:13–16, Pearson makes the following statement: "With respect to the situation in Thessalonica at the time of the writing of 1 Thessalonians ... that the Thessalonian Christians were actually suffering systematic persecution in the apostolic period is very much in doubt" (1971, 87). Agreed! There *is* no evidence of "systematic persecution" (Still 1999, 39). Pearson seems to misunderstand Paul's reference to suffering (πάσχειν) in verse 14d as precisely that, and uses this as further evidence for an interpolation. He refers to Hare for support which is ironic because Hare does not read verse 14 in the same way (1967, 63):

> Paul was able to visit the Jerusalem church at widely scattered intervals and find a stable, continuing organization. It is therefore not wise to exaggerate the meaning of ἐπάθετε, which may refer to public insults, social ostracism and other kinds of non-violent opposition.

Yet, this is the kind of exaggeration that Pearson employs in order to reinforce his interpolation hypothesis. If the reference to "suffering" (a better translation than "persecution" for the πασχ- word group)[70] in verse 14 is authentic, to what does Paul refer when he mentions the suffering of the Judean Christians? The remainder of this section will examine this question in an attempt to emphasise the suitability of Paul's comparison between the Thessalonians and the Judeans.

Paul uses Ἰουδαία four times — each instance in a geographical sense.[71] Although the term may be used to differentiate an area of Palestine other than Samaria, Galilee, Perea and Idumea, there is no reason for Paul to use it in this restricted sense. He

---

[66] Bouttier 1966, 53–54; Bruce 1982, 45; Green 2002, 141; Richard 1995, 119; see von Dobschütz 1909, 109.

[67] *Contra* de Boer 1962, 99–103; Larsson 1991, 429.

[68] Merk 1989, 193; see Clarke 1998, 337; Elias 1992, 126–128. Thus, for Clarke, the example motif in 1:8 is very significant since the Thessalonians are now examples because they have imitated how Paul lives (1998, 338). He looks to 2:1–12 for further support of this thesis (338–339). See also Pobee 1985, 69–71.

[69] Brant 1993, 292–293; Larsson 1991, 429; so also Fowl 1993, 430; Frame 1912, 110; see Davis 1971, 291–462. Although unnecessarily lengthy, Davis does a thorough job of giving a history of research of the *mimēsis* motif and in his discussions of active and passive imitation.

[70] The distinction between "suffering" and "persecution" is perhaps a false dichotomy since both may refer to sporadic criticism, discrimination, ostracism, and physical abuse (Tellbe 2001, 95; see BDAG 785, §3.b), although the latter term usually carries anachronistic connotations.

[71] Rom 15:31; 2 Cor 1:16; Gal 1:22; 1 Thess 2:14.

is probably referring to all of Palestine, i.e. to the land of the Judeans (Jews).[72] The qualification τῶν ἐκκλησιῶν τοῦ θεοῦ (v. 14b) indicates nothing as to location and has significance beyond the scope of this investigation.[73] Against the assessment of Pearson are a number of indications that suggest at least the possibility of suffering among Judean *ekklēsiai*: (1) There was no inconsiderable unrest between Roman authorities and Jews prior to the writing of First Thessalonians, including the suppression by procurator Cuspius Fadus (44–46 C.E.) of an uprising under Theudas, and confrontations between Jews and Romans under Ventidius Cumanus (48–52 C.E.) involving a massacre where thousands of Jews were killed. Moreover, the widespread famine in Judea during the mid forties C.E. probably contributed to mounting unrest.[74] (2) In addition to political instability there was also religious unrest and this is far more significant because there is some evidence that Christians in Judea prior to 50 C.E. underwent suffering at the hands of Zealots (Bruce 1982, 46). Jewett makes an excellent case for reconstructing a situation in Judea where an underground Zealot movement was essentially in control of the political and religious situation (1971a; followed by Wanamaker 1990, 113). He argues that Gal 6:12–13 indicates that circumcision was central to the conflict (see also Jewett 1986, 39). Jewett concludes (1971a, 205):

> My hypothesis therefore is that Jewish Christians in Judea were stimulated by Zealotic pressure into a nomistic campaign among their fellow Christians in the late forties and early fifties. Their goal was to avert the suspicion that they were in communion with lawless Gentiles. It appears that the Judean Christians convinced themselves that circumcision of Gentile Christians would thwart Zealot reprisals.

E. P. Sanders is more cautious when he says that "at least some non-Christian Jews persecuted (that is, punished) at least some Christian Jews in at least some places" (1985, 191). But he agrees with Jewett that the central issue was circumcision and further suggests that the references to suffering may actually refer to Jewish punishments (Sanders strenuously highlights the fact that this cannot be decisively proved to be the case).[75] Perhaps the best attested fact towards this conclusion is that Paul himself contributed to such suffering (191).[76] Furthermore, it is reasonable to suggest that Paul's zealousness was not an isolated instance; there still would have been lingering hostility.[77] (3) Another telling point against Pearson's argument is that there is no reason for limiting Paul's reference to the present or near past

[72] Examples of this broader usage may be found in antiquity, including Strabo 16.2.21, 34; Josephus *Ant.* 1.160; *B.J.* 3.48–58; *C. Ap.* 1.179, 195; Luke 1:5; Acts 10:37; Gal 1:22; see BDAG 477–478, esp. §2; Best 1972, 114; Betz 1991, 192; Brandon 1951, 91–92; Green 2002, 141; Gutbrod 1965, 382; Hengel 1991, 73–74; Holtz 1998, 99–100; Malherbe 2000, 168; Morris 1959, 89; Schlier 1972, 39; von Dobschütz 1909, 108–109.

[73] See Cerfaux 1959a, 95–117; Donfried 1996c, 404–407; Lindemann 1995, 40–42.

[74] For primary references to these events, see discussion in §III.d.4 below.

[75] So also Setzer 1994, 169; cf. 2 Cor 11:24; Gal 5:11; 6:12; 1 Thess 2:16.

[76] So also Tellbe 2001, 108; Wortham 1995, 41; cf. 1 Cor 15:9; Gal 1:13–14; Phil 3:6; Acts 5:17–8:3.

[77] Eadie 1877, 82; Okeke 1981, 129; Sanders 1985a, 298; 1999, 278.

(Simpson 1988, 122). In particular, Paul uses the aorist (ἐπάθετε) which means that he could be referring to any number of events in the past (constative). This makes irrelevant Pearson's assertion that there is no evidence for persecution of *ekklēsiai* in Judea between 44 C.E. and the war against Rome — even if true.[78]

The charge that Paul is inaccurate in his reference to Judean persecution is no longer tenable (*contra* Baur 1875, 87). Essentially, the argument has been from silence anyway. Not only does the evidence from Paul's letters (including suffering instigated by him as well as his own suffering at the hands of others) but also the political and religious situations in Judea prior to Paul's writing of First Thessalonians *individually* admit the conclusion that some Jewish Christians suffered in Judea. It is unnecessary to conclude that Paul exaggerates the situation in Judea in order to use their experience as an example for exhorting the Thessalonians (*contra* Schlueter 1994, 51–53).

4. Paul makes a comparison between the Judeans who suffered ὑπὸ τῶν Ἰουδαίων (v. 14e) and the Thessalonians who suffered τὰ αὐτά ... ὑπὸ τῶν ἰδίων συμφυλετῶν (v. 14d). The comparison should be understood in terms of other references to affliction and suffering in First Thessalonians.[79] My primary aim here is to build a case for the authenticity of 2:13–16 and so build a platform on which I may develop an interpretation of one of the most significant eschatological statements in First Thessalonians (v. 16d). However, a short examination of conflict language in Paul aids in situating the pericope in its proper historical context. The letter contains a number of words that refer to instances of distress and conflict, relating either to Paul and his co-workers, or to the community. The most frequent is θλῖψις (1 Thess 1:6, 3:3 and 3:7);[80] the cognate verb, θλίβειν, appears in 3:4, only in the passive.[81] Paul uses the noun and verb in a figurative sense and they are usually translated "affliction" and "to suffer affliction", respectively. The notion of θλῖψις is viewed as an inheritance of Christians from Israel (Court 1982, 60), or more directly, as a continuation of the παθήματα τοῦ Χριστοῦ (2 Cor 1:5; Schlier 1965, 143–144).[82] In this sense, θλῖψις and πάθημα are synonymous; Paul uses the two interchangeably in 2 Cor 1:4–8. In First Thessalonians the latter appears only in 2:14 (ἐπάθετε) of which the passive form is the only example in Paul (Michaelis 1967b, 920). Implicit in the word group is Paul's understanding of affliction/suffering as an inevitable part of Christian fellowship (κοινωνὶα παθημάτων, Phil 3:10; cf. 2 Cor 1:7). For the Philippians, Paul characterises suffering for the sake of Christ as a grace (ὅτι ὑμῖν ἐχαρίσθη τὸ ὑπὲρ Χριστοῦ ... τὸ ὑπὲρ αὐτοῦ πάσχειν, Phil 1:29; Kremer 1993c, 51). Elsewhere, suffering is not only linked to this present age

[78] Malherbe 2000, 173–174; *contra* Pearson 1971, 86–87; see Frame 1912, 109; Simpson 1988, 120.

[79] For an introduction to the secondary literature on conflict in First Thessalonians, see Chapter 1, §IV.e.

[80] Cf. Rom 2:9; 5:3*bis*; 8:35; 12:12; 1 Cor 7:28; 2 Cor 1:4*bis*, 8; 2:4; 4:17; 6:4; 7:4; 8:2, 13; Phil 1:17; 4:14; cf. also 2 Thess 1:4, 6*bis*; Eph 3:13; Col 1:24.

[81] Cf. 2 Cor 1:6; 4:8; 7:5; cf. also 2 Thess 1:6, 7; 1 Tim 5:10.

[82] Cf. Phil 3:10; 1 Pet 4:13; Col 1:24.

(τὰ παθήματα τοῦ νῦν καιροῦ, Rom 8:18), but is a precondition for participation in glory (εἴπερ συμπάσχομεν ἵνα καὶ συνδοξασθῶμεν, Rom 8:17).[83] In 1 Thess 2:2 (προπάσχειν) Paul specifically includes himself in suffering (cf. 2 Cor 1:6–7). His statement is formulated in a context of declaring the gospel of God in the face of great opposition (λαλῆσαι πρὸς ὑμᾶς τὸ εὐαγγέλιον τοῦ θεοῦ ἐν πολλῷ ἀγῶνι), which recalls his labour (κόπος, 2:9), toil (μόχθος, 2:9) and specific hindrances (κωλύειν, 2:16; ἐγκόπτειν, 2:18; Dautzenberg 1990, 26). Further, Paul refers to affliction as an anticipated accompaniment to the Christian life (αὐτοὶ γὰρ οἴδατε ὅτι εἰς τοῦτο κείμεθα, 3:3), and indeed as common to the acceptance of his proclamation (1:6; Kremer 1991, 152). Similar phrases to the one in 1 Thess 3:7, ἐπὶ πάσῃ τῇ ἀνάγκῃ καὶ θλίψει ἡμῶν, are common in Paul.[84] It is quite probable that Paul considers θλῖψις as an eschatological tangent to the present distress (… τὴν ἐνεστῶσαν ἀνάγκην, 1 Cor 7:26) since the appointed time has grown very short (ὁ καιρὸς συνεσταλμένος ἐστίν, 7:29).[85] In this connection, the association of θλῖψις with death and resurrection is expected (147; Simundson 1992, 224).[86]

Assuming that the Thessalonians were suffering public insults, social ostracism and other kinds of non-violent opposition, with whom are the συμφυλέται to be identified? The word appears to be coined by Paul (σύν + φυλέτης)[87] and is a *hapax legomenon* although there are several references to cognate nouns, including σύμφυλος and συμφυλία.[88] Danker gives a descriptive definition of συμφυλέτης as

[83] Kremer 1993b, 1; Michaelis 1967b, 934.

[84] E.g. 2 Cor 1:4; 4:8; 7:4, 5.

[85] Schlier 1965, 144–145; see Strobel 1990, 78–79.

[86] Cf. Rom 8:35–36; 2 Cor 1:8–9; 11:23.

[87] In antiquity, other references to συμφυλέτης are rare and probably dependent on 1 Thess 2:14. The lexicographer Hesychius (5th century C.E.) lists the word and gives the synonym: ὁμοέθνος (see M. Schmidt 1965, vol. 4, 97. But ὁμοέθνος is more specific than ὁμόφυλος [LSJ 1223].). Hermias Alexandrinus Philosophus (5th century C.E.) uses the word when referring to the old tribes (ἡ παλαιά φυλή) and to specific members of that tribe: καὶ οἱ τούτου συμφυλέται σεμνοὶ καὶ σιωπηλοὶ (*Irrisio gentilium philosophorum* 16; see Diels 1879, 655, line 8). Finally, the lexicon *Suda* (10th century C.E.), gives ὁμοεθνῶν and συγγενῶν as synonyms of συμφυλετῶν (see Adler 1967–1971, vol. 4, 462); see also entries in BDAG and LSJ.

[88] For σύμφυλος, see Aristotle *Mund.* 4.19, … τε καὶ πνευμάτων διαφοραὶ βρονταί τε καὶ ἀστραπαὶ καὶ πρηστῆρες καὶ κεραυνοὶ καὶ τὰ ἄλλα ἃ δὴ τούτοις ἐστὶ σύμφυλα ("… the winds and various breezes, thunder and lightning, fiery bolts and thunderbolts and all the other things of the same class" [Forster/Furley 1955]); *Part. an.* 6.10, οἷον αἵ τε μέλιτται καὶ τὰ σύμφυλα ζῷα ταύταις ("such are the bees and the kindred tribes" [Peck/Forster 1937]); Plutarch *Brut. an.* 8, πρῶτον μὲν γὰρ ἑκάστῳ γένει ζῴου μία τροφὴ σύμφυλός ἐστι, τοῖς μὲν πόα τοῖς δὲ ῥίζα τις ἢ καρπός ("In the first place each species of animal has one single food proper to it, grass or some root or fruit" [Cherniss/Helmbold 1927–1976]); *Quaest. conv.* 8.2, (with reference to the Egyptian's hatred of the sea), ὡς ἀσύμφυλον ἡμῖν καὶ ἀλλότριον ("as an element unrelated and alien" [Minar/Sandbach/Helmbold 1927–1976]); furthermore (in the same paragraph and also of the Egyptians), ὅθεν οὔτε τὸ ὕδωρ πότιμον αὐτῆς οὔθ' ὧν τρέφει τι καὶ γεννᾷ καθαρὸν ἡγοῦνται καὶ οἰκεῖον, οἷς μήτε πνεύματος κοινοῦ μήτε συμφύλου νομῆς μέτεστιν ("Hence they neither consider sea-water potable, nor any of the creatures it nourishes as ritually pure or edible, since they do not partake of air in common with us nor live in our congenial habitat" [Minar/Sandbach/Helmbold 1927–1976]); *Tu. san.* 26, ἀλλὰ καὶ ταῦτα δεῖ μνημονεύειν, τὰ σύμφυλα καὶ πρόσφορα τῷ σώματι, καὶ τοὐναντίον ἐν ταῖς καθ' ὥραν μεταβολαῖς καὶ ταῖς ἄλλαις περιστάσεσιν εἰδότας οἰκείως προσαρμόττειν ἑκάστῃ τὴν δίαιταν ("But we must keep in mind both those things that are congenial and suitable to the body, and, conversely,

"one who is a member of the same tribe or people group" (BDAG 960); the definition of LSJ is similar: "of the same φυλή" (1688). Considering that Aristotle, Epicurus, Plutarch and Babrius (see footnotes above) use cognates for descriptions of animals and natural phenomena, generic terms like "kind" and "group" seem more appropriate than "tribe" or "people group". However there are fixed uses of the root words φυλέτης and φυλή which likely nuance the use of συμφυλέτης in First Thessalonians. The word φυλέτης does not appear in the LXX or NT. But it is commonly used elsewhere in descriptions of social groups and organisations of cities — often with other words of socio-political delimitation, including: δημότης,[89] συγγενής,[90] κωμήτης[91] and πολίτης.[92] It is important to note that many of these

---

as changes attendant on the season occur and different circumstances arise, we should, in full knowledge of the facts, suitably adjust our mode of living to each" [Babbitt 1927–1976]). Finally, see Babrius (2nd century C.E.) 101.1–4,

> Λύκος τις ἁδρὸς ἐν λύκοις ἐγεννήθη,
> λέοντα δ᾽ αὐτὸν ἐπεκάλουν. ὁ δ᾽ ἀγνώμων
> τὴν δόξαν οὐκ ἤνεγκε, τῶν δὲ συμφύλων
> ἀποστατήσας τοῖς λέουσιν ὡμίλει.
>
> "A wolf grown oversized among his fellow-wolves
> was nicknamed 'Lion.' Having no sense,
> he knew not how to bear such glory but deserted his kinsmen
> and went about in the company of lions" (Perry 1965).

For συμφυλία, see Epicurus 2.115, who gives several alternative explanations of what produces falling stars, including: καὶ κατὰ σύνοδον δὲ ἀτόμων πυρὸς ἀποτελεστικῶν, συμφυλίας γενομένης εἰς τὸ τοῦτο τελέσαι ... ("or else by the meeting of atoms productive of fire, when a gathering of kindred materials occurs to cause this ..." [Bailey 1926]).

89 See Aristotle *Eth. nic.* 8.9.5, ὁμοίως δὲ καὶ φυλέται καὶ δημόται ("and similarly the members of a tribe or parish" [Rackham 1926]); Isocrates *Panath.* 145, τὰς ἀρχὰς τοὺς προκριθέντας ὑπὸ τῶν φυλετῶν καὶ δημοτῶν ("the magistracies those who had been selected beforehand by the members of their respective tribes and townships" [Norlin 1928–1945]).

90 See Lysias 21.6, οὔτε φίλος ὢν οὔτε συγγενὴς οὔτε φυλέτης ("as [he was] neither my friend nor my relative nor a member of my tribe" [Lamb 1930]); Josephus *Ant.* 4.14, καὶ γὰρ φυλέτης ὢν ἐτύγχανεν αὐτοῦ καὶ συγγενής ("for he was of the same tribe and indeed his kinsman" [Marcus 1926–1965]). Paul also uses the word in Rom 9:3; 16:7, 8, 21.

91 See Plato *Leg.* 956c, δὲ κωμῆταί τε καὶ φυλέται ("villagers and tribesmen" [Bury 1914–1935]).

92 See Aristotle *Eth. nic.* 9.2.9–10, καὶ συγγενέσι δὲ καὶ φυλέταις καὶ πολίταις καὶ τοῖς λοιποῖς ἅπασιν ἀεὶ πειρατέον τὸ οἰκεῖον ἀπονέμειν, καὶ συγκρίνειν τὰ ἑκάστοις ὑπάρχοντα κατ᾽ οἰκειότητα καὶ ἀρετὴν ἢ χρῆσιν. τῶν μὲν οὖν ὁμογενῶν ῥᾴων ἡ σύγκρισις, τῶν δὲ διαφερόντων ἐργωδεστέρα ("Kinsmen also, fellow-tribesmen, fellow-citizens, and the rest — to all we must always endeavour to render their due, comparing their several claims in respect of relationship and of virtue or utility. Between persons of the same kind discrimination is comparatively easy; but it is a harder matter when they are differently related to us" [Rackham 1926]); see also *Pol.* 2.1.12, where, in a discussion of what is to be common (κοινωνεῖν) among citizens (πολῖται) of a city (πόλις), Aristotle comments on the different relationships between citizens: ὁ μὲν γὰρ υἱὸν αὑτοῦ ὁ δ᾽ ἀδελφὸν αὑτοῦ προσαγορεύει τὸν αὐτόν, ὁ δ᾽ ἀνεψιὸν ἢ κατ᾽ ἄλλην τινὰ συγγένειαν ἢ πρὸς αἵματος ἢ κατ᾽ οἰκειότητα καὶ κηδείαν αὑτοῦ πρῶτον ἢ τῶν αὑτοῦ, πρὸς δὲ τούτοις ἕτερος φράτορα ἢ φυλέτην ("[F]or the same person is called 'my son' by one man and 'my brother' by another, and another calls him 'nephew,' or by some other relationship, whether of blood or by affinity and marriage, the speaker's own in the first place, or that of his relations; and in addition someone else calls him 'fellow-clansman' or 'fellow-tribesman'" [Rackham 1932]); in Dio Chrysostom *Diffid.* 3, φυλέτης appears in close juxtaposition with συμπολιτεύειν, δημότης and συγγενής. Cf. also συνπολίτης in Eph 2:19.

references provide examples of groups of people bound by categories other than blood relationships — this despite the fact that φυλή appears repeatedly in the LXX as a fixed term to describe the tribal system of Israel (Maurer 1974, 246). Consequently, even though many NT references often follow this fixed use,[93] the translations "tribe" and "family" are misleading in some contexts (245).[94] The word group, therefore, should be described more generally as referring to a socio-political subgroup of people (see BDAG 1069, §2).[95] The point of this investigation has a significant bearing on one aspect of the discussion among Thessalonian commentators: Paul's reference to the συμφυλέται of the Thessalonian Christians cannot be taken in an ethnic sense.[96] Whether the Christian community consisted of non-Jews only or also contained some Jewish Christians is irrelevant to the identity of those causing πάθημα.[97] Some scholars seek to harmonise Paul's account with Acts 17 by proposing that Jews instigated unrest among non-Jews (cf. Acts 17:5, 13) such that both Jews and non-Jews are the cause.[98] Although this is possible, it does not adequately explain the hostility that the largely non-Jewish community experienced after Paul and his co-workers left Thessalonica (Wanamaker 1990, 113). Others argue that the polemic against οἱ Ἰουδαῖοι makes little sense unless Jews were also involved in Thessalonica[99] although the emphatic ἰδίων expresses contrast and possibly mitigates against this.[100] Regardless of these arguments, the socio-political connotations of the cognates φυλέτης and φυλή strongly support the conclusion that Paul uses συμφυλέτης in a local rather than ethnic sense.[101] The precise relationships between members of a φυλή and especially between members of different φυλαί are largely unknown (MacMullen 1974, 131–132). The investigation of συμφυλέτης by vom Brocke, in terms of the various known φυλαί in Thessalonica at the time of Paul is most interesting and well-informed (2001, 156–159). He argues that the reference to φυλέτης demands a more specific interpreta-

[93] Matt 19:28; Luke 2:36; 22:30; Acts 13:21; Rom 11:1; Phil 3:5; Heb 7:13–14; Jas 1:1; Rev 5:5; 7:4–8; 21:12.

[94] E.g. Gen 12:3; 28:14; Ezek 20:32; Matt 24:30; Rev 1:7; 5:9; 7:9; 11:9; 13:7; 14:6; see Holtz 1998, 102; vom Brocke 2001, 155–156.

[95] Findlay 1904, 53; Nilsson 1951, 143, 149; Reinmuth 1998, 129.

[96] *Contra* Green 2002, 142; Malherbe 2000, 168; Meeks 1989, 691; Moffatt 1910, 29; Staab 1965, 20; Still 1999, 218–226; von Dobschütz 1909, 109–110; Ward 1973, 73.

[97] Marshall 1983, 78–79; *contra* Bornemann 1894, 109; von Dobschütz 1909, 109–110.

[98] So Best 1972, 114; Donfried 1984, 247–248; Milligan 1908, 29; Sandnes 1991, 186; Tellbe 2001, 114; Thomas 1978, 258; Vawter 1960, 42; Ward 1973, 73.

[99] Morgan Gillman 1990, 44; see Manus 1990, 36; Marshall 1983, 78; Richard 1995, 120; Riesner 1998, 352; Tellbe 2001, 113.

[100] Alford 1958, 260; Auberlen/Riggenbach 1869, 41; Bornemann 1894, 109; Eadie 1877, 81; Frame 1912, 110; Morris 1959, 89; Still 1999, 224.

[101] Donfried 1993, 18–19; Légasse 1999, 144; Milligan 1908, 29; Morris 1959, 89; P.-G. Müller 2001, 144; Riesner 1998, 352; Rigaux 1956, 443. The statement by de Vos that such a conclusion (i.e. taking συμφυλέτης in a local sense) is motivated solely from a need to harmonise Paul with the account of Acts is not entirely correct (1999, 157–158; see also Still 1999, 220; 2004, 61–62). With regard to the comparative nature of Paul's point, Weatherly not only accepts a local sense for συμφυλέτης, but argues for the implication that οἱ Ἰουδαῖοι is also local (1991, 85).

tion than Holtz's comment, "die Mitglieder des sozialen Lebensbereichs" (1998, 102), and takes the term as a reference to the cultic life of urban Thessalonica (162). Attention is drawn to the link between citizenship and active participation in a φυλή with its patron god(s); vom Brocke proceeds to argue that Jews and non-Jews could not have been co-members. If there is any evidence of co-membership then it is of non-Jews and former Jews (163–164).[102] But vom Brocke is too preoccupied with associating the Thessalonian Christians with a particular φυλή thereby accommodating the reference to the εἴδωλα in 1:9; this is now a reference to cultic gods — probably Asclepius and Dionysius (162). The formation of a φυλή, as has been shown above, does not depend solely on pre-existing boundaries of citizenship. It may be formed on a number of bases: blood relation, local association, patron gods. Thus, it is conceivable that Paul considers his Thessalonian converts as forming a new kind of φυλή bound together ἐν θεῷ πατρὶ καὶ κυρίῳ Ἰησοῦ Χριστῷ (1 Thess 1:1).[103] To conclude: the possibility that Jews may be included among the συμφυλέται does not make this a historical probability. However and pending further evidence, the best interpretations of 2:14 make allowance for the presence of some Jews among the φυλαί associated with the Thessalonian Christians.[104] References to Jews may no longer be used to justify an interpolation theory (*contra* Richard 1995, 120).

5. In the analysis of 1 Thess 2:13–14 above, I have emphasised issues pertaining to compilation and interpolation hypotheses. In this regard, the implications of my conclusions are presented at length elsewhere (§IV below). However, assuming for the time being that these verses are authentic, there is one particular feature that I want to highlight as relevant for my thesis, namely, the connection between accepting the word of God and suffering. Paul expresses a correlation between the two whereby suffering is understood as an unavoidable outcome of accepting Paul's *kērygma*, a view which he reiterates a few verses later (see 1 Thess 3:3–4). I find the connection important because it illustrates the interrelation between the negative and positive aspects of Paul's pattern of exhortation. As an interpreter, one would

[102] Although the term φυλή does not appear (groups were formed under βούλευται), Judge draws attention to a marble *stēlē* dated approximately 150–200 C.E. which clearly portrays partnerships "between Gentile sympathisers, proselytes and Jews for specified end" (2002, 78). Against vom Brocke, it does appear possible that non-Jews and Jews could have been associated in the same group.

[103] The φυλαί were often grouped together under their own god (Glotz 1929, 5–6) and members often had to tolerate different ethnicities within them (24); see Humphreys 1978, 193–208; Oakes 2002, 246–247. Although entirely removed from this discussion, the terminology of the Thessalonian community as a new "family of God" is consistent with this thesis (see Johnson 2002; Malherbe 1995).

[104] Tellbe 2001, 115; *contra* Barclay 1993, 514. For Still, the inclusion of Jews and non-Jews in συμφυλέτης is inconsistent with Paul's usually careful distinction between the "ethnic" groups, both elsewhere and in First Thessalonians (1999, 221–223). He concludes that συμφυλέτης refers "to non-Jewish, Thessalonian townsfolk" (1999, 223). However, Paul's interest in First Thessalonians is not between the dichotomy Jew/non-Jew but insider/outsider (cf. 1 Thess 4:5, 12, 13; 5:6, 7). This terminology allows Paul to transcend previous social boundaries even while maintaining an ethnic identity. Despite my disagreement with Still on the matter, his discussion of the lexical and historical issues is thorough (218–227). Tellbe (2001, 112–115) provides some correctives to Still's discussion.

presumably associate accepting the word of God, or turning to God from idols, with the positive aspect, as a means for community identity and existence. Likewise, one would also presumably associate suffering and conflict with the negative aspect, as part of understanding or explaining experiences of social disintegration. But Paul alludes to the opposite associations, through the correlation between acceptance and suffering. Indeed, notions of suffering are viewed by Paul as a means for eschatological existence. His reference to the *mimēsis* motif has rhetorical significance in effecting a positive exhortation, for in that motif he invokes an identity and solidarity with the Judean *ekklēsiai* that rises above suspicions of historicity and authenticity. In my view, the arguments outlined above, that the reference to μιμητής in verse 14 is historically possible, advances a defence against interpolation charges, but does not add to modern interpretations of the text. Rather, by considering how these verses contribute to the eschatological discourse of the letter, it is possible to discern in a new way what Paul is attempting to say. In summary: Paul invites the Thessalonians to embrace their affliction as something to be expected, and further, offers them support not only from himself and his co-workers, but from the Lord, and from other *ekklēsiai*. The references to the *mimēsis* motif and to suffering are thus to be interpreted as paradigms for a new identity.

c. The Judeans – Who Killed, Drove Out, Displease and Oppose (2:15)

1. Paul moves on to a cascade of accusations (vv. 15a–e) against οἱ Ἰουδαῖοι (v. 14e) and the interpretation of that phrase is the first issue for discussion (§III.c.2), the outcome of which not only has ramifications for the interpretation of verse 15–16 but particularly for the charge that Paul is anti-Semitic (Excursus 4). Once the antecedent to the accusations is established the charges will be dealt with in order. As is evident, each charge is caustic enough to be controversial and nearly every aspect of verse 15 is challenged by interpolation hypothesisers: οἱ Ἰουδαῖοι killed the Lord Jesus (§III.c.3) and the prophets (§III.c.4), drove out Paul and his co-workers (§III.c.5), do not please God and oppose all men (§III.c.6). Thus, in the analysis of this verse, the aims are to present pertinent information in order to make an informed choice about whether Paul wrote it or not, and also, as the subject matter becomes increasingly eschatological, to focus more on the themes pursuant to that topic.

2. It is not helpful to open and close an investigation of the phrase οἱ Ἰουδαῖοι by observing that since Paul himself is a "Jew" then he cannot be making sweeping statements against all Jews in general. The plethora of definitions and debate over the use of the phrase indicates the problematic nature of the discussion. The entry in BDAG highlights the difficulties of translating οἱ Ἰουδαῖοι as "the Jews". A general definition is given as: "one who identifies with beliefs, rites, and customs of adherents of Israel's Mosaic and prophetic tradition" (478). But the term can

be equally applied to persons who claim a genealogical connection and those who become proselytes; it can describe adherents of Moses who reject Jesus as the *Kyrios*, and those who recognise Jesus as such.[105] Consequently, the designation Ἰουδαῖος must not be translated "Jew" without careful assessment of historical circumstances and contemporary ethnic, religious and social realities (478).[106] Such an assessment of the context of 1 Thess 2:14 immediately suggests the translation "the Judeans" rather than "the Jews" for οἱ Ἰουδαῖοι (478, §2.c; Lowe 1976, 130). But this does not end the matter. If Paul speaks of specific Jews only – the very Judeans who killed the Lord Jesus (v. 15a) – then an anti-Jewish charge is avoided. But it seems that Paul is unreserved with the rest of the charges (vv. 15b–e) and the conclusion that he is really referring to all Jews in general is strangely unavoidable. Gutbrod recognises this difficulty in that somehow Paul can use Ἰουδαῖος at once as a concrete description of those who killed the Lord Jesus, and, as a "supratemporal" description of those who always "decide against, and reject, both God and His community" (1965, 380). Thus, it appears that Paul uses οἱ Ἰουδαῖοι both in a restrictive and non-restrictive sense — but that comment is getting ahead of the discussion.

The article by Gilliard (1989) is a turning point in the discussion of whether οἱ Ἰουδαῖοι is restrictive or not (i.e. specifically "the Judeans", or generally "the Jews"). The first part of his article examines the significant presence of a comma between verses 14 and 15 (481–488). He argues that since punctuation is not in the earliest manuscripts (at least there is no hint of punctuation between 1 Thess 2:14, 15) and since the comma has an "anti-Semitic" consequence, then it should be removed from modern versions of the Greek text (486–487).[107] The second part of his article seeks to demonstrate that the participial phrase immediately following the phrase οἱ Ἰουδαῖοι is restrictive (488–502).[108] If taken in this way, Gilliard argues that the charges are finally properly understood as "not against *the* Jews, but against *those* Jews whom he specified" (498). The article by Gilliard is well researched and well written. Moreover, he is correct to reject the comma reading at the end of verse 14. And technically, he is correct to maintain that Paul often uses participial

[105] See Frankfurter 2001, 409; Kuhli 1991, 195. Murray seeks to narrow the definition of "Jewish" and "Judaism": "... these terms are really appropriate for those who looked to Jerusalem as their focus of identity, while a distinct term is needed for those who were hostile to the Jerusalem of the Second Temple" (1982, 195); he suggests "dissenting Hebrew" be used (198–199).

[106] Again, Murray suggests a number of terms to differentiate various groups. Thus, besides using the terms "Jew" and "(dissenting) Hebrew" for those who are for and against (respectively) the Jerusalem of the Second Temple, he proposes that, in view of the increasing number of converts to Christianity from outside the Israelite world, the terms "Judaistic" (= proselytes to Judaism who then become Christians) and "Hebraistic" (= proselytes to Christianity who have closer affinities to the "dissenting Hebrew") may be appropriate (1982, 205–206).

[107] Note however that Koenig has already argued this thesis (1979, 47).

[108] The presence of the comma, or any other kind of punctuation (e.g. slash, colon, semi-colon, period), prevents such an interpretation since it produces "relative clauses or other constructions that do not limit the nouns they modify" (Gilliard 1989, 482); hence the second part of his article depends on the first.

phrases in a restrictive sense.[109] A problem arises however with his thorough-going identification of the various charges (vv. 15a–e) with *those* Jews, or more precisely, with different groups of Jews. Thus, for Gilliard, one group killed Jesus, one group killed the prophets (though possibly the same group), another drove Paul out, and still another group displeases God and opposes all men (498–500). But he concludes (500–501):

> The four or five groups, past and present, are logically not discrete, and Paul may have thought that some Jews belonged in more than one, even in every, group. In fact, given the anger that is rhetorically evident in this passage and given that only one article is expressed for the several participles, it is likely that Paul in no wise had clearly distinct groups or numbers in mind.

This is where Gilliard's thesis seems to unravel. The text makes no indication whatsoever that Paul was thinking of different groups when he wrote the series of charges in verse 15 (Broer 1991, 329); even Gilliard points out that there is only one article and therefore one long clause which defines οἱ Ἰουδαῖοι. The alternative, also seemingly advocated by Gilliard, is to take the charges as all referring to the same group of Jews. But the probability of this stretches the historical context of 1 Thess 2:13–16 to breaking point: Paul could not possibly be saying that the Jews who killed Jesus are the *same* Jews who killed the prophets, and that these Jews are the *same* Jews who drove Paul out *and* displease God *and* oppose all men (Simpson 1988, 144). The charges are too encompassing to limit the reference to just one group (Broer 1983, 74–75).[110] These problems have not been addressed by Malherbe who follows Gilliard without reservation (2000, 169).[111] Paul's understanding of οἱ Ἰουδαῖοι must be coloured by his contextual reference to the geographical location Ἰουδαία. Those Jews from Judea are in mind; i.e. Judeans. Thus, the group of Jews to which Paul refers is finite[112] — at least initially. But the text does not just give a geographical location. It goes on to specify particular charges some of which only particular Jews would have been guilty (e.g. vv. 15b, c) and some of which appear to be more general accusations (e.g. vv. 15d, e). Accordingly, some scholars argue for an opposite view to Gilliard's, that despite the specificity of some of the charges

---

[109] 1 Cor 2:6, 2 Cor 1:6 and 1 Thess 2:14 are the only problematic references sighted by Gilliard (1989, 490–491). However, see rebuttal by Verhoef (1995, 42–44).

[110] Sandmel highlights one aspect of the problem: "How broadly were 'the Jews' responsible? Were Jews in Alexandria in Egypt involved or those in Athens or in Galilee? The Sanhedrin numbered 71. Add leading priests, say 50. Add the crowd in Jerusalem, say 100. Can the total have been more than 250? The Jewish population of the world in the age of Jesus is estimated as between 2 and 4 million. Do the Christian Scriptures intend to convey that the Jews – all the Jews, of every age and region – killed Jesus?" (1978, 136); see Isaac 1964, 119–120. That a larger timeframe is in view is evident from the change of tense (aorist to present) in v. 15 (Broer 1991, 329).

[111] A number of other scholars are also entirely convinced by Gilliard's thesis: Feldman 1996, 285; Johanson 1995, 520; Smith 2000, 703; see Koenig 1979, 46–48.

[112] See Weatherly 1991, 85–86; so also Ben-Chorin 1980, 205; P.-G. Müller 2001, 145.

Paul's comments really encompass all Jews who reject the proclamation that Jesus is the *Kyrios*.[113]

In conclusion to this section on οἱ Ἰουδαῖοι, although the better translation may well be "the Judeans", with its emphasis on a geographical location, the context of 1 Thess 2:13–16 indicates a more general reference as well.[114] But "general reference" does not mean all Jews every where and of every time as if οἱ Ἰουδαῖοι is purely an ethnic designation. Rather, the essential thrust of the polemic is against all outsiders; it just so happens that these outsiders are Jews (deSilva 1996, 74).[115] This makes sense in view of Paul's apocalyptic orientation: a historical group of Jews, the Judeans, are typologically interpreted as representatives of those guilty of the charges outlined by Paul (Giblin 1970, 13; see Hurd 1986, 33–35). If this is the case, there is then no need to pedantically reconstruct groups of Jews who are to be held responsible for each individual charge (Simpson 1988, 142).

3. The first charge, against the Jews καὶ τὸν κύριον ἀποκτεινάντων Ἰησοῦν (v. 15a), is used by Pearson in his argument against authenticity. He supposes that such a charge with its blame directed at Jews is a post-70 C.E. development and provides numerous references to apostolic fathers who link the destruction of Jerusalem with God's punishment of Jews for the killing of Jesus (1971, 83–84; Beck 1994, 79). If authentic, then it remains a singular statement among Paul's letters. Actually, Acts is the only other NT document to make a similar claim (2:36; 3:15; 5:30; 7:52; 10:39) although the Gospels do portray that the Jews had a role to play in Jesus' death (Simpson 1988, 98–100). The discussion usually revolves around an apparent discrepancy between 1 Thess 2:15 and 1 Cor 2:8 where Paul comments that the rulers of this age (οἱ ἄρχοντες τοῦ αἰῶνος τούτου) crucified the Lord of glory (τὸν κύριον τῆς δόξης ἐσταύρωσαν). Again, Pearson serves as an example proponent of the argument against authenticity (1971, 85):

> [Paul] never attributes the death of Jesus to the Jews. 1 Corinthians 2:8 is the best example of Paul's own view: Jesus was brought to his death by the demonic "rulers of this age" who did not know that by so doing they would defeat themselves in the process. And even if one wants to take the phrase οἱ ἄρχοντες τοῦ αἰῶνος τούτου in 1 Corinthians 2:8 as a reference to purely human agencies, then one can credit Paul with historical accuracy in pointing to the Roman imperial authorities as responsible for the crucifixion rather than the Jewish people.

Unfortunately, Pearson does not acknowledge that the identification of οἱ ἄρχοντες is strongly disputed (Clarke 1993, 114–117). It is debated whether Paul is referring

[113] Davies 1978, 8; Hagner 1993, 133–134; Holtz 1989, 122–123; 1998, 103; Mussner 1984, 152; see Lamp 2003, 422–424; Meeks 1985, 105; Reinbold 1994, 291; Richard 1995, 120; Smith 2000, 703.

[114] Bruce 1982, 46; de Jonge 1979, 134; Still 1999, 41–42.

[115] See Holtz 1998, 103; Patte 1983, 126–127; *contra* Still 1999, 222.

to supernatural authorities,[116] human authorities[117] or a double reference to both.[118] The text is not clear enough to make a definitive judgment on the matter (Wenham 1995, 364); to be sure, no few scholars allow for 1 Cor 2:8 to include a reference to Jews,[119] or a more general reference.[120] As well, most scholars conclude as far as is possible to reconstruct from the Gospel accounts and other sources that there was some co-operation between Jewish and Roman authorities.[121] Consequently, it is possible that Paul emphasises one party (οἱ ἄρχοντες in 1 Cor 2:8) on one occasion and another party (οἱ Ἰουδαῖοι in 1 Thess 2:15) on a different occasion (Weatherly 1991, 84). Indeed οἱ ἄρχοντες is merely a larger group inclusive of some Ἰουδαῖοι. Flannery rightly comments that the problem of apportioning responsibility "is not properly the historian's task but one upon which he stumbles in presenting his materials" (1965, xiii). This is a welcome corrective to a discussion which often fails to account for the theological aspect of Jesus' execution. It is an eschatological event of divine salvation (Wenham 1995, 148; cf. 1 Thess 5:9–10) such that it is not so appropriate to attempt to apportion guilt therein (*contra* Blinzler 1959, 292–293). In conclusion, the first charge (v. 15a) may not be rejected as an interpolation.

4. The second charge is an extension of the first and also problematic: the Judeans also killed the prophets (καὶ τοὺς προφήτας, v. 15b). The word order of verse 15a – τῶν καὶ τὸν κύριον ἀποκτεινάντων Ἰησοῦν – makes sense only if the verb has a double object.[122] Hence the translation, "*both* the Lord Jesus and the prophets". The alternative, which takes οἱ προφῆται with the following verb (ἐκδιώκειν, v. 15c), is designed to alleviate the logical inconsistency of referring first to Jesus, then prophets (presumably OT prophets), then Paul (the expected order would be prophets, Jesus, Paul) rather than making the most sense of the word order.[123] The unusual rupture between ὁ κύριος and Ἰησοῦς should not be taken as evidence for a non-Pauline interpolation but as a way of emphasising the fact that Jesus is

[116] Barrett 1971, 70–72; Conzelmann 1975, 61; Davies 1984, 193; Delling 1964a, 489; Héring 1962, 16; Merk 1990, 168.

[117] Carr 1977; Fee 1987, 104; Horsley 1998, 58; Miller 1972; Parry 1926, 52.

[118] Cullmann 1957, 63; see Bruce 1982, 47; Thrall 1965, 25–26.

[119] Carr 1977, 21; Clarke 1993, 116; Fee 1987, 104; Parry 1926, 52; Robertson/Plummer 1911, 36–37; Weatherly 1991, 83; see Miller 1972, 528.

[120] Calvin 1960, 53; Horsley 1998, 58; Jewett 1986, 38.

[121] Crossan 1995, 147; Isaac 1964, 139; Parkes 1974, 46–47; Ward 1973, 73; Wenham 1995, 140–141; see Brown 1994, 328–397; Sanders 1985a, 286, 294–318; *contra* Isaac 1964, 140–144. Lenski goes too far when he says with reference to the killing of Jesus, "... the Jews forced the Gentile Pilate to act as their tool" (1937, 265).

[122] See Eadie 1877, 84–85; Fee 1994, 49; Michel 1967, 54.

[123] *Contra* Bornemann 1894, 111–112; Findlay 1904, 54; Thomas 1978, 259; see Milligan 1908, 30. Best observes that the aorist tense of ἐκδιώκειν is another reason for taking οἱ προφῆται with that verb. The past rather than present tense then makes sense – "who killed the Lord, i.e. Jesus, and persecuted the prophets and us" – even though he does not consider this the best solution (1972, 116). Rigaux (1956, 447) notes that the addition of a subject or object at the end of a phrase or clause is not uncommon in Paul (cf. καὶ τοῦ κυρίου in 1:6; καὶ ὁ θεός in 2:10). See von Dobschütz' extensive discussion (1909, 111–112); he takes οἱ προφῆται with ἀποκτείνειν.

none other than ὁ κύριος.[124] Alternatively, Gilliard argues that Ἰησοῦς should not be taken with ὁ κύριος but with οἱ προφῆται such that Ἰησοῦν καὶ τοὺς προφήτας becomes a parenthetical phrase added for emphasis. This explains the unusual word order of verse 15a and, if correct, would support the notion that Paul is referring to Christian prophets (1994, 266). This is one way to resolve the logical inconsistency alluded to (above): Paul refers to Jesus, then to Christian prophets and finally to Paul and his co-workers (so also Koenig 1979, 47; Thomas 1978, 260). Such candidates as John the Baptist, Stephen and James the son of Zebedee could be in Paul's mind when he refers to the charge of killing the prophets (Gilliard 1994, 263).[125] At least such an interpretation cannot, *a priori*, be ruled out (Dautzenberg 1997, 505; cf. 1 Thess 5:19–20).[126] Conversely, in light of the text's ambiguity, the opposite interpretation that Paul is referring to Jewish prophets must also be considered. Thus, the variant reading, τοὺς ἰδίους προφήτας "their own prophets",[127] is probably an early attempt to clarify the phrase — it would then refer to Jewish prophets.[128] Actually, regardless of difficulties in word order or logical consistency, the pervasive influence of Deuteronomic tradition on the development of early and later Christian thought is a convincing reason for understanding οἱ προφῆται as a reference to Jewish prophets.[129] Paul appears to refer to one aspect of that tradition, namely, to Israel's rejection of the message of the prophets and which often includes the perception that Israel also persecuted and killed them. Such a *perception* (whether any prophets were killed or not is irrelevant)[130] is pre-Christian in origin.[131] The widespread development of this tradition and its association with the killing of Jesus is clearly evident from a variety of different strands of tradition.[132] In conclu-

---

[124] Frame 1912, 111; Morris 1959, 90; Thomas 1978, 259. Furthermore, *contra* Schmidt (1983, 273), Weatherly is correct to point out other examples where a verb form separates a noun from an attributive adjective (1991, 95; cf. 1 Cor 7:7, 12; 10:4; 12:24; 2 Cor 7:5; Phil 2:20).

[125] Note however that the identification of the earliest Christian martyrs as "Christian prophets" is tenuous at best (Fee 1994, 49–50).

[126] For rebuttal, see Verhoef 1995, 45–46.

[127] Manuscript witnesses to this variant include D[1] Ψ 𝔐 sy; Mcion[T] (see NA[27]).

[128] Best 1972, 115; Malherbe 2000, 169; Morris 1959, 91; Ward 1973, 74; see Metzger 1994, 562.

[129] For discussion of the Deuteronomic tradition, see esp. Schoeps 1950, 126–143; Steck 1967; but see also Scott 1993; Schade 1984, 128–130.

[130] So Alford 1958, 260; Geiger 1986, 157; Pobee 1985, 70–71; see Freudmann 1994, 191–192; Sanders 1999, 275. Schlueter argues, in view of the lack of evidence that Jews actually killed any prophets, that Paul is exaggerating (1994, 67–68).

[131] For references to killing of the prophets, cf. 1 Kgs 19:10; Neh 9:26; Jer 2:30; Rom 11:3; cf. also *Jub.* 1:12; *1 En.* 89:51; *Mart. Ascen. Isa.* 5:1–14; for references to persecution of the prophets, cf. 2 Chr 36:16; Jer 9:7–9; Hos 9:7–9; Sir 49:7.

[132] Tuckett 1990, 167; see Broer 1983, 72–73; de Jonge 1988, 174; Hagner 1993, 135; Simpson 1990, 42. Thus, cf. Matt 23:34–36 (par.); 23:37–39 (par.); Mark 12:1–12 (par.; see explicit reference in Matt 21:46); Luke 13:33; Acts 7:52; Heb 11:36–38; *Barn.* 5.11. The last reference does not make an explicit link between the killing of Jesus and the prophets. However *Barn.* 5.11, which reads, οὐκοῦν ὁ υἱὸς τοῦ θεοῦ εἰς τοῦτο ἐν σαρκὶ ἦλθεν, ἵνα τὸ τέλειον τῶν ἁμαρτιῶν ἀνακεφαλαιώσῃ τοῖς διώξασιν ἐν θανάτῳ τοὺς προφήτας αὐτοῦ ("So then the Son of God came in the flesh for this reason, that he might complete the total of the sins of those who persecuted his prophets to death" [Lake 1912–1913]), does have striking

sion, it is probable that Paul capitalises on an established motif such that his reference to οἱ προφῆται is none other than to Jewish prophets.[133]

5. The third charge is more personal, καὶ ἡμᾶς ἐκδιωξάντων (v. 15c). The discussion revolves around who is signified by ἡμεῖς and how ἐκδιώκειν should be rendered. Regarding the first issue, ἡμεῖς could just as easily refer to Paul and his co-workers specifically,[134] to Paul and apostles generally (cf. 2:6; Schlueter 1994, 71–73), or to Paul and followers of Jesus even more generally (de Jonge 1979, 134). The first option, however, is most probable because Paul often employs the first person plural pronoun when referring to himself and his co-workers.[135] The second issue is difficult to resolve simply because ἐκδιώκειν (*hapax legomenon* in the NT)[136] can be legitimately rendered in different ways. BDAG has two descriptive definitions: (1) "to use tactics that cause the departure of someone from a place" and (2) "to annoy persistently" (301). But the distinction is not very helpful since definition two is a perfect example of the "tactics" mentioned in definition one although there may be a difference in motives. The question in 1 Thess 2:15 is whether Paul is referring to the action of persons being generally and persistently annoying, or else being persistently annoying with the express motive of driving him and his co-workers from their mission work. Several scholars argue that ἐκδιώκειν should be translated "to persecute",[137] because it fits with the theme of persecution of the prophets.[138] Yet, there are numerous reasons to opt for the translation "to drive out" (Tellbe 2001, 107): it is the more typical definition of the verb;[139] it makes sense of the sudden change to the aorist tense since it points to a specific event (Wanamaker 1990, 115); it accords with the passive voice of ἀπορφανίζειν in 2:17 which implies that Paul had no choice in the matter;[140] finally, it supports a reading of ἡμεῖς that refers to Paul and his co-workers rather than generally to followers of Jesus since these would not fulfil the circumstances of the charge (Still 1999, 132).

---

similarities to 1 Thess 2:16a, c. On the possible relationship between Paul and Q regarding the redaction of Deuteronomic tradition, see de Jonge 1988, 35; Kloppenborg 2000, 82–84; Wenham 1995, 321.

[133] Best 1972, 116; Sandnes 1991, 199–200; Steck 1967, 274–279; *contra* Schlueter 1994, 67–68.

[134] Best 1972, 116; Eadie 1877, 86; von Dobschütz 1909, 113. Schlueter rightly questions whether Timothy is included in this reference since he is an unlikely target for persecution because he is a non-Jew (so also Sanders 1996, 1940). She concludes: "While the Paul of Acts has Timothy circumcised, it is doubtful that the Paul of the letters would have done so (Gal. 2.3; 5.11; Phil. 3.3; 1 Cor. 7.18–20). Therefore, if Paul is implying that Timothy is part of the group being persecuted, he was exaggerating: as far as we know, the synagogue did not go about persecuting Gentiles for not obeying the Jewish law" (1994, 71).

[135] See Excursus 1 for discussion.

[136] Cf. textual variant in Luke 11:49.

[137] Balz 1990a, 408; Frame 1912, 112; Oepke 1964c, 230; Schlueter 1994, 69.

[138] Best 1972, 116; Ruether 1974, 90; cf. LXX of Ps 36:28; 43:17; 68:5; 118:157; Sir 30:19; *T. Jud.* 18:4.

[139] Richard 1995, 121; Still 1999, 134; cf. Deut 6:19; 1 Par 8:13; 12:16; Ps 100:5 (LXX); Jer 27:44; 30:13; Dan 4:25θ, 32θ, 33θ; 5:21θ; Joel 2:20; Thucydides 1.24.5; Demosthenes *Zenoth.* 6; Aristotle *Hist. an.* 8(9).31; Josephus *C. Ap.* 1.292; Lucian *Tim.* 10.

[140] *Contra* Freudmann (1994, 208) and Schlueter (1994, 68–70), this is possible evidence for Paul being driven from Thessalonica.

6. The fourth and fifth charges, καὶ θεῷ μὴ ἀρεσκόντων καὶ πᾶσιν ἀνθρώποις ἐναντίων (vv. 15d, e), are often construed to be examples of the kind of anti-Jewish polemic that Paul would never use (Baur 1875, 87; Pearson 1971, 83, 85). Closer scrutiny reveals however that ἀρέσκειν is a verb commonly used by Paul.[141] Its occurrence in 2:4 and 4:1 provides a contrast to 2:15; the present tense for all three occurrences shows that Paul considers "pleasing God" to be an ongoing activity (Best 1972, 117). For Paul, who is seeking to present the gospel (cf. 2:4, 16a), opposition to him (2:15e, 16a) is taken to be not pleasing to God (2:15d; Broer 1983, 80–81). In this context then, the charge that οἱ Ἰουδαῖοι do not please God is a specific statement about the actions of those Jews who seek to hinder Paul's mission to the *ethnē* (2:16a–b; Richard 1995, 121; Simpson 1988, 119). Paul probably relies on statements used traditionally as non-Jewish anti-Semitic slander. But his reformulation is not slander but polemic.[142] Thus, when he says that οἱ Ἰουδαῖοι are πᾶσιν ἀνθρώποις ἐναντίων this is to be understood to refer to "all" those who are hindering his mission to the *ethnē* (Malherbe 2000, 176).[143] Malherbe's statement that such polemic is theological rather than sociological may underemphasise the negative social interaction Paul must have had with his opponents (2000, 170).[144] It is possible to observe the differences between Jews and non-Jews without necessarily making anti-Jewish implications (Haacker 1988, 408). Thus, Simpson argues that it is substantially more correct to refer to verse 15e as a well-known slogan rather than as a piece of anti-Jewish polemic — this acknowledges that descriptions of the Jews could be and were put to different uses (1988, 106).[145]

d. God's *Orgē* Is Going to Come (2:16)

1. The last verse of this section begins with an explanation of why οἱ Ἰουδαῖοι are "against all men" and concludes with an enigmatic, if not ardent, eschatological pronouncement. The analysis now turns, increasingly, towards eschatological *topoi* including the proclamation of the gospel to non-Jews (τὰ ἔθνη), salvation (σωτηρία), sin/s (ἁμαρτία/ι) and *orgē* (ὀργή), to name a few. Thus, Paul provides the substance of the conflict, κωλυόντων ἡμᾶς τοῖς ἔθνεσιν λαλῆσαι (v. 16a), with an attendant

---

[141] Rom 8:8; 15:1, 2, 3; 1 Cor 7:32, 33, 34; 10:33; Gal 1:10; 1 Thess 2:4, 15; 4:1; cf. 2 Cor 5:9; 2 Tim 2:4.

[142] Flannery 1965, 7–8; Haacker 1988, 407–408; Johanson 1995, 520; see Boring/Berger/Colpe 1995, 492; Schaller 1998, 557; cf. also Diodorus Siculus 34.1; Josephus *C. Ap.* 2.148; Tacitus *Ann.* 15.44; *Hist.* 5.5; Juvenal *Sat.* 14.96–106; Philostratus *Vit. Apoll.* 5.33. Conzelmann provides numerous other references (1992, 45–49).

[143] Alford 1958, 260–261; Baumbach 1983, 70. Kampling amply shows that this is how the polemic was understood by the church fathers (1993).

[144] See Hurd 1986, 34–35. In an article on Christian anti-Judaism, Blanchetière examines the nature of the Jewish-Christian split as predominately socio-cultural rather than "religious" (1998, 194–198).

[145] For extensive primary references to various attitudes towards the Jews, see Whittaker 1984, 14–35; see also Daniel (1979, 47–48) for a short list of positive references regarding Jews.

ἵνα-clause, ἵνα σωθῶσιν (v. 16b), where the verb σῴζειν immediately invokes a link to 1:10 and 5:9 (§III.d.2). He then supplies the results of the hindering, ἀναπληρῶσαι αὐτῶν τὰς ἁμαρτίας πάντοτε (v. 16c), and uses traditional wording to do so (§III.d.3). The concluding clause, ἔφθασεν δὲ ἐπ' αὐτοὺς ἡ ὀργὴ εἰς τέλος (v. 16d), must be analysed as a whole even though there are extensive discussions centring on each of three components: φθάνειν, ἡ ὀργή and εἰς τέλος. That is, the translation and interpretation of the phrase is greatly effected by the results of each of those discussions (§III.d.4–7). Forthwith, there is a short conclusion to round out the analysis of this verse as well as a preliminary synthesis of the analysis of verses 15–16 (§III.d.8).

2. There is no successive καί for the participle κωλυόντων which indicates that it is subordinate to the preceding charge[146] and perhaps even to the fourth charge (Haufe 1999, 47; Still 1999, 136). Again, ἡμεῖς (v. 16a; cf. v. 15c) refers to Paul and his co-workers (Still 1999, 136; Wanamaker 1990, 115). Why οἱ Ἰουδαῖοι are thought to be hindering Paul's mission – probably because of his proclamation of a law-free gospel to the *ethnē* (see Broer 1983, 82; Sanders 1996, 1938–1939) – is not as important as the recognition that Paul is not referring to an isolated incident but to an attitude of opposition against his whole missionary proclamation and therefore (for Paul) against God himself.[147] Although a connection would be tempting in view of Paul's subsequent letters, Donaldson is right to reject any causal link between the *orgē* experienced by οἱ Ἰουδαῖοι and the offer of salvation to the *ethnē*. Thus, the Jewish activity is a response to, and not a cause of, Paul's mission to the *ethnē* (1997, 227).[148] Paul's purpose is no less than the salvation of the *ethnē* (ἵνα σωθῶσιν, v. 16b);[149] and this motivation is personal and probably does not reflect traditional material.[150] In this connection Paul becomes an agent or initiator of salvation, so to speak.[151] The significance of verse 16b should not be underestimated — it carries eschatological implications in that σῴζειν is primarily a future occurrence for Paul.[152] It is possible that Paul has 1 Thess 1:10 and 5:9 in

[146] Best 1972, 117; Malherbe 2000, 170; Wanamaker 1990, 115.

[147] This is emphasised by the change to the present tense. It is important however to realise that the persecution the Judean *ekklēsiai* underwent may have been for an entirely different reason (Sanders 1985a, 282). See analogous use of κωλύειν in Luke 11:52 (Légasse 1991a, 333).

[148] Wenham 1995, 301; see de Lacey 1993, 337–338; *contra* Scott 1993, 656–657. "It is not until Romans, probably the last of Paul's surviving letters, that he reflects on the failure of the mission to Israel. It is striking that the charge against the Jews in 1 Thess. 2:14–16 has nothing to do with their rejecting Paul's gospel. Their fault, rather, was opposing Paul's mission to the Gentiles" (Sanders 1985, 184). On the relationship between Israel's rejection and the Gentile mission, see Donaldson 1993, esp. 87.

[149] Cf. Rom 10:1; 11:14; 1 Cor 9:22; 10:33; Foerster 1971, 992. Whether the clause expresses purpose or result is debated. Some commentators suggest both here (Best 1972, 118; Wanamaker 1990, 116).

[150] Davies 1978, 7; see Gaston 1991, 311. Note the recurrence of the theme of hindrance in 2:18, although there Paul uses ἐγκόπτειν.

[151] Morris 1993, 859; O'Collins 1992, 910; Radl 1993, 319.

[152] Foerster 1971, 992; Larsson 1985, 620; see Bammel 1959, 308; Frame 1912, 112–113; Richardson 1969, 105. Of the nineteen references to σῴζειν in Paul, seven are future passive indicative forms (Rom 5:9, 10; 9:27; 10:9, 13; 11:26; 1 Cor 3:15; cf. 1 Tim 2:15), three are future active indicative forms (Rom 11:14;

mind (Best 1972, 118) or else that he is thinking of the future life (cf. 2:12).[153] If so, the denouncement of verse 16d would be doubly acerbic in contrast to the salvation from *orgē* offered to the *ethnē*.[154] Otherwise, the immediate context of his mission emphasises that σῴζειν initially refers to membership in the *ekklēsia* and thus ἐν Χριστῷ (cf. 1:1; 4:16; 5:18) and only subsequently to one's destiny (θεῖναι, 5:9; Radl 1993, 321).

3. Although the consensus is that Paul more or less depends on tradition – regarding the formulation, εἰς τὸ ἀναπληρῶσαι αὐτῶν τὰς ἁμαρτίας πάντοτε (v. 16c) – there is little agreement as to his source(s). Thus, Orchard (1938), Schippers (1966) and Wenham (1981) for example, argue that there are direct parallels between 1 Thess 2:15–16 and Matt 23:29–38 (or at least vv. 32–36). Conversely, Tuckett (1990) rejects as "insignificant ... any clear link between Paul and the synoptic tradition at this point" (167; see Rigaux 1956, 445–446). It cannot be denied however that Matt 23:32–36 shows some similarities.[155] Orchard (1938, 20–21) and Schippers (1966, 232) highlight four words shared between 1 Thess 2:15–16 and Matt 23:32–36: ἀποκτείνειν (1 Thess 2:15a; Matt 23:34; cf. v. 37); προφήτης (1 Thess 2:15b; Matt 23:31, 34; cf. v. 37); (ἐκ)διώκειν (1 Thess 2:15c; Matt 23:34); (ἀνα)πληροῦν (1 Thess 2:16c; Matt 23:32). Furthermore, Orchard points out the following similarities in thought sequence:[156]

	1 Thess 2:15–16		Matt 23:32–36
2:15c	οἱ Ἰουδαῖοι τῶν ... καὶ ἡμᾶς ἐκδιωξάντων	23:34	... καὶ διώξετε ἀπὸ πόλεως εἰς πόλιν
2:16c	εἰς τὸ ἀναπληρῶσαι αὐτῶν τὰς ἁμαρτίας πάντοτε	23:32	καὶ ὑμεῖς πληρώσατε τὸ μέτρον τῶν πατέρων ὑμῶν
2:15a–b	οἱ Ἰουδαῖοι τῶν καὶ τὸν κύριον ἀποκτεινάντων Ἰησοῦν καὶ τοὺς προφήτας	23:34	ἐγὼ ἀποστέλλω πρὸς ἡμᾶς προφήτας ... ἐξ αὐτῶν ἀποκτενεῖτε καὶ σταυρώσετε
2:16d	ἔφθασεν δὲ ἐπ' αὐτοὺς ἡ ὀργὴ εἰς τέλος	23:36	ἀμὴν λέγω ὑμῖν, ἥξει ταῦτα πάντα ἐπὶ τὴν γενεὰν ταύτην

1 Cor 7:16*bis*; cf. 1 Tim 4:16; 2 Tim 4:18), one is a present passive indicative form (1 Cor 15:2) and one is an aorist passive indicative form (Rom 8:24; cf. Titus 3:5); even this last passage has a reference to hope (cf. also v. 25). Thus, even though the past tense looks to the beginning of the Christian life there is also a future orientation looking to a future fulfilment (Morris 1993, 860; see O'Collins 1992, 911; Sanders 1977, 449). The remaining references are to verbs whose moods do not convey a temporal element (1 Cor 1:18, 21; 5:5; 9:22; 10:33; 2 Cor 2:15; 1 Thess 2:16; cf. Eph 2:5, 8; 1 Tim 1:15; 2:4; 2 Tim 1:9).

[153] Wanamaker 1990, 116; i.e. against 1 Thess 1:10, "σώζειν ist positiver" (von Dobschütz 1909, 114).

[154] "The biblical texts focus on the Gentiles as the objects of divine wrath, but Paul's expression identifies the Jews as the object of divine wrath. Might we not see in this a kind of eschatological reversal?" (Collins 1991a, 145–146); similarly, Best 1972, 121; Johanson 1995, 529.

[155] Konradt comments that the affinity between the texts is "jedenfalls frappierend" (2003, 81).

[156] See Johanson 1995, 523–524; Wanamaker 1990, 116. Neirynck (1986, 279–281) also supports a link between Paul and the gospel tradition. He reproduces the text of 1 Thess 2:15–16 (and 4:14–17 and 5:1–7 for that matter) and lists parallels to the Synoptics. Even Pearson observes parallels though he uses them to argue for a post-70 C.E. historical situation for 1 Thess 2:13–16 (1971, 92–94).

At least the Matthean verses seem to give a telescopic view of Jewish history not unlike 1 Thess 2:15–16 (Wenham 1981, 361–362). Thus, those whose fathers had shed the blood of prophets before them (Matt 23:30) were guilty of the same acts such that these crimes fill up the measure of righteous blood (cf. v. 35). The parallel passage, Luke 11:47–52, makes this aspect (of culminating judgment) even more specific: ἵνα ἐκζητηθῇ τὸ αἷμα πάντων τῶν προφητῶν τὸ ἐκκεχυμένον ἀπὸ καταβολῆς κόσμου ἀπὸ τῆς γενεᾶς ταύτης (v. 50). It is not necessary to demand "direct parallels" or insist on a common tradition between the Matthean and Pauline texts (*contra* Goulder 1974, 165), whether as part of a (pre-synoptic?) πληροῦν tradition or not. Rather the similarities may be explained by independent use of stereotypical material — and the situation in which Paul found himself made it appropriate here.[157]

The construction εἰς τό + infinitive signifies either a purpose or result clause; the presence of πάντοτε suggests the latter.[158] Paul can use this adverb because he is not thinking of all Jews in general but of a group who "always" acts contrariwise to God (Broer 1990, 154–155; Simpson 1988, 148). Although Paul often uses this type of construction to express purpose, and even though such an interpretation would fit well with the election motif (ἐκλογή) in Rom 9:11 and 11:5, 7, 28 (cf. 1 Thess 1:4), the context does not warrant such a determinative interpretation here. There is no hint (in First Thessalonians) that God is arranging a predetermined Jewish response to Paul's mission.[159] Paul makes these charges and conclusions against οἱ Ἰουδαῖοι as a result of his experience in Thessalonica and elsewhere.[160] However, the filling of their sins to the full measure is not something οἱ Ἰουδαῖοι are looking to do and it is in this sense that Paul expresses the result of hindering as a component of God's purpose.[161] It is not surprising that Paul refers to sins in the plural (αἱ ἁμαρτίαι, v. 16c) — although ἡ δύναμις τῆς ἁμαρτίας (1 Cor 15:56) is principal to Paul's view of sin. Outside of Romans the programmatic singular appears only at 1 Cor 15:56, Gal 2:17 and 3:22 (Dunn 1998, 111).[162] To be sure, he refers to the plural a number of times.[163] With relation to the connection between the filling up of sins and the hindering of Paul's missionary efforts, it is instructive to note that

[157] Cf. Gen 15:16; Jer 32:34; Dan 4:34; 8:23; 9:24; 11:36; 2 Macc 6:14–15; Wis 19:4; Herm. *Vis.* 2.2.2. See Davies 1978, 7–8; Donfried 1984, 248–249; Hübner 1993, 109; Malherbe 2000, 174–175; Orchard 1938, 20–23; Schippers 1966, 232–233; Tuckett 1990, 165–167; Wenham 1995, 321.

[158] Best 1972, 118; see *GGBB* 594; *contra GNTG* vol. 3, 143; Morris 1959, 91.

[159] *Contra* Alford 1958, 261; Frame 1912, 113; Marshall 1983, 80; Milligan 1908, 31; Morris 1959, 91; Stuhlmann 1983, 105; von Dobschütz 1909, 114; Ward 1973, 75.

[160] Green 2002, 147; Lenski 1937, 267; Malherbe 2000, 176; Richard 1995, 122; Richardson 1969, 103; Stott 1991, 56.

[161] Auberlen/Riggenbach 1869, 42; Denney 1892, 90; Eadie 1877, 88–89; Frame 1912, 113; Malherbe 2000, 170–171; Thomas 1978, 259; Wanamaker 1990, 116; see Bammel 1959, 308.

[162] The references to the singular form in 2 Cor 5:21 and 11:7 refer to a change of reign (then under sin, now under righteousness of God) and to committing particular sins, respectively (Fiedler 1990, 67).

[163] Cf. Rom 3:25; 4:7; 7:5; 11:27; 1 Cor 15:3, 17; Gal 1:4; 1 Thess 2:16; cf. also Eph 2:1; Col 1:14; 1 Tim 5:22, 24; 2 Tim 3:6.

Paul's own imperfection arises, διότι ἐδίωξα τὴν ἐκκλησίαν τοῦ θεοῦ (1 Cor 15:9; cf. also Gal 1:23; Phil 3:6). At least from a present and practical viewpoint αἱ ἁμαρτίαι emphasises the breakdown of human relationships and active hostility to God.[164] Thus, Paul may refer to a quantity of sins in the sense that there is a predetermined number after which comes judgment.[165] Otherwise, keeping in mind Paul's view of sin (sing.), there is a continuity of sins in the past and present such that Paul expresses that the complete filling of these sins is accomplished.[166] That Paul leaves no room for completing this fulfilment of sins – it is accomplished already – bears witness to the immediacy of *orgē* (Simpson 1988, 286; 1990, 45).

4. The verb φθάνειν appears seven times in the NT.[167] According to BDAG there are three descriptive definitions for it: (1) "to be beforehand in moving to a position"; (2) "to get to or reach a position"; (3) "to come to or arrive at a particular state" (1053, §1–3). Virtually all commentators agree that 1 Thess 4:15 contains the only NT reference to the first definition; hence, "to come before", "to precede". More to the point, such a transitive definition is entirely ruled out in 1 Thess 2:16d because there is no direct object.[168] Paul uses the third definition, translated "to attain", in Rom 9:31 and Phil 3:16. This leaves the other references (arguably) for the second definition, usually translated "to come", "to arrive", "to reach" (Fitzer 1974, 90). Actually, there is extensive literature on the semantic range of φθάνειν — but with specific reference to its contact with ἐγγίζειν in the formulations, ἡ βασιλεία τοῦ θεοῦ[169] and ἡ βασιλεία τῶν οὐρανῶν.[170] That specific and technical discussion is beyond the scope of this analysis although it is instructive to take note of the apparent ambiguity of the verb. The proposed distinction between the *arrival* of the kingdom and the *coming* of the kingdom – giving rise to the term "realised" (a term used to sustain an uncomfortable juxtaposition between the present and future) – is difficult to maintain.[171] Thus for example, the Aramaic מְטָא (BDB 1100) in Dan 4:11, 22 (MT) is translated with ἐγγίζειν in Dan 4:11, 22 (LXX) but with φθάνειν in Dan 4:11θ, 22θ (Berkey 1963, 179–182). Moving back to φθάνειν in 1 Thess 2:16, it is not possible to prove whether or not the verb signifies nearness or actual

---

[164] Grundmann 1964a, 308–309; see Dunn 1998, 124; Morris 1993a, 877.

[165] Best 1972, 118; Simpson 1988, 146; see Pobee 1985, 89; cf. Gen 15:16; Dan 8:23; 2 Macc 6:14.

[166] Broer 1983, 82–83; Bruce 1982, 48; so Delling: "... the reference here is not to the extreme limit of God's patience after the attainment of which His wrathful judgment will break on pious Judaism, but to the constant (πάντοτε) augmentation of sin by Judaism in its conflict with the free Gentile mission" (1968, 306); see Milligan 1908, 31; Smith 2000, 704.

[167] Matt 12:28 (par. Luke 11:20); Rom 9:31; 2 Cor 10:14; Phil 3:16; 1 Thess 2:16; 4:15; cf. προφθάνειν in Matt 17:25.

[168] Eadie 1877, 89; Richard 1995, 122; cf. τοὺς κοιμηθέντας in 1 Thess 4:15 (BDAG 1053, §1). Buck/Taylor (1969, 147) have missed this point since they insist on an anticipatory meaning. Their translation for v. 16d, "But the wrath for the end has come upon them ahead of time!", stands alone.

[169] Matt 12:28 (par. Luke 11:20); Mark 1:15; Luke 10:9, 11.

[170] Matt 3:2; 4:17; 10:7. For an introduction to ἐγγίζειν (and ἐγγύς), see Kümmel 1961, 19–25.

[171] For a classic statement of a "realised" kingdom of God, see Dodd 1935; Kümmel 1961. Gräßer's discussion of the "Gegenwart und Zukunft der Gottesherrschaft" (1974, 21–26) is illustrative of the difficulty; see with reference to ἔφθασεν, esp. 22–23.

contact (*contra* Clark 1940). As Clark himself has shown (though unintentionally), even if the original sense of definition one (above) has *not* been lost (55–57; but see MM 666–667), the use of φθάνειν cannot be limited to a meaning of nearness in view of the varied uses of the verb.[172] Berkey concludes: "Imminent nearness and actual arrival do frequently overlap; thus it is extremely difficult to speak of the one without also speaking of the other, and practical distinctions break down" (1963, 184). How then, is φθάνειν in 1 Thess 2:16 to be translated? First, the syntax of verse 16d must be analysed particularly with reference to both prepositional phrases: ἐπ' αὐτούς acts as an adverbial qualifier while εἰς τέλος appears to furnish a temporal quality (see further discussion below). Second, Fitzer notes that definitions two and three (above) are especially clear in texts which have a temporal element (1974, 88–89).[173]

The *crux interpretum* is unquestionably the aorist tense. The problem is not in the aorist itself since Paul always uses that tense of φθάνειν but with its translation in context. What does Paul mean when he says, "the *orgē* came on them ..."; or, "the *orgē* reached them"?[174] To what is he referring? Can Paul refer to *orgē* as a contemporary event or *zeitgeschichtliches Ereignis*? I think not, or at least not exclusively (see §III.d.5 below). But in order to examine the arguments of many of my conversation partners it is necessary to explore this alternative — namely, that φθάνειν refers to an event (or events) in Paul's (and the Thessalonians') past. For some, there is no doubt that the destruction of the temple is the obvious and only candidate.[175] Thus, so the argument goes, since Paul did not make the reference clear the only candidate for an unambiguous historical reference must be to 70 C.E. Hence 1 Thess 2:16d is an interpolation. But if existing interpolation theories are taken as unconvincing this argument can be turned on its head such that (in view of its authenticity) φθάνειν must not have a historical reference at all since there is no obvious candidate (see §III.d.6 below).[176] Alternatively, and rightly, Hurd rejects the assumption that the author (Paul or an interpolator) must have

---

[172] So Johanson 1995, 521; *contra* Best 1972, 119; Thomas 1978, 260. But neither can it be made to mean (exclusively) arrival, as if it were synonymous with ἐγγίζειν (*contra* Dodd 1935, 43–44). The article by Clark (1940) is invaluable for its copious references to ἐγγίζειν and φθάνειν in papyri, pseudepigrapha, Philo and Plutarch; see also Kümmel 1961, 105–109.

[173] E.g. 1 Esd 3:1; 2 Esd 7:73 (ὁ μὴν ὁ ἕβδομος); 2 Par 28:9; Eccl 12:1; Dan 4:11θ; 6:25θ; 7:13θ; 8:7θ (ἕως); Cant 2:12; Dan 7:22θ ([ὁ] καιρός); Dan 12:12θ (εἰς ἡμέρας).

[174] It is curious that scholars universally avoid these two renderings for v. 16d (see for example, Marshall 1983, 82; Milligan 1908, 32; similarly, Giblin 1970, 14; Hasler 1993, 422; Okeke 1981, 130). Although the context does warrant a different translation I find it helpful to consider these alternatives. The perfect variant ἔφθακεν (see NA[27] for mss. evidence) is an attempt to remove the harshness of the statement (Best 1972, 121; Metzger 1994, 563). The evident need to resolve the *crux* of the aorist drives some scholars to support this variant reading (so Jowett 1859, 63; Munck 1967, 63) even though the textual witnesses favour the aorist.

[175] Baur 1875, 88, 340; Moffatt 1910, 29; Orchard 1938, 22; Pearson 1971, 83; Scott 1909, 228–229; see Schoeps 1950, 144–183, esp. 154.

[176] So Best 1972, 120; Simpson 1988, 154. Hengel/Barrett are not convinced that any text of the NT explicitly refers to that event; they make no reference to 1 Thess 2:16 (1999, 32–33).

been referring to "the most obvious candidate" (i.e. the destruction of the temple). Clearly, in the absence of a clear referent in the text *any* number of events known to the Thessalonians *could* have been in Paul's view here (1986, 35).[177] Suggested candidates are wide-ranging:[178] the destruction of the temple in 587 B.C.E. (Scott 1993, 652); the death of Jesus in 27–32 C.E.;[179] the aftermath of the death of Herod Agrippa I in 43/44 C.E. (Bacon 1922, 360);[180] the insurrection of Theudas under Cuspius Fadus in 44–46 C.E.;[181] the famine in Judea under Claudius in 46–47 C.E. (Buck/Taylor 1969, 148–149);[182] the disturbance among the Jews in Jerusalem under the Roman governor Ventidius Cumanus during the Passover of 49 C.E. (Bruce 1982, 46);[183] the expulsion of the Jews from Rome under Claudius in 49/50 C.E.;[184] the renewed Zelotic terror in 50–52 C.E. (Gaston 1970, 456). Of these, the destruction of 587 B.C.E. seems rather remote, the event of Jesus' death would be a novel way of understanding *orgē* (Schlueter 1994, 59) and there is some debate about the relevance of the Jewish expulsion from Rome since it appears to have had nothing to do with the persecution of Christians in Judea.[185] Jewett concludes: "the important fact is that there were large-scale disasters that someone might have described in terms of wrath upon the Jews at the time of writing 1 Thessalonians" (1986, 38).[186]

---

[177] The acceptance or rejection of a reference to the destruction of the temple is tied to whether one views this passage to be an interpolation or not — unless of course, Paul is making a prophetic/proleptic announcement (see discussion below).

[178] For discussions of various events, including natural phenomena, and political and social occurrences during the period prior to the writing of First Thessalonians, see McLaren 1998, 21–35, esp. 127–149 (history of research on Judea); Rhoads 1976, 47–93; Smallwood 1981, 144–292.

[179] Cranfield 1979, 218–219; Donfried 1984, 252; Lamp 2003, 426.

[180] Cf. Josephus *Ant.* 19.343–350; Acts 12:20–23; see Schwartz 1990, 145–175. Incidentally, Bacon's thesis about the significance of 12 years after the crucifixion is ingenious but not convincing (1922, 372–376), although he is followed by Johnson (1941).

[181] Cf. Josephus *Ant.* 20.97–99; see Smallwood 1981, 257–263.

[182] As partial support for their choice, Buck/Taylor note that famine is one of the traditional "woes of the end" (cf. Mark 13:8; Rom 8:35) and makes excellent sense in view of the context. It appears that the famine in Judea (cf. Josephus *Ant.* 20.51–53, 101; 3.320–321; Eusebius *Hist. eccl.* 2.3, 8, 12; Orosius *Hist.* 7.6.12) occurred about a year after a severe famine in Egypt (cf. Pliny *Nat.* 5.58; Strabo 17.1.3–4). Gapp provides a cogent argument for taking the proclamation of a great famine in Acts 11:27–30 to be a reference to these conjoining occurrences (1935); see also Kasher 1988, 192–194; 1990, 245–254; Leaney 1984, 113–114; Wortham 1995, 40.

[183] Cf. Josephus *Ant.* 20.105–117; *B.J.* 2.223–231; see Green 2002, 149; Jewett 1971a, 205; Smallwood 1981, 263–269; Wenham 1995, 300. The statistics of 20 000 (*Ant.* 20.112) and 30 000 (*B.J.* 2.227) given for the incident by Josephus are probably exaggerations.

[184] Cf. Suetonius *Claud.* 25.4; Acts 18:2; so Bammel 1959, 295–301; Brown 1994, 380; Green 2002, 149; Wenham 1995, 300–301.

[185] Best 1972, 120; Broer 1990, 149–150; Jewett 1971a, 205; 1986, 37–38; Wenham 1995, 300–301; see esp. Pobee who builds a case against such a reference (1985, 90).

[186] This is disputed by Johanson 1995, 522. Further, von Dobschütz is against this view: "Die mannigfachen Versuche der Exegese, ihn auf ein bestimmtes historisches Ereignis zu beziehen, zeigen nur die Unmöglichkeit präteritaler Auffassung ..." (1909, 116).

5. A few scholars however are not convinced that φθάνειν refers to the past at all, particularly because of the questionable identification of *orgē* with a contemporary event. If it can be shown that Paul's reference to *orgē* is predominately to the future then this will nullify the problem of finding a suitable historical event to which Paul is referring (Steck 1967, 276–277). An introduction to Paul's understanding of *orgē* has already been presented in the analysis of 1 Thess 1:10 (Chapter 3, §III.b.7). There is little doubt *à propos* the present and future orientation of the concept. But which is predominate here in 2:16? Wanamaker proposes that the presence of the definite article (ἡ ὀργή) suggests a reference to 1:10 and therefore an emphasis on the future aspect (1990, 117).[187] Yet the use of the article may have been Paul's custom.[188] Indeed the only two indefinite references to ὀργή are Rom 2:8 and 4:15 and these can hardly be to anything other than part of the ὀργὴ θεοῦ discussion beginning in Rom 1:18.[189] Rather than attempting to find a specific reference to the past some scholars look to a hardening motif in Romans.[190] Thus, the act of hindering (1 Thess 2:16a) and the completion of the full measure of sins (v. 16c) are evidences of divine hardening in the present.[191] But such an explanation seems excessively dependent on Romans and tangential to the purposes of Paul in this letter (Best 1972, 119; Schlueter 1994, 57) although there is a clear link between the act of hindering and *orgē* (Richardson 1969, 104).[192] Perhaps the discussion may be simplified by observing that past or present *orgē* does not inevitably admit a contemporary reference.[193] It is possible that Paul is referring to eschatological categories of a culminating salvation history (positive) and an imminent day of judgment (negative; Geiger 1986, 157; Holtz 1998, 106). Hence, moving the discussion away from a distinction between past, present and future, Kuck (1992, 223–225) is able to distinguish between Paul's references to judgment designed to bolster his followers' confidence in their own salvation (1 Thess 1:10; 5:2–5, 9) and references used to denounce opponents or outsiders (1 Thess 2:16; 4:6).[194] In

[187] So also Best 1972, 119; see Johanson 1995, 522.

[188] Cf. Rom 3:5; 5:9; 9:22; 12:19; 13:5; 1 Thess 1:10.

[189] The other references to *orgē* are made definite from the prepositional phrases in which they appear: Rom 2:5 (ἐν); 13:4; 1 Thess 5:9 (εἰς). For a discussion of Rom 1:18, see Eckstein 1987. He makes some pertinent comments regarding the future aspect of *orgē* (esp. 82–86).

[190] Cf. σκληρότης (2:5); σκληρύνειν (9:18); πωροῦν (11:7; cf. 2 Cor 3:14); πώρωσις (11:25).

[191] Brown 1994, 380; Dunn 1998, 507; Munck 1967, 63–64; Wanamaker 1990, 117; Wenham 1995, 301; Witherington 1992, 103, 111.

[192] Wenham argues that there is a "three-way parallelism" between 1 Thess 2:16, Rom 11:25 and Luke 21:23, 24 (1995, 321–326).

[193] *Contra* Dahl 1977, 137; Elias 1992, 125–126; Kvalbein 2000, 57. Wenham may be correct in his assessment that Rom 13:4–5 is an example of an "in-history" reference to *orgē* (1995, 300). Lehnert provides numerous references to *orgē* as a present reality (2002, 19). But this does nothing to prove that 1 Thess 2:16 is of the same type of reference. Thus, rightly: "... wenn Paulus sonst von Gottes Zorn redet, meint er nie ein geschichtliches Ereignis" (Reinmuth 1998, 130). Broer argues that Paul's view does not reflect "ein zeitgeschichtliches Ereignis" (1990, 157); so also Dibelius 1925, 11; Thomas 1978, 261.

[194] For further discussion of the parallels between 2:16 and 4:6, see Wick 1994, 21–22. The idea that *orgē* is not remedial but retributive is well developed by Crockett (1991).

this sense, *orgē* is neither past, nor present, nor future; it is eschatological (Broer 1990, 151–153). The temporal qualification provides an implication of Paul's spatial relation to the *eschaton* — the aorist tense in verse 16d is an explicit statement to the Thessalonians that the consummation of the end is at hand (Watson 1999, 68).[195] As well, the aorist demonstrates that God's *orgē* is inevitably decided.[196]

6. So far in the discussion it has been assumed (and this is the assumption of the vast majority of commentators working on this passage) that the aorist signification of φθάνειν demands a past-time reference. In particular, the examination of possible *zeitgeschichtliche Ereignisse* to which Paul could be referring works towards this end (§III.d.4 above). The conclusion of the discussion in the last section (§III.d.5 above), however, proposes that Paul's conception of *orgē* resists a purely past, present or future connotation. The context indicates a future reference but ἔφθασεν seems to block this interpretation. The aim of this section of the discussion is to demonstrate the *possibility* that the aorist signification can encompass a future-time. Whether this is *probable* or not depends very much on the entire discussion at hand – not to mention the phrase εἰς τέλος (§III.d.7 below) – and such argument is reserved for the conclusion (§III.d.8 below).

The fact that the tense of a Greek verb refers primarily to aspect (i.e. imperfective, aoristic, perfective) rather than to time (i.e. past, present, future), so often pointed out by Greek grammarians of the NT,[197] is often neglected in exegetical discussions. There are all sorts of uses for the aorist tense, including (not exhaustive): ingressive, effective, constative, gnomic, epistolary, dramatic and prophetic/proleptic aorists.[198] None of these uses necessarily demands a decision as to the time of action of the verb. Indeed Porter argues that the time of action is entirely *independent* of the verb form and must be established on other grammatical grounds, i.e. "at the level of larger grammatical or conceptual units, such as the sentence, paragraph, proposition, or even discourse" (1994, 21; see also Dana/Mantey 1955, 200). The precise relationship between tense form and aspect of a verb is not at issue here.[199] Even if only a partial severing between tense and time of action is admitted this means that there is scope for discussion regarding the time of action of ἔφθασεν despite its aorist tense form (Black 1998, 105).

Before moving directly to a discussion of 1 Thess 2:16d, it is first instructive to examine other instances of the aorist where there may be a future (i.e. prophetic/

[195] See Gaston 1970, 456–457; Pobee 1985, 89–90; Roetzel 1972, 79–81.

[196] Broer 1983, 85; Bruce 1982, 48; Morris 1959, 92. In this connection, one of Bammel's reasons for finding an event in the past as a reference to *orgē* is because Paul cannot otherwise be so certain about the Jewish fate (1959, 308).

[197] See Black 1994, 9–15; Porter 1994, 20–49; *GGBB* 494–512. For a more extensive discussion of verbal aspect, see Fanning 1990; Porter 1989.

[198] In this discussion "prophetic" and "proleptic" are used synonymously. Although I prefer the precision of the term "proleptic" in a technical discussion of Greek aspect, many commentators use "prophetic" in a similar sense, and so I use both to avoid confusion.

[199] See for example the debate between Porter (1989) and Fanning (1990); see also Carson 1993; Fanning 1993; Porter 1993; Schmidt 1993; Silva 1993.

proleptic) signification of the verb. In this connection, several relevant NT references exist. In Rom 8:30 Paul concludes, οὓς δὲ ἐδικαίωσεν, τούτους καὶ ἐδόξασεν, where the aspect of ἐδόξασεν may be either dramatic (present) or proleptic (future). In Mark 11:24, Jesus is made to say, πάντα ὅσα προσεύχεσθε καὶ αἰτεῖσθε, πιστεύετε ὅτι ἐλάβετε, καὶ ἔσται ὑμῖν, where ἐλάβετε appears to have a proleptic aspect.[200] Another example is in Rev 10:7, which reads, ὅταν μέλλῃ σαλπίζειν, καὶ ἐτελέσθη τὸ μυστήριον τοῦ θεοῦ,[201] where the RSV translates the aorist: "the mystery of God ... should be fulfilled".[202] That this last reference involves a temporal particle of condition is immaterial as far as the aspect of the aorist is concerned even though other examples of the proleptic aorist may be sighted which involve conditional clauses.[203] Schlueter is forced to be selective in her references in order to reject the proleptic aorist on that basis (1994, 55–56; i.e. that proleptic aorists only exist in conditional clauses).[204] Finally, Boring/Berger/Colpe draw attention to several instances in the Dead Sea Scrolls where the *orgē* of God comes upon Jews (not part of an eschatological remnant) "to the uttermost" (עד כלותם).[205] In particular, they refer to 1QM 3:9 as an example where the perfect tense is used in a prophetic sense (1995, 493).[206] Hopefully it is clear that the proleptic (future-time) aorist is at least *possible* in 1 Thess 2:16d (Berkey 1963, 185).[207] This opens the way for an interpretation which emphasises the certainty of *orgē* rather than its timing.[208] Quite a number of scholars take ἔφθασεν as a prophetic/proleptic aorist.[209]

Johanson (1995) moves the discussion of 1 Thess 2:16d in a wholly new direction. He argues that the future signification of the aorist verb is made clear in the pragmatic dimension of the text, that is, "the rhetorical, reader-impacting dimension of textual strategies" (522). He argues that if 1 Thess 2:14e–16 is similar to the specific form or *Gattung* of prophetic speech then this will greatly enhance the *probability* that ἔφθασεν is either dramatic or proleptic (523). Accordingly,

---

[200] The alternative readings for ἐλάβετε, including λαμβάνετε and λή(μ)ψεσθε underscore the paucity and semantic force of the proleptic aorist (*GGBB* 564).

[201] Again, the alternative readings indicate the significance of the aorist (see NA[27]).

[202] For other examples of the proleptic aorist, see BDF 171–172, §333; *GGBB* 563–564; Porter 1994, 37. On Rev 10:7, Turner comments: "Moreoever, aorist appears for the future in 10[7], on the basis of the Hebrew *waw* converting the normal perfect to the imperfect, and so it is not 'it was fulfilled,' but 'it shall be fulfilled' (*GNTG* vol. 4, 152).

[203] Eg. Matt 12:26, 28; 18:15; John 15:6; 1 Cor 7:28.

[204] See Best 1972, 120. In fact, although Schlueter depends solely on the examples in Robertson's grammar for her argument (cf. *GGNT* 846–847) she has overlooked one of his references that demonstrates the fallacy of her argument, namely, John 13:31; see also Lenski 1937, 268; Milligan 1908, 32.

[205] Cf. 1QM 4:1–2; 1QS 2:15–17; 4:13–14; 5:12–13.

[206] They conclude: "Thus the ἔφθασεν of 1 Thessalonians need not point or look back to the Jewish war and the destruction of Jerusalem" (Boring/Berger/Colpe 1995, 493).

[207] *Contra* Green 2002, 148–149; Munck 1967, 63; Pearson 1971, 82; Simpson 1990, 71.

[208] See Hagner 1993, 132–133; Haufe 1999, 47–48; Johanson 1995, 522; Marshall 1983, 155–156; Morris 1959, 92; Richardson 1969, 105; von Dobschütz 1909, 16, 117.

[209] Dibelius 1925, 11; Findlay 1904, 56; Frame 1912, 114; Malherbe 2000, 177; Nicholl 2004, 95–96; Oepke 1970, 165; Orchard 1938, 22; Rigaux 1956, 452; von Dobschütz 1909, 116; Ward 1973, 77; Williams 1992, 48–49; see also Gaston 1970, 456; Wenham 1981, 373.

Johanson examines the woe-oracle form in the LXX in terms of text-syntactic, text-semantic and text-pragmatic features (525–528). He contends that such woe-oracles generally have three elements, including the woe cry, one or more indictments and a corresponding judgment (527). Furthermore, he has found that the judgment component of the oracles may be expressed either with the imperfect or perfect verb in Hebrew (and therefore either with a corresponding future or aorist verb in Greek).[210] In particular, Isa 5:13–15, 31:2 and Hab 2:16–17 demonstrate the general interchangeability of the LXX translation of the Hebrew imperfect or perfect (either with a future or aorist tense verb; 530). Johanson proceeds to argue that 1 Thess 2:14e–16c corresponds to the indictment element of the woe-oracle form, and that 2:16d corresponds to the judgment element (528–529). The fact that there is no οὐαί in 1 Thess 2:15–16 does not pose a problem for Johanson in view of the pericope's function in First Thessalonians. On this matter, he concludes (529):

> ... in 2:15–16 Paul is using what Greco-Roman rhetoricians would understand as a vituperative digression. Consequently, the main point he was trying to make does not lie in the digression. To have ended the sentence at 2:14 with Ἰουδαίων and started 2:15 with οὐαὶ αὐτοῖς, ὅτι, κτλ. would have given the digressive material the kind of prominence it was not meant to have.

Even if Johanson has not shown conclusively that 1 Thess 2:16 is a woe-oracle he has been able to show that 1 Thess 2:15–16 has similarities with that form which makes a proleptic ἔφθασεν somewhat more *probable*.

7. In view of the preceding discussions (esp. §III.d.4–6) it is now appropriate to ask how εἰς τέλος should be translated. There are so many variations in translation between scholars that it is not helpful to list them all here.[211] Instead, this analysis is structured around two options based on the grammatical functionality of the phrase: εἰς τέλος is an adverbial phrase referring to ἔφθασεν either in a temporal or modal sense.[212] In the first instance, the phrase is considered to be parallel to πάντοτε (v. 16c) and thus variously translated, "at last", "finally", "at/to/until the end", "for ever".[213] These translations however are not synonymous; the first two indicate something of a result while the latter two indicate duration, either limited

[210] Johanson (530) gives a list of examples from the MT and LXX, including: Isa 5:9, 24; 28:3; 31:3; Zeph 3:5 (Hebrew imperfect transl. as Greek future); Isa 31:2; Hab 2:16 (Hebrew imperfect transl. as Greek aorist); Isa 28:2, 4; 30:5; 31:2 (Hebrew perfect transl. as Greek future); Isa 5:13 (Hebrew perfect transl. as Greek aorist); Isa 30:4 (Hebrew perfect transl. as Greek present).

[211] Marshall (1983, 81) provides as good a summary as can be found in the literature.

[212] The phrase could be taken adjectivally and therefore as a qualification of ἡ ὀργή. This would support a translation like "(the wrath) that leads up to the end"; see Marshall 1983, 81; Wenham 1981, 362. Alford's translation, "to the end of it, i.e. the wrath: so that it shall exhaust all its force on them" (1958, 261), appears to take εἰς τέλος adjectivally even though he specifically rejects ἡ ὀργή as its object of qualification. An adverbial sense is preferable.

[213] Best 1972, 121; Donfried 1984, 252; Frame 1912, 114–115; Malherbe 2000, 171; Milligan 1908, 32; Schlueter 1994, 21; Simpson 1988, 152; Stott 1991, 57; Wanamaker 1990, 117.

or unlimited.[214] A temporal sense for εἰς τέλος is well attested.[215] In the second instance, εἰς τέλος is translated as a final clause, thus, "completely", "decisively", "to the uttermost".[216] The modal sense is also well attested.[217] Ackroyd (1969, 126) and Marshall (1983, 81) solve the dilemma by suggesting that both a temporal and modal sense are present in the phrase (cf. John 13:1).[218]

Any translation of εἰς τέλος must embrace the problematic nature of its context.[219] But it appears that there is no definite argument to tip the favour decisively either way. Some scholars look to references like Mark 13:13 to support their arguments for a temporal sense (par. Matt 24:13; cf. Matt 10:22).[220] But in the Markan passage, as Sandnes rightly points out, εἰς τέλος is linked to the durative verb ὑπομένειν whereas in 1 Thess 2:16d it is linked to a punctiliar one (1991, 193). Thus, if the translations "until the end" or "right to the end" are insisted upon, Sandnes notes that this translation naturally raises the question, "What will then follow?" (193), which is beyond the scope of Paul's thought here (regardless of what he says in Rom 11).[221] Actually, this question is irrelevant in relation to Paul's sense of urgency regarding the end (Okeke 1981, 130–131). In conclusion, since the linguistic evidence is equivocal, and since I have argued for a prophetic/proleptic aspect of φθάνειν, I am inclined to support a translation of εἰς τέλος which seems most appropriate for a future reference of *orgē*. The translation "finally" is able to

---

214 Wanamaker (1990, 117–118) prefers "until the end" because it does not make *orgē* absolute but limits it (cf. ἕως τέλους in 1 Cor 1:8; 2 Cor 1:13). In this sense, it is similar to εἰς τὸ αἰῶνα (Pobee 1985, 90). See Fitzer 1974, 91; Munck 1967, 64–65; Stählin 1967, 434.

215 Gen 46:4; Num 17:28; Deut 31:24, 30; Josh 8:24; Ps 17:36; 48:10; Job 14:20; 23:3, 7; Hab 1:4; Ezek 36:10; Matt 10:22; Mark 13:13; John 13:1; 2 Cor 3:13; Heb 6:8.

216 Bruce 1982, 48; Court 1982, 64; Delling 1972, 56; Findlay 1904, 57; Haufe 1999, 48; Hübner 1993a, 348; Lenski 1937, 269; Moule 1959, 70; Schade 1984, 127–128; Schlueter 1994, 57–58; see also BDF 112, §207(3); *GNTG* vol. 3, 266.

217 Josh 3:16, 20; 10:13; 1 Par 28:9; 2 Par 12:12; 31:1; Job 6:9; 20:7, 28; Ps 9:7, 19, 32; 12:2; 15:11; 43:24; 51:7; 67:17; 73:1, 3, 10, 11, 19; 76:9; 78:5; 88:47; 102:9; Ezek 15:4, 5; 20:40; 22:30; Dan 2:34θ; 3:19θ, 34 (cf. Odes 7:34 [LXX]); 11:13θ; Amos 9:8; Jdt 7:30; 14:13; 2 Macc 8:29; Sir 10:13; 12:11; Luke 18:5; *Pss. Sol.* 1:1; 2:5.

218 With reference to *T. Levi* 6:11, Baarda suggests that εἰς τέλος ought to be translated "finally" with both a temporal and modal aspect present (1992, 61). Similarly, Lamp argues for a temporal-modal combination (2003, 426). Even Danker exhibits some hesitancy in making a choice; BDAG has 1 Thess 2:16 under εἰς as a marker of degree (thus "completely", "fully", "absolutely"; BDAG 289, §3) *and* under τέλος as an adverbial expression with temporal connotations (thus "forever", "through all eternity"; 998, §2.b.γ).

219 "The context must decide whether the expressions are to be taken temporally or quantitatively" (Delling 1972, 56). Thus for example, Elliger first notes that εἰς τέλος indicates a temporal goal, "until the end", but rejects this translation for "finally, ultimately" in 1 Thess 2:16 (1990, 398), presumably because of the context.

220 Donfried 1984, 250–252; Munck 1967, 64.

221 Sandnes goes on: "The comparison with Mark 13:12–13, in fact, proves our point. There εἰς τέλος is immediately followed by σωθήσεται. The best translation of εἰς τέλος in 1 Thess 2:16c is thus 'finally' or 'at last'. This means the ὀργὴ is the eschatological wrath of God" (1991, 193); cf. *2 Clem* 19.3. Wenham's view is distinctly opposite: "If Paul is referring to an imminent eschatological judgment, he probably does not mean the end of all things, but a particular judgment on the Jews (ἐπ' αὐτούς), after which the Gentile mission (just mentioned – as hindered by the Jews) may go on" (1981, 374).

encompass both a temporal and modal sense (Baarda 1992, 61). Thus, Paul refers to *orgē* in terms of a sweeping catalogue of deeds which displease God — in this sense εἰς τέλος means "finally", "at last". At the same time, Paul refers to a culmination of God's displeasure which is evident in the fulfilment of sins — in this sense εἰς τέλος refers to that kind of judgment which is "final".

Before the conclusion (§III.d.8 below), it is necessary to consider the striking parallel of *T. Levi* 6:11.[222] For the sake of comparison I present both verses together:

T. Levi 6:11 ἔφθασε δὲ ἡ ὀργὴ κυρίου ἐπ' αὐτοὺς εἰς τέλος
1 Thess 2:16d ἔφθασεν δὲ ἐπ' αὐτοὺς ἡ ὀργὴ εἰς τέλος

The similarities are too close not to accept some sort of literary relationship between the verses.[223] Baarda provides a list of options in order to explain the relationship: (1) Paul is dependent on *T. Levi*; (2) author of *T. Levi* is dependent on Paul; (3) phrase is borrowed from *T. Levi* by an interpolator in Paul; (4) phrase is borrowed from Paul by an interpolator in *T. Levi*; (5) Paul and author of *T. Levi* are dependent on a common source (1992, 62). Baarda proceeds to work through these options (62–71).[224] He begins by rejecting option three as conjecture (62);[225] option four is more difficult but Baarda is confident that the phrase is not an interpolation in *T. Levi* either (63–65).[226] He briefly examines options one and two but finds both rather inconclusive since it is not clear why either author would choose this particular phrase for inclusion in his own work (65–67).[227] This leaves option five

[222] See de Jonge's critical edition of *T. 12 Patr.* (1978, 32). Charles' text of *T. Levi* 6:11 differs slightly: ἔφθασε δὲ αὐτοὺς ἡ ὀργὴ τοῦ θεοῦ εἰς τέλος (1966, 41; this is similar to 1 Thess 2:16d in some mss. [see NA[27]]). Lamp (2003, 416) sets out the three texts (Charles, de Jonge and NA[27]) in a handy table. Baarda's examination of the manuscripts concurs with de Jonge's, that ἡ ὀργὴ κυρίου is original (1992, 60). The variation in placement of ἐπ' αὐτοὺς is most likely due to influence from 1 Thess 2:16 (Hollander/de Jonge 1985, 147).

[223] Argyle 1952, 257; Baarda 1992, 59–73; Charles 1908, 42; 1966, 41; de Jonge 1975a, 260; Frame 1912, 115; Marshall 1983, 82; see Schade 1984, 127; *contra* Bammel 1959, 309; Becker 1970, 258 (see 1974, 24); Fitzer 1974, 91; Michel 1967, 58. Although a literary connection is evident, the contexts are different and care must be taken not to extort Paul by making 1 Thess 2:16d conform to *T. Levi* 6:11 or *vice versa* (Sandmel 1962, 5).

[224] See also the valuable discussion by Frame 1912, 115–116.

[225] For Baarda's arguments regarding the authenticity of 1 Thess 2:13–16, see 1984, 22–30.

[226] A number of factors seems to point to this conclusion: Baarda notes a play on words between *T. Levi* 6:11 and 7:1, the latter text which has μὴ ὀργίζου (1992, 64). Hollander/de Jonge note an *inclusio* between 6:11 and v. 8b (1985, 148). Furthermore, although Rigaux (1956, 455) argues that the lack of the phrase in the Armenian α-recension indicates that it was not in the original Greek mss., it is relevant to note that the latter part of v. 10 is also missing (see critical edition by Stone 1969, 141; for the Armenian β-recension, cf. 77). On the basis of Stone's conclusion that the peculiarities of the α-recension are suspect (unless supported by the Greek) when compared to the β-recension (163), Baarda is correct to reject the Armenian witnesses as supportive of an interpolation at *T. Levi* 6:11 (1992, 64–65); on the matter, see de Jonge 1995, 112–113.

[227] Charles (1966, 42) and Moffatt (1910, 29) settle on option one (see Argyle who also asserts that Rom 1:32 is a direct quotation of *T. Ash.* 6:2 [1952, 257]) and de Jonge on option two but none gives good reason for their decisions. De Jonge argues: "On the basis of what is found elsewhere I am inclined to think that the present wording of *T. Levi* 6:11 did indeed undergo influence from 1 Thess 2:1–16" (1995, 113).

for which a number of commentators previously argue;[228] but this is conjecture as well. At least there is no other known parallel of the phrase (69–70). Ultimately, Baarda settles on option one since he can envisage that "Paul had in mind a Greek version of the Shechem episode in which mention was made of the final wrath to which he refers in 1 Thess. 2:16c" (72).[229] Thus, just as the Sichemites/Canaanites hindered (cf. κωλύειν in *T. Levi.* 6:8) the other men and women (*T. Levi* 6:9), so too did οἱ Ἰουδαῖοι hinder Paul's mission. The expression of *orgē* becomes a pronouncement in both texts which is motivated under similar circumstances (71–72). Lamp's comparison of the two texts yields an even closer picture of similarity (2003, 420–422). He finds similar wording and a similar progression of thought between *T. Levi* 6 and 1 Thess 2:13–16. Thus, Lamp argues that the conceptual parallel of *T. Levi* 6:11 may be used to interpret 1 Thess 2:16d. Despite explicit caveats to his discussion which emphasise the differences between the texts, Lamp's interpretive conclusions regarding the identity of "the Jews", the tone of the indictment against "the Jews" and the judgment against "the Jews" (422–427), make too much of the similarities.

8. Often Paul's zeal (Phil 3:6) shows through in his letters, such that Frame's statement is apt: "The letters of Paul reveal not a machine but a man" (1912, 111). Gager emphasises the polemic in 2:16 too sharply when he refers to "Paul's anger" and to "feelings nowhere in evidence in the other letters" (1983, 255–256). Indeed, Paul can be very hostile against his opponents[230] and he speaks strongly of οἱ Ἰουδαῖοι elsewhere.[231] It goes without further argument that Paul *is* capable of making the kind of statement found in 1 Thess 2:16d. It is part of an *eschatologische Zuspitzung* of which Paul's statements are somewhat milder than others (Geiger 1986, 157).[232]

In summary of the analysis for 1 Thess 2:16d, it is argued that φθάνειν does not specifically distinguish between "imminent nearness" and "actual arrival"; nor is it to be taken in an anticipatory sense as in 4:15. Rather if it refers to a *zeitgeschichtliche Ereignis*, then there is a list a possible candidates other than the destruction of the temple (so §III.d.4 above). But if *orgē* is not fixed in a contemporary setting but assigned a future orientation – and this makes sense in view of Paul's references to

---

But it is not at all clear why the author of *T. Levi* (or a later redactor for that matter) would be influenced by the Pauline text "[o]n the basis of what is found elsewhere".

[228] Best 1972, 122–123; Dibelius 1925, 11; Holtz 1989, 122; Malherbe 2000, 177; Marshall 1983, 82; Michel 1967, 58. Friedrich claims, "Auch die Wendung ‚auf sie ist der Zorn völlig gekommen' ist im Judentum anscheinend geläufig", but only gives *T. Levi* 6:11 as evidence (1976, 227). See Milligan's reference to "a half-stereotyped Rabbinical formula" (1908, 32); de Jonge ventures along this line but very tentatively (1975a, 260).

[229] Baarda himself emphasises the note of conjecture in his suggestion which is made particularly problematic in view of the Christian influence on the transmission of *T. 12 Patr.* (see de Jonge 1993).

[230] E.g. 2 Cor 11:13–15; Gal 5:2–12; Phil 3:2, 18–19.

[231] E.g. Rom 2:17–29; 3:1–8; 9:1–3; 10:1–4, 18–21; 11:8–32. So Donfried 1984, 252–253; Dunn 1998, 507; Holtz 1989, 123; Jewett 1986, 38–39; Still 1999, 42–44.

[232] Cf. for example, 1QM 1:1–2, 5; 3:9; 4:12; 9:5; 1QS 2:12–18 (Kuhn 1992, 344–346).

orgē elsewhere in First Thessalonians – then a past reference for φθάνειν is unsuitable (so §III.d.5 above). Thus, the analysis turns to an examination of the prophetic/proleptic aorist and how it is possible that Paul intended ἔφθασεν to have a future reference. To this end, a short presentation of verbal aspect is given along with a consideration of Johanson's thesis that 2:15–16 is part of a woe-oracle *Gattung* (so §III.d.6 above). Finally, an examination of εἰς τέλος reveals its ability to express a temporal and modal sense (so §III.d.7 above).

These individual conclusions lead to the following translation of verse 16d: "But *orgē* is going to come on them finally". The choice of the periphrastic construction, "is going to come", is an attempt to portray the future time of action of ἔφθασεν without over-emphasising it.[233] It is important to keep the notion of prolepsis wholly in mind. Paul anticipates – in the present – the unfolding of a future occurrence. In this connection, it is not inappropriate to note the specific background of the proleptic statement. Explicitly, this is the hindering of his own mission (v. 16a). Implicitly, other triggers may have contributed to the emphatic tone of Paul's statement. Thus, without admitting a *zeitgeschichtliche Ereignis* for *orgē*, Paul could have considered any number of incidents as harbingers of the future. Consequently, the historical trajectory of Paul's mission is paramount (Schlier 1972, 41).[234]

Finally, the rhetorical effect of 1 Thess 2:15–16 becomes more noticeable when compared to the eschatological discourse found elsewhere in First Thessalonians. In particular, I draw attention to the insider/outsider cues which serve to promote an eschatological identity: the συμφυλέται and οἱ Ἰουδαῖοι become representative of those who reject Jesus as the *Kyrios*, or more personally, reject Paul's *kērygma*. In contrast, members of the *ekklēsia* in Thessalonica accept the *kērygma*, and are therefore distinguished. Furthermore, the two groups are representative of Paul's pattern of exhortation. The one group, despite experiences of suffering, await deliverance from *orgē* (1 Thess 1:10); for them, there is hope of an eschatological existence. The other group consists of Jews and non-Jews who have no deliverance. Paul describes their completion of the full measure of their sins and offers an eschatological existence consisting only of *orgē* which is going to come on them finally.

IV. The Authenticity of 1 Thess 2:13–16

1. First Thessalonians 2:13–16 is one of two pericopes in First Thessalonians whose authenticity is questioned (the other is 5:1–11).[235] Since it contains eschatological

[233] Porter uses the "going to" phrase: "There is no English equivalent for translational purposes, since the English future tense with 'will' is too strong" (1994, 37).

[234] Thus, Best prefers to emphasise the immediacy of the future judgment based on the "inner logic" between the Jewish response to Paul's mission and the fact that "the End is only a short time away" (1972, 120).

[235] The (untenable) thesis of Fuchs (1964) that 1:2–10 is also an interpolation is all but forgotten (see Collins 1984, 13–14; Friedrich 1973, 290).

elements relevant to my thesis, a thorough investigation of its authenticity is vitally important, and the outcome of this discussion (whether authentic or not) greatly affects the interpretation of the pericope. As indicated in the introduction to the analysis (above), the discussion of various interpolation hypotheses has been postponed until after the analysis because that analysis will help determine the worth of each argument. An adequate history of research of this topic has been recently provided by Schlueter and is not attempted below (1994, 13–38; see also Collins 1984, 96–135). Rather, it is more helpful to summarise and critically discuss the main lines of pursuit used to question the authenticity of 2:13–16.[236] Specifically, this discussion is divided into textual evidence (§2), historical (§3), form critical (§4) and theological arguments (§5), and conclusion (§6).

2. The textual evidence for an interpolation is meagre but certainly *not* non-existent. There is a reference to a Latin manuscript in NA^{27}, omitting verse 16d, which is ignored by virtually all scholars.[237] The reference is to Vatic. lat. 5729 (11th century), first hand, the second correcting to the Vulgate text, but with *enim* instead of *autem*. There are at least two (extreme) explanations of this witness. On the one hand, the omission may be an oversight on the part of the first copier or perhaps even a purposeful rejection of verse 16d which was then corrected by a second hand to the Vulgate text. In such case, the witness is irrelevant for an interpolation hypothesis. On the other hand, the omission may reflect a recension of Latin manuscripts whose trajectory is preserved only by this Latin witness and which may be traced back to an original Greek manuscript. In such case, the witness would be vitally important for an interpolation hypothesis and worth consideration. Since neither scenario may be proved it is the conjecture of this writer that the omission probably reflects a previous decision by a copyist to reject the clause on theological grounds. Since the witness is exceptionally isolated it is unlikely that the trajectory of this decision goes back to a Greek manuscript.[238] In view of Vatic. lat. 5729, regardless of whether it is (in)significant for an interpolation hypothesis, it is nevertheless a minor oversight that scholars continue to assert that there is "no manuscript evidence".[239]

Baarda (1985), in an article on 2:14–16, suggests that the name Rodrigues, but not Ritschl, should be eliminated from the critical apparatus of NA^{26}. Accordingly, NA^{27} (5. korrigierter Druck) has made the correction but now replaces the name of Rodrigues with P. W. Schmiedel. I would think that the listing of *any* names defeats the purpose of a critical apparatus designed to identify manuscript evidence

[236] For other summaries, see Coppens 1975, 91–93; Holmstrand 1997, 42–46; Weatherly 1991, 79–91.

[237] The only exceptions I can find are Hagner, who mentions the Latin manuscript in a footnote but without further discussion (1993, 130), and Tomson, who mentions the manuscript in passing (2001, 173–174).

[238] Sincere thanks must go to Klaus Wachtel for his correspondence on this issue.

[239] *Contra* Beck 1994, 82; Bell 1994, 332; Brown 1994, 378; Buck/Taylor 1969, 148; Davies 1978, 6; Green 2002, 143–144; Koenig 1979, 47; Scott 1993, 651; Smith 2000, 703; Stott 1991, 55; Tellbe 2001, 105; Thomas 1978, 258; Wenham 1995, 319–320.

for alternate readings.[240] Historical, form critical and theological arguments are of lesser value in a critical apparatus of the NT — such arguments probably should be confined to the domain of textual critical discussion (*contra* Beck 1994, 82).

3. A number of so-called "historical" arguments are often proposed in order to support an interpolation hypothesis, which may be summarised as follows:

- Paul would not have used the Judean *ekklēsiai* as an example.[241]
- There is no evidence of persecution of Christians in Judea prior or during the time of writing of First Thessalonians.[242]
- Paul nowhere else attributes the death of Jesus to the Jews. To the contrary, it seems that he attributes that blame to others (1 Cor 2:8).[243]
- There is no appropriate historical event to which ἡ ὀργή could refer other than the destruction of the temple in 70 C.E.[244]

The first two arguments are from silence — the one based on the difficulty of explaining why Paul chose those *ekklēsiai* for comparison (§III.b.2 above) and the other based on the fact that there is little evidence of persecution in that time and place (§III.b.3–4 above). Besides, Paul himself was a persecutor. The third argument is more substantial since the charge that οἱ Ἰουδαῖοι killed the Lord Jesus (v. 15a) *is* remarkable. However, an interpretation that makes οἱ ἄρχοντες (1 Cor 2:8) entirely exclusive of Jews remains doubtful which means that 1 Thess 2:15a does not necessarily contradict 1 Cor 2:8 (§III.c.3 above). The fourth argument is based on the assumption, *a priori*, that the destruction of 70 C.E. is the only historical event that could fit the statement of verse 16d. But many other events present themselves as possible candidates (§III.d.4 above).[245] Further, the future oriented *orgē* suggests that the aorist tense does not necessarily refer to a contemporary event. The alternative ways of interpreting verse 16d, particularly in terms of the eschatological discourse in First Thessalonians, demonstrate the inefficacy of argument four (§III.d.5–7 above).

4. Form critical arguments in the scholarly discussion are frequent and repetitive:

- First Thessalonians 2:13–16 constitutes a second *letter-thanksgiving* and therefore must be an interpolation. Furthermore, the interpolator slavishly copied 1:2–5.[246]

---

[240] Unfortunately, there is no discussion whatsoever in the introduction of NA[27] as to the criteria used for the inclusion and exclusion of names in their critical apparatus.

[241] Baur 1875, 87; Pearson 1971, 87; Richard 1995, 119.

[242] Baur 1875, 319; Pearson 1971, 86–87.

[243] Beck 1994, 79; Havener 1983, 25; Pearson 1971, 84; Richard 1995, 121; see Sandmel 1978, 14–15.

[244] Baur 1875, 88; Moffatt 1910, 29; Pearson 1971, 82–83; see Bailey 1955, 279–280.

[245] The numerous candidates for a historical reference are plain even for a scholar who argues, on other grounds, that 1 Thess 2:14–16 is an interpolation (Moffatt 1901, 625–626).

[246] Beck 1994, 77–78; Eckart 1961, 32; Havener 1983, 25; Koester 1979, 38; Pearson 1971, 91; Refshauge 1971, 4; Schmidt 1983, 269–270; see Boers 1976, 151–152.

- The abrupt transition between 2:12 and 2:13, the lack of a formal *transition* between 2:16 and 2:17, and the fact that 2:11–12 forms an introduction to the *apostolic parousia* in 2:17–3:13, points to 2:13–16 as an interpolation.[247]
- There are numerous un-Pauline words and turns of phrases.[248]

An extensive discussion of the epistolary and rhetorical forms of Paul's letters (with special reference to First Thessalonians) has been presented in order to substantially rebut the first argument (Chapter 2; see summary in §II.c above). That there is a thanksgiving formula in 2:13 absolutely constitutes no evidence for an interpolation.[249] Moreover, neither does the repetition of material in 1:2–10 furnish means for convincing support. Numerous scholars have shown that 2:13–16 is an integral part of First Thessalonians overall — besides, it is not a slavish copy in view of the distinguishable rhetorical effects of each pericope (§II.b above). The second argument is of the weakest and most subjective type.[250] Since there is, to date, no formal analysis of introductory passages to the *apostolic parousia* in Paul's letters, then the conclusion that 2:11–12 forms an introduction to 2:17 is an assumption requiring substantiation (Coppens 1975, 95; Simpson 1988, 78–79). Alternatively, 2:11–12 not only makes an appropriate conclusion to 2:1–12, but 2:13–16 is by no means an unexpected part of the letter's progression (Tellbe 2001, 106; Weatherly 1991, 81). The third form critical argument for an interpolation is multifaceted. The (implicit) reasoning advances along these lines: Paul's vocabulary and style are sufficiently known and distinctive so as to make apparent those texts which are written by him and those texts which are written by another. (I say "implicit" because most scholars are not quite audacious enough to couch their methodology in such positivistic terms!) Yet, it is difficult to establish a norm for Paul's letters by which they may be measured, as is made amply clear by the struggles between scholars in the assessment of the structure of his letters (again, see Chapter 2).[251]

---

[247] Koester 1979, 38; Pearson 1971, 88–90; Schmidt 1983, 270; see Eckart 1961, 33–34.

[248] Richard 1995, 17 (cf. 119–123); Schmidt 1983; 271–276.

[249] Koester argues: "... as part of Paul's effort to create a Christian form of the conventional proem, this section makes no sense whatsoever. A polemic against the Jews, consisting of statements from a traditional topos, is completely unwarranted in a proem that makes every effort to reshape the theme of the writer-recipient relation in the conventional proem of the private letter. A polemic against a third party would destroy the very result which Paul wants to accomplish" (1979, 38). This argument is based on nothing more than a preconceived (however well) idea of what ought and ought not to be incorporated into Paul's created "Christian form of the conventional proem". *Contra* Koester, the polemic of 2:13–16 may be understood in terms of Paul's agenda, which, among other things, is to maintain a community polarised between those who accept Jesus as the *Kyrios* and those who do not (§III.c.2 above).

[250] "This is the weakest argument that can be offered, for on almost any page of the Bible one can omit some verses and find a smooth sequence without them" (Brown 1994, 380).

[251] See also Simpson 1990, 50; 1993, 936. Murphy-O'Connor astutely concludes: "... the argument from style, which has been used to determine the authenticity and inauthenticity of certain letters, can no longer be considered valid ... Our inability to determine in precise detail the contribution of a coauthor, to set out the extent of secretarial involvement, and to fix the number of secretaries employed makes it impossible to define Paul's style in such a way as to permit the detection of significant variations from that norm. This conclusion is confirmed by recent stylistic studies" (1995, 34–35).

Consequently, there is no further attempt in this discussion to address linguistic issues raised by scholars like Schmidt (1983; but see critique by Weatherly 1991) or compilation theorists (§II.d above). Perhaps the most crucial aspect of the debate – regarding the phrase καὶ διὰ τοῦτο (v. 13a) – is taken up in the analysis. The reader is directed to the somewhat extensive discussion for a conclusion (§III.a.2 above).[252]

5. Some of the theological arguments remain formidable:

- Paul never uses the *mimēsis* motif other than of himself thereby making (at least) verse 14 an interpolation.[253]
- Paul would not have used non-Jewish anti-Jewish polemic (v. 15e).[254]
- The εἰς τέλος implies that God's *orgē* is final thereby making verse 16d incompatible with Rom 9–11, esp. 9:1; 11:26.[255]

The first argument, regarding the *mimēsis* motif, is by far the weakest of this trio. In reiteration, there is simply not enough evidence to make such a strong statement. Furthermore, Paul has no problem referring to different *ekklēsiai* as examples (cf. esp. 1 Cor 16:1; 2 Cor 8:1–6; 9:2). I suspect that the real difficulty with the *mimēsis* motif is not so much with the fact that Paul has used the motif of someone/thing other than himself but with his choice of *ekklēsiai* for imitation — i.e. Judean *ekklēsiai* (vv. 14b, c), and is thus related to the first historical argument (§IV.3 above).[256] The validity of the second argument depends on one's view of whether Paul is guilty of making statements which condemn all Jews in general. I conclude that he is not (§III.c.2 above). Nevertheless, his statements do possess an anti-Semitic "effect" (Excursus 4 below). Johnson (1989) and Schlueter (1994) provide adequate rhetorical models to accommodate Paul's polemic (§III.c.6 above). Finally, the third theological argument has, in terms of history of research, received the most attention. How can the Paul of 1 Thess 2:13–16 be the same Paul of Rom 9–11? An initial assessment might include several alternatives. (1) It is possible that Paul has radically changed his view regarding the fate of Israel; this cannot be

[252] One relevant argument that does not come up in the above discussion is raised here. Schmidt's suggestion that the καὶ διὰ τοῦτο of 2 Thess 2:11 is an imitation of 1 Thess 2:13 (1983, 273) puts an untenable historical strain on his interpolation theory for 1 Thess 2:13–16, since this would require the insertion to be accomplished and accepted *prior* to the composition of Second Thessalonians. It would seem, on the basis of probability, that either there is no allusion between the letters at this point (Koester 1979, 38), or that 1 Thess 2:13 at least, is authentic (Still 1999, 32; Weatherly 1991, 93). Similarly problematic is Richard's observation that Second Thessalonians follows the compiled form of First Thessalonians. He states, in the context of his argument that 1 Thess 2:14–16 is an interpolation: "One should note briefly that this editorial activity has left traces in 2 Thessalonians (two thanksgivings; see 1:3 and 2:13) while 2:14–16 and its anti-Judaism have not" (1995, 125). Again, against all probability, this would mean that the compilation of First Thessalonians would have had to have been accomplished and accepted very quickly (even if a late date for Second Thessalonians is admitted).

[253] Beck 1994, 77; Koester 1979, 38; Pearson 1971, 87–88; Richard 1995, 119.

[254] Baur 1875, 87; Brandon 1951, 93; Pearson 1971, 85; Richard 1995, 121–122, 126.

[255] Beck 1994, 80–81; Brandon 1951, 92–93; Havener 1983, 25–26; Koester 1979, 38; Moffatt 1910, 29; 1918, 72–73; Pearson 1971, 81.

[256] For further discussion, see §III.b.2 above.

summarily ruled out. Yet, there is no need to emphasise inconsistency or charge Paul with crude contradiction — he simply reflects on various topics at different times and with different agendas.[257] More than that, Paul's explicit use of the mystery motif in Rom 11:25 (cf. 1 Cor 15:51) emphasises the different agendas between the two texts.[258] (2) Perhaps the disparate statements should be harmonised through some process of synthesis? But far from being helpful, synthesis can impede and often does impede critical exegesis since foreign elements are unknowingly and sometimes knowingly(?) incorporated into the interpretation. Schlueter examines this tendency of scholars towards theological harmonisation (1994, 54–64). Thus, some scholars feel the need to resolve any contradiction between First Thessalonians and Romans.[259] In reality, each text ought to be interpreted in its own right (63–64).[260] Along this line, much more significance should be attached to arguments that 1 Thess 2:13–16 is inconsistent *within* First Thessalonians. Broer indirectly makes this point when he comments that many of the interpolation theories are (wrongly) based on comparisons of 1 Thess 2:13–16 with passages outside First Thessalonians, especially Rom 11 (1990, 149). Consequently, I have sought to pay more attention to the epistolary and rhetorical structure of the letter overall rather than on parallels to Paul's other letters (see Chapter 2 and §II.c–d above). Beck (1994, 80) and Havener (1983, 25–26) argue that the orientation of *orgē* is opposite in 1:10 (see Binder 1990, 91). This alleged contradiction is cleared up on the basis of a prophetic/proleptic verb in 2:16d (§III.d.6 above). (3) Alternatively, perhaps Paul is not dealing with the same topics in these texts and so comparisons between them is like comparing apples and oranges. Paul refers to οἱ Ἰουδαῖοι (specifically those who fit the charges so outlined) in 1 Thess 2:13–16; he refers to πᾶς Ἰσραήλ

[257] Collins 1984, 128; see Hagner 1993, 135; Okeke 1981, 132–135. Thus, the issue may not at all be Paul's different outlook with respect to the imminence of the *parousia*. Rather, Simpson suggests that Paul's missionary understanding has developed: "The time remaining is allowed to have a more definite content than just *waiting* (cf. 1 Thess 1:10)" (1990, 48).

[258] Whether Paul knew about the salvation of all Israel (καὶ οὕτως πᾶς Ἰσραὴλ σωθήσεται, Rom 11:26), at the time of writing First Thessalonians, is impossible to ascertain (*contra* Sandnes 1991, 193–194). Although μυστήριον can have the sense of disclosure or revelation (O'Brien 1993, 622), it is acknowledged that the term is a technical description of the saving acts of God (Brown 1968, 50), and in the context of Rom 11:25–26, more a reference to Paul's understanding (or lack thereof) of God's election of Israel in the face of a contradictory present than an appeal to a special disclosure or revelation (Bornkamm 1967, 822–823; Krämer 1991, 447–448); *contra* Kim 2002, 239–257. Thus, to be more precise, the insight of Paul which is conveyed in the sequence of Israel's partial hardening (v. 25) and Israel's salvation (v. 26) with οὕτως as the logical connector, *is* the mystery (Bockmuehl 1990, 173). Thus, "... in 1 Thessalonians there is no sign of the remarkable recombination that we find in Romans" (Gager 2000, 149). For a more detailed discussion of the link between "mystery" and "revelation", see Harvey 1980.

[259] See for example, Simpson 1988, 89–91, 123–133. As well, Scott is insistent on finding a future hope for the Jews in 1 Thess 2:16 so as to "soften" the apparent contradiction between it and Rom 11:25–32 (1993, 655–657). Munck's exegesis of 1 Thess 2:16 is ruled by his view of Romans (1967, 62–65; see analysis of Munck's exegesis by Schlueter 1994, 55–58); see also Mussner 1991.

[260] So rightly, Malherbe 2000, 178–179; Okeke 1981, 134–135; Still 1999, 40–41; see also Geiger 1986, 158, who supports an interpolation theory; *contra* Beck 1994, 80.

in Rom 11:25–26, and throughout Rom 9–11.[261] There can be, therefore, no point-for-point comparison.[262] (4) Finally, in the last instance, it is argued by many that 1 Thess 2:13–16 is an interpolation. This alternative is rejected on the strength of the analysis above.

6. In Ingo Broer's introduction to an article on the *Interpolationshypothese* stands these sobering words (1990, 138):

> Es liegt nahe, in dieser Situation der Bibelwissenschaft, die mit den divergierenden Stellungnahmen zu 1 Thess 2,14–16 noch sehr schmeichelhaft gekennzeichnet ist, die Hoffnung auf die neueren Methoden der Literaturwissenschaft zu richten und von ihnen eine größere Objektivität für unsere Arbeit zu erhoffen. Allerdings läßt bei etwas näherer Betrachtung schon die unterschiedliche Nomenklatur diese Hoffnung wieder schwinden und die Tatsache, daß die beiden vorliegenden linguistischen Analysen von 1 Thess 2,14–16 in unserer Frage zu genau entgegengesetzten Ergebnissen kommen, zeigt, daß diese Hoffnung naiv ist.

Consequently, in no way is it possible to conclude that the authenticity of 1 Thess 2:13–16 is defensible beyond doubt. But if Pearson's article (1971) may be taken as *the* definitive statement for an interpolation hypothesis,[263] then I have at least provided a thorough analysis of all arguments under discussion. At the very least a basis has been established for taking the pericope as Pauline which means that the statements it contains – especially the problematic verse 16d – find a place in an examination of the eschatology of First Thessalonians. Consequently, an excursus on Paul's so-called anti-Semitism is in order.[264]

Excursus 4
Paul's So-Called Anti-Semitism

1. It is quite pertinent to briefly consider the charge that 2:13–16 is anti-Semitic especially in view of the conclusion that the pericope is authentic. Principal to this discussion is a right definition of "anti-Semitism", and whether either "anti-Judaism" or "anti-Jewish" ought to be used instead (§2). Forthwith, an alternative category, that Paul is "anti-anyone-against-

---

[261] Cf. Rom 9:6, 27, 31; 10:19, 21; 11:2, 7.

[262] Bruce 1982, 49; Donfried 1984, 252–253; Holtz 1989, 130; Lindemann 1995, 41–42; Smith 2000, 703.

[263] His article is unreservedly followed by a number of scholars: Boers 1976; Gager 1983, 255; Idinopulos/Ward 1977, 198–200; Koester 1979, 38; 1980, 292; Schmidt 1983.

[264] The need for discussion of 1 Thess 2:13–16 in monographs on anti-Semitism in Paul or in the NT – esp. in the face of an inconclusive interpolation hypothesis – is obvious. This is proved simply from the fact that nearly every monograph on the subject deals with it in a significant way. Thus, it is a misjudgment that Hall, III, in his monograph entitled, *Christian Anti-Semitism and Paul's Theology* (1993), relegates his comments on 1 Thess 2:13–16 to a mere footnote and immediately dismisses it as an interpolation. To make matters worse, he misrepresents Ernst (*sic*) Best and F. F. Bruce as supporting these verses as not by Paul (164). His monograph receives a fitting review (Siker 1994).

Jesus-as-the-*Kyrios*" is examined (§3) before a summary of Patte's helpful distinction between *intentionality* and *effect* (of a text) is presented as a conclusion (§4).

2. Scholars remain in a quandary when it comes to the applicability of the terms "anti-Semitism", "anti-Judaism" and "anti-Jewish" chiefly because none of them is exactly appropriate for describing Paul's polemical outbursts in 2:13–16 and elsewhere. Strictly speaking, it could be argued that Paul is not "anti-Semitic" because such a term implies a type of racial distinction which is irrelevant in antiquity — that is, it implies a type of genetic racial distinction which is contrasted with other types of prejudice, e.g. social, political, religious. Furthermore, it seems entirely inappropriate to use a term which is equally applicable to Babylonians, Arabs and Jews alike.[265] Yet a look at the literature shows how difficult it is to distance the term "anti-Semitism" from the discussion (Daniel 1979, 46). Part of the difficulty arises, possibly, from a confusion between the ancient and modern categories of "race" (Meagher 1979, 4). Buell argues that the ancient conception of race (unlike modern conceptions) includes the notion of mutability and that it is demarcated by how one worships. Consequently, the *locus* of one's "race" changes with "conversion" or change of one's religious practice. Such a thesis allows for scholars to rethink the boundaries between Christians and Jews in antiquity — not in terms of birth or physiology, but in terms of practical/theological issues like the Law or the identity and significance of Jesus (2001, 467). Only then is it possible to reformulate an ancient view of "anti-Semitism" which is not limited to race but also includes those other categories – social, political, religious – and therefore moves away from previously mutually exclusive categories (Patte 1988, 32; see Geiger 1986, 154).[266] But are the terms "anti-Judaism" or "anti-Jewish" more accurate?[267] Sevenster argues that the former term is preferable since it is more specific and focuses on a religion and an attitude rather than on those who practice that religion (1975, 2; see Poliakov 1966, 6).[268] But it remains problematic in that it presupposes a level of divergence between Jews and Christians beyond that attained in the first century — the boundaries of Judaism(s) are more fluid.[269] On some level

[265] See Broer 1983, 60; Colpe 1996, 790; Daniel 1979, 45–46; de Lange/Thoma 1978, 114; Dunn 1992a, 179–180; Flannery 1965, 23; Isaac 1964, 21; Klassen 1986, 6; Sevenster 1975, 1.

[266] Crossan's distinction between religious and racial prejudice is no longer concrete: "Anti-Judaism is religious prejudice: a Jew can convert to avoid it. Anti-Semitism is racial prejudice: a Jew can do nothing to avoid it. They are equally despicable but differently so" (1995, 32). More appropriately, Theißen comments: "Juden treten, sofern sie das Evangelium nicht annehmen, in die Rolle der unerlösten Heiden. Heiden, sofern sie dem Evangelium glauben, treten in die Rolle von Juden. Einige Belege für diesen Rollentausch seien aufgeführt" (1991, 337–338).

[267] Finding "anti-Semitism" an inapplicable term, Flannery searches for another word which describes "those oppositions intellectual in nature, whether theological or apologetical, which are bereft of hatred or stereotyping of Jews as persons or as a people"; he concludes: "The choice of the word 'anti-Judaic' is by no means a felicitous one, but until a better one is found it must fill the semantic void" (1973, 583).

[268] Thus, for Sevenster (1975, 4), the radical social expression ("anti-Semitism") is an unnecessary development of a theological conviction ("anti-Judaism").

[269] See Daniel 1979, 45–46; de Kruijf 1978, 124; Dunn 1992a, 180; *contra* Ruether, who does not seem to acknowledge this: "Paul's position was unquestionably that of anti-Judaism. This does not, of course, mean that Jews, as a people, are excluded from becoming members of the community of salvation (Christians). The polemic against 'the Jews' in Paul, as in the New Testament generally, is a rejection of *Judaism*, i.e., 'the Jews' as a religious community. Judaism for Paul is not only *not* an ongoing covenant of salvation where men continue to be related in true worship of God: it *never* was such a community of faith and grace" (1974, 104), although later in her book she comments rightly, "When Christians were still Jews, operating as a Jewish sect that still hoped to be accepted by its parental faith, it might have seemed meaningful to rail against those 'hypocrites and blind guides.' However onesided these judgments appear

however, it is clear that Paul is in theological disagreement with some Jews. Thus, is it best to refer to Paul as "anti-Jewish"? The observation that Paul was himself a "Jew" should not rule out consideration of this term (Bruce 1982, 51). Dunn for example shows that the diverse connotations of יהודי/Ἰουδαῖος make it possible for Paul to reject the identity of "Jew" in terms of ethnicity and lifestyle and yet, at the same time, affirm a positive overtone of the term (1999, 182).[270] Be that as it may, Paul still views his *kērygma* as a (the!) emerging legitimate fulfilment of the Judaisms of his time (Fee 1994, 50). So the imprecision of the term "anti-Jewish", at least as it applies to Paul, makes it less useful (Dunn 1992a, 180).[271]

3. It appears that none of the three terms, "anti-Semitism", "anti-Judaism" and "anti-Jewish" is entirely suitable to describe Paul's polemic in his letters. This is indisputable on the basis that Paul is not wholesale against Semites or Judaism or Jews (Patte 1988, 44). His real apology is for Christ and him crucified (1 Cor 2:2). That is, Paul is "anti-anyone-against-Jesus-as-the-*Kyrios*".[272] Such a category transcends distinctions between Jews, non-Jews, or otherwise (Gal 3:28), and all boundaries – racial, social, political, religious – are insignificant in view of this over-riding criterion (White 1999, xxii). Consequently some scholars, like E. P. Sanders, prefer to use the term "intra-Jewish" rather than "anti-Jewish" when it comes to describing Paul's polemical statements in his letters. Just because Paul is critical of some Jews or of some forms of Judaism does not make him "anti-Jewish" or "anti-Judaic" (1999, 268–269).[273] Such criticism was common (Broer 1991, 347–350).[274] Paul merely wanted to redefine traditional forms of Judaism in terms of his *kērygma* (Sanders 1999, 274).[275] Johnson provides especial insight into Jewish rhetoric at the time of Paul (1989, esp. 430–441). He concludes that strong polemic which often had nothing to do with the specific actions of an opponent was used to maintain rivalry between opposing parties (430). Such maintenance was for the edification of one's own school. Consequently, it is possible that Paul, in 1 Thess 2:13–16, is not interested in whether his polemical statements, indeed out right slander, are based on fact or not. He may not even be thinking specifically of the persecution he had just received at the hand of Jews (so also Haacker 1977, 169).[276] Rather, he is

in retrospect, they did express the deep disappointment of early Christian experience" (232). Yet, Murray highlights the imprecision inherent in the terms "Jewish" and "Judaism", simply because "[t]oo many and too diverse groups are included under the terms" (1982, 196).

[270] Rom 2:28–29; 3:1; 1 Cor 9:20; cf. Rom 9:1–5; see Dunn 1992a, 182–187; Trocmé 1985, 152.

[271] Furthermore, as Barton points out, Paul's rejection of any other "*kērygma*" should not be considered either anti-Jewish or an example of intolerance. "What Paul sought was not their tolerance but their conversion to the truth" (1998, 125).

[272] See Bammel 1959, 307–308; Feldman 1996, 286; Gager 1983, 186; Michel 1967, 53; Ryrie 1959, 41; Wright 1991, 199–200. Geiger comments: "Der Gegensatz liegt dann gar nicht zwischen ‚Jude' und ‚Nicht-Jude', sondern zwischen den Angehörigen des wahren Gottesvolkes und seinen Gegnern" (1986, 156).

[273] So also Broer 1983, 87–89; 1991, 331–332; see Boccaccini 1991, 214–216; Fransen 1957, 69; Geiger 1986, 159; Haacker 1977, 168–169; Malherbe 2000, 179; Ruether 1979, 232; Wright 1991, 207.

[274] E.g. Sir 50:25–26; Wis 14:22–30; *Pss. Sol.* 2:11–13; 4:1–12; 8:9–13; 1QH 2:31; 4:9, 19; *Let. Aris.* 152. Schlueter notes that the harshest polemic is often reserved for insiders (1994, 176–185).

[275] Becker argues that the specific focus of 2:13–16 in connection with the whole letter is not on Jewish/non-Jewish categories but on elect/non-elect categories. Thus, by examining the theme of election (*Erwählung*) in First Thessalonians, Becker is able to conclude that Paul, without openly saying it, is able to designate some Jews as non-elect in 2:13–16 (1986, 98–99); similarly, see Tellbe 2001, 134–135.

[276] However, Patte may be right when he says: "... despite the diatribe against the Jews (2:16), the convictional pattern demands that this same harsh judgment be applied to the persecutors at each stage of the pattern, that is, to the Gentile fellow citizens of the Thessalonians as well as to the Jews (in the same

dealing with a school of thought — an attitude of people (not necessarily Jews but including them) who are against Jesus as the *Kyrios* and against the *Christianoi* (Johnson 1989, 433; see Grieb 1996, 767). Johnson provides examples of intra-Jewish polemic in Josephus, Qumran material and other ancient sources (434–440).[277]

4. It is a disgrace to scholarship that some scholars are unable to suppress their own prejudices in their observations of other's prejudices. Sandmel's anti-German slander is as loathsome as the anti-Semitism he is against (1978, 158), although his experiences during World War 2 should be taken into account:

> The erudition of the German scholars, their copious citations of scholarship, and their learned footnotes should not conceal the simple fact that their repeated misinterpretations of Judaism rest on condescension. One must ascribe to the succession of German scholars a hostility against Jews and Judaism as extreme as it has been repetitious and a presentation of Judaism that is not a picture but a travesty (1978, 158).[278]

Likewise, in the course of his arguments from ancient texts, Isaac's polemic against "Catholics" may only be described as a cheap shot: "But Catholics rarely read Holy Scripture; how many of them know that the first Christians were all Jews, and that primitive Christianity was Judeo-Christianity?" (1964, 120–121). Although these two quotations may represent an extreme in scholarly expression, Patte (1988), in what (I think) is a pivotal article, warns that anti-Semitism still lurks in scholarly works — even in those works which are attempting to address the very issue.[279] Patte distinguishes between the *intentionality* of a text and the *effect* of a text on its readers.[280] He draws from his theory of structural semiotics but purposely uses non-technical language to make his point (1988, 33). Patte qualifies what he means by the intention of a discourse: "*That which governs, orients, and structures our discourses* as well as our actions is not merely our conscious intentions but rather our *intentionality*, which is not necessarily self-conscious" (40). Further, there is also an effect of the same discourse (41):

---

way that in the letter to the Galatians both the Gentile idolators and the Jews are under a curse). Thus this passage is not, in Paul's mind, anti-Semitic but rather 'anti-persecutor'" (1983, 145; so also Lyons 1985, 205). M. S. Taylor (1995) argues against "conflict theories" and removes her discussion of anti-Judaism from the social to the theological realm. "As I have already argued ... the Christian writings on Judaism betray a preoccupation with matters of intra-mural significance rather than a concern with justification and defence vis-à-vis contemporary Jews" (161). Although Taylor's point is well taken, I am convinced that, as indicated in texts like 1 Thess 2:13–16, polemical statements against Jews did stem from initial social conflict (see criticism by McKnight 1996; see also Broer 1991, 331). Thus, I agree with Schäfer when he refers to a "kernel of truth" in Jewish polemic whereby he notes that justifiable and legitimate statements can slide into the unjustifiable and illegitimate (1997, 205). But I disagree with his conclusion that Paul is therefore guilty of an anti-Semitic attitude (206); Paul is simply guilty of strong intra-mural polemic.

[277] See also Hester 1996, 276; Mayer 1976, 311–312.

[278] The sentiments in this quotation are hardly moderated by the disclaimer: "Not all these people were blatantly anti-Semitic" (Sandmel 1978, 158).

[279] On this theme, see Klein 1978, who first attempts to identify a widespread anti-Jewish vein in the secondary literature and then to synthesise its influence in Christian theology. In addition, see Vos 1984, who examines the influence of *Antijudaismus/Antisemitismus* on articles in *TDNT* 1–4 (ed. by G. Kittel).

[280] Gaston voices a similar view in his definition of anti-Judaism: "Just as individuals can be relatively free of personal prejudice and still participate actively in a system of racism, so anti-Judaism has to do with words and their objective effects whether or not the people who speak them subjectively hate Jews" (1979, 50); so also Barth: "All too often, though not always, what Christians have made of Paul gave good reason to the Jews to consider him an anti-Semite" (1968, 89).

> In the universe of discourses that we share with our audiences, our discourses have unintended effects. This is what, for the purpose of this paper, I will simply call the "*effect upon the readers*" of our written discourses, or their *rhetoric*. The "effect upon the readers" might be quite far removed from what we intended. But, in most instances, we do not even notice it, especially in the case of our written discourses, because we are satisfied that our discourses express our good intentions and thus we have a clear conscience. When we discover this unexpected effect upon readers, we simply complain that we have been misunderstood, without noticing that the rhetoric of our discourse generated this unexpected effect.

It is possible to conclude that Paul is intentionally not anti-Semitic — his letters convincingly reveal a person who considers his life and thought as "within Judaism" (44).[281] But Paul's texts may well have an anti-Semitic effect.[282] Further, Patte warns against making exclusive an inherent definition of Christianity as over against Judaism (39). It must not be forgotten that in 2:13–16 Paul does not rail only against Jews since the phrase ὑπὸ τῶν ἰδίων συμφυλετῶν (v. 14d) does not limit the persecutors to Jews only (§III.b.4 above). But a proper representation of the text does include an acknowledgement of a polemic against some Jews — that is, acknowledgement of the anti-Semitic effect of the text.[283] In conclusion, there is no doubt that Paul, Sandmel and Isaac are intentionally *not* anti-Semitic, anti-German nor anti-Catholic, respectively; this is made clear from the overall thrust and tenor of their writings. But like Paul, there are isolated texts which clearly have an effect on its readers: for Paul, the effect might be anti-Semitism; for Sandmel, it might be anti-Germanism; for Isaac, it might be anti-Catholicism. The point of relevance is that despite the effect of a text like 1 Thess 2:13–16, Paul remains, intentionally and therefore absolutely, not anti-Semitic, not anti-Judaic and not anti-Jewish.

End of Excursus

V. Conclusion

1. As in 1 Thess 1:9–10, Paul formulates a positive and negative pattern of exhortation, although the negative aspect takes up most of 1 Thess 2:13–16. It is decisive for the interpretation, however, that Paul begins the pericope positively, with a reference to thanksgiving (v. 13) for the Thessalonians' reception and acceptance of the word of God (λὸγος θεοῦ). Once again there is a close relationship between Paul's entrance to the community and his *kērygma*. Thus, the Thessalonians have accepted the true (ἀληθῶς) word which is working in them (ἐνεργεῖν), and their new existence is characterised by imitation of the *ekklēsiai* of God (v. 14). The reference

[281] So also Kim 2002, 250; Manson 1953, 437; Mussner 1984, 140; Sanders 1999, 276.

[282] See Kampling's thorough article (1993) on the history of interpretation of 1 Thess 2:14–16 ranging from the earliest church to Theodoret. Thus (rightly): "Paul and the other writers of the NT who engaged in this struggle for a separate identity, using vituperation directed at the Jewish people as a tool in the struggle ... never dreamed of the consequences of their statements on subsequent generations" (Wanamaker 1990, 118–119).

[283] It is a pity that Beck, in his important section on "practical considerations" (in the context of a discussion on anti-Jewish polemic in the letters of Paul), does not distinguish between the intentionality and effect of the pericope under discussion; see his *intentionally* pure but misguided conclusions (1994, 81–84).

to the Judean *ekklēsiai*, in particular, is designed to encourage the followers of Jesus in Thessalonica that they are not alone in their experiences. Others are experiencing suffering too. Such an association of solidarity invokes a powerful and positive sense of identity.

2. Paul then turns to increasingly eschatological motifs which illustrate the Thessalonians' current social disintegration. The emphasis on the list of accusations against "the Jews" (οἱ Ἰουδαῖοι), and on the eschatological statement about *orgē*, is considerable, especially since verses 14–16 form an *eschatological climax* of a much larger epistolary unit of First Thessalonians (i.e. 2:1–16). However, with eschatology as a hermeneutical key, it becomes clear that the antipathy between the Thessalonians and "the Jews" is a typological portrait of the struggle between those who have accepted Jesus as the *Kyrios* and those who have not. The negative aspect of Paul's pattern of exhortation, despite the controversial nature of its expression here, must be balanced with the positive aspect. Paul uses specific examples of social disintegration, between the Thessalonians and their own countrymen (συμφυλέται), between the *ekklēsiai* of God and "the Jews" and between Paul and those who hinder his mission, to provide a means for community identity and existence. The eschatological statement of verse 16d is to be interpreted in these terms, not absolutely.

Chapter 5
First Thessalonians 4:13–18

1. First Thessalonians 4:13–18 is quintessential of early Pauline eschatological and apocalyptic thought. Nowhere else does Paul relate such a detailed portrayal of the *parousia* of the Lord. Nor does he often use many of the themes which are found here, including a description of resurrection as a bringing in (v. 14), a reference to a word of the Lord (v. 15), apocalyptic details of a descending Lord using terms like κέλευσμα, ἀρχάγγελος and σάλπιγξ (v. 16), the employment of a translation motif and a meeting of the Lord using the analogy of Hellenistic formal receptions (v. 17). Each of these themes is worthy of careful consideration in its own right as is the traditional hope of the resurrection in the face of death. But the most challenging factor in the interpretation of 1 Thess 4:13–18 is not the elucidation of complex themes and their interrelation, although individual contributions in the analysis advance a more coherent synthesis of the text. Rather, as the history of research confirms (Excursus 5), the *crux interpretum* is the problematic horizon of the Thessalonians' life-situation and Paul's attendant solution by way of consolation. A component of the problematic comprises finding a balanced approach to the competing influence of Jewish traditions and popular Hellenistic culture.

2. This is the third fundamental representative of the eschatological discourse of the letter which has been chosen for analysis. One the one hand, this pericope poses no difficulties for the argument that eschatology is the best hermeneutical key for understanding First Thessalonians. Paul explicitly sets out to address the problem of death which is an obvious exponent of social disintegration. His pattern of exhortation, which includes references to eschatological motifs, provides a way for the Thessalonians to understand what happens to those who are asleep (4:13). His words of comfort (4:18) reinforce community solidarity. On the other hand, those references to eschatological motifs pose all sorts of difficulties for the exegete, because many of the motifs (esp. in 4:16–17) can be interpreted in different ways. As well, some of the argumentation is not clear (e.g. the logic of 4:14). A better understanding of the exegetical problems of the text leads to a more critical appropriation of how Paul's pattern of exhortation provides a means for integration into an eschatologically identifiable existence.

3. At regular intervals the reader will find a number of preliminary syntheses of the analysis in which, as in other chapters, I draw out various implications for my thesis. These syntheses are more important than ever because of the length of

this chapter, which is due in part to the problematic nature of 1 Thess 4:13–18 and subsequently, to the associated secondary literature. Despite the necessity to probe deeply into numerous exegetical problems in order to intepret the text according to the historical-critical approach, the goal is to keep focussed on the thesis that eschatology is the best hermeneutical key for understanding First Thessalonians.

I. Arranged Text and Translation

13a Οὐ θέλομεν δὲ ὑμᾶς ἀγνοεῖν, ἀδελφοί,
13b περὶ τῶν κοιμωμένων,
13c ἵνα μὴ λυπῆσθε
13d καθὼς καὶ οἱ λοιποὶ οἱ μὴ ἔχοντες ἐλπίδα.
14a εἰ γὰρ πιστεύομεν
14b ὅτι Ἰησοῦς ἀπέθανεν καὶ ἀνέστη,
14c οὕτως καὶ ὁ θεὸς τοὺς κοιμηθέντας διὰ τοῦ Ἰησοῦ ἄξει σὺν αὐτῷ.
15a Τοῦτο γὰρ ὑμῖν λέγομεν
15b ἐν λόγῳ κυρίου,
15c ὅτι ἡμεῖς οἱ ζῶντες
15d οἱ περιλειπόμενοι εἰς τὴν παρουσίαν τοῦ κυρίου
15e οὐ μὴ φθάσωμεν τοὺς κοιμηθέντας·
16a ὅτι αὐτὸς ὁ κύριος
16b ἐν κελεύσματι,
16c ἐν φωνῇ ἀρχαγγέλου
16d καὶ ἐν σάλπιγγι θεοῦ,
16e καταβήσεται ἀπ᾽ οὐρανοῦ
16f καὶ οἱ νεκροὶ ἐν Χριστῷ ἀναστήσονται πρῶτον,
17a ἔπειτα ἡμεῖς οἱ ζῶντες
17b οἱ περιλειπόμενοι ἅμα σὺν αὐτοῖς ἁρπαγησόμεθα
17c ἐν νεφέλαις εἰς ἀπάντησιν τοῦ κυρίου εἰς ἀέρα·
17d καὶ οὕτως πάντοτε σὺν κυρίῳ ἐσόμεθα.
18a Ὥστε παρακαλεῖτε ἀλλήλους
18b ἐν τοῖς λόγοις τούτοις.

13a We do not want you to be ignorant, brothers,
13b about those who are asleep,
13c that you may not grieve
13d as also the others who have no hope.
14a For if we believe
14b that Jesus died and rose up,
14c even also God will bring with him, through Jesus, those who have fallen asleep.
15a For this we say to you
15b by the word of the Lord,
15c that we who live
15d who remain until the coming of the Lord

15e will not precede those who have fallen asleep;
16a for the Lord himself
16b with a command,
16c the voice of an archangel
16d and the trumpet of God
16e will descend from heaven
16f and the dead in Christ will rise first,
17a then we who live
17b who remain, will be caught up at the same time with them
17c in the clouds to meet the Lord in the air;
17d and so we will always be with the Lord.
18a Therefore comfort each other
18b with these words.

II. Preliminary Issues

1. As usual, justification for the arrangement of the text (§I above) is set out verse by verse (§II.a.1–6 below). Perhaps more so than in previous chapters, questions of structure are dominant even if only because the pericope to be analysed is longer. Thus, in an endeavour to understand the flow of Paul's thought various features of the text have been identified including chiastic structures, repetitions, parallelisms, *inclusiones* as well as extensive structural links to 5:1–11 (§II.a.7). A number of scholars have found other parallels in Paul (2 Cor 4:13b–14; 1 Cor 15:1–58) and in the Synoptic Gospels (Matt 24–25) although the contributing significance of these parallels remains to be seen (§II.b). One dominant feature of the verses is surely the reference, ὑμῖν λέγομεν ἐν λόγῳ κυρίου (vv. 15a–b), and a preliminary investigation of the phenomenon of referring to words of the Lord (§II.c) sharpens the subsequent analysis, particularly with reference to the controversial sources (§II.c.2–3). Another dominant feature in this pericope as throughout the letter is Paul's reference to the *parousia* of the Lord. An investigation of the term appears here by way of introduction rather than digressing to an excursus later (§II.d). However, there is an excursus at the end of the preliminary issues which provides a detailed survey of the literature on 1 Thess 4:13–18. It is set out in table form and is intended to orient the reader to exegetical issues past and present (Excursus 5).

a. Arrangement of the Text

1. The pericope begins with a recognisable marker, οὐ θέλομεν δὲ ὑμᾶς ἀγνοεῖν, ἀδελφοί (v. 13a), which often appears in Paul's letters with constituents of θέλειν, ἀγνοεῖν and ἀδελφός. A different marker with χρεία and ἔχειν also appears in First Thessalonians (1:8; 4:9; 5:1); there may be a significant link between the

two (Malbon 1983). The transitional marker, δέ, and an element of direct address, ἀδελφοί, telegraph the beginning of a new section.[1] The preposition περί (v. 13b) first introduces the subject of verse 13, those who are asleep (v. 13b), and second introduces the rest of the pericope. The ἵνα clause (v. 13c) resumes the opening statement and is functionally equivalent to ὅτι (BDAG 476, §2.a.α).[2] The remainder of verse 13 begins with the comparative καθὼς καί (v. 13d) which is similar to καθάπερ καί in 4:5. The subject οἱ λοιποί is characterised by a negatived substantive participle of ἔχειν.

2. Verse 14 begins with a protasis of a first class condition (v. 14a) but with no corresponding apodosis. Paul could have constructed an apodosis such as καὶ πιστεύομεν ὅτι οὕτως or καὶ πιστεύειν δεῖ ὅτι (Eadie 1877, 149). He chooses rather an ellipsis of thought whereby he expresses a comparative clause beginning with οὕτως καί (v. 14c). Paul seems to move easily from a subjective statement, "if we believe that ...", to an objective statement, "even also God will ...", a move designed to provide a reason for not grieving as is made clear by the post-positive γάρ (v. 14a). The conjunction, ὅτι, introduces a short traditional formula, Ἰησοῦς ἀπέθανεν καὶ ἀνέστη (v. 14b), with Jesus as subject. The οὕτως καί clause then introduces a shift of subject to God (v. 14c). This shift is highlighted in the arrangement by placing the names Ἰησοῦς and ὁ θεός under each other. The parallelism is further strengthened by the presence of two aorist verbs ἀποθνῄσκειν and κοιμᾶσθαι (Malherbe 2000, 266). The last part of the verse (v. 14c) is arranged on one line even though there are two verbs, κοιμᾶσθαι and ἄγειν, and two prepositional phrases, διὰ τοῦ Ἰησοῦ and σὺν αὐτῷ. The Greek text is ambiguous and may be arranged in a number of ways depending on the grammatical function of the phrase διὰ τοῦ Ἰησοῦ. It may be taken as an instrumental genitive which governs the whole clause.[3] Or it may be taken as a modifier of the substantive τοὺς κοιμηθέντας. That it is a modifier of the following verb ἄγειν is also possible. Scholars remain evenly divided over the function of the prepositional phrase.[4] However, there is an argument for taking διὰ τοῦ Ἰησοῦ with the substantive participle which is based on a structural observation of parallelism. The text may be set out as follows:

Ἰησοῦς ἀπέθανεν	καὶ ἀνέστη
τοὺς κοιμηθέντας διὰ τοῦ Ἰησοῦ	ἄξει σὺν αὐτῷ

[1] The pair also appear in 1 Thess 2:17; 4:10; 5:1, 4, 12, 14.

[2] Except for 2 Cor 1:8 (which is followed by ὑπέρ), the other instances of οὐ θέλομεν δὲ ὑμᾶς ἀγνοεῖν are all followed by ὅτι. Although possible, there is no need to insist that ἵνα implies purpose (Haufe 1999, 82; *contra* Eadie 1877, 148; Frame 1912, 167; Howard 1988, 169; Malherbe 2000, 263; Richard 1995, 225; Ward 1973, 103). Including the specific formula with θέλειν and ἀγνοεῖν, instances where θέλειν is followed by a ἵνα construction yield mixed results: in Matt 7:12, Mark 6:25, 9:30, 10:35, Luke 6:31 and 2 Cor 11:12, ἵνα is declarative; in Mark 14:12, John 5:40, 17:24, Rom 1:13, 11:25, 1 Cor 14:19, Gal 4:17, 6:12, 13 and Phlm 14, ἵνα expresses purpose; in 1 Cor 14:5 and 2 Cor 5:4, ἵνα expresses result. Luke 18:41 is not relevant since ἵνα is used there to express an imperative idea.

[3] This possibility is rarely suggested (see RSV; Reinmuth 1998, 145; Ward 1973, 103).

[4] Bailey (1955, 303) and Best (1972, 189) leave the question open.

This arrangement picks up on the repetition of the name Ἰησοῦς[5] in the first pair as well as the conceptual parallel between ἀποθνῄσκειν and κοιμᾶσθαι. The second pair is more loosely related; ὁ θεός as the subject of the second verb ἄγειν is the implied actor of the first verb ἀνιστάναι despite the active voice. At this preliminary stage I am not advocating or rejecting this reading of διὰ τοῦ Ἰησοῦ but merely pointing out a common way of expressing verse 14.[6]

3. Verse 15 opens with τοῦτο γάρ (v. 15a) where γάρ identifies verse 15 as an explication of the previous verse (rather than another ground for the prohibition in v. 13)[7] while τοῦτο directs the argument towards what follows,[8] i.e. a word of the Lord, ὑμῖν λέγομεν ἐν λόγῳ κυρίου (vv. 15a, b). Although a similar phrase appears in 1 Thess 1:8 (ὁ λόγος τοῦ κυρίου, cf. also 2 Thess 3:1), elsewhere Paul does not employ such a formulation (cf. 1 Cor 7:10; 9:14; 11:23). More striking is the plural expression, λέγομεν (v. 15a). The precise placement of the "word" remains problematic. If a specific word is given at all then it is introduced by ὅτι either at verses 15c or 16a. The alternative placement becomes a summary and emphasis of what is contained in the word itself. The double articulated participles, οἱ ζῶντες οἱ περιλειπόμενοι (vv. 15c, d), are repeated in verses 17a, b, and express a direct contrast to τοὺς κοιμηθέντας (vv. 14c, 15e). Later, Paul refers to the sleeping ones as οἱ νεκροὶ ἐν Χριστῷ (v. 16f). The emphatic ἡμεῖς (v. 15c) makes it clear that Paul is thinking of different groups; he and his co-workers fit into the same group as the Thessalonians to which he is writing (Fuerbringer 1942, 648). The participles are governed by a temporal prepositional phrase articulated by εἰς (v. 15d). The parallelism in structure between verses 15c, d and verses 17a, b prompts the question of whether ἅμα σὺν αὐτοῖς ἁρπαγησόμεθα (v. 17b) ought to be understood in terms of εἰς τὴν παρουσίαν τοῦ κυρίου (v. 15d). The last part of verse 15 begins with οὐ μή (v. 15e), a rare combination in Paul.[9]

4. Verse 16 begins with ὅτι and functions as a marker of subordination furthering the argument of the previous verse. As such, it is not parallel with the ὅτι in verse 15c but is governed by ὑμῖν λέγομεν ἐν λόγῳ κυρίου (vv. 15a, b). The αὐτός (v. 16a) is emphatic and accentuates ὁ κύριος (v. 16a) as the subject of the verse which is tacitly prepared for by two preceding qualitative references (κυρίου, vv. 15b, d). This verse is dominated by three prepositional phrases headed by ἐν (vv. 16b, c, d). In fact, such structure is a recurring feature of the whole pericope (vv. 15b, 17c, 18b). In verse 16, the phrases express attendant circumstances to the subject (ὁ κύριος, v. 16a) and the verb (καταβαίνειν, v. 16e). The first two are asyndetic in arrangement while the last one is linked via a coordinating conjunction. The presence of καί

[5] The articulated form of the name in v. 14c emphasises that Paul is referring to *that* Jesus who died and rose (Findlay 1904, 97; Lenski 1937, 329).

[6] See esp. von Dobschütz 1909, 191, but also Eadie 1877, 152; Frame 1912, 170; Jowett 1859, 81; Thomas 1978, 280.

[7] Eadie 1877, 153; Frame 1912, 171; Malherbe 2000, 267; Wanamaker 1990, 170.

[8] Ahn 1989, 204; Bruce 1982, 98; Fuerbringer 1942, 646.

[9] Other than here, it occurs only in Rom 4:8, 1 Cor 8:13, Gal 5:16 and 1 Thess 5:3.

(v. 16d) along with the observation that the latter two phrases have qualifying genitives, suggest to some commentators that these three phrases refer to the same idea. Although it is tempting to move ἐν Χριστῷ (v. 16f) to the next line in order to line it up with the other ἐν phrases in this verse, such a move would de-emphasise the importance of its qualification of a new subject, οἱ νεκροί (v. 16f). The καί in verse 16f is more consecutive than coordinating since it provides a consequence of the apocalyptic details so presented. There is some measure of parallelism between verses 16f and 14c:

καὶ	οἱ νεκροὶ ἐν Χριστῷ	ἀναστήσονται πρῶτον,
οὕτως καὶ	ὁ θεὸς τοὺς κοιμηθέντας διὰ τοῦ Ἰησοῦ	ἄξει σὺν αὐτῷ

Indeed, the conceptual parallelism between the verses, οἱ νεκροί and τοὺς κοιμηθέντας, ἐν Χριστῷ and διὰ τοῦ Ἰησοῦ, and ἀναστήσονται and ἄξει σὺν αὐτῷ, supports the notion that ἀνιστάναι completes the ellipsis of thought back in verse 14. Finally, Paul sometimes places the adverb of time, πρῶτον (v. 16f), in an initial position.[10] Its ultimate position lends even stronger emphasis to the sequence: "first" (πρῶτον, v. 16f) and "then" (ἔπειτα, v. 17a).

5. Verse 17 begins with the adverb, ἔπειτα (v. 17a), proceeds with the same double articulated participles as in verses 15c, d, οἱ ζῶντες οἱ περιλειπόμενοι, and then provides a third sequential marker, ἅμα σύν (v. 17b; Plevnik 1997, 82). Whether these markers are intended to be temporal or, particularly in the case of ἅμα σύν, to describe events which are simultaneous (so for example, Richard 1995, 227) is to be determined below. There is yet another prepositional phrase with ἐν (v. 17c) which gives attendant circumstances of being caught up, σὺν αὐτοῖς. This is followed by two prepositional phrases with εἰς. The first, εἰς ἀπάντησιν τοῦ κυρίου (v. 17c), provides a goal for the verb ἁρπάζειν (v. 17b), while the second, εἰς ἀέρα (v. 17b), provides an extension of the ἀπάντησις, "in the air". It is common for the substantive ἀπάντησις and cognates to take the genitive case in order to express association although the dative is also extant (*GGNT* 528). The last part of the verse (v. 17c) is reminiscent of the structure in verse 14c, with its corresponding καὶ οὕτως (οὕτως καί, v. 14c), σὺν κυρίῳ (σὺν αὐτῷ, v. 14c) and future tense verb, ἐσόμεθα (ἄξει, v. 14c). The combination καὶ οὕτως (v. 17c) does more than make reference to what precedes (BDAG 742, §1.b); it is a climax to the whole argument and summarises Paul's answer to those Thessalonians who are grieving.[11]

6. Verse 18 begins with ὥστε which introduces an independent clause followed by an imperative form of παρακαλεῖν (v. 18a). The conjunction performs a rather similar function to τοιγαροῦν (4:8) and διό (5:11), all of which provide a practical consequence to preceding statements (Malherbe 2000, 278). The prepositional phrase with ἐν is to be understood instrumentally; with these very words the

[10] Cf. Rom 1:8; 3:2; 1 Cor 11:18.

[11] Frame 1912, 177; Malherbe 2000, 277; Richard 1995, 228.

Thessalonians are to comfort each other (ἐν τοῖς λόγοις τούτοις, v. 18b). The exhortation forms an *inclusio* with verse 13 (Gillman 1985, 272; Plevnik 1997, 68):

v. 13 οὐ θέλομεν δὲ ὑμᾶς ἀγνοεῖν, ἀδελφοί, περὶ τῶν κοιμωμένων,
ἵνα μὴ λυπῆσθε …
v. 18 ὥστε παρακαλεῖτε ἀλλήλους ἐν τοῖς λόγοις τούτοις

Or to put it another way, both statements refer to the cognitive attitudes of the Thessalonians with regard to those who are asleep. The first statement describes the Thessalonians before Paul addresses the subject (i.e. the Thessalonians are ignorant and grieving) and the second describes an expected outcome or transformation (i.e. the Thessalonians are informed and comforted; Patte 1983a, 119).

7. Besides the preliminary identification of a number of repetitions, parallelisms and an *inclusio*, there are some further details of structure. Jeremias (1958, 148) identifies a chiastic structure in 4:15–17:

a οἱ ζῶντες οἱ περιλειπόμενοι …
b τοὺς κοιμηθέντας …
b' οἱ νεκροὶ …
a' οἱ ζῶντες οἱ περιλειπόμενοι

Hurd (1998, 67) attempts a more ambitious arrangement of 4:15–18:[12]

a Τοῦτο γὰρ ὑμῖν λέγομεν ἐν λόγῳ
b κυρίου,
c ὅτι ἡμεῖς οἱ ζῶντες οἱ περιλειπόμενοι εἰς τὴν παρουσίαν τοῦ κυρίου
d οὐ μὴ φθάσωμεν
e τοὺς κοιμηθέντας·
f ὅτι αὐτὸς ὁ κύριος
ἐν κελεύσματι,
ἐν φωνῇ ἀρχαγγέλου καὶ
ἐν σάλπιγγι θεοῦ,
καταβήσεται ἀπ᾽ οὐρανοῦ
e' καὶ οἱ νεκροὶ ἐν Χριστῷ
d' ἀναστήσονται πρῶτον,
c' ἔπειτα ἡμεῖς οἱ ζῶντες οἱ περιλειπόμενοι ἅμα σὺν αὐτοῖς
ἁρπαγησόμεθα ἐν νεφέλαις εἰς ἀπάντησιν τοῦ κυρίου εἰς ἀέρα·
b' καὶ οὕτως πάντοτε σὺν κυρίῳ ἐσόμεθα.
a' Ὥστε παρακαλεῖτε ἀλλήλους ἐν τοῖς λόγοις τούτοις.

Hurd admits some uncertainty about whether this structure is the "conscious intention" of Paul (67). Vena argues for a similar structure but expresses no reservations (2001, 121).[13] He asserts that the central statement (d for Vena; f for Hurd): "…

[12] Hurd gives his arrangement in English and identifies direct and indirect verbal parallels with bold and italics typefaces respectively. These correlate to the solid and broken underlines in my arrangement which is presented in Greek.

[13] Vena combines lines d (d') and e (e') in his arrangement.

addresses, in a nutshell, the Thessalonians' concern. It is the apostle's main thought, which is developed by the other letters in the structure" (121; so also Harvey 1998, 273). Putting that claim aside, Harvey criticises Hurd's placement of κυρίου (b) on a line by itself when it clearly belongs to its head noun λόγῳ. Further, the parallel with b' is strained since a single word (κυρίου) is set against an entire clause (καὶ οὕτως πάντοτε σὺν κυρίῳ ἐσόμεθα). Instead, Harvey suggests a less detailed approach whereby ἡμεῖς οἱ ζῶντες οἱ περιλειπόμενοι (vv. 15c, d, 17a, b) forms a ring-composition that frames verses 15–17 (273).[14] Different again is Gillman's arrangement which maintains a chiastic structure for the whole of 4:13–18. Rather than setting out the text on the basis of repetitions or verbal parallels, he builds his arrangement on a two-step progression in thought whereby Paul presents kerygmatic material and then draws an implication from it (1985, 272):[15]

4:13	A Introduction: may you not grieve
4:14	B The *kērygma* and its implication
4:14a	a *Kērygma*: Jesus died and rose
4:14b	b The dead with Jesus
4:15–17	B' The word of the Lord and its implication
4:15–17a	a The word of the Lord
4:17b	b The living and the dead with the Lord
4:18	A' Conclusion: comfort one another

Collins and Malbon arrange 4:13–18 using structural considerations other than those previously mentioned, though each scholar's methodology is entirely different (i.e. respectively based on thematic observations and structural exegesis).[16]

	Collins (1984, 157)[17]	Malbon (1983, 62)
4:13	Announcement of the topic and purpose of its exposition	An inversion of the "you know" marker
4:14	Recollection of the creed and a statement of its implications	Demonstration/explanation of the asserted knowledge
4:15–17(c)	Explanation based on a word of the Lord	Elaboration of a word of the Lord
4:(17d)–18	Final exhortation	Implications of the asserted belief

First Thessalonians 4:13–18 is not an isolated text but an integral part of the *paraenesis* of the letter. As such it has links with what precedes (4:9–12) and follows (5:1–11). Although Paul begins a new *topos* in 4:13, the transition is not as abrupt

---

[14] Harvey summarises his structure as follows: A = the living Christ; B = the dead in Christ; A' = the living in Christ (1998, 273).

[15] This arrangement is followed by Légasse 1999, 243.

[16] The only difference in arrangement is that Malbon separates 4:17d from 4:15–17c and includes it as one of the implications of the asserted belief. In view of the significance of the statement in 4:17d, it cannot be included in the subset of 4:15–17. Thus, Malbon's arrangement is preferred.

[17] Followed by McNicol 1996, 18; cf. Bickmann 1998, 138; Johanson 1987, 189; Jurgensen 1994, 86; Lüdemann 1980a, 232.

as some commentators suggest.[18] The opening statements about not needing to be written to (4:9; 5:1) are contrasted with Paul's wish that they not be ignorant (4:13). Additionally, the phrase πρὸς τοὺς ἔξω (4:12) is a parallel designation to οἱ λοιποί (4:13) drawing the two pericopes closer (Green 2002, 218).

The structural links between 4:13–18 and 5:1–11 are extensive. Both pericopes have an assertion of knowing or not knowing: οὐ θέλομεν δὲ ὑμᾶς ἀγνοεῖν (4:13a); οὐ χρείαν ἔχετε ὑμῖν γράφεσθαι (5:1b). Both have an element of direct address: ἀδελφοί (4:13a; 5:1a). Both introduce a *topos* with similar formulation: περὶ τῶν κοιμωμένων (4:13b); περὶ δὲ τῶν χρόνων καὶ τῶν καιρῶν (5:1a). In each there is a contrast of ἐλπίς: οἱ μὴ ἔχοντες ἐλπίδα (4:13d) and ἐλπίδα σωτηρίας (5:8c) — a concept which is immediately qualified in both instances with an interpretive statement about God's action through Jesus: ὁ θεὸς ... διὰ τοῦ Ἰησοῦ (4:14c); ὁ θεὸς ... διὰ τοῦ κυρίου ἡμῶν Ἰησοῦ Χριστοῦ (5:9a, c).[19] Both pericopes refer to the death of Jesus: ἀπέθανεν (4:14b); τοῦ ἀποθανόντος (5:10a; Howard 1988, 188). The phrases οἱ λοιποί (4:13d; 5:6a), σὺν αὐτῷ (4:14c; 5:10c) and ἅμα σύν (4:17b; 5:10c) appear in each (Lambrecht 2000, 169). Additionally, just as 4:17 contains a recapitulation of the preceding discussion in 4:13–16, so too does 5:10 (ἵνα εἴτε γρηγορῶμεν εἴτε καθεύδωμεν ἅμα σὺν αὐτῷ ζήσωμεν) appear to be a recapitulation of the same discussion begun in 4:13 (Holtz 1998, 182; Plevnik 1979, 77). There is a reiteration in 5:11 of an imperative *inclusio* structure in 4:18:

4:18 ὥστε παρακαλεῖτε ἀλλήλους ἐν τοῖς λόγοις τούτοις
5:11 διὸ παρακαλεῖτε ἀλλήλους καὶ οἰκοδομεῖτε εἷς τὸν ἕνα,
καθὼς καὶ ποιεῖτε

These observations of structure support a literary unity of 1 Thess 4:13–5:11.[20] The direct contrast of subject matter to the surrounding *paraenesis* merely reinforces this position (Hoffmann 1966, 229; Johanson 1987, 118).

b. Parallels with Other Texts

1. A discussion of the relationship between 1 Thess 4:13–18 and other texts, including provenances, quotations, allusions and thematic similarities, rightly belongs to the analysis of individual verses. However, the number of candidates and the complexity of alleged parallels (esp. Matt 24–25) make it helpful to present a preliminary summary here. At this stage only larger pericopes are considered.

2. Plevnik (2000) asserts that 1 Thess 4:14 and 2 Cor 4:13b–14 are close parallels. In his article he argues that the latter text clarifies the elusive thought in 1 Thess

[18] *Contra* Best 1972, 180; Malherbe 2000, 262; von Dobschütz 1909, 184.

[19] Malherbe 2000, 266; see Howard 1988, 188; Lambrecht 2000, 170; May 1981, 62; Reinmuth 1998, 142.

[20] For further discussion, see Collins 1980a; Howard 1988. In connection with the outline of 4:13–18 presented by Collins (see above), McNicol finds a similar outline for 5:1–11 (1996, 18).

4:14, particularly about the destination of the apostle and of the faithful. Plevnik set out the texts as follows (84):[21]

	1 Thess 4:14		2 Cor 4:13–14
		4:13a	Ἔχοντες δὲ τὸ αὐτὸ πνεῦμα τῆς πίστεως κατὰ τὸ γεγραμμένον· ἐπίστευσα, διὸ ἐλάλησα,
4:14a	εἰ γὰρ πιστεύομεν	4:13b	καὶ ἡμεῖς πιστεύομεν, διὸ καὶ λαλοῦμεν,
		4:14a	εἰδότες
	ὅτι Ἰησοῦς ἀπέθανεν καὶ ἀνέστη,		ὅτι ὁ ἐγείρας τὸν κύριον Ἰησοῦν
4:14b	οὕτως καὶ ὁ θεὸς τοὺς κοιμηθέντας διὰ τοῦ Ἰησοῦ ἄξει σὺν αὐτῷ.	4:14b	καὶ ἡμᾶς σὺν Ἰησοῦ ἐγειρεῖ καὶ παραστήσει σὺν ὑμῖν.

The connection between the pericopes is one of content rather than form (85). But this does not stop Plevnik from drawing inferences from 2 Cor 4:13b–14 for the interpretation of 1 Thess 4:14.

3. A more commonly cited parallel is 1 Cor 15:1–58 or some part therein. Gillman provides an extensive arrangement of the parallels (1985, 273–275):[22]

	1 Thess 4:13–18		1 Cor 15:1–58
4:13	ἵνα μὴ λυπῆσθε	15:1–2	ἐκτὸς εἰ μὴ εἰκῇ ἐπιστεύσατε.
4:14a	εἰ γὰρ πιστεύομεν ὅτι Ἰησοῦς ἀπέθανεν καὶ ἀνέστη,	15:3–4	παρέδωκα γὰρ ὑμῖν ἐν πρώτοις, ὃ καὶ παρέλαβον, ὅτι Χριστὸς ἀπέθανεν ... ὅτι ἐγήγερται
		15:6	... τινὲς δὲ ἐκοιμήθησαν
		15:11	... καὶ οὕτως ἐπιστεύσατε.
4:14b	οὕτως καὶ ὁ θεὸς τοὺς κοιμηθέντας διὰ τοῦ Ἰησοῦ ἄξει σὺν αὐτῷ.	15:18–20	... οἱ κοιμηθέντες ἐν Χριστῷ ... Νυνὶ δὲ Χριστὸς ἐγήγερται ἐκ νεκρῶν ἀπαρχὴ τῶν κεκοιμημένων.
		15:23	ἔπειτα οἱ τοῦ Χριστοῦ ἐν τῇ παρουσίᾳ αὐτοῦ,
4:15a	Τοῦτο γὰρ ὑμῖν λέγομεν ἐν λόγῳ κυρίου,	15:51a	ἰδοὺ μυστήριον ὑμῖν λέγω·

[21] Plevnik sets out the two texts in English, either with quotations or thematic headings. I prefer to present the verses in Greek since this provides a more precise indication of whether there are parallels or not. The underlines are mine.

[22] See also Merklein who provides a similar arrangement (1992, 414–415). As with the presentation of Plevnik's parallels above, I have set out the two texts in Greek. Again, the underlines are mine. For further discussion of the parallels, see Luedemann 1980, 198–199.

4:15b	ὅτι ἡμεῖς οἱ ζῶντες οἱ περιλειπόμενοι εἰς τὴν παρουσίαν τοῦ κυρίου οὐ μὴ φθάσωμεν τοὺς κοιμηθέντας	15:51b	πάντες οὐ κοιμηθησόμεθα, πάντες δὲ ἀλλαγησόμεθα,
4:16–17	ὅτι αὐτὸς ὁ κύριος ἐν κελεύσματι, ἐν φωνῇ ἀρχαγγέλου καὶ ἐν σάλπιγγι θεοῦ, καταβήσεται ἀπ᾽ οὐρανοῦ καὶ οἱ νεκροὶ ἐν Χριστῷ ἀναστήσονται πρῶτον, ἔπειτα …	15:52	ἐν ἀτόμῳ, ἐν ῥιπῇ ὀφθαλμοῦ, ἐν τῇ εσχάτῃ σάλπιγγι· σαλπίσει γὰρ καὶ οἱ νεκροὶ ἐγερθήσονται ἄφθαρτοι καὶ ἡμεῖς ἀλλαγησόμεθα.
4:18	Ὥστε παρακαλεῖτε ἀλλήλους ἐν τοῖς λόγοις τούτοις	15:58	Ὥστε, ἀδελφοί μου ἀγαπητοί, ἑδραῖοι γίνεσθε, ἀμετακίνητοι, περισσεύοντες ἐν τῷ ἔργῳ τοῦ κυρίου πάντοτε,

He proposes that these points of contact (structure, themes, vocabulary) suggest an implicit theme of transformation in 1 Thess 4:15–17 (275–276). That proposal remains to be examined below. Even though the verbal parallels are few, these texts refer to similar ideas and therefore deserve to be compared.[23] In fact, the "wesentliche Unterschiede" may provide more insight into the interpretation of 1 Thess 4:13–18 (Verburg 1996, 226–227).

4. Aside from parallels within the Pauline letters, there have been many attempts to identify traditional material in 1 Thess 4:13–5:11 which derives from the Synoptic Gospels or from other common sources (e.g. Q, proto-synoptic Apocalypse, collection of Jesus-sayings).[24] Much of the discussion concentrates on the source(s) of λόγος κυρίου, and this aspect will be dealt with below. Here, the discussion is more introductory and limited to perceived parallels between 1 Thess 4:13–18 and Matt 24–25.

For McNicol (1996, 34), a parallel exists between 1 Thess 4:16 and Matt 24:30–31:

	1 Thess 4:16		Matt 24:30–31
4:16a	ὅτι αὐτὸς ὁ κύριος (4:16e καταβήσεται ἀπ᾽ οὐρανοῦ)	24:30b	τὸν υἱὸν τοῦ ἀνθρώπου ἐρχόμενον ἐπὶ τῶν νεφελῶν τοῦ οὐρανοῦ
4:16b	ἐν κελεύσματι,		μετὰ δυνάμεως καὶ δόξης πολλῆς·
4:16c	ἐν φωνῇ ἀρχαγγέλου	24:31a	καὶ ἀποστελεῖ τοὺς ἀγγέλους
4:16d	καὶ ἐν σάλπιγγι θεοῦ,		αὐτοῦ μετὰ σάλπιγγος μεγάλης,

[23] Just the reference to a λόγος κυρίου and a μυστήριον (cf. also Rom 11:25–26) sets these texts apart (so Bockmuehl 1990, 171; see Holtz 1998, 184; Malherbe 2000, 268).

[24] See Aejmelaeus 1985; Howard 1988, 180–186; McNicol 1996, 15–44; Orchard 1938, 23–30; Rigaux 1975; Wenham 1981; 1995, 305–316, 329–336; for opposing view, see Tuckett 1990, 169–182.

On the basis of key terminology hardly found elsewhere, coupled with alleged extensive sequential parallelism between the two texts (apart from 4:16e), McNicol is confident that Paul and Matthew are drawing on a common tradition. A case for a direct literary relationship however, is not warranted (34–35).[25] Howard (1988) promotes a more elaborate hypothesis of sixteen parallels between 1 Thess 4:16–5:7 and Matt 24–25. The following list includes only alleged parallels for the text under discussion (181):[26]

1. Christ himself returns:
   αὐτὸς ὁ κύριος … καταβήσεται (1 Thess 4:16)
   τὸν υἱὸν τοῦ ἀνθρώπου ἐρχόμενον (Matt 24:30)
2. From heaven:
   καταβήσεται ἀπ᾽ οὐρανοῦ (1 Thess 4:16)
   ἐπὶ τῶν νεφελῶν τοῦ οὐρανοῦ (Matt 24:30)
3. With a shout:
   ἐν κελεύσματι (1 Thess 4:16)
   μετὰ δυνάμεως καὶ δόξης πολλῆς (Matt 24:30)
4. Accompanied by angels:
   ἐν φωνῇ ἀρχαγγέλου (1 Thess 4:16)
   καὶ ἀποστελεῖ τοὺς ἀγγέλους αὐτοῦ (Matt 24:31)
5. With the trumpet of God:
   καὶ ἐν σάλπιγγι θεοῦ (1 Thess 4:16)
   μετὰ σάλπιγγος μεγάλης (Matt 24:31)
6. Believers are supernaturally gathered to Christ:
   ἔπειτα ἡμεῖς οἱ ζῶντες οἱ περιλειπόμενοι ἅμα σὺν αὐτοῖς ἁρπαγησόμεθα (1 Thess 4:17)
   καὶ ἐπισυνάξουσιν τοὺς ἐκλεκτοὺς αὐτοῦ ἐκ τῶν τεσσάρων ἀνέμων ἀπ᾽ ἄκρων οὐρανῶν ἕως τῶν ἄκρων αὐτῶν (Matt 24:31)
   τότε δύο ἔσονται ἐν τῷ ἀγρῷ, εἷς παραλαμβάνεται καὶ εἷς ἀφίεται· δύο ἀλήθουσαι ἐν τῷ μύλῳ, μία παραλαμβάνεται καὶ μία ἀφίεται (Matt 24:40–41)
7. Believers meet the Lord:
   εἰς ἀπάντησιν τοῦ κυρίου εἰς ἀέρα (1 Thess 4:17)
   τότε ὁμοιωθήσεται ἡ βασιλεία τῶν οὐρανῶν δέκα παρθένοις, αἵτινες λαβοῦσαι τὰς λαμπάδας ἑαυτῶν ἐξῆλθον εἰς ὑπάντησιν τοῦ νυμφίου (Matt 25:1)
   ἰδοὺ ὁ νυμφίος, ἐξέρχεσθε εἰς ἀπάντησιν αὐτοῦ (Matt 25:6)
8. In the clouds:
   ἐν νεφέλαις (1 Thess 4:17)
   ἐπὶ τῶν νεφελῶν (Matt 24:30)

Howard asserts that the principal themes are the same and the order is substantially the same (181). He argues that the "moderate dissimilarity" of imagery indicates use

[25] *Contra* Orchard 1938, 19–20; Waterman 1975, 107.

[26] The English headings are Howard's. It should be noted that I do not agree with some of the terminology (e.g. "returns"; "supernaturally"). The Greek text additions are mine.

of a more dynamic tradition (i.e. oral) to suit each writer's own individual purposes (182). Wenham previously identified parallels as per points four, five, six and eight above (1981, 348). He admits that "the verbal parallelism is not very impressive" since ἀπάντησις (1 Thess 4:17; Matt 25:6) is the only one of significance (349). Yet he concludes that the thematic parallels are too extensive to be accidental and are best explained as indicating common tradition (348–349).[27] I agree with Tuckett who is not persuaded by the evidence, least with ἀπάντησις. The word occurs too often in the LXX (over 100 times) to draw any conclusions of parallels. In addition, Tuckett argues that its appearance in the parable of the ten virgins (Matt 25:1–13) may be a Matthean construct and therefore unavailable to influence Paul's wording (1990, 176–177).[28] Tuckett also takes issue with point six above. The link between ἁρπάζειν and Matt 24:31, 40–41 is tenuous, particularly to the latter verses. The contrast between those "taken" and those "left" is alien to 1 Thess 4 (177). Besides these specific objections, Tuckett generally finds difficulty accepting any of the proposed parallels between 1 Thess 4:13–18 and Matt 24–25 on the basis of commonly accepted results of source criticism. Some of the parallels alluded to are to texts usually regarded as Matthean redactions of Mark (e.g. Matt 24:30–31) while others are to texts usually regarded as a redactional combination of Markan and Q material (177). Consequently, alleged parallels between the texts must take into account the redaction history of Matthew, making such parallels difficult to establish (Aejmelaeus 1985, 79–86).[29] Even if the objections thus far are deemed unconvincing, there appears to be no reason why Paul would give a quotation of the material in Matt 24:30–31 (or material along the line of its trajectory), in 1 Thess 4:13–18. The situation that Paul addresses, and to which his reference to a λόγος κυρίου presumably relates, has no link to the Matthean text. The issues about Christians dying, about who will participate in the *parousia* of the Lord, and whether the living will have precedence over the dead are not addressed in Matthew.[30] Consequently, Tuckett (1990, 180) concludes rightly:

---

[27] So also Kim 1993, 476; see Peterson 1930, 699; Schenk 1978, 295–296; Witherington 2006, 135–136.

[28] This point is irrelevant for Wenham who argues that Paul is able to draw on a variety of traditions (1995, 310–311). In reply, I find an argument (for or against a parallel between Paul and Matthew) which is based on a construct of pre-synoptic traditions to be unhelpfully subjective; see Tuckett 1990, 177 n. 85.

[29] Kim attempts to solve the problem by moving the parallel from Matt 24:30–31 to Mark 13:26–27, since the only substantial difference is the reference to "trumpet" in Matt 24:31 (2002a, 233). This solution does not address the fact that the only verbal parallels between 1 Thess 4:16–17 and Mark 13:26–27 are the references to "heaven" and "clouds", neither of which is used in the same way.

[30] Kim endeavours to discredit Tuckett's argument by attempting to show how Paul could have "interpreted the idea of the Son of Man 'gathering his elect' from the four corners of heaven or of heaven and earth through his angels (Matt 24.31/Mark 13.27) as implying the resurrection of the dead believers in view of the concerns of the Thessalonians" (2002a, 234). This solution only deals with the one issue about Christians dying; there is still nothing in the Matthean or Markan texts which explains who will participate in the *parousia*, or how that participation will unfold (see Patterson 1991, 30).

Thus the source-critical analysis of 1 Thes 4,16–17 itself, and the general irrelevance of Mt 24,30–31 to the Thessalonian situation, make it improbable that the saying adduced by Paul here is a tradition related in some way to Mt 24,30–31.

c. Words of the Lord

1. The phenomenon of referring to a λόγος κυρίου is uncommon in Paul. References which strictly contain λόγος and κύριος in some combination are few: λέγομεν ἐν λόγῳ κυρίου (1 Thess 4:15) which possibly refers to a saying of Jesus; and, ὁ λόγος τοῦ κυρίου (1 Thess 1:8; cf. 2 Thess 3:1) which is used as a synonym of Paul's *kērygma* (Cerfaux 1959, 37–38; Kittel 1967, 115).[31] There are a few parallels however, which may be grouped semantically with λόγος κυρίου phrases. These are listed by Boring (1982, 73–74): 1 Cor 7:10, 12, 25; 9:14; 11:23–26; 14:37.[32] None of these follows the formulation of 1 Thess 4:15a, where Paul uses a prepositional phrase with an instrumental dative to modify λέγειν.[33] The phrase ἐν λόγῳ κυρίου does occur in the LXX a number of times,[34] as does ἐν ῥήματι κυρίου (3 Kgdms 13:18), ἐν λόγῳ (τοῦ) θεοῦ (2 Kgdms 16:23; 1 Par 15:15), ἐν λόγῳ αὐτοῦ (Sir 39:17; 43:26)[35] and ἐν λόγῳ ὑψίστου (Sir 48:5). Henneken (1969, 73–98) demonstrates that λόγος κυρίου is a *terminus technicus* in the LXX for a prophetic word (92–95; see Davies 1963, 106). He concludes that although Paul's reference to a λόγος κυρίου is not strictly formal in character, it is clear that he is speaking as a prophet (95) and that the contents of the saying come from the exalted Lord (98). More recently, Hofius provides a short summary of the various views concerning the λόγος κυρίου in 1 Thess 4:15–17, and gives special emphasis to the LXX parallels (1991, 339–340). He concludes, mainly on the basis of 3 Kgdms 12:33–13:34, 21:35 and 1 Par 15:15, that Paul is referring to a saying of the exalted Lord that he personally received (339; so also Neirynck 1986, 311).

2. The sources of λόγοι κυρίου are diverse and often difficult to identify in particular instances. One reason for this is that oral and written traditions developed

---

[31] Similarly, Paul uses other combinations with λόγος to refer to his *kērygma* or to scripture: ὁ λόγος τοῦ θεοῦ (Rom 9:6; 1 Cor 14:36; 2 Cor 2:17; 4:2; cf. Col 1:25; 2 Tim 2:9; Titus 2:5); τὸν λόγον λαλεῖν (Phil 1:14); ὁ λόγος (Rom 9:9; 1 Thess 1:6; cf. 2 Tim 4:2); cf. ὁ λόγος αὐτοῦ (Titus 1:3).

[32] On 1 Cor 7:10, 12, 25 and 9:14, see the monograph by Dungan (1971) who examines Paul's use of particular sayings in a church setting and compares this with the handling of the same/similar traditions in synoptic texts. Although outside this discussion, Acts 20:35 is striking: οἱ λόγοι τοῦ κυρίου Ἰησοῦ ὅτι αὐτὸς εἶπεν. "Echoes" of alleged sayings are rightly to be separated from texts which make explicit reference to a saying of Jesus (regardless of whether the saying is given or not); see Hunter 1961, 46–51; Roetzel 1991, 77–79.

[33] Rom 14:14 contains ἐν κυρίῳ Ἰησοῦ which modifies the phrase οἶδα καὶ πέπεισμαι. But this is not a reference to a saying of Jesus and the terminology is too far removed from 1 Thess 4:15 to be of use.

[34] 3 Kgdms 13:1, 2, 5, 32; 21(MT 20):35; 2 Par 30:12; Sir 48:3; cf. ἐν λόγῳ κύριος λέγων in 3 Kgdms 13:9, 17.

[35] Cf. Wis 9:1; *Pss. Sol.* 17:24, 25.

alongside each other and were transmitted in a variety of ways: through missionary propaganda, *praxis*, liturgy, teaching and polemic (e.g. isolated sayings in Paul and Acts); through specific theological and sociological life situations (e.g. Gospels, P. Oxy. 840, P. Eg. 2); and through the emergence of other collections (e.g. *Gos. Thom.*, *1 Clem.* 13.2; 46.8).[36] Paul's references to the sayings of Jesus were certainly to an oral tradition (Holtz 1991, 383). An attempt to determine source(s) of the λόγος κυρίου referred to in 1 Thess 4:15 (and of like references in Paul) must include a consideration of the following options:

First, Paul may be referring to a saying of the earthly Jesus, if not to a saying preserved elsewhere, then to a so-called *agraphon* (i.e. a saying of Jesus not found in the Gospels), or combination of *agrapha*. Assuming that the point at issue in 1 Thess 4:15–17 is the participation of the living and dead at the *parousia*, and the relative order of the two, it appears that Paul is not referring to a saying found elsewhere (Tuckett 1990, 180). There are no theories of a plausible *Sitz im Leben* for Jesus to make such a statement (Best 1972, 191). If the saying is genuine, it cannot have been referring to Jesus' *parousia* (Gaston 1970, 407–408). Despite this, some scholars still prefer to find parallels in the Synoptic Gospels or John (and accordingly relegate the assumed points at issue to Pauline redaction; Allison 1982). Proposed parallels include: a saying about a heavenly figure with angels in Matt 16:27 and 24:30 (McNicol 1996, 34–37; Sanders 1985a, 146); a saying about the Son of Man in Mark 13:26–27 (par.);[37] a saying about "one taken" and "one left" in Matt 24:40–41 (par.; Wenham 1995, 306); a saying about some who will not taste death before they see the kingdom of God come with power in Mark 9:1 (Gewalt 1982);[38] a saying about the dead and the living in John 11:25–26;[39] a saying about equality in Matt 20:16 (Michaels 1994, 186–188). A totally different suggestion comes from R. Steck (1883) who argues that the *Herrnwort* stems from *4 Ezra* 5:42. Alternatively, the λόγος κυρίου could be an *agraphon*, with no recognisable parallel, but still regarded as a saying of the earthly Jesus.[40] References to 1 Thess 4:15–17 rarely appear in articles on *agrapha*.[41] Due to the nature of *agrapha*,[42] it is difficult to prove that Paul is referring to a saying of Jesus at all (despite the efforts of some; see esp. Jeremias 1963, 32–45), although this observation is insufficient to dismiss the option altogether (Patterson 1991, 30). If there is a saying of Jesus here, there remains the problem of the plural verb (λέγομεν, v. 15a) of introduction since the saying is then a formulation of the Christian *ekklēsia* (Kümmel 1961, 52).

---

[36] For discussion, see Koester 1982, 59–70.

[37] Jeremias 1963, 78–79; Kim 2002a, 233; Wenham 1981, 367–368.

[38] For links between Mark 9:1, 13:30 and Matt 10:23, see Crawford 1982, 228–230.

[39] Gundry 1973, 102–103; 1987, 164–165; Nepper-Christensen 1965, 151–153; cf. John 6:39.

[40] Holtz 1991, 389; 1998, 184; Lohse 2000, 34; Nicholl 2004, 40–41; Wilcke 1967, 131.

[41] But see Jeremias 1957, 177–178; Schmid 1957, 206; Stroker 1992, 92.

[42] See methodological comments by Gundry 1987, 165; McNicol 1996, 37.

Second, Paul may be referring to a saying of the exalted Jesus.[43] Like the option of taking the λόγος κυρίου as an *agraphon*, this option immediately resolves the problem of finding an appropriate parallel. Uncertainty emerges however, over whether the saying is mediated by Paul himself,[44] or another Christian prophet.[45] There is certainly no question about whether Paul could have undertaken a prophetic role.[46] A parallel between 1 Thess 4:15–17 and 1 Cor 15:51–52, the latter of which contains the word μυστήριον and refers to a "prophetische Erkenntnis", is sometimes used to support Paul's mediation of the λόγος κυρίου.[47] This approach is beside the point despite similarities between the texts, because μυστήριον and λόγος κυρίου are not synonymous (U. B. Müller 1975, 223–225; see Wolter 2005, 185–186). Further, while Paul claims to receive the gospel δι᾽ ἀποκαλύψεως Ἰησοῦ Χριστοῦ in Gal 1:12, this only attests to his ability to receive revelations and cannot be used to prove mediation here. In conclusion and whether the first or second option is supported, a distinction between a saying of Jesus (i.e. "tradition") and a saying of the exalted Lord ought to be maintained. Richardson defines a number of criteria for characterising such a distinction (1980, 71).

Third, Paul may be referring to a statement claiming the authority of the exalted Jesus, either based on an unspecified saying or group of sayings, or else based entirely on Paul's own understanding.[48] This option solves a different problem, where scholars are unable to agree on the precise placement of an alleged saying in verses 15–17, by abandoning any attempt to find such a saying or sayings (Hofius 1991, 339 n. 16). Rather for Hartman, Paul uses ἐν λόγῳ κυρίου to refer to a tradition common to this text and to Mark 13 (par.) which stems from a midrashic structure based on Dan 7:13 and 12:2–3 (and other Danielic texts). Such an underlying structure explains the similarities between the Gospel texts and 1 Thess 4 (1966, 181–190).[49] Hyldahl essentially agrees with Hartman's thesis although he finds that the saying behind Matt 24:30–31 is identical with 1 Thess 4:16–17 (1980, 130). Goulder also observes extensive similarities between the Synoptics and First Thessalonians; he sees direct dependence of Matthew on Paul as a high probability (1974, 167). He understands the statement, οἴδατε γὰρ τίνας παραγγελίας ἐδώκαμεν ὑμῖν διὰ τοῦ κυρίου Ἰησοῦ (1 Thess 4:2), as "teaching based on that of Jesus and interpreted by the OT through the inspired mind of the apostle" (1974, 147). Thus, in verse

[43] Best 1972, 189–193; Collins 1984, 159; Davies 1963, 106–107; Dunn 1990, 326; 1998b, 174; Jurgensen 1994, 88.

[44] Donfried 2000a, 57; Henneken 1969, 73–98; Hofius 1991, 339–340; Mearns 1981, 140–141; P. Müller 1988, 26; Neirynck 1986, 311; Steck 1883, 511.

[45] Baumgarten 1975, 94; Boring 1982, 11; Harnisch 1973, 40; Hoffmann 1966, 218–220; Kramer 1966, 160; Luz 1968, 328–329; Siber 1971, 42–43.

[46] For a definition of a Christian prophet and the characterisation of Paul as one, see Ashton 2000, 179–197; Aune 1983, 189–231; Boring 1982, 15–21, 30–36; Hill 1979, 2–9, 111–118.

[47] Dautzenberg 1999, 64; see Merklein 1992, 418; Theobald 1991, 40.

[48] Giblin 1970, 21; Giesen 1985, 133; Hofius 1978, 104; Lenski 1937, 332; Merklein 1992, 412–413; see also Becker 1976, 51–54; Konradt 2003, 129–130 n. 591; Schlier 1963, 21.

[49] See Kieffer 1990, 213; Wanamaker 1990, 171.

15 Paul may only be making reference to tradition glossed with standard Jewish teaching (147; Brown 1964, 45). However, the specific nature of the problem Paul addresses seems to rule out such a suggestion (Löhr 1980, 271). Paul does not say that he gives a quotation (*Anführung*) of a word of the Lord but that he speaks *by* (ἐν) a word of the Lord (Merklein 1992, 413).

3. The current discussion among scholars about the λόγος κυρίου in 1 Thess 4:15–17 does not satisfactorily characterise the source(s) used by Paul. The proposal of a saying or sayings behind the verses from the earthly Jesus cannot be ruled out (Hengel 2002, 356). But neither can the proposal that Paul is relying on a saying of the exalted Jesus (Löhr 1980, 271). A decision between the two is often predicated upon a methodological predilection regarding a minimalist or maximalist inclination of each scholar (Boring 1983, 107–108).[50] The question of whether there was a distinction between the sayings of the earthly and exalted Jesus further complicates the discussion.[51] Although that question is beyond the scope of the inquiry here, the difficulty in developing criteria for the distinction serves to discourage a definitive solution in the case of 1 Thess 4:15–17. Rather, Boring makes a plea for using the qualifications of possibility and probability (even very high probability) rather than proof (1983, 108). He observes that choosing between options one and two (from above) is too simplistic (109):

> … Christian prophets contributed to the tradition of Jesus' words in a variety of ways: both primarily (creating new sayings) and secondarily (modifying traditional sayings), both directly (by contributing to it) and indirectly (by influencing the ways others contributed to it), and at more than one moment in the trajectory of a saying.[52]

In conclusion, Kramer suggests that the phrase gives the same note of authority that is gained from a quotation of the LXX. The authority and validity of the statement is thereby reinforced (1966, 159–160). Similarly, Richard argues that Paul uses the phrase to describe a way of speaking. In the OT it designates God's law or will and frequently describes prophetic activity (1995, 240). Consequently, Paul refers not to a saying but to "a message from the Lord" (240; Smith 2000, 724). But there is still plenty of scope for debate and it cannot be certain that Paul's use corresponds to the LXX (Siber 1971, 42). My conclusion is to downplay the possibility of isolating

[50] For example, compare the strongly opposing views of Kim (2002a, 231–241) and Tuckett (1990, 176–182) on the question of sources. Note Kim's attacks against Tuckett (and Walter 1985): "… they try to weaken" (231); "… a desperate argument born of excessive scepticism" (232).

[51] See Aune 1983, 233–245; Boring 1982, 1–14; Dunn 1978; Hill 1979, 160–185; Schröter 2004. Walter gives his opinion: "Aber man sollte sich jedenfalls klarmachen, daß die uns geläufige Unterscheidung von 'irdischem' und 'erhöhtem' Kyrios von Paulus weder hier noch sonst hervorgehoben wird" (1985, 500).

[52] See similar comments by Walter 1985, 507–508. Nicholl appears to have overlooked Boring's extensive and important examinations (Boring 1982 [cf. 1991]; 1983; cf. other ref. in the previous n.) of the problems regarding the mingling of prophetic and Jesus-sayings, when he says: "historical evidence that prophetic words were integrated into Jesus tradition is lacking" (2004, 39). Incidentally, none of the works of Aune, Boring or Hill appears in Nicholl's bibliography.

a saying behind 1 Thess 4:15–17 and concomitantly emphasise Paul's own role in the prophetic statement (Schneider 2000, 234–240).[53] If there is a saying, then Paul transmits it with apostolic authority and freedom (Hengel 2002, 356). Failing the discovery of a new variant in the Synoptic Apocalypse or a new *agraphon* which identifies the λόγος κυρίου as from the earthly Jesus, *one* solution is to interpret Paul's reference as an indication that he received a word from the exalted Lord, paraphrased it into his own words and uses it as an authoritative solution to the Thessalonians' question about those asleep (Hofius 1991, 339–340).

d. *Parousia* in Paul[54]

1. The noun, παρουσία, appears twenty-three times in the NT.[55] The corresponding verb (παρεῖναι) also appears[56] but since it is not used for the coming of Jesus it rarely figures in the discussion (although cf. John 7:6; 11:28). Dictionary articles generally draw attention to the double connotation of *parousia* as presence/arrival. The NT writers had many other terms at their disposal for describing the coming of Jesus (Riggans 1995).[57] However, none perhaps so clearly invokes a much larger

---

[53] Nicholl argues that Paul would not have referred to a prophetic saying "in light of the Thessalonians' apparently low opinion of prophecy as reflected in 1 Thess. 5:19ff." (2004, 39). This is more than negated by Paul's own claims to authority (so 1 Thess 2:1–12).

[54] This section is intended to provide a preliminary introduction to the use of παρουσία in First Thessalonians and esp. in 4:15, with only a brief overview of the secondary literature. For a more detailed introduction to this important Pauline term, the reader is directed to the following literature (by no means exhaustive). Dictionary articles include: Braumann 1976; Brown 1976; Conzelmann 1961; Karrer 1992; Oepke 1967; Pax 1963; Radl 1993; 1998; Rowland 1990; 1992; cf. BDAG and MM s.v. Articles on various aspects of the *parousia* include: Aune 1975; Beasley-Murray 1991; Best 1972, 349–371; Cerfaux 1959, 31–68; Cullmann 1956, 141–162; Dunn 1997; 1998, 294–315; Dupont 1952, 49–64; Glasson 1988; Guntermann 1932, 28–85; Jurgensen 1994; Kennedy 1904, 158–221; Kreitzer 1987, 93–129; Milligan 1908, 145–151; U. B. Müller 2001; Owen 1959; Plevnik 1975a, 199–277; Riggans 1995; Scott 1972; Selby 1999; Sleeper 1999; Smalley 1964; 1964a; Vos 1953, 72–93; Ware 1979; Witherington 1992, 147–180. Monographs on the *parousia*, focusing on First Thessalonians include: Ahn 1989; Burkeen 1979; Jurgensen 1992; and/or otherwise: Fison 1954; Glasson 1947; Holleman 1996; Maxwell 1968; Minear 1954; Moore 1966; Plevnik 1997; Robinson 1957; Vena 2001.

[55] If a variant reading of 1 Cor 1:8 is admitted there would be twenty-four references to παρουσία in the NT; but ἡμέρα τοῦ κυρίου is the better reading (see NA[27]). In the Gospels it appears only in Matthew: once of Jesus (24:3) and several times of the Son of Man (24:27, 37, 39). In the rest of the NT it appears predominately in Paul but also in some of the later epistles: of Christ (1 Cor 15:23), of the Lord (1 Thess 4:15; Jas 5:7, 8; cf. 2 Pet 3:4), of the Lord Jesus (1 Thess 2:19; 3:13; 2 Thess 2:8), of our Lord Jesus Christ (1 Thess 5:23; 2 Thess 2:1; 2 Pet 1:16), of the Son (1 John 2:28). It is used once to refer to the coming day of God (2 Pet 3:12). Paul also uses παρουσία to refer to the presence/arrival of himself (2 Cor 10:10; Phil 1:26; 2:12), of Stephanas, Fortunatus and Achaicus (1 Cor 16:17) and of Titus (2 Cor 7:6, 7).

[56] Matt 26:50; Luke 13:1; John 7:6; 11:28; Acts 10:21, 33; 12:20; 17:6; 24:19; 1 Cor 5:3; 2 Cor 10:2, 11; 11:9; 13:2, 10; Gal 4:18, 20; Col 1:6; Heb 12:11; 13:5; 2 Pet 1:9, 12; Rev 17:8.

[57] These include among others (see Robinson 1957, 18; Vena 2001, 108): ἔρχεσθαι (Matt 10:23; 11:3 [par.]; 16:27 [par.], 28 [par.]; 24:30 [par.], 39, 42, 44 [par.]; 25:31; 26:64 [par.]; John 4:25; 7:27, 31; 14:3; 21:22, 23; Acts 1:11; 1 Cor 4:5; 11:26; 2 Thess 1:10; Heb 10:37; Rev 1:7; 22:20; cf. 1 Thess 1:10; 5:2); ἀποκαλύπτειν (Luke 17:30); ἀποκαλύψις (1 Cor 1:7; 2 Thess 1:7; 1 Pet 1:7, 13; cf. 1 Pet 4:13); ἐπιφάνεια (2

complex of eschatological ideas, including resurrection and judgment (Rowland 1990, 513).[58] The trajectory of the term traverses multiple strands of tradition. It is influenced by the literature of Second Temple Judaism and continues to develop through the time of the first Christians, the Gospel writers and beyond.[59] The word is a well established technical term for the presence/arrival of a king or emperor (Deissmann 1995, 368–373). Its Hellenistic flavour must be reckoned with when it comes to an interpretation of the word in the NT. However, it is problematic to impose the technical meaning onto the NT use (because it is not used consistently), leading many scholars to argue that it is not a *terminus technicus* there.[60] Since it is used in a consistent manner in First Thessalonians, perhaps the designation "quasi-technical" is appropriate (Collins 1993, 67–68; see Gundry 1987, 162). Whether and how παρουσία is connected to the historical Jesus is difficult to say although the rise of the expectation of Jesus' *parousia* cannot be severed from the Jesus tradition altogether (Holleman 1996, 95–122; Owen 1959).[61]

2. Paul's own varied use illustrates the term's flexibility (Minear 1954, 111), and it is difficult to determine just how much political Hellenistic contact plays a part, particularly when Paul's language is often influenced by theophany texts of the OT (Glasson 1947, 157–171, and esp. 1988).[62] In particular, Paul's descriptions of the *parousia* of the Lord resemble descriptions of the Day of the Lord in the OT (e.g. Exod 19; Isa 26–27; Zech 14).[63] The notion of a personal *parousia* is a later development which Paul sharpens with his identification of the *parousia* Jesus as the resurrected one (Beasley-Murray 1991). Such a sharpening redefines *parousia* as

Thess 2:8; 1 Tim 6:14; 2 Tim 4:1, 8; Titus 2:13); μαράνα θά or μαρὰν ἀθά (1 Cor 16:22; Mundle 1976); φανεροῦν (Col 3:4). Vena provides a handy table defining the use by NT writers of various terms for the coming of Jesus, organised into three separate time periods of 49–65 CE, 65–85/90 CE and 90–120/130 CE (2001, 112–113).

[58] On the *parousia* and final judgment, see Kreitzer 1987, 93–129, and esp. 99–112; Plevnik 1997, 221–243. On the *parousia* and resurrection (re 1 Cor 15), see Holleman 1996.

[59] See Ahn 1989, 71–179; Moore 1966, 7–34; Vena 2001, 33–104. For apocalyptic references, see for example: *T. Jud.* 22:2; *T. Levi* 8:15; *T. Ab.* 13:4, 6 (rec. A); *1 En.* 38:2; 49:4; *2 En.* 32:1.

[60] Koester 1990, 445–446; Plevnik 1999, 539; Popkes 2002, 854; *contra* Laub 1973, 33; 1976, 21; Radl 1993, 44; 1998, 1402; Theißen 1999, 160. Vena rightly recognises that παρουσία is never used as a technical term in the NT since it is always followed by a qualifying phrase. He points out that the word was used in a Christian context for the first time as a technical term by Clement of Alexandria in the 3rd century CE (2001, 107–108), and that of the incarnation. Later in his monograph, Vena inconsistently refers to Paul's use of παρουσία in First Thessalonians as the "first mention of the parousia as a technical term" (115).

[61] See discussion by Glasson (1947, 63–150) and Robinson (1957, 36–82) who argue that the *parousia* does not go back to the authentic Jesus.

[62] This question is central to the interpretation of *parousia* in 1 Thess 4:15–17, where the word ἀπάντησις (v. 17) perhaps hints at a technical use for the arrival of a king or an emperor (Peterson 1930; Koester 1997, 158–159). For opposing views, see for example, Dupont 1952, 49–73; Plevnik 1999. For other examples of Hellenistic use, see Connolly 1987; Horsley 1981; Vena 2001, 33–57; MM 497 s.v. For a review of the literature and discussion of the possible influence of Hellenistic formal receptions, see §III.e.6 below.

[63] See Chapter 6, §III.a, for further discussion of the phrase ἡμέρα κυρίου.

christocentric to some extent (Scott 1972; Ware 1979).[64] The "presence" aspect of *parousia* (or the "already") expressed by the resurrection is not invalidated by delay but provides extended expectation of the "not yet", or a fresh articulation of hope (Dunn 1997).[65] Thus, a motif of delay became a basis for some exhortations (Snyder 1975). The apocalyptic imagery often surrounding references to *parousia* are indicative of the discontinuity between Paul's statements and the subject matter being articulated via the language of vision, or symbol (Smalley 1964a). The thesis that Paul changed his view regarding whether he would be alive at the *parousia* is closely linked to a chronology of Paul's letters and will be discussed below (§III.c.4). That Paul's interest (or the Thessalonians' interest) in First Thessalonians regarding the *parousia* of Jesus exceeds that of his other letters (and recipients) is clear because, of the five references in the authentic Paul, four are found in this letter (not counting the variant reading in 1 Cor 1:8).

Excursus 5
Monographs and Articles on 4:13–18 (in table form)

1. Many attempts at expressing Paul's thought in these verses are crippled by the sizeable task of engaging the, often *not* mutually exclusive, theses of different authors. In general, articles on the pericope only address one topic or aspect of the discussion; scholars can struggle to engage the text on a systematic level. This is not the fault of individual authors but the limiting nature of articles themselves. In addition, the commentary format often does not admit extensive surveys of the literature. Commentators sometimes operate from an inadequate consultation base with previous work.[66] Consequently, this leaves monographs to fill the gap. I am aware of only three specifically on 1 Thess 4:13–18: one in German (Harnisch 1973) and another in French and never published (Jurgensen 1992), both including 5:1–11; one in English (Mason 1992) but focusing only on the aspect of resurrection.

2. The table which follows is arranged in chronological order (earlier to more recent), with a list of scholars and dates appearing vertically at the side of each row. Although it is not immediately obvious how many different theses exist for the interpretation of 1 Thess 4:13–18,[67] the strength of this arrangement is that it shows the chronological development of various approaches, and allows for a fuller expression of the systematic thought of each scholar. All entries have only one date after a name which indicates the first significant contribution to the discussion by an author. Sometimes further dates appear at the beginning of individual footnotes. These indicate subsequent contributions by an author, and/or noteworthy developments in an author's thought. References are always to the first date unless indicated otherwise.

[64] Gundry comments: "The first hard evidence of the Christian use of παρουσία for the second coming appears, then, in 1 Thessalonians. This datum creates a presumption that Paul was responsible for introducing the term into Christian vocabulary as a technical designation" (1987, 162).

[65] See Aune 1975; Smalley 1964.

[66] A notable exception is Rigaux's (1956) commentary; the introduction is a massive 340 pages.

[67] For summaries, see Marshall 1983, 120–122; Merk 1997.

3. The table is arranged on a double page into columns containing four foci by which material is arranged. Thus, columns one and two outline an assessment of the Thessalonians' problem(s) and Paul's answer(s) or response(s), respectively, while columns three and four separate two issues which I think are helpful for distinguishing theses — namely, an author's view on the λόγος κυρίου and what influence predominately inspires Paul's thought, respectively. Hopefully, this arrangement aids the clarity of presentation of an author's thesis and also aids the use of the table as a reference guide to a history of research on 1 Thess 4:13–18. In addition, footnotes appear periodically at the bottom of each page and these contain commentary and references to alert the reader to points of contact between theses, whether of rejection, dependency or development. Sometimes a footnote appears on a facing page in relation to its reference, and this is done to utilise the available space below the table. A quick glance at these footnotes reveals numerous cross references, often to scholars whose names appear as entries in their own right. Thus, lines of thought are linked together or distinguished by this system. Sometimes compartments in the table are left blank (signified by a centred *m-dash*). This occurs only when an author offers little or no comment in the category represented by that column. In a few cases, an author is included in the table even when a comprehensive analysis of 1 Thess 4:13–18 is not given. This is because some aspect of a thesis may have made a significant contribution to the discussion and the reader is made aware of this in an explanatory footnote for those references.

	The Thessalonians' Problem(s)	Paul's Answer(s)
E. Peterson 1930[1]	—	Paul views the Thessalonians meeting the Lord at his *parousia*, in the same manner as an important dignitary or king was accorded upon arrival to a city (683). A significant portion of Peterson's article (683–692) consists of references to ancient texts: die Papyrustexte, die Inschriften, die literarischen Belege.
J. Dupont 1952, 39–113[2]	—	Paul uses terminology, which, despite contact with Hellenism, should be interpreted in the context of the LXX, and particularly the theophany text of Exod 19:10–18.
W. Schmithals 1965[3]	Some Thessalonians had been made doubtful about the resurrection of the dead (which was part of Paul's founding *kērygma*), probably by gnostic agitators, who denied the resurrection (115–119).	—
U. Luz 1968[4]	—	—

[1] See also Peterson 1964. Peterson's *Einholung* thesis is rejected by: Cosby 1994; Dupont 1952; Plevnik 1999. It is followed by: Baumgarten 1975, 96; Cerfaux 1959, 39–42; Collins 1984, 345; Gorman 2004, 160; Green 2002, 226–228; Gundry 1987; 1996; Lincoln 1981, 188; Lüdemann 1980a, 252–253; Marshall 1983, 131; Mason 1992, 105–109; Merklein 1992, 412; Mundle 1975; Nicholl 2004, 43–44; Wilckens 1988, 145; Witherington 1992, 158; see Bruce 1982, 102–103; Dibelius 1925, 24; Holtz 1986, 203; Richard 1995, 246–247.

[2] Dupont does not develop a new interpretation of 4:13–18. However, his view that Paul's language is situated in the Judaism(s) of the LXX rather than in Hellenism is decisive in the history of research. He is followed by Wilcke (1967, 141–147). His critique of Peterson (1930) is representative of scholars who do not find Hellenistic formal receptions a compelling analogy for Paul's use of ἀπάντησις.

λόγος κυρίου	Jewish/Hellenistic Influence?
Although there is no Gospel text corresponding to Paul's λόγος κυρίου, Peterson finds an implicit reference to a "feierliche Einholung" in Matt 25:1ff. (699).	The *Einholung* of the κύριος "sich eines Bildes aus staatsrechtlichem Brauch bedient" (698).
—	The terminology of παρουσία (49–64), εἰς ἀπάντησιν (64–73) and ἐπιφάνεια (73–77) is understood fundamentally in the contexts of primitive Christianity and Jewish traditions (78).
—	—
Luz reconstructs the λόγος κυρίου as follows (329): "Der Herr mit Befehlswort mit der Stimme des Erzengels und mit der Posaune Gottes wird herabsteigen vom Himmel. Die Toten im Herrn werden auferstehen. Die Übrigbleibenden werden zusammen mit ihnen entrückt werden mit den Wolken zur Begegnung mit dem Herrn in der Luft."	—

[3] See also Schmithals 1960; 1964; 1984; 1988. For Schmithals, 1 Thess is a compilation of multiple letters (4 different letters [1964; 1965]; 5 different letters [1984]; n.b. 1 Thess is a unity in an earlier article [1960]). Further, 4:15–18 is considered as redaction (1984, 111) and secondary (1988, 194). The thesis that Gnostic agitators were behind the Thessalonians' denial of the resurrection is formulated by Lütgert (1909) and developed by Schmithals. Harnisch (1973) reiterates the thesis with minor nuances.

[4] Luz' reconstruction of the λόγος κυρίου in 4:16–17 is decisive for many subsequent studies. He is more or less followed by: Baumgarten 1975, 94; Harnisch 1973, 42–43.

	The Thessalonians' Problem(s)	Paul's Answer(s)
W. Marxsen 1969 [5]	The near-expectation of the *parousia* is so strongly emphasised in 1 Thess that despite Paul's awareness of the resurrection of the dead idea, it was not emphasised in his founding *kērygma*. Consequently, when some Thessalonians died, hopelessness ensued for those who had died and also for themselves (26–28). "Das Datum ihres möglichen Todes stand in Konkurrenz mit dem Datum der Parusie" (34).	Paul formulates a solution to the Thessalonians' problem in terms of *Entrückung*; the resurrection of the dead is inserted into this solution and in no way becomes a *Thema* on its own. The emphasis remains on the *parousia* (30). Paul intends radically to expand the Thessalonians' faith (cf. the key phrase, διὰ τοῦ Ἰησοῦ, in v. 14) by showing that the *parousia* hope is grounded in the salvation act of God in Jesus (34–35).
J. Plevnik 1975a [6]	Paul previously described the Thessalonians' involvement in the *parousia* of the Lord in terms of assumption. Since persons undergoing assumption had to be alive (so Lohfink 1971) the Thessalonians may have thought those who had died could not take part in the *parousia* (272). Consequently, they were unable to properly relate the resurrection to the *parousia* (203).	Paul clarifies the relationship between the resurrection and the *parousia* by emphasising that everyone, dead and alive will take part in the *parousia*. Although Plevnik refers to Lohfink in his 1975a article, the thesis that Paul explains resurrection as a restoration to the earthly life is not made explicit until his later articles (1984, 281; 1989, 265). For Paul, the assumption "is not the *Einholung* of Jesus but rather the *Einholung* of the faithful, who are brought up to 'be with the Lord forever' (v. 18)" (2000, 95).
H. Koester 1979 [7]	Koester finds it an awkward exercise to look for specific problems behind 4:13–18 and 5:1–11. Rather, he understands the entire eschatological section as an example of "Paul's effort to transform the conventional genre of the letter into a Christian medium of communication" (40). In order for Paul to express the message of the Christian gospel – "the gospel announced the end of the world, the coming of a new age, an expectation that the future of God which was at hand would make everything new" (40) – he had to expand the traditional genre. "In 1 Thessalonians, as well as in later Christian letters, the eschatological section became the most distinctive mark of the new genre, be it as the typical final paragraph as in 1 Cor 15 or 2 Pet 3, or as the primary corpus of a letter as in Romans 3:21–11:36" (40).	

[5] See also Marxsen 1979. The thesis that the resurrection of the dead was not part of Paul's *kērygma* (to the Thessalonians) is asserted by: Becker 1976, 39, 46; 1993, 140–141; Jewett 1986, 94–95; Lüdemann 1980a, 229–230; 1993, 34–35; Moffatt 1910, 37; Nicholl 2004, 35–38; Schnelle 1986, 210; 2003, 191; Wilckens 1988, 143–144. For Wilckens, Paul proceeds "... ad hoc eine Lehre von der Auferweckung der vor den Endereignissen Entschlafenen zu entwerfen beginnt" (1988, 143). Lüdemann also de-emphasises a resurrection hope in preference to a *parousia* hope (1980, 196–197). The concept of resurrection is auxiliary to Paul's older idea of translation (1993, 35–36). See also Kegel 1970, 35–36; Merklein 1992, 407; Schnelle 1986, 210; Sellin 1986, 37–46.

Further, Lüdemann argues that Paul implicitly makes the connection "as Christ – so the Christians" for the first time in 1 Thess. Consequently, 1 Thess is accorded a much earlier date (see 1980a, 220– 264). On this connection, see also: Hyldahl 1980, 133–134; Oepke 1970, 172; Sellin 1983, 227; 1986, 45–46; Stanley 1961, 87.

λόγος κυρίου	Jewish/Hellenistic Influence?
The λόγος κυρίου is located in 4:16–17 (already summarised in v. 15), and it is "ein urchristliches Prophetenwort als Herrenwort", but modified by Paul (35–36).	—
Plevnik argues that Paul acted as a prophetic interpreter (of a word attributable to Jesus) by creatively adapting the word to a new situation (232). As such, Plevnik locates the λόγος κυρίου in 4:16–17 (231). Plevnik changes his view in a subsequent publication: "The question here deals with post-Easter anxieties, rather than with a problem that Jesus faced before Easter. Thus, the best possibility for the origin of this saying is a special revelation of the Lord to Paul" (1997, 81).	Plevnik locates the predominant influence of Paul in Jewish apocalyptic and OT sources (233).
—	Koester understands 1 Thess as the "creation of the first Christian letter" which must be understood in terms of letters from the late Hellenistic and Roman Imperial period (34). Paul reshapes literary conventions (34–40) and interprets traditional material (40–44).

[6] See also Plevnik 1984; 1989, 263– 266; 1990, 56–59; 1997; 1999; 2000. Plevnik follows Dupont's (1952) emphasis on the importance of theophany texts and applies the work of Lohfink (1971) to 4:13–18. Plevnik (1999) thoroughly rejects Peterson's *Einholung* thesis (1930) and is followed by: Giesen 1985, 135–136; Johanson 1987, 124–125; Jurgensen 1994, 85 (with reservations); Kreitzer 1987, 179–180; Richard 1995, 237; Wanamaker 1990, 166; see Meyer 1987.

[7] Smith also rejects interpretations of 4:13–18 which look for a specific problem. Rather, Paul gives examples of how the Thessalonians can exhibit "good form" (εὐσκημόνως, 4:12) in the face of difficulties (e.g. untimely deaths). Paul secures the permanent prestige of community members with a consoling message of *parousia* (1995, 87–90).

	The Thessalonians' Problem(s)	Paul's Answer(s)
R. F. Collins 1980a[8]	The Thessalonians were grieving for the dead *and* for their own future, exhibiting a "pagan anxiety" in the face of death (328). It is possible that the deaths were a result of persecution, and that these deaths had led the community to question the "coming triumph of God" (1993, 161–162). "Will not those who have died be deprived of an opportunity to participate in the parousia? And isn't that all the more tragic if those who have died did so precisely because of their faith?" (1993, 162).	The Thessalonians are reminded that the resurrection of Jesus is the ground of salvation for both the living and the dead (330). Paul uses traditional apocalyptic themes to explain how even οἱ κοιμηθέντες can be σὺν κυρίῳ. On such a basis, the Thessalonians are exhorted to encourage one another (333). Paul may allude to the Jewish speculation that those alive at the *parousia* would be better off than those dead. By using the traditions of resurrection and rapture, Paul is able to show that the dead will not be disadvantaged (1993, 163–165).
N. Hyldahl 1980[9]	The nearness of the *parousia* and the notion that Paul would be alive at the *parousia* were emphasised in Paul's *kērygma*. The death of some community members shattered the Thessalonians' *parousia*-hope (122–123), some of whom began to question Paul's *kērygma* altogether (129).	Paul emphasises the *parousia* and its nearness in 1 Thess, including a discussion of the "Zeitpunkt der Parusie" (122). He combats the Thessalonians' hopelessness by connecting the resurrection of Jesus (and his *parousia*) with the resurrection of those who had died (133). Paul reassures the Thessalonians that just as God raised Jesus from the dead, so too will he raise dead Christians (134).
G. Löhr 1980[10]	—	—

[8] See also Collins 1993. Herman (1980) also emphasises the significance of the death and resurrection of Jesus for those who had died.

[9] Hyldahl's thesis has certain contacts with Marxsen (1969), esp. concerning the connection between the resurrection of Jesus and the hope that Christians will also be raised (see ref. to Lüdemann, under Marxsen 1969). Sellin also asserts that the problem of the Thessalonians centres on *parousia*, not on

λόγος κυρίου	**Jewish/Hellenistic Influence?**
The λόγος κυρίου is "a *dictum* of early Christian prophecy ... to be found in vv. 16–17" (330). Collins (331–332) follows the reconstruction of Harnisch (1973, 39–46).	Paul uses Jewish apocalyptic traditions, but recasts them to suit his own purposes. Since his audience was Hellenistic, it is not improper to note the dual-level language, whereby Paul drew on Jewish motifs and terminology, but which made sense to a Hellenistic audience (1993, 166).
Hyldahl follows Hartman's (1966) theory that a midrash of Daniel stands behind the so-called "synoptic apocalypse" (Mark 13 [par.]). He identifies the λόγος κυρίου in 4:16–17 as identical to Matt 24:30–31 (130). Although the synoptic texts lack a connection between the resurrection and the *parousia*, Paul's addition to the apocalyptic tradition may be attributed to a Danielic influence (131). Sand also suggests that the apocalyptic thought has been influenced by Daniel (1972, 171).	—
Löhr's article only examines the "Herrenwort" of 4:15–17 with little comment on the Thessalonians' problem(s). The λόγος κυρίου is located in 4:16–17 which contains "allgemeines apokalyptisches Gedankengut" and provides a background to Paul's concrete situation-specific summary in v. 15 (269). The similarity between 1 Thess 4:15–17 and 1 Cor 15:51–52 must mean that they go back to the same tradition, albeit probably an oral one. The differences are attributed to a changed community situation. Löhr reconstructs the λόγος κυρίου into two units (271–273): 1. ὅτι ἐν ἀτόμῳ, ἐν σάλπιγγι θεοῦ, ἐν κελεύσματι ὁ κύριος καταβήσεται ἀπ' οὐρανοῦ καὶ τοὺς κοιμηθέντας ἐγερεῖ. 2. καὶ ἡμεῖς οἱ ζῶντες ἀχθησόμεθα ἐν νεφέλαις εἰς ἀπάντησιν τοῦ κυρίου εἰς ἀέρα. An original application of the saying might be reconstructed as: οἱ νεκροὶ καὶ ἡμεῖς οἱ περιλειπόμενοι σὺν κυρίῳ ἐσόμεθα (270). Löhr does not eliminate the first person plural formulation because it is doubtful whether a more primitive form can be accurately identified; this is probably the form circulated in early Christianity (271). The second unit may have a background in a theophany text (cf. Exod 19; 272). The "apokalyptisch-eschatologische" character of the text does not fit with a gnostic background in 1 Thess (273).	

resurrection. Cases of death brought about an "Infragestellung des Glaubens überhaupt" which Paul addresses through an "apokalyptische Motiv der endzeitlichen Totenerweckung" contained in the λόγος κυρίου of vv. 16–17 (1986, 39).

[10] See Gewalt 1982.

	The Thessalonians' Problem(s)	Paul's Answer(s)
D. Gewalt 1982 [11]	—	—
A. F. J. Klijn 1982 [12]	A question arose regarding the fate of Christians at the *eschaton*, particularly about a supposed inequality between those still alive and those who had died (67). The problem of the living being in a more advantageous position is common to apocalyptic literature (68), and arises from a problematical merging of two different traditions, viz. surviving to the end (prophetic eschatology) and a resurrection and judgment of all humans (apocalyptic tradition; 69). Such uncertainty raised questions about the applicability of Paul's *paraenesis* for the two groups (68).	Paul's answer addresses an issue of *paraenesis*, not of doctrinal misunderstanding (68). Using apocalyptic traditions, Paul shows that both those who survive to the end and those who die beforehand must remain vigilant and persevere (5:1–11). There is no difference between the two groups: both those awake and asleep (5:10) will live ἅμα σὺν Jesus (72). Paul provides *paraenesis* using apocalyptic material (4:16–17) and assumes that the Thessalonians are intimately familiar with a notion of the coming Day of the Lord (5:1–2; 69).
K. P. Donfried 1985 [13]	Paul's *kērygma* could be seen as a violation of the "decrees of Caesar" (344). Deaths among the Thessalonians are to be understood in a context of persecution and political opposition. These deaths are a result of persecution and the question arises: "what is the status of those who have died in Christ prior to the parousia?" (348; see 347–352).	Paul uses terminology from mystery cults and royal theology for protreptic purposes (353). Such terminology has continuity and discontinuity with the Thessalonians' "pagan past". Paul summarises his answer to the problem of death (including the status issue) in 5:9–10 (352–353).

[11] Gewalt is not the only one to identify the λόγος κυρίου in 4:15b(–16a). See 106–107 n. 9 for ref., and: Donfried 1993, 39–41; Gundry 1987, 165; Hartman 1966, 188; Hofius 1991, 338–341; Holtz 1991, 385–386; 1998, 183–185; Merklein 1992, 410–415; Michaels 1994, 183–185; Reinmuth 1998, 142; von Dobschütz 1909, 193–194; Wilcke 1967, 132–133.

[12] The thesis that the Thessalonians were concerned about an apparent inequality between the living and the dead, based on Jewish apocalyptic texts, is often taken up by scholars: Boring/Berger/Colpe 1995, 494–495; Delobel 1990; Howard 1988, 168; see already, Cerfaux 1959, 38–39; Magnien 1907; Schweitzer 1953, 90–97; Scott 1972. However, Klijn's emphasis on *paraenesis* and the importance of ἅμα in 4:17 and 5:10 is not developed (see Gillman 1985, 270–271; Richard 1995, 242).

<table>
<tr><th>λόγος κυρίου</th><th>Jewish/Hellenistic Influence?</th></tr>
<tr><td colspan="2">Gewalt builds on an article by Löhr (1980) but compares 1 Thess 4:15–17, 1 Cor 15:51– 52 and Mark 9:1 (see esp. synopsis, 109). He finds a "Grundstruktur" common to all three texts, formulated as:
Eine Gruppe von (uns) Christen
wird (sicherlich) nicht sterben,
bevor die eschatologische Wende eintritt.
The differences between the three periphrastic "Performanztexten" are borne out in the various syntactic, semantic and pragmatic functions in context (111). The identification of the Grundstruktur supports the thesis that the λόγος κυρίου is to be located in 4:15–16a (106–107).</td></tr>
<tr><td>—</td><td>Jewish apocalyptic affords a special privilege to those who survive until the end (Dan 12:12–13; Pss. Sol. 17:50; 18:7; Sib. Or. 3:370). Such persons will be present at the final justification of Israel (4 Ezra 6:25; 7:27; 9:8). Further, survivors are compared favourably over those who have died (4 Ezra 13:16–24). However, elsewhere it is made clear that judgment occurs at the same time (4 Ezra 5:41–45; 70–71). Klijn emphasises the importance of "in unum" (v. 45), which is equated to ἅμα in 1 Thess 4:17; 5:10. The aspect of simultaneity is found elsewhere (2 Bar. 30:2; 51:13; 4 Ezra 6:20; L.A.B. 19:12). He concludes: "1 Thess. 4.13–18 can be explained entirely against the background of apocalyptic thinking" (72).</td></tr>
<tr><td>Donfried follows Merklein (1992) in the identification of the λόγος κυρίου in 4:15b (1993, 39–41). It is "a prophetic word transmitted by the heavenly Lord to the prophet Paul" (1993, 40).</td><td>—</td></tr>
</table>

[13] Donfried 1985 = 1997 with minor changes. See also Donfried 1989; 1990; 1993; 2000a, 56–58. Edson (1940; 1948) provides an extensive background to Donfried's views. Scholars who agree that the Thessalonians underwent persecution related deaths include: Collins 1993, 161–162; Lindars 1985, 771; Pobee 1985, 113. The possibility is entertained by: Bruce 1970, 1159; Chapa 1994, 156; Green 2002, 222; Hester 1996, 277; Marxsen 1972, 245; Nepper-Christensen 1965, 138; Riesner 1998, 386–387; Still 1999, 215–217.

To compose this table I read (in date order) everything each author had published on First Thessalonians. To my surprise I found that Donfried's original article on cults in Thessalonica (1985) appears in a longer article on the theology of First Thessalonians (1993, 12–26), with subtle changes and omissions. Some of

	The Thessalonians' Problem(s)	Paul's Answer(s)
H. Giesen 1985 [14]	The Thessalonians were uncertain about how the resurrection of Jesus related to those who had died (126); they had probably misunderstood Paul's *kērygma* (135). Paul had previously taught that the *parousia* could occur at any time according to a "Modell der Entrückung" (135). Paul probably also included the eschatological resurrection in his *kērygma*, but this would have been irrelevant for cases of death since models of translation require resurrection as a return to an earthly life (136).	Paul explains that cases of death provide no reason to give up hope (128). Paul reiterates the *kērygma* regarding the death and resurrection of Jesus as a grounding for his thesis in vv. 15b, 17a, about those already dead and those who are alive at the *parousia* (134). Paul clarifies that for those already dead there is a return to life before translation (136). The apocalyptic details (v. 16) serve to guarantee equality at the *parousia*; the dead are raised first (138). Thus, Paul is able to comfort the Thessalonians and exhort them to be ready for the *parousia* when it should come (146).
R. Jewett 1986 [15]	A reconstruction of the Thessalonian situation includes eight issues which were troubling the community (91–109) including the death of church members (94–96). Some radicals among the Thessalonians interpreted the situation, with its apocalyptic orientation, in terms of realised eschatology (see 176–178). Coupled with the fact that the Thessalonians were unaware of a resurrection hope is the notion of cooptation between the Cabirus and civic cults, whereby a *parousia*-expectation of a new redeemer figure included a divinisation of community members (176; cf. 123–132). Thus, death could only be interpreted as permanent (94).	Jewett does not provide an exegesis of 4:13–18. Consequently, he understands Paul's answer to the Thessalonians' problem (i.e. 4:13–18) in general terms: "Paul responded to the crisis of a radicalized and hence vulnerable millenarism by writing 1 Thessalonians" (177).

these changes are a cut and paste of other articles previously published (including footnotes). Incidentally, the article (1985) is published *again* with minor changes, but under a new title (1997), and *yet again* (without changes) in a volume of essays by Donfried (2002, 21–48).

In the references below, and for the convenience of the reader, I have used an arrow (→) to show where substantially the same material is located. Out of one hundred thirteen pages (i.e. Donfried 1993 and 1993a), there are forty-two pages of previously published material. Indeed, parts of the remaining seventy-one pages serve as a source for subsequent publications. Donfried does make statements as follows: "As we have already suggested ..." (1993, 19); "Earlier we attempted to indicate the importance of the religious cults of Thessalonica ..." (1993, 48); "In several of our previous discussions ..." (1993, 64). But such comments would normally be understood to refer to an earlier part of the current article, not to unacknowledged previously published material. The last reference below refers to two publications in the same year where the same material with minor differences was published without acknowledgement.

1984, 249, 251–253 → 1993, 69–70 | 1985, 338 → 1993, 15 | 1985, 336 → 1997, 215 | 1985, 336–341 → 1993, 12–14 | 1985, 342–346 → 1993, 15–18 | 1985, 342–352 → 1997, 215–223 | 1985, 347–350 → 1993, 19–23 | 1985, 350–351 → 1993, 24–26 | 1989, 242–244 → 1993, 18–19 | 1989, 256–257 → 1993,

λόγος κυρίου	Jewish/Hellenistic Influence?
Paul uses the formulation ἐν λόγῳ κυρίου to identify his *kērygma* as authoritative, not to identify a particular saying (132–134).	—
—	—

23–24 \| 1989, 259–260 → 1993, 26–27 \| 1990, 5–7; 1992, 1017–1020 → 1993, 9–12 \| 1990, 9–13 → 1993, 31–35 \| 1990, 16–23 → 1993, 64–69 \| 1990, 23–26 → 1993, 70–72 \| 1991a, 196 → 1993, 8–9 \| 1993, 3–7 → 2000a, 38–42 \| 1993, 51–53 → 2000a, 55–56 \| 1993a, 84–89 → 1993b, 129–136.

[14] Giesen, whose thesis is far removed from Plevnik's, nevertheless agrees with him on the issue of *Entrückung* (cf. Plevnik 1984). He asserts that Paul did not maintain a near expectation (*Naherwartung*) of the *parousia*, as if that were the source of the Thessalonians' loss of hope (135). This is made clear by the double participles οἱ ζῶντες οἱ περιλειπόμενοι where Paul differentiates between those alive now (in contrast to the dead) and those who survive to the *parousia* (136–139).

[15] See also Jewett 1972. Jewett originally developed a thesis of "enthusiastic radicalism" for the Thessalonian situation (1972), based on the previous work of Lütgert (1909). But he critiques his own earlier thesis (1986, 146–147) and develops a new, millenarian model (161–178). The model is adopted by: Murphy-O'Connor 1996, 114–129 (with reservations); Stacy 1999, 186–188; cf. Meeks 1983a. Wanamaker (1987) examines the emergence of apocalyptic Christianity at Thessalonica in terms of millenarianism, apparently independently of Jewett.

	The Thessalonians' Problem(s)	Paul's Answer(s)
R. H. Gundry 1987 [16]	Paul may have so emphasised the imminent return of Jesus that his teaching on the future resurrection was "swallowed up", if indeed he taught it at all (167).	Paul's reference to a sequence of events (πρῶτον ... ἔπειτα, 4:16–17) emphasises the surety of the resurrection (168). Paul hellenised dominical tradition to strengthen his consolation to the Thessalonians (168–169).
T. H. Olbricht 1990 [17]	"All believers share the hope of the Parousia through Christ's care. The believers who have died continue in Christ's care. Therefore, the believers who have died share in the Parousia. All believers will be caught up by Christ to be with God. The believers who have died will be raised. Therefore, they will be caught up with Christ to be with God. No one knows the time when Christ will return, so everyone must be ready. The Thessalonians do not know when Christ will come. Therefore, the Thessalonians must be ready for the return of Christ" (232).	
M. D. Goulder 1992 [18]	The Thessalonians received a conflicting *kērygma*, one from Paul and the other from Silas (101–104). The problem of death arose from a notion that the kingdom had arrived (90–92), a notion which also spawned controversy over other issues: giving up work (88–90), celibacy (93), questions about Paul's *kērygma* countered in 2:1–12 (94–96). Goulder argues that Silas was able to proclaim his gospel during the founding visit, after Paul had left Macedonia (101).	Paul counters false ideas with a letter. He reminds the Thessalonians that the kingdom is a future reality, something he, at least, taught them during the founding visit (91–92; cf. 5:1–2). Paul attempts to repair the damage caused by Silas' different *kērygma* by emphasising co-authorship, esp. through the dominating first person plural "we" (102).

[16] See also Gundry 1996. Gundry develops Peterson's (1930) thesis particularly in his second article (1996) where he rejects Cosby's (1994) critique of Peterson; see Tellbe 2001, 123–130. The idea that Paul may not have emphasised the prospect of death before the *parousia*, in preference of a thoroughly emphasised and proximate *parousia*, is also asserted by Still (1999a, 196–197).

[17] Olbricht sets out the Thessalonians' implied problems and Paul's answers (4:13–5:11) in terms of enthymemes and their underlying syllogisms — according to Aristotelian rhetorical analysis.

λόγος κυρίου	Jewish/Hellenistic Influence?
Regarding the λόγος κυρίου, Paul draws on a dominical saying, most likely the same one recorded in John 11:25–26. He does not give a quotation of the saying, but revises it according to contextual needs in 1 Thess 4:15–17 (164–165). The point of the saying appears in v. 15, while vv. 16–17 provide further details (165). The identification of the λόγος κυρίου as a saying of Jesus also recorded in John 11:25–26 is previously developed by Nepper-Christensen, who also sees the same saying behind 1 Cor 15:51–52 (1965, 151– 154).	Gundry concludes that Paul has hellenised dominical tradition about the *parousia* of Jesus (162–163). Paul equates the παρουσία of Jesus with ἡμέρα κυρίου (cf. 5:1–11), and in the process christianises Jewish tradition (169–172). Gundry rejects Dupont's (1952) theory that 4:16–17 has the theophany text of Exod 19:10–18 as its background (161). Regarding the Hellenistic custom of meeting (ἀπάντησις) a visiting emperor, Gundry comments: "... joining the Lord in his descent corresponds so closely to hellenistic practice that hellenistic readers could hardly have missed the correspondence and a hellenistic author could hardly have failed to intend it" (166– 167).
—	—
—	—

[18] Goulder acknowledges the problems of assuming Pauline authorship of 2 Thess, but still suggests that Paul's references to a "forged letter" (2 Thess 2:2) and specific postscript (3:17) may be understood as evidence that Silas wrote his own letter (possibly prefaced with: "Silvanus, Paul and Timothy") of which contents Paul did not approve (103). For another theory involving Silvanus, see Binder 1983; 1990.

	The Thessalonians' Problem(s)	Paul's Answer(s)
H. Merklein 1992[19]	The Thessalonians do not require new information about the resurrection. Otherwise Paul would have supplied a straightforward apodosis in 4:14, and his statement in 4:15 about the living not preceding those asleep would not have made sense. The Thessalonians were unclear about the connection between the resurrection and the *parousia* (405–406). They feared that the resurrection would occur after the *parousia*. Thus, it is not that the Thessalonians have no hope. Rather, deaths of community members is incompatible with an intense near expectation (408–409).	Paul informs the Thessalonians not by emphasising the resurrection but by stressing that it occurs first (πρῶτον). Only then does the *parousia* itself occur; Paul concludes that both the dead and the living will be together with him (407). The solution to the Thessalonians' problem is essentially answered in 4:15b, 17b, while 4:16–17a is an explication and elucidation (410).
C. A. Evans 1993	—	—

[19] Börschel (2001, 224–241) relies heavily on Merklein.

<table>
<tr><th>λόγος κυρίου</th><th>Jewish/Hellenistic Influence?</th></tr>
<tr><td colspan="2">Merklein concludes that the λόγος κυρίου is to be found in 4:15b (410), and that Paul does not cite a Herrenwort but a Prophetenwort which he himself speaks (412–413). "Die Annahme eines direkten Zitats erscheint aber als wenig wahrscheinlich" (412).
Merklein supports his first conclusion on semantic and pragmatic grounds. If 4:15b is a summary as many commentators suppose then Paul would have located it after the citation of the saying or else before its introduction. Only 4:15b contains the information regarding the discursive sequence of the resurrection and the parousia. Word statistics may not be used to determine the location of the saying since both 4:15b and 4:16–17 contain apocalyptic ideas and presumably traditional material (410–411). On pragmatic grounds, Merklein asserts that the Thessalonians already knew many of the details of the parousia since the statements in 4:16–17a would be a strange way of introducing new information; Paul brings only the πρῶτον (v. 16) and the ἅμα σὺν αὐτοῖς (v. 17) as new (411–412).
Merklein supports his second conclusion by examination of texts which distinguish between a Herrenwort and a "durchaus pneumatischem" Wort, and by the observation that Paul does not cite a λόγος κυρίου but says that he speaks ἐν λόγῳ κυρίου (412–413). "Er spricht in der Autorität des Herrn", and as such probably refers to a Prophetenwort which he himself speaks (413). Merklein confirms his interpretation by noting a structural correspondence with 1 Cor 15:50–58 (414–417) including: an introductory formula (1 Thess 4:15a; 1 Cor 15:50, 51a), "ein kurzes thetisches Wort" (1 Thess 4:15b; 1 Cor 15:51b), "bekannte apokalyptische Motive" using similar prepositional formulation (1 Thess 4:16a; 1 Cor 15:52a), comparable contents and the same function (1 Thess 4:16–17; 1 Cor 15:52b–57) and similar "paränetische Schlußfolgerung" (1 Thess 4:18; 1 Cor 15:58).</td></tr>
<tr><td>Evans proposes (tentatively) that Chrysostom may have recognised Ps 46:6 (LXX) behind the λόγος κυρίου (246). Regardless, the original λόγος κυρίου may have reflected the tone of the Psalm. That is, related to Jesus, his resurrection and ascension were a cause of rejoicing. In 1 Thess, the saying is transformed into an apocalyptic image of the Lord's return, making an element of judgment necessary. "Although not cited as a prooftext, or as a prophecy fulfilled, Ps. 47.6 has, nevertheless, made a significant contribution to the eschatological ideas of 1 Thessalonians" (252).</td><td>Evans argues that Ps 46:6 (LXX) lies behind the language and imagery of 1 Thess 4:16. He notes the principal parallels and differences (240–241). There is also significant evidence for the connection in patristic (242–246) and Jewish (246–250) exegesis. Finally, Evans looks to the dominical and prophetic traditions in 5:1–11, and the links to eschatological judgment (251–252), to explain the replacement of ἀλαλαγμός (Ps 46:6 [LXX]) with κέλευσμα (1 Thess 4:16), "the only important difference" between the texts (241).</td></tr>
</table>

	The Thessalonians' Problem(s)	Paul's Answer(s)
J. R. Michaels 1994	Michaels does not explicitly outline the problem(s) of the Thessalonians. But his view of the situation is probably best formulated as: the Thessalonians were concerned about parity between the dead and the living at the *parousia*.	Paul avoids a detailed presentation of the traditional (Jewish) hope of resurrection by appealing to the precedent of Jesus (which the Thessalonians already accepted) and to one of Jesus' sayings: "the last will be first and the first last". Paul offers to the Gentile Christians an understandable answer regarding parity at the *parousia*, i.e. there will be equity and equality between the living and the dead (194).
R. E. Otto 1997	The problem behind this pericope stemmed from the Thessalonians' own Greek religious milieu, particularly the perceived power exercised by cultic gods and demons over those who had died. A fear arose for their fate and spread to those still alive, such that an assurance of salvation became suspect (198, 206).	Paul responds by asserting that Jesus died and rose, and emphasises (*viz.* διὰ τοῦ Ἰησοῦ, v. 14) that those who have died are still in communion with Christ (198–199). Victory over spiritual powers is assured through a metaphor of assumption which depicts "a rapture of the sons of light after the manner of 1QM and certain other pseudepigraphical texts" (202–203). The Thessalonians are assured of being the Lord's possession through the metaphor of "meeting in the air", the air being the very signification of the powers of darkness over which the "conquering king" has "granted victory" (206).
A. J. Malherbe 2000 [20]	The Thessalonians were unable to contextualise apocalyptic expectations of resurrection and *parousia* into a systematic whole (284). Their grief stemmed from uncertainty about the relationship between the living and the dead at the *parousia* (261), fuelled by Jewish apocalyptic speculations that those alive would have an advantage over the dead (284).	For the first time, Paul brings together the ideas of eschatological resurrection and *parousia*. He affirms that the dead will not be disadvantaged at the *parousia* (284). Paul's answer clarifies the issues the Thessalonians are struggling with, and thereby provides consolation to his readers (286; cf. 1983, 254–255).

[20] See also Malherbe 1983. Similarly, Wilcke argues that Paul put forward "keinen eschatologischen Zeitplan" (1967, 122). Luz argues that in Thessalonica there was "nicht eine systematisierte apokalyptische Eschatologie" (1968, 322); cf. Frame 1912, 163–164; Haufe 1986, 446–454; 1999, 80–81.

λόγος κυρίου	Jewish/Hellenistic Influence?
Michaels follows Gundry (1987) and Merklein (1992) in identifying the λόγος κυρίου in 4:15b (183–185), but proposes that Matt 20:16 with its notion of equality (186–188), which arises again in *Gos. Thom.* 4 (188–189), forms the background to Paul's reference. Paul does not give a quotation of the saying; its visibility appears only in the reference to πρῶτον in 4:16 (191–192), although the idea of the "first and the last" is understood by Paul to be the end of distinctions and dualities (190–191).	Michaels agrees with Gundry (1987) that Paul hellenised dominical eschatological and apocalyptic tradition in 1 Thess (194).
Allowing that Paul may be referring to an *agraphon*, Otto asserts that "there cannot be wide divergence between this parenetic midrash and Matthew 24:29–31, 40–44" (199).	Otto understands the pericope esp. in light of the 1QM tradition (cf. 14:2–17) and consequently also Zech 14:1–5 since the idea of "descent" is implicit there (1QM 14:4). Otto also allows for the possible background of theophanic texts from the OT (200).
Malherbe takes the λόγος κυρίου to be a prophetic revelation received by Paul from the exalted Lord (268–269). As such, Paul does not give a quotation of a word (267). The activity of Christian prophets (5:20–21) in the community may be one reason why Paul chose to identify his own teaching as a "message from the Lord" (284).	Malherbe makes few comments regarding whether Paul is drawing on Jewish apocalyptic tradition or a Hellenistic background. For example, Malherbe accepts the possibility that παρουσία may have certain connotations for Greek readers (272), but rejects the notion that Paul uses ἀπάντησις in its technical sense of meeting a visiting dignitary (277).

	The Thessalonians' Problem(s)	Paul's Answer(s)
J. R. Harrison 2002[21]	The problem of "whether those living at the end-time would be in a more advantageous position than the dead" (72) arises in a context of persecution (76), developing out of the provincial loyalty oaths to the Caesars (79; see Judge 1971).	Paul critiques imperial eschatology and Augustan apotheosis traditions by using and reinterpreting political terms like: κύριος, παρουσία, ἀπάντησις, εἰρήνη καὶ ἀσφάλεια, σωτηρία, and ἐλπίς (cf. esp. 88–95).
S. Kim 2002a[22]	The Thessalonians' excitement about the *parousia* and grief about the dead arose from misunderstandings of Jesus tradition which Paul delivered as part of his *kērygma* (231). These sayings, like Matt 24:30–31/Mark 13:26–27, may have been misinterpreted since they do not refer to the resurrection of the dead. The Thessalonians grieved because they could not see how those who had died could take part in the *parousia* and salvation (239–240). Paul did teach the resurrection of the dead; it is just that the Thessalonians did not understand it adequately (230).	Since the problem came about from misunderstandings of Jesus tradition (throughout 4:13–5:11), Paul proceeds to correct the Thessalonians' anxiety by citing the problematic saying of Jesus and expounding its full implications. He interprets it in light of the kerygmatic death and resurrection of Jesus (237–241).
R. S. Ascough 2004[23]	The Thessalonians were previously members of a voluntary association (see Ascough 2000), and like most associations in antiquity were involved in the burial of their members (510–515). An important social implication of burial within an association included a sense of belonging and group identity even of dead members (515–520). The acceptance of Paul's *kērygma* about deliverance from the coming *orgē* probably meant that the Thessalonians ceased planning for a proper burial and pattern of commemoration. After all, the *parousia* was imminently expected (523–524). A crisis developed when some members died since there was now no social implication of belonging and no hope of salvation for dead members (525).	Paul addresses the problem of belonging and identity of dead members by assuring the Thessalonians that those who had died are still part of the association. He emphasises that they are only asleep and have not died (525). Further, Paul elaborates on how the dead take priority over the living at the *parousia* of the Lord (526). Part of Paul's apocalyptic language consists of reassurance that death before the coming *orgē* does not affect the social implications of membership. Therefore, there is no reason to give up hope or to discontinue burial practices, esp. since such practices reaffirm the membership of the deceased (526–530).

[21] Scholars who also emphasise Paul's critique of imperial ideology include: Hendrix 1991; Khiok-Khng 1998; Koester 1990 (=1997 with changes). Alternatively, Krentz argues that Paul's use of cultic language emphasises Paul's point that the *kērygma* is not a political threat (1988, 336).

λόγος κυρίου	JEWISH/HELLENISTIC INFLUENCE?
—	Paul combines "a blend of traditional Jewish apocalyptic" with "a radical subversion of Roman eschatological imagery and terminology" both reflecting Paul's Jewish roots and stripping away the ideological power of imperial eschatology (92–93).
Kim argues that Paul definitely referred to Jesus tradition as part of his *kērygma* because in 5:2 (thief motif; preserved in Matt 24:43–44/Luke 12:39–40), Paul assumes that the Thessalonians already know the tradition (238). In 5:1–11, Paul cites Jesus tradition in order to correct an inadequate understanding of it (239). Kim argues that 4:15–17 is to be interpreted in the same way (239). Thus, Paul refers to a word of the earthly Jesus (235–237), in 4:16–17, which "is really a paraphrase of the Jesus tradition made to apply to the Thessalonian situation" (237).	Kim bypasses the background issue altogether except to comment: "It has long been suspected that some eschatological sayings of Jesus are echoed in our passage" (231). In a previous article (1993), Kim refers favourably to Gundry's thesis (1987) but still asserts that Paul is referring to Jesus tradition.
—	According to Ascough's theory, the Thessalonians were predominately Gentile (526). Thus, Ascough interprets Paul's use of apocalyptic images in terms of social practices at Thessalonica, not from Jewish apocalyptic literature. To this end, Ascough draws attention to elements of eschatological and apocalyptic ideas in Greek culture and philosophical traditions (526–527). Paul's *kērygma* of a coming *orgē* correlates with a pagan notion that the world is under threat of annihilation (528). The language used by Paul attempts to answer social questions, not theological ones (529).

[22] See also Kim 1993. Similarly to Kim, Longenecker asserts that since Paul alludes to the sayings of the historical Jesus in 5:1–11 (and 2 Thess 2:1–12), he therefore also alludes to a saying in 1 Thess 4:16–17 (1985, 91).

[23] See also Ascough 2000, 2003.

III. Analysis

a. Concerning Those Who Are Asleep (4:13)

1. The analysis of 1 Thess 4:13 begins with an examination of a *disclosure* formula which introduces the pericope of 4:13–18 (§III.a.2) and a περί formula which introduces a new *topos* (§III.a.3). The remainder of the verse takes the form of a ἵνα clause expressing a negative purpose (§III.a.4). Besides the identification of the precise meaning of κοιμᾶσθαι (v. 13b), Paul's perspective on οἱ λοιποὶ οἱ μὴ ἔχοντες ἐλπίδα (v. 13d) is fundamental to a correct understanding of the verse (§III.a.5). Finally, there is a short statement on *how* Paul expects the Thessalonians to grieve (§III.a.6).

2. The pericope opens by way of a *disclosure* formula, with an initial verb of *disclosure* (θέλειν), a negative noetic verb in the infinitive (ἀγνοεῖν), personal address (ἀδελφοί) and information introduced by περί (v. 13b; Mullins 1965, 46). The phrase is mainly a Pauline expression (BDAG 12, §1.a), with minor variations of particles,[68] although γινώσκειν σε θέλω does appear in the papyri (MM 286). The word θέλειν is synonymous with βούλεσθαι (BDF 52, §101); Paul uses it in a similar formulation, γινώσκειν δὲ ὑμᾶς βούλομαι, ἀδελφοί (Phil 1:12; cf. Josephus *Ant.* 13.354). The negative inference that ἀγνοεῖν confers onto 1 Thess 4:13–18 is made all the stronger by its contrast with numerous occurrences of εἰδέναι as well as other statements of knowing and remembering elsewhere in the letter (P.-G. Müller 2001, 182; Green 2002, 217). Thus, Paul emphasises the material which follows (Schrenk 1965, 49; see Harnisch 1973, 22), but whether or not he is signalling the introduction of new information is debatable. Some scholars argue that Paul does use the formula to introduce new information.[69] Hurd asserts that Paul uses other forms including a γνωρίζειν phrase[70] and οὐκ οἴδατε ὅτι in First Corinthians[71] to introduce information which is already known (1998, 76). Nevertheless, none of the five occurrences of the negative formulation unequivocally demonstrates that Paul is introducing new information (*contra* Lüdemann 1980a, 232–233; Nicholl 2004, 21).[72] In addition, Paul's repeated references to eschatological motifs increase

[68] Cf. Rom 1:13 (with ὅτι); 1 Cor 10:1 (with ὅτι); Rom 11:25 (with accusative); 1 Cor 12:1 (with περί); 2 Cor 1:8 (with ὑπέρ and ὅτι); *2 Clem.* 14.2 (with ὅτι); *L.A.E.* 18:1. Paul also uses a positive formulation (1 Cor 11:3; cf. Rom 16:19); cf. also Col 2:1; Acts 17:20; Jas 2:20. Only 2 Cor 1:8 also has θέλομεν. The rest have the usual singular form (θέλω); the textual variation in 1 Thess 4:13 is due to harmonisation and therefore rejected (Zimmer 1893, 63).

[69] Donfried 1985, 348; Hurd 1998, 76; Lüdemann 1980, 195–196; 1980a, 232–233; Nicholl 2004, 20–22; see Frame 1912, 166.

[70] 1 Cor 12:3; 15:1; Gal 1:11.

[71] 1 Cor 3:16; 5:6; 6:2, 3, 9, 15, 16, 19; 9:13, 24; cf. Rom 6:16.

[72] Richard (1995, 232) rightly points out that either there is not enough information about an audience's prior knowledge (Rom 1:13; 2 Cor 1:8) or the formula concerns a proper understanding of an issue under discussion (Rom 11:25; 1 Cor 10:1; 12:1). Malherbe observes that Paul's varied use of the formulae "makes it impossible to draw rigid conclusions about their significance" (2000, 262).

the probability that Paul spoke at length on such subjects during his founding visit. The exhortative character of the pericope serves to further support the notion that the material is not new (Haufe 1999, 82; Smith 2000, 723).[73] Consequently, 4:13–18 is more likely a clarification of certain points than a first communication.[74]

3. Along with the *disclosure* of verse 13a, the presence of δὲ … περί (vv. 13a, b) accentuates an introduction of a new *topos*, περὶ τῶν κοιμωμένων. Although some manuscripts have the perfect form, κεκοιμημένων (see NA[27]), the present is to be preferred because it is more likely that κοιμωμένων has been changed to κεκοιμημένων, not because the latter is the usual expression (*contra* Metzger 1994, 565),[75] but due to probable conformation to 1 Thess 4:14, 15 (Zimmer 1893, 63). It always appears in the middle voice.[76] The literal sense of the term, "to be asleep", appears in only a few NT references.[77] The remainder of instances are a figurative extension, "to be dead", and this is the only way Paul uses κοιμᾶσθαι (BDAG 551).[78] Such use appears extensively in both Jewish[79] and non-Jewish traditions[80] (LSJ s.v.; Bultmann 1965, 14; Hoffmann 1966, 186–206); the concept of sleep as a "sleep

---

[73] The *disclosure* serves to strengthen a previous relationship and therefore prepares for *petitions* which follow (Snyder 1972, 357–358).

[74] Plevnik 1990, 56; Richard 1995, 233; see Siber 1971, 15; Wilcke 1967, 113.

[75] Metzger appears to base his comment about κεκοιμημένων being "the usual expression" on Matt 27:52 and 1 Cor 15:20. This is strange considering that the NT exhibits a broad range of verb forms for κοιμᾶσθαι, including: aorist passive indicative (Acts 7:60; 13:36; 1 Cor 15:6; 2 Pet 3:4); perfect middle indicative (John 11:11, 12); present middle indicative (1 Cor 11:30); future passive indicative (1 Cor 15:51); aorist passive subjunctive (1 Cor 7:39); present middle participle (Matt 28:13; Acts 12:6; 1 Thess 4:13); aorist active participle (Luke 22:45); aorist passive participle (1 Cor 15:18; 1 Thess 4:14, 15).

[76] Even in the LXX, the active form only appears at Gen 24:11 and 3 Kgdms 17:19.

[77] Matt 28:13; Luke 22:45; John 11:12; Acts 12:6.

[78] References with an explicit note of resurrection include: Matt 27:52 (ἠγέρθησαν); 1 Cor 15:20 (Χριστὸς ἐγήγερται ἐκ νεκρῶν), 51 (πάντες δὲ ἀλλαγησόμεθα); 1 Thess 4:14 (ὁ θεὸς τοὺς κοιμηθέντας διὰ τοῦ Ἰησοῦ ἄξει σὺν αὐτῷ), 15 (see v. 16, οἱ νεκροὶ ἐν Χριστῷ ἀναστήσονται); cf. John 11:11, 12 (σωθήσεται). References without an explicit note include: Acts 7:60; 13:36; 1 Cor 7:39; 11:30; 15:6, 18 (ἐν Χριστῷ); 1 Thess 4:13; 2 Pet 3:4. John 11:11–13 is interesting not least because of the enigmatic phrase, περὶ τῆς κοιμήσεως τοῦ ὕπνου (v. 13; cf. Wis 17:14; *T. Zeb.* 10:6), but because it highlights the emergence of the figurative extension from the literal sense of κοιμᾶσθαι (cf. Job 14:12). Although the context indicates that Lazarus is dead (v. 14), this does not stop the author of John from describing his death as κοιμᾶσθαι and resurrection as ἐξυπνίζειν (v. 11). The eschatological connotations of sleep/death (cf. decisive statement in v. 4) are missed by the disciples (v. 13; see Balz 1972, 555; Coenen 1975, 443); cf. also Herm. *Mand.* 4.4.1; *Sim.* 9.16.6–7.

[79] Many of the LXX references include the common phrase, κοιμᾶσθαι … μετὰ τῶν πατέρων (Gen 47:30; Deut 31:16; 2 Kgdms 7:12; 3 Kgdms 1:21; 2:10; 11:21, 43; 14:31; 15:8, 24; 16:6, 28; 22:40, 51; 4 Kgdms 8:24; 10:35; 13:9, 13; 14:16, 22, 29; 15:7, 22, 38; 16:20; 20:21; 21:18; 24:6; 1 Par 17:11; 2 Par 16:13; 21:1; 26:2, 23; 27:9; 28:27; 32:33; 33:20; 36:8; cf. *T. Sim.* 8:1). There are also many references to the figurative "sleep of death" (Judg 5:27; 2 Par 9:31; Ps 40:9 [LXX]; Job 3:13; 14:12; 21:11, 13, 26; 22:11; 27:19; Isa 14:18; 43:17; 65:4; Ezek 31:18; 32:20, 21, 27, 28, 29, 30, 32). For a list of Hebrew language euphemisms for "death", see Schorch 2000, 215–218, esp. "Der Tod als Schlaf" (216–217).

[80] Homer *Il.* 11.241; Sophocles *El.* 509. Catullus 5.4–6 uses an analogous figure: *soles occidere et redire possunt: nobis cum semel occidit brevis lux, nox est perpetua una dormienda* ("Suns may set and rise again. For us, when the short light has once set, remains to be slept the sleep of one unbroken night" [Cornish 1912]). See McAlpine (1987) and van der Horst (1991, 115–118) for further references.

of death" is not distinctively Jewish or Christian, probably because the figurative association of "sleep" with "death" is so intuitive (Green 2002, 217). Consequently, neither previous use nor Paul's use of the term may be definitively confined to either tradition.[81] Paul gives κοιμᾶσθαι a Christian stamp in 1 Cor 15:18 (οἱ κοιμηθέντες ἐν Χριστῷ)[82] and 1 Thess 4:14 (ὁ θεὸς τοὺς κοιμηθέντας διὰ τοῦ Ἰησοῦ ἄξει σὺν αὐτῷ), but there are probably no semantic implications associated with the word (Lattimore 1962, 164–165)[83] either with regard to a hope for a future resurrection[84] or to a so-called intermediate state.[85] Neither does the present tense of the participle support either association;[86] at best it is ambiguous on this point (Völkel 1991a, 302).[87] Paul prefers the present tense because it serves to introduce the subject of the pericope (περὶ τῶν κοιμωμένων, v. 13b) much better than the perfect would have (Richard 1995, 225).[88] Is Paul being euphemistic with his use of κοιμᾶσθαι instead of ἀποθνήσκειν or οἱ νεκροί (so Frame 1912, 167)?[89] This is possible although the concepts of sleeping and death are not wholly synonymous (see οἱ νεκροί in v. 16f). The suggestion that Paul is using terminology stemming from the Thessalonians themselves is plausible (Richard 1995, 224–225). Paul does

---

[81] Horsley 1983b, 93; see Hoffmann 1966, 202; Schneider 2000, 129–145 (n.b. Schneider's discussion is given with a view to an exegesis of 1 Cor 15:51). Although I do not agree with the conclusions of Jackson (esp. with regard to an intermediate state), his preliminary work on κοιμᾶσθαι is valuable (1996, 20–95). On the problems associated with identifying whether an inscription may be considered Jewish or not, see van der Horst 1991, 16–18. The fact that κοιμᾶσθαι is only applied to "church members" in the NT is incidental (*contra* Moore 1966, 109; Völkel 1991a, 302).

[82] A similar phrase is found in *1 En.* 49:3, "fallen asleep in righteousness" (Isaac 1983); cf. Herm. *Sim.* 9.16.5, 7.

[83] Thus, Hoffmann: "Es ist aber mit Recht zu fragen, ob nicht die neutestamentlichen Schriftsteller mit diesem überkommenen Ausdruck einen neuen speziell christlichen Sinn verbunden haben. Dies kann nur eine Untersuchung der einzelnen Stellen entscheiden" (1966, 202). Bailey agrees, commenting that although the term does illustrate the concept of death and an associated awakening or resurrection, it does so by contextual inference and interpretation only (1964, 166).

[84] Baumgarten 1975, 115; Coenen 1975, 443; Howard 1988, 167, n. 13; Marshall 1983, 119; *contra* Nicholl 2004, 22–23. The majority of references in the LXX and apocalyptic literature give no indication of a hope for a future resurrection (see list of references above; cf. *Jub.* 23:1–3; 36:18; 45:15; *1 En.* 49:3; 100:5; *T. Mos.* 1:15; 10:14; *T. Reub.* 3:1; *T. Jos.* 20:4; *2 Bar.* 11:4; 85:3). In conjunction with references which *do* give an inference (2 Macc 12:44–45; *1 En.* 91:10; 92:3; *4 Ezra* 7:32, cf. 37; *2 Bar.* 30:2; Dan 12:2 is only indirectly relevant because it has καθεύδειν instead of κοιμᾶσθαι), Paul's use of the term in this regard is impossible to discern. For a summary of the use of the term for death, see Bailey 1964, 162.

[85] Bailey 1964, 166; Best 1972, 185; Kennedy 1904, 268–269; Vos 1953, 146; Wanamaker 1990, 167; *contra* Jackson 1996, 4.

[86] *Contra* Jackson 1996, 130; Milligan 1908, 55; Otto 1997, 193–194.

[87] Frame attempts to limit the ambiguity by noting that believers are οἱ κοιμηθέντες ἐν Χριστῷ (1 Cor 15:18), in some undefined sense (1912, 166). With reference to a notion of "Zwischenzustand", Michel (rightly) argues that κοιμᾶσθαι and καθεύδειν are not to be understood in an anthropological sense (1936, 287–288).

[88] Or, it may point to more than one death although the interpretation that "a large number of deaths keep on occurring" is unwarranted (*contra* Whiteley 1974, 269).

[89] Bruce's argument that Paul does not use κοιμᾶσθαι (or καθεύδειν) for the death of Jesus because he "probably intended to stress the reality of his [Jesus'] death, as something not to be alleviated by any euphemism" (1982, 97), seems contrived (see Vos 1953, 145).

not refer to the dead in general, nor are the Thessalonians grieving about anyone other than their deceased community members (P.-G. Müller 2001, 182; Schlier 1963, 20). If there *is* any question about the fate of outsiders (e.g. ancestors, non-believing friends), Paul does not answer it here (Giesen 1985, 134; Paddison 2005, 144).[90] That Paul is referring to deaths as a result of persecution is highly unlikely (*contra* Donfried 1985 et al.).[91] There is certainly no thought of martyrdom in the sense of the later (2nd century) development that a "martyr" (μάρτυς, μαρτυρεῖν) is such because he/she dies (see Strathmann 1967, 504–508).

4. The remainder of the verse forms a final clause; ἵνα μή expresses a negatived purpose of the pericope, ἵνα μὴ λυπῆσθε (v. 13c), and καθὼς καί introduces a comparative subclause, καθὼς καὶ οἱ λοιποὶ οἱ μὴ ἔχοντες ἐλπίδα (v. 13d). There is no need to make ἵνα consecutive as Paul expresses results in verse 18. Although καθώς is an adverb either of comparison or degree (BDAG 493) some commentators opt for the former but without justification (so Eadie 1877, 148; Fuerbringer 1942, 644). Others argue that Paul is referring to a prohibition of grieving, not to degrees of grieving.[92] This seems a superficial handling of λυπεῖν which Paul elsewhere uses as a legitimate emotion of Christian experience (Nicholl 2004, 24–25). In 2 Cor 7:9–11, Paul refers to the Corinthians' grief unto repentance (ἐλυπήθητε εἰς μετάνοιαν, v. 9) which he further describes as a godly grief unto salvation (ἡ γὰρ κατὰ θεὸν λύπη μετάνοιαν εἰς σωτηρίαν, v. 10a). This is opposed to a worldly grief which produces death (ἡ δὲ τοῦ κόσμου λύπη θάνατον κατεργάζεται, v. 10b). It is conceded that Paul does not champion λυπεῖν, *per se*, but only the results of it (ἰδοὺ γὰρ αὐτὸ τοῦτο τὸ κατὰ θεὸν λυπηθῆναι πόσην κατειργάσατα ὑμῖν σπουδήν ..., v. 11; see Balz 1991, 364). But it is still a part of the Christian life (Bultmann 1967a, 320–321). In addition, Paul refers to the mercy God showed Epaphroditus in keeping him from death, lest he should have sorrow upon sorrow (ἵνα μὴ λύπην ἐπὶ λύπην σχῶ, Phil 2:27). Consequently, it seems sensible to understand 1 Thess 4:13c not as a prohibition but as a final clause negatively describing *how* the Thessalonians are to regard those who are asleep (Green 2002, 218; Richard 1995, 234). If U. B. Müller is correct in identifying a "Heilsorakel" beginning with μὴ λυπῆσθε (cf. *1 En.* 102:4–5; *4 Ezra* 12:44–46), and continuing with "einer futurischen Heilsankündigung" (v. 14), this indicates that Paul is dealing with a concrete grief among community members (1975, 220–225).[93] The interpretation of Harnisch (1973, 24; followed by Mason 1993, 124; P. Müller 1988, 21–23), whereby the reference

---

[90] It is not clear what Kaye means when he says, "Apparently a problem arose because christians had died", and then further comments in a footnote, "Although perhaps not necessarily believers" (1975, 48).

[91] See discussion in Chapter 4, §III.b.3.

[92] The interval between death and the *parousia* for the Thessalonians is considered so short as to justify such an absolute statement (Frame 1912, 167). They are not to grieve at all, in accordance with the religious value of death (Barclay 2000a, 37; n.b. although here and elsewhere I give page numbers to Barclay's article in modern Greek [2000a], I am working from an unpublished English manuscript which Barclay kindly provided [2000]).

[93] On the application of apocalyptic traditions to a crisis situation, see U. B. Müller 1993, 293–294.

to grief is nothing more than to an inevitable consequence of future deaths in the community, is rejected. It is unlikely that Paul would go to such lengths to comfort the Thessalonians without unusual extenuating circumstances such as the actual death of some community members. The verb λυπεῖν itself means, "be sad", "distressed", "grieve", as opposed to the active idea of causing severe mental or emotional distress (BDAG 604).[94] It does not offer any clues as to how Paul wants the Thessalonians to grieve. These are found in the adverbial clause of verse 13d.

5. The antecedents of the substantive adjectival phrase, οἱ λοιποί, are difficult to identify precisely. Paul uses the phrase again in 5:6[95] and both instances initially refer to all non-followers of Jesus.[96] Thus, it may be compared to (but not equated with) οἱ ἔξω of 4:12 and τὰ ἔθνη of 4:5.[97] Unlike the unqualified reference in 5:6 (cf. Eph 2:3) however, οἱ λοιποί appears in 1 Thess 4:13d with a dependent adjectival phrase consisting of an articulated negatived participle and an object, οἱ μὴ ἔχοντες ἐλπίδα.[98] This adjectival phrase acts as a restricting relative clause in a similar way that τὰ μὴ εἰδότα τὸν θεόν restricts τὰ ἔθνη (v. 5; Malherbe 2000, 264). Consequently, οἱ λοιποί refers to a subset of non-followers of Jesus, namely, those who have no hope,[99] including Jews.[100] The word group ἐλπίς/ἐλπίζειν represents an important part of Paul's theology despite its relatively infrequent appearance in his letters. Paul uses both noun and verb in a variety of ways.[101] References to ἐλπίζειν of a non-

[94] Paul uses both the passive (Rom 14:15; 2 Cor 2:2, 4; 6:10; 7:9*ter*, 11; 1 Thess 4:13) and active forms (2 Cor 2:5*bis*; 7:8*bis*; cf. Eph 4:30).

[95] Cf. 1 Cor 9:5; Gal 2:13; cf. also Eph 2:3; 1 Tim 5:20.

[96] Mayer states (1990, 438): "In two passages the Gentiles are said to be excluded from the hope of salvation (Eph 2:12; 1 Thess 4:13)". This statement is incomprehensible, first because it wrongly assumes an equation between οἱ λοιποί and τὰ ἔθνη and second, because it does not account for the restricting relative clause to follow. The view of Freed (2005) that οἱ λοιποί refers to "other members of the brotherhood who have not yet reached the status of 'in Christ' (4.16)" (91) is rejected on the basis of Paul's use here and the clear parallels in 4:5, 12. Freed's assertion that "[t]here is not one passage in the undisputed letters of Paul where *hoi loipoi* refers to non-converts" (91), is mitigated by the fact that there are only two other instances of use in Paul. Certainly, just because Paul uses the phrase of converts in 1 Cor 9:5 and Gal 2:13 does not mean that this is how he uses it here.

[97] Fendrich 1991, 360; Frame 1912, 168; Green 2002, 218; Marshall 1983, 119; Milligan 1908, 56.

[98] A similar statement, ἐλπίδα μὴ ἔχοντες, appears in Eph 2:12. Otherwise, the motif of "having hope" remains positive (Hanse 1964, 824; cf. Acts 24:15; Rom 15:4; 2 Cor 3:12; Eph 2:12; 1 John 3:3).

[99] Haufe 1999, 82; P.-G. Müller 2001, 182; Richard 1995, 234.

[100] Holtz 1998, 189; Malherbe 2000, 265; Wilcke 1967, 116–117; *contra* Nicholl 2004, 23; von Dobschütz 1909, 188. Despite Jewish beliefs in an afterlife, and the negative rhetoric against οἱ Ἰουδαῖοι elsewhere in the letter (2:14–16), Paul has no problem gathering Jews and non-Jews under the phrase οἱ λοιποί (Barclay 2000a, 36).

[101] The noun is usually articulated (Rom 5:4, 5; 8:24*ter*; 12:12; 15:4, 13*bis*; 2 Cor 1:7; Phil 1:20; 1 Thess 4:13; cf. Eph 1:18; Col 1:5, 27; 1 Tim 1:1; 2:13); non-articulated references also appear (2 Cor 3:12; 10:15; Gal 5:5; 1 Thess 2:19; cf. Eph 2:12; 2 Thess 2:16). Paul sometimes uses ἐλπίς in a prepositional phrase, particularly with ἐπί (Rom 4:18; 5:2; cf. 8:20; 1 Cor 9:10; Titus 1:2), but also with παρά (Rom 4:18) and ἐν (Rom 15:13); cf. Eph 4:4; Col 1:23; Titus 3:7. The formulaic triad, ἐλπίς, πίστις and ἀγάπη is not very common in Paul (1 Cor 13:13; 1 Thess 1:3; 5:8; although cf. Rom 5:1–5; Gal 5:5–6; Eph 4:2–5; Col 1:4–5; Heb 6:10–12; 10:22–24; 1 Pet 1:3–8, 21–22; *Barn.* 1.4; 11.8; Pol. *Phil.* 3.2–3; Hunter 1938, 428).

soteriological kind (e.g. to his travel plans; expressions of concern) may be grouped together (Mayer 1990, 439).[102] Other references more directly develop the Pauline concept.[103] Paul essentially projects the OT use of hope although the development of trust as part of the concept is more closely aligned to the LXX use (Hoffmann 1976, 240).[104] Thus, in 1 Cor 13:7, ἡ ἀγάπη is characterised as an attitude which πάντα πιστεύει, πάντα ἐλπίζει, πάντα ὑπομένει. Consequently, hope fixed on God requires a trust and patience to wait (Bultmann 1964a, 530).[105] The emphasis on waiting should not be overemphasised (*contra* Prendergast 1992, 284) and ἐλπίς/ἐλπίζειν no longer contains an aspect of fear (i.e. ἐλπὶς πονηρά, Isa 28:19). Rather, hope is a hope of salvation (σῴζειν, Rom 8:24; σωτηρία, 1 Thess 5:8) and deliverance (ῥύεσθαι, 2 Cor 1:10; Mayer 1990, 438–439). Such hope is enabled by the spirit (πνεῦμα) – in which it finds its source of power (δύναμις, Rom 15:13) – and by faith (πίστις, Gal 5:5). Its connection to God's act of salvation (ἐν Χριστῷ)[106] emphasises hope as an eschatological blessing (Bultmann 1964a, 532; Hanse 1964, 825). But the content of hope remains unseen (εἰ δὲ ὃ οὐ βλέπομεν ἐλπίζομεν, Rom 8:25) and waiting with patience (δι' ὑπομονῆς ἀπεκδεχόμεθα, 8:25) is an ongoing act of faith (see Rom 4; see Stuhlmacher 2000, 325).

Paul's conception of ἐλπίς/ἐλπίζειν is so strongly coloured by his *kērygma* that he is able to characterise all non-followers of Jesus as those οἱ μὴ ἔχοντες ἐλπίδα (1 Thess 4:13d). As a result, the category specified by the articulated negatived clause is not restricted much; all οἱ λοιποί (v. 13d) are lumped together (Weder 1986, 489). This is not surprising since the word group is used extensively in the LXX to distinguish between the righteous (δίκαιοι) and ungodly (ἀσεβεῖς). Thus, the hope of the ungodly is κενή (Wis 3:11; Job 7:6; cf. 5:14), it is ἐν νεκροῖς (Wis 13:10), and the ungodly die without hope (Prov 11:7; Wis 3:18). Such hope comes to an end (ὀλέσθαι, Prov 10:28; 11:7) and perishes (ἀπολέσθαι, Job 8:13; Prov 11:23).[107] In contrast, there is hope to the godly (ἐλπὶς τῷ εὐσεβεῖ, Isa 24:16 [LXX]), whose hope is fixed on God[108] as σωτήρ.[109] It extends to the resurrection (2 Macc 7:14; Bultmann 1964a, 529). The statement of 1 Thess 4:13d must be understood with this background in mind: specifically the polarising effect of ἐλπίς/ἐλπίζειν on

---

[102] Apart from 2 Cor 5:11 (with a perfect infinitive following) and 8:5 (absolutely), these references occur either with an aorist infinitive (Rom 15:24; 16:7; Phil 2:19, 23) or with ὅτι following (2 Cor 1:13; 13:6; Phlm 22; cf. 1 Tim 3:14; BDAG 319). In addition, all these references are to the present active indicative form of the verb except for 2 Cor 8:5 and 1 Tim 3:14 which have the aorist active indicative and present active participle forms, respectively.

[103] The distribution of tense and voice forms in Paul is fairly even: present active indicative (Rom 8:24, 25; 1 Cor 13:7); future active indicative (Rom 15:12; although this is a quotation of Isa 11:10); perfect active indicative (2 Cor 1:10; cf. 1 Tim 4:10; 5:5); perfect active participle (1 Cor 15:19); cf. perfect active infinitive (1 Tim 6:17).

[104] For references, see Bultmann 1964a, 521–523.

[105] For an outline of the "Grund der Hoffnung" in Paul, see Luz 1968, 323–324.

[106] 1 Cor 15:19; cf. Phil 2:19; 1 Thess 1:3.

[107] Cf. Job 11:20; Wis 5:14.

[108] Sir 34:13; *Pss. Sol.* 5:11; 8:31; 17:34, cf. v. 39; Ps 17:3 (LXX); 30:7, 15, 25 (LXX), etc.; Jer 17:7.

[109] *Pss. Sol.* 17:3; cf. Ps 16:7 (LXX); 36:40 (LXX); 85:2 (LXX); Sus 60θ; *Pss. Sol.* 15:1.

humanity. Commentators fail to grasp Paul's meaning when they interpret the statement as if non-followers of Jesus had *no* hope at all. This line of questioning often leads to investigations about conceptions of an afterlife among οἱ λοιποί (Best 1972, 185–186), usually with reports of a hopelessness in general.[110] Even when such conceptions are found (Wanamaker 1990, 167) they are often explained away as practical hopelessness.[111] Rather, the meaning of the phrase, οἱ λοιποὶ οἱ μὴ ἔχοντες ἐλπίδα, is a thoroughly Christian one as the context dictates (Henneken 1969, 76; see Plevnik 1975a, 204). Paul focuses on the qualitative description, καὶ οὕτως πάντοτε σὺν κυρίῳ ἐσόμεθα (v. 17d). Members of οἱ λοιποί may or may not have a resurrection hope (even this is no real hope; Bultmann 1952, 320), but they certainly have no hope of being with Christ (Phil 1:23),[112] only *orgē* (1 Thess 1:10; 2:16; 5:9; Rom 1:18–32).[113] Faith and hope constitute the Christian existence both in life and death.[114]

6. Finally, the question of how Paul intends the Thessalonians to grieve is worth investigating a little further. Malherbe argues that it is an absolute prohibition, but one which responds to a specific question the Thessalonians had addressed to him (2000, 264). For Plevnik, the issue at stake was hope for participation in the *parousia*. If the remaining Thessalonians had lost such hope then their grief would resemble οἱ λοιποί who also have no hope in the *parousia* (1975a, 204–205). Paul's argument would then address the hope that οἱ νεκροὶ ἐν Χριστῷ (v. 16f) have not been abandoned (Barclay 1992, 51–52). If there is an element of hopelessness with regard to resurrection then this could include the possibility that the Thessalonians (still alive) feared death.[115] But this remains conjecture. Regardless of the possibilities, Paul addresses λυπεῖν across a number of arenas. First, he refers to outsiders who do not enjoy community solidarity with Paul and his followers, and contrasts them with Jesus-followers who are able to confess in theological terms the source and nature of hope. Second, Paul develops the eschatological identity of the community by referring to specific actions of Jesus the *Kyrios*, and therefore to the destiny of members. Third and finally, the social aspect of grief is taken up directly in the final admonition, παρακαλεῖτε ἀλλήλους ἐν τοῖς λόγοις τούτοις (1 Thess 4:18), and far from being an absolute prohibition, Paul acknowledges a grief common to humanity which is experienced at the death of ἀδελφοί and ἀδελφαί. In this way, Paul introduces the *topos* of death with associated grief, including a rationalisation of current experiences of grief arising from deaths among community members as

---

[110] Bruce 1982, 96; Milligan 1908, 56; Witherington 2006, 126–132; see Deissmann 1995, 176–178.

[111] Green 2002, 218–219; Marshall 1983, 119; Morris 1959, 137.

[112] Frame 1912, 167; Otto 1997, 195. This distinction is similar to Luedemann's categories of *parousia*-hope and resurrection-hope (1980, 196–197; followed by Donfried 1990, 13). For Nebe, the categories are even simpler: *Christen* and *Nichtchristen* (1983, 94).

[113] Giesen 1985, 127; Watson 1999, 73. Becker comments: "Es geht also nicht um ihre subjektive Hoffnung, sondern um das vom christlichen Standpunkt aus gefällte Urteil, daß für sie wegen des Zornes Gottes keine Zukunft offen ist (1,10; 2,16) — trotz ihrer möglichen eigenen Erwartungen" (1976, 47–48).

[114] Bultmann 1964a, 532; Wilcke 1967, 118–119; see Mackintosh 1914, 115–116.

[115] Kieffer 1990, 212; Marshall 1990, 260; see Best 1972, 186; Richard 1995, 234.

well as picturing a special future where death and grief are left behind in preference of a utopian eschatological existence.

b. Believing That Jesus Died and Rose (4:14)

1. There are several exegetical problems associated with this verse. Some may be dealt with independently while others require a synthesis of various investigations. As noted in the preliminary issues (§II.a.2 above), Paul begins with a first class condition but provides no apodosis. Instead, εἰ γὰρ πιστεύομεν (v. 14a) is awkwardly completed with οὕτως καί (v. 14c; §III.b.2). He refers to a traditional formula, Ἰησοῦς ἀπέθανεν καὶ ἀνέστη (v. 14b); the very unusual reference to the verb ἀνιστάναι with the active voice (as opposed to more usual references to ἐγείρειν) requires explanation (§III.b.3). But how Paul construes the jumble of phrases in verse 14c is the most challenging exegetical problem here. It is not clear how διὰ τοῦ Ἰησοῦ should be interpreted, particularly whether it should be construed with τοὺς κοιμηθέντας or with ἄξει (§III.b.4). Finally, these problems along with the question of how to interpret ἄξει in the context of the Thessalonians' grief, are brought to a close with a short (synthetic) discussion (§III.b.5).

2. Verse 14 begins with a conditional clause (introduced by εἰ) which is linked to the previous verse by γάρ (v. 14a), a marker used absolutely by Paul to introduce his argument (BDAG 189, §1.a). Paul proceeds to explain why the Thessalonians do not need to grieve (i.e. ἵνα μὴ λυπῆσθε, v. 13c). Although a condition in the first class may be translated "since" (BDF 189, §372[1]), the translation "if" better expresses the confessional aspect of the statement (*GGBB* 694). The plural "we believe" applies to all followers of Jesus, including (presumably) the Thessalonians who had died, and for whom Paul's addressees are grieving (Best 1972, 187; Jurgensen 1994, 87). Paul uses the formulation πιστεύειν ὅτι rarely[116] and whether it is part of the confession to follow is open to question (Holtz 1983, 59–60). It is used in the same sense as πιστεύειν εἰς (cf. Gal 2:16) as an abbreviation or summary statement of the proclaimed (1 Cor 15:11) and confessed (Rom 10:9) *kērygma* (Bultmann 1968, 203–204; Stanton 2003, 175). For Paul, Rom 10:9 expresses the content of πίστις which includes the acknowledgement of Jesus' resurrection and the acknowledgement that Jesus is Lord: ὅτι ἐὰν ὁμολογήσῃς ἐν τῷ στόματί σου κύριον Ἰησοῦν καὶ πιστεύσῃς ἐν τῇ καρδίᾳ σου ὅτι ὁ θεὸς αὐτὸν ἤγειρεν ἐκ νεκρῶν, σωθήσῃ. The two confessions go together as Bultmann highlights: "The resurrection is not just a remarkable event. It is the *soteriological* fact in virtue of which Jesus became the κύριος" (1968, 209; emphasis added). Although the traditional formula in 1 Thess 4:14b does not contain a reference to Jesus as κύριος, the πιστεύειν ὅτι statement is followed by no fewer than four references to κύριος (vv. 15d; 16a; 17c,

[116] Rom 6:8; 10:9; cf. Jas 2:19; 1 John 5:1, 5; BDAG 816, §1.a.β. Paul prefers constructions with εἰς, ἐπί and with the dative case; for discussion, see *GNTG* vol. 1, 67–68.

d). Paul does not comfort the Thessalonians with a psychological reassurance but reminds them of their acceptance of a *kērygma* tied to history, or to a salvation history made accessible in the πίστις and ὁμολογία of Jesus as resurrected *Kyrios* (217). This includes a πίστις which is provisionally temporal, but primarily oriented to the future. The ὁμολογία begins with what God has already done (Rom 10:9; 1 Thess 4:14b) and looks to the future of what God will do (1 Thess 4:14c).[117]

3. I have already dealt with the typical formula, "he [God] raised him [Jesus] from the dead" which is found repeatedly in Paul.[118] The double reference to Ἰησοῦς (vv. 14b, c), the second articular, is a standard example of anaphora[119] and possibly indicates a Palestinian origin of the expression here (Best 1972, 187; Stanley 1961, 86). Paul uses the name by itself relatively infrequently (Foerster 1965, 289).[120] The statement here, ὅτι Ἰησοῦς ἀπέθανεν καὶ ἀνέστη (v. 14b), is not typical because Paul hardly ever uses ἀνιστάναι and this is the only place where Ἰησοῦς is the subject of a statement about his death (Collins 1984, 158; Kramer 1966, 199). Of the four occurrences of the verb in Paul, two refer to a mundane meaning: rising as opposed to sitting down (καθίζειν, 1 Cor 10:7) and rising to rule (ἄρχειν, Rom 15:12 which gives a quotation of Isa 11:10). The other two appear here in 1 Thess 4:14, 16 (cf. also Eph 5:14).[121] If there is a semantic difference for Paul between ἐγείρειν and ἀνιστάναι, then it is difficult to define.[122] The idea that ἐγείρεν refers predominantly to what happened at Easter while ἀνιστάναι and ἀνάστασις are reserved especially for the resurrection of Jesus-followers (Coenen 1978, 276) is not borne out by Paul's interchangeable use of the verbs/noun in 1 Cor 15:12–13, 42 (Kreitzer 1993a, 807). As well, nowhere else does Paul use the active voice to describe the resurrection of Jesus.[123] But there is no implication of agency on the part of Jesus in his own resurrection; nor is it possible to read personal agency into the verb: "aus eigener Kraft" (Kremer 1992, 9). This is made clear in verse 16f

[117] Cf. similarly, Rom 6:8; Bruce 1982, 96; Bultmann 1968, 221.

[118] For references and discussion, see Chapter 3, §III.b.5.

[119] In the epistles and Revelation the name Jesus stands without the article in all cases except: 2 Cor 4:10, 11; 1 Thess 4:14; Eph 4:21; 1 John 4:3 (*GNTG* vol. 3, 167).

[120] Rom 3:26; 8:11 (cf. synonymous Χριστός); 1 Cor 12:3 (cf. κύριος); 2 Cor 4:10*bis*, 11*bis*; 11:4; Gal 6:17; Phil 2:10; 1 Thess 1:10; 4:14; cf. Eph 4:21.

[121] Paul uses ἀνάστασις (Rom 1:4; 6:5; 1 Cor 15:12, 13, 21, 42; Phil 3:10; cf. 2 Tim 2:18) but not ἔγερσις (cf. Matt 27:53; Frame 1912, 169). This is particularly noteworthy in 1 Cor 15:12, 13, 42 where Paul uses ἐγείρειν but not the corresponding noun — instead he uses ἀνάστασις.

[122] So much so that Kremer considers them as "gleichbedeutend" (1993, 1178). The two verbs appear to have a similar use at times, esp. between 1 Thess 4:14 and Rom 8:34; 1 Cor 15:3b–4; 2 Cor 5:15. Hofius comments: "Es liegt nahe, in den unterschiedlichen Formulierungen – ἀπέθανεν καὶ ἀνέστη einerseits und ἀπέθανεν καὶ ἐγήγερται/ἠγέρθη andererseits – lediglich sprachliche Varianten des Bekenntnisses zu erblicken, daß Jesus 'gestorben und auferstanden' ist" (2002a, 96). O'Donnell investigates ἐγείρειν and ἀνιστάναι using collocation analysis. He highlights some differences with regard to the frequency of specific words in company as well as with regard to tense and voice (1999). For a discussion of O'Donnell's article, see §III.d.8 below.

[123] Similarly, ἐν ᾗ καὶ ὁ Ἰησοῦς ἀνέστη ἐκ νεκρῶν καὶ φανερωθεὶς ἀνέβη εἰς οὐρανούς (*Barn.* 15.9). Incidentally, ἀνιστάναι probably does not appear in the passive voice in the NT though there are some morphologically ambiguous forms between the middle and passive voice (O'Donnell 1999, 142).

where the middle voice of ἀνιστάναι (οἱ νεκροὶ ἐν Χριστῷ ἀναστήσονται) refers to phenomenological fact only, not agency (Havener 1981, 113–114; Hogg/Vine 1929, 135).[124] If agency must be found, then God is the agent of resurrection as the change of subject from Jesus (v. 14b) to God (v. 14c) indicates (Giesen 1985, 131; see Plevnik 1975a, 206–207). Paul often refers to the formulation, Χριστὸς ἀπέθανεν,[125] but not so often to a combination of dying and rising. When he does, it is expressed without a fixed form.[126] The confession-like introduction, the name Ἰησοῦς without qualification, the presence of ἀνιστάναι instead of ἐγείρειν, the active voice construction with Jesus as subject, and the summary-like formulation about Jesus' death and resurrection, all point to 1 Thess 4:14b as a pre-Pauline traditional formula (Havener 1981, 111–113). Whether Paul altered the formula by omitting a ὑπὲρ/περὶ ἡμῶν phrase is unknown; its omission certainly cannot be used to reject the identification of a pre-Pauline formula here (*contra* Harnisch 1973, 32–33).

4. The adverbial phrase, οὕτως καί, marks the inference Paul makes from his previous confession, εἰ γὰρ πιστεύομεν (v. 14a).[127] The aorist signification of τοὺς κοιμηθέντας, especially in the participial mood gives no temporal indication and should not be understood as referring to the moment of the Thessalonians' falling asleep.[128] The translation, "was put to sleep" (*GNTG* vol. 1, 162; followed by Robertson 1934, 816–817), overemphasises the passive voice. Such a translation probably puts too much importance on the διά phrase.[129]

The remainder of the verse is translated in different ways by commentators because it is not clear how διὰ τοῦ Ἰησοῦ functions. There are two options: (1) διὰ τοῦ Ἰησοῦ modifies the substantive τοὺς κοιμηθέντας, or (2) διὰ τοῦ Ἰησοῦ modifies the verb ἄγειν. Each is dealt with in turn (below), but first it is helpful to note how Paul uses διά in conjunction with various combinations of Jesus, Christ and Lord. According to BDAG, διά with the genitive has five extended definitions: (1) marker of extension through an area or object; (2) marker of extension in time; (3) marker of instrumentality or circumstance whereby something is accomplished or effected; (4) marker of personal agency; (5) finally, at times διά with the genitive seems

---

[124] O'Donnell (1999) raises some interesting questions about "ergavity" and the Greek voices. It may be noted in passing that if O'Donnell has correctly identified ἀνιστάναι as an ergative verb (he leaves the identification open to question), then the verbal construction may omit entirely any reference (explicit or implicit) to an agent (159). Again, see §III.d.8 for details.

[125] Cf. Rom 5:6, 8; 14:9, 15; 1 Cor 8:11; 15:3; 2 Cor 5:15; Gal 2:21; 1 Thess 5:9–10; although with a slightly different formulation, see also Rom 6:10; 8:34; 2 Cor 5:14. For a discussion of the "dying formula" in literature before and during Paul's time, albeit applied to figures other than Jesus, see Gibson 2005; Kramer 1966, 26–28.

[126] Cf. Rom 4:25; 8:34; 14:9; 1 Cor 15:3–5; 2 Cor 5:15. For a discussion of the variations of form and of their development, see Kramer 1966, 32–33.

[127] The variant, ὁ θεὸς καί (B 1739 *pc*) instead of καὶ ὁ θεός is inconsequential to this analysis.

[128] *Contra* Askwith 1911, 61; Bruce 1982, 98; Wanamaker 1990, 169.

[129] I.e. a passive verb may receive the action that is expressed by διά with the genitive, although here the agent named is intermediate, not ultimate (Wallace 1996, 433–434).

to have causal meaning (224–225, §A). Of these definitions, the third and fourth are pertinent for the analysis here, although the relevant subset of the third definition (of means or instrument, §3.a) has little semantic difference (in this case) to the fourth definition because of the agency implied in the personal name. Paul uses διὰ τοῦ Ἰησοῦ only here, but other combinations do occur: διὰ Ἰησοῦ Χριστοῦ (τοῦ κυρίου ἡμῶν) appears a number of times,[130] as do διὰ τοῦ Χριστοῦ (2 Cor 1:5; 3:4) and διὰ Χριστοῦ (Rom 2:16; 2 Cor 5:18); as well, there is διὰ τοῦ κυρίου Ἰησοῦ (1 Thess 4:2; cf. Heb 2:3) and διὰ τοῦ κυρίου ἡμῶν Ἰησοῦ Χριστοῦ,[131] not to mention δι᾽ αὐτοῦ[132] and δι᾽ οὗ.[133]

If διὰ τοῦ Ἰησοῦ is taken with the participial phrase, τοὺς κοιμηθέντας, then it would serve as a qualifying phrase to the object of the clause (option one above).[134] In such capacity the phrase serves as a genitive of attendant circumstances. Although Best explores the possibilities of such an interpretation, he gives five possible explanations all of which he rejects (1972, 188–189). The majority view is to understand διὰ τοῦ Ἰησοῦ as virtually synonymous with ἐν Χριστῷ. It would then give a qualification about the union between those who had fallen asleep and Jesus (cf. 1 Cor 15:18). They had died as Jesus-followers.[135] The demonstration that διά can be made to function in such capacity is secondary only,[136] which makes comparisons between τοὺς κοιμηθέντας διὰ τοῦ Ἰησοῦ (1 Thess 4:14c) and οἱ νεκροὶ ἐν Χριστῷ (v. 16f) somewhat inconsequential. The decision for taking διὰ τοῦ Ἰησοῦ with the participle rests squarely on the arguments of word order and parallelism in the pericope.[137] As outlined in the preliminary issues of this pericope (see §II.b.2 above) the grammatical and conceptual parallels in the structure of verse 14 are clear enough, but not so compelling as to rule out any other option. Further, it is misleading to argue that διὰ τοῦ Ἰησοῦ should not be taken with the principal verb because the predicate already has a prepositional phrase, i.e. σὺν αὐτῷ.[138] Paul is

[130] Rom 1:8; 5:21; 7:25; 16:27; Gal 1:1; Phil 1:11; cf. Eph 1:5; John 1:17; Acts 10:36; Titus 3:6; Heb 13:21; 1 Pet 2:5; 4:11; Jude 25.

[131] Rom 5:1, 11; 15:30; 1 Cor 15:57; 1 Thess 5:9.

[132] Rom 5:9; 11:36; 1 Cor 8:6; 2 Cor 1:20; cf. Eph 2:18; Col 1:16, 20; 3:17.

[133] Rom 1:5; 5:2, 11; 1 Cor 8:6; cf. Gal 6:14.

[134] So Alford 1958, 273–274; Askwith 1911, 61–63; Auberlen/Riggenbach 1869, 73; Bruce 1982, 97; Calvin 1961, 363; Dibelius 1925, 21; Findlay 1896, 102; Frame 1912, 170; Milligan 1908, 57; Morris 1959, 139–140; Richard 1995, 226; Rigaux 1956, 535–537; Staab 1965, 34–35; Stanley 1961, 87; Thomas 1978, 280; von Dobschütz 1909, 191; Williams 1992, 82.

[135] Ahn 1989, 203; Askwith 1911, 62–63; Egelkraut 1984, 90; Green 2002, 221; Moule 1959, 57; Plevnik 1975a, 211; Witherington 2006, 133. Similarly, Turner understands διά as expressing manner with a corresponding translation of, "with Jesus" (*GNTG* vol. 3, 267). Although possible, διά as expressing manner would be highly unusual here since that mode of expression is usually reserved for verbs of saying (BDAG 224, §A.3.b).

[136] Jowett (1859, 81), Frame (1912, 170) and Rigaux (1956, 536) bypass the problem of equating διά with ἐν by noting that the equivalence is one of conception only, not of grammar.

[137] Bruce 1982, 97; Dupont 1952, 42; Frame 1912, 170; Marshall 1983, 124; Milligan 1908, 57; Stanley 1961, 87; Thomas 1978, 280; von Dobschütz 1909, 191.

[138] *Contra* Bruce 1982, 97; Otto 1997, 198; Tellbe 2001, 102; von Dobschütz 1909, 191.

able to use more than one prepositional phrase to modify a principal verb (Nicholl 2004, 28; Wilcke 1967, 127).[139] The fact that διὰ τοῦ Ἰησοῦ precedes the verb is unusual, since a prepositional phrase which modifies a verb generally takes a post-positive position (*GNTG* vol. 3, 349). However, changes in word order for oratorical effect are common practice in Paul[140] and a prepositional phrase before the verb is an acceptable grammatical construction (*contra* Wanamaker 1990, 169).

Alternatively, if διὰ τοῦ Ἰησοῦ is taken with the verb, ἄξει, then it would serve as an adverbial phrase of instrumentality, whereby Jesus is an intermediate agent of God's action (option two above).[141] Thus, the translation would run: "even also, through/by Jesus, God will bring with him those who have fallen asleep". Despite the awkward construction in Greek such an interpretation makes excellent sense of Paul's thought.[142] Paul often uses διά to express agency (Oepke 1964d, 67), and in the various formulations of διά with Jesus, Christ and Lord, *this is exclusively the case* (see Siber 1971, 27). Thus, salvation from *orgē* is δι᾽ αὐτοῦ (Rom 5:9) and διὰ τοῦ κυρίου ἡμῶν Ἰησοῦ Χριστοῦ (1 Thess 5:9); resurrection is effected δι᾽ ἀνθρώπου (1 Cor 15:21) and victory over death is given διὰ τοῦ κυρίου ἡμῶν Ἰησοῦ Χριστοῦ (1 Cor 15:57); peace with God is mediated διὰ τοῦ κυρίου ἡμῶν Ἰησοῦ Χριστοῦ (Rom 5:1); being reconciled to God is διὰ Χριστοῦ (2 Cor 5:18; cf. Rom 5:11); eternal life is mediated διὰ Ἰησοῦ Χριστοῦ τοῦ κυρίου ἡμῶν (Rom 5:21); creation is mediated δι᾽ αὐτοῦ (1 Cor 8:6); Paul receives grace and apostleship δι᾽ οὗ (Rom 1:5; sc. Ἰησοῦ Χριστοῦ from v. 4; cf. Rom 5:2); God judges the secrets of men διὰ Χριστοῦ Ἰησοῦ (Rom 2:16); finally, at the day of Christ (εἰς ἡμέραν Χριστοῦ), the Philippians are filled with the fruits of righteousness τὸν διὰ Ἰησοῦ Χριστοῦ (Phil 1:11).

In summary, there is no grammatical argument which rules out either option: διά with the genitive may be functioned either as a qualifying genitive expressing attendant circumstances or as an adverbial phrase expressing instrument. But an "eindeutige Entscheidung" is possible (*contra* Laub 1973, 126). While the structure of the sentence more naturally leads to the first option, the preponderance of evidence regarding Paul's use of διά with Jesus, Christ and Lord makes the second option far more compelling.[143]

5. All that remains for discussion here is the principal verb, ἄγειν, and a second prepositional phrase, σὺν αὐτῷ, which modifies the principal verb. Specifically, what is the significance of ἄγειν in the context of the pericope? Elsewhere Paul uses the verb sparingly[144] and always in a sense of "to lead/guide morally or spiritually"

---

[139] E.g. Rom 1:8; 2:16; 5:1, 11, 21; 2 Cor 3:4.

[140] BDF 248, §472(2); *GGNT* 417; *GNTG* vol. 3, 349.

[141] So Best 1972, 189; Bornemann 1894, 201; Giesen 1985, 130; Hoffmann 1966, 213–216; Holtz 1998, 193; Kegel 1970, 34–35; Konradt 2003, 131; Kremer 1992, 19; Lenski 1937, 329–330; Luz 1968, 326; Malherbe 2000, 266; Moffatt 1910, 36–37; Reinmuth 1998, 145; Schade 1984, 158; Schlier 1963, 21; 1972, 77; Ward 1973, 103.

[142] See Collins 1984, 159; Hoffmann 1966, 215–216; Malherbe 2000, 266; Saunders 1981, 26–27; Wilckens 1988, 144.

[143] Lüdemann's suggestion that διά has a causal nuance is probably correct (1980a, 239).

[144] Rom 2:4; 8:14; 1 Cor 12:2; Gal 5:18.

(BDAG 16, §3; Ellingworth 1974, 430). Most commentators do not interpret ἄξει in 1 Thess 4:14 like this but take it literally, as implying a direction of movement of an object from one position to another (BDAG 16, §1.a). Consequently, the discussion tends to concentrate on the implied direction of movement (Ellingworth 1974) and the goal of the verb (Plevnik 2000). Plevnik argues that 2 Cor 4:14 (εἰδότες ὅτι ἐγείρας τὸν κύριον Ἰησοῦν καὶ ἡμᾶς σὺν Ἰησοῦ ἐγερεῖ καὶ παραστήσει σὺν ὑμῖν) makes the goal of ἄξει explicit: God will bring the dead into his presence by taking them up (2000, 94–95). The debate at this point (*viz.* direction of movement and goal of verb) often includes the remainder of the pericope (1 Thess 4:15–17) and especially interpretative decisions about ἀπάντησις (v. 17c). As such, the theses of Ellingworth, Plevnik and others are engaged later in this analysis. At this point, it is possible to interpret 1 Thess 4:14c both in terms of its own grammatical structure and also in conjunction with the previous verse. Namely, the apodosis, to have any connection whatever with the protasis, must address ἐγείρειν (ἀνιστάναι) in some sense. Those who had died undergo the same experience as Jesus, and σὺν αὐτῷ (BDAG 962, §1.b.γ) they are both raised and brought into God's presence (see Borse 1990, 25; Kim 2002a, 228). With regard to the resurrection, what is explicitly described in 1 Cor 6:14 is only implicitly described here.[145] But Schade is right to recognise that the unbalanced protasis/apodosis leaves room for a translation idea; thus, ἄγειν corresponds to resurrection *and* translation (1984, 145; so also Kegel 1970, 34). Regardless of the details to come, Paul already gives a reason why there is no need to grieve. Christian hope is ultimately to be with him (vv. 14c, 17d); being alive at the *parousia* is really only an expectation, not part of the kerygmatic hope.[146] The οὕτως καί construction implies the notion of resurrection in the clause, ἄξει σὺν αὐτῷ (v. 14c; see Plevnik 1975a, 209). But emphasis remains on the *parousia* and the Thessalonians' relationship to the *parousia* Jesus Christ (as is made clear in 1 Thess 4:15–17), not on the resurrection (Hoffmann 1966, 217–218).[147] Otherwise Paul would have repeated the verb ἀνέστη (or used ἐγείρειν) in a properly constructed apodosis (Wanamaker 1990, 169). Thus, Paul does give the analogy: what happened to Jesus will also happen to believers (Lüdemann 1980a, 232–242).[148] Although the formula seems atypical for Paul, the connection

[145] Giesen 1985, 129; Konradt 2003, 130; see Lüdemann 1980a, 233; P. Müller 1988, 24.

[146] See Luz 1968, 323; Schade 1984, 157; similarly, Becker 1980.

[147] The argument is consecutive (Wilcke 1967, 124–125): "Hier in 1 Thess 4,14 ist die Auferweckung Jesu verstanden als Voraussetzung für die Begegnung mit dem Herrn bei seiner Parusie" (Giesen 1985, 129).

[148] Cf. esp. Rom 8:11, 1 Cor 6:14 and 2 Cor 4:14 for a similar analogy. Wilson argues that Paul failed to make this connection during his founding visit and that οὕτως καί (v. 14c) introduces a new conclusion (1968, 102–103). He makes this assertion by noting that Paul does not refer to his previous teaching but gives new information, ἐν λόγῳ κυρίου in successive verses. Although there are implications for the resurrection of dead Christians, the *crux* of the pericope is not on resurrection, but as Koester points out, on the communal question of whether (and how) the dead will be united with the living to meet the Lord at the *parousia* (1997, 159).

between the resurrection of Jesus and the resurrection of believers is Pauline (de Jonge 1988, 38; Hays 1991, 233).

Finally, it is instructive for the thesis to emphasise that verse 14 is not a didactic proof for the resurrection of Jesus-followers; it is a misreading of the text to reduce the discussion only to this. Rather, Paul has purposefully avoided technical resurrection language in verse 14c in order to highlight solidarity between *ekklēsia* members and Jesus. As such, attempts to elicit a direction from the verb ἄγειν misses the point.

c. A Word of the Lord (4:15)

1. Paul gives another reason why the Thessalonians are not to grieve by addressing the *topos* περὶ τῶν κοιμωμένων (4:13b) with a λόγος κυρίου. The phenomenon of and sources for words of the Lord have received a preliminary discussion (§II.c above). There I concluded that Paul has paraphrased a received word from the exalted Lord. Consequently, the analysis of this verse (and vv. 16–17) does not proceed primarily on the basis of reconstructing earlier layers of tradition as though a specific λόγος κυρίου is embedded in the Pauline text. Rather, Paul directly addresses an issue raised by the Thessalonians, in his own words, and uses traditional material to do so. He provides a comparison between the living and the dead — a comparison which has a point of reference in the significant phrase, εἰς τὴν παρουσίαν τοῦ κυρίου (v. 15d). The preliminary investigation of *parousia* in Paul (§II.d above) provides a springboard for an analysis of several exegetical issues here. After a brief consideration of verse 15a and its connection to the rest of the pericope (§III.c.2), a survey of the word παρουσία in First Thessalonians is presented (§III.c.3). It is often assumed that Paul implies he would be alive at the *parousia* (see the emphatic first person plural pronoun, ἡμεῖς in v. 15c), an assumption which is critically assessed here (§III.c.4). Finally, regardless of whether verse 15 is identified as a λόγος κυρίου or as Pauline redaction, the verse gives insight into the possible issues or questions about which the Thessalonians' needed information (§III.c.5).

2. Again, Paul uses γάρ to continue his argument on the *topos*. The use of οὗτος referring to what precedes (antecedent) or follows (postcedent) is so common as to require no further comment.[149] The question here is whether τοῦτο (v. 15a) is purely resumptive or whether it refers to the following ὅτι (v. 15c). Both options are grammatically possible and therefore should be kept open. Richard observes that "almost without exception and without discussion" commentators argue that τοῦτο only refers to what follows (1995, 240). Capitalising on the fact that τοῦτο often has an antecedent reference in classical Greek, Richard asserts that this is how Paul often uses it. Further, "More precisely the expression *touto gar* (used also in 2 Cor 8:10 and 1 Thess 4:3, 15; 5:18) always refers back to what has been

[149] BDAG 740–741, §1.b.α–β; BDF 151, §290(2, 3); *GGBB* 333–334.

discussed" (240). This is hardly the case. There is no reason why τοῦτο γάρ should be limited to an antecedent reference in 1 Thess 4:3 especially since the apposition, ὁ ἁγιασμὸς ὑμῶν, provides a postcedent one (*contra* Richard 1995, 187).[150] The other two references besides 1 Thess 4:15 cited by Richard (2 Cor 8:10; 1 Thess 5:18) do have an antecedent reference, as indicated by the syntax.[151] But the reference of τοῦτο cannot be determined on the basis of one grammatical aspect (i.e. with γάρ following) but must include all syntactic elements of the context. In 1 Thess 4:15, τοῦτο γάρ is part of a syntactic structure with ὅτι (v. 15c) which admits a postcedent reference.[152] I have kept the discussion solely to instances of τοῦτο γάρ, since for Richard the presence of γάρ is the determining factor for deciding on an antecedent reference for τοῦτο.[153] However, in the case of 1 Thess 4:15, another syntactical element (ὅτι) is decisive.[154] The subordinating conjunctions in verse 15c and verse 16a may function in a number of different ways (*GGBB* 453–461; BDF 202–205, §396–397); but each option outlined here depends on a subordinate and dependent relationship with τοῦτο. First, ὅτι may introduce direct discourse (i.e. ὅτι *recitativum*) in which case it would be represented by a colon (or quotation marks), following the thought introduced in 1 Thess 4:15a–b: "For this we say to you by the word of the Lord: we who live ..." (v. 15c) and: "the Lord himself ..." (v. 16a). In either instance, this option would only make sense if Paul's λόγος κυρίου stems from a saying of the earthly Jesus (so Gewalt 1982, 108), which while possible is not the best alternative for understanding the source(s) of the saying (§II.c above).[155] Further, it is highly unlikely that both statements in verses 15c–e and verses 16a–f (or even to v. 17c) are to be included as part of the saying. Second, ὅτι may stand in apposition to the demonstrative pronoun, τοῦτο (v. 15a). As such, the pronoun is postcedent or even *kataphoric* since its content is described in what follows (*contra* Richard 1995, 240; see Merklein 1992, 418). Taken in this way, the first conjunction would identify the λόγος κυρίου as beginning in verse 15c, and the translation would be: "For this we say to you by the word of the Lord, namely that we who live ...". There is no reason to reject this interpretation other than that the highly debatable location of the λόγος κυρίου is often identified as beginning in verse 16a not in verse 15c.[156] Although

[150] Another example where τοῦτο γάρ is in an appositional construction, and with a postcedent reference, appears in 1 Pet 2:19. On οὗτος in apposition, see *GGNT* 698–700.

[151] So also Rom 12:20; cf. Acts 27:34; Eph 6:1; Col 3:20; 1 Tim 4:16; 5:4; Heb 7:27.

[152] So also Eph 5:5; Col 3:20.

[153] On a similar issue, see the discussion of καὶ διὰ τοῦτο (1 Thess 2:13) in Chapter 4, §III.a.

[154] Ironically, Richard argues that καὶ διὰ τοῦτο in 1 Thess 2:13 has a forward directed meaning because of the following ὅτι (1995, 111–112). This reading serves Richard's compilation hypothesis, just as a backwards meaning in 1 Thess 4:15 serves his thesis that Paul does not give a quotation of a dominical saying (240).

[155] *Contra* BDF 246–247, §470(1), the ὅτι *recitativum* does not necessarily imply that Paul is giving a saying verbatim (*GGBB* 454–455; *GGNT* 1027–1028).

[156] But note the following references where the saying is assigned to v. 15: Donfried 1993, 39–41; Gewalt 1982, 108–113; Gundry 1987, 165; Hartman 1966, 188; Hofius 1991, 338–341; Holtz 1991, 385–386; 1998, 183–185; Merklein 1992, 410–415; Michaels 1994, 183–185; Reinmuth 1998, 142; von Dobschütz 1909, 193–194; Wilcke 1967, 132–133.

the second ὅτι (v. 16a) could also be taken this way – "... namely that the Lord himself ..." – the intervening statement (vv. 15c–e) between τοῦτο (v. 15a) and ὅτι (v. 16a) goes against this identification. Third, ὅτι may introduce indirect discourse (i.e. declarative ὅτι). The conjunction is often used this way to recast a saying or thought into reported form, but again does not imply that there must have been an original statement underlying the indirect discourse (*GGBB* 456). Such a function may be assigned to either ὅτι, depending on where the λόγος κυρίου is situated, and is commonly adopted in the NT especially after verbs like λέγειν.[157] Finally, the context allows one further option for translation of the subordinating conjunction, namely, as an epexegetical marker. This interpretation, where ὅτι is rendered "that" or even "to the effect that", would only suit one of the instances of the conjunction. It would then function to explain the statement introduced by the other ὅτι. In summary, Paul continues his answer from verse 14 (antecedent reference) and prepares for his next instalment (postcedent or resumptive reference) with τοῦτο. Assuming that Paul paraphrases the λόγος κυρίου starting at verse 16a, the second ὅτι is best understood as declarative, while the first ὅτι (v. 15c) is best understood as epexegetical. In so saying this, it is explicitly admitted that alternative grammatical solutions are possible for the interpretation of each ὅτι, and my solution is based on deciding factors relating to the source, form and location of Paul's λόγος κυρίου.

Paul often uses λέγειν in the first person singular form[158] but only twice in the first person plural form (here and Rom 4:9). Whereas in Rom 4:9 the plural λέγομεν is collective of a Jewish dialogue partner, in 1 Thess 4:15a it is used to refer to a statement made to the Thessalonians (ὑμῖν) by Paul and his colleagues (whether Silvanus only or both Silvanus and Timothy). There is no need to find a literary plural here (Excursus 1).

3. As previously noted, First Thessalonians contains four of the five Pauline references to the noun παρουσία (when used of Jesus/Lord)[159] in 2:19, 3:13, 4:15 and 5:23. Paul also uses other words to express eschatological manifestation in the letter: ἔρχεσθαι, of *orgē* (1:10) and of the Day of the Lord (5:2); ἀναμένειν, of the Son from heaven (1:10); φθάνειν, of *orgē* (2:16); καταβαίνειν, of the Lord (4:16); and ἐφιστάναι, of sudden destruction (5:3). These demonstrate that Paul's references to *parousia* are not isolated but emerge from a thoroughgoing expectation of God in salvation history. A survey of pericopes in First Thessalonians where παρουσία occurs is instructive to how Paul uses it in 1 Thess 4:15.

---

[157] The conjunction often appears after numerous different verbs that "denote mental or sense perception, or the transmission of such perception, or an act of the mind, to indicate the content of what is said, etc." (BDAG 731); cf. *GGNT* 1032–1036.

[158] The various forms include: λέγω (Rom 6:19; 9:11; 10:18, 19; 11:1, 11, 13; 12:3; 15:8; 1 Cor 6:5; 7:6, 8, 12, 35; 10:15, 29; 15:51; 2 Cor 6:13; 7:3; 8:8; 9:4; 11:16, 21; Gal 1:9; 3:15, 17; 4:1; 5:2, 16; Phil 4:11; Phlm 19, 21; cf. Eph 4:17; 5:32; Col 2:4; 1 Tim 2:7; 2 Tim 2:7); ἐρῶ (2 Cor 12:6; Phil 4:4); ἔλεγον (2 Cor 9:3; Phil 3:18; cf. 2 Thess 2:5); εἴπω (1 Cor 11:22).

[159] The title *Kyrios* and its significance is discussed in the analysis on 1 Thess 4:16 (§III.d.2 below).

In 1 Thess 2:19–20, Paul refers to the *parousia* of the Lord Jesus, and uses catchwords – ἐλπίς, χαρά, στέφανος καυχήσεως and δόξα – to describe how Paul feels about the Thessalonians despite not being able to see them (cf. vv. 17–18).[160] The question and answer posed in the text is well balanced (Harvey 1998, 269–270; see Rigaux 1956, 88 n. 3):

τίς γὰρ ἡμῶν ἐλπὶς ἢ <u>χαρὰ</u> ἢ στέφανος καυχήσεως
– ἢ οὐχὶ καὶ ὑμεῖς –
ἔμπροσθεν τοῦ κυρίου ἡμῶν Ἰησοῦ ἐν τῇ αὐτοῦ παρουσίᾳ;
ὑμεῖς γάρ ἐστε ἡ δόξα ἡμῶν καὶ ἡ <u>χαρά</u>.

Paul does not refer to the *parousia* of the Lord Jesus because he is looking to the future but because he is seeking a confirmation of success for his efforts in the present (Collins 1984, 205), and concomitantly, because it provides a basis for exhortation (Simpson 1998, 21–22). This is confirmed by verse 20 with its present tense verb (ἐστέ). Further, Paul elsewhere refers to χαρά[161] and καύχημα (2 Cor 1:14; Phil 2:16) in connection with success of his mission (see Bultmann 1965a, 650–652), which is verified in an apocalyptic reference to God's call (καλοῦντος ὑμᾶς εἰς τὴν ἑαυτοῦ βασιλείαν καὶ δόξαν, 1 Thess 2:12). Again, the verb is in the present tense and not only links this age with the age to come (Watson 1999, 68) but emphasises the present and continuing nature of the event (Donfried 2002, 241). The στέφανος imagery is extensive in the ancient world, the LXX and later Jewish literature, and in the NT (Grundmann 1971; see excursus by Richard 1995, 132–134). In the authentic Paul, the word appears only here, in Phil 4:1 and in 1 Cor 9:25. The last reference, which finds its background in the *agōn* motif (see Pfitzner 1967, 76–129; cf. 1 Thess 2:2) is of lesser relevance here (*contra* Malherbe 2000, 185); likewise, the LXX phrase, στέφανος καυχήσεως (Prov 16:31; Ezek 16:12; 23:42) is not germane to Paul's use (Collins 1984, 206; Wanamaker 1990, 123–124). The background to Paul's boasting is more closely situated to those places where boasting is given eschatological significance;[162] such boasting is "finally actualised in the time of salvation" (Bultmann 1965a, 647), a time in which Paul considers himself to be living. Some Hellenistic texts refer to crowns as a part of the preparation for the *parousia* of a king (see MM 497; 589). The Thessalonians could not have missed the link between στέφανος and *parousia*, but Paul turns the imagery on its head: Paul is not thinking of a crown to be won but of the Thessalonians *as* his crowning achievement (Richard 1995, 134).[163] They are his glory and hope (Deissmann

[160] The link between πάθημα and δόξα, where the latter is an eschatological goal of the former (Michaelis 1967b, 921; cf. Rom 8:17–18), may have some bearing in this text since Paul has just made reference to his hindrance by Satan (καὶ ἐνέκοψεν ἡμᾶς ὁ σατανᾶς, v. 18) and to the suffering of the Thessalonians (ἐπάθετε, v. 14).

[161] 2 Cor 7:4; Phil 2:2; 4:1; 1 Thess 3:9.

[162] Zech 10:12; Ps 149:5; 1 Chr 16:33.

[163] Crown-imagery should not be limited to its associations with the *parousia* of a king. Special headgear is also important for the cults of Roma, Cabirus and Dionysus (Donfried 1985, 341).

1995, 369; Morris 1959, 97). In this regard, Phil 4:1 is a striking parallel where the Philippians are also Paul's joy and crown, (χαρὰ καὶ στέφανός μου). A note of judgment is implicit in Paul's preoccupation for recognition of a successful mission (Conzelmann 1969, 267; cf. 2 Cor 1:14; Phil 2:16) and perhaps reiterated with the repetition of ἔμπροσθεν (1 Thess 2:19; 3:13; cf. 2 Cor 5:10).[164] There is an eschatological inference in στέφανος which is missing in Hellenistic texts (Harrison 2002a; Pfitzner 1967, 105–106).

The judicial element of 1 Thess 2:19 is strengthened by an allusion to Zech 14:5 in 1 Thess 3:13:

Zech 14:5	καὶ ἥξει κύριος ὁ θεός μου καὶ πάντες οἱ ἅγιοι μετ᾽ αὐτοῦ
1 Thess 3:13	εἰς τὸ στηρίξαι ὑμῶν τὰς καρδίας ἀμέμπτους ἐν ἁγιωσύνῃ ἔμπροσθεν τοῦ θεοῦ καὶ πατρὸς ἡμῶν ἐν τῇ παρουσίᾳ τοῦ κυρίου ἡμῶν Ἰησοῦ μετὰ πάντων τῶν ἁγίων αὐτοῦ

In Zech 12–14, the phrase "with all his holy ones" is part of an extended description of the Day of the Lord and almost certainly refers to angels. In 1 Thess 3:13, there is some confusion about whether οἱ ἅγιοι refers to angels or Christians.[165] Paul never uses ἅγιος (substantively or otherwise) for angels or any other beings besides humans (unless here).[166] Consequently, a number of commentators take the reference to be to humans despite the apparent inconsistency between Christians accompanying the Lord Jesus in 3:13 and meeting the Lord in 4:15–17. Most of the attempts to resolve this difficulty are superficial or forced.[167] Holleman also provides an argument for identifying οἱ ἅγιοι as humans (1996, 96). He refers to

[164] See Brandenburger 1984, 475; Kreitzer 1993, 261. Konradt is against the idea that ἔμπροσθεν contains a note of judgment and argues that Paul's perspective in 2:19 and 3:13 is wholly other (2003, 183–186). Certainly, ἔμπροσθεν is not always judicial, even when used of persons who come before God/Lord (cf. 1 Thess 1:3; 3:9; 1 John 3:19; BDAG 325, 1.b.β). But Konradt has not considered the force of Paul's boasting here, with its implicit reference to judgment and reward.

[165] Some commentators avoid the issue by taking οἱ ἅγιοι as a reference to angels and Christians; so Alford 1958, 267; Eadie 1877, 120–122; Milligan 1908, 45; Morris 1959, 115; Rigaux 1956, 492.

[166] Rom 1:7; 8:27; 12:13; 15:25, 26, 31; 16:2, 15; 1 Cor 1:2; 6:1, 2; 7:14; 14:33; 16:1, 15; 2 Cor 1:1; 8:4; 9:1, 12; 13:12; Phil 1:1; 4:21, 22; Phlm 5, 7; cf. 2 Thess 1:10; Eph 1:1, 15, 18; 2:19; 3:5, 8, 18; 4:12; 5:3; 6:18; Col 1:2, 4, 12, 26; 3:12; 1 Tim 5:10.

[167] Ellingworth (1974), in an article which focuses on the verb ἄγειν (1 Thess 4:14) as implying upward movement, struggles to resolve the inconsistency of identifying οἱ ἅγιοι as saints. He translates 3:13 as, "... when our Lord Jesus comes, to be with all who belong to him" (428). At best, this is an uncritical and unnecessary translation of the Pauline phrase (μετὰ πάντων τῶν ἁγίων αὐτοῦ), as Ross ably observes (1975, 444). Thomas attempts to solve the problem by stretching the double connotation of *parousia*. For him, 4:15–17 emphasises the "coming" or "arrival" of the Lord, while 3:13 emphasises the "presence" aspect of the *parousia* (1978, 268–269). But this appears to be a distinction of convenience which is not reflected in the text. Otto suggests that διὰ τοῦ Ἰησοῦ (4:14) emphasises a communion with Christ – "alive in soul and in communion with the risen Christ" – thereby interpreting 3:13 as a testimony to the fact that the "enrobed" saints (cf. Rev 6:9–11) are with Jesus at his *parousia* (1997, 199). But this suggestion is too synthetic and misunderstands the function of the problematic διά-phrase in 4:14. See Findlay (1891, 91; 1904, 77), Lenski (1937, 300–301), Mason (1992, 107–108 n. 50) and Simpson (1998, 15) who also argue that οἱ ἅγιοι refers to saints.

4 Ezra and particularly to references to God's eschatological agent who will come with "those who are with him" (7:28; 13:52). These are understood to include those "who from their birth have not tasted death" (6:26) as well as special righteous ones who "shall be taken up from among men" after their deaths to live with God's eschatological agent (14:9 [Metzger 1983]). Holleman comments: "Just like the author of 4 Ezra, Paul proves to be familiar with the tradition according to which special righteous ones are taken up to heaven soon after their deaths" (1996, 96 n. 2). Since this tradition is quite distinct from any notion of eschatological resurrection, Holleman does not find any inconsistency in the reference to an archangel in 1 Thess 4:16 (96). The fact that *4 Ezra* is dated to the late 1st century CE does not pose a problem for Holleman who finds the roots of the tradition in many earlier texts — the roots being the heavenly vindication of the martyr tradition (144–157). But Holleman's thesis fails on a fundamental point: namely, he seems to assume that the heavenly vindication of the martyr tradition includes a promise of resurrection *and* accompaniment with the *parousia* Lord. His extensive survey of the heavenly vindication of the martyr tradition cites such diverse texts as 2 Maccabees, Josephus, Wisdom of Solomon, *Liber antiquitatum biblicarum* (Pseudo-Philo) and *Testament of Job*, but not once does he demonstrate that these texts include a tradition of martyrs accompanying God's eschatological agent. Pobee is more careful: "The eschatological fate of the martyr presents a very diverse array of ideas. They are to be rewarded. But the nature of the reward is of great variety" (1985, 41). Indeed, the notion of martyr accompaniment is a later development of the heavenly vindication of the martyr tradition (cf. *Did.* 16.7, *Mart. Ascen. Isa.* 4:14).[168] Holtz (1998, 147) rightly comments of the *Didache* reference (in which the later development is esp. clear):

> Indessen ist das doch offenbar erst eine spätere Stufe der Entwicklung, die für 1Thess nicht ohne Gründe vorausgesetzt werden kann. Kein Grund jedenfalls ist, daß nach der literarischen Überlieferung des Judentums der Messias nicht von Engeln begleitet wird.[169]

Consequently, Holleman's thesis is rejected. In conclusion to this issue, a right interpretation of οἱ ἅγιοι might be found along the line of interpretation of Zech 14:5, of which 1 Thess 3:13 and *Did.* 16.7 are part (Hunzinger 1968, 75). In Matt 25:31, the wording of the LXX text (καὶ πάντες οἱ ἅγιοι μετ' αὐτοῦ) is changed (καὶ πάντες οἱ ἄγγελοι μετ' αὐτοῦ),[170] identifying οἱ ἅγιοι as οἱ ἄγγελοι (Goulder 1974, 166). But by the time of *Did.* 16.7, οἱ ἅγιοι are identified with those resurrected from the dead. Thus, the Didachist qualifies a reference to the resurrection of the

[168] It is improbable that a tradition of martyr accompaniment arose during the time of Paul simply because there were not enough martyred Christians to accommodate the tradition. Dunn comments: "There was no thought yet clearly expressed, so far as we can tell, of the vindicated righteous returning in triumph to earth or of their vindication being displayed on earth" (1998, 295).

[169] See Dibelius (1925, 16–17) for further references and P.-G. Müller (2001, 166–167) for corroborating discussion.

[170] Note the variant reading (cf. NA[27]), οἱ ἅγιοι ἄγγελοι, in some witnesses.

dead by saying, οὐ πάντων δέ, ἀλλ᾽ ὡς ἐρρέθη, followed immediately by the Zecharian text. The trajectory of interpretation for 1 Thess 3:13 is decidedly reflected in the older identification of οἱ ἅγιοι as angels,[171] and not in a later development of that trajectory (Ross 1975; *contra* Nicholl 2004, 30). This is confirmed by 1 Thess 4:16 where dead Christians are not with the Lord (Dibelius 1925, 17; Holtz 1998, 146–147). That this identification is the only exception to Paul's use of ἅγιος is tempered by the presence of several references to such an identification elsewhere in the NT and LXX[172] and significantly in the context of the *parousia* of the Son of Man.[173] As well, 1 Thess 3:11–13 is highly structured (Jewett 1969) and consists of somewhat traditional material which may contain expressions used in a different way to other Pauline references (Havener 1983, 19).

One feature of 1 Thess 3:13 which has not been discussed and which arises again in connection with a *parousia* text in 5:23 is a motif of holy living.[174] In 1 Thess 3:13, Paul prays that God will establish the hearts of the Thessalonians as unblamable in holiness (τὰς καρδίας ἀμέμπτους ἐν ἁγιωσύνῃ). Paul employs ἁγιωσύνη but rarely (see also Rom 1:4; 2 Cor 7:1). Rendered as "sanctification" or "holiness", it refers to a quality rather than a state (Procksch 1964, 114) and expresses Paul's theological assumption of the Thessalonians' position before God (Porter 1993a, 398).[175] So too, ἄμεμπτος is an explicit verdict of eschatological judgment (Grundmann 1967, 573; cf. Phil 2:15). A cognate, ἀμέμπτως, appears in 1 Thess 2:10 where Paul sums up his behaviour towards the Thessalonians (cf. ὁσίως), as well as in 5:23 where Paul prays that they will be kept blameless at the coming of the Lord Jesus (ἀμέμπτως ἐν τῇ παρουσίᾳ τοῦ κυρίου ἡμῶν Ἰησοῦ Χριστοῦ τηρηθείη).[176] The verb ἁγιάζειν appears in 5:23, where Paul expresses an active construction requesting God to effect a state of sanctification for the Thessalonians (Balz 1990b, 17; Procksch 1964, 112).[177]

[171] So Bornemann 1894, 155–156; Green 2002, 181; Haufe 1999, 65; Légasse 1999, 197–198; Procksch 1964, 109; P.-G. Müller 2001, 166–167; von Dobschütz 1909, 152–153; Wanamaker 1990, 145.

[172] Acts 10:22; Rev 14:10; cf. also Deut 33:2; Job 5:1; 15:15; Ps 67:18 (LXX); 88:6–7 (LXX); Dan 4:13θ; 8:13θ; Tob 11:14; 12:15 (BA).

[173] Mark 8:38 (par.); cf. Jude 14; Vos 1953, 137–138.

[174] The pervasive character of this motif has led Weima to venture the suggestion that "holiness is the most important theme of 1 Thessalonians" (1996, 98). Lyons observes: "1 Thess. has a higher density of explicit holiness terms than any other Pauline letter. With 1,482 words in the Greek text (Nestle-Aland 26), 1 Thess. makes up only 4.6% of the total words in the Pauline corpus (32,440). Yet its percentage of explicit holiness words is more than twice the corpus average (.675 compared to .327). ... These statistics are based on *Gramcord*" (1995, 188).

[175] With regard to the motif of judgment, the word "theological" is purposefully employed (see Neyrey 1980, 223). Note the interplay between ὁ θεὸς καὶ πατὴρ ὑμῶν and ὁ κύριος ἡμῶν Ἰησοῦς (1 Thess 3:11). The Thessalonians are to stand before the former (v. 13) while the latter (ὁ κύριος, v. 12) is their rescuer (1:10) who establishes their hearts' blameless in holiness (3:13), and who even died for them (5:9–10).

[176] Interestingly, ἀμέμπτως often appears in funerary texts (Horsley 1987a, 141) which is suggestive of its relevance for the Thessalonians even if they did die before the *parousia*.

[177] A question of Pauline anthropology regarding the unusual combination of πνεῦμα, ψυχή and σῶμα is beyond the scope of discussion here. I suspect Weima is on the right track when he links the phraseology to his thesis regarding the function of Paul's *letter-closings*. Paul emphasises wholeness at the coming of the Lord Jesus Christ (cf. ὁλοτελής, ὁλόκληρος, v. 23) to allay fears and questions regarding those who had died

Finally, Paul refers to ἁγιασμός three times in the letter, typically in a prepositional construction, ἐν ἁγιασμῷ (4:4, 7), and in a statement of the will of God, ὁ ἁγιασμὸς ὑμῶν (4:3).[178] The latter word emphasises "sanctifying" as a comprehensive goal for the conduct of the Thessalonians (Balz 1990b, 17; cf. εἰς ἁγιασμόν in Rom 6:19). Thus, ἁγιασμός is an explicit qualification of how the Thessalonians ought to live and please God (τὸ πῶς δεῖ ὑμᾶς περιπατεῖν καὶ ἀρέσκειν θεῷ, 1 Thess 4:1). This is not to imply that holiness received as sanctification is anything other than dependent on χάρις (Lattke 1987, 356–357). That sanctification, however, may be worked out in imperative living (Collins 1984, 309).[179]

In each of these texts an imperative aspect of holy living is immediately followed by an indicative eschatological statement.[180] Hence, when Paul refers to his behaviour in 1 Thess 2:10 and exhorts the Thessalonians to lead a life worthy of God, he makes an apocalyptic reference to kingdom and glory (v. 12). When Paul refers to the Thessalonians' acceptance of the word of God, and to their imitation of the *ekklēsiai* of God which are in Judea in Christ Jesus (2:13–14), he goes on to refer the *parousia* of the Lord Jesus (v. 19). When Paul prays that the Thessalonians may increase and abound in love (3:12), again he immediately refers to the *parousia* of the Lord Jesus (v. 13). Paul's prayer in 5:23 is followed by another reference to the *parousia* of the Lord Jesus Christ. As well, Paul's reiterations to holy living in 4:3, 4 and 7 are balanced by an indicative statement of judgment for those who transgress (ὑπερβαίνειν) these imperatives: διότι ἔκδικος κύριος περὶ πάντων τούτων (v. 6; cf. Rom 12:19). Indeed, the *letter-paraenesis* beginning with λοιπὸν οὖν (1 Thess 4:1) is preceded by a direct statement about the *parousia* (3:13). Even the exhortations implied in the imagery of day/night, light/darkness, awake/asleep and sobriety/drunkenness (5:4–8) are followed by a reference to *orgē* and salvation: ὅτι οὐκ ἔθετο ἡμᾶς ὁ θεὸς εἰς ὀργὴν ἀλλὰ εἰς περιποίησιν σωτηρίας (v. 9; cf. Rom 13:12–13). Schnelle (1990, 301–302) highlights the importance of Paul's (indicative) eschatological statements:[181]

> Während sich in den späteren Paulusbriefen christologische, sakramentale, pneumatologische und eschatologiche Begründungen für die Zuordnung von Indikativ und Imperativ

---

prior to the *parousia* (1995, 193–194). Wholeness is also emphasised *à propos* a trichotomous statement in an early Christian amulet (Horsley 1981c, 102–103). For further discussion of the Pauline text, see monographs by Gundry 1976; Jewett 1971; further, see Bultmann 1952, 191–227; Conzelmann 1969, 173–184; Dunn 1998, 51–78; Horsley 1987, 38–39; Langevin 1965; Schweizer 1953; van Stempvoort 1961.

[178] As well, Paul refers to τὸ πνεῦμα τὸ ἅγιον (1 Thess 1:5, 6; 4:8) and τὸ πνεῦμα (5:19). As with the anthropological question (previous footnote), the problematic issue regarding the proper interpretation of σκεῦος in the exhortation of 4:4 goes beyond the discussion here. Besides referring to the various commentaries, the reader is directed to the following literature: Baltensweiler 1963; Bassler 1995; Baumert 1990; Carras 1990; Collins 1983a; 1983b; Elgvin 1997; Konradt 2001; Maurer 1971; McGehee 1989; Ulonska 1987; Weima 1996; Whitton 1982; Yarbrough 1999.

[179] For extensive bibliography on *Heiligkeit* in the NT, see Lattke 1985, 706–708.

[180] See Cerfaux 1959, 57–60; Evans 1968, 170–200; Schnelle 1990; more generally, see Gnilka 1989.

[181] Similarly, Donfried 1990, 14–15; see Schnelle 1986, 209; 2003, 193–196.

> finden, fungiert im 1 Thessalonicherbrief die Parusie als die Begründung des ethischen Wandels schlechthin. Paulus verweist zur Motivation seiner Forderung nach Heiligung und untadeligem Leben (vgl. 1 Thess 3,13; 5,23; ferner 4,3.4.7) auf das Kommen Christi, d.h. der Imperativ resultiert nicht aus dem vergangenheitlichen Christusgeschehen, sondern aus der unmittelbar bevorstehenden Parusie.

This brief survey of *parousia* in First Thessalonians demonstrates that Paul uses a motif of *parousia* in his pattern of exhortation. This holds true even for the *parousia* reference in 1 Thess 4:15–17 despite the theological and didactic elements of the text (Witherington 1992, 156). This is consistent with the positioning of 4:13–5:11 in the *letter-paraenesis* of First Thessalonians and with the clearly paraenetic-oriented material in 4:1–12 and 5:12–22 (see Kümmel 1962, 223). This does not mean that Paul's view of *parousia* is nothing more than *paraenesis*. But the context should always be kept in mind. Thus, Paul's exhortations are essentially grounded in an eschatological expectation — not so much in the future as in an eschatological salvation work in Christ which encompasses the present and future (see Luz 1981, 156–162).[182] The theme of judgment implicit in the *parousia* reinforces the social behaviour required by Paul[183] although the connection between the eschatological discourse and exhortation should not be too crudely made (*contra* Fatum 1997, 187; see Okorie 1994, 60). According to Meeks, Paul's apocalyptic expectations also reinforce solidarity of the community, which itself would promote behaviour consistent to the maintenance of the community (1989, 694; see also Koester 1990, 446–447).

4. The question of whether Paul expected to be alive at the *parousia* of the Lord is often muddied by the debate over a possibility of development in Paul's thought. The latter topic is dealt with only incidentally here. Whereas the verb λέγομεν (v. 15a) refers to Paul, Silvanus and Timothy, the pronoun ἡμεῖς (v. 15c) emphatically includes Paul (Silvanus and Timothy) *and* the Thessalonians to whom he is writing. Paul emphasises his solidarity with the living Thessalonians with the striking participial phrases, οἱ ζῶντες οἱ περιλειπόμενοι (vv. 15c, d), repeated several verses later (vv. 17a, b). The ζάω/ζωή word group appears five times in First Thessalonians (1:9; 3:8; 4:15, 17; 5:10). The reference in 3:8 is to an emotional quality of life; in 1:9 and 5:10 Paul refers to an eschatological and eternal quality. Although the double reference in 4:15, 17 is in an eschatological context, it has a different conception: of being physically alive as a contrast to death (van der Watt 1990, 357–358). The phrase (ἡμεῖς) οἱ ζῶντες also appears with a similar contrast elsewhere in Paul (cf. 2 Cor 4:11; 5:15). The term does not yet emphasise the (Pauline) nuanced apocalyptic overtones of Rom 5–8, with the connection to the powers of sin (ἁμαρτία) and death (θάνατος),[184] although present and future connotations are merged in 1 Thess

[182] Collins rightly points out that each of the three references to the call of God (2:12; 4:7; 5:24) are made in a manifestly eschatological context (1984, 290).

[183] See Selby 1999; Sleeper 1999, 132–133; Wanamaker 1990, 145.

[184] For a discussion of ζῆν and ζωή as a soteriological category in Paul, see Schottroff 1991, 106–107.

4:17 with the conclusion: καὶ οὕτως πάντοτε σὺν κυρίῳ ἐσόμεθα (see Bultmann 1964b, 866–870; esp. 869). The phrase οἱ περιλειπόμενοι occurs elsewhere with the same context of surviving death (4 Macc 12:6; 13:18; Josephus *Ant.* 7.9) and περιλείπεσθαι is often used this way,[185] especially by Josephus.[186] The construction with εἰς τὴν παρουσίαν τοῦ κυρίου (v. 15d) is significant since it gives a temporal limitation to περιλείπεσθαι in the present (Frame 1912, 173); the use of εἰς instead of ἐν is unparalleled in Paul (cf. 1 Thess 2:19; 3:13; 5:23; 1 Cor 15:23). The connotation of surviving to a future reference is found in Jewish apocalyptic and such connection fuels some speculations about the background of the pericope (e.g. Klijn 1982). An association of a survival motif with remnant (λεῖμμα) theology is obtuse at best;[187] a connection to the eschatological woes expected in some strands of Jewish theology finds little more substantiation (see Pobee 1985, 115).

The alignment of Paul with those who are expected to survive until the *parousia* offers the possibility that he himself expected to be alive. Indeed, a sizeable number of commentators convert the possibility to probability. When Paul refers to the possibility of death in his later letters, this is understood to indicate that he changed his mind on the matter.[188] The implicit possibility remains despite attempts to moderate his expectation with an argument that Paul views humanity as consisting of two groups – living and dead – in which he quite naturally places himself in the former.[189] In so doing Paul unavoidably equates the survivors with concrete community members (Hoffmann 1966, 221). Nor is it possible to insulate Paul from the expectation by asserting that he is *only* referring to those Christians who will be alive at the time,[190] or that he only identifies himself with the surviving generation in order to strengthen his exhortations.[191] Paul could have easily avoided the implication in 1 Thess 4:15, 17 by using the impersonal third person (Otto 1997, 199; Wanamaker 1990, 172). A correct interpretation of Paul's intention on the matter at this time in his missionary career must account for other statements

[185] 2 Macc 1:31; 8:14; Euripides *Hel.* 426; Herodian 2.1.7.

[186] Josephus *Ant.* 1.96; 5.228; 6.146, 364; 7.113, 117; 9.102; 10.112; 13.5; *B. J.* 2.90, 397, 497; 3.20; *C. Ap.* 1.35.

[187] See Holtz 1998, 195; Malherbe 2000, 271; Richard 1995, 226. For background information on remnant, see Herntrich 1967, 196–209 (OT) and Schrenk 1967, 209–214 (Paul).

[188] Alford 1958, 274–275; Bruce 1982, 99; Frame 1912, 172–173; Jurgensen 1994, 93; Plevnik 1975a, 203; Wanamaker 1990, 172.

[189] Eadie 1877, 157–158; Green 1958; Hogg/Vine 1929, 138–139; Witherington 1992, 24–25; 2006, 134; see Dysinger 1944, 568.

[190] *Contra* Cranfield 1982a, 506; Morris 1959, 141–142; Uprichard 1979, 155. Giesen argues that the second participle, οἱ περιλειπόμενοι (vv. 15d, 17b) has "eine spezifizierende Funktion" (1985, 137) in relation to the first participle, (ἡμεῖς) οἱ ζῶντες (vv. 15c, 17a). Giesen gives the translation: "Wir, die Lebenden, werden, insofern wir bis zur Parusie des Herrn zurückbleiben, den Entschlafenen nichts voraus haben" (137). While this is possible, the argument remains hypothetical and makes the best sense if understood in the context of Giesen's rejection of *Naherwartung* in Paul. For a similar argument, but where *Naherwartung* is not at issue, see Hoffmann 1966, 220–221; Wimmer 1955, 285–286.

[191] *Contra* Calvin 1961, 364–365. There are many and various other arguments attempting to avoid Paul's being proved to be wrong; see Best 1972, 194–195; Malherbe 2000, 270–271.

in First Thessalonians on his relation to the *eschaton*; all other statements (in Paul's subsequent letters) which may or may not lead to developmental theories are of secondary relevance. After the emphatic statements in 1 Thess 4:15, 17, Paul goes on in 5:1–11 to assert that no one knows when the Day of the Lord will come (v. 2), and hortatively exhorts the Thessalonians not to sleep (καθεύδειν) but to keep awake (γρηγορεῖν) and be sober (νήφειν, v. 6). Further, he concludes that the Lord Jesus died for Paul and the Thessalonians so that, whether awake or asleep, they might live with him (vv. 9–10). It is possible that Paul uses γρηγορεῖν and καθεύδειν in verse 10 as referring to categories of being alive and dead, respectively.[192] If so, then in closest proximity to his assertion that he would survive until the *parousia*, Paul acknowledges the possibility that he might also die (Best 1972, 195–196; Green 1958, 285–286). Granted, elsewhere in First Thessalonians Paul betrays an expectation of an imminent *parousia* (*contra* Giesen 1985). The motif of waiting implies nearness (1:9); so does the identification of the Thessalonians as a present substantiation of glory and joy at the *parousia* (2:19–20). But Paul cannot be made into a fanatic regarding hope in an imminent *parousia* (Hanhart 1969, 449). Nor are his expectations to be taken to mean that he thought the *parousia* would occur while he lived, just that it could occur.[193] The phrase οἱ περιλειπόμενοι could even be taken to imply that survival until the end is the exception rather than the rule (Richard 1995, 241–242), although this interpretation does not really fit with the fact that the deaths among the Thessalonians are unexpected (Holtz 1998, 195–196).[194] Paul's other letters leave the matter open, and he consistently asserts that he may either be alive[195] or dead[196] at the *parousia* of the Lord (Oropeza 2000, 176; Richard 1995, 241).

5. The remaining phrase (v. 15e) consists of a negative construction (οὐ μή) followed by a verb in the aorist active subjunctive (φθάσωμεν) and a substantive participle (τοὺς κοιμηθέντας). Such a construction, with οὐ μή + aorist subjunctive expresses emphatic denial (BDF 184, §365). It occurs rarely in Paul but is found

[192] The question of how the two verbs are to be understood in 5:1–11 is very difficult to answer. I allude only to one possibility here and direct the reader to Chapter 6 which deals extensively with the issues. At this stage, all I am willing to say is that Paul's exhortations in 5:3–8 are best understood in terms of his broader pattern of exhortation to help the Thessalonians understand that the community has an eschatological existence (similarly, Wanamaker 1990, 189).

[193] Moore 1966, 110; Rösch 1918, 494; Stott 1991, 100–101.

[194] That Paul is dealing with two groups of people (one group is worried about those who had died; another group is proud of the fact that they would survive to the *parousia*) is a hypothesis based on the speculation that οἱ ζῶντες οἱ περιλειπόμενοι reflects a proud boast made by the second group (see argument by Green 1958, 286; 1970, 267). In order to rebut their claims, Paul "allies himself, almost ironically, with their outrageous claims, only to reverse with devastating effectiveness their ideas of priority" and therefore uses terminology "wholly conditioned by the Church situation in Thessalonica" (286). There is no doubt that Paul uses appropriate terminology according to a situational need. But the hypothesis that Paul is dealing with two groups as outlined by Green is not sustained by the text.

[195] 1 Cor 7:29–31; 15:51–52; Rom 13:11–12; cf. Phil 3:20; 4:5.

[196] 1 Cor 6:14; 2 Cor 1:9; 4:14; 5:1–10; Phil 1:20–23.

frequently elsewhere in the NT, sometimes in quotations of the LXX;[197] the emphasis is consistent with classical use (Smyth 1916, 394). A previous discussion of φθάνειν appears elsewhere in connection with its reference to *orgē* in 1 Thess 2:16d (Chapter 4, §III.d.4). As noted there, 1 Thess 4:15e is the only reference in the NT where φθάνειν appears with the definition "come before", "precede", with the accusative of the person preceded (BDAG 1053, §1).[198] Despite such rare use in the LXX (cf. Wis 4:7; 6:13; 16:28) this older definition is widespread in Josephus[199] and elsewhere (Fitzer 1974, 88–90).[200] But why has Paul used this precise formulation to address whatever it is that caused the Thessalonians grief concerning τοὺς κοιμηθέντας? Is φθάνειν a key word for the Thessalonians (so Richard 1995, 227)? If so, this would explain why Paul makes such a strong negative formulation (Malherbe 2000, 272–273). The problem has something to do with the relationship between those dead and those still living; it is not so much about the fact that some had died (Moore 1966, 109). But it is difficult to be more precise at this point because the nuance of φθάνειν can only be determined by the context. Does the notion of precedence refer to a question of survival with the attached connotations of advantage?[201] If so, φθάνειν is to be understood in terms of the emphatic οἱ ζῶντες οἱ περιλειπόμενοι (vv. 15c–d, 17a–b). Or is Paul perhaps referring to a presupposed sequence of resurrection? If so, φθάνειν is to be understood in terms of the temporal sequence of πρῶτον ... ἔπειτα (vv. 16f, 17a). These and other options for the interpretation of 1 Thess 4:15 are left open until such time as the analysis for verses 16–17 is complete.

In summary, in the analysis I show just how significant the eschatological motif of the *parousia* of the Lord is for Paul's pattern of exhortation in First Thessalonians. The paraenetic connection, where Paul associates imperatives for holy living, is unmistakeably present. Consequently, with eschatology as a hermeneutical key, I argue that the *parousia* reference in 1 Thess 4:15 has a strongly paraenetic force, despite the fact that the reference is part of a larger sequence of thought in verses 16–17. Thus, the *parousia* of the Lord invokes an important message of solidarity and promotes holy living.

---

[197] Rom 4:8 (Ps 31:2 [LXX]); 1 Cor 8:13; Gal 5:16; 1 Thess 4:15; 5:3; cf. Gal 4:30 (Gen 21:10). See further, statistical comments in *GNTG* vol. 1, 187–192.

[198] Cf. προφθάνειν in Matt 17:25.

[199] For example, *Ant.* 6.228; 7.64, 176, 247, 263; 9.70; *B. J.* 2.546.

[200] Homer *Il.* 21.262; Hesiod *Op.* 554, 570; Herodotus 7.188; Euripides *Heracl.* 120; *Iph. taur.* 669; Diodorus Siculus 15.61.4; *Let. Aris.* 137; Philo *Leg.* 3.215; cf. MM 666–667.

[201] In this regard, Mark 9:1 (par.) and 13:30 (par.) are not insignificant parallels since they may also allude to surviving to the *eschaton*; see Collins 1993, 164–165; Klijn 1982; Malherbe 2000, 283–285; Marshall 1983, 127. For further references, see Excursus 5 above (esp. under Klijn in the table).

d. The Lord Himself Will Descend (4:16)

1. Almost every word in 1 Thess 4:16 requires more than a passing comment because Paul redacts traditional material to present a complex apocalyptic scenario, always with his stated purpose of consolation in mind. He rarely uses the terms that appear here, or else they are found in unusual combinations. The sources of Paul's traditional material are diverse and it is sometimes difficult to determine which context is uppermost. This will become more obvious as the analysis proceeds but a prime example of this difficulty is the competing contexts of theophanies and Hellenistic *parousiai* for the interpretations of the various components of the verse.

This verse may be divided into two statements (see arrangement in §I above): the Lord himself will descend from heaven (vv. 16a, e) and the dead in Christ will rise first (v. 16f). The remaining phrases (vv. 16b–d) are attendant circumstances describing the first statement. After a short introduction on the Pauline title ὁ κύριος (§III.d.2), attention is turned first to the individual terms which make up the three prepositional phrases (§III.d.3) and second to the question of the relationship between the phrases (§III.d.4). The initial goal of the discussion in §III.d.3–4 is to critically assess why and how Paul uses particular terminology and the nature of its contribution to the overall intention of the pericope. The significance of the governing verb, καταβαίνειν (v. 16e), is also considered with particular attention given to the imagery of the Lord descending from heaven (§III.d.5). The second half of the verse is tackled in two parts: regarding the topic of those asleep (τοὺς κοιμηθέντας, v. 15e), what connotations have the christologically loaded phrase, οἱ νεκροὶ ἐν Χριστῷ (v. 16f; §III.d.6)? As with the investigation of ἐν Χριστῷ (see below), I do not provide a general history of research regarding "resurrection" in Paul. Rather, Kremer's extensive analysis of resurrection in *Resurrectio mortuorum* (1992) is used as a comprehensive introduction to the subject and as a platform for asking further questions arising from the text. These include: Does Paul here for the first time make a connection between Jesus' resurrection and the resurrection of believers? In addition, what is the relationship between the *parousia* of Jesus and the resurrection of the dead in Christ (§III.d.7)? What is the significance of the middle form of ἀνιστάναι (§III.d.8)? It appears that the motif of resurrection in this pericope only serves a more important process of translation. Even if this is not the case, what is the nature of the resurrection envisaged: does it include transformation (§III.d.9)?[202] Of course, the final goal of the analysis is to explain how Paul uses these motifs, which are all eschatological, to develop his pattern of exhortation. As I have done previously, I draw together some conclusions by way of a preliminary synthesis at the end of the analysis of this verse (§III.d.10).

[202] The significance of the emphatic πρῶτον (v. 16f) will be discussed in the analysis of the next verse (§III.e.2 below).

2. Pursuant to the previous discussion on the function of ὅτι (§III.c.2 above), verse 16a opens a subordinate declarative clause with a new subject ὁ κύριος preceded by the intensive pronoun αὐτός in apposition. The title (ὁ) κύριος is Paul's favourite for Jesus in a *parousia* connection, either by itself[203] or in a more complete formulation (Kramer 1966, 173).[204] The question of how Jesus came to be called *Kyrios* in pre-Pauline tradition need not be entered into here. The earlier idea that the *Kyrios* title originated out of Hellenistic Gentile Christianity[205] has been thoroughly rejected in view of its links with pre-Christian terms of address, רַבִּי and מָרִי (אָדוֹן?) applied to Jesus, although influence of Hellenistic *kyrios* traditions chiefly manifesting itself in an emphasis on Jesus' exaltation (Rom 8:34; 1 Cor 15:25; cf. Ps 110:1) cannot be discounted.[206] There is widespread debate about whether and how much the earliest Christians transferred the status described by the *Kyrios* title for God to Jesus.[207] For Hahn, there is no initial transference (1969, 79); rather the expression of Jesus' exaltation is a far reaching christological development (103–114). At least the development raises questions about early Jewish Christian interpretations of a monotheistic tradition leading Hurtado to speak of a distinctive "binitarian" adjustment of that tradition (Hurtado 1993a, 563; see Hengel 1995, 383–389). Dunn, in an article which examines the use of *kyrios* in Acts, notes that the author of Luke-Acts is able to use the title for both God and Jesus (1997, 377), a use which is "indicative of an unreflective stage in early christology" (378). Dunn finds Acts 2:34–36 most instructive, where a Christian reading of Ps 110:1 enables the author to speak of God as Lord and Jesus as Lord in the same breath; but the lordship of Jesus is derivative of the lordship of God (378). Thus, the *Kyrios* title invests authority in Jesus because he now exercises the same authority with God. In this connection, it is not surprising to find the title in close association with traditions of resurrection, exaltation and *parousia* (Whiteley 1974, 108), each successive of the former. Thus, if by Jesus' resurrection he is considered *Kyrios* then exaltation is confirmation of that lordship (Dunn 1998, 245). Further, Jesus as *Kyrios* at his *parousia* emphasises his role as eschatological agent, exercising God's authority, which Paul makes explicit in his reference to ἡμέρα κυρίου in 1 Thess 5:2 (Witherington 1992, 164–165). In 1 Thess 4:16a, the intensive marker, αὐτός, primarily serves to emphasise the identity of the descending one; the Lord is none other than Jesus, who died and rose (v. 14b).

3. A stand out feature of verse 16 is three prepositional phrases headed by ἐν (vv. 16b, c, d), the first two asyndetic and the last one coordinated with καί.

---

[203] 1 Thess 4:15, 16, 17; 5:2; 1 Cor 4:5; 5:5; 11:26; cf. Phil 4:5.

[204] So τοῦ κυρίου (ἡμῶν) Ἰησοῦ (Χριστοῦ) in 1 Thess 2:19; 3:13; 5:23; 1 Cor 1:7, 8; 2 Cor 1:14.

[205] Bousset 1970; Bultmann 1952, 51–52; cf. Lohmeyer 1927.

[206] Fitzmyer 1991a; Foerster 1965a; Hahn 1969; Hurtado 1998; Kramer 1966; Schnelle 2000, 181–182.

[207] Important for this aspect of the discussion are Paul's references to *kyrios* texts which originally applied to יהוה: Rom 10:13 (Joel 3:5); 1 Cor 1:31 (Jer 9:23–24); 10:26 (Ps 24:1); 2 Cor 10:17 (Jer 9:23–24); for further discussion, see Hurtado 2003, 194–195; Kreitzer 1987, 113–129; Whiteley 1974, 106–108.

Before attempting to answer pertinent questions about the grammatical function of the phrases and their overall interpretation within the context of the verse, it is essential to examine the pre-tradition of the terminology used. The first phrase, ἐν κελεύσματι (v. 16b), appears without a qualifying genitive as the others. The noun κέλευσμα does not appear elsewhere in the NT and occurs only once in the LXX as part of a fixed expression, ἀφ' ἑνὸς κελεύσματος (Prov 30:27) in a dissimilar context. According to Schmid, κέλευσμα (cf. similar nouns, κέλευσις, ἐγκέλευσις) can "range from a specific command, through a terse order, to an inarticulate cry" (1965, 657). He gives references to such broad use as the command of a deity, a cry of encouragement to animals, the call of the κελευστής who sets the rhythm for rowing on board a ship, and a cry of a baby at night (656–657). The verb κελεύειν appears more widely in the NT and LXX, with similar significance.[208] In none of these cases is there a clear parallel to Paul's use in 1 Thess 4:16.

The relative sparsity of the term has led some commentators to find semantic parallels rather than verbal ones. Thus, Plevnik examines the so-called "command call" motif in contexts resembling 1 Thess 4:16–17, of which he considers depictions of theophanies and the Day of the Lord to be the most pertinent (1975a, 235). In particular, he examines texts with גָּעַר, a word often translated in the LXX by ἐπιτιμᾶν or ἐπιτίμησις, and which often appears in theophany texts but also in later pseudepigraphal and Qumran literature (235–243). Plevnik also looks at NT texts with references to ἐπιτιμᾶν (243–245).[209] He concludes: "In the light of this motif study, we suggest that the expression *en keleusmati* in 1 Thes 4:16 has the function of characterizing Christ's coming in power in the end-time as the act of establishing God's rule and kingdom" (245–246). Plevnik's conclusion is similar in a later publication (1997) where he further asserts: "The basic notion underlying this motif is the power and authority of the coming Lord to remove what does not conform to the kingdom of God" (85), and in this way associates the "command call" with the resurrection, although Plevnik thinks it unlikely that it deals directly with the resurrection of the dead (84–85). I am cautious of Plevnik's conclusions particularly because the background of 1 Thess 4:16–17 cannot be conclusively proved to be theophany texts (there are multiple influences here). Besides, there are quite a few references which Plevnik does not consider.

The word κέλευσις is often used in a political context to denote an official "order", "decree" or "resolve" issued by government officials or the emperor himself (Schmid 1965, 657).[210] It is possible that Paul intentionally uses the word to make a statement against the ideology of imperial eschatology by contrasting the κέλευσις

---

[208] These references appear mostly in 1–4 Macc, but see also 1 Esd 9:53; Bel 14; Sus 32θ, 56θ; Jdt 2:15; 12:1; Tob 8:18. The NT references are found in Matthew and Acts (except for Luke 18:40); for references, see Balz 1991b; Denis 1987.

[209] It is surprising that Plevnik does not pick up on the presence of ἐπιτιμᾶν in Jude 9, esp. since in the same verse the author refers to Michael, the archangel.

[210] E.g. Plutarch *Mor.* 32C; Josephus *Ant.* 17.65; cf. *B.J.* 1.134.

of imperialism with the κέλευσμα associated with the coming of the Lord.[211] Less probable are links to a military context (e.g. Aeschylus *Pers.* 397; Thucydides 2.92); these probably have little influence on Paul's use of κέλευσμα because there is minor emphasis on judgment here (Bruce 1982, 100; Wilcke 1967, 138). Putting these suggestions aside, there are many other contexts where κέλευσμα or κελεύειν is used. Thus, in several texts God makes commands (ὁ δεσπότης ἐκέλευσεν, *T. Ab.* 15:9): of Baruch (κελεύματι θεοῦ, *3 Bar.* [intr.]);[212] of death who awaits a command (ὁ θάνατος ... ἐλθὼν ...ἀπεκδεχόμενος τὴν κέλευσιν τοῦ δεσπότου, *T. Ab.* 16:3); of holy archangels (ὁ ὕψιστος ἐκέλευσε τοῖς ἁγίοις ἀρχαγγέλοις, *1 En.* [Greek] 9[B]:4); of Michael the commander-in-chief (ὁ ὕψιστος κελεύει τὸν ἀρχιστράτηγον Μιχαήλ, *T. Ab.* 9:8 [rec. A]) and of Michael the archangel (ὁ κύριος ἐκέλευσε τῷ ἀρχαγγέλῳ Μιχαήλ, F. *Jub.* [Greek] 10:7). In another context, Philo refers to the one command (ἑνὶ κελεύσματι, *Praem.* 117) of God gathering together exiles from the very ends of the earth (cf. a similar notion in John 5:25). Thus, theophanies are not the only plausible background for Paul's use of κέλευσμα. On the strength of the references outlined here, the command probably stems from God himself. But this suggestion must meet with the analysis of the other two ἐν phrases and especially with the question of whether the voice of the archangel and the trumpet of God are epexegetical descriptions of the command (see below).

The second phrase contains a reference to an archangel, ἐν φωνῇ ἀρχαγγέλου (v. 16d). The noun ἀρχάγγελος appears only here and in Jude 9 in the NT and LXX. Other references to ἀρχάγγελοι are abundant elsewhere (cf. Philo *Her.* 205) especially in the Pseudepigrapha.[213] But very few of these references predate Paul.[214] There are many other possible references to archangels where other descriptive terms are employed, including: (ὁ) ἀρχιστράτηγος,[215] Μιχαηλ εἷς τῶν ἀρχόντων τῶν πρώτων (Dan 10:13), Μιχαηλ ὁ ἄγγελος ὁ μέγας,[216] μετ᾽ ἀγγέλων δυνάμεως αὐτοῦ (1 Thess 1:7), ἄγγελος ἰσχυρός (Rev 5:2; 10:1; 18:21), and ἀρχιχιλιάρχος (*Pr. Jos.* 7 [fragment A]). The name Michael is associated with many of these references (cf. also 1QM 17:6–7) but alternative names are used (Reid 1993, 22–23).[217] Thus, it is impossible to determine the identity of the archangel in 1 Thess 4:16 (Wilcke 1967, 136–137; *contra* BDAG 137). In the Pauline context, the reference to an archangel is consistent with the association of angels with the

---

[211] On this theme, see Excursus 5, under Harrison (2002) in the table.

[212] An older form of κέλευσμα is κέλευμα, with no appreciable difference in meaning (Schmid 1965, 656).

[213] These include: F. *Jub.* (Greek) 2:1; 10:7; 48:1; *1 En.* (Greek) 9(B):1, 4; 20:7; 20(B):7; *Apoc. Mos.* (preface); 3:2, 3; 13:2; 22:1, 2; 37:4; 38:1; 40:1; 43:1, 2; *Pr. Jos.* 7 (fragment A); *4 Ezra* 4:36; *T. Ab.* (rec. A): 1:4, 6; 5:7; 10:1; 13:10, 11; 14:10; 15:14; 16:6; 20:10; *3 Bar.* 10:1; 11:8; 12:4; *Apoc. Sedr.* 14:1; *Gk. Apoc. Ezra* 1:3.

[214] F. *Jub.* (Greek) 2:1; 10:7; 48:1; possibly also *1 En.* (Greek) 9(B):1, 4; 20:7; 20(B):7.

[215] Josh 5:14, 15; Dan 8:11; cf. *2 En.* 22:6; 33:10; *Jos. Asen.* 14:8; *T. Mos.* 10:2; *T. Ab.* (multiple ref.).

[216] Dan 12:1; cf. ὁ ἄρχων in 12:1θ.

[217] For further references, see Kittel 1964, 87; Newsom 1992, 252.

eschaton.[218] Particularly relevant are those texts which describe the Son of Man coming with his (holy) angels[219] who gather his elect (Mark 13:26–27 [par. Matt 24:30–31]). Further, it is said that the Lord Jesus will be revealed from heaven with his mighty angels (2 Thess 1:7). This text is made less relevant by the overt emphasis on judgment, a motif which is further in the background for 1 Thess 4:16 (Plevnik 1997, 86–87). The connection between φωνή and ἄγγελος is common.[220] Although the pseudepigraphal *Apocalypse of Moses* is too late to influence Paul, one text is an interesting parallel to 1 Thess 4:16 because of its similar terminology. In *Apoc. Mos.* 37:1–6, the author describes the taking of Adam to Paradise: an angel sounded the trumpet (ἰδοὺ ἐσάλπισεν ὁ ἄγγελος, v. 1); other angels cried out with a fearful voice (οἱ ἄγγελοι ... ἐβόησαν φωνὴν φοβερὰν λέγοντες, v. 1); Adam was snatched away (ἥρπασεν τὸν Ἀδάμ, v. 3); the Father of all gave him to the archangel Michael (ὁ πατήρ τῶν ὅλων ... παρέδωκεν αὐτὸν τῷ ἀρχαγγέλῳ Μιχαήλ, v. 4), saying to take Adam up to Paradise (ἆρον αὐτὸν εἰς τὸν παράδεισον, v. 5). Several verses prior to this description an angel had informed Eve that Adam had gone out of his body and commanded her: "Rise and see his spirit borne up to meet its maker" (ἀνάστα καὶ ἴδε τὸ πνεῦμα αὐτοῦ ἀναφερόμενον εἰς τὸν ποιήσαντα αὐτὸν τοῦ ἀπαντῆσαι αὐτῷ, 32:4 [Johnson 1985]). For certain, it cannot be stressed strongly enough that there are far too many differences in the texts for *Apoc. Mos.* 37:1–6 to be of more than general use for illuminating Paul's thought. But the common elements – context of death, trumpet, voice of angels, being snatched away, the presence of an archangel, meeting God – demonstrate how ancient authors use apocalyptic imagery to serve a purpose. In the case of the *Apocalypse of Moses*, the images are part of a presentation of the coming of God (ἐρχόμενος, 33:2); Paul's use of similar imagery is also given in the context of the coming of the Lord. In both cases, the references serve to emphasise the eschatological power of the coming one (see Kittel 1964, 87). While angelology is of increasing significance in the first century, Paul's reference to an archangel probably serves only to emphasise the significance of the φωνή (Broer 1990b 15–16).

The third phrase, ἐν σάλπιγγι θεοῦ (v. 16d) is connected to the second with καί. The term σάλπιγξ has a complex trajectory through Jewish, intertestamental and early Christian literature (see Bockmuehl 1991; Friedrich 1971). The older conception of σάλπιγξ where it appears as an LXX translation of the Hebrew שֹׁפָר, "horn", as an instrument blown in battle, is no longer present in the NT except perhaps at 1 Cor 14:8 where it appears as a metaphor.[221] The instrument is used as

---

[218] Kittel 1964, 84; Plevnik 1975a, 254–256; Watson 1992, 254.

[219] Cf. Matt 25:31; Mark 8:38 (par.); 1 Thess 3:13; Jude 14.

[220] Ps 102:20 (LXX); Job 38:7 (LXX); Rev 5:2, 11 (φωνὴν ἀγγέλων); 7:2; 8:13 (with ref. to σάλπιγξ; so also Rev 9:13; 10:7; 11:15); 14:9, 15, 18; 19:17.

[221] There are other Hebrew words represented in the LXX by σάλπιγξ as well as alternative translations for שֹׁפָר. For references and discussion, see Friedrich 1971, 76–78; Lichtenberger 1993a, 225.

a signal in battle[222] as well as a signal acknowledging dependence on God.[223] It is used at solemn occasions often in a cultic sense,[224] and appears in theophanies.[225] But it is the eschatological significance of the trumpet which is of more relevance for Paul. In this connection, the σάλπιγξ is associated with the judgment motif of the Day of the Lord.[226] It appears again in a battle context, but this time symbolically in the last battle between the sons of light and the sons of darkness.[227] The term has various connections in the intertestamental literature including: angels and judgment,[228] salvation (cf. *Pss. Sol.* 11:1; *Apoc. Ab.* 31:1–4), resurrection,[229] and as part of a description of God (*Apoc. Sedr.* 11:2, 13). The closest formulation to ἐν σάλπιγγι θεοῦ in 1 Thess 4:16 are a few apocalyptic references to ἐν (τῇ) σάλπιγγι,[230] of which God blows the trumpet himself (Zech 9:14) or else the archangel Michael blows it.[231] Throughout the trajectory of the term there is a developing transference of the instrument from a human to a heavenly sphere. As such it is difficult to characterise a reference to trumpet as anything more than "a literary device to underline the importance of the themes portrayed" (Bockmuehl 1991, 207; see Williams 1999, 234–235). The question of who blows the trumpet therefore recedes into the background despite the genitive θεοῦ (Best 1972, 197; Vos 1953, 141).[232]

4. The three prepositional phrases with ἐν (vv. 16b–d) express attendant circumstances. Such use is found elsewhere with verbs of movement to denote an accompanying state.[233] Many commentators rightly recognise that ἐν κελεύσματι without a genitive of qualification functions semantically as the head phrase of the other two phrases. Thus, ἐν φωνῇ ἀρχαγγέλου καὶ ἐν σάλπιγγι θεοῦ (v. 16c, d) becomes a doublet of epexegetical phrases, each with a genitive and linked via

---

[222] Num 31:6; 1 Kgdms 13:3; 2 Kgdms 2:28; Job 39:24, 25; 1 Macc 6:33; 7:45; 9:12; 16:8.

[223] Num 10:2, 8, 9; Josh 6:5, 8, 13, 20; 2 Par 13:12, 14; 1 Macc 3:54; 4:40; 5:31, 33; 2 Macc 15:25; Jer 6:1, 17; 28:27; 49:14.

[224] Lev 23:24; 25:9; Num 10:10; 2 Kgdms 6:15; 4 Kgdms 11:14; 12:14; 1 Par 13:8; 15:24, 28; 16:6, 42; 2 Par 5:12, 13; 7:6; 15:14; 20:28; 23:13; 29:26, 27, 28; 1 Esd 5:57, 61, 62, 63; 2 Esd 3:10; 18:15; 22:35, 41; Ps (LXX) 46:6; 80:4; 97:6; 150:3; Dan 3:5, 7, 10, 15; Sir 50:16.

[225] Exod 19:13, 16, 19; 20:18; cf. Aristob. 8.10.13, 16, 17; Heb 12:19.

[226] Isa 27:13; Ezek 7:14; 33:3, 4, 5, 6; Hos 5:8; Joel 2:1, 15; Zeph 1:16; Zech 9:14; cf. Jer 4:5, 19, 21; Amos 2:2; 3:6.

[227] Cf. multiple references in 1QM (for discussion, see Bockmuehl 1991, 208–210; Friedrich 1971, 82); cf. also *Sib. Or.* 5:253.

[228] *Pss. Sol.* 8:1; *Apoc. Mos.* 38:2; *T. Ab.* 12:10 (rec. A); *4 Bar.* 3:2; *Sib. Or.* 8:239.

[229] *Gk. Apoc. Ezra* 4:36; cf. *Sib. Or.* 4:174; *Tg. Ps.-J.* (Exod 20:15); *Did.* 16.6.

[230] Ezek 7:14; *Pss. Sol.* 11:1; cf. ἐν τῇ ἐσχάτῃ σάλπιγγι, 1 Cor 15:52.

[231] *Apoc. Mos.* 22:1–4; cf. *4 Bar.* 4:1; *Apoc. Zeph.* 9:1; 10:1; 11:5; 12:1.

[232] See Aristob. 8.10.13, 16, 17, where the author is unable to find the specific source of the trumpet sounds: "The trumpet blasts were quite strongly audible at the same time as the exhibition of the lightning-like fire, although no such instruments were present nor any to sound them, but all things happened by divine arrangement" (8.10.16 [A. Yarbro Collins 1985]).

[233] Oepke 1964e, 538; so also Fuerbringer 1942, 649. Examples include: ἐν ῥάβδῳ ἔλθω πρὸς ὑμᾶς (1 Cor 4:21); ὅταν δὲ ἔλθῃ ὁ υἱὸς τοῦ ἀνθρώπου ἐν τῇ δόξῃ αὐτοῦ (Matt 25:31); τὸν υἱὸν τοῦ ἀνθρώπου ἐρχόμενον ἐν τῇ βασιλείᾳ αὐτοῦ (Matt 16:28); οὗτός ἐστιν ὁ ἐλθὼν ... Ἰησοῦς Χριστός, οὐκ ἐν τῷ ὕδατι μόνον ἀλλ' ἐν τῷ ὕδατι καὶ ἐν τῷ αἵματι (John 5:6). For further examples of ἐν as expressing attendant circumstances, including classical, LXX and other NT references, see *GGNT* 588–589.

a coordinating καί.[234] Although the grammatical structure of the text does not require this interpretation (the three prepositional phrases could be understood individually), this option dispenses with the difficulty of distinguishing the functions of the command, voice and trumpet: all audible acts (Wanamaker 1990, 173–174). The translation represents this interpretation by the omission of the second and third "with": "with a command, [i.e.] the voice of an archangel and the trumpet of God". The more general conclusion that these phrases of attendant circumstances provide an overarching emphasis on God's powerful entrance into the human sphere is probably the least that could be said (see Minear 1954, 199–200). More to the point is the notion that the *parousia* of the Lord often coincides with themes of judgment and salvation. The association of judgment (particularly with reference to the archangel)[235] need not be rejected just because it does not accord with Paul's purpose of consolation. On the one hand, Paul consoles the Thessalonians regarding those who have died, especially about how the dead are involved in the *parousia*. No element of threat or judgment is presupposed. On the other hand, because the subject matter involves the *parousia* which itself contains an element of judgment, it is impossible for Paul not to use language which contains that element. Another, more appropriate connection to Paul's terminology is the implicit reference to waking up the dead at the resurrection. In John 5:28–29, the hour is coming when those in tombs will hear the voice (φωνῆ) of the Son of Man and come forth (ἐκπορεύεσθαι) either to the resurrection of life (εἰς ἀνάστασιν ζωῆς) or to the resurrection of judgment (εἰς ἀνάστασιν κρίσεως). Taken in this way, the command in 1 Thess 4:16b may be a signal for the resurrection of the dead in Christ (v. 16f). The parallel between the texts might be strengthened by the observation that κελεύσματι appears in close juxtaposition to the phrase αὐτὸς ὁ κύριος (v. 16a). The Lord therefore signals the resurrection (Wanamaker 1990, 173). In addition, the trumpet of God is symbolic of a call to resurrection.[236] In 1 Cor 15:52, the sound of the trumpet is so defined (σαλπίσει γὰρ καὶ οἱ νεκροὶ ἐγερθήσονται), as similarly in Matt 24:31.[237] Finally, in verses 16b–d Paul may be influenced by Hellenistic *parousiai* (Cerfaux 1959, 32–35) where the attendant circumstances may hint at an imperial celebration (Beare 1962a, 625; Gundry 1987, 162–163). If so, then this prepares the way for the thesis that Paul is alluding to formal Hellenistic receptions.[238] But Cosby does point out that while the voice

[234] Frame 1912, 174; Howard 1988, 183; Malherbe 2000, 274; Nicholl 2004, 42; Siber 1971, 46; von Dobschütz 1909, 195; Wilcke 1967, 138; see Vos 1953, 140. Thus: "Das traditionelle Material ist aufgenommen, um ein allgemeines Bild von der Parusie zu zeichnen, nicht aber, um den Ablauf im einzelnen darzustellen" (P. Müller 1988, 27).

[235] See primary references above.

[236] An inscription of the late 2nd or 3rd century CE vividly depicts the enduring symbolism of the trumpet: οὐ χρυσὸς οὐκ ἀργύ[ρ]ιν ἀλ<λ>' ὀστέα κατακίμενα, περιμένοντα φωνὴν σάλπιγγος ("Neither gold nor silver but bones lie here awaiting the trumpet of God" [Pryor 2002, 102]).

[237] Other references in this connection are listed above; see Balz 1991a, 280; Frame 1912, 174; Vos 1953, 138–139; Wanamaker 1990, 174.

[238] See discussion of ἀπάντησις in §III.e.6 below.

of the archangel and the trumpet of God could be construed as referring to the loud shouts and heralding of Hellenistic receptions (Gundry 1987, 165–166),[239] the symbolism of the trumpet in Paul's presentation is not identical: the trumpet is blown by a heavenly being not by one of a welcoming crowd (Cosby 1994, 29–30). In a later article, Gundry moderates Cosby's criticism by noting that the differences between Paul's presentation and Hellenistic formal receptions, regarding the function of the trumpet, are understandable in view of a need for supernatural action required for the resurrection of dead Christians, the snatching up of them and the meeting in the air. "At least the Parousia and Hellenistic formal receptions share the element of happy noise" (1996, 40).

5. The reference to καταβαίνειν in verse 16e invokes a strongly symbolic motif of ascending/descending. Along with its opposite (ἀναβαίνειν), the verb is often used of a geographical or spatial sense because of the high elevation of Jerusalem and the temple (Fendrich 1991a, 254). But a religious significance is applied to the symbolism in multifarious ways as portrayed in the LXX references: θεός/κύριος descends at Mt. Sinai;[240] the notion of an ascending and descending God[241] overlaps with the ascending and descending angels;[242] the act of descending is one of benevolence,[243] judgment[244] and deliverance;[245] it certainly has cultic overtones (P. Müller 1988, 27).[246] In some references there is an eschatological aspect present (Schneider 1964, 523): the spirit descends like a dove on the baptised Jesus (Mark 1:10 [par.]; cf. John 1:32–33); the angel of the Lord descends from heaven to roll back the stone (Matt 28:2); descending angels of heaven play a part in the unfolding drama of Revelation (10:1; 18:1; 20:1) and καταβαίνειν appears in conjunction with the restoration of the holy city Jerusalem (Rev 21:2, 10). Reference to a cloud motif is common throughout.[247] The only other occurrence of the verb in Paul appears in Rom 10:7 (discounting Eph 4:9, 10) in a quotation of Deut 30:11–14, as part of a complex argument for the validation of the gospel (see Käsemann 1980,

---

[239] For primary text references, see Peterson 1930. Witherington (1992, 158) even suggests that κέλευσμα may refer to the command to open the city gates at the *parousia* of a visiting monarch (cf. Ps 24:7–10).

[240] Exod 19:11, 18, 20; 24:16; 33:9; 34:5; 2 Esdras 19:13; similarly, see the transfiguration accounts in Mark 9:9 (par).

[241] Prov 30:4; cf. John 3:13, with ref. to the Son of Man, and Acts 14:11, of the gods descending; cf. also Eph 4:9, 10.

[242] Gen 28:12; cf. John 1:51; *T. Ab.* 7:8 (rec. A).

[243] Gen 11:5, 7; Num 11:17, 25; 12:5; Deut 31:15; cf. *1 En.* 25:3.

[244] Thus, θεός/κύριος descends in anger (2 Kgdms 22:10; Ps 17:10 [LXX]; 143:5 [LXX]) and judgment (Gen 18:21; Mic 1:3, 12; cf. *Sib. Or.* 3:308); otherwise theophanic images assume a role of judgment, including: fire from heaven (4 Kgdms 1:10, 12, 14; cf. Luke 9:54; Rev 13:13; 20:9; *T. Ab.* 12:4 [rec. B]), supernatural rain (Deut 28:24; cf. Rev 16:21), and a sword (Isa 34:5).

[245] Gen 46:4; Exod 3:8 (cf. Acts 7:34); Isa 31:4; with reference to angels, so 3 Macc 6:18. In the Gospel of John, Jesus is the (living) bread (of God/life) which comes down from heaven (6:33, 41, 42, 50, 51, 58). In Jas 1:17, every good and perfect gift from above descends from the father of lights.

[246] 2 Par 7:1, cf. v. 3; 2 Macc 2:10; *Liv. Pro.* 21:10.

[247] E.g. Exod 24:16; 34:5; Num 11:25; 12:5; Deut 31:15; 2 Kgdms 22:10.

288–290; Byrne 1996, 317–318). Although the presence of the verb is contributed to Paul's redaction (i.e. the Deuteronomic text is altered to a form reminiscent of Ps 106:26 [LXX]), this connection bears little relevance to the text at hand. Thus, while there are numerous references in the biblical tradition connecting καταβαίνειν with an action of God, Paul's choice to link it with his presentation of the *parousia* of the Lord is rarely investigated. One exception is an article by Glasson (1988) who argues that OT theophanies lie behind Paul's conception of the *parousia* of the Lord. While Glasson is able to find virtually all the apocalyptic elements of 1 Thess 4:16 in theophanic texts of the LXX, he is only able to cite Mic 1:3 and Isa 31:4 (cf. 2 Esdras 19:13) as parallels to Paul's use of καταβαίνειν (1988, 261). But of *these* texts there is only one other common element (φωνή, in Isa 31:4) and that with a different function to the φωνή in 1 Thess 4:16. Fortunately, C. A. Evans (1993) has filled this gap with the observation that Ps 46:6 (LXX) could lie behind the wording of 1 Thess 4:16 (see table in Excursus 5). Evans provides convincing reasons for the differences between the texts and defines a relevant trajectory of interpretation through patristic (242–246) and Jewish exegesis (246–250). This does not mean that Paul consciously uses the Psalm since the reference may be embedded within an inherited tradition which Paul uses here (251). However, the portrayal of the Lord as a great and fearful king (Ps 46:3), who subdues peoples and nations (46:4) and provides an inheritance (46:5), and of God who reigns over the nations and sits on his holy throne (46:9) all in a context of celebration (46:2, 10), coheres with Paul's apocalyptic portrait in First Thessalonians (1993, 252). According to Evans, the element of judgment (n.b. κέλευσμα instead of ἀλαλαγμός, cf. Ps 46:6) poses no problem here because other ancient interpreters understood Ps 46:6 as referring to judgment, which also forms part of the context of 1 Thess 4:16, *vis-à-vis* 1 Thess 5:1–11 (252). The phrase ἀπ' οὐρανοῦ (v. 16e) contrasts the place of departure from the destination of the Lord's descending.[248] Nothing more needs to be added from the previous discussion of οὐρανός elsewhere (Chapter 3, §III.b.4).

6. The last clause of the verse, καὶ οἱ νεκροὶ ἐν Χριστῷ ἀναστήσονται πρῶτον (v. 16f), articulates a consequence of the apocalyptic details presented so far and consists of a subject (with dative phrase), finite verb and adverb. The substantive adjective νεκρός occurs almost exclusively in the NT in the plural and refers to "the dead" in contrast to those alive (Bultmann 1967, 893; Dabelstein 1991, 459). Besides the numerous references to νεκρός in the formulaic statement that God raised Jesus from the dead (Chapter 3, §III.b.5), Paul often refers to "the dead" in connection to resurrection[249] or else with reference to God's ability to raise the dead (Rom 4:17; 11:15; 2 Cor 1:9). Thus, Christ is Lord of the dead and the living (Rom 14:9). Paul's figurative use of the word does not appear in First Thes-

[248] Whether that destination is other than ἀήρ (v. 17c), either to the earth or back up to heaven cannot be decided at this point but must await the discussion of 4:17 (§III.e.6 below).

[249] 1 Cor 15:13, 15, 16, 21, 29, 32, 35, 42, 52; Phil 3:11; cf. Heb 6:2.

salonians.[250] But the reference in 1 Thess 4:16 is different to all of those so far mentioned because Paul does not merely refer to "the dead", but rather "the dead ἐν Χριστῷ". The only similar formulations in the NT are οἱ κοιμηθέντες ἐν Χριστῷ (1 Cor 15:18) and οἱ νεκροὶ οἱ ἐν κυρίῳ (Rev 14:13). While neither are irrelevant for Paul's reference in 1 Thess 4:16, the presence of the thoroughly Pauline ἐν Χριστῷ makes it more difficult to furnish a satisfying interpretation. In part, this is because ἐν Χριστῷ is used so often by Paul with different connotations, of locality, of instrumentality and of manner (Seifrid 1993, 433–434).[251] But even this is an over-simplification. Since Paul's use is so varied no attempt is made in this analysis to examine the occurrences of ἐν Χριστῷ in Paul, nor to discover the origin of the phrase, nor even whether and how the phrase expresses a Pauline mysticism. To these questions the reader is directed to an extensive history of research (not exhaustive).[252] The ἐν-construction appears to give no indication of how it is to be interpreted (Wedderburn 1985, 87) and there is no clue as to how Paul uses the phrase in 1 Thess 4:16 from the other occurrences in the letter.[253] The conceptual parallelism between διὰ τοῦ Ἰησοῦ (v. 14c) and ἐν Χριστῷ (v. 16f) possibly suggests that ἐν Χριστῷ is used instrumentally (Donfried 1996c, 400; Kim 2002a, 226); this admits the provocative interpretation: "the dead will be raised by Christ".[254] It is more probable however, that Paul intends another significance more along the lines of comforting his followers.[255] Thus, the phrase characterises a realm of existence (Elliger 1990a, 448; see Schnelle 1986, 212–213) such that οἱ νεκροὶ ἐν Χριστῷ takes on an ecclesiological sense as an abbreviation of the expression ἐν (τῷ) σώματι (τοῦ) Χριστοῦ (cf. 2 Cor 5:17; Gal 3:28). In this way Paul emphasises the death, resurrection and exaltation of Christ (see Barrett 1953, 149; Hahn 1993a, 483). Whether Paul uses ἐν Χριστῷ to indicate that those who are raised in verse 16 belonged to Christ at the time of their deaths[256] or whether he infers some kind of relationship between dead believers and Christ in their state of death is debatable (see Hoffmann 1966, 236–238). Paul does elsewhere only use νεκρός to refer to the state of death rather than to the event (Thrall 2002, 293).[257] The emphasis remains

[250] Cf. Rom 6:11, 13; 7:8; 8:10; cf. also Eph 2:1, 5; Col 2:13; Heb 6:1; 9:14.

[251] See the five categories of Oepke (1964e) which identify nuances of the three general senses indicated by Seifrid. Wedderburn (1985) gives a survey of the various uses outlined by the major grammars. For references to the uses of Χριστός with prepositions in Paul, including ἐν, διά, εἰς, and σύν, see Cerfaux 1959a, 212–213; Grundmann 1974, 550–551. The significance of σὺν κυρίῳ (v. 17d) is considered in the analysis of that verse (§III.e.7 below).

[252] Bousset 1970; Bouttier 1966; Büchsel 1949; Dupont 1952; Neugebauer 1958; 1961; Pelser 1998; Schweitzer 1953; Turner 1965, 118–122; Wedderburn 1985; 1986.

[253] 1 Thess 2:14; 5:18; cf. ἐν κυρίῳ in 3:8; 4:1; 5:12.

[254] As such, ἐν would not be understood to express personal agency, but to indicate means as in 1 Cor 12:13 (see *GGBB* 373–374 for a discussion of ἐν + dative as used to express means).

[255] I admit that the association of ἐν Χριστῷ with οἱ νεκροί and not with ἀναστήσονται is an interpretative decision. From a grammatical viewpoint, either association is possible.

[256] Best 1972, 197; Dabelstein 1991, 459; Wanamaker 1990, 174.

[257] In Rev 14:13 the reference is explicitly to the event as signified by the repetition of the definite article (οἱ νεκροὶ οἱ ἐν κυρίῳ ἀποθνήσκοντες); cf. 4 Macc 16:25 for a similar reference.

however on the resurrection and participation (cf. *2 Bar.* 30:1), and there is no reference to some kind of intermediate state here (*contra* Bailey 1964, 166).

7. The resurrection is always the action of God[258] or his spirit.[259] A number of verbs are used including: ἐγείρειν,[260] ἀνιστάναι,[261] ζῳοποιεῖν,[262] ἀναζῆν[263] (cf. ζῆν). The resurrection of Jesus is no mere resuscitation or return to the earthly life entailing the prospect of another death in a world under the law of death. Rather, the resurrection of Jesus is an overcoming of death ("Überwindung des Todes"; Rom 6:9; Acts 13:34) whereby the crucified one is no longer under the power of death (Kremer 1992, 10). Besides those verbs listed above, the authors of the NT also describe the resurrection of Jesus with terms like "exalt",[264] "bring up",[265] and even "glorify" (11).[266] The resurrected one is now the Son of God (Rom 1:4) made to be Christ and Lord (Acts 2:36), exalted to the right hand of God,[267] the first fruits of the resurrected (1 Cor 15:20) and a life giving spirit (1 Cor 15:45; 1992, 11–12). The resurrection of the dead is understood by Paul only in close dependence on the resurrection of Jesus and mostly in the context of the *parousia* (12). Paul does not speak about the resurrection of all the dead despite such language elsewhere (e.g. Acts 24:15), where such references usually include a general judgment (13).[268] Further, in the later text of Ephesians, the resurrection of the dead is associated with the language of "Bekehrung"/"Taufe" (Eph 5:14). The emphasis shifts from a future aspect to a present one (13–14).[269]

Paul reassures the Thessalonians that the dead in Christ will also overcome death by God's action through Jesus (v. 14c) including the resurrection of Jesus (v. 14b), and by the statement that the dead in Christ will rise (see the repetition of ἀνιστάναι in vv. 14b, 16f).[270] Is the connection between the resurrection of Jesus and the resurrection of believers made here by Paul for the first time (so Nicholl 2004, 35–38; Schnelle 1986, 210)? Oepke finds a balance: "Die Missionspredigt hatte vielleicht, alles auf die Lebenden zuspitzend, den Zusammenhang zwischen der Auferstehung Christi und derjenigen der gläubig Verstorbenen nicht aus-

---

[258] Rom 4:17; 10:9; 1 Thess 1:10; cf. 2 Kgs 5:7.

[259] Rom 8:11–13; 1 Pet 3:18. The following discussion is dependent on Kremer 1992, esp. 8–23.

[260] For references and discussion of ἐγείρειν, see Chapter 3, §III.b.5.

[261] For references and discussion of ἀνιστάναι, see §III.b.3 above; the significance of the middle voice is the subject of the following paragraph (§III.d.8 below).

[262] Rom 4:17; 8:11; 1 Cor 15:22, 36, 45; 2 Cor 3:6; Gal 3:21; cf. John 5:21; 6:63; 1 Pet 3:18; Judg 21:14B; 3 Kgdms 5:7; 2 Esd 19:6; Job 36:6; Ps 70:20 (LXX); Eccl 7:12.

[263] Luke 15:24; cf. Rom 7:9.

[264] John 3:14; 8:28; 12:32, 34; Acts 2:33; 5:31.

[265] Rom 10:7; Heb 13:20.

[266] John 7:39; 8:54; 11:4; 12:16, 23, 28; 13:31, 32; 16:14; 17:1, 5; 21:19.

[267] Acts 2:33; cf. Mark 16:19.

[268] E.g. Acts 10:42; 17:31; Luke 14:14; cf. John 5:29 with its parallel statements: εἰς ἀνάστασιν ζωῆς and εἰς ἀνάστασιν κρίσεως.

[269] Cf. also John 5:24–25; 11:25–27; 1 John 3:14.

[270] Thus, resurrection theology primarily has "eine Hoffnung begründende und tröstende Funktion" (Schrage 1997, 33).

drücklich betont. Paulus trägt das hier nach" (1970, 172). Stanley agrees with Oepke and further suggests that Paul immediately supplies a word of the Lord in order to support his developed connection between the two occurrences (1961, 87).[271] It is not that Paul hits on the idea "for the first time" but that he makes the connection stronger than previously made, and stronger still in a later letter (1 Cor 6:14).[272] The emphasis on being with him (see recurring σὺν αὐτῷ in vv. 14c, 5:10b and σὺν κυρίῳ in v. 17d) links the resurrection with the *parousia* of the Lord.[273] The resurrection of the dead is envisaged only in connection with the *parousia* which strongly suggests that the Thessalonians did not have a problem with the resurrection as such but with some aspect of the *parousia* (Börschel 2001, 234).

8. An introduction to Paul's use of ἀνιστάναι has already been given (§III.b.3 above). Whereas Paul refers to the resurrection of Jesus previously (1:10; 4:14), this is the first time he makes the explicit statement that Christians will also be raised although this conclusion is intimated already in verse 14. Paul's use of the verb (instead of ἐγείρειν) may show conformity to a pre-Pauline formula in verse 14b. The opposite view, that Paul uses a pre-Pauline formula in verse 16f (to which v. 14 shows conformity in choice of verb) is less likely since it requires Paul to have thought out the entire pericope before writing (Havener 1981, 111; *contra* Luz 1968, 325–326), and because the phrase in verse 16 is clearly redacted to serve the context at hand (n.b. the Pauline ἐν Χριστῷ and the emphatic πρῶτον). But this does not rule out the possibility that Paul is relying on traditional material here as well (Bruce 1982, 101). The future middle indicative form and its implications are often ignored by commentators probably because of the difficulty in defining the precise signification of the middle voice.[274]

The usual definitions of voice in Greek focus on the role of the grammatical subject in relation to the process described by the verb form (see O'Donnell 1999, 156–157). Is the grammatical subject the agent of the process so described (active voice) or the recipient (passive voice)? O'Donnell (1999), in a linguistic study of ἐγείρειν and ἀνιστάναι, uses *collocational* analysis to describe the semantic value of voice forms especially for *ergative* verbs (see below for a definition of "ergative"). The following is a summary of pertinent parts of O'Donnell's article:

> In short, such analysis involves the examination and classification of words found in close proximity to each other and a characterisation of a verb's transivity (137). After a critical review of previous classifications of the two verbs (esp. transitive/intransitive and active/passive categories) in the RSV translation, BAGD, *TDNT* and *EDNT* (140–144), and in various grammars (145–147), O'Donnell examines ἐγείρειν and ἀνιστάναι as keywords and compiles a list of words occurring within a specified span (in this case four words before and after each keyword). A table showing the first forty collocates ordered in

[271] Stanley refers to the 4th ed. of Oepke's commentary (1949).

[272] Lüdemann 1980a, 256–260; see Bultmann 1952, 81; Sellin 1983, 227; 1998, 918.

[273] Kremer 1992, 19; 1993, 1178; Sellin 1986, 39.

[274] In his article on ἀνιστάναι, Oepke (1964a) does not refer to the distinctive voice form used in the NT.

terms of frequency of occurrence is provided (162–163). Such results show differences in the company the two verbs keep (only the most pertinent differences for Paul's use of ἀνιστάναι in 1 Thess 4:16 are given here): νεκρός is the third most frequent collocate of ἐγείρειν, but only the eighth most frequent collocate of ἀνιστάναι; θεός is the twelfth most frequent collocate of ἐγείρειν, but only the twenty-first most frequent collocate of ἀνιστάναι (similarly, thirteenth and twenty-fourth, respectively for the name Ἰησοῦς); Χριστός is the fifteenth most frequent collocate of ἐγείρειν, but is not a significant collocate of ἀνιστάναι; finally, πρῶτον is not a significant collocate of ἐγείρειν, but is the thirty-second most frequent collocate of ἀνιστάναι (see O'Donnell's table, 162–163). In a preliminary way, this analysis shows that ἐγείρειν is more likely to state the actor/recipient than is ἀνιστάναι, as shown by the comparisons of θεός, Ἰησοῦς and Χριστός as collocates for each verb. O'Donnell then proceeds to examine grammatical patterns of co-occurrence of words with respect to ἐγείρειν and ἀνιστάναι. Such an examination is sometimes called *colligational* analysis (152–153). He finds that ἀνιστάναι is used primarily with the perfect aspect (realised by the aorist and future tense forms) and rarely with any other aspect (only three times with the imperfect aspect, realised by the present tense form). In contrast, ἐγείρειν uses all three aspects (perfect, imperfect and stative). This is quite significant because it shows that ἀνιστάναι is used almost exclusively with a background, summary aspect (153). Likewise, different grammatical patterns come to light regarding voice distribution. O'Donnell finds that ἀνιστάναι is used with the active voice (96 times) and the middle voice (12 times), but not with the passive voice (according to the GRAMCORD database),[275] whereas ἐγείρειν significantly is used with the middle/passive voice (86 times) more often than with the active (58 times). Further, all instances of the middle/passive forms are in clauses where the verb is intransitive (154–155).

The delineation of a link between the grammatical co-occurrence of voice forms and transitive/intransitive clauses paves the way for a better understanding of why Paul uses ἀνιστάναι with the middle voice in 1 Thess 4:16. Bypassing the technical discussions of transivity (see 155 for references), O'Donnell goes on to describe ergative verbs, which are verbs able to have the same thing as object (when transitive) or as subject (when intransitive; 156). For example, in the verbal pair, "I closed the door/the door closed", the first clause is transitive and identifies the agent as grammatical subject while the second clause is intransitive and gives no clue as to the agent (the grammatical object "the door" is now subject; 155–159). Using the concept of ergavity, O'Donnell is able to explain why Paul uses ἐγείρειν but not ἀνιστάναι with the passive form. If the latter is an ergative verb then it can be used to avoid any reference to whom or what does the action. As such, ἀνιστάναι is never used with the passive voice since that form contains an implicit reference to the agent of the process and negates the special ability of ergative verbs to state phenomenological fact without any reference to agency whatsoever (159). These observations add another dimension to the question of Paul's choice of ἀνιστάναι over ἐγείρειν in 1 Thess 4:16f. He may well have been following the choice of verb

[275] There are three morphologically ambiguous references which could be taken as passive (Rom 15:12; Heb 7:11, 15) but for which GRAMCORD tags as middle forms (O'Donnell 1999, 154).

contained in the traditional formula of verse 14b. But if O'Donnell is correct in his identification of ἀνιστάναι as possibly an ergative verb, then Paul purposely avoids any reference to the agent of resurrection. In this way, Paul de-emphasises the resurrection which suggests that the Thessalonians are not concerned about it (i.e. there is no need to identify the agent or verify his credentials). Rather, the emphasis is squarely placed on the grammatical subject and on the adverbial modifier following the verb.

9. The question of whether transformation is inherently a part of resurrection in 1 Thess 4 is often asked with an eye on Paul's statement: ἰδοὺ μυστήριον ὑμῖν λέγω· πάντες οὐ κοιμηθησόμεθα, πάντες δὲ ἀλλαγησόμεθα (1 Cor 15:51). An answer in the negative does not necessarily entail the view that transformation is not expressed at all in the pericope. Transformation might be connoted in other aspects of the text like the translation (v. 17c) or the statement about being with the Lord always (v. 17d). The question at hand is this: When Paul refers to the resurrection of the dead in Christ (v. 16f), is there any notion of transformation? For some, the motif of resurrection serves only to facilitate Paul's description of translation as a means to comfort the Thessalonians.[276] Luedemann comments (1980, 197):

> The resurrection of the Christians is produced by Paul in order to enable him to say that both the previously dead Christians and the survivors are lifted up in the air to be with Christ. One could even say that the disadvantage of having died is made up for by the resurrection which is here a reconstitution of the old body.

He concludes, "resurrection is revivication [*sic*] of the corpse" (201). The view of resurrection as revivification is found elsewhere in antiquity, usually in connection with a renewed or restored earth ("erneuerte Erde"; Kremer 1992, 10).[277] Lüdemann finds *2 Bar.* 50:2–3 particularly relevant since by resurrection the dead are made to be on equal footing with the living. That a transformation is described separate from the resurrection (51:1) and that the dead are not changed by the resurrection but are still recognised by the living (see ἅμα σὺν αὐτοῖς in 1 Thess 4:17b), is evidence for Lüdemann that Paul did not conceive of resurrection as transformation in 1 Thess 4:13–18 (1980a, 260).[278] Similarly, Plevnik argues that Paul does not envisage a mixed group of believers, some raised to a new and transformed life and others still living and remaining to the *parousia*, as being translated to meet the Lord (1984, 277): "… in 1 Thess 4, 16 the resurrection seems to be a resumption of life on earth, not a transformation as described in 1 Cor 15, 51–55" (1989, 265). As such, it is not to be compared with a general or eschatological resurrection (Giesen 1985, 136). In contrast, Meyer argues that Paul could not have understood resurrection apart from transformation (1987). Yet his discussion is perhaps over-biased towards a

[276] See Kegel 1970, 35–36; Lüdemann 1993, 35–36; Merklein 1992, 407; Schnelle 1986, 210; Sellin 1986, 37–46.

[277] 1 Kgs 17:17–24; 2 Kgs 4:18–37; Mark 5:21–43 (par.); Luke 7:11–16; John 11:1–46; Acts 9:36–41; 20:9–12; cf. 2 Macc 7:11; 14:46; *Sib. Or.* 4:181–182; Ps.-Phoc. 100–104.

[278] On *2 Bar.* 49–51, see discussion by Harrington 2002, 30–31.

synthesis of Paul's view of resurrection; he hardly engages the text here.[279] Vos also gives a synthetic discussion and comes to the same conclusion as Meyer. But he notes rightly that the question of transformation is beside the point in 1 Thess 4 (1953, 207). In conclusion, it is clear that Paul's reference to the confession in verse 14 centres on the kerygmatic hope of overcoming death. When it comes to the resurrection of the dead in Christ, it is logical that Jesus' death and resurrection becomes an analogy for believers' death and resurrection; the recurrence of the same verb seems important in this regard. Lüdemann certainly makes the point well that resurrection as revivification fits the context of the envisaged translation and meeting the Lord. But the hope of resurrection cannot be relegated wholly as a support motif for translation. Kremer rightly emphasises that resurrection is more than just life after death ("Fortleben") and includes an emphasis on community life with the Lord (1992, 18). This emphasis is not so much that resurrection facilitates a translation motif but that both the resurrection and translation facilitate Paul's emphasis on being with the Lord (19–20).

10. Commentators often refer to 1 Thess 4:16 at length either because of the interesting apocalyptic details, or because it is often thought to contain some form of a λόγος κυρίου. While both of these aspects of the verse are interesting and even important considerations for a correct interpretation of the pericope – hence significant space in the analysis has been allotted to their investigations – they are not the focus of my attention. In contrast, I find the motif of a descending Lord and of resurrection far more pertinent to the thesis. In particular, with Ps 46:6 (LXX) as a background to the verse, connotations of celebration and rejoicing fit well into Paul's positive pattern of exhortation. So too does the motif of resurrection which is no mere resuscitation, but a re-creation of the Thessalonian community. As such, Paul uses eschatological and apocalyptic imagery and motifs to weave together a new eschatological existence which rises above social conflict and even death. A new identity emerges which consists of celebrating a returning Lord (or King) and which obliterates distinctions between death and life.

e. Always with the Lord (4:17)

1. First Thessalonians 4:17 continues with temporal markers peppering the apocalyptic details of the descending Lord. The question of whether Paul lays out these details with temporal (i.e. the occurrence of one aspect specifically before or after another) or sequential (i.e. the mere enumeration of occurrences) significance and its answer plays a role of wherein the emphasis is placed on the problem of the

[279] Meyer asks the question: "Does Paul understand the dead to return by resurrection to the conditions of the present life?" (1986, 375). By his own admission, however, he limits the relevance of his conclusions on the problematic issue: "For present purposes there is no need to offer ... a fully detailed exegesis of the Pauline texts" (374).

Thessalonians (§III.e.2). On a related issue, ἅμα σύν can be understood either as expressing "temporality" or "association" (or both). The support for one over the other is influenced by the interpretation of the relationship between resurrection and translation (§III.e.3). With regard to the translation motif, the scholarly debate continues as to whether ἁρπάζειν is to be understood in terms of Jewish apocalyptic or otherwise (§III.e.4); similarly, the reference to clouds may be interpreted variously and therefore must be weighed accordingly. Consequently, questions like whether the clouds are to be understood as vehicles of translation, or whether a process of transformation is implied in the motif, are not straightforward (§III.e.5). Even more problematic is the division in scholarship over whether εἰς ἀπάντησιν is to be understood in terms of LXX usage (esp. with reference to the Sinai theophany) or in terms of Hellenistic formal receptions. The approach taken here is to examine afresh both sides of the debate including an assessment of the primary data, and develop a balanced interpretation of the issues in terms of what associations the Thessalonians themselves would have intuitively read into Paul's use. The issue of an implied direction of movement is also discussed (§III.e.6). The remainder of the verse summarises Paul's answer to the Thessalonians' grief (§III.e.7).

2. Markers of time/sequence appear with significance throughout the pericope. These markers may be variously interpreted and include in particular the future tense verb φθάσωμεν (v. 15e), a prepositional phrase of temporal limitation beginning with εἰς (v. 15d), the adverbial pair πρῶτον/ἔπειτα (vv. 16f, 17a)[280] and ἅμα (σύν) in verse 17b. Their interpretation comes to a head especially in connection to the adverbial pair πρῶτον/ἔπειτα where Paul places the adverbs one after another for emphasis. Arguments from grammar cannot be used to decide whether Paul intends to separate described events into a temporal sequence or whether he simply delineates a sequential relationship with no temporal element.[281] The neuter adjective, πρῶτον, may be used as an adverb to show chronological sequence, to delineate a sequence of enumerations, or to distinguish degrees or prominence. Paul arguably uses the adverb in all three ways (BDAG 893–894). Similarly, ἔπειτα may be used to indicate what is next in order, either without specific indication of chronological sequence or with such indications (e.g. as with πρῶτον; BDAG 361). It does not help to examine other texts in Paul which contain one or other of πρῶτον and ἔπειτα.[282] For example, Paul's use of πρῶτον in Rom 1:16 (Ἰουδαίῳ τε πρῶτον καὶ Ἕλληνι) may be taken either as one of temporal priority (Langkammer 1993, 188) or as establishing sequence (Michaelis 1968, 869). Similarly, Paul uses ἔπειτα sometimes in an ambiguous way.[283] Even where Paul uses the adverbial pair, the significance

[280] The textual variation πρῶτοι (see NA[27]) is rejected as a likely conformation to νεκροί earlier in the verse (Bruce 1982, 94).

[281] See Robertson: "The context must often decide the exact idea of an adverb" (*GGNT* 549).

[282] For πρῶτον, see Rom 1:8, 16; 2:9, 10; 3:2; 15:24; 1 Cor 11:18; 12:28; 15:46; 2 Cor 8:5; for ἔπειτα, see 1 Cor 12:28; 15:6, 7, 23, 46; Gal 1:18, 21; 2:1.

[283] For example, on 1 Cor 15:5–8 Balz comments: "Taken as a whole, the sequence in vv. 5–8 is

of the markers is determined by the context. Thus, in 1 Cor 12:28, ἔπειτα is used to denote a next position in an enumeration of items begun with πρῶτον, but in 15:46 the pair is used to give a chronological sequence.[284] Besides 1 Thess 4:16–17 and the references just cited, Paul does not employ the adverbs elsewhere. Consequently, only the context of 1 Thess 4:13–18 is helpful in determining on a systematic level whether Paul intends for πρῶτον/ἔπειτα to mark temporal significance in addition to sequence. It is not surprising that commentators are divided on the issue. On the one hand, the various elements of the apocalyptic scenario (e.g. descent, resurrection, translation, meeting) may be telescoped into the ultimate goal of being with the Lord (v. 17d);[285] the adverbial pair πρῶτον/ἔπειτα has qualitative not chronological significance.[286] On the other hand, the Thessalonians may not require an outline of the *parousia* with the associated occurrences as much as they need assurance that those who have died will take part in the *parousia*. That is, Paul reassures them that the resurrection is temporally before the translation to meet the Lord.[287] The formulation with φθάνειν (v. 15e) seems to support the latter interpretation (Börschel 2001, 236–237). The conclusion of Nicholl, that φθάνειν reflects absolute advantage (and concomitantly disadvantage) can only be held with his parallel assertion that the Thessalonians did not know about the resurrection of the dead (2004, 33–35), an assertion that has already been rejected (§III.d.7 above).

3. The double articulated participles, οἱ ζῶντες οἱ περιλειπόμενοι (vv. 17a, b), are repeated from verses 15c, d.[288] Paul emphasises the relationship between the living and the dead at the *parousia*. There is a discernable progression of thought between verses 15c–d and 17a–c. First Paul refers only to those alive, who remain until the *parousia* of the Lord (vv. 15c–d). Second he includes those sleeping as subject along with those alive, who remain (v. 17a–b); these are the dead in Christ who will be raised (v. 16f). Third he explains the *parousia* of the Lord in terms of translation (ἁρπάζειν) with an emphasis on ἅμα σύν (v. 17b). Finally Paul concludes that both the living and the dead who are raised will always be with the Lord (v. 17c).

---

temporal (cf. esp. v. 8), but among the individual parts of the list the emphasis may lie on various witnesses and groups of witnesses, and not on the temporal sequence" (1991c, 20).

[284] The BDAG entry under ἔπειτα illustrates the difficulty in determining the marking value of the adverbs. BDAG puts 1 Cor 15:46 and 1 Thess 4:17 under a section where ἔπειτα is used with indications of chronological sequence (i.e. πρῶτον ... ἔπειτα, §1.b), while 1 Cor 12:28 is put in a different category, as referring to a next position of an enumeration of items (§2), even though it also has the adverbial pair (πρῶτον ... ἔπειτα). There is no justification provided for the distinction.

[285] Schmid comments: "The ultimate goal of all events at the *parousia* is the πάντοτε σὺν κυρίῳ εἶναι of believers (v. 17; cf. Phil. 1:23). Other points have no independent significance; they are simply means to an end or embellishing details which may fluctuate. This insight is essential to a true understanding of the eschatological statements of Paul" (1965, 658–659).

[286] Best 1972, 198; Hoffmann 1966, 224; see Mason 1993, 114–119.

[287] Bruce 1982, 101; Eadie 1877, 168–169; Wanamaker 1990, 174.

[288] There is no plausible explanation for the omission of οἱ περιλειπόμενοι in some manuscripts (see NA[27]), and is here considered with Metzger as an "accidental oversight" (1994, 565).

First Thessalonians 4:17 builds to one of the most fundamental and systematic statements of the pericope (cf. v. 17d); the marker ἅμα (v. 17b) serves an important function in emphasising progression towards that statement, καὶ οὕτως πάντοτε σὺν κυρίῳ ἐσόμεθα (v. 17d), especially since it anticipates the inclusive ἐσόμεθα. Generally as an adverb, ἅμα expresses simultaneous occurrence, "at the same time" (BDAG 49, §1). Paul uses it this way in Phlm 22. The presence of σύν in 1 Thess 4:17b (cf. 5:10) however, opens the possibility that ἅμα expresses association, "together with" (similar to *una cum*).[289] As such it would function grammatically as an improper preposition with the dative (pleonastic in this instance). Whether ἅμα should be taken as an adverb[290] or as improper preposition[291] is difficult to determine. The significance of the repeated σύν in verse 17d must not be underestimated and its associative idea would suggest ἅμα is used as an improper preposition. But if my analysis is correct, in regard to an emphasis placed on the temporal relationship between resurrection/translation rather than between sequential relationships of various elements in the apocalyptic scenario (§III.e.2 above), this could suggest ἅμα is used as an adverb — the translation of the living and the resurrected dead in Christ is at the same time, or simultaneous. Although Klijn (1982) is able to cite apocalyptic texts which use equivalents to the Greek ἅμα (see esp. *4 Ezra* 5:45), even in a similar context (for references, see Excursus 5), those texts are not determinative for Paul's use of ἅμα as either adverb or improper preposition. There is no quantitative time indication regarding the occurrences of resurrection and translation, just a qualitative sequential indication that the one occurs before the other. But the associative idea is too strongly present in verses 17b, d, to be ruled out altogether. Thus, either translation – "at the same time" or "together" – is acceptable since both contain opposite (but not mutually exclusive) emphases of temporality and association.

4. The reference to ἁρπάζειν (v. 17b) is a stand-out feature of 1 Thess 4:13–18, first because Paul rarely uses the word in an eschatological context (cf. apocalyptic reference in 2 Cor 12:2, 4), and second because there is little use of the verb to depict a translation idea in pre-Pauline tradition.[292] The verb is used fourteen times in the NT with several connotations including: the taking or snatching of one's property (Matt 12:29; cf. John 10:12); the taking or snatching of someone, either by force[293] or with no resistance offered;[294] metaphorically with regard to

[289] See BDF 104, §194(3); Findlay 1904, 101; cf. Rom 3:12 where ἅμα is used as an adverb of association, but without σύν.

[290] Best 1972, 198; Moule 1959, 81–82; MM 24–25.

[291] BDAG 49, §2.b; *GGNT* 638.

[292] It is difficult to describe precisely the semantic domain of ἁρπάζειν and ἁρπαγμός, giving rise to many different English glosses. The term "translation" is used generically to include technical descriptions of heavenly ascent and various assumptions of the soul and of the person. The appropriate gloss for the verb as used in 1 Thess 4:17, whether that be "caught up", "taken up", "assumed", "translated", "raptured", etc., is determined by a contextual interpretation of the pericope (see below).

[293] John 6:15; 10:28, 29; Acts 23:10; Jude 23.

[294] Acts 8:39; 2 Cor 12:2, 4; 1 Thess 4:17; Rev 12:5.

the kingdom of heaven.[295] The noun, ἁρπαγμός appears only in Phil 2:6, but with different significance (Abramowski 1981). The verb is hardly used for translations in the LXX although the famous ascensions of Enoch (Gen 5:21–24) and Elijah (2 Kgs 2:2–15) depict a similar translation idea;[296] it appears in Wis 4:11 in a text which is clearly about Enoch though his name is not mentioned.[297] There are some parallels in the OT Pseudepigrapha but rarely with ἁρπάζειν (see Lohfink 1971, 51–74; Segal 1980).[298] The verb is used of the gods snatching up people (see Strelan 2004, 88).

Lohfink has analysed the differences between *Himmelsreisen* and *Entrückungen* in antiquity. Terminology for the latter includes verbs expressing disappearance (ἀφανίζειν, ἀφανίζεσθαι, ἀφανὴς γίγνομαι and ἄφαντος γίγνομαι), verbs expressing suddenness and unexpectedness (ἁρπάζειν, ἀναρπάζειν, ἐξαρπάζειν and συναρπάζειν) and sometimes the verb μεθιστάναι. The substantives, ἀφανισμός, ἁρπαγή and μετάστασις are also used (for primary references, see 1971, 41–42). As a type of *Himmelfahrt*, the *Entrückung* may be summarised with the following points (see 37–41): (1) there is no accent placed on the journey but only on the starting and finishing points; (2) the standpoint is one of an earthly perspective; the *Entrückung* may be likened to a *Verschwinden*; (3) descriptions of the *Entrückung* scene as well as details of spectators or witnesses are often present; (4) the whole man is involved; it is a *leibliche Entrückung*; (5) it is always initiated and carried out by the miraculous intervention of God; (6) it is always exclusive and only ever includes reports of an individual.

Lohfink isolates important motifs of *Entrückung* accounts which never appear all together but which belong to different stages of development in antiquity: mountain, funeral pyre, lightning, whirlwind, chariot, eagle, cloud, etc. (for details and primary references, see 42–49). In 1 Thess 4:17, the motif of translation is announced not only through the verb ἁρπάζειν but also by a reference to clouds and an implicit statement of direction, εἰς ἀέρα (at least initially the direction is upward; see §III.e.5 below).

There has been some discussion about the interpretation of ἁρπάζειν in 1 Thess 4:17. While it is possible to establish a link to Jewish apocalyptic tradition, the link

---

[295] Matt 11:12 (par.); 13:19. Regarding this difficult application of the verb, see introductory discussion by Trilling (1990, 156–157); see also BDAG 134, §2.b; Foerster 1964; Hoffmann 1972, 50–79; Schrenk 1964.

[296] Cf. αἴρειν in 3 Kgdms 18:12; 4 Kgdms 2:16; ἐξαίρειν in Ezek 3:14; ἀναλαμβάνειν in Ezek 3:12; Sir 49:14; ἐπιλαμβάνειν in Bel 36 (cf. v. 39); μετατιθέναι in Wis 4:10 (cf. ἁρπάζειν in v. 11); Sir 44:16. For a detailed examination of translation accounts of Elijah and Enoch, see Schmitt 1976, 47–151 and 152–192, respectively.

[297] On Enoch see also Sir 44:16; 49:14; *Jub.* 4:23; *T. Isaac* 4:2; *1 En.* 39:3; 52:1; 70:1–4; *2 En.* 3:1; 7:1; Josephus *Ant.* 1.85; 9.28; *L.A.B.* 1:16. For discussion of these and other references to the Enoch tradition, see Betz 1982, 684–685; Haufe 1961, 105–108.

[298] *Jos. Asen.* 12:8; *Apoc. Mos.* 37:3; *Gk. Apoc. Ezra* 5:7. For an introduction to texts of Hellenistic Judaism which refer to notions of translation of Abraham, Moses, Baruch, Ezra and Zephaniah, see Colpe et al. (1994) 443–445.

is slender. Rowland (1982, 386) refers to Wis 4:11 as especially significant (because of the occurrence of ἁρπάζειν):

> This passage offers us clear evidence of the use of *harpazo* in connection with the heavenly ascent of a figure who plays a central role as the pseudonymous recipient of heavenly visions in Jewish apocalyptic literature.[299]

However, such a motif is applied only to individual and exceptional figures (Segal 1980, 1354).[300] Haufe (1999, 85) comments:

> Griechen und Juden wissen nur um die Entrückung einzelner von der Erde in den Himmel, nicht aber von einer apokalyptischen Kollektiventrückung. Sie ist ein singulärer Zug im Text. Wie schon bei der Auferstehung verrät dieser auch jetzt nichts über den eigentlichen Akteur des Geschehens. Man wird an Gott denken müssen.

Consequently, Plevnik's application of an individual translation to a collective one may be justified on the basis of a resurrection context; Plevnik overlooks the discrepancy (1984, 279–280). But it does raise the question of whether and how Paul intended to invoke a motif of Jewish apocalyptic and whether the Thessalonians made the association. Plevnik seizes on the observation that one has to be alive to be assumed and suggests that the Thessalonians were grieving about those who had already died because they would be unable to take part in the assumption and therefore in the *parousia* (280–283). Although this interpretation neatly explains the grief of the Thessalonians over those who had died, it requires that Paul included a translation motif as part of his original presentation of the *parousia*; there is no evidence for this (Malherbe 2000, 276; Nicholl 2004, 46–47). Again, it should not be assumed that Paul uses the motif in line with Jewish apocalyptic thought. Another discrepancy (or development?) in the tradition is found in the theme of translation in Matt 24:37–44 (par.) where one is taken and one is left (εἷς παραλαμβάνεται καὶ εἷς ἀφίεται, v. 40; cf. v. 41). In this text those left are the ones who are saved whereas in 1 Thess 4:17 it is those translated who are saved (Collins 1984, 162).[301] Further, it is not clear how the motif of translation relates to the meeting of the Lord (v. 17c). Betz (1982, 686) for example, argues that the translation depicted by Paul is not a final (eschatological) ascent into heaven

[299] As an aside, in the case of Enoch there is a connection between being found pleasing and being translated (cf. εὐηρέστησεν δὲ Ενωχ τῷ θεῷ in Gen 5:22; εὐάρεστος θεῷ in Wis 4:10; Ενωχ εὐηρέστησεν κυρίῳ in Sir 44:16). Is there any significance in the fact that Paul begins the *letter-paraenesis* with an exhortation to please God (ἀρέσκειν θεῷ, 1 Thess 4:1) and then proceeds to explain the fate of the dead and the living at the *parousia* in terms of translation? Moffatt (1910, 38) notes the connection but otherwise makes no comment. Yet pleasing God is significant enough in the context of his letter writing for Paul to refer to his own conduct (1 Thess 2:4) as well as to the negative conduct of οἱ Ἰουδαῖοι (1 Thess 2:15).

[300] The exceptional nature of translations is emphasised in Sir 49:14, οὐδεὶς ἐκτίσθη ἐπὶ τῆς γῆς τοιοῦτος οἷος Ενωχ καὶ γὰρ αὐτὸς ἀνελήμφθη ἀπὸ τῆς γῆς. But note an exception in *4 Ezra* 6:26 where there is a reference to a collective translation; cf. also *T. Mos.* 10:8–9.

[301] Wenham suggests that Paul is playing on the words and ideas of Matt 24:40 (par.) when he emphasises that it is those "who are left" who are translated and therefore saved (1995, 306). This is a remote possibility.

but a motif employed to introduce the ceremonial *Einholung* of the coming Lord (see §III.e.6 below for a discussion of εἰς ἀπάντησιν). Alternatively, rather than a translocation from an earthly to a heavenly sphere, there are a number of references to the motif which shows that the verb is used to depict a transportation generally, from one place to another, particularly by the action of the Spirit (Strelan 2004, 88–89).[302]

Malherbe argues against the standard interpretation that Paul uses ἁρπάζειν in a context of Jewish apocalyptic. Rather, he finds the consolation tradition to be of special interest because it demonstrates how Paul could have used ἁρπάζειν to console the Thessalonians. There are numerous references amassed by Malherbe (e.g. in epitaphs, Lucian, Plutarch, Seneca, Ovid, Cicero, Horace, Pliny) where deceased persons have been snatched away to death, including the verb and its cognates as well as the Latin *rapio* and *eripio* (see 1983, 255 n. 80; 2000, 275–276). He concludes (1983, 256):

> Paul's use of ἁρπάζω in v. 17, when seen in this context, represents a neat twist. Whereas the word usually denoted the separation from the living, Paul uses it to describe a snatching to association with the Lord and other Christians.

This interpretation would suit Paul's intention to comfort the Thessalonians (v. 18). Concomitantly, a rationalisation of *Entrückung* as an important picture and symbol for the assumption of the soul (*Seelenaufstieg*) and immortality (*Unsterblichkeit*) is constantly met in antiquity (Lohfink 1971, 49). Lohfink refers to Cicero (*Resp.* 1.16) as representative: *Quibus quidem Romulum tenebris etiamsi natura ad humanum exitum abripuit, virtus tamen in caelum dicitur sustulisse.* The spiritualisation of the motif was an elegant way to express reserve regarding *Entrückungsgeschichten* but still maintain an *Entrückungsglauben* (49).[303] Thus, if Paul uses ἁρπάζειν as a motif of consolation – as a kind of apology or rationalisation against death – then there is a lesser need to locate the motif in traditions of Jewish apocalyptic.[304] Further, just as there is no suggestion that Paul uses ἁρπάζειν with connotations of attacking or violence because it does not fit the context (see BDAG 134, §1), there is also no need to import the verb's overtones of suddenness. After commenting that the verb means "snatch, seize, i.e., take suddenly and vehemently" (Gillman 1985, 276) and referring to its nuance of "suddenness" in Acts 8:39 and Rev 12:5,

[302] Cf. Homer *Il.* 3.380–383; 20.443; 21.597; Dio Chrysostom *Troj.* 90.

[303] Another alternative is proposed by Otto who argues that ἁρπάζειν invokes a metaphorical motif "as divine assurance of protection and victory over evil in eschatological conflict" (1997, 203). In particular, Otto looks to 1QM 14:2–17 where a hymn of victory includes praises to God for a victory over evil through a metaphor of assumption. As well, he refers to *1 En.* 96:2 and *T. Mos.* 10:8–9, which both refer to the exaltation of Israel over its enemies (202–203). While I agree with Otto (203) that the translation motif in 1 Thess 4:17 is not intended to be understood literally, his interpretation of ἁρπάζειν, including references to victory texts, is too far removed from the purpose of the Pauline text.

[304] Although on a different aspect of 1 Thess 4:13–18, Ascough acknowledges the likely influence of Jewish apocalyptism on Paul's thought, but then concludes: "The point is that the Thessalonians need not have been aware of Jewish apocalyptic thought for Paul's words to make sense" (2004, 528).

Gillman makes the following statement about its use in 1 Thess 4:17: "No time lapse at all is indicated during the rapture experience" (277). But the importing of connotations gained from other contexts onto the verb here is exactly the kind of erroneous exegesis Barr (1961) previously exposed. Time indications are expressed by verbs of time and by grammatical constructions; regarding 1 Thess 4:16–17, these have already been analysed (§III.e.2–3 above). Paul does not make any statement regarding the violence, suddenness, or instantaneity about the translation process. Rather, he uses the motif of translation along with other motifs (e.g. the descending Lord, resurrection of the dead in Christ, meeting the Lord in the air) to support his final statement, καὶ οὕτως πάντοτε σὺν κυρίῳ ἐσόμεθα (v. 17d).

5. The translation verb is immediately followed by a prepositional phrase, ἐν νεφέλαις (v. 17c). A reference to clouds is not unexpected due to its established associations with motifs of ascending and descending (including theophanies) as well as with the motif of translation. What is distinctive here is Paul's choice of preposition and the association of clouds with those being translated rather than with the *parousia* of the Lord. Numerous different prepositions are used by the NT authors including: ἐν, ἐπί and μετά in sayings about the Son of Man,[305] ἐκ to signify the source of a voice in a transfiguration account (Matt 17:5 [par.]); ὑπό with reference to the guiding cloud of the Exodus account (1 Cor 10:1; cf. ἐν in v. 2); μετά in a saying about the coming (ἔρχεσθαι) of Jesus (Rev 1:7); ἐν in a statement about the ascension of the two witnesses (Rev 11:12). Otherwise, the noun νεφέλη occurs without a preposition in a reference to natural phenomena (Luke 12:54) and metaphorically (Jude 12; cf. 2 Pet 2:17); it is also the subject of the verb ὑπολαμβάνειν of Jesus' ascension (Acts 1:9) and the object of the verb περιβάλλειν of a mighty angel (Rev 10:1).

The cloud motif has a number of antecedent references which are more or less reflected in Paul's use. In the OT, the motif often accompanies theophanies as an expression of the power of אלהים (e.g. Exod 19:16) and the glory of יהוה.[306] It also appears repeatedly in the story of the covenant characteristically as the pillar of cloud, עַמּוּד עָנָן, in which God conceals and manifests himself (Oepke 1967a, 905; see Minear 1954, 119–122).[307] Although the motif is not explicitly mentioned in the translation accounts of Elijah and Enoch, the storm cloud probably stands behind the סְעָר or whirlwind in 2 Kgs 2:11 (cf. Sir 48:9, 12; *1 En.* 39:3); the cloud motif is directly attested in later pseudepigraphic elaborations.[308] The ascension of Jesus (Acts 1:9) is somewhat apotheotic and the cloud serves as a revelatory element in the narrative (Strelan 2004, 36). The cloud motif also appears in Greek and Roman ascension myths, with "the idea of clouds enveloping, transporting,

[305] So ἐν: Mark 13:26; Luke 21:27; ἐπί: Matt 24:30; 26:64; cf. Rev 14:14, 15, 16; μετά: Mark 14:62; cf. Rev 1:7.

[306] E.g. Exod 24:15–18; cf. 34:5; *T. Job* 42:3.

[307] Exod 13:21–22; 14:19, 24; 33:9, 10; Num 12:5; 14:14; Deut 31:15; Neh 9:12, 19; Ps 99:7; cf. *Sib. Or.* 3:251; *Liv. Pro.* 2:16, 18.

[308] *1 En.* 14:8; cf. *T. Ab.* 8:3 (rec. B); 10:1 (rec. A); 10:2 (rec. B); 12:1, 9 (rec. B).

and even transforming significant figures" (38).[309] In an apocalyptic context, the motif appears again in a translation account (Rev 11:11–12). Similarly to 1 Thess 4:17, there are the consecutive elements of resurrection, a loud voice calling, and a translation of the two witnesses (see Plevnik 1975a, 271). But it would be premature to interpret Paul's reference to the cloud motif only in terms of theophanies or translation accounts. There is also a consistent association of clouds with the *parousia* which undoubtedly stems from Dan 7:13 and associated traditions. Thus, the Son of Man comes with clouds of heaven (עִם in MT; μετά in Dan 7:13θ; cf. ἐπί in Dan 7:13 [LXX]). It is difficult to make anything of the variations of prepositions.[310] Scott notes that in every NT reference to Dan 7:13, the word order (of the Aramaic, LXX and Theodotion traditions) has been changed so that the phrase including a reference to clouds now immediately follows the verb of coming (1959, 130–131). Another development includes the notion of descent, either to the earth (cf. John 3:13; Acts 1:11) or to a region visible from the earth.[311] Scott suggests that these developments arose from a reinterpretation of eschatological materials whereby the Son of Man came to be thought of as a supernatural being and therefore associated with theophany accounts of יהוה. The interpretation of his *parousia* as a descent (καταβαίνειν) in the same manner as יהוה[312] is attested in the NT with the same verb only at 1 Thess 4:17 (131–132). Thus, even though the clouds are now associated with humans undergoing translation rather than with the *parousia* Lord (see Gaston 1970, 407; Wanamaker 1990, 175), there is still likely to be some influence of Dan 7:13 reflected in Paul's use (Hartman 1966, 189–190).

Many commentators understand the cloud motif in 1 Thess 4:17c as a reference to the means of the translation process, even as a vehicle of translation.[313] Such an interpretation enjoys some support in apocalyptic traditions.[314] However, in view of the convergence of numerous motifs in 1 Thess 4:15–17, including the descending Lord, resurrection of the dead in Christ, translation, clouds and meeting the Lord in the air, an interpretation of ἐν νεφέλαις as a vehicle of ascension only accounts for the translation motif. Paul's reference to clouds must surely be understood, in some sense, as evocative of all these motifs. Paul thus emphasises the meeting of the Lord as an event beyond any single level of reality or phenomenon (see Minear 1954, 115–127, esp. 117). Koester is right to emphasise the mythological aspect where the motif "serves to transcend the horizon of the earthly realm and to describe the eschatological meeting of the Lord in cosmic dimensions" (1997, 160).

---

[309] For primary references, see Strelan 2004, 37–38.

[310] For a discussion of the various Greek renderings of the preposition עִם, see Scott 1959, 128.

[311] Cf. Matt 24:30 (par.); 1 Thess 4:17; Rev 1:7.

[312] Exod 34:5; Num 11:25; 12:5; Ps 17:10 (LXX).

[313] Best 1972, 198–199; Frame 1912, 175; Gillman 1985, 277–278; Plevnik 1997, 63; Sabourin 1974, 309; Rigaux 1956, 547; von Dobschütz 1909, 198; Wilcke 1967, 146.

[314] E.g. *1 En.* 18:5; *T. Ab.* 9:8 (rec. A); 10:2 (rec. B); 12:1, 9 (rec. B); 15:2, 12 (rec. A); *Gk. Apoc. Ezra* 5:7.

The question of whether a transformation is implicitly (or even explicitly) included in the translation motif is external to the analysis of the text. There is no doubt that transformation is associated with heavenly journeys. But just how so is a difficult question to answer.[315] First Corinthians 15:51–52 is hard to ignore on this point. However, since Paul only refers to the resurrection in passing and since he does not linger in the least on the nature of the resurrection existence, there is no reason to interject the agenda of 1 Cor 15 onto this pericope (similarly, Smith 2000, 725). Furthermore, the reference to σῶμα in 1 Thess 5:23 is included in a peace benediction and may not be used to import an idea of transformation in 1 Thess 4:17 (*contra* Gillman 1985, 279). Therefore, speculations that Paul's reference to translation and clouds implies some kind of transformation are rejected.[316] Certainly, entering the heavenly realm requires transformation; but Paul stops short of stating that the dead and the living are translated *into heaven*, only that they are to meet the Lord in the air (1 Thess 4:17c). It cannot be determined whether Paul omits an explicit statement of transformation because he (and/or the Thessalonians) are not interested in such details or because he has not thought through sufficiently the implications of being with the Lord (v. 17d). It may well be both.

6. The presence of the noun ἀπάντησις in the phrase, εἰς ἀπάντησιν τοῦ κυρίου εἰς ἀέρα (1 Thess 4:17c),[317] is another *crux interpretum* for all commentators of this pericope. Since the article of Peterson on the *Einholung* of the Lord (1930) and the response by Dupont (1952), the question has raged whether or not Paul uses εἰς ἀπάντησιν in a technical sense to refer to a civic custom of welcoming important visitors to a city. The formulation εἰς ἀπάντησιν is commonly used in the LXX,[318] as is εἰς ἀπαντήν[319] and εἰς συνάντησιν,[320] but less so εἰς ὑπάντησιν[321] and εἰς συναντήν.[322] In addition, there are numerous references to the verbs ἀπαντᾶν,[323]

[315] For a short discussion, see Himmelfarb 1991, 87–90.

[316] See Best 1972, 198; Bornemann 1894, 209; Bruce 1982, 102; Jurgensen 1994, 89; *contra* Betz 1982, 686; Findlay 1891, 106; Gillman 1985, 277; Plevnik 1997, 88; Vena 2001, 119.

[317] The minor variation εἰς ὑπάντησιν (see NA[27]) is a common mix-up of ὑπ- and ἀπ- prefixes.

[318] Judg (A) 4:18; 11:31, 34; 14:5; 15:14 (cf. εἰς συνάντησιν); 19:3; 20:25, 31; 1 Kgdms 4:1; 6:13; 9:14; 13:10, 15; 15:12; 25:32, 34; 30:21*bis*; 2 Kgdms 6:20; 19:26; 1 Par 12:18; 14:8; 19:5; 2 Par 12:11; 15:2; 19:2; 20:17; 28:9; 1 Esd 1:23; Jer 28:31*bis*; 34:3; 48:6; Jdt 5:4; 1 Macc 12:41; Tob 11:16; cf. *T. Job* 9:7; Matt 25:6; Acts 28:15; ἀπάντησις occurs less frequently in other formulations: 1 Sam 16:4; 21:2; Esth 8:12k; 2 Macc 12:30; 14:30; 15:12; 3 Macc 1:19; Sir 19:29; *Let. Aris.* 91.

[319] Judg 4:22A; 2 Kgdms 10:5; 15:32; 16:1; 19:16, 17, 21, 25; 3 Kgdms 2:8, 19, 35n; 12:24k; 20:18; 21:27; 4 Kgdms 4:26, 31; 5:21; 8:8, 9; 9:18, 21; 10:15; 16:10; 23:29.

[320] Gen 14:17; 18:2; 19:1; 24:17, 65; 29:13; 30:16; 32:7; 33:4; 46:29; Exod 4:14, 27; 5:20; 18:7; 19:17; Num 20:18, 20; 21:33; 22:34, 36; 24:1; 31:13; Deut 1:44; 2:32; 3:1; 29:6; Josh 8:5, 14, 22; 9:11; Judg 6:35; 7:24; 15:14; Judg (B) 4:18, 22; 11:31; 14:5; 19:3; 20:25, 31; 1 Kgdms 17:48; 18:6; 23:28; 2 Kgdms 2:25; 5:23; 3 Kgdms 18:7, 16; 4 Kgdms 1:3, 6, 7; 14:9; 2 Par 35:20; Ps 58:5; 151:6; Prov 7:15; Isa 7:3; 21:14; Zech 2:7; Jdt 2:6; 1 Macc 3:11, 16, 17; 5:39, 59; 6:48; 7:31; 9:11, 39; 10:2, 59, 86; 16:5; 3 Macc 5:2; Tob 11:16. For συνάντησις in other formulations, see Num 23:3; 1 Kgdms 25:20; 3 Kgdms 12:24l.

[321] Judg 11:34B; cf. Matt 8:34; 25:1; John 12:13.

[322] 3 Kgdms 18:16; 4 Kgdms 2:15; 5:26.

[323] Gen 28:11; 33:8; 49:1; Judg (A) 8:21; 15:12; 18:25; Ruth 1:16; 2:22; 1 Kgdms 10:5; 15:2; 22:17, 18; 25:20; 28:10; 2 Kgdms 1:15; 3 Kgdms 2:32, 34; 1 Esd 9:4; Job 4:12; 21:15; 36:32; Prov 26:18; Jer 13:22;

συναντᾶν[324] and ὑπαντᾶν.[325] I have attempted to provide an exhaustive list of references to ἀπάντησις and its cognates in the LXX to illustrate the magnitude of Peterson's omission of any references to the LXX in his article, especially since in many of these references the word group is used similarly as in descriptions of Hellenistic *Einholungen*. The entry in *TDNT* (s.v.) also contains the omission (Peterson 1964). This oversight mars an otherwise groundbreaking interpretation of εἰς ἀπάντησιν in 1 Thess 4:17 and understandably leaves the way open for a thorough examination of biblical texts leading to the possibility of a counter thesis, *viz*. Dupont.

Although others saw a parallel between NT references to ἀπάντησις and an ancient custom in antiquity,[326] it was Peterson who first thoroughly investigated the occurrences of use in papyri, inscriptions and literary sources. He asserts (1930, 683):

> Die ἀπάντησις (resp. ὑπάντησις) in v. 17 ist nicht ein zufälliges Sich-Treffen mit dem Kyrios, sondern es handelt sich um einen staatsrechtlichen Brauch, wonach hochgestellte Personen (besonders Könige oder ihre Vertreter) bei ihrer παρουσία durch die Bevölkerung nach einem vorgeschriebenen Zeremoniell eingeholt werden.

After an extensive examination of numerous primary documents (683–692) Peterson provides a *Zusammenfassung* (693–702). He observes that there is a whole series of terms for the *Einholung*, including: συναντᾶν, ἀπαντᾶν, ὑπαντᾶν, ἀπάντησις, ὑπαπάντησις and ὑπάντησις. The variation between ὑπάντησιν and ἀπάντησιν in 1 Thess 4:17 is irrelevant since both are considered to be *termini technici* for a formal meeting of a king, another important person, or a bishop (693). The *Einholung* is usually formal and is signalled by the announcement of a formal resolution (693). Members of the community would go outside the city walls an accustomed distance to meet the important visitor (694). Typically there would be a cross section of representatives from all parts of city life including religious, political, administrative and military personnel as well as teachers and their students, citizens, women, virgins etc. (694). Participants of an *Einholung* wear wreaths, carry torches and burn incense; even the city is adorned with wreaths and perfumed. Sometimes a sacrifice is made to the gods in which the visitor naturally took part

---

34:18; Dan 10:14θ; Hos 13:8; Jdt 3:4; 7:15; 1 Macc 5:25; 10:56, 58, 60; 11:15, 22, 60, 68; 12:25; 14:40; 2 Macc 7:39; 3 Macc 3:20; Sir 31:22; 33:1; 40:23; 43:22; Tob 14:4; Wis 8:16; cf. Mark 14:13; Luke 17:12.

[324] Gen 32:2, 18; 46:28; Exod 4:24, 27; 5:3, 20; 7:15; 23:4; Num 23:16; 35:19, 21; Deut 22:6; 23:5; 31:29; Josh 2:16; 11:20; Judg (B) 8:21; 15:12; 18:25; 20:41; 2 Kgdms 2:13; 18:9; 2 Esd 22:38; 23:2; Job 3:12, 25; 4:14; 5:14; 27:20; 30:26; 39:22; 41:18; Ps 84:11; Prov 7:10; 9:18; 12:13a, 23; 17:20; 20:30; 22:2; 24:8; Eccl 2:14, 15; 9:11; Isa 8:14; 14:9; 21:14; 34:14, 15; 64:4; Jdt 1:6; 10:11; 1 Macc 4:29; 5:25; 7:39; 10:74; 11:2, 6, 64; cf. Luke 9:37; 22:10; Acts 10:25; 20:22; Heb 7:1, 10.

[325] Dan 10:14; Sir 9:3; 12:17; 15:2; Tob 7:1; Wis 6:16; cf. Matt 8:28; 28:9; Mark 5:2; Luke 8:27; 14:31; John 4:51; 11:20, 30; 12:18; Acts 16:16.

[326] E.g. Moulton comments: "It seems that the special idea of the word was the official welcome of a newly arrived dignitary — an idea singularly in place in the NT exx." (*GNTG* vol. 1, 14; cf. MM s.v.). Moulton is followed by Frame (1912, 177).

(695). Repeatedly, references include the carrying of cult objects, either images of wood and sculptures or in the case of Christian references, crosses; there is also clapping and shouting along with commendations and warm greetings (696–697). Calls of acclamation and extending hands are accompanied by pronouncements, sometimes of good omen, sometimes of bad (697). Peterson understands Paul's reference to ἀπάντησις in 1 Thess 4:17 according to the antique idea found across many texts (698):

> Die Christen verlassen die Tore der Welt und eilen dem Kyrios bei seiner Παρουσία auf Wolken entgegen. Feierlich holen sie ihren König bei seinem Einzug ein. Es ist charakteristisch, daß Paulus, resp. der λόγος Κυρίου, den er zitiert, sich eines Bildes aus staatsrechtlichem Brauch bedient. Man weiß sich in der ältesten Christenheit als Bürger einer πόλις, die einen König einholt, aber diese πόλις ist nun nicht eine irdische Stadt, sondern die in das Kosmische ausgeweitete *Civitas Dei*.

Peterson refers to Phil 2:10–11 as another example of Paul adapting the ceremonial *Einholung* to describe the future *parousia* of the Lord, where the inhabitants of the future city of God including angels (ἐπουρανίων), dead Christians (καταχθονίων) and those still alive (ἐπιγείων), greet the Lord with an acclamatory call: κύριος Ἰησοῦς Χριστὸς εἰς δόξαν θεοῦ πατρός (v. 11; 698–699).[327] As well, Peterson finds a similar use of ἀπάντησις in Matt 25:1–12 where some elements of a typical *Einholung* are used: παρθένοι (Matt 25:1, 7, 11); λαμπάδες (Matt 25:1, 3, 4, 7, 8) and κραυγή (Matt 25:6; see 699). Finally, he notes that the exegetical tradition of 1 Thess 4:15–17 reflects his observations regarding the technical significance of the word group (esp. by John Chrysostom and Theodore of Mopsuestia; 700–701).[328]

Dupont (1952, 64–73) takes issue with Peterson's thesis on a number of points, but none more so than for Peterson's failure to examine Jewish sources. He acknowledges the existence of the Hellenistic custom and finds two descriptions of Hellenistic *parousiai* in Josephus to which Peterson refers (cf. *Ant.* 11.325–328; *B.J.* 7.100–103) particularly suggestive (64–65). However, despite the fact that Chrysostom found the analogy significant and regardless of the fact that Peterson's explanation "paraît si simple et si cohérente" (67), Dupont does not find his interpretation of 1 Thess 4:17 convincing. In particular, although the word ἀπάντησις is associated with descriptions of "parousies royals hellenistiques", this is not the only explanation of Paul's use of the word particularly since the same terminology and similar analogies may be found elsewhere. This leads to the question from whence Paul draws his inspiration (67). Dupont argues: "Avant de conclure à la dépendance de Paul à l'égard de l'hellénisme, il eût fallu se demander si le judaïsme ne pouvait pas, lui aussi, fournir une explication valable de la manière dont l'Apôtre s'exprime" (67). Dupont is surprised that Peterson does not examine the LXX references to ἀπάντησις, particularly when there are numerous examples

---

[327] The presence of ἁρπαγμός in this context (Phil 2:6) is not irrelevant. See Abramowski 1981, 1–17.

[328] Besides the numerous references to the *Einholung* in antiquity supplied by Peterson, see also Cicero *Att.* 8.16.2; 16.11.6.

of the εἰς construction with considerable correspondence to the ceremonial bringing in of Hellenistic *parousiai* (67–68). After highlighting two examples (Gen 14:17; 2 Kgdms 19:16, 21) Dupont asserts: "Il n'y a pas de raison, semble-t-il, de demander à un usage hellénistique l'explication d'une terminologie et d'une coutume bien connues du monde juif" (68). Further, since Dupont finds that Paul's terminology in 1 Thess 4:15–17 clearly contains elements of the Sinai theophany (particularly the trumpet of God), it stands to reason that the source of inspiration for the eschatological coming of the Lord is precisely the Sinai theophany. Thus (69):

> Si le peuple dut sortir de l'enceinte du camp pour aller à la rencontre du Seigneur descendant sur le Sinaï, il n'en sera pas autrement à la fin des temps. Comment s'étonner dès lors que Paul parle à son tour d'aller à la rencontre du Seigneur?

Dupont not only opposes Peterson's *Einholung* thesis, but when Paul refers to the Thessalonians as his crown of boasting (στέφανος καυχήσεως, 1 Thess 2:19) he finds no reference whatsoever to Hellenistic *parousiai* (71–72). In conclusion, Dupont asserts: "La 'venue' en gloire du Seigneur Dieu sur le Sinaï apparaît ainsi, dans notre passage, comme le prototype de la 'venue' eschatologique (παρουσία) du Seigneur Jésus" (73).

The ensuing scholarly debate about the inspiration of ἀπάντησις in 1 Thess 4:17 is polarised between the influences of Hellenistic *parousiai* and the Sinai theophany. In recent times, Cosby (1994), Gundry (1996) and Plevnik (1999) have continued the discussion. Cosby argues that ἀπάντησις (and cognates) is used very widely in antiquity and is not to be understood as a technical term for the Hellenistic formal reception (1994, 21). Moreover, he asserts that there are no correlations between the description of the *parousia* in 1 Thess 4:15–17 and the elements normally associated with receptions (28–31):

> (1) there is no announcement by decree of the coming; (2) there is no mention of special garments or wreaths to be worn at the reception; (3) there are no descriptions of enthusiastic greetings and cheers; (4) there is no encouragement of donations or taxes levied; (5) the element of judgement associated with the *parousia* has no correlation in Hellenistic formal receptions; (6) there is no mention of the coming dignitary offering sacrifices as in Hellenistic custom.

Cosby does admit that the custom of Hellenistic formal receptions is a part of Paul's cultural background. But the notion that ἀπάντησις is a technical term is wholly rejected (31). Gundry (1996) rightly criticises Cosby's article as confusing. Cosby asserts on the one hand: "Ironically, 1 Thess 4:14–17 does not specifically mention any of the elements normally associated with receiving dignitaries" (1994, 22), but on the other hand: "In 1 Thess 4:13–17, the custom of the Hellenistic formal reception is part of the cultural background for Paul's thinking" (31). Again, Cosby asserts on the one hand: "An analysis of the ancient descriptions of these receptions shows that most of their usual elements are actually the opposite of what we find in Paul's description of the Parousia" (1994, 15), but on the other hand: "The various descriptions of receptions reveal diversity in the way such meetings were conducted" (31, n. 45; see Gundry 1996, 39). Gundry then proceeds to show that Cosby's contention that there are no correlations between the description of the *parousia* in 1 Thess 4:15–17 and the elements normally associated with Hellenistic formal receptions, is incorrect (see Gundry's point by point rebuttal; 39–41). Gundry concludes: "… Paul's description of the Parousia in 1 Thess 4:15–17 comes closer to what we know of Hellenistic formal receptions than Cosby allows" (41). Alternatively, Plevnik (1999) is critical of both Peterson and Dupont. He observes that in Hellenistic formal receptions the meeting of a coming dignitary is actively planned and executed. But in 1 Thess 4:17 those meeting the Lord play an entirely passive role (ἁρπαγησόμεθα, v. 17b). Further, Plevnik doubts whether going up from the earth is an appropriate analogy for going out of a city. As well, the notion that Christians are to receive the Lord and accompany him back to the earth does not fit with Plevnik's understanding of 1 Thess 4:14 (where, it is argued, the direction of movement is upward; see 1999, 541). But neither is Plevnik convinced by Dupont's explanation since Dupont's dependency on the Sinai theophany is strained (542–543). With Best (1972, 199), Plevnik observes that the two accounts are not parallel: the cloud motif is used in a different way; the people ascend rather than being translated and there is nothing comparable in 1 Thess 4:15–17 regarding the giving of the Ten Commandments (1999, 543). Plevnik leaves behind the theses of Peterson and Dupont and returns to his interpretation of 1 Thess 4:13–18 in terms of assumption/exaltation (1984; 1997; 1999, 544–545). Ironically, in his haste to justify his thesis that Paul had previously described the *parousia* to the Thessalonians in terms of assumption (and that this was the source of the Thessalonians' problem regarding those who had died), Plevnik does not refer to εἰς ἀπάντησιν again. Rather, it appears that he subsumes whatever significance the phrase may have in his understanding of translation as a taking up which itself involves a transformation and permanent change of existence (1999, 545–546).

This review of Peterson, Dupont, Cosby, Gundry and Plevnik provides some basis for comment on how Paul uses εἰς ἀπάντησιν in 1 Thess 4:17. It is apparent that the primary evidence does not support a technical meaning ("die technische Bedeutung"; Peterson 1930, 683) for ἀπάντησις and its cognates; it is incorrect to refer to the word group as a *terminus technicus* (*contra* 693; Koester 1997, 160).[329] However, the evidence does show "the existence and form of an ancient custom" (Lattke 1990, 115) and Peterson should be acknowledged as the first to demonstrate extensively a *theme* of *Einholung* in the same way Funk (1967) first demonstrated a theme of *apostolic parousia* (Chapter 2, §V.2). Dupont's contribution is significant since he analysed the primary text evidence for εἰς ἀπάντησιν in the LXX. Further,

[329] The fact that there is no clear reference to Hellenistic formal receptions in LSJ (s.v.) supports this conclusion. In LSJSup (s.v.) there is only the additional statement, "*the action of going out to meet* an arrival, esp. as a mark of honour" and the inclusion of several references to Cicero (*Att.* 8.16.2; 9.7.2; 16.11.6).

he raised the important issue of identifying Paul's main source of inspiration (1952, 69). But the nature of a theme with its inconsistency of expression,[330] makes it very difficult to distinguish the confluence of the same theme in one source or set of traditions (e.g. "le judaïsme") and another (e.g. "le hellénisme").[331] Consequently, Dupont errs by his insistence to show that 1 Thess 4:15–17 can be understood in terms of the LXX references to εἰς ἀπάντησιν and particularly in terms of the account of the Sinai theophany, because he does not go on to demonstrate how "la source d'inspiration" may be usefully integrated under Paul's purpose of consolation. Repeatedly he acknowledges the existence of a theme of Hellenistic formal receptions but refuses to accept that Paul or any of the NT authors intentionally evoked the custom (70–72). His statement, "L'expression elle-même, nous l'avons dit, est trop commune dans la littérature biblique pour suffire à attester une inspiration grecque" (70) betrays his agenda to undercut Peterson's thesis. But it "cuts" both ways; the theme of *Einholung* is sufficiently fluid to preclude conclusive comparisons between 1 Thess 4:15–17 and either LXX descriptions or Hellenistic formal receptions. And Dupont seems to forget that Paul is writing primarily to recently converted Gentiles (see 1 Thess 1:9–10; Harrison 2002, 85 n. 54).

Even if Paul has the Sinai theophany (and the LXX tradition) solely in mind when he uses the phrase εἰς ἀπάντησιν, the influence of Hellenistic formal receptions is significant. Rigaux rightly comments: "Une influence n'exclut pas l'autre. Paul ne vit pas en vase clos" (1956, 234). The analysis of the text comes to a head in the identification of all connotations which the Thessalonians probably would have associated with the theme. The picture painted by Paul of meeting the descending Lord "... corresponds so closely to hellenistic practice that hellenistic readers could hardly have missed the correspondence and a hellenistic author could hardly have failed to intend it" (Gundry 1987, 166–167). An association of Paul's reference with Hellenistic formal receptions cannot be rejected. Such receptions remain an important analogy. However, since Paul provides very few details about the *Einholung* it is not necessary to go beyond Best's cautious conclusion: "its use therefore assists in building up the atmosphere already created in v. 16" (1972, 199). Furthermore, εἰς ἀπάντησιν τοῦ κυρίου (1 Thess 4:17c) imparts a communal element; both the resurrected dead and the living will together meet the Lord in celebration of his *parousia* (see Koester 1990, 447). The political overtones carried in the combination of the terms, παρουσία, κύριος and ἀπάντησις, provide a powerful and positive statement against imperial ideology. Paul seems to deliberately reverse conventional expectations in order to console a marginalised Christian community (see Tellbe 2001, 128–129; Vena 2001, 116–117).

[330] See Mullins (1973, 357) for a distinction between "form" and "theme".

[331] The distinction between Judaism and Hellenism is Dupont's (67). I find it somewhat misleading since the LXX is itself a witness to the pervasive influence of Hellenism (see Koester 1995, 237–240).

The first of two phrases, τοῦ κυρίου, which follows ἐν νεφέλαις εἰς ἀπάντησιν (1 Thess 4:17c) serves to identify the Lord as the one who is met while the second phrase locates the place of meeting, εἰς ἀέρα. The choice of preposition is another example of a common use of εἰς in place of ἐν in a local sense (BDF 110, §205). The ancient world-view distinguishes the sphere above the earth as the ἀήρ and αἰθήρ, the latter of which is not found in biblical texts. It is tempting to view the reference as Gundry does, in terms of Hellenistic formal receptions whereby the air becomes a place to meet the coming Lord — not too far from the world-city (1987, 168). Such an interpretation, however, takes Paul's reference perhaps too literally. Otto may be correct when he sees the reference to the air in terms of pagan associations with demonic powers (see Eph 2:2 and perhaps also *4 Bar.* 9:17).[332] Thus, Paul comforts the Thessalonians with the reassurance that the Lord is even Lord of the air and all that is in it (1997, 204–205).

Some commentators have sought to reject any notion of Hellenistic formal receptions in 1 Thess 4:17 because it does not fit with their understanding of the implied direction of movement (of both those translated and of the Lord). The existence of the theme does not mean that Paul necessarily envisaged a literal return to earth (i.e. city) as part of an *Einholung*. Such an interpretation makes too much of the connection (Otto 1997, 203). Rather, Paul does not say where the final destination of the faithful will be (Friedrich 1976, 244), whether as a return to earth[333] or else as an eschatological translation into heaven.[334] Perhaps the issue did not matter to the first Christians since a similar ambiguity exists for statements of the coming Son of Man (see Bruce 1982, 103; Richard 1995, 246). The difficulty in First Thessalonians is the incompatible movements of a descending Lord and ascending faithful. This is compounded by other seemingly incompatible elements, including the influence of Hellenistic formal receptions on the one hand (with its implicit downward movement), and the upward movement implied in ἄγειν (1 Thess 4:14c) and in ἁρπάζειν (v. 17b). Commentators like Plevnik (2000) and Ellingworth (1974) too quickly gloss over these incompatible elements in order to reach a definitive answer on the implied movement.[335] Concomitantly, other commentators too quickly supply unnecessary details to the text, *à propos* of an earthly kingdom or *interregnum* (see rightly, Räisänen 2002, 6–10; *contra* Turner 2003). Paul does not give a systematic or necessarily coherent explanation of the motifs employed; he provides rather a solution to a concrete problem of grief (Hoffmann 1966, 227).

---

[332] For further references, see Merklein 1990.

[333] Foerster 1964a, 166; Gundry 1987, 175 n. 29; Sanders 1991, 30; Witherington 1992, 158; 1994, 194.

[334] Frame 1912, 176; Mason 1992, 106–109; Plevnik 2000; Räisänen 2002, 6–10; Wanamaker 1990, 175.

[335] There is certainly no need to complicate the issue by understanding ἄγειν (v. 14c) as making a statement of movement at the *parousia* (Vos 1953, 138), not even as a part of the *parousia* occurrence (see Hoffmann 1966, 217). For a different interpretation of the verb, see discussion in §III.b.5 above.

7. The purpose of consolation is explicitly revealed in 1 Thess 4:18 as the conclusion to the pericope; but the climax of Paul's argument is stated in 1 Thess 4:17d. Only van der Horst (2000) raises the question of whether καὶ οὕτως may be better understood in a temporal sense ("only then", "thereafter") rather than the more commonly explained modal sense ("and so", "thus"). In his short article, van der Horst provides sufficient evidence for the possibility that καὶ οὕτως can express temporality.[336] He does not push either sense in the case of 1 Thess 4:17 and concludes (524):

> ... after the descent of Jesus Christ from heaven "the dead in Christ will rise *first*; *thereafter* we who are alive, who are left, will be caught up in the clouds together with them to meet the Lord in the air; *and* [*only*] *then* we will be with the Lord forever" ... This translation makes at least as much sense as the traditional 'and so,' if only because the text so unambiguously indicates that the apostle is speaking about a temporal order: first A, therafter [*sic*] B, and finally (but *only then*) C.

I agree that the temporal elements are clearly indicated here, but a modal sense still dominates because 1 Thess 4:17d is not only the conclusion to verses 16–17 but also verses 14–15. Thus, Paul is able to summarise his whole argument in terms of being with the Lord. That this is the right emphasis for καὶ οὕτως seems to be supported by the corresponding structure between verses 14c and 17d (§II.a.5 above).

The presence of σύν κυρίῳ in his statement about being with the Lord always, is significant because it is part of a recognisable "with Christ" motif in Paul. While he uses ἐν Χριστῷ in verse 16f, here he uses σύν (cf. also σύν αὐτῷ in v. 14c and 5:10b). Elsewhere, Paul refers to a future reference of being σύν Χριστῷ either implicitly in heaven (Phil 1:23; cf. Col 3:3) or ἐν δόξῃ (cf. Col 3:4; 1 Thess 4:14). Otherwise, Paul rarely refers to dying σύν Χριστῷ (Rom 6:8; cf. Col 2:20; Rom 8:32) or being raised in the future σύν Ἰησοῦ (2 Cor 4:14; for being made alive σύν αὐτῷ in the present, see Col 2:13). There is also a reference to Christ's weakness and power as an analogy for Paul's weakness ἐν αὐτῷ and yet by God's power he shall live σύν αὐτῷ (2 Cor 13:4; Dunn 1998, 401–402). Understanding the difference between ἐν and σύν in these phrases in terms of present and future descriptions is too simplistic (*contra* Koester 1990, 448; Uprichard 1981, 109–110). Dunn draws attention to the plethora of συν- compound verbs throughout Paul (many of which appear only in Paul in the NT).[337] The emphasis is always communal (Elliger 1993, 291–292). Unlike ἐν Χριστῷ formulations, σύν Χριστῷ does not always entail a mystical dimension but can simply refer to being in the company of Christ. As such, it is not necessary to see a present/future distinction between ἐν Χριστῷ of verse 16f and σύν κυρίῳ of verse 17d.[338] Thus, it is important to distinguish between

[336] While van der Horst's article (2000) primarily deals with Rom 11:26, the evidence adduced is relevant for the discussion here.

[337] See Dunn 1998, 402–403; similarly, Bouttier 1962, 42–43.

[338] Ellis rightly points out (regarding Phil 1:23) that "Paul does not desire to die *in order* to be σύν Χριστῷ", but because he would rather be delivered from his severe afflictions (2000, 144).

an association of the living and the dead with Christ which is effected through baptism, and the eschatological association which is effected through resurrection and *parousia*.[339] This latter association probably also includes participation in his (i.e. Christ's) life and glory and victory (Grundmann 1971a, 783). The reference to κύριος instead of Χριστός in 1 Thess 4:17d is understandable because of the just mentioned ἀπάντησις as well as its correlation to the descending Lord (v. 16).

In conclusion, 1 Thess 4:17 contains the climax of the pericope and the strongest affirmation of the Jesus-followers in Thessalonica. When Paul employs the motifs of translation, meeting the Lord and of always being with him, he offers a basis for community identity and existence which transcends the current social disintegration — even death. I spend some time in the analysis examining how Paul structures the verse, particularly with various markers of time/sequence. I conclude that the emphasis is temporal rather than sequential because the Thessalonians are not asking Paul to explain the relationship between the resurrection of Christians and the *parousia* of the Lord as much as they are seeking consolation in the face of death. Thus, Paul ultimately informs the *ekklēsia* that despite instances of death, the inclusion of the whole community in the celebration of the *parousia* of the Lord is effected by resurrection of the dead in Christ, both in terms of revivification and recreation, and by the translation of the community into a new existence. The description of the celebratory meeting between members and the Lord, in terms of Hellenistic formal receptions, contributes to the consolatory tone of Paul's message. On this issue, I seek to find a right balance between competing sources of inspiration. By keeping in mind Paul's *use* of eschatological motifs in the verse, as throughout First Thessalonians, attention is directed away from examinations of individual motifs *per se*, which sometimes lead to conflicts in interpretation, and towards examinations of discourse which yield a more cohesive reading of the text. Thus, despite interesting observations about significant apocalyptic details of "clouds" and "air" (v. 17c), for example, I focus on the overall intent of the verse which is unquestionably verse 17d, namely, "so we will always be with the Lord".

f. Comfort One Another (4:18)

1. The *finale* of 1 Thess 4:13–18 is anticlimactic given that Paul's theological and christological argument culminates in verse 17d. However, the statement of verse 18 underscores Paul's purpose of consolation, a purpose which is reiterated in 5:11 (for a comparison, see §II.a.7 above). The conjunction, ὥστε, introduces an inferential independent clause containing an imperative form of παρακαλεῖν (v. 18a). Paul could have used other inferential conjunctions (e.g. διό in 5:11; τοιγαροῦν in 4:8) although ὥστε often appears in eschatological contexts (Malherbe 2000,

[339] Similarly, Holleman 1996, 171–172; see Best 1972, 201; Bouttier 1962, 53.

278).[340] The exhortation is to comfort or encourage each other; the verb is used this way repeatedly in antiquity (BDAG 765, §4). Paul uses the verb (παρακαλεῖν) and the noun (παράκλησις) in a similar way elsewhere.[341] In some sense, Christian exhortation is always grounded in *kērygma* (Schmitz 1967, 794); here, Paul refers to the statements just made in verses 14–17 (Frame 1912, 177) with the instrumental phrase, ἐν τοῖς λόγοις τούτοις (v. 18b).

2. The evidence is inconclusive whether First Thessalonians takes the form of a "letter of consolation" or not (Chapa 1994).[342] Despite Malherbe's observations that nearly all the elements in 1 Thess 4:13–18 are reflected in Hellenistic letters of consolation (1983, 254–256), Chapa is not convinced that such a background best illustrates the purpose of the pericope (1990, 224–226). He does agree that παρακαλεῖτε ἀλλήλους has a "strong Hellenistic flavor" (227), but in view of the vastly different sources and natures of consolations (between the Graeco-Roman world and Christian hope),[343] Chapa is more inclined to find an underlying "Jewish mentality expressed in Greek form" (227). For example, 2 Macc 7 suits admirably the context of consolation in 1 Thess 4:13–18 (228). Regardless of formal rhetorical descriptions, there is no doubt that in this text, Paul offers consolation as part of his pattern of exhortation.

IV. Conclusion

1. In the introduction to this chapter I say that Paul explicitly sets out to address the problem of death in 1 Thess 4:13–18, a problem which is obviously an exponent of social disintegration. I also claim that a better understanding of the exegetical problems of the text would lead to a more critical understanding of how Paul's pattern of exhortation offers a means for integration into an eschatologically identifiable existence. At the end of this chapter I now invite the reader to assess the results of the analysis to see how well this claim has been fulfilled.

2. The questions and concomitant answers surrounding the λόγος κυρίου, including its nature, extent and location, have significant bearing on how best to interpret 1 Thess 4:15–17, which is a substantial portion of the pericope. Of the alternative sources for the λόγος κυρίου, including a saying of the earthly Jesus, a

[340] 1 Cor 4:5; 10:12; 11:33; 15:58; Phil 2:12.

[341] 1 Cor 14:31; 2 Cor 1:4, 6; 2:7; 7:6, 7, 13; 1 Thess 3:2, 7; 5:11; cf. Eph 6:22; Col 2:2; 4:8; 2 Thess 2:17; cf. also παραμυθεῖσθαι in 1 Thess 2:12; 5:14. For the noun, see Rom 15:4, 5; 1 Cor 14:3; 2 Cor 1:3, 4, 5, 6, 7; 7:4, 7, 13; Phil 2:1; Phlm 7; cf. 2 Thess 2:16.

[342] Chapa concludes: "If we should not formally classify 1 Thessalonians as a 'letter of consolation', we may, nevertheless, be justified in calling it a consoling letter without intending to exclude other valid purposes" (1994, 160).

[343] One difference is obvious: Paul refers to λόγοι not as "menschliche Trostworte" but as "Gottes Wort" (Henneken 1969, 67). Further, Paul does not address the topic of grieving as much as he does erroneous eschatological convictions which give rise to grieving (Nicholl 2004, 20).

saying of the exalted Jesus, or a statement from Paul claiming the authority of the exalted Jesus, I prefer the last alternative because it appears to accord with Paul's purpose of consolation. This purpose is served well enough by the invocation of the Lord and his authority and there is no need to attempt to isolate a saying or group of sayings. This frees up the interpretation considerably as there is no longer a need to employ source, form and redaction criticism to find an elusive saying. Rather, throughout the analysis above, I emphasise the Pauline redaction of the text, being mindful that there may well be numerous references to pre-Pauline traditions, but keeping the rhetoric or purpose of the text in the foreground.

3. The motif of the *parousia* of the Lord appears in this pericope and I deal with it both in a preliminary way and also in the analysis of verse 15. While the question of how Paul is influenced by the use of the motif – either in terms of OT theophanies or Hellenistic *parousiai*– is an important consideration, that question is caught up in the sources of influence for other motifs in 1 Thess 4:13–18. The issue of sources will be summarised briefly below. Rather, the point I wish to make here is the paradigmatic association between Paul's use of the motif and his pattern of exhortation. An analysis of 1 Thess 2:19–20, 3:13 and 5:23 shows that Paul employs the *parousia* of the Lord as part of a comprehensive *paraenesis* in the letter. An assessment of Paul's use at a discourse level is often neglected when it comes to 1 Thess 4:15, a neglect which is perhaps understandable in light of the immediate context of apocalyptic details. However, I propose a new reading of the *parousia* reference in this context. Instead of representing a stereotyped formula as part of a λόγος κυρίου, Paul's reference invokes a pattern of exhortation designed to address positively the Thessalonians' grief in the face of death. From a systematic point of view, the grandeur and power of the *parousia* of the Lord becomes both a rallying point for community solidarity, and also an imperative for holy living which offers further maintenance of a community identity into the future.

4. The prominence of the kerygmatic hope plays an important part in the synthesis of the pericope. Paul subtly promotes a pattern of exhortation by building on commonly accepted beliefs, and he does so through a carefully developed argument. Unlike outsiders, Jesus-followers in Thessalonica can depend on the proclamation of Jesus' death and resurrection, on the connection between the resurrection of Jesus and the resurrection of the dead in Christ, on the *parousia* of the Lord with power and celebration, on meeting the Lord, and finally on the ultimate goal of always being with the Lord. By referring to those who have no hope (v. 13d), Paul offers a negative backdrop in front of which he interprets the problem of death wholly in positive terms.

The question of how to translate διὰ τοῦ Ἰησοῦ (v. 14c), either with τοὺς κοιμηθέντας or with ἄξει, is answered definitively by examining how Paul uses διά with Jesus, Christ and Lord elsewhere. In every case, Paul uses διά to express agency which strongly supports taking διὰ τοῦ Ἰησοῦ with the verb. This is an important conclusion because of the systematic correlation with "deliverer" references elsewhere in First Thessalonians. Thus, in 5:9, the Lord Jesus Christ is the agent of salvation from *orgē* and in 1:10, Jesus is the delivering one, who delivers the Thessalonians from the *orgē* which comes. Thus, the interpretation of Jesus as the agent of God's action in 4:14 is in agreement with the rest of the letter.

5. Most commentators do not traverse verbal theory very often. Yet, in the case of how best to interpret the middle voice of ἀνιστάναι (v. 16f), detailed interaction with verbal theory yields important results for establishing Paul's purpose for addressing the *topos* of death in 1 Thess 4:13–18. Through the application of *collocational* and *colligational* analysis of ἐγείρειν and ἀνιστάναι, O'Donnell shows how the latter performs as an ergative verb, or a verb which is able to express phenomenological fact only. Any agent of the resurrection, implied or not, is de-emphasised. It follows, therefore, that the Thessalonians are not necessarily concerned about the resurrection. I find such analysis and conclusions a very compelling reason to reject Marxsen's (and followers) reconstruction of a Thessalonian community where the resurrection of the dead is not part of Paul's founding *kērygma*, but an afterthought to address the situation of deaths among community members.

6. The results of the analysis of the apocalyptic details in 1 Thess 4:16–17 show how important it is to correctly identify the source or sources of influence for each of the motifs employed by Paul. This is one of the chief reasons why I offer an extended analysis of those verses. Several systematic observations are now in order.

First, the atomistic results of some exegeses offer a misleading interpretation of motifs which are not meant to be understood individually or literally. One example of this comes from examinations of the three prepositional phrases with ἐν, regarding the command, the voice of an archangel and the trumpet of God (vv. 16b–d). Plevnik's attempts to turn the command, or κέλευσμα, into a highly theologised term referring to Christ's coming in power ignores the wider and more generic uses of the motif in antiquity. Likewise, a fixation on attempting to identify the archangel obscures the usefulness of provocative texts like *Apoc. Mos.* 37:1–6, which while not being a direct parallel, is quite illuminating regarding the purposes of apocalyptic imagery.

Second, where two or more sources of influence are clearly present, the interpretation should be coherent and contribute to a picture of the situation to which Paul is writing. In this regard, I invoke the rule that the source or sources of influence most closely associated with the context, both in the letter and in the first-century community, are given precendence despite the existence of clear trajectories and links to historical texts or cultures of a previous era. The two examples which follow are ample illustrations of this point. (1) Much energy has been expended in attempts to explain why and how Paul uses the verb, ἁρπάζειν (v. 17b), in the context of the pericope. It is possible to explain the motif in terms of the famous ascensions of Enoch and Elijah, and/or in terms of Jewish apocalyptic tradition (cf. esp. Wis 4:11). Some commentators on this passage even develop a thesis built around the peculiar necessity to be alive in order to be eligible for translation (so Plevnik). But by keeping in mind the immediate context of death, Malherbe goes against the standard interpretation and finds numerous links between Paul's use of the motif and its use in the consolation tradition. I think he gets it right. Along with Lohfink's provocative suggestion that *Entrückung* is symbolic of the assumption of the soul and immortality, I suggest that Paul employs the motif of translation as an apology or rationalisation against death. Such an interpretation finds support in the analysis and fits very well with my thesis that Paul uses eschatological motifs to promote a pattern of exhortation; in this case, to promote an eschatological existence beyond death. (2) Perhaps an even clearer example of how this rule applies comes from the extensive examination of εἰς ἀπάντησιν (v. 17c) and the competing influences of OT theophanies and Hellenistic *parousiai*. After working through the relevant primary and secondary literature on the matter, I conclude that either source of influence may have inspired Paul's use. Since there is no technical meaning for the phrase (only a reference to an ancient custom), and adequate references to the secondary literature exist to support both sides of the debate, the issue is decided for me on systematic and contextual grounds. Despite my argument in an earlier chapter that the *ekklēsia* in Thessalonica could conceivably consist of Jews and non-Jews, the probability remains that the community is composed entirely of non-Jews. This notwithstanding, as Hellenistic readers, the association of Hellenistic formal receptions with Paul's depictions of a *parousia* Lord is undeniable. The fact that some details between the two are incompatible (e.g. the question of the direction of movement implied by Paul, either up or down) is irrelevant in view of an interpretation of the text which emphasises the eschatological discourse inherent in it. The Hellenistic reading of ἀπάντησις supports the celebratory overtones of hope against the face of death, and the subversive political overtones of terms like παρουσία and κύριος reinforce the alternative security of an otherwise marginalised Christian community.

7. With eschatology as a hermeneutical key, the interpreter is more easily able to see how various motifs in the pericope are fit together to serve Paul's pattern of exhortation. This is particularly the case when the results of the analysis from other parts of the eschatological discourse found throughout First Thessalonians are applied to the more specific conclusions found here. For example, the insider/outsider rhetoric in 2:13–16 augments the thesis that Paul deliberately uses political language in an anti-imperial way. Part of his pattern of exhortation no doubt includes strengthening a sense of solidarity, positively and negatively. The references to *orgē* in the letter function in a similar way; one reference offers a positive deliverance from *orgē* (1:10; see also 5:9) while another offers a negative characterisation of those who are against Paul and therefore against the *ekklēsia* in Thessalonica (2:16). But most important, perhaps, is the context of affliction and conflict of which deaths is a part. In 4:13–18, Paul does not address the problem of death as if the *topos* is an isolated opportunity for didactic theologising.

Indeed, Paul's pattern of exhortation is here brought fully to bear on the problem of affliction and conflict, which initially arose from the conversion experience and finds ultimate expression in death. Along these lines, it is instructive to examine the grammatical structures to see how Paul uses eschatological motifs in the pericope. The progression of argument in verse 14, despite the lack of a properly constructed apodosis, reveals the importance of solidarity. Paul employs ἄγειν to offer a generic description of resurrection, translation and meeting the Lord. The authority invoked in the λόγος κυρίου reference in verse 15 offers reassurance to community members who have lost loved ones. The temporal markers peppered throughout the text, particularly the future tense verb φθάσωμεν (v. 15e), the adverbial pair πρῶτον/ἔπειτα (vv. 16f, 17a) and the special use of ἅμα σύν (v. 17b), offer clues as to how Paul uses the eschatological motifs found in the pericope. Each motif helps construct an increasingly hopeful existence in the face of death: There exists a higher power, the *Kyrios*, who is above death and whose authority exceeds the imperial ideology and power. Those who have died are not lost in the eschatological schema, but take part in a new creation of resurrection. The integration of the community is then confirmed through members' translation to meet the Lord in the air. The celebratory connotations via Hellenistic formal receptions, express an appropriate picture of the transformed community. Where once community members were experiencing social disintegration, they now look forward to an eschatological existence *par excellence* which includes always being with the Lord.

Chapter 6
First Thessalonians 5:1–11

First Thessalonians 5:1–11 introduces a new section in the *letter-paraenesis* and follows the *topos* on those who are asleep (4:13–18). Paul begins the pericope with a familiar περὶ δέ, but with regard to the *topos* on the times and the seasons, instead of saying that he does not want the Thessalonians to be ignorant (4:13), he asserts that they have no need to be written to (5:1). Despite the structural unity of 1 Thess 4:13–5:11, including the link between the *parousia* and the day of the Lord (ἡμέρα κυρίου), the eschatological motifs in the latter pericope serve a different function in Paul's pattern of exhortation in First Thessalonians.

In 1 Thess 4:13–18, Paul interprets the problem of death wholly in positive terms. That is, he uses eschatological motifs not to address or explain the Thessalonians' social disintegration (as he does, for example, in 2:13–16), but to offer a positive means for community identity and existence. Thus, the motifs of hope of resurrection, *parousia* of the Lord, meeting and being with the Lord, and so forth, are all intended to encourage solidarity and identity. The issue of judgment, either associated with instances of death and conflict or with some of the motifs themselves (e.g. *parousia*), is downplayed.

Quite the reverse occurs in 1 Thess 5:1–11. Here, eschatological motifs are used to address both the negative and positive aspects of Paul's pattern of exhortation, and a motif of judgment is now explicitly introduced into the discourse. Negative similes of a thief and birth pains of a woman are applied to the day of the Lord, along with a reference to destruction and to the fact that there will be "no escape" (5:2–3). As the argument unfolds, however, Paul begins to shift to the positive aspect of his pattern of exhortation by emphasising the insider/outsider distinction found elsewhere in the letter. The rhetorical pairs of day/night, light/darkness, awake/asleep, sober/drunk, salvation/*orgē*, some of which are repeated a number of times, reinforce social disintegration and at the same time, community identity. The soldier talk – putting on a breastplate and a helmet (5:8) – sustains the theme of judgment, as does the reference to *orgē* (5:9). But the function of these motifs is positive. The Thessalonian community is characterised by the triad of faith, love and hope, and is destined for salvation, and especially to be with the Lord Jesus Christ (5:9–10).

But there is a more significant difference between 5:1–11 and 4:13–18 regarding the function of eschatological motifs. In 4:13–18, the eschatological discourse is unequivocally shaped around the *topos* of death — a topic of immediate social concern for the Thessalonian Jesus-followers. Similarly, in the other pericopes examined, social disintegration is understood in the context of current or recently passed experiences. Thus, in 2:13–16, it is related to suffering and conflict experienced by the Thessalonian *ekklēsia* and indeed by the Lord Jesus himself. In 1:9–10, it is related to the conversion experience. But in 5:1–11, Paul does not overtly address the Thessalonians' social disintegration by linking it to current or recently passed experiences. Rather, the pattern of exhortation is more indirect. Social disintegration is now understood symbolically, in terms of the day of the Lord. Far from understanding this motif as referring to something literally expected in the future, the day of the Lord expresses an ongoing tension of being a Jesus-follower. According to Paul, at some time whether contemporary or future, everyone faces *orgē* or salvation. Consequently, Paul substantially increases the rhetorical power of his paraenetic statements by creating a crisis (i.e. the day of the Lord) and then addressing that crisis. However, in no way does this mean that 5:1–11 is general *paraenesis*, or to be understood as independent of the situation of the Thessalonian Jesus-followers.[1]

As I show in the analysis below, using eschatology as a hermeneutical key to interpet Paul's pattern of exhortation offers a way forward concerning some of the problematic issues facing the modern interpreter. The eschatological motif of the day of the Lord, and the unusual terminology employed in the pericope are no longer to be understood as referring to Paul's original or founding message. Nor do the references to sleep need to be interpreted according to the previous *topos* on death. Further, this approach – where Paul's pattern of exhortation is understood in terms of his use of eschatological motifs to enhance community solidarity – offers a breakthrough for solving the sleep/awake conundrum in 5:10.

In what follows I offer a discussion of preliminary issues and a comprehensive analysis of 1 Thess 5:1–11. The analysis follows the arrangement of the text given below. I examine the historical context – whether social, political or theological – of each motif encountered, and then interpret Paul's use of the motifs in First Thessalonians. It is obvious that these motifs are formulated or redacted by Paul out of eschatological and apocalyptic traditions.[2] In the case of 5:1–11, eschatological motifs and Paul's pattern of exhortation meet in an unusually concentrated way. Thus, along with numerous exegetical discussions, there are three preliminary syntheses which draw together some of the results of the analysis, as well as begin to address the question of how Paul uses eschatological language to exhort the Thessalonians. By the end of this chapter I hope to explain why Paul felt the need to write to the Thessalonians about the times and the seasons.

[1] See Chapter 2.
[2] See esp. Collins 1980a; Plevnik 1979; Rigaux 1975.

I. Arranged Text and Translation

1a περὶ δὲ τῶν χρόνων καὶ τῶν καιρῶν, ἀδελφοί,
1b οὐ χρείαν ἔχετε ὑμῖν γράφεσθαι,
2a αὐτοὶ γὰρ ἀκριβῶς οἴδατε
2b ὅτι ἡμέρα κυρίου ὡς κλέπτης ἐν νυκτὶ οὕτως ἔρχεται.
3a ὅταν λέγωσιν·
3b εἰρήνη καὶ ἀσφάλεια,
3c τότε αἰφνίδιος αὐτοῖς ἐφίσταται ὄλεθρος
3d ὥσπερ ἡ ὠδὶν τῇ ἐν γαστρὶ ἐχούσῃ,
3e καὶ οὐ μὴ ἐκφύγωσιν.
4a ὑμεῖς δέ, ἀδελφοί,
4b οὐκ ἐστὲ ἐν σκότει,
4c ἵνα ἡ ἡμέρα ὑμᾶς ὡς κλέπτης καταλάβῃ·
5a πάντες γὰρ ὑμεῖς υἱοὶ φωτός
5b ἐστε καὶ υἱοὶ ἡμέρας.
5c οὐκ ἐσμὲν νυκτὸς
5d οὐδὲ σκότους·
6a ἄρα οὖν μὴ καθεύδωμεν ὡς οἱ λοιποί
6b ἀλλὰ γρηγορῶμεν καὶ νήφωμεν.
7a οἱ γὰρ καθεύδοντες νυκτὸς καθεύδουσιν
7b καὶ οἱ μεθυσκόμενοι νυκτὸς μεθύουσιν·
8a ἡμεῖς δὲ ἡμέρας ὄντες νήφωμεν
8b ἐνδυσάμενοι θώρακα πίστεως καὶ ἀγάπης
8c καὶ περικεφαλαίαν ἐλπίδα σωτηρίας·
9a ὅτι οὐκ ἔθετο ἡμᾶς ὁ θεὸς εἰς ὀργὴν
9b ἀλλὰ εἰς περιποίησιν σωτηρίας
9c διὰ τοῦ κυρίου ἡμῶν Ἰησοῦ Χριστοῦ
10a τοῦ ἀποθανόντος ὑπὲρ ἡμῶν,
10b ἵνα εἴτε γρηγορῶμεν εἴτε καθεύδωμεν
10c ἅμα σὺν αὐτῷ ζήσωμεν.
11a διὸ παρακαλεῖτε ἀλλήλους καὶ οἰκοδομεῖτε εἷς τὸν ἕνα,
11b καθὼς καὶ ποιεῖτε.

1a About the times and the seasons, brothers,
1b you have no need to be written to,
2a for you yourselves know accurately
2b that the day of the Lord comes as a thief in the night.
3a When they say:
3b "peace and security",
3c then sudden destruction comes on them
3d just as the birth pains on the pregnant [woman],
3e and they shall not escape.
4a But you, brothers,
4b are not in darkness,
4c so that the day shall catch you unawares as a thief;
5a for you are all sons of light
5b and sons of the day.
5c We are not of the night
5d nor of darkness;
6a so then let us not sleep as the others
6b but let us keep awake and be sober.
7a for the ones sleeping sleep at night
7b and the ones getting drunk are drunk at night;
8a but because we belong to day, let us be sober
8b by having put on a breastplate of faith and love
8c and a helmet, a hope of salvation;
9a for God destined us not for *orgē*
9b but for obtaining salvation
9c through our Lord Jesus Christ
10a who died for us,
10b so that whether we are awake or asleep
10c we might live together with him.
11a Therefore encourage each other and build up one another,
11b just as you are doing.

II. Preliminary Issues

a. Arrangement of the Text

1. First Thessalonians 5:1–11 begins very similarly to the previous pericope, and markers include περὶ δέ, ἀδελφοί and the formulaic οὐ χρείαν ἔχετε... (vv. 1a, b). Whether περὶ δέ indicates that Paul is responding to a letter written by the Thessalonians has been discussed elsewhere.[3] Regardless, he emphasises what is known, with a second assertion of "knowing", οἴδατε (v. 2a). The conjunction, γάρ, links the first two verses, and Paul clarifies the general phrase, οἱ χρόνοι καὶ οἱ

[3] Chapter 2, §VI.5.

καιροί (v. 1a), with a more specific assertion (see ὅτι, v. 2b) about the ἡμέρα κυρίου (v. 2b). The assertion is made more intensive with the personal pronoun, αὐτοί (v. 2a), which also appears in combination with γάρ elsewhere in the letter (1:9; 2:1; 3:3; 4:9). The particle and adverb, ὡς ... οὕτως (v. 2b), provide a correlation, "as ... so". The correlation is strengthened by the prepositional phrase, ἐν νυκτί (v. 2b), which acts substantially as an adverb of ἔρχεται (v. 2b; so *GGNT* 550): "as a thief in the night comes, so comes the day of the Lord". The phrase ὡς κλέπτης appears twice (cf. vv. 2b, 4c). Verse 3 is somewhat disjunctive of the previous verses,[4] but certainly cannot be taken with verse 4, which has distinctive markers. Rather, the complex sentence, syntactically structured around ὅταν and τότε, is understood as demonstrating or explaining commonly known information held by Paul and the Thessalonian community (see Malbon 1983, 63). The temporal conjunction, ὅταν, and the present subjunctive verb, λέγωσιν (v. 3a), express in this case, a non-iterative (*contra* Best 1972, 207), indefinite action which is contemporaneous with the verbal idea found in the main clause, beginning with the correlative adverb, τότε (v. 3c; see *GNTG* vol. 3, 112).[5] The conjunction conveys future contingency, the present subjunctive that of progressive or continuous action (*GGBB* 518–519). The ὥσπερ clause (v. 3d) offers further information. The phrase τῇ ἐν γαστρὶ ἐχούσῃ (v. 3d) gives the same idea as εἶναι ἔγκυος (Frame 1912, 182), and this is reflected in the translation.[6] Finally, the Pauline use of οὐ μή is notable.[7] The negative plus the subjunctive, ἐκφύγωσιν (v. 3e), rules out a potentiality, which is much stronger than οὐ plus the indicative which merely rules out a certainty (*GGBB* 468). As decisively as possible, Paul is saying that there is no escape.

2. The insertion of direct address, ὑμεῖς δέ, ἀδελφοί (v. 4a), along with the inclusion of another instance of δέ, indicate a new syntactical unit, but one which continues the *topos* introduced in verse 1. Paul has already referred to the metaphors of "thief" and "night" (v. 2b); now he refers to "darkness", οὐκ ἐστὲ ἐν σκότει (v. 4b), as a metaphor extension of the ἡμέρα κυρίου. The "day" is now also "daylight" as opposed to "darkness" and the "night" (v. 5). Further, he uses ὑμεῖς twice (vv. 4a, 5a) which makes a strong contrast between the Thessalonian community and those for which there shall be no escape. The conjunction, ἵνα (v. 4c), plus the subjunctive, καταλάβῃ (v. 4c), take the place of an infinitive of result. It is translated "so that" to indicate a consecutive use (see BDAG 477, §3);[8] the consequence of the verbal action – to be caught unawares – is not intended (*GGBB* 473). The post-positive conjunction, γάρ (v. 5a), introduces, by way of clarification, the chiastic structure in verse 5, which is clearly observable (see arrangement above): φῶς (v. 5a)/σκότος

[4] See NA[27] for manuscript evidence alternatively supplying a transitional δέ or γάρ.

[5] The translation "whenever" for ὅταν, expresses an iterative idea, which is out of place here.

[6] It is typical of ὥσπερ clauses to require supplementation to fill out the meaning (for examples, see BDAG 1107, §b); in this case, γυναικί is supplied (see ET above).

[7] See discussion in Chapter 5, §III.c.5.

[8] For debate on whether ἵνα can have a consecutive meaning in the NT, see Moule 1959, 142; BDF 197–198, §391(5); *GGNT* 997–998; *GNTG* vol. 1, 209–210.

(v. 5d); ἡμέρα (v. 5b)/νύξ (v. 5c). The Semitisms, υἱοὶ φωτός and υἱοὶ ἡμέρας, are not so strange to *Koinē* Greek as to be unintelligible (*GNTG* vol. 2, 441; MM 649 s.v.), although there is ambiguity about whether the genitives are subjective or objective (*GNTG* vol. 4, 90). Half way through the chiastic structure is a change of person (from second to first), and now Paul includes himself in the metaphor descriptions. The negative conjunction, οὐδέ (v. 5d), joins two negative clauses, where ἐσμέν (v. 5c) is to be supplied in the second. Paul probably prepares for the exhortations of the following verses. The combination of ἄρα οὖν (v. 6a) is rare in the NT;[9] ἄρα is inferential and οὖν marks a transition. In this way Paul introduces direct exhortation as a result or consequence of his previous statements. The change from the indicative to subjunctive mood is typical. The volitive, hortatory subjunctives appear in quick succession, καθεύδωμεν (v. 6a), γρηγορῶμεν (v. 6b), νήφωμεν (v. 6b), and all three are repeated in the verses which follow (vv. 10b, 10b, 8a, respectively). Paul emphasises solidarity with his exhortations and with the Thessalonian community by including himself — "let us…" (*GGBB* 464–465). The use of μή (v. 6a) as the particle of negation is typical, as is the adversative particle, ἀλλά (v. 6b). The phrase, ὡς οἱ λοιποί (v. 6a), has more than a passing resemblance to the previous phrase, καθὼς καὶ οἱ λοιποί (4:13d), although whether there is any connection is still to be determined. As in verse 5a, γάρ (v. 7a) is a marker of clarification which expresses a continuation in the text, more strongly than a particle like δέ. The genitive of νύξ (vv. 7a, b) is sometimes used to express a kind of time (see *GGBB* 122–124). When do "the others" sleep and get drunk? … νυκτός, "at night".

3. The second half of the eschatological *paraenesis* begins with another personal pronoun, ἡμεῖς (v. 8a), and the particle, δέ (v. 8a), marking a strong contrast with the previous verse. The repetition of the hortatory subjunctive, νήφωμεν (v. 8a), elevates the theme of "sobriety" as one of the more important exhortations in this pericope. The awkward transition between νήφωμεν (v. 8a) and ἐνδυσάμενοι (v. 8b) suggests that verse 7 may be parenthetical, and Paul is now attempting to continue the exhortation left off in verse 6 (Wanamaker 1990, 185). Regardless, the verb stands at the head of a long, complex sentence which includes two adverbial participles, ὄντες (v. 8a) and ἐνδυσάμενοι (v. 8b).[10] The first is a present participle indicating a cause or reason for the exhortion (see *GGBB* 631; *GNTG* vol. 3, 157), as well as expressing belonging or association (BDAG 285, §9). Consequently, ἡμεῖς ἡμέρας ὄντες (v. 8a) is translated "because we belong to the day…". The second is an aorist participle indicating the means by which the exhortation is to be carried out. Usually, this would be expressed with the present participle, showing contemporaneity with the main verb, but in this case the participle conveys antecedent action (which encroaches on the domain of the causal participle, "let us be sober *because* you have put on …"), and contemporaneous action, "let us be sober

[9] Rom 5:18; 7:3, 25; 8:12; 9:16, 18; 14:12, 19; Gal 6:10; see also Eph 2:19; 2 Thess 2:15.

[10] From a grammatical perspective, the division between verses 8a and 8b by Rigaux (1975) is impossible (so also Wanamaker 1990, 177).

by having put on ..."). Although the latter translation is somewhat awkward, it properly expresses the adverbial participle, ἐνδυσάμενοι (v. 8b), as used here. The rest of verse 8 consists of two direct objects of the participle, θώρακα (v. 8b) and περικεφαλαίαν (v. 8c). The former has a pair of qualifying genitives while the latter has a more unusual appositional construction, ἐλπίδα σωτηρίας (v. 8c; see *GGNT* 498). The sentence, begun in verse 8a, continues into verses 9–10, organised around ὅτι (v. 9a) and ἵνα (v. 10b). Unlike the previous instance of ὅτι (see v. 2b), which merely serves as a marker of narrative content, here the conjunction introduces a subordinate, causal clause which provides an explanation of why the Thessalonians are to take up the exhortation to sobriety.[11] This observation is important when considering arguments, for and against, about whether a pre-Pauline formula is to be found here. The middle voice form of the verb, τιθέναι (v. 9a), can have an active meaning (*GNTG* vol. 3, 55). Here it appears with a double accusative, εἰς ὀργήν (v. 9a) and εἰς περιποίησιν σωτηρίας (v. 9b), expressing mutual exclusivity: οὐκ (v. 9a) ... ἀλλά (v. 9b). The arrangement shows the parallel between the two accusatives (with εἰς). While the translations "for" and "to", respectively, poorly express the parallel, they are preferred as idiomatic. The second accusative is qualified with an adverbial phrase of means beginning with διά (v. 9c). Although it is possible to understand the phrase as a qualification of ἔθετο (v. 9a), the word order suggests the association promoted here. Thus, one obtains salvation *through* the Lord Jesus Christ (v. 9c). Paul goes on to describe this Lord as one "who died for us" (v. 10a), with an articulated participle performing the function of an attributive adjective. Following this is a consecutive, ἵνα clause (v. 10b), where the conjunction serves as a marker of result. The εἴτε ... εἴτε pair (v. 10b) expresses contingency: "whether ... or". The change from the present subjunctive, γρηγορῶμεν and καθεύδωμεν (v. 10b), to the aorist subjunctive, ζήσωμεν (v. 10c), after ἵνα occurs occasionally.[12] The significance of ἅμα σύν (v. 10c) for the interpretation of the pericope should be considered (see 4:17b).

4. The similarity in structure between 4:18 and 5:11 leads to the observation that the latter verse may serve as a conclusion not only to the *topos* on the times and seasons (5:1–11), but also to the previous *topos* on those who are asleep (4:13–18). The inferential conjunction, διό (v. 11a), articulates two imperative mood verbs, παρακαλεῖτε and οἰκοδομεῖτε (v. 11a). The subject and object of the second verb, εἷς τὸν ἕνα (v. 11a), is an unusual construction and it is debated whether it should be understood as synonymous with ἀλλήλους (v. 11a), the object of the first verb. Paul concludes the verse with the phrase, καθὼς καὶ ποιεῖτε (v. 11b). Other structural parallels with 4:13–18 have been noted elsewhere.[13]

5. Additional observations of structure include the chiasm in 1 Thess 5:5 (Milligan 1908, 67):

---

[11] On the translation of ὅτι with "for", see BDAG 732, §4.b.

[12] See Zimmer 1893, 66, for textual variants.

[13] See Chapter 5, §II.a.7.

a ὑμεῖς υἱοὶ φωτός
 b ἐστε καὶ υἱοὶ ἡμέρας
 b' οὐκ ἐσμὲν νυκτὸς
a' οὐδὲ σκότους·

As with 4:13–18, Hurd (1998, 68) is again ambitious with regard to his identification of a chiastic structure in 5:2–8:

a ἡμέρα κυρίου
 b ὡς κλέπτης ἐν νυκτὶ οὕτως ἔρχεται.
  c ὅταν λέγωσιν· εἰρήνη καὶ ἀσφάλεια, τότε αἰφνίδιος αὐτοῖς ἐφίσταται ὄλεθρος ὥσπερ ἡ ὠδὶν τῇ ἐν γαστρὶ ἐχούσῃ, καὶ οὐ μὴ ἐκφύγωσιν.
   d ὑμεῖς δέ, ἀδελφοί, οὐκ ἐστὲ ἐν σκότει, ἵνα ἡ ἡμέρα ὑμᾶς ὡς κλέπτης καταλάβῃ·
    e πάντες γὰρ ὑμεῖς υἱοὶ φωτός
    e' ἐστε καὶ υἱοὶ ἡμέρας
   d' οὐκ ἐσμὲν νυκτὸς οὐδὲ σκότους· ἄρα οὖν μὴ καθεύδωμεν ὡς οἱ λοιποί
  c' ἀλλὰ γρηγορῶμεν καὶ νήφωμεν.
 b' οἱ γὰρ καθεύδοντες νυκτὸς καθεύδουσιν καὶ οἱ μεθυσκόμενοι νυκτὸς μεθύουσιν·
a' ἡμεῖς δὲ ἡμέρας ὄντες νήφωμεν

The chiastic arrangement as set out in English by Hurd is hardly defensible, but in Greek it is obvious that no such structure exists in the text (regardless of whether Paul was conscious of it or not; *contra* 1998, 68). None of the *stichoi* match very well, and some not at all. In particular, Hurd ignores the significant thief motif in the b/b' parallel by comparing ἐν νυκτί with νυκτός, rather than drawing attention to the κλέπτης references in b/d. The parallel in e/e' of φῶς/ἡμέρα is not as good as the φῶς/σκότος and ἡμέρα/νύξ parallels outlined previously. Finally, what of the c/c' parallel? Hurd has nothing to say here because there are no parallels to be found. The idea that "through the whole passage runs a steady alternation between words associated with 'day' and those connoting 'night'" (68) is not sustained in the text. Harvey attempts to develop this idea, but his arrangement (see 1998, 266) goes against the identification of any alternations.[14]

Finally, the parallelism of verse 7 displays *paronomasia*, or the repetition of the same verb stems:

καθεύδοντες νυκτὸς καθεύδουσιν
μεθυσκόμενοι νυκτὸς μεθύουσιν·

[14] To be fair, Harvey does offer a critique of Hurd's chiastic structure, and is realistic regarding ambiguities in his proposal of an alternating structure (1998, 275).

b. Traditional Background and Parallels with Other Texts

1. Much has been discussed about the traditional background of 1 Thess 5:1–11, not least with regard to the authenticity of the pericope. Notwithstanding compilation theories,[15] the question of integrity essentially arises with the article of Friedrich (1973), who argues that the pericope is entirely an interpolation. But unlike the extensive discussion of the authenticity of 2:13–16 which has numerous proponents for and against,[16] scholars have generally rejected Friedrich's arguments involving vocabulary, style and theology (reiterated in his commentary of 1976).[17] Assuming that 5:1–11 is authentic does not explain the peculiarities of the text, however, which are significant enough to warrant a preliminary discussion of possible reasons for the peculiarities, especially allusions, quotations and/or material sharing a common trajectory or social setting.

2. Pursuant to that discussion, attention is rightly drawn to Rom 13:11–14, which has some parallels to 1 Thess 5:1–8 (see below):[18]

	1 Thess 5:1–8		Rom 13:11–14
5:1a	περὶ δὲ τῶν χρόνων καὶ τῶν καιρῶν (5:9b) εἰς περιποίησιν σωτηρίας	13:11	καὶ τοῦτο εἰδότες τὸν καιρόν, ὅτι ὥρα ἤδη ὑμᾶς ἐξ ὕπνου ἐγερθῆναι, νῦν γὰρ ἐγγύτερον ἡμῶν ἡ σωτηρία ἢ ὅτε ἐπιστεύσαμεν.
5:2	αὐτοὶ γὰρ ἀκριβῶς οἴδατε ὅτι ἡμέρα κυρίου ὡς κλέπτης ἐν νυκτὶ οὕτως ἔρχεται.	13:12	ἡ νὺξ προέκοψεν, ἡ δὲ ἡμέρα ἤγγικεν. ἀποθώμεθα οὖν τὰ ἔργα τοῦ σκότους, ἐνδυσώμεθα δὲ τὰ ὅπλα τοῦ φωτός.
5:4	ἡμεῖς δέ, ἀδελφοί, οὐκ ἐστὲ ἐν σκότει, ἵνα ἡ ἡμέρα ὑμᾶς ὡς κλέπτης καταλάβῃ·	13:13	ὡς ἐν ἡμέρᾳ εὐσχημόνως περι- πατήσωμεν, μὴ κώμοις καὶ
5:5	πάντες γὰρ ὑμεῖς υἱοὶ φωτός ἐστε καὶ υἱοὶ ἡμέρας. οὐκ ἐσμὲν νυκτὸς οὐδὲ σκότους·		
5:6	ἄρα οὖν μὴ καθεύδωμεν ὡς οἱ λοιποὶ ἀλλὰ γρηγορῶμεν καὶ νήφωμεν.		
5:7	οἱ γὰρ καθεύδοντες νυκτὸς καθεύδουσιν καὶ οἱ μεθυ- σκόμενοι νυκτὸς μεθύουσιν·		μέθαις, μὴ κοίταις καὶ ἀσελγείαις, μὴ ἔριδι καὶ ζήλῳ,

[15] See Chapter 4, §II.d.

[16] For a summary, see Chapter 4, §IV.

[17] For critiques of the interpolation hypothesis, see Collins 1979a; Plevnik 1979; Rigaux 1975. With reference to Friedrich's article, Vögtle asserts that the question of the authenticity of 1 Thess 5:1–11 must remain open (1976, 560).

[18] For the parallels, see esp. Friedrich 1973, 305–307; Rigaux 1975, 337–338.

5:8	ἡμεῖς δὲ ἡμέρας ὄντες νήφωμεν ἐνδυσάμενοι …	13:14	ἀλλὰ ἐνδύσασθε τὸν κύριον Ἰησοῦν Χριστὸν καὶ τῆς σαρκὸς πρόνοιαν μὴ ποιεῖσθε εἰς ἐπιθυμίας.

The arrangement above shows that there are verbal and thematic parallels between Rom 13:11–14 and 1 Thess 5:1–8.[19] The former text is generally considered to come from a baptismal context which leads to the conjecture of the same for the Thessalonian pericope.[20] Certainly, the motifs of light/darkness and the exhortation to put on armour are significant for this conclusion.[21] But many commentators remain unconvinced (Collins 1984, 145–153), or use circumspect language such that the motifs serve as indirect allusions to baptismal liturgy.[22] Dunn rightly points out that texts should not be interpreted in terms of a baptismal context just because certain elements sometimes associated with baptism happen to be present. Inevitable distortions in the interpretation surely follow (1970, 104).[23] Therefore, while it is acknowledged that Rom 13:11–14 may have a baptismal context, and that there are a number of parallels between it and 1 Thess 5:1–11, the latter text is not necessarily to be regarded as also having a baptismal context (Holtz 1983, 70; Plevnik 1979, 85).

Also significant are the alleged parallels between 1 Thess 5:1–11 and synoptic texts:[24] 1 Thess 5:1–2 (Matt 24:36); 1 Thess 5:2, 4 (Matt 24:42–44; Luke 12:39–40); 1 Thess 5:3 (Matt 24:37–39; Luke 17:26–30; 21:34–36); 1 Thess 5:5–6 (Matt 24:42; Mark 13:34–36; Luke 12:36–38); 1 Thess 5:6–7 (Matt 24:45–50; Luke 12:42–46).[25] The most certain of these alleged parallels, according to a majority of commentators, are the motif of the day of the Lord coming like a thief in the night and the motif of sudden destruction coming upon unaware outsiders. The relevant texts are set out below:

---

[19] Thompson (1991, 143 n. 2) also notes the parallel phrases, περιπατῆτε εὐσχημόνως (1 Thess 4:12) and εὐσχημόνως περιπατήσωμεν (Rom 13:13).

[20] On Rom 13:11–14, see among others Byrne 1996, 397–401; Cranfield 1979, 679–690; Jewett 2007, 816–828; Käsemann 1980, 362–364; Schlier 1977, 396–400; Vögtle 1976.

[21] See Fuchs 1965; Harnisch 1979; U. B. Müller 1975, 156–157. Harnisch also finds the confessional formula of 1 Thess 5:9–10 to be a significant indicator of a baptismal context (see 142–152).

[22] See Jewett 2007, 817–818; Laub 1973, 157–167; Pax 1971, 259–260.

[23] Freed's interpretation that First Thessalonians is written by Paul to a baptised group and an unbaptised group is nearly incomprehensible (see 2005, 50–97). There is simply no evidence in the letter for such a systematic application of the theme of baptism.

[24] For identification and discussion of parallels, see Howard 1988, 181; McNicol 1996, 19–29; Orchard 1938, 24–30; Waterman 1975, 109–111; Wenham 1981, 347, 353–356; 1995, 307–316.

[25] For a helpful, thematic arrangement, see Tuckett 1990, 169.

"the day of the Lord comes like a thief in the night"

1 Thess 5:2, 4

5:2 αὐτοὶ γὰρ ἀκριβῶς οἴδατε ὅτι ἡμέρα κυρίου
ὡς κλέπτης ἐν νυκτὶ οὕτως ἔρχεται.

5:4 ὑμεῖς δέ, ἀδελφοί, οὐκ ἐστὲ ἐν σκότει,
ἵνα ἡ ἡμέρα ὑμᾶς ὡς κλέπτης καταλάβῃ·

	Matt 24:42–44		Luke 12:39–40
24:42	γρηγορεῖτε οὖν, ὅτι οὐκ οἴδατε ποίᾳ ἡμέρᾳ ὁ κύριος ὑμῶν ἔρχεται.		
24:43	ἐκεῖνο δὲ γινώσκετε ὅτι εἰ ᾔδει ὁ οἰκοδεσπότης ποίᾳ φυλακῇ ὁ κλέπτης ἔρχεται, ἐγρηγόρησεν ἂν καὶ οὐκ ἂν εἴασεν διορυχθῆναι τὴν οἰκίαν αὐτου.	12:39	τοῦτο δὲ γινώσκετε ὅτι εἰ ᾔδει ὁ οἰκοδεσπότης ποίᾳ ὥρᾳ ὁ κλέπτης ἔρχεται, οὐκ ἂν ἀφῆκεν διορυχθῆναι τὸν οἶκον αὐτοῦ.
24:44	διὰ τοῦτο καὶ ὑμεῖς γίνεσθε ἕτοιμοι, ὅτι ᾗ οὐ δοκεῖτε ὥρᾳ ὁ υἱὸς τοῦ ἀνθρώπου ἔρχεται.	12:40	καὶ ὑμεῖς γίνεσθε ἕτοιμοι, ὅτι ᾗ ὥρᾳ οὐ δοκεῖτε ὁ υἱὸς τοῦ ἀνθρώπου ἔρχεται.

"sudden destruction comes upon unaware outsiders"

	1 Thess 5:3		Luke 21:34–36
5:3	ὅταν λέγωσιν· εἰρήνη καὶ ἀσφάλεια, τότε αἰφνίδιος αὐτοῖς ἐφίσταται ὄλεθρος ὥσπερ ἡ ὠδὶν τῇ ἐν γαστρὶ ἐχούσῃ, καὶ οὐ μὴ ἐκφύγωσιν.	21:34	προσέχετε δὲ ἑαυτοῖς μήποτε βαρηθῶσιν ὑμῶν αἱ καρδίαι ἐν κραιπάλῃ καὶ μέθῃ καὶ μερίμναις βιωτικαῖς καὶ ἐπιστῇ ἐφ᾽ ὑμᾶς αἰφνίδιος ἡ ἡμέρα ἐκείνη
		21:35	ὡς παγίς· ἐπεισελεύσεται γὰρ ἐπὶ πάντας τοὺς καθημένους ἐπὶ πρόσωπον πάσης τῆς γῆς.
		21:36	ἀγρυπνεῖτε δὲ ἐν παντὶ καιρῷ δεόμενοι ἵνα κατισχύσητε ἐκφυγεῖν ταῦτα πάντα τὰ μέλλοντα γίνεσθαι καὶ σταθῆναι ἔμπροσθεν τοῦ υἱοῦ τοῦ ἀνθρώπου.

There can be little doubt regarding the importance of these parallels for an identification of pre-Pauline traditions. The parallels above, particularly the motif of the thief, cannot be easily dismissed — even Tuckett (who is representative of a minimalist approach to the problematic) concedes that Paul is dependent on Jesus tradition here (1990, 182; see Dunn 1998b, 176–177). Other commentators are more positive, and find a cumulation of parallels such that Paul is specifically and generally dependent on Jesus tradition.[26] But whether this is Jesus tradition found in the Synoptics or a pre-synoptic form is an open question which need not be investigated further here.[27]

There is much more that could be said about the background of 1 Thess 5:1–11, especially regarding LXX and Qumran parallels (see the analysis below). But it is unnecessary, for my purposes, to go beyond the general conclusion of Rigaux who notes that Paul extensively redacts and uses traditional images, both eschatological and apocalyptic, to exhort his audience in a time (or aeon) bounded by the death and resurrection of Jesus Christ, on the one hand, and the day of the Lord or the *parousia* of the Lord, on the other (1975, 339–340).

III. Analysis

a. Concerning the Times and the Seasons (5:1–3)

1. Clues to Paul's purposes in writing 1 Thess 5:1–11 are offered in the first verses, although the matter of their determination cannot be ultimately decided without recourse to the conclusions of the analysis of the whole pericope. However, a number of initial observations may be given here, especially regarding the relation between Paul's purposes and the statement (see v. 1b) that the Thessalonians have no need to be written to (§III.a.2). The *topos*, περὶ δὲ τῶν χρόνων καὶ τῶν καιρῶν (v. 1a), is understood to be none other than the ἡμέρα κυρίου (v. 2b). Numerous attempts have been made to define this *topos*, in terms of Jewish and early Christian apocalyptic and eschatological traditions, and there is no need to contribute at length to that discussion. Rather, in the context of 1 Thess 5, of more relevance is how Paul uses this motif to promote his pattern of exhortation (§III.a.3). In this regard, it is important to take into account the peculiar language and emphases afforded in verse 3. The phrase, εἰρήνη καὶ ἀσφάλεια (v. 3b), is a more significant example of the unusual language to be found here, especially because its interpretation has far-reaching ramifications for the political and therefore social situation of the Thessalonian *ekklēsia* (§III.a.4). In a concluding section, I offer a synthesis of the analysis to date. In particular, the historical context in which Paul introduces a *topos* on the times and seasons is developed, including a discussion of how the various motifs encounted in 1 Thess 5:1–3 are used by Paul (§III.a.5).

[26] See for example, Dunn 1998b, 173–180; Kim 2002a; Wenham 1984; 1995, 385–388.

[27] Thus, there is a history of interpretation which argues that Luke is dependent on Paul (see esp. Aejmelaeus 1985, followed by Tuckett 1990; see also Best 1972, 207; Orchard 1938), rather than Paul being dependent on pre-synoptic traditions that are utilised only in Luke's gospel (see Hartman 1966, 192–193; März 1992; McNicol 1996, 28–29, 43–44; Wenham 1984). Bauckham argues for the priority of the Q version of the thief parable in Luke, because there the image is not connected with the image of staying awake at night. Presumably, such a connection is a later development (1977, 169 n. 2).

2. About the times and the seasons, Paul states that the Thessalonians have no need to be written to. Some commentators have argued, on the basis of the fact that he goes on to address the *topos*, that Paul implies that he is responding to a question or questions, stemming either from Timothy's oral report (3:6) or from a letter from the Thessalonian *ekklēsia* to Paul.[28] I have already offered a discussion of the latter option; my opinion is that the *letter-paraenesis* is contingent not on a letter from the Thessalonians but only on an oral report from Timothy.[29] An important presupposition of this judgment is the assumption that 1 Thess 5:1–11 *is* contingent — an assumption not without some justification. Previously, I concluded that although Paul extensively uses stereotypical language, this language has been redacted for a specific context or purpose.[30]

The double assertion of knowing in verses 1–2, οὐ χρείαν ἔχετε ὑμῖν γράφεσθαι (v. 1b) and αὐτοὶ γὰρ ἀκριβῶς οἴδατε (v. 2a), suggests that Paul is not introducing new material unknown to his converts at Thessalonica. Yet, in a similar way to the question of whether Paul is responding to specific questions, another question inevitably arises: why does Paul go on to present information on the very topic about which he just said the Thessalonians know? Malbon (1983, 60) provides an answer to this question by observing a paradigmatic structure which is repeated throughout First Thessalonians, including 5:1–11:

(1) assertion of knowing (vv. 1, 2; also vv. 2–8),
(2) demonstration or explanation of knowing (vv. 3, 5, 7),
(3) assertion of explanation or axiom (vv. 9–10a),
(4) implication(s) of assertion or axiom (vv. 6, 8, 10b, 11; see further, 62–63).

Malbon's analysis distinguishes between objective and subjective knowledge, or knowing a fact and knowing a person, respectively. She concludes that Paul's purpose in 1 Thess 5:1–11 is to develop and encourage subjective or personal knowing, of each other and of God (70). Thus, the question of whether Paul is presenting new information or not is not necessarily very helpful. Rather, a starting point for analysis is recognising the paraenetic purpose of the text. Paul uses the introduction to express confidence in the Thessalonians (Malherbe 1992, 293) and to prepare for exhortations to follow (Watson 1999, 74). These somewhat methodological questions may now be put to one side in favour of the analysis of various motifs found in verses 1–3.

3. According to the limited number of references available, the two words for time in the phrase, οἱ χρόνοι καὶ οἱ καιροί (v. 1a), are to be understood synonymously (Yoder-Neufeld 1997, 75) despite the fact that χρόνος and καιρός individually can

[28] So Frame 1912, 178–179; Green 2002, 230; Nicholl 2004, 50.

[29] *Contra* those who reject any contingency: Collins 1984, 163; Malherbe 2000, 288. See Chapter 2, §VI.5.

[30] See Chapter 2, §VI.4; *contra* Koester (1997, 161) who asserts that 1 Thess 5:1–11 "must be read as a deliberate exposition by Paul that does not have any specific reference to concerns of the readers".

have very different meanings.[31] That one is dependent on the other (hendiadys) is not necessarily the case.[32] Further, even though the phrase appears in very different contexts, it may have a technical meaning (Best 1972, 204; Frame 1912, 180). It is possible to import a connotation of judgment associated with καιρός, especially with regard to OT, intertestamental and NT references.[33] This would certainly fit the context here. Alternatively, the phrase may be interpreted according to the special Pauline definition of καιρός (see for example, 2 Cor 6:2) as referring to "the eschatological time that began with the sending of Christ" (Baumgarten 1991, 233). More to the point is the parallel in Rom 13:11, where the term is used to describe an awareness of salvation history, whereby salvation is ever nearer (νῦν γὰρ ἐγγύτερον ἡμῶν ἡ σωτηρία). Harnisch is correct when he refers to "die bis zum Eschaton noch ausstehende Zeitspanne" (1973, 54). This interpretation is consistent with the synonymous use of the terms found in the literature, especially in eschatological contexts.[34]

The phrase, ἡμέρα κυρίου (1 Thess 5:2b), appears a number of times in the NT[35] and the LXX (MT: יום יהוה).[36] A number of variations arise in the NT,[37] including ἡμέρα κυρίου Ἰησοῦ (2 Cor 1:14), ἡμέρα κυρίου Ἰησοῦ Χριστοῦ (1 Cor 1:8), ἡμέρα Χριστοῦ (Phil 1:10; 2:16), ἡμέρα Χριστοῦ Ἰησοῦ (Phil 1:6), even just ἡ/ἐκείνη ἡμέρα. The last variation has too many references to list here, although it should be noted that Paul easily adopted the shorter formulation,[38] as well as ἡμέρα ὀργῆς (Rom 2:5) and ἡμέρα σωτηρίας (2 Cor 6:2*bis*).[39] The last two phrases, with ὀργή and σωτηρία, well illustrate the double reference Paul inherited from the OT, both as a day of *orgē* and judgment as well as a day of salvation and deliverance (see 1 Thess 1:10; 5:9; Haufe 1999, 92). Plevnik traces the history of development of יום יהוה in his extensive survey of the OT and Jewish apocalyptic writings including *1 Enoch*, *4 Ezra*, *2 Baruch* and the *Testament of the Twelve Patriarchs* (1997, 11–39).[40] He notes that in addition to the ambivalence (i.e. judgment and salvation) inherent in the term, a transference of association developed, from God to his agent (usually a messianic figure). This development culminates, for Paul, in iden-

---

[31] See BDAG & MM s.v.; Bruce 1982, 108–109. Examples where the two terms are synonymous, or nearly so, include: Eccl 3:1; Dan 2:21; 4:37; 7:12; Sir 29:5 (cf. 43:6); Tob 14:4; 14:5s; Wis 8:8 (cf. 7:18); P. Lond. 42.23; Acts 1:7; cf. 2 Esd 20:35; 23:31; Acts 3:19–21.

[32] *Contra* Collins 1984, 163; Hübner 1993b, 488; Lucchesi 1977, 537; Malherbe 2000, 288; Nicholl 2004, 50; Rigaux 1975, 322; Stuhlmann 1983, 47.

[33] Wanamaker 1990, 178; so also Baumgarten 1991, 233; Delling 1965, 461.

[34] The conclusion of Lucchesi (1977, 540), that the NT use of the terms is inspired by Philo rather than Daniel *et alii*, is rejected.

[35] Matt 7:22; Acts 2:20; Rom 14:6; 1 Cor 5:5; 1 Thess 5:2; 2 Thess 2:2; 2 Pet 3:10.

[36] Isa 2:12; 13:6, 9; Jer 32:33; Ezek 7:10; 13:5; 30:3; Joel 1:15; 2:1, 11; 3:4; 4:14; Amos 5:18, 20; Obad 1:15; Zeph 1:7, 14*bis*; Mal 3:19, 22; cf. Jer 26:10.

[37] Whether these variations include ἡμῶν or not (the manuscript evidence is often divided) has not been indicated in this list.

[38] Rom 2:16; 13:12; 1 Cor 3:13; 1 Thess 5:4, 8; cf. 2 Thess 1:10; 2 Tim 1:12, 18; 4:8.

[39] Similarly, cf. ἡμέρα ἀπολυτρώσεως in Eph 4:30.

[40] See also the excursus, "sur l'origine du 'Jour de Yahvé'", by Langevin 1967, 154–167.

tifying the *parousia* of the Lord (Jesus) as identical with the day of the Lord (1997, 43–44),[41] although there is a different emphasis associated with each (n.b. celebration in 1 Thess 4:15–17; judgment in 5:1–3).[42] Consequently, Delling concludes that the day of the Lord is wholly future, since it is not only a day of judgment but "the revelation of the glory of Jesus at His *parousia*" (1964b, 952–953). Such a definition forces Delling to interpret the ἡμέρα references in 1 Thess 5:5, 8, independently of the ἡμέρα κυρίου phrase in verse 2, because the Thessalonians supposedly cannot be υἱοὶ ἡμέρας in the present age (953 n. 50). But Delling has conceived his definition of the day of the Lord too narrowly. The motif is able to encompass a significant tension between past, present and future, such that its original identification with Israel's past is expanded into a concept of cosmic significance (von Rad 1965, 124). This tension is well expressed in the parallel texts of 1 Thess 5 and Rom 13. In the one, Paul exhorts his audience to live appropriately because they are sons of the day. In the other, he exhorts his audience to live appropriately because the day is near (ἐγγίζειν).[43] Thus, "der 'Tag' als paränetischer Begriff" is even emphasised by Radl (see 1981, 163–166).

The metaphoric description of the day of the Lord – ὡς κλέπτης ἐν νυκτὶ οὕτως ἔρχεται (1 Thess 5:2b; cf. v. 4c) – is of a Christian origin. Although the thief imagery appears in a number of LXX texts,[44] the association to the *parousia* of the Son of Man and to the day of the Lord is attested only in the new era and never outside Christian texts (Best 1972, 205).[45] The broad attestation of the image (in Paul, the Synoptics, 2 Peter and Revelation) supports a pre-Pauline traditional source or sources, but whether it may be traced back to a Q source, or to Jesus himself, is disputed.[46] The connection between the thief (ὁ κλέπτης) and the exhortation to watch (γρηγορεῖν) certainly does not originate with Paul. The consensus view is that Paul employs the image of the thief to express an element of surprise; the coming of the day cannot be foreseen (Holtz 1998, 214). Stanley offers an insightful article on the negative social impact the image may have had on first-century women. He observes that the image of a thief has strong ethical implications attached. "The image works by playing on the fears of the audience: who would want to end up on the wrong side of the divine judgment?" (2002, 470). Yet Stanley's extensive examination of the activities of burglars in the first century shows that women had more to fear than men, such that the imagery of the thief in the night is some-

[41] Best 1972, 206; Delling 1964b, 952; Malherbe 2000, 291; Witherington 1992, 168. Trilling asserts that Paul is the first to clearly articulate this connection between the *parousia* and the day (1991, 121; so also Gundry 1987, 169).

[42] Despite the traditional nature of the motif of the day of the Lord, in view of the development of the motif, it is not likely that κύριος = "God" (*contra* Collins 1990a, 778).

[43] Malherbe 2000, 289; Roetzel 1972, 83; see also Mayhue 1991.

[44] Exod 22:1; Deut 24:7; Job 24:14; 30:5; Ps 49:18; Prov 29:24; Isa 1:23; Jer 2:26; 30:3; Hos 7:1; Joel 2:9; Obad 1:5; Zech 5:3–4; Ep Jer 57; Sir 5:14; 20:25.

[45] Matt 24:43 (par. Luke 12:39); 1 Thess 5:2, 4; 2 Pet 3:10; Rev 3:3; 16:15; *Gos. Thom.* 21 (cf. 103).

[46] In particular, see extensive discussion by Aejmelaeus 1985, 28–37; Harnisch 1973, 84–116; Konradt 2003, 139–143; Lövestam 1963, 95–107; März 1992; Smitmans 1973.

what andro-centric (485). In 1 Thess 5:1–3, this gender difference is reinforced by another image, that of birth pains.[47] Stanley concludes: "Perhaps Paul meant to strike fear into the hearts of his female listeners; more likely he simply took over a common simile without thinking about its implications" (483). Incidentally, this is the only place where the phrase ἐν νυκτί is mentioned in this connection. Malherbe's suggestion (2000, 290), that in this way Paul prepares for the exhortations to follow (viz. νύξ in vv. 5c, 7a, b), is plausible.

4. In addition to the disjunctive transition between verses 2 and 3, there is also a change of address from the second to the first person. Paul first affirms that the Thessalonian *ekklēsia* knows accurately that the day of the Lord comes as a thief in the night, and then continues with an assertion about what others (or outsiders) are saying. The Thessalonians already know this, and Paul simply reminds them here. The fomulation which follows, εἰρήνη καὶ ἀσφάλεια (v. 3b), contains a very strange way, for Paul, of referring to εἰρήνη, an important concept for him. Although it appears in First Thessalonians only here and in typical epistolary structures (cf. 1:1; 5:23), it is commonly found elsewhere in his letters.[48] Paul usually connects peace with his understanding of salvation; by faith humanity no longer stands under *orgē* but under righteousness (see for example, Rom 5:1–11).[49] But in 1 Thess 5:3, it appears to have a general connotation and is coupled with ἀσφάλεια which, while not unknown in biblical tradition,[50] is by no means well attested in the NT (Luke 1:4; Acts 5:23).[51] Paul's use of the slogan has been traditionally understood either in the context of the false peace sayings in Ezek 13:10 and Jer 6:14 (cf. 8:11 [MT])[52] or else in the context of imperial Roman propaganda, or *pax Romana*. Although the Thessalonian formulation is reminiscent of the alleged prophetic parallels,[53] there is nothing in the contexts to suggest a connection. Nor is there yet a plausible reason for Paul to change the second εἰρήνη to ἀσφάλεια.[54] More problematic is the lack of parallels of such a phrase in an apocalyptic context.[55] In contrast, the political

[47] See discussion of Gempf (1994), below.

[48] Besides the epistolary formulations (Rom 1:7; 15:13?, 33; 16:20; 1 Cor 1:3; 2 Cor 1:2; 13:11; Gal 1:3; 6:16; Phil 1:2; 4:9; Phlm 3), see Rom 2:10; 3:17; 5:1; 8:6; 14:17, 19; 1 Cor 7:15; 14:33; 16:11; Gal 5:22; Phil 4:7.

[49] For further details, see Foerster 1964b; Hasler 1990.

[50] Lev 26:15; Deut 12:10; 1 Esd 8:51; Ps 103:5; Prov 8:14; 11:15; 28:17; Isa 8:15; 18:4; 34:15; 1 Macc 14:37; 2 Macc 3:22; 4:21; 9:21; 15:1, 11; 3 Macc 5:5; Tob 14:7s; Wis 8:18, 19.

[51] See also ἀσφαλής in Acts 21:34; 22:30; 25:26; Phil 3:1; Heb 6:19.

[52] So Best 1972, 207–208; Bruce 1982, 110; Frame 1912, 181; Holtz 1998, 215–216; Nicholl 2004, 54.

[53] Thus: ... λέγοντες εἰρήνη εἰρήνη καὶ οὐκ ἦν εἰρήνη (Ezek 13:10); λέγοντες εἰρήνη εἰρήνη καὶ ποῦ ἐστιν εἰρήνη (Jer 6:14).

[54] *Contra* Holtz (1998, 215 n. 364), ἀσφάλεια cannot be understood as a variation of εἰρήνη, particularly because the word appears in the literature with very specific connotations. Nicholl's suggestion that ἀσφάλεια "would seem to capture well the sense of the Hebrew שלום in Jer. 6:14/8:11" (2004, 54), is wishful thinking. He fails to offer critical discussion on the matter.

[55] Koester 1997, 161; vom Brocke 2001, 170–171; *contra* Holtz 1998, 215. The suggestion of Harnisch, that Paul uses the slogan to counter gnostic-oriented enthusiasts (1973, 78–82), is unsubstantiated.

association is well documented (*contra* Nicholl 2004, 53–54).[56] The numismatic evidence shows that the *pax Romana* was a program as much as it was a statement.[57] Hendrix (1991) provides textual parallels, as well as architectural, sculptural and other types of evidence to reconstruct a peculiar relationship between the inhabitants of Thessalonica and Roman rule.[58] In particular, the city's inhabitants had a tendency to imitate imperial Roman propaganda, and Roman benefaction was very important for understanding the political context.[59] This makes the thesis, that Paul is overtly referring to such propaganda, very plausible.[60] But such an association does not necessarily imply a specific attack on the Roman establishment (Oakes 2005, 318), and Paul's reference in 1 Thess 5:3 falls short of supporting this interpretation (*contra* Donfried 1985, 344; Still 1999, 261–262). It does, however, confirm Paul's dualistic view when it comes to the Thessalonian *ekklēsia* — those who say "peace and security" are clearly outside the community, and are among those who are thought to experience the day of the Lord in a negative way (Hendrix 1991, 118). In this sense Paul does take up the phrase with polemical intent, for the outsiders are now identified with imperial Rome (Bammel 1984, 378). A more specific identity, where the outsiders are none other than the συμφυλέται of 1 Thess 2:14, is not incompatible with this identification (Johanson 1987, 131–132).

Malherbe rejects the political association of the slogan "peace and security" on the grounds that the hypothesis implies a persecuted church, for which he finds no evidence in First Thessalonians. In addition, he rejects political connotations for terms like παρουσία and ἀπάντησις in the previous pericope and therefore finds no support for a political interpretation here. Finally, Malherbe argues that such an interpretation does not give sufficient weight to the apocalyptic context in which the slogan is cited (2000, 304). This last point is ironic considering that Malherbe himself offers no further comments on the apocalyptic context of the slogan. With regard to the first two arguments, I draw attention to previous examinations of conflict language,[61] and of political terms[62] in First Thessalonians. We disagree sharply on the issues. The alternative view espoused by Malherbe is that the slogan "peace and security" is "Paul's own ironic formulation to describe the views of false teachers that he is countering" (1999, 137). Malherbe offers numerous examples of Epicurean uses of ἀσφάλεια, and argues that Paul uses apocalyptic traditions and Epicurean characterisations to speak against false prophets in the community (see

---

[56] See Bammel 1960; Hendrix 1991; Konradt 2003, 145 nn. 672–673; vom Brocke 2001, 174–176; Wengst 1987, 19–21, 76–79.

[57] For refs., see Hendrix 1991, 113 n. 16; see also vom Brocke 2001, 176–178.

[58] Hendrix is followed closely by Still (1999, 263–266).

[59] See Hendrix 1984; 1992a; see also Chapter 1, §IV.e.

[60] There is an increasing number of scholars who support a political association; see among others: Bammel 1960, 837; Green 2002, 233–234; Harrison 2002, 86–87; Haufe 1999, 93; Hendrix 1991, 112–118; Koester 1997, 162; Konradt 2003, 145–146; Oakes 2005, 318; Still 1999, 262; Wengst 1987, 78; Witherington 2006, 146–147.

[61] See Chapter 1, §IV.e; Chapter 4, III.b.

[62] See for example, Chapter 5, §II.d, §III.d.3, §III.e.6.

1 Thess 5:20–21) and to remind his followers of their eschatological identity (2000, 304–305). Despite the Epicurean parallels, I agree with Harrison who concludes that (2002, 86 n. 61),

> the prominence of both εἰρήνη and ἀσφάλεια – whether individually or combined – in the imperial propaganda would have ensured that the "hidden transcript" at Thessaloniki was imperial in its reference rather than Epicurean.

Paul asserts that when they say "peace and security", τότε αἰφνίδιος αὐτοῖς ἐφίσταται ὄλεθρος (v. 3c). There is little to say about these terms. As with ἀσφάλεια, ὠδίν and γαστήρ, the terms αἰφνίδιος[63] and ἐφιστάναι[64] are *hapax legomena* in Paul, and ὄλεθρος only occurs twice (here and in 1 Cor 5:5).[65] The idea of suddenness follows well the imagery of the thief. The motif of destruction introduced here is general and differs from the absolute use in the phrase, ὄλεθρος αἰώνιος (2 Thess 1:9). If ὄλεθρος does not refer to annihilation, then the usage probably implies ruin or "the loss of all that gives worth to existence" (MM 445),[66] or else it is opposite to σωτηρία (Frame 1912, 182).[67]

The next motif, ὥσπερ ἡ ὠδὶν τῇ ἐν γαστρὶ ἐχούσῃ (v. 3d), also expresses the idea of suddenness, although now the inescapability of the coming destruction is in view (Radl 1993b, 506; see Bertram 1974, 672). The image of birth pains is well known in prophetic and apocalyptic literature (Rigaux 1975, 325), and is often associated with the day of the Lord and/or judgment.[68] It is probably remotely (if that) related to the messianic birth pains (Mark 13:8 [par. Matt 24:8]).[69] Paul uses the metaphor of labour pangs several times, but each instance is not easily comparable (Gal 4:19, 27; Rom 8:22), and the often associated word, τίκτειν, occurs only once in his letters (Gal 4:27) despite its common occurrence in the LXX.[70] The singular form of ὠδίν in 1 Thess 5:3 is unusual, but does not seem to have any significance here or elsewhere.[71] The next phrase, ἐν γαστρὶ ἔχειν, is commonly found in the medical writers from Hippocrates onwards to refer to a woman who is pregnant.[72] Gempf (1994) offers a discussion on the imagery of birth pains in the NT, and explores the question of why Jewish and Christian literature employs

---

[63] For the only other biblical references, see 2 Macc 14:17; 3 Macc 3:24; Wis 17:14; Luke 21:34.

[64] The word occurs more often, but in the NT predominantly in Luke-Acts. The use, as here of the coming or happening of an event (esp. a misfortune), is rare; see Wis 6:8; 19:1; Luke 21:34 (BDAG 418, §2).

[65] The word is common in the LXX, and used to refer to eschatological destruction: Jer 31(48):3; 4 Macc 10:15; Wis 1:14 (Schneider 1967, 168).

[66] So also, Malherbe 2000, 292; Milligan 1908, 65.

[67] Due to a lack of evidence, Best leaves the matter open (1972, 208).

[68] See for example, Isa 13:8; 21:3; 26:17–18; Jer 6:24; 13:21; 15:9; 22:23; Hos 13:13; *1 En.* 62:4; *4 Ezra* 2:27; 4:40, 42; see also 1QH 3:7–10; 5:30–31; 9:29–32.

[69] For discussion, see Harnisch 1973, 62–72.

[70] For references where ὠδίν and τίκτειν appear, see 1 Kgdms 4:19; 4 Kgdms 19:3; Ps 47:7; Isa 13:8; 21:3; 26:17; 37:3; 66:7; Jer 6:24; 8:21; 13:21; 22:23; 27:43; Hos 13:13; Mic 4:9; Odes 5:17.

[71] See also Isa 26:17; 37:3; Jer 22:23; Odes 5:17; *Pss. Sol.* 3:9; *T. Job* 18:4.

[72] For refs. see BDAG & MM s.v.

such imagery in a predominately andro-centric culture. He finds a multifaceted use of the image to depict intense, helpless, productive and cyclical pain.[73] Its appeal may well be the fact that it can be used broadly as a metaphor with which everyone can identify, even if not experience first-hand (134). Gempf argues rightly that in 1 Thess 5:3, Paul uses the pangs of childbirth as a metaphor for helplessness in the face of judgment. In this sense, there is no thought (or joy) of a coming child, but rather, only a negative sense of suffering and destruction (124–126).

The concluding phrase of 1 Thess 5:1–3, καὶ οὐ μὴ ἐκφύγωσιν (v. 3e), again refers to outsiders. In this instance it is the day of the Lord that outsiders will not escape. Otherwise, the verb is used of being unable to escape God,[74] judgment,[75] sin[76] and darkness (Job 15:30). The parallel text in Luke 21:34–36 uses ἐκφυγεῖν with quite a different implication, for there insiders are exhorted to keep watch, δεόμενοι ἵνα κατισχύσητε ἐκφυγεῖν ταῦτα πάντα τὰ μέλλοντα γίνεσθαι (v. 36). A positive formulation is also found in cases of escaping illness or death (2 Macc 9:22; 3 Macc 6:29). But the combination of being able/unable to escape childbirth is exceedingly rare. In Isa 66:7, the writer refers to the escape of childbirth even before the onset of labour pangs. Otherwise, the combination occurs only in a papyrus letter, provenance unknown, which is reproduced in *NewDocs* 9 (see Llewelyn 2002a, 57–58).[77] The letter is written by a mother to her children and offers insight into the fear and apprehension associated with childbirth during that time. The letter makes it clear that the mother considered her daughter's life in danger; she prayed daily to the gods for her daughter's sake (57, lines 8–9). The report of a successful birth is understood as an "escape" (ἐκφυγεῖν, line 10). Llewelyn draws a parallel to 1 Thess 5:3 (58), where the physical danger and apprehension associated with childbirth is now an analogy for the destruction coming on those who say "peace and security",[78] or better, on those who identify with Roman rule. Only this time, unlike the daughter in the letter whose escape occasions great joy (see 57, lines 10–12), Paul makes it unmistakably clear to his readers that there is no escape from the day of the Lord.

5. By way of summarising the results of the analysis so far, it is worth considering, even if only in a preliminary way, why a *topos* on the times and the seasons is at all relevant for the Jesus-followers in Thessalonica. Or to put it another way: regardless of whether the Thessalonians asked about the topic or whether Paul raises it of his own accord, how does it fit into historical reconstructions of the Thessalonian

---

[73] Gempf (1994) offers numerous references in the ancient literature to support these emphases.

[74] 2 Macc 6:26; Tob 13:2.

[75] 2 Macc 7:35; 4 Macc 9:32; *Pss. Sol.* 15:8; Rom 2:3; Heb 12:25.

[76] Prov 10:19; cf. 12:13; Sir 16:13.

[77] Apparently, there are no other instances of the combination: "Though one can speak of escaping death or illness, there is no other documentary evidence, as far as I am aware, that uses ἐκφεύγω of childbirth" (Llewelyn 2002a, 58).

[78] It is (interesting) coincidence that the letter contains a reference to ἀσφαλῶς (57, lines 16–17), but in a different context compared to Paul's use of ἀσφάλεια.

ekklēsia of the first century? I previously argue that First Thessalonians is a letter written to a community in conflict. The sources of this conflict are many, but the immediate context indicates (1 Thess 4:13–18) that the problem of death is the most pressing issue to which Paul writes. This is confirmed by the similarities in structure between 4:13–18 and 5:1–11 (Johanson 1987, 129–130). In particular, both pericopes conclude with very similar statements (including παρακαλεῖν). There is no inconsistency in translation, when ὥστε παρακαλεῖτε ἀλλήλους (4:18a) is translated, "therefore comfort each other", and διὸ παρακαλεῖτε ἀλλήλους (5:11a) is translated, "therefore encourage each other", first because both nuances are equally possible (see BDAG s.v.), and second, because Paul's emphasis in each pericope is different. In 4:13–18, Paul deliberately addresses the *topos* of death, and comforts and reassures the community. In 5:1–11, he leaves behind literal occurrences of death and addresses the situation both negatively and positively. In the first three verses, the emphasis is on the negative aspect of his pattern of exhortation. I suggest, therefore, that Paul continues to address the problem of death among community members, but only in an indirect way.

When Paul refers to the times and the seasons, and to the day of the Lord, he addresses the question of when the *parousia* of the Lord will occur (Harrison 2002, 72). It is quite natural for this question to come up, especially since Paul has just finished portraying a vivid hope even in the face of death. I can imagine the Jesus-followers in Thessalonica asking: "When is it that we will be with the Lord?" (see 4:17; 5:10). The question stems from a social concern and has nothing to do with the so-called "delay of the *parousia*" (see Koester 1990, 454; *contra* Richard 1995, 249). Despite the impression that Paul only refers to *how* the Lord will come, he also addresses the *when* question. No one knows when the day of the Lord will come because it comes unexpectedly, indeed, like a thief in the night. Paul asserts that the Thessalonians already know this accurately. The use of εἰδέναι (5:2a) here is to be understood according to Malbon's analysis (see above, §III.a.2); in no way does Paul indicate that he had previously presented a Jesus-saying on the coming of the Son of Man, much less that the Thessalonians had an inadequate understanding of the saying and that Paul seeks to correct this (*contra* Kim 2002a, 238–239). With regard to the reference to ἀκριβῶς, Malherbe (2000, 289) may well be correct to draw attention to the Danielic use of the adjectival and verbal forms (cf. Dan 2:45; 7:16) although the context of "accurate" interpretations of visions may not be as closely related to Paul's text as he suggests. The adverb, and its cognates, is widely used[79] in a number of contexts such that I do not think anything can be made of it (for illustrative references, see MM s.v.), except perhaps to draw attention to other references which also contain a time element (Matt 2:8, 16; Luke 1:3). Paul offers a syntactical structure which develops his answer to when the day of the Lord will come (ὅταν ... τότε; vv. 3a, c) although the present subjunctive, λέγωσιν (v. 3a), can be misleading. It is not as though sudden destruction comes only and

[79] It is not used by Paul; see Eph 5:15.

literally "when they say…", although the impersonal verb makes it clear that it is outsiders who receive the eschatological *Vernichtung* (see Konradt 2003, 144). Yet the contingency of Paul's formulation invites his readers to interpret the motif of the day of the Lord as contemporary judgment (Hendrix 1991, 111; Tellbe 2001, 125–126), and the political overtones of the slogan "peace and security" drive home the relevance of the day in the social life of community members. If anything, Paul further heightens expectations of the *parousia* and therefore develops the symbolism of the day of the Lord as a powerful rhetorical platform for exhortation.

Such an interpretation of 1 Thess 5:1–3 prepares the way for understanding Paul's other references to "the day" in the pericope (vv. 4c, 5b, 8a). Thus, there is no tension regarding Paul's designation of community members as υἱοὶ ἡμέρας (v. 5b), because that "day" is realised in the present both in the metaphor of battle and in the presence of faith, love and hope (v. 8; Koester 1997, 163; Popkes 2002, 854). But more will be said about these issues in the analysis of those verses (below).

b. Eschatological *Paraenesis* (5:4–10)

1. The eschatological *paraenesis*, as I have described the bulk of the remainder of 1 Thess 5:1–11, contains numerous hortatory subjunctive verbs to impart a forceful and sustained exhortation. Although ἡμεῖς δέ (v. 8a) constitutes a structural break in this unit, the analysis of verses 8–10 is included with the preceding verses because in them Paul continues his exhortation to sobriety. As has already been noted, there are several changes of person throughout the pericope. First, the change to the second person in verses 4–5b is in contrast (δέ, v. 4a) to the third person of verse 3. Then there is the change to the first person in verses 5c–10. In this way, Paul offers a transition between the negative judgment statements of verse 3 and the positive exhortative statements of verses 5–10, and at the same time extends the metaphor of the day of the Lord. Now the "day" is used somewhat synonymously with "light" as a contrast to "darkness" and "night". Paul's pattern of exhortation is characterised by numerous rhetorical pairs,[80] many of which are constituent of eschatological imagery.

In the analysis of 1 Thess 5:4–10, I offer concise investigations of these pairs: day/night and light/darkness (§III.b.2); awake/asleep and sober/drunk (§III.b.3). The last pair, salvation/*orgē*, is discussed in conjunction with the formulaic statements in verses 9–10. The results of these investigations are informative for understanding the eschatological *paraenesis* of the pericope and how it applies to the Thessalonian *ekklēsia*. Then there is a concluding comment on the traditional background discussion as it pertains to the soldier imagery in verse 8 (§III.b.4). Finally, I draw

[80] For a list of these pairs, set out according to the two groups, οἱ λοιποί and ὑμεῖς/ἡμεῖς/ἀδελφοί, see Focant 1990, 353.

attention to the problematic use of γρηγορεῖν and καθεύδειν (v. 10b) and show how Paul uses eschatological motifs to reinforce his pattern of exhortation (§III.b.5).

2. The first two rhetorical pairs are palpably connected, for it is usually "light" during the "day" and "dark" during the "night".[81] As such, the imagery would have been readily understood (Best 1972, 209). Paul asserts that his brothers and sisters in Thessalonica are not "in darkness" (ἐν σκότει, v. 4b) so that the day shall catch them unawares as a thief.[82] He provides an explanation for his confidence in them; it is because they are "sons of light" and "sons of the day" (vv. 5a, b), not of the night nor of darkness (vv. 5c, d).[83] The dualistic images of light and darkness are common in the NT as they (phenomenologically) are everywhere (see Ritt 1993, 447). Their well-known and extensive use in the ancient world has been documented elsewhere.[84] Paul does not use φώς very often,[85] and when he does, the term usually refers to a conversion context (Rom 2:19; 2 Cor 4:6),[86] or to exhortations of Christian living (Rom 13:12; 2 Cor 6:14).[87] The opposite term, σκότος, has no special significance in Paul's letters and reflects common Jewish use. Other than the references just cited in relation to φώς, Paul uses the term elsewhere only in 1 Cor 4:5,[88] which incorporates the notion of judgment on "things hidden in darkness" (τὰ κρυπτὰ τοῦ σκότους). The overt eschatological connection, however, lies with the day/night pair (Conzelmann 1971, 442). The question of whether ἡμέρα is used consistently or means different things (cf. 1 Thess 5:4c, 5b, 8a) is dealt with shortly in connection with the distinctive phrase, υἱοὶ ἡμέρας (v. 5b; see below). The references to νύξ go beyond a simple antonymic definition. Paul does not use it as a literal description of the day of the Lord, as in Joel 2:2 (cf. Amos 5:18, 20), but rather as a figurative image of judgment (see Conzelmann 1974a, 322); it is symbolic of death.[89] Such an association (a.k.a. κοιμᾶσθαι in 1 Thess 4:13b) was

---

[81] That is, unless a person lives in the extremes of north (Arctic Circle) or south (Antarctic Circle), which Paul did not!

[82] The textual variation, κλέπτας, instead of κλέπτης in v. 4c is found in several manuscripts (see NA[27]; Zimmer 1893, 66). Förster's thesis (1916; see similarly Frame 1912, 184; Milligan 1908, 66), that Paul is referring to those who will be caught like thieves is unsustainable (Preisker 1965, 756).

[83] For a connection between thieves and the night, see Euripides *Iph. taur.* 1025–1026. In the play, Iphigeneia asks: ὃς δὲ σκότον λαβόντες ἐκσωθείμεν ἄν; to which Orestes replies: κλέπτων γὰρ ἡ νὺξ τῆς δ᾽ ἀληθείας τό φῶς.

[84] For example, see Aalen 1951; Conzelmann 1971; 1974a; Delling 1964b; 1967a; Hackenberg 1993; Lövestam 1963, 8–24; P.-G. Müller 1991; Ritt 1993; Trilling 1991.

[85] Cf. φωστήρ in Phil 2:15; φωτισμός in 2 Cor 4:4, 6.

[86] See also *Jos. Asen.* 8:9.

[87] See also the apocalyptic reference to Satan as an ἄγγελος φωτός (2 Cor 11:14); cf. Eph 5:8*bis*, 9, 13, 14; Col 1:12.

[88] Cf. σκοτίζεσθαι in Rom 1:21; 11:10; cf. also Eph 5:11; 6:12; Col 1:13.

[89] Cf. Plutarch *Mor.* 296A, B; *IGUR* 1154 (in *NewDocs* 4, 149); *T. Ash.* 5:2–3. Williams describes the dangers of life in the city after dark (1999, 8).

probably not lost on Paul's readers, but it is clear that Paul only applies νύξ and σκότος to outsiders (5:5c, d).[90]

As part of his use of the day/night and light/darkness imagery, Paul employs the Jewish traditional formulation, "sons of … light" (υἱοὶ φωτός, v. 5a) and "… day" (υἱοὶ ἡμέρας, v. 5b), although the latter phrase appears to be coined by Paul himself (Best 1972, 210). Paul probably understood υἱοὶ φωτός and υἱοὶ ἡμέρας synonymously (Bruce 1982, 111). The Hebraistic formulation is well represented in the Pauline literature,[91] but whether its provenance is purely from LXX use, or also by analogy in the Greek language, is immaterial here.[92] What is important is that Paul uses the phrases to identify his readers as insiders in contrast to outsiders; as such the construction is a genitive of quality (*GNTG* vol. 3, 207–208; vol. 4, 90). The predicate use of νυκτός (v. 5c) and σκότους (v. 5d; sc. υἱοί) is clearly related (BDF 89, §162[6]). The compressed language is quite ambiguous, since υἱοὶ φωτός could be translated "lightful sons", "enlightened sons", "sons who dwell in the light" or "sons characterised by light", only to name some of the alternatives. Due to the strong contrast in 1 Thess 5, and the emotive force associated with the theme of "sonship", the latter translation is probably closest to Paul's intention (*GGBB* 79–81). There is an emphasis on community solidarity such that Paul emphasises that all members of the Thessalonian *ekklēsia* are sons of light and sons of the day (see πάντες, v. 5a; Best 1972, 210). Even the faint-hearted (ὀλιγόψυχοι, v. 14) are included (Frame 1912, 184).

The inherent dualism of the light/darkness imagery is abundantly illustrated in the apocalyptic literature,[93] but, perhaps suprisingly, υἱοὶ φωτός and its parallel τέκνα φωτός, are not nearly so well attested. Besides the references in Luke 16:8, John 12:36 and Eph 5:8, the phrases occur nowhere else in the NT or LXX.[94] There certainly is no technical meaning here (Conzelmann 1974a, 345). Although there are a few gnostic references these appear in an entirely different context.[95]

---

[90] This, despite the fact that "night" is not generally associated with "death" in the OT, NT or Rabbinic literature (Daube 1968, 629–630).

[91] See υἱοὶ θεοῦ (Rom 8:14, 19; Gal 3:26; cf. τέκνα [τοῦ] θεοῦ, Rom 8:16, 21; Rom 9:8; Gal 2:15); υἱοὶ θεοῦ ζῶντος (Rom 9:26, quotation of Hos 2:1); υἱοὶ Ἰσραήλ (Rom 9:27, quotation of Isa 10:22; 2 Cor 3:7, 13); υἱοὶ Ἀβραάμ (Gal 3:7; cf. Ἀβραὰμ πάντες τέκνα, Rom 9:7); τὰ τέκνα τῆς σαρκός and τὰ τέκνα τῆς ἐπαγγελίας (Rom 9:8; cf. Gal 4:28); τὰ τέκνα τῆς ἐρήμου (Gal 4:27); cf. υἱοὶ τῆς ἀπειθείας (Eph 2:2; 5:6; cf. Col 3:6?); υἱοὶ τῶν ἀνθρώπων (Eph 3:5); τέκνα ὀργῆς (Eph 2:3); τέκνα φωτός (Eph 5:8). The singular formulation also occurs in Paul: ὁ υἱὸς τῆς παιδίσκης (Gal 4:30; cf. v. 31); ὁ υἱὸς τῆς ἐλευθέρας (Gal 4:30); cf. υἱὸς τῆς ἀπωλείας (2 Thess 2:3).

[92] *GGNT* 496; *GNTG* vol. 2, 441; MM 649; "… this construction is probably a Hebraism in the main, but would not appear barbaric" (BDAG 1025, §2.c.β).

[93] For example, see *T. Levi* 19:1; *T. Jos.* 20:2; *1 En.* 41:8; 108:11–15; *T. Job* 43:6.

[94] Kuhn comments (in the English summary of his paper): "… there is no clear evidence that the expression 'children of light' is used in any early Jewish writings other than the Qumran library. To the best of my knowledge, this genetive [*sic*] construction also does not appear in the rabbinic literature. In fact, apart from Gnosis, i.e. Gnosticism, only the texts from the Qumran library offer any extra-Christian parallels. This is not usually recognized clearly enough" (1992, 341).

[95] See for example, NHC II,*4*,97,13–14; V,*3*,25,17–18; VII,*3*,78,25–26; XIII,*1*,37,19–20.

In contrast, the extensive parallels in the Qumran literature are much nearer in context to Paul's use (Kuhn 1992, 352; Reicke 1988, 94). The Community Rule wastes no time laying down an imperative of loving all "sons of light" and hating all "sons of darkness" (1QS 1:9–10).[96] Those who enter the community duplicitously shall be cut off from the "sons of light" (2:16). Behind this dualism is the apocalyptic distinction between the "Prince of light" who rules the "children of righteousness" and the "Angel of Darkness" who rules the "children of injustice" (3:20); the "spirits of light and darkness" further distinguish the two groups (3:24–25).[97] The "master" instructs the "sons of light" with regard to these spirits (3:13–15). Indeed, the metaphor of the two spirits plays an important role of exhortation in the community, and the ways of each are explicitly enumerated (see 1QS 4). It is significant that in the Community Rule, the phrases "sons of light" and "sons of heaven" are associated with an election motif (1QS 3:15; 4:22), which is an additional parallel to 1 Thess 5:9 (Kuhn 1992, 348). Similarly, Paul's reference to the putting on of armour (5:8) may have as its background the numerous references to war between the "sons of light" and the "sons of darkness" (1QM 1:1–5, 6, 10–15; 3:7, 9; 13:15; 14:16). This possibility is strengthened by further parallels to 1 Thess 5:

> ... [for the sons] of darkness there shall be no escape. [The sons of righteous]ness shall shine over all the ends of the earth; they shall go on shining until all the seasons of darkness are consumed and, at the season appointed by God, His exalted greatness shall shine eternally to the peace, blessing, glory, joy, and long life of all the sons of light (1QM 1:6–8; transl. by Vermes 1995, 125).

Despite the similarities between 1 Thess 5:8 and Isa 59:17, the extensive and relevant nature of the parallels to 1QS and 1QM is impressive.

Getting back to 1 Thess 5:5, it is impossible to escape the conclusion that Paul uses υἱοὶ φωτός and υἱοὶ ἡμέρας in a similar way to the Qumran community (Koester 1990, 450–451). The War Scroll, in particular, emphasises a definitive separation between the "sons of light" and the "sons of darkness". The identities of each group are characterised by their differences, especially with regard to their respective destinies. Thus, rhetoric of a contemporary war merges, in an anticipatory way, with the rhetoric of a final war (Conzelmann 1974a, 326).[98] This leads to the question of how Paul's use of ἡμέρα in 1 Thess 5:4c, 5b and 8a, relates to the day of the Lord (v. 2b). In the first place, Paul's repetition of the phrase, ὡς κλέπτης (v. 4c; cf. v. 2b), clearly indicates that the reference to "day" in verse 4 is still to the day of the Lord. However, the phrase, ἐν σκότει (v. 4b), immediately preceding this reference, shows that Paul alludes as well to the double connotation of ἡμέρα, to the day of the Lord and to daylight (Malherbe 2000, 294). Thus, Paul

[96] The formulation "sons of light" also appears in 4Q174 1:8–9; 4Q510 1:6–7; cf. 4Q544.

[97] Cf. the "company of Satan" and the "company of God" in 1QM 13:5.

[98] See references to the "day of vengeance" (1QM 7:6), "battle of God" (9:6; 15:13) and "day of revenge" (15:3, 6, 15); cf. also 1QM 17:1–9.

uses the motif in a transitional way (Lövestam 1963, 48). Then in verse 5, ἡμέρα is wholly subsumed by the dualistic images of day/night and light/darkness, which he expresses chiastically. The tension between a description of the Thessalonian *ekklēsia* as υἱοὶ ἡμέρας and the identification of this "day" as referring to the day of the Lord is resolved by remembering that this pericope is above all, eschatological *paraenesis*. This is made unmistakeably clear by the way Paul proceeds, especially with his use of ἄρα οὖν (v. 6a), and the presence of numerous hortatory subjunctives (vv. 6–8a). But unlike Lövestam (1963, 51), who offers an unusually clear discussion of how to interpret the reference to ἡμέρα in verse 5 (48–53), I do not use the adjective "eschatological" to refer to a future time, such that the day is somehow *literally* associated with the *parousia* of the Lord. Indeed, such a literal association misunderstands Paul's employment of eschatological images.[99] It is important to distinguish between the phenomenological expectation inherent of eschatological imagery – the *parousia* of the Lord and the day of the Lord – and the significant rhetorical impact of Paul's *paraenesis* on his readers.[100] By including the singular phrase, υἱοὶ ἡμέρας, Paul cleverly incorporates the eschatological image of the day of the Lord into his pattern of exhortation. In so doing, he brings to bear a powerful and negative (judgment) image onto the social situation of the Thessalonians but inverses it. They escape the destruction of the day of the Lord precisely because they belong to the day. Such a reading of 1 Thess 5:5 makes it unnecessary to resort to comments about "eschatological completion" (*contra* Plevnik 1979, 80) or "eschatological condition" (*contra* Collins 1984, 167), neither of which means much of anything.[101] In conclusion, Paul employs day/night and light/darkness imagery to effectively heighten the contrast between insiders and outsiders and therefore buttress community identity and existence (deSilva 1996, 66). The change of person between verses 5b and 5c further serves to reinforce Paul's own solidarity with the community by invoking the imitation motif (Watson 1999, 76–77). Although the Qumran references are far more hostile in outlook, the motifs there serve a similar function (Wanamaker 1990, 182). The eschatological *paraenesis* forces an equally eschatological decision (indicative-imperative; cf. Rom 13:12–14), and as such, emphasises the importance of holy living.[102]

3. The second set of rhetorical pairs, awake/asleep and sober/drunk, is governed by the inferential and transitional phrase, ἄρα οὖν (v. 6a), which introduces a series of hortatory subjunctive verbs: καθεύδωμεν (v. 6a), γρηγορῶμεν (v. 6b), νήφωμεν (v. 6b; cf. v. 8a). The question of why Paul uses καθεύδειν instead of κοιμᾶσθαι (cf. 4:13b, c, 15e) is important, especially with regard to the problematical use of

[99] Thus, there is no need to distinguish between "light" as present and "day" as future, a distinction which is not supported by the text (*contra* Lövestam 1963, 52).

[100] Nicholl fails to recognise this distinction and attempts, at some length, to establish the future temporal connotation of the "day" in verse 5 (2004, 58–59).

[101] Nor is it less ambigiuous to refer to the "provisional" status of being sons of the day (*contra* Witherington 2006, 148).

[102] P.-G. Müller 1991, 482; see Chapter 5, §III.c.3; see also *T. Levi* 19:1; *T. Benj.* 5:3.

καθεύδειν in verse 10b. The primary issue there, is whether καθεύδειν is to be understood as referring to vigilance (as opposed to indolence), or to death (as opposed to being alive; see §III.b.5, below). More pertinent to the discussion here is the semantic range signified by καθεύδειν and, subsequently, how Paul uses it in verses 6a and 7b. Paul only uses the verb in this pericope so there is no possibility of establishing a customary definition.[103] Elsewhere in the NT and LXX, καθεύδειν is used literally (i.e. to cease to be awake),[104] and metaphorically as a figurative extension, to refer to indolence,[105] to sexual relations (Gen 39:10; Jdt 4:14) and to refer to death.[106]

The pairing of καθεύδειν with γρηγορεῖν (and νήφειν) confirms that Paul refers to the figurative extension of indolence in 1 Thess 5:6a. The motif of being awake or keeping watch is rare in Paul (1 Cor 16:13; cf. Col 4:2) but common in the Synoptics.[107] LXX references to γρηγορεῖν are sparse.[108] Nützel observes that the figurative sense, "be alert" or "be vigilant" (extended from the literal sense of "not sleeping"), is predominant in the NT, and appears in several well defined contexts, including being prepared for the *parousia* of the Lord (or the Son of Man) and being watchful for negative developments in the *ekklēsia* (1990, 265). In contrast, νήφειν appears hardly at all in the biblical tradition,[109] although it is well represented in antiquity to express literally, "sobriety", and figuratively, "self-control".[110] The NT use is quite narrow (n.b. references in Philo are not particularly relevant),[111] and refers to the predicament of being a Jesus-follower, with associated imperatives (see Bauernfeind 1967, 938–939). Paul clearly refers to μεθύσκεσθαι and μεθύειν

[103] There is also a reference in Eph 5:14, ἔγειρε, ὁ καθεύδων, καὶ ἀνάστα ἐκ τῶν νεκρῶν, καὶ ἐπιφαύσει σοι ὁ Χριστός, where the term is used to refer to vigilance. This is made clear by the remainder of the verse and also by the following exhortations (Edgar 1979, 348; followed by Howard 1985, 338 n. 4).

[104] Gen 28:13; 1 Kgdms 3:2, 3, 5*bis*, 6, 9; 19:9; 26:5*bis*, 7*bis*; 2 Kgdms 4:5, 6, 7; 12:3; 3 Kgdms 18:27; 1 Esd 3:6; 4:11; Prov 3:24; 6:22; Cant 5:2; Ezek 4:9; Dan 4:10; Amos 6:4; Jonah 1:5; Sir 22:9; Tob 8:13; Matt 8:24 (par. Mark 4:38); Matt 13:25; 25:5; 26:40 (par.), 43, 45; Mark 4:27. For further refs. to the literal use, see BDAG & LSJ s.v.; Jackson 1996, 20–29; Oepke 1965, 431–432.

[105] Isa 51:20; Mark 13:36; Eph 5:14; for further refs., see Oepke 1965, 432.

[106] Ps 87:6 (LXX); Dan 12:2 (cf. 12:2θ; Matt 9:18, 23–24 (par.); cf. Homer *Il.* 14.482–483; Aeschylus *Cho.* 906; Sophocles *Oed. col.* 621–622; Plato *Apol.* 40c, d; *EG* 559.7–8. These texts are reproduced in full, in §III.b.5, below.

[107] Matt 24:42 (par.), 43; 25:13; 26:38 (par.), 40 (par.), 41 (par.); Mark 13:34, 37; Luke 12:37; cf. Acts 20:31; 1 Pet 5:8; Rev 3:3, 4; 16:15.

[108] 2 Esd 17:3; Jer 5:6; 38:28*bis*; Lam 1:14; Dan 9:14θ; Bar 2:9; 1 Macc 12:27; *Pss. Sol.* 3:2.

[109] See *Let. Aris.* 209; 2 Tim 4:5; 1 Pet 1:13; 4:7; 5:8; cf. ἐκνήφειν in Gen 9:24; 1 Kgdms 25:37; Joel 1:5; Hab 2:7, 19; Sir 31:2; 1 Cor 15:34.

[110] See BDAG & LSJ s.v.; Bauernfeind 1967. Horsley (1982b, 69) observes a parallel use of νήφειν in a private letter, with a figurative meaning of "self-control" (see 66, line 37 for the text).

[111] But see, for example, Philo *Somn.* 2.160–161: ... τῷ γὰρ ὄντι ὁ μὴ τὴν δι' οἴνου μέθην μᾶλλον ἢ τὴν δι' ἀφροσύνης ἐπιτηδεύων, ὀρθότητι καὶ ἐγρηγόρσει δυσχεραίνων, ὥσπερ οἱ κοιμώμενοι καταβέβληται καὶ παρεῖται καὶ καταμέμυκε τὰ τῆς ψυχῆς ὄμματα, οὐδὲν εὔθ' ὁρᾶν οὔτ' ἀκούειν τῶν θέας καὶ ἀκοῆς ἀξίων οἷός τε ὤν· ("For indeed he who gives way to the intoxication which is of folly rather than of wine bears a grudge against upright standing and wakefulness, and lies prostrate and sprawling like sleepers with the eyes of his soul closed, unable to see or hear aught that is worth seeing or hearing" [Colson/Whitaker 1929–1962]).

(1 Thess 5:7b) as literal antonyms to νήφειν, where the former verb is the process, "become drunk", of the latter state, "be drunk" (BDAG s.v.).[112] However, it is doubtful whether a real distinction between the verbs can be maintained (MM 394), although μεθύσκεσθαι appears in the NT only in the passive voice.[113] The purpose of verse 7 is to emphasise the contemporary aspect of the exhortations to vigilance and sobriety (v. 6). It is surely significant that the comparative phrase, ὡς οἱ λοιποί (v. 6a; cf. 4:13d), appears here. The subtle link to κοιμᾶσθαι in 1 Thess 4:13 raises the possibility that Paul uses καθεύδειν not only as a negative exhortation against indolence, but also as a reminder that the Thessalonians do not sleep the sleep of death as those who have no hope (οἱ μὴ ἔχοντες ἐλπίδα, 4:13d). This possiblity hinges on the acceptance of καθεύδειν as referring, figuratively, to the sleep of death. And there are enough ancient references to such a use that, despite whatever problems commentators have with such an interpretation of καθεύδειν in verse 10, it must be allowed here as a possibility. In terms of a positive exhortation, the Thessalonians are to maintain hope (see vv. 8c, 9b) precisely by keeping awake and being sober.

In 1 Thess 5:6–7, Paul offers a provocative statement of Christian living, summarised in a few words of eschatological *paraenesis*. Just as the day of the Lord is one of the more important motifs in 1 Thess 5:1–8, so too is the motif of "night" (Best 1972, 212). The Thessalonian *ekklēsia* is not of the night (v. 5c), and this quite naturally invokes, for Paul, the metaphor of sleeping. The unusual terminology here implies that he is relying, at least indirectly, on traditional material.[114] This is particularly evident in the connection between sleeping and watching, as found in the synoptic references given above.[115] Both γρηγορεῖν and νήφειν have multifaceted associations with Paul's pattern of exhortation. Thus, insiders are not surprised by the day of the Lord. Instead, they are watching for that day. Likewise, insiders are not sleeping, nor indolent. They do not sleep the sleep of death as others

[112] For an example of the contrast between drunkenness and sobriety, see Plutarch *Mor.* 781D: ὁ δ' Ἐπαμεινώνδας, εἰς ἑορτήν τινα καὶ πότον ἀνειμένως τῶν Θηβαίων ῥυέντων, μόνος ἐφώδευε τὰ ὅπλα καὶ τὰ τείχη, νήφειν λέγων καὶ ἀγρυπνεῖν ὡς ἂν ἐξῇ τοῖς ἄλλοις μεθύειν καὶ καθεύδειν ("Epameinondas, when all the Thebans crowded to a certain festival and gave themselves up utterly to drink, went alone and patrolled the armouries and the walls, saying that he was keeping sober and awake that the others might be free to be drunk and asleep" [Babbitt 1927–1976]), although here the synonym ἀγρυπνεῖν (instead of γρηγορεῖν) is used; see also *Cor. Herm.* 1.27: Ὦ λαοί, ἄνδρες γηγενεῖς, οἱ μέθῃ καὶ ὕπνῳ ἑαυτοὺς ἐκδεδωκότες καὶ τῇ ἀγνωσίᾳ τοῦ θεοῦ, νήψατε, παύσασθε δὲ κραιπαλῶντες καὶ θελγόμενοι ὕπνῳ ἀλόγῳ ("Hearken, ye folk, men born of earth, who have given yourselves up to drunkenness and sleep in your ignorance of God; awake to soberness, cease to be sodden with strong drink and lulled in sleep devoid of reason" [Scott 1968]).

[113] Luke 12:45; John 2:10; Eph 5:18; 1 Thess 5:7; Rev 17:2. For μεθύειν in the NT, see Matt 24:49; Acts 2:15; 1 Cor 11:21; 1 Thess 5:7; Rev 17:6. For LXX and other refs., see Preisker 1967, 545–547.

[114] Yoder-Neufeld draws attention to the use of καθεύδειν and μεθύειν to identify those who are under judgment (see Isa 19:14; 24:20; 28:1, 3, 7–8; 29:9, 10; 51:17, 21–22; 63:3, 6; 65:11; Joel 1:5; Amos 6:4) as part of the cosmic drama of the divine warrior's intervention (1997, 82–83).

[115] Wenham 1995, 308–311; cf. Best 1972, 211–212; Wanamaker 1990, 184. The association holds despite the reservations put forward by Tuckett (1990, 169–170).

who have no hope. Instead, they are alert, and wakeful, and are exhorted to live accordingly. Finally, insiders belong to the day, because they are sons of light and sons of the day, and therefore they are exhorted to sobriety, or self-control (v. 8a). Paul emphasises the contrast between insiders and outsiders by referring, literally, to the activities of the latter: they sleep and get drunk (v. 7). But even here the figurative extensions of the motifs are present (see Wanamaker 1990, 185). Readings of this verse which refer to prohibitions of Christians sleeping until the *parousia* of the Lord, or to prohibitions against inbibation of wine (οἶνος), are eisegetical in nature (see for example, Jewett 1986, 190). Similarly, Lövestam's interpretation of νύξ as a metaphor for "the present age", where the children of light live "in the time of the prevailing night" (1963, 54), is an over-interpretation of the motif. The night is no more present than the day is future. In so saying, however, there is probably still an apocalyptic notion of the aeons inherent in the rhetorical pair (see Hahn 1975a, 421), although see Rom 13:12 (Jewett 2007, 821). Paul merely uses both motifs, metaphorically, as negative and positive elements of his eschatological *paraenesis*.

4. Paul returns to the motif of sobriety, or self-control in verse 8, and appears to continue the exhortations left off in verse 6. As I indicated in the preliminary examination of the verse's structure (see §II.a.3 above), νήφειν is complemented with two adverbial participles. Paul exhorts the Thessalonian converts to be sober because they belong to the day. This is the last reference to the "day" in 1 Thess 5:1–11, and here, more than ever, the contemporaneous quality comes to the fore: the Thessalonians are exhorted to act out the day through the metaphor of battle. Despite the presence of faith, love and hope, the Thessalonians are still undergoing considerable affliction. Therefore, such soldier imagery in verse 8 reinterprets, in eschatological language, the social, political and theological realities of being a Jesus-follower and serves to augment Paul's positive pattern of exhortation. The use of the aorist participle, ἐνδυσάμενοι, of antecedent action, does not necessarily refer to conversion or baptism (*contra* Paulsen 1990, 452; rightly, Best 1998, 591). Wanamaker (1990, 185–186) suggests that finer details like this may be irrelevant for the use of the imagery here.

Paul alludes to Isa 59:17, which reads in part:

> καὶ ἐνεδύσατο δικαιοσύνην ὡς θώρακα καὶ περιέθετο περικεφαλαίαν σωτηρίου ἐπὶ τῆς κεφαλῆς καὶ περιεβάλετο ἱμάτιον ἐκδικήσεως.

The two texts contain a number of similarities, including ἐνδύεσθαι, θώραξ, περικεφαλαία and σωτηρία.[116] Paul's use of the triadic formula (cf. 1 Thess 1:3), πίστις, ἀγάπη and ἐλπίς (σωτηρίας) in place of δικαιοσύνη and σωτήριον is awkward because of the disproportionate elements in the trito-Isaian text. The context of judgment is shared between the texts, although in trito-Isaiah God dons the armour

[116] Cf. ἐνδυσάμενοι τὸν θώρακα τῆς δικαιοσύνης (Eph 6:14); τὴν περικεφαλαίαν τοῦ σωτηρίου (Eph 6:17); cf. also Wis 5:18–23.

as an act of war/judgment whereas in First Thessalonians it is those who belong to the day that put on armour (Kreitzer 1987, 126–128). There are a number of other possible associations which are helpful for understanding Paul's use of the armour motif. In light of the previously identified links to Qumran literature, it is a possibility that Paul also alludes to the battle imagery of that community, despite the lack of a specific parallel to the putting on of armour. There is no doubt that images of armour are relevant for Paul's readers.[117] Donfried observes numismatic evidence in Thessalonica of coins with the helmeted head of Roma on the obverse side. But his suggestion that 1 Thess 5:8 would have invoked associations with the Cabirus wearing a laurel crown, as well as with the importance of crowns in the cult of Dionysus, is dubious (see 1985, 341). Paul uses ἐνδύεσθαι a number of times, of which Rom 13:12 (ἐνδυσώμεθα δὲ τὰ ὅπλα τοῦ φωτός) is the closest parallel to 1 Thess 5:8.[118] He also uses it to refer to putting on (the Lord Jesus) Christ (Rom 13:14; Gal 3:27), and putting on imperishability (ἀφθαρσία) and immortality (ἀθανασία, 1 Cor 15:53, 54).[119] Thompson shows that while the motifs of light and darkness are shared between the Thessalonian and Roman texts, Paul uses the clothing motif in a fundamentally different way in Romans (1991). There, "putting on the armour of light" is subsumed under a more striking concept: ἐνδύσασθε τὸν κύριον Ἰησοῦν Χριστόν (Rom 13:14). Such an act invokes a goal of imitating Christ and ties in well with Paul's exhortations to renewal and transformation (12:1–2).[120] But the context is somewhat different in 1 Thess 5, where Paul uses the motif of putting on armour to describe how the Thessalonian *ekklēsia* is to act out sobriety (*contra* Richard 1995, 254–255). In his monographic study of the "Divine Warrior" motif, Yoder-Neufeld observes that Paul refers to the motif to reinforce identity with associated task (1997, 75). It is not that the Thessalonians are to be ready for battle in relation to the day of the Lord, but that they are to identify themselves with the security and identity afforded to those who wear the armour of the divine warrior (76). Yoder-Neufeld agrees that the day is metaphorical and not entirely future (78–79) such that υἱοὶ ἡμέρας is a designation of contemporaneous reality, but one which does not abrogate the need for exhortation (84). Indeed, the divine warrior motif represents judgment as a divine intervention, with implications for the Thessalonian *ekklēsia* (86). Paul uses the imagery of the divine warrior in Isaiah 59, including various elements of armour, but reapplies those elements with the triad of faith, love and hope. Yoder-Neufeld notes however, that the militancy associated with the motif is not diminished by this reapplication, and the implications of status and task are still present:

[117] See Williams (1999, 220–221) for a detailed description of the armour worn by Roman soldiers.

[118] See also Eph 6:11: ἐνδύσασθε τὴν πανοπλίαν τοῦ θεοῦ.

[119] In addition, see ἐκδύεσθαι (2 Cor 5:3, 4); ἐπενδύεσθαι (2 Cor 5:2, 4); ἀπεκδύεσθαι (Col 2:15; 3:9); ἀπέκδυσις (Col 2:11). The un-compounded form, δύειν, does not appear in the NT.

[120] Jewett 2007, 823; Thompson 1991, 151. See also Thompson's general discussion of the clothing motif in Paul (149–158).

> ... faith, love, and hope are pulled into the picture of the coming of the Divine Warrior as associated with the fearsome day of the Lord. Not only that, these virtues are exercised by a community which puts them on as the armour of *God* (88).

Thus, Paul's motif of sobriety goes beyond specific exhortations to holy living (e.g. 1 Thess 4:3–8; 5:12–22), or to avoid temptations of the flesh (*contra* Fuchs 1965, 361). Rather, Paul refers to a more global dimension in his eschatological *paraenesis*, where the breakdown of justice depicted in Isaiah now augments the social and political context of the Thessalonians (Georgi 1991, 28–30). This interpretation of 1 Thess 5:8 fits well with my thesis that Paul only indirectly addresses the Thessalonians' social disintegration in this pericope. The crisis rhetorically generated by the motif of the day of the Lord is developed by the allusion to trito-Isaiah's divine warrior, and, as I shall show next, heightened by the dichotomous rhetorical pair: salvation/*orgē*.

5. The final two verses of the eschatological *paraenesis* are a continuation of 1 Thess 5:8, where ὅτι (v. 9a) expresses another reason for the Thessalonians to be sober, and ἵνα (v. 10b) expresses the result. In 1 Thess 5:9, Paul uses τιθέναι, a verb he uses a number of times elsewhere,[121] to refer to the destiny of humanity, either to receive *orgē* or σωτηρία (cf. Rom 5:9). The themes of election and calling appear several times in First Thessalonians and cannot be easily passed over here (see Chapter 1, §IV.b). The Thessalonian *ekklēsia* is the object of God's choice (ἐκλογή, 1:4; τιθέναι, 5:9) and calling (καλεῖν, 2:12; 4:7; 5:24). Besides this explicit terminology, Marshall also finds implicit references to election, including concern about the danger of falling away (3:5), and Paul's prayers for the *ekklēsia* (3:10, 11–13), to name only two (see 1990, 259 n. 2). A key question is how Paul uses τιθέναι here. Often, the answer is formulated in exclusive terms of God's choice (before the creation of the world) on those whom he has destined for salvation regardless of human response, or of God's choice as a result of human response to the "good news" (εὐαγγέλιον). Thus, the motifs of election and calling are reduced to the issue of perseverance.[122] But such an approach to this text unduly ignores anthropological considerations, whereby the decision of faith is based on, and made in response to, the proclamation of the λόγος or εὐαγγέλιον.[123] Such a decision is neither lessened by the acknowledgement of the prior (eschatological) occurrence of Jesus' death (5:10) and resurrection (1:10; 4:14), which implicitly includes God's foreknowledge (cf. Rom 8:29–30), nor is it made decisive in the acceptance of the proclamation (cf. Bultmann 1952, 329–330). Rather, for Paul, the eschatological *paraenesis* serves to reinforce the desirability and even necessity

---

[121] Rom 4:17; 9:33; 14:13; 1 Cor 3:10, 11; 9:18; 12:18, 28; 15:25; 16:2; 2 Cor 3:13; 5:19; cf. 1 Tim 1:12; 2:7; 2 Tim 1:11.

[122] On the one side, see esp. Gundry Volf 1990, 21–27; see also Frame 1912, 187–188; Kaye 1975, 51; on the other side, see Marshall 1990.

[123] Paul refers to these terms repeatedly in First Thessalonians; see Chapter 1, §III.2. Maurer comments: "The verb has in view here the point at which God's transcendent decision and man's real existence converge" (1972, 157).

of sobriety, and in so doing, reinforces a transformed community identity — the corporate hope of salvation is expected to be salvation itself. This is expressed by the phrase, εἰς περιποίησιν σωτηρίας (5:9b), where σωτηρίας is an objective genitive (BDAG 804, §2). Such vocabulary is unusual for Paul (περιποίησις only occurs here),[124] but Havener has shown that the phrase εἰς περιποίησιν is used elsewhere in similar contexts (1981, 118–119). The debate over whether "obtain" or "receive" is the better translation, with active and passive nuances, often raises the question of how much human involvement is to be included in the acquisition of salvation (e.g. Gundry Volf 1990, 23–27; followed by Nicholl 2004, 64–65). This question, however, does not reflect the rhetorical purpose of verses 9–10, where Paul offers an explanation for his exhortations. The emphasis on the two destinies, *orgē* for outsiders and salvation for insiders, reinforces an eschatological identity which is no longer based on social or political concerns. Both ὀργή and σωτηρία as significant eschatological terms in First Thessalonians have been discussed elsewhere.[125]

Paul continues the eschatological *paraenesis* with an adverbial phrase of means beginning with διά, which is often used in a stereotypical phrase, διὰ τοῦ κυρίου ἡμῶν Ἰησοῦ Χριστοῦ (v. 9c),[126] and which here introduces another traditional formula: τοῦ ἀποθανόντος ὑπὲρ ἡμῶν (v. 10a). Paul has already referred to what may be called a "resurrection formula" in 1 Thess 1:10 (see Chapter 3, §III.b.5) and a "death and resurrection formula" in 1 Thess 4:14 (see Chapter 5, §III.b.3). In 1 Thess 5:10, Paul uses a "dying formula" most likely adapted from the stereotypical form, Χριστὸς ὑπὲρ ἡμῶν ἀπέθανεν, which includes a reference to Χριστός, the aorist form of ἀποθνῄσκειν and the interpretation of his death as being for someone or something.[127] Kramer notes that the formula is always associated with the title Χριστός (except John 11:51) and leaves open (ὑπὲρ ἡμῶν) whether Christ's death is to be understood as substitution or atonement or both (1966, 26–27). Neither of these terms properly expresses Paul's thought here, and Hooker suggests that "participation" and even "sharing of experiences" are more accurate descriptions of the relationship between Christ and the believer. In particular, the additional outcome of living σὺν αὐτῷ (1 Thess 5:10c) indicates that the interchange expressed here is one-sided with an emphasis on human dependence (1978, 462–463). There is no thought of Christ and the believer changing places (1995, 29). Finally,

[124] Cf. 2 Thess 2:14; Eph 1:14.

[125] On ὀργή, see Chapter 3, §III.b.7; Chapter 4, §III.d.5; on σωτηρία, see Chapter 3, §III.b.6–7; Chapter 4, §III.d.2.

[126] For analysis and discussion, see Kramer 1966, 84–90.

[127] Froitzheim 1979, 31; Wengst 1972, 78; followed by Havener 1981, 116. See Χριστὸς ὑπὲρ (ἡμῶν) ἀπέθανεν (Rom 5:6, 8; 14:15); Χριστὸς ἀπέθανεν ὑπὲρ τῶν ἁμαρτιῶν ἡμῶν (1 Cor 15:3); ὃ (Χριστὸς) ἀπέθανεν (Rom 6:10; 1 Cor 8:11); Χριστὸς (Ἰησοῦς) ὁ ἀποθανών (Rom 8:34); (εἷς) ὑπὲρ πάντων ἀπέθανεν (2 Cor 5:14, 15); Χριστὸς ἀπέθανεν (Gal 2:21). These references show that the textual variation in 1 Thess 5:10, of περί instead of ὑπέρ in a minority of manuscripts, is to be rejected (*contra* de Jonge 1990, 230), despite the fact that περί is probably the more difficult reading (see *GNTG* vol. 1, 105). There is probably not much difference in meaning between the prepositions (BDAG 1031, §A.3; Best 1972, 218). Could the variation be an assimilation to περὶ τῶν κοιμωμένων in 1 Thess 4:13 (so Reese 1980, 215)?

it is unlikely that there is a larger pre-Pauline tradition here, whether similar to the reconstruction of Harnisch (1973, 124), or otherwise.[128] While parts of 1 Thess 5:9–10 are stereotypical, those verses remain essentially Pauline redactions (similarly, Collins 1984, 168–170; Plevnik 1979, 86–87).

The result of this death ὑπὲρ ἡμῶν is expressed in the conclusion of the eschatological *paraenesis*: ἵνα εἴτε γρηγορῶμεν εἴτε καθεύδωμεν ἅμα σὺν αὐτῷ ζήσωμεν (vv. 10b–c). The syntax of this clause is straight forward; rather, it is Paul's choice of vocabulary that is difficult to interpret. As I remarked earlier, the problem rests squarely on the question of how γρηγορεῖν and καθεύδειν are to be understood. If Paul uses the pair of verbs to refer to the categories of being "alive" or "dead" then it is probable that 1 Thess 5:10 alludes to the *topos* of death (1 Thess 4:13–18). The repetition of the marker, ἅμα σὺν (v. 10c; cf. 4:17b), seems to support this allusion. This would mean that regardless of whether the Thessalonians are alive or dead at the *parousia* or the day of the Lord, both will live together with him (sc. the Lord Jesus Christ). But if Paul uses the pair to refer to categories of vigilance or indolence then the significance of the verse changes dramatically. Now Paul refers to the fact that it does not matter whether the Thessalonians are indolent or not, they would still live together with the Lord. That γρηγορεῖν and καθεύδειν are used in a similar way earlier in the pericope (vv. 6, 7) seems to support this view. These alternatives are substantially different and worthy of careful examination in order to determine the significance of the eschatological *paraenesis* in 1 Thess 5:10.

First, the ridiculous claim that καθεύδειν is rarely or never used to refer to death, needs to be put away once and for all. Edgar concedes that the verb is used of death twice in the LXX (Ps 87:6; Dan 12:2), but asserts with regard to the NT: "None of the instances unequivocally refers to physical death" (1979, 348). Hogg and Vine (1929, 172) emphasise that the verb is used of death only once in the NT (Matt 9:24 [par.]). In a weighty article on 1 Thess 5:10, Lautenschlager rejects all references where καθεύδειν alledgedly refers to death. He asserts that in such cases, the context supplies the notion of being dead — it has nothing to do with the metaphorical meaning of the verb (1990, 42). In this way, Lautenschlager reviews Eph 5:14, several synoptic references including Matt 9:24 (par.), Ps 87:6 (LXX), Dan 12:2, and numerous references in the Pseudepigrapha and profane Greek texts including grave inscriptions (43–49). Amongst other conclusions, he states:

> *Nur* κοιμᾶσθαι eignet darüber hinaus der metaphorische Sinn des Todesschlafs. In der *gesamten griechischen Literatur* gibt es m. W. *keinen einzigen Beleg* dafür, daß auch καθεύδειν "tot sein" bzw. "entschlafen" hieße, wohl aber Belege, die diesen Sinn ausschließen (49).[129]

It is widely recognised that καθεύδειν is not well attested for the figurative meaning of death.[130] However, there are a number of references, including the NT, LXX

[128] See extensive critique of Harnisch by Havener 1981, 118–120.

[129] Lautenschlager is followed by Heil 2000, 465.

[130] Oepke's assessment that καθεύδειν "is often used for death" (1965, 435) is misleading, esp. when he is only able to cite two references (rightly pointed out by Edgar 1979, 347).

and extra-biblical literature, which cannot be dismissed altogether. These include at least the following:

Ps 87:5–6 (LXX) προσελογίσθην μετὰ τῶν καταβαινόντων εἰς λάκκον, ἐγενήθην ὡς ἄνθρωπος ἀβοήθητος ἐν νεκροῖς ἐλεύθερος, ὡσεὶ τραυματίαι ἐρριμμένοι καθεύδοντες ἐν τάφῳ, ὧν οὐκ ἐμνήσθης ἔτι καὶ αὐτοὶ ἐκ τῆς χειρός σου ἀπώσθησαν.

Dan 12:2 (cf. 12:2θ) καὶ πολλοὶ τῶν καθευδόντων ἐν τῷ πλάτει τῆς γῆς ἀναστήσονται, οἱ μὲν εἰς ζωὴν αἰώνιον, οἱ δὲ εἰς ὀνειδισμόν, οἱ δὲ εἰς διασπορὰν καὶ αἰσχύνην αἰώνιον.

Matt 9:18, 23–24 (par.) ἰδοὺ ἄρχων εἷς ἐλθὼν προσεκύνει αὐτῷ λέγων ὅτι ἡ θυγάτηρ μου ἄρτι ἐτελεύτησεν· ἀλλὰ ἐλθὼν ἐπίθες τὴν χεῖρά σου ἐπ᾽ αὐτήν, καὶ ζήσεται.

καὶ ἐλθὼν ὁ Ἰησοῦς εἰς τὴν οἰκίαν τοῦ ἄρχοντος καὶ ἰδὼν τοὺς αὐλητὰς καὶ τὸν ὄχλον θορυβούμενον ἔλεγεν· ἀναχωρεῖτε, οὐ γὰρ ἀπέθανεν τὸ κοράσιον ἀλλὰ καθεύδει. καὶ κατεγέλων αὐτοῦ.[131]

Homer *Il.* 14.482–483 φράζεσθ᾽ ὡς ὑμῖν Πρόμαχος δεδμημένος εὕδει[132] ἔγχει ἐμῷ ("Consider how your Promachus sleeps, vanquished by my spear" [Murray 1999]).

Aeschylus *Cho.* 906 ἕπου, πρὸς αὐτὸν τόνδε σὲ σφάξαι θέλω. καὶ ζῶντα γάρ νιν κρείσσον᾽ ἡγήσω πατρός· τούτῳ θανοῦσα ξυγκάθευδ᾽, ἐπεὶ φιλεῖς τὸν ἄνδρα τοῦτον, ὃν δ᾽ ἐχρῆν φιλεῖν στυγεῖς ("Come, this way! By his very side I mean to kill thee. And since, while he lived, thou heldest him better than my father, sleep with him in death, since he is the man thou lovest, but hadst hate for him whom thou wast bound to love" [Smyth 1922–1926]).

Sophocles *Oed. col.* 621–622 ἵν᾽ οὑμὸς εὕδων καὶ κεκρυμμένος νέκυς ψυχρός ποτ᾽ αὐτῶν θερμὸν αἷμα πίεται ("Then shall my dead body, sleeping and buried, cold as it is, drink their warm blood" [Lloyd-Jones 1994–1996]).

Plato *Apol.* 40C, D δυοῖν γὰρ θάτερόν ἐστιν τὸ τεθνάναι· ἢ γὰρ οἷον μηδὲν εἶναι μηδὲ αἴσθησιν μηδεμίαν μηδενὸς ἔχειν τὸν τεθνεῶτα, ἢ κατὰ τὰ λεγόμενα μεταβολή τις τυγχάνει οὖσα καὶ μετοίκησις τῇ ψυχῇ τοῦ τόπου τοῦ ἐνθένδε εἰς ἄλλον τόπον. καὶ εἴτε μηδεμία αἴσθησίς ἐστιν, ἀλλ᾽ οἷον ὕπνος, ἐπειδάν τις καθεύδων μηδ᾽ ὄναρ μηδὲν ὁρᾷ, θαυμάσιον κέρδος ἂν εἴη ὁ θάνατος ("For the state of death is one of two things: either it is virtually nothingness, so that the dead has no consciousness of anything, or it is, as people say, a change and migration of the soul from this to another place. And if it is unconsciousness, like a sleep in which the sleeper does not even dream, death would be a wonderful gain" [Fowler 1914–1935]).

EG 559.7–8 καὶ λέγε Ποπιλίην εὕδειν, ἄνερ· οὐ θεμιτὸν γὰρ θνήσκειν τοὺς ἀγαθούς, ἀλλ᾽ ὕπνον ἡδὺν ἔχειν ("You must say, sir, that Popilia is asleep: for it would not be right for good people to die, but to sleep sweetly" [Lattimore 1962, 59]).

---

[131] There are minor variations in the parallels of this text; it is significant that Luke adds the phrase εἰδότες ὅτι ἀπέθανεν (8:53) as an editorial remark indicating the reason for the crowd's laughter (Howard 1985, 340). Edgar (1979, 348) argues that Jesus could not have used καθεύδειν to refer to death because Jesus would then have said, "she is not dead (ἀποθνήσκειν), but she is dead (καθεύδειν)" (see also France 2002, 239). But this view does not take into account the subtle play on words here, nor that Jesus was indicating that he was about to bring the girl back to life (Davies/Allison 1991, 132; *contra* Lautenschlager 1990, 45). For further discussion of the use of καθεύδειν in Matt 9:24 (par.), see Jackson 1996, 104–107; Luz 2001, 43.

[132] The simple form, εὕδειν, arguably has the same meaning as καθεύδειν (Oepke 1965, 431).

Reconstructing the meaning of καθεύδειν via its associations with such words as ἀποθνήσκειν, νεκρός among others – far from being "der Kardinalfehler bisheriger semantischer Untersuchungen" (Lautenschlager 1990, 42) – is a perfectly acceptable linguistic approach. This has been amply shown by the application of collocational analysis in another context (see Chapter 5, §III.d.8). In drawing attention to these texts, I am by no means suggesting that they decide the question of how Paul uses καθεύδειν in 1 Thess 5:10. But it should be conceded that the sleep of death is within the semantic range of καθεύδειν.

Second, in examinations of 1 Thess 5:10, not enough attention has been paid to the semantic range of γρηγορεῖν. For those commentators who argue that γρηγορεῖν and καθεύδειν refer to being vigilant and indolent, respectively, it is commonplace to observe that γρηγορεῖν is never used to refer to being "alive" (so Edgar 1979, 349; Lautenschlager 1990, 40–42).[133] This should be a considerable problem for commentators who argue that γρηγορεῖν and καθεύδειν refer to being "alive" and "dead", respectively. But this problem is rarely taken up as the discussion usually focuses on the semantic range of καθεύδειν. For example, Howard concludes (1985, 347):

> ... after evaluating both the lexical and contextual data the conclusion is consistently drawn that the meaning of καθεύδω in 1 Thess 5:10 is "death." ... As a result, I also conclude that γρηγορέω in 5:10 should be interpreted metaphorically as "alive" in order to achieve balance semantically with καθεύδω in the grammatical construction.

This conclusion, without discussion or examination of a single text with γρηγορεῖν used in this way, does not suffice.[134] Although BDAG (208, §3) and LSJ (s.v.) assert that the verb can have the meaning of being alive, the only text cited to support this assertion is 1 Thess 5:10. Further, it is amazing that Lövestam, in a monographic length study of ἀγρυπνεῖν and γρηγορεῖν (1963), does not offer any commentary on this verse. Sometimes reference is made to Philo *Somn.* 1.150, ἄλλοτε μὲν ζῶν καὶ ἐγρηγορώς, ἄλλοτε δὲ τεθνεὼς ἢ κοιμώμενος ("sometimes alive and wakeful, sometimes dead or asleep" [Colson/Whitaker 1929–1962]), but the use of the adverb in that text is inconclusive.

The linguistic data above shows that the "alive/dead" interpretation for γρηγορεῖν and καθεύδειν is a difficult assumption to make (Völkel 1991, 222). But the

---

[133] Milligan (1908, 70) refers to Plato *Symp.* 203A for a reference to γρηγορεῖν as "alive", but the use of the verb (with καθεύδειν) is ambiguous.

[134] Typical is Malherbe's conclusion (which he arrives at without any further discussion): "These two verbs [γρηγορεῖν and καθεύδειν] do not normally describe life and death ... but their use here is suggested by their appearance in the exhortation in vv 6–8 and by the use of euphemism in consolation" (2000, 300). The point is well made by Edgar (1979). Besides those he lists as guilty of failing to engage in "independent original study" (345), see also Holtz 1998, 230–231; Jurgensen 1994, 103–104 n. 42; Légasse 1999, 304–305; Mayer 1974, 67; P.-G. Müller 2001, 197; Nicholl 2004, 66; Plevnik 1979, 90; Selby 1999, 405; Smith 2000, 727; Witherington 2006, 153. The problem is particularly highlighted when the metaphor is dispensed with altogether and a commentator offers the translation (without discussion): "*Ob wir leben oder ob wir sterben, wir sind des Herrn*" (Stolina 2002, 102).

alternative vigilance/indolence interpretation is perhaps even more difficult to explain in the context of 1 Thess 5:1–11.[135] Such a reading appears to negate the exhortations of verses 6–7 such that it does not matter what the Thessalonians do — ultimately they will live together with him (v. 10c). Thus, Edgar translates the latter part of verse 10 with: "who died for us, that whether we watch or fail to watch we shall live together with him" (1979, 349). He asserts that Paul's point is to emphasise the certainty of hope, which depends on Christ's death, not on watchfulness. But Edgar does not address the apparent problem of how this conclusion correlates (or not) with the rest of the pericope. Lautenschlager (1990, 49–50) comments:

> Das Verbpaar γρηγορεῖν – καθεύδειν ist damit *keine* der vielfältigen Möglichkeiten, den Gegensatz von Leben und Tod zum Ausdruck zu bringen. Folglich ist – vor allem auch im Blick auf den unmittelbaren Kontext (5,6) – in 1Thess 5,10 die Interpretation "sei es, daß wir in Erwartung der Parusie heilig leben, sei es, daß wir nachlässig werden" die sprachlich gebotene.

Further, Lautenschlager understands the tension between the imperative (vv. 6–7) and the indicative (vv. 9–10) as expressing a paradox. Even in the event of extreme cases of ethical failure, the eschatological saving power of God prevails (56). This view is somewhat similar to Edgar's, although Lautenschlager does attempt to address the tension inherent in his reading. He does not say that the Thessalonians are now free of ethical decision, just that their faith in the death and resurrection of Jesus guarantees rescue from *orgē* (56). Alternatively, Heil offers an original thesis to explain Paul's use of γρηγορεῖν and καθεύδειν in 1 Thess 5:10:

> The hortatory context of 5.9–10 indicates that "whether we may be awake or whether we may be asleep" implies that if some should presently be found to be ethically "asleep", then they must be "awakened" to vigilance before the parousia (2000, 466).

In particular, he observes a temporal difference between the aorist subjunctive verbs (ἐκφυγεῖν, v. 3; καταλαμβάνειν, v. 4; ζῆν, v. 10) and the present subjunctive verbs (καθεύδειν, v. 6; γρηγορεῖν, vv. 6, 10; νήφειν, vv. 6, 8). Thus, if some are currently asleep, but destined for salvation and living with the Lord in the future, then the inference is that those now asleep must be awakened (468). In this way Heil is able to take seriously the exhortations to holy living found throughout First Thessalonians. For Heil, a number of other features in First Thessalonians point to a pattern of some community members (the vigilant ones) encouraging other community members (the indolent ones), including the peculiar wording of 5:11, the very specific commands in 5:14, and the exhortations to pray constantly (5:17) and avoid evil (5:22). All of these are now references to the indolent members of the

---

[135] Konradt finds the difficulty of this alternative so great that he feels compelled to go against the lexical evidence (see 2003, 178–179). Giesen appears not even to be aware that an alternative exists: "Daß καθεύδειν und γρηγορεῖν hier leiblich tot bzw. lebendig heißen muß, ist wohl unbestritten" (1985, 145 n. 84).

community who need to be awakened before the coming of the day of the Lord (469–470).

In response to Edgar, Lautenschlager and Heil, who have all attempted to solve the conundrum of γρηγορεῖν and καθεύδειν in 1 Thess 5:10, I draw attention once again to the thesis that eschatology is the best hermeneutical key to interpret Paul's pattern of exhortation in First Thessalonians. In this instance, emphasising the eschatological discourse, and especially its function,[136] avoids the conflicting picture obtained from form-critical studies and linguistic analyses. Accordingly, it is important to reconsider how Paul employs various eschatological motifs as part of his purposes in writing 1 Thess 5:1–11. While Paul refers to the times and the seasons in response to an oral report from Timothy, he does not raise this issue specifically because the Thessalonians asked about the *topos*. Rather, Paul goes on to address the times and the seasons, and indeed, the day of the Lord, because the Thessalonian *ekklēsia* is in fundamental need of encouragement and exhortation in the face of conflict. The motif of the day of the Lord is a preeminently applicable motif as it expresses both aspects of his pattern of exhortation: negative (judgment) and positive (salvation). Paul emphasises the relevance of the motif by linking it to a well-known political slogan, "peace and security", by which he confirms the identity of outsiders upon whom the negative aspects of that day will fall. Far from being a threat, 1 Thess 5:1–3 serves initially to distinguish between insiders and outsiders, and offers a strongly negative outcome for the very ones who are afflicting the Jesus-followers in Thessalonica. Then in the eschatological *paraenesis* of 1 Thess 5:4–10, Paul promotes the positive aspect of his pattern of exhortation, using multiple rhetorical pairs. The Thessalonians are sons of light, and sons of the day; therefore Paul expects them to keep awake and be sober. Because they are not in darkness, the day of the Lord shall not "catch them unawares" (v. 4). The verb, καταλαμβάνειν, is a strengthened form which is sometimes used to express an element of surprise and/or hostile take over (Delling 1967, 10; Malherbe 2000, 294).[137] It is significant that Paul does not allow for any division of status within the community. All (πάς, v. 4) are sons of light and sons of the day. None shall be surprised by the day. There is no problem with Paul's identification of community members as sons of the day because this day is not some future occurrence as much as it is a powerful rhetorical statement reversing the negative social situation of the Thessalonians. The emphasis is on eschatological *paraenesis*. Thus, Paul applies the indicative of belief to a community struggling for identity and solidarity; such application has attendant imperatives in the present.

[136] Jaquette proposes a similar approach: "The material in 4:13–5:11 functions to comfort the Thessalonians (4:18; 5:11) and console them in their grief. Focus on the eschatological *content* of 4:13–5:11 should not distract us from seeing the consolatory *function* of this pericope, a function quite at home in both philosophical and rhetorical traditions" (1996, 39).

[137] It is often used this way for the catching (by surprise) of someone in the act of adultery (BDAG 520, §3.a). For a parallel use, see John 12:35, where there is a warning against darkness (σκοτία).

The tendency to interpret Paul's use of eschatological motifs as expressing a realised eschatology is curbed by remembering that these motifs serve as exhortations, not as some kind of literal expectation of the future. This is a mistake Heil makes in the formulation of his interpretation of 1 Thess 5:10. It is a serious misreading of Paul's purposes in this pericope to attempt to distinguish between present and future elements (*contra* Heil 2000, 468). In particular, Heil points to a number of present and aorist subjunctive verbs to support his thesis. Yet, he seems unaware that subjunctive verbs do not have a temporal element as do indicative verbal forms. The present and aorist tenses, rather, express different aspects of the verbal action, imperfective and aoristic, respectively.[138] Koester correctly observes the ambiguity inherent in the aorist subjunctive verb, ζήσωμεν (v. 10; *contra* Holtz 1998, 230). Paul could have supplied the future indicative if he had wanted to refer to the future (Koester 1990, 452).

That 1 Thess 5:8–10 is a long, complex sentence is significant, and often forgotten amongst efforts to identify tradition and redaction in these verses. But an examination of the eschatological discourse of First Thessalonians emphasises the rhetorical message of the text as it stands. In other words, it is instructive to look between the traditional elements, at the grammatical structures on which various eschatological motifs are hung. Consequently, it is revealing to note the importance of the verb, νήφειν (v. 8a), which is modified by two adverbial participles, ὄντες (v. 8a) and ἐνδυσάμενοι (v. 8b). The imperative command to sobriety arises *because* the Thessalonians belong to the day (Richard 1995, 254). Furthermore, the command is carried out by having (previously) put on a breastplate of faith and love and a helmet, a hope of salvation (vv. 8b, c). The sentence continues in verses 9–10, and is organised around ὅτι (v. 9a) and ἵνα (v. 10b). The problematic clause, ἵνα εἴτε γρηγορῶμεν εἴτε καθεύδωμεν ἅμα σὺν αὐτῷ ζήσωμεν (v. 10b, c), is directly linked to verse 8. That is, the status of belonging to the day, with the associated imperative of sobriety, leads to the result of living together with him. The change from the present subjunctive (γρηγορῶμεν and καθεύδωμεν) to the aorist subjunctive (ζήσωμεν) is best explained according to aspectual theory. Paul hereby distinguishes between imperfective action (community members are in a durative state of vigilance or indolence) and aoristic action (community members live, point of fact, with the Lord). Many commentators fail to realise, however, that living with the Lord is independent of whether the Thessalonians are vigilant or indolent. Rather, Paul explains that the command to sobriety is carried out through the putting on of faith, love and hope, which are characteristics of a community destined for salvation. The motif of the divine warrior does not primarily represent some kind of eschatological battle in which the Thessalonian *ekklēsia* must take

[138] It is ironic that Heil gives a reference to Porter's monograph on verbal aspect (1989; not 1993 as Heil 2000, 468 n. 13, indicates), a book which thoroughly addresses the fallacies of reading temporal distinctions into the tenses. For a discussion of the significance of tense and aspect for interpreting Greek verbs, see my discussion of ἔφθασεν (1 Thess 2:16) in Chapter 4, §III.d.6.

up arms, whether offensively or defensively.[139] Instead, it is a literary or rhetorical device for emphasising the triad of faith, love and hope (Rigaux 1975, 332). This triad (cf. 1:3) identifies a community for which the Lord Jesus Christ has already died. The motif of the divine warrior refers to, more than anything, a community status and identity (Yoder-Neufeld 1997, 91).

In summary: γρηγορεῖν and καθεύδειν are to be understood as referring to vigilance/indolence. The "sleep of death" is certainly within the semantic range of καθεύδειν, but the association of "being awake" with γρηγορεῖν has no support in the ancient literature. This fact cannot be ignored for the majority view.[140] The problem of how to get around the apparent tension between 5:10 and previous exhortations is solved by recognising the purposes of Paul's pattern of exhortation. Koester's conclusion is instructive:

> The terms γρηγορεῖν and καθεύδειν are chosen in verse 10 because Paul does not only intend to say that to be alive or to have died at the time of the coming of the Lord is irrelevant – all will go out to meet the Lord – he also wants to emphasize that the believers' existence is not determined by the watchfulness that is focussed on the "day of the Lord" (1990, 453).

The "believers' existence" is contrasted over against "the others" (v. 6a) such that insiders are sons of light and sons of the day — both in a contemporary and future sense. Paul's references to mundane sleeping and drunkenness in verse 7 drive home the contemporary status of insiders. Outsiders are sleeping and getting drunk right now, not in some "eschatological future".[141] Such insider status holds even when Paul refers to eschatological categories of *orgē* and salvation. In other words, there is no thought whatsoever whether the Thessalonians are insiders or not — past, present or future. Through the exercise of faith, love and hope, insiders live with the Lord. Of course, there is always the possibility that insiders may lose their status as insiders (Nützel 1990, 265), and this is a real motivating factor (Gorman 2004, 162). Thus, *contra* Nicholl, the motivation for obedience has nothing to do with the "certainty of eschatological status" (2004, 61). On the contrary, Paul clearly asserts that insiders live with the Lord. The motivation comes about through the necessity of remaining an insider. Selby recognises this when he says that the Thessalonians "have nothing to fear regarding the day of the Lord coming as a thief in the night *as long as* they remain as 'children of light'" (1999, 404). Thus, Paul's

---

[139] The question of whether the armour of breastplate and helmet is to be understood as offensive (cf. Eph 6:13) or defensive misunderstands Paul's use of the motif (*contra* Malherbe 2000, 297; Plevnik 1979, 86; Vena 2001, 125).

[140] It is strange that Richard observes this fact but does not unambiguously translate γρηγορεῖν and καθεύδειν as referring to vigilance/indolence. After referring to Dan 12:2, Richard offers the following translation: "whether we are alert (and waiting for the Lord's day) or whether we are asleep (in the dust of the earth) we will live together with him" (1995, 257). It appears that Richard wants to have it both ways.

[141] Commentators seem unsure of what to do with verse 7. See, in particular, Witherington, who comments: "V. 7 is a sort of gloss on or illustration of what Paul has just said ..." (2006, 149).

pattern of exhortation is designed to keep the community intact and is not a threat to its integrity.

There is, therefore, no incompatibility between these exhortations and the obliteration of vigilance/indolence.[142] Just as with life and death (cf. 1 Thess 4:17), notions of vigilance and indolence are ἀδιάφορα (see Jaquette 1996, 38–42, although he misunderstands the significance of 1 Thess 5:10).[143] Incidentally, this is how one should interpret the parallels between 1 Thess 5:10 and 1 Thess 4:13–18, both in conceptual (cf. καθεύδειν and κοιμᾶσθαι) and linguistic (cf. repetition of ἅμα σύν) terms. The parallels do not serve to support the interpretation of γρηγορεῖν and καθεύδειν as referring to being "alive" or "dead" as some kind of crude reference to the *topos* of death in 4:13–18 (*contra* Kim 2002a, 228; Schlier 1963, 30). Nor is it helpful to surmise why Paul did not use ζῆν and ἀποθνήσκειν (see Tarazi 1982, 163). Rather, the parallel between the texts is found in the community solidarity and identity of Jesus-followers in Thessalonica: whether a member dies before the *parousia* or survives, and whether a member is vigilant or not, every member will always be with the Lord (4:17) and live together with him (5:10).

c. Encourage and Build Up Each Other (5:11)

Little needs to be said about this verse. That the inferential conjunction, διό, introduces a conclusion to the exhortations of 5:1–11 is clear. Whether this conclusion constitutes a summary of 4:13–18 as well is somewhat irrelevant as a decision either way makes little difference to the interpretation. Although there is similar wording (cf. παρακαλεῖτε ἀλλήλους, 4:18a, 5:11a), the differences between the verses are important. In 4:18b, Paul includes the instrumental phrase, ἐν τοῖς λόγοις τούτοις, which appears to be a very specific reference to his argument in 4:14–17. Likewise, in 5:11a, b, Paul adds, καὶ οἰκοδομεῖτε εἷς τὸν ἕνα, καθὼς καὶ ποιεῖτε, which may also be a very specific reference to the exhortations in 5:1–11. The phrase also looks forward to further exhortations in 5:12–22 (Malherbe 2000, 287).

The phrase, εἷς τὸν ἕνα is more problematic. It is not clear whether it is synonymous with ἀλλήλους (so BDF 129, §247[4]; Frame 1912, 191) or whether it has some further nuance. For example, it may bring out the mutual relations involved in οἰκοδομεῖν (*GGNT* 692). Thus, it may place emphasis on the individual (Malherbe 1983, 245; 1990a, 388–389). It is interesting to note that the verb has connotations of spiritual growth (Freed 2005, 68), both of the community and of the individual (see particularly Paul's use in First Corinthians), but this should

[142] *Contra* Bruce 1982, 114; Holtz 1998, 231; Howard 1985, 343–344; P.-G. Müller 2001, 98; Nicholl 2004, 66; von Dobschütz 1909, 213; Witherington 2006, 243.

[143] For a similar interpretation of γρηγορεῖν and καθεύδειν in 1 Thess 5:10, but with a greater emphasis on the tension between the "objektiv" statement of salvation (v. 9) and the "subjektiv" statement of hope (ἐλπίς, v. 8), see Nebe 1983, 103–104.

not be applied too rigidly (see Michel 1967a, 140–141). The exhortations here are most likely designed to enforce and maintain group control over the community as a means for developing solidarity and identity (Wanamaker 1990, 190). Heil's interpretation, that each one (εἷς) is to build up the other (τὸν ἕνα) as a reference to the one who is "awake" awakening the one who is "asleep" (see 2000, 469), only makes sense if his thesis regarding 1 Thess 5:10 is accepted. It is more likely that just as Paul exhorted each of the Thessalonians (cf. ὡς ἕνα ἕκαστον ὑμῶν, 2:11), he now wants them to exhort and build up each other individually (Malherbe 2000, 301).

IV. Conclusion

1. So, why does Paul address the Thessalonians about the times and the seasons? The answer lies in the mixing of eschatological motifs where images and metaphors roll into each other to express powerful exhortations. The *topos* of the times and the seasons is reformulated in terms of the day of the Lord which comes as a thief in the night. This, in turn, is linked to the imperial slogan, "peace and security", and to the apocalyptic image of birth pains of a pregnant woman. Paul develops the rhetorical crisis of the day of the Lord in negative and positive terms, and utilises numerous metaphors, of day and night, light and darkness, being awake and asleep, and sobriety and drunkenness. Difficulties in interpreting these metaphors arise from the way Paul uses them differently, even in adjacent verses. Thus, the day of the Lord in verse 2 becomes "day" as opposed to "night" in verse 4, which makes the subsequent phrase, "sons of the day" in verse 5 somewhat ambiguous. Does this reference to "day" mean that the day of the Lord has come such that the Thessalonians are now fully part of it, or that the Thessalonians are sons characterised by light rather than darkness? Even more difficult is the problem of how Paul uses καθεύδειν. In verse 6, he appears to use a figurative meaning of the verb, to refer to indolence as an antonym to being awake and sober. In verse 7, the literal meaning comes to the fore, where sleep (which is done at night) is associated with drunkenness (which also occurs at night). Then in verse 10, Paul uses καθεύδειν for a third time, in a result clause: "so that whether we are awake or asleep we might live together with him". Whether Paul uses the verb (in conjunction with γρηγορεῖν) to refer to being dead (and alive) or to indolence (and vigilance) is difficult to decide. In addition to determining how Paul uses eschatological motifs, there is also the challenge of correctly identifying tradition and redaction throughout. Finding a probable balance between competing trajectories for traditional elements adds to the complexity of the pericope.

2. Paul uses eschatological motifs to address both the positive and negative aspects of his pattern of exhortation. But unlike the other pericopes examined, in 1 Thess 5:1–11 Paul does not overtly address the Thessalonians' social disintegration

by linking it to current or recently passed experiences. Rather, the day of the Lord becomes a symbolic representation of the Thessalonians' social disintegration. Instead of identifying a specific precipitant for disintegration (e.g. conversion experience, suffering and conflict, death of community members), Paul alludes to the oppressive social and political atmosphere of the Roman rule. The political import of the slogan, "peace and security" (v. 3), and the political connotations inherent in the divine warrior motif (v. 8) are important. In this way, insiders are distinguished from outsiders without Paul ever quite saying exactly who the outsiders are. In no uncertain terms, these outsiders shall not escape destruction (v. 3), for their destiny is *orgē* (v. 9). In contrast, the Jesus-followers in Thessalonica are not surprised by the day of the Lord because they are sons of light and sons of the day (v. 5). They have already put on faith, love and hope (v. 8), and are destined to obtain salvation through the Lord Jesus Christ (v. 9). There is nothing gained by debating the merits of "predestination" and "free will" in this context. The point here is to recognise that Paul refers to two groups whereby the Thessalonians are now offered a means for integration into an eschatologically identifiable existence. This existence is defined as living together with the Lord Jesus Christ (v. 10).

When I say that the eschatological *paraenesis* is indirectly related to the social disintegration of the Thessalonians, this does not mean that the pericope is general *paraenesis*, without "specific reference to concerns of the readers" (*contra* Koester 1997, 161). When Paul introduces the motif of the day of the Lord its relevance is not made less because the Thessalonians did not ask about it. Rather, social and political conflict is an essential context of this pericope, as is the association to the *topos* of death (4:13–18). More than that, the relevance of the eschatological *paraenesis* is grounded in the symbolic crisis of the day of the Lord, with its implications of judgment and deliverance. Paul exploits the negative and positive aspects of the motif to build his pattern of exhortation in 1 Thess 5:1–11. Thus, the rhetorical pairs throughout the text (day/night, light/darkness, awake/asleep, sober/drunk, salvation/*orgē*), reinforce social disintegration and at the same time, community identity. The relevance, or contingency of the pericope, is not diminished by recognising the symbolic nature of the day of the Lord. Indeed, I assert that Paul chose this eschatological motif precisely because of its application to his pattern of exhortation.

3. On another matter, there is a temporal tension inherent in the employment of eschatological motifs in *paraenesis*. On the one hand, the phenomenological expectation associated with references to eschatological (and apocalyptic) motifs sometimes leads to the erroneous conclusion that the occurrences depicted (e.g. the apocalyptic end of the world, or the resurrection of the just and the unjust, etc.) are literally expected. On the other hand, Paul uses eschatological motifs to develop a contemporary and powerful rhetorical message for his recipients. Thus, just as the *parousia* of the Lord is a metaphor expression of eschatological expectation (see Chapter 5, §III.c.3), so too the day of the Lord motif is an essential

element of Paul's pattern of exhortation. In this way, Paul does not necessarily promote a "realised eschatology" even though he is able to characterise the Jesus-followers at Thessalonica as "sons of the day". Rather, the theological significance of the day of the Lord as an eschatological occurrence to be hoped for is to be separated from the rhetorical or paraenetic impact of being described as sons of the day. But in terms of eschatological *paraenesis*, some elements in 1 Thess 5:1–11 are "realised". Paul refers to contemporary judgment on the Roman rule in verse 3, and reinforces the present nature of his exhortations with literal references to sleeping and getting drunk in verse 7. Finally, Paul relativises present and future by using the aorist subjunctive, "we might live" (ζήσωμεν), in verse 10.

4. The phrase, εἴτε γρηγορῶμεν εἴτε καθεύδωμεν (v. 10b), is one of the most difficult to interpret in First Thessalonians.[144] I have shown that the matter of how to understand this phrase cannot be decided from the semantic range of καθεύδειν, which clearly extends to the figurative sleep of death. As a matter of fact, that γρηγορεῖν is never used to refer to being alive would seem to decide the matter. Although the alternative interpretation is difficult, where the phrase refers to vigilance or indolence, this does not warrant the ignoring of the literary evidence. Thus, the onus of responsibility now falls heavily on proponents of the majority view that Paul uses the phrase to refer to being alive or dead.

Going beyond the attempts by Edgar (1979), Lautenschlager (1990) and Heil (2000), I propose a new interpretation of 1 Thess 5:10. The eschatological discourse of the text reveals that the result of living together with the Lord Jesus has little to do with vigilance or indolence. Rather, the result of living with "him" has everything to do with being an insider. This insight comes from recognising how the ἵνα clause fits into, and concludes, the eschatological *paraenesis* of the pericope, rather than bogging down in discussions of tradition and redaction.[145] Paul says *all* Jesus-followers in Thessalonica are sons of light and sons of the day (v. 5; *contra* Freed 2005, 79).[146] It is because they are insiders (see ἄρα οὖν in v. 6) that Paul exhorts them to keep awake and be sober. Similarly, it is because they belong to the day that Paul repeats the exhortation to sobriety or self-control. Indeed, the Thessalonian *ekklēsia* has proved its status by having put on faith, love and hope (v. 8). Finally, insiders expect to obtain salvation through the Lord Jesus Christ (v. 9). Consequently, the Thessalonians' motivation to respond to Paul's eschatological *paraenesis* comes from the necessity of remaining an insider. The result is that

[144] It perhaps competes with the textual issue of 2:7 (νήπιοι/ἤπιοι), the proleptic aorist of 2:16 (ἔφθασεν) and the problematic debate of 4:4 (regarding the correct translation of σκεῦος).

[145] Paddison (2005) takes Edgar (1979) to task for being distracted by the different verbs for sleep in 1 Thess 4:13–5:11. He asserts that "Edgar pays scant attention to the theological logic of 5:9–10: Jesus died 'for us' *so that* whether 'we are dead or alive we might live with him'" (186); this makes it clear that Paul returns once again to the issue of death (186). For sure, I do not think Paul ever stopped addressing the issue of death, but Paddison himself fails to recognise the interplay between insiders/outsiders and how the ἵνα clause reveals a conclusion for insiders only.

[146] Furthermore, the characterisation of two groups by Freed (2005, 62–65), where one consists of baptised members and one does not, is rejected.

regardless of whether a brother or sister is vigilant or indolent, all shall live together with the Lord Jesus Christ.

This does not mean that vigilance counts for nothing. If I have understood Paul correctly, that in verses 8–10 he is saying that insiders obtain salvation, with the concomitant result of living with the Lord Jesus Christ, then it is helpful to reverse this logical sequence. Insiders belong to the day (v. 8) because they are sons of light and sons of the day (v. 5). Insiders are not caught unawares by the day of the Lord (v. 4). Nor are they surprised by the coming of the day because they know accurately about its coming (v. 2). By working backwards in this manner, it is possible to delineate in the first instance, the difference between insiders and outsiders: knowledge (εἰδέναι).[147] Elsewhere in First Thessalonians, Paul makes it clear that he expects actions to accompany such knowledge. Thus, in 1 Thess 1:4–10, there is a progression of sequence: Paul knows about the Thessalonians' calling; the Thessalonians know what kind of men Paul and his companions proved to be on the founding visit. This results in the Thessalonians becoming imitators of Paul and the Lord, and in receiving the word. In 2:1–16, Paul asserts that his visit was not in vain with the result being that the Thessalonians not only received the word, but received it as the word of God not as the word of men. In 3:1–10, the Thessalonians are expected to stand fast despite the knowledge that suffering affliction is to be their lot. In 4:1–12, knowledge of instructions given to the Thessalonians is expected to result in following a number of exhortations given by Paul through the Lord Jesus. Similarly, in 5:1–11, Paul expects an appropriate response to knowledge about the day of the Lord; hence the exhortations to sleep not, to keep watch and remain sober. If knowledge or lack thereof distinguishes insiders from outsiders, then using this knowledge to follow Paul's exhortations maintains insider status.

Why Paul exhorts the Thessalonians specifically to watchfulness and sobriety probably stems from their association with the day of the Lord. It is not necessary to look for special connections, whether gnostic (Harnisch), millenarian (Jewett), Epicurean (Malherbe), imperial (Donfried) or otherwise. The paraenetic application of the day of the Lord overrides these other alleged associations such that the traditional connection between the coming "day" and watching is a sufficient explanation for the presence of these exhortations here. Although the motif of sobriety is rarely attested in the NT, its presence here is probably due to its link to the motif of drunkenness which has long been part of the biblical tradition.

---

[147] See also 1 Thess 1:4, 5; 2:1, 2, 5, 11; 3:3, 4; 4:2, 4, 5; 5:12.

Chapter 7
Conclusion

1. Eschatology is the best hermeneutical key to interpret Paul's pattern of exhortation in First Thessalonians. Paul employs eschatological motifs in such a pervasive manner that it is accurate to refer to the eschatological discourse of the letter. This discourse plays a prominent role in the epistolary structure of the letter and the motifs are found in every significant pericope. The references to affliction in First Thessalonians show that Paul is responding to a community in conflict. Consequently, one of the central purposes of the letter is to provide exhortations which are relevant to this community.

2. Paul's pattern of exhortation provides a way to understand the Thessalonians' current social disintegration. Paul uses the ideological and paradigmatic aspects of eschatological motifs to help the Thessalonians understand the inevitable negative consequences of accepting his *kērygma*.

3. Paul's pattern of exhortation also provides a means for integration into an eschatologically identifiable existence. Many of the same eschatological motifs are used for this aspect of his pattern. Paul makes it clear that a proper understanding of why the Thessalonians are experiencing conflict is, in fact, the means for integration. The parameters of community identity are transferred from the anthropological to the theological realm. Paul uses eschatological motifs extensively to carry out these two aspects of his pattern of exhortation and this demonstrates the applicability of the hermeneutical key proposed here.

4. The analyses of 1:9–10, 2:13–16, 4:13–18 and 5:1–11 provide the first monograph-length examination of these fundamental representatives of the eschatological discourse in the letter. There are monographs on 2:14–16 (Schlueter 1994) and 4:13–18,[1] but these focus primarily on one text or the other. In contrast, the comprehensive presence of eschatological motifs in the letter makes it more appropriate to acknowledge the extensive relationships between the pericopes. Consequently, the epistolary structure of the letter was examined (Chapter 2) as a preparation for the exegetical chapters.

5. Among the more important conclusions of the epistolary analysis are the resolution of the "thanksgiving problem" and the characterisation of the *letter-paraenesis* (4:1–5:22) as bearing directly on the situation of the Thessalonian community. The first conclusion comes about by recognising that the thanksgiving reiterations

[1] Harnisch 1973; Jurgensen 1992; Mason 1993; Schneider 2000.

(2:13–16; 3:9–10) have a rhetorical purpose and do not mark successive formal *letter-thanksgivings* nor require an extension of the *letter-thanksgiving* (1:2–10). This permits a simpler epistolary analysis of the form and function of 2:1–16 (a *disclosure* of a past-present relationship). The description of 2:13–16 as a legitimate part of the epistolary and rhetorical structure of First Thessalonians makes the numerous interpolation/compilation theories unnecessary. As well, the position of 1:9–10 at the close of the *letter-thanksgiving* implies a greater literary significance for the *eschatological climax* it contains. This lends credence to Munck's thesis (1963) that these verses anticipate other pericopes in First Thessalonians. The second conclusion came out of a re-evaluation of the epistolary label "*letter-body*" (usually 2:1–12). The label is rejected in preference to the designation *main part* (1:2–5:22) which embraces the epistolary arrangement of the letter without constricting its rhetorical freedom. Thus, the main purpose statements of First Thessalonians are not limited to any one structure, whether to 2:1–16, 2:17–3:13 or 4:1–5:22, for example. This opens the way for understanding the *letter-paraenesis* as a subsection of the *main part* and therefore as not being "tacked" onto the end of the letter. The *topoi* in the *letter-paraenesis*, including on those who are asleep (4:13–18) and on the times and the seasons (5:1–11), are definitely to be understood as consisting of material which bears directly on the situation of the Thessalonian community.

The results of the epistolary analysis reveals that in virtually every epistolary section of First Thessalonians, Paul uses, systematically, eschatological motifs to promote his pattern of exhortation. Paul carefully constructs and integrates eschatological motifs which consistently provide a paraenetic function. Such a conclusion highlights the importance of eschatology and the function of eschatological discourse in First Thessalonians.

6. The first pericope for analysis (1:9–10) contains numerous eschatological motifs. Some of these motifs, including references to Paul's entrance into the community, conversion, dualism between idols and God and waiting for the son from heaven, are distinctive to this text. The others, including resurrection, deliverance and *orgē*, are programmatic for the remainder of First Thessalonians. Paul refers to a report of what others are saying about his converts in Thessalonica and formulates statements using traditional material (perhaps stemming from *Missionsverkündigung*). The Thessalonians' current social disintegration is directly linked to their turning to God, since conversion includes a theological realignment with social ramifications. For example, they no longer worshipped the gods which was a part of municipal living in first-century Macedonia. Paul emphasises an apocalyptic dualism between God (who is "living and true") and idols (who are "dead and dumb"). The juxtaposition of the pair serves to heighten the social disintegration of the Thessalonians who now embark on a new life of service, which is paradoxically, freedom. The new community identity is characterised by waiting. This is understood in eschatological terms of resurrection, deliverance and *orgē*. The confession that God raised Jesus from the dead is a central basis of Paul's

hope of resurrection for those who have fallen asleep (4:13–18); Jesus' resurrection is analogous of the new life of the community, as new creation. In contrast, the previous life of the Thessalonians remains under a coming *orgē*, an eschatological motif which Paul uses to differentiate between those who have accepted the word of God and those who have not (2:13–16). Thus, Paul emphasises the solidarity of the new community which is to be delivered from *orgē*, and which is destined to obtain salvation (5:9).

7. The second pericope for analysis (2:13–16) has been shown to be an authentic part of First Thessalonians. Not only are the epistolary and rhetorical arguments for its inclusion convincing, but all aspects of interpolation hypotheses – especially the arguments put forward by Pearson (1971) – have been examined on historical-critical grounds. There is no case for an interpolation here, neither for 2:13–16 or 2:14–16, nor even just 2:16. The reference to suffering (2:14) is to be included among the other eschatological references to killing the Lord Jesus and the prophets, the displeasure of God, the full measure of sins, the hinderance of Paul's mission to non-Jews, and the pronouncement of a coming *orgē*. On the one hand, the Thessalonians' current social disintegration involves significant levels of suffering and affliction, particularly arising out of the conversion process. On the other hand, Paul promotes the development of a new eschatological existence as a necessary outcome of that disintegration. This new existence also involves significant levels of suffering and affliction, as is clear from Paul's own experiences (e.g. 2:2; 3:1–10). Paradoxically, both the negative (disintegration) and the positive (integration) aspects of Paul's pattern of exhortation are characterised by these same categories.

The questions of whether the Thessalonians' "countrymen" (συμφυλέται) should be taken in an ethnic sense (i.e. inclusive or exclusive of Jews) or not, and whether "the Jews" (οἱ Ἰουδαῖοι) refer to a subset of Judeans or to all Jews in general, take up considerable space in the analysis (Chapter 4, §III.b.4 & §III.c.2). However, with eschatology as the hermeneutical key, the interpretation of these terms is simplified. Paul is not so concerned with specific struggles between citizens in Thessalonica, or with a precise delimitation of the very Jews who are guilty (according to Paul) of the deeds catalogued in 2:15–16. Rather, he is primarily concerned with the development of a community identity in the face of conflict. The conclusions in the analysis show that these terms refer to those who are against Jesus as the *Kyrios*. Paul reinforces a community identity with a polemic against all outsiders, whether non-Jews or Jews. These outsiders, which are typologically and apocalyptically represented by a historical group of Jews, are under *orgē* (2:16).

The conclusion that this judgment is prophetic/proleptic and not past (Chapter 4, §III.d.4–8), is supported by recognising that *orgē* in the eschatological discourse of First Thessalonians refers to the future, despite some impingement on the present. As such, *orgē* is a complementary category to salvation (σωτηρία, 5:9), which is also envisaged in the future. Both categories represent negative and positive aspects of the Thessalonians' new eschatological existence. Consequently, the present aspect of *orgē* is certainly not given the same emphasis as in Rom 1:18. This highlights a difference between the Paul of First Thessalonians (his earliest letter), and the Paul of Romans (a much later letter).

8. The results of the analysis of the third fundamental representative of the eschatological discourse in First Thessalonians (4:13–18), when combined with the results obtained from the first two pericopes, provide a basis for reconstructing the Thessalonians' problems and Paul's solutions.

The Thessalonian Christian community is composed of mostly non-Jews (though not exclusively so),[2] such that their exposure to Jewish eschatological and apocalyptic traditions is limited. Consequently, *a priori*, they would have found Paul's *kērygma* somewhat unfamiliar, in form and content. Paul's letter, with its theme of affliction (θλῖψις) indicates that the Thessalonians are suffering, but to what extent is difficult to determine (Chapter 1, §IV.e). The political overtones of Paul's *kērygma* probably contribute to the picture (Chapter 1, §IV.a).[3] Into this background comes the issue of death with theological and social implications. What happens to the dead? How are they delivered from *orgē* (1:10)? Do they take part in the *parousia* of the Lord? Clearly, Paul proclaimed the *parousia* of the Lord. But did he proclaim the resurrection of the dead? I think he did (*contra* Marxsen 1969 et al.). So why are the Thessalonians grieving over those who have died? There is not enough evidence to sustain a gnostic hypothesis (*contra* Schmithals 1965; Harnisch 1973). Rather, two pivotal phrases, "we will not precede those who have fallen asleep" (οὐ μὴ φθάσωμεν τοὺς κοιμηθέντας, 4:15e) and, "and so we will always be with the Lord" (καὶ οὕτως πάντοτε σὺν κυρίῳ ἐσόμεθα, 4:17d), as well as the temporal markers in the text (Chapter 5, §III.e.2–3), show that the Thessalonians misunderstood the relationship between the resurrection and the *parousia* (Malherbe 2000). Paul is not so naïve as to think there would be no deaths before the near expected *parousia* (*contra* Gundry 1987; Hyldahl 1980). The Thessalonians feared that the dead would only be raised after the *parousia* (Merklein 1992). In addition to these theological implications, there are also social implications for community members who died (as well as for members still living). Is not the patron God of the Christians strong enough to preserve his members? There is probably a hint of fear on the part of those still alive,[4] and the Thessalonians are struggling to maintain community identity as a result (see Ascough 2004). They are also living under an imperial system unsympathetic to minority religious sects. The hope of a better existence both in life and death is strongly linked to the *parousia* of the Lord. When inevitable deaths begin to occur, the Thessalonians think there is no hope of being σὺν κυρίῳ always, with the associated celebratory connotations (*viz.* ἀπάντησις) and release from earthly afflictions.

---

[2] See discussions of 1 Thess 1:9c (Chapter 3, §III.a.5–7) and 2:14d (Chapter 4, §III.b.4).

[3] Donfried 1985; Harrison 2002; Koester 1997.

[4] Collins 1980a; Kieffer 1990; Otto 1997.

With regard to questions of source and location of the λόγος κυρίου (Chapter 5, §II.c), I argue that Paul does not introduce a recognisable saying with the phrase, "by the word of the Lord" (ὑμῖν λέγομεν ἐν λόγῳ κυρίου, 4:15a–b). Instead, he invokes authority for his solution to the Thessalonians' problems. The wording in 4:15c–17c is no doubt traditional, but the presence of repetitions throughout along with the identification of numerous redactions dependent on the Thessalonians' specific situation, make it unlikely that Paul relies on anything other than a prophetic saying of the exalted Lord. Since Paul does not give a quotation of a saying here, there is no need to decide whether 4:15 contains a summary of a word and 4:16–17 contains the word itself, or the other way around.

A key to understanding 4:13–18 is to recognise that Paul uses Jewish traditions out of which Christian *kērygma* developed, to console a largely non-Jewish Hellenistic community in Thessalonica. Since Paul himself is a Hellenistic author, it is appropriate to refer to Paul's hellenisation of Jewish tradition (Gundry 1987). An interpretation of the pericope must involve a sifting between the trajectories of the motifs employed, in order to emphasise properly what associations the Thessalonians themselves would have made when reading Paul's letter. If this is a valid hermeneutical rule,[5] then the interpretations of Dupont (1952), Klijn (1982) and Plevnik (1984), for example, must be rejected on the basis that they are not intuitive solutions to the Thessalonians' problems. It is unlikely that ἀπάντησις is best understood in terms of its use in the LXX traditions when the thesis of Peterson (1930) and others so elequently describes a context for the term which is much closer to the situation in Thessalonica (Chapter 5, §III.e.6). It is also unlikely that the community is caught up in the Jewish problem of whether survivors have an advantage over the dead. Just because the Sinai theophany might be behind the motif of the descending Lord, does not mean that the other motifs (particularly the one of translation) must also be interpreted in that context (Chapter 5, §III.e.4). Nor is it likely that the Thessalonians understood the subtle distinctions between *Entrückungen* and other types of *Himmelfahrten*. Rather, Paul begins to rebuild communal identity by invoking a *kērygmatic* confession about Jesus (4:14a–b) and emphasising that through Jesus (as intermediate agent) God will bring with him, those who have fallen asleep (4:14c). Paul concludes his sustained argument with a parallel statement about being with the Lord always (4:17d); the community is once again complete since the living and the dead are now together (see v. 17b). Paul consoles the Thessalonians with a series of eschatological motifs including the *parousia* of the Lord and subsequent ἀπάντησις, the resurrection of the dead in Christ and the translation of the living and the dead in the clouds. The motif of the descending Lord with apocalyptic details (4:16a–e) is a description of the *parousia*

[5] The observations of Cook (2006) cast some doubt on the validity of this hermeneutical rule, although his observations apply more to "pagan" outsiders' interpretations of Paul, rather than to "pagan"-turned-"Christian" insiders.

in traditionally Jewish terms as a way of emphasising the power of the Christian Lord. But the dual-level language throughout must be understood primarily in Hellenistic terms. Thus, the *parousia* of the Lord is comparable to the *parousiai* of imperial representatives; the resurrection of the dead is expressive of God's power to provide communal identity even beyond the grave; the translation of the living is an apology or rationalisation against death — even a social vindication of the patron God of the Christians; meeting the Lord is a celebratory subversion against the prevailing imperial ideology. Paul makes it clear that both the dead and the living will take part in the *parousia* of the Lord and that ultimately, all members will be with the Lord always.

A systematic view of the eschatological discourse in the letter informs how Paul uses a number of eschatological motifs in 4:13–18. From among the many conclusions arising from the analysis I draw attention here to two only. First, there is a paradigmatic association between Paul's use of the *parousia* of the Lord motif and his pattern of exhortation such that the imagery, in association with Hellenistic *parousiai*, reinforces community solidarity and provides an eschatological imperative for holy living. Second, Paul uses the problem of death as a negative backdrop against which he promotes a pattern of exhortation by presenting commonly accepted beliefs. In particular, the confession of the death and resurrection of Jesus (4:14) and the connection between the resurrection of Jesus and the resurrection of the dead in Christ (4:14, 16) interprets the problem of death wholly in positive terms. A careful delineation of the grammatical structures of the pericope, including how Paul employs eschatological motifs within that structure, results in a reading of the text which reveals a message of an increasingly hopeful existence in the face of death — a message which concludes with a utopian statement of always being with the Lord.

9. The final pericope for analysis (5:1–11) is different to its neighbour text (4:13–18) in two significant ways. First, in terms of his pattern of exhortation, Paul employs eschatological motifs to promote negative and positive aspects, or disintegration and integration, whereas in 4:13–18 he only develops the positive aspect. Second, unlike all the other pericopes analysed, the pattern of exhortation in 5:1–11 is indirect, such that it is not based on current or recently passed experiences. This leads to a new interpretation for the day of the Lord motif which is symbolic of the Thessalonians' social disintegration. By creating a rhetorical crisis, Paul substantially increases the rhetorical power of his *paraenesis*. Thus, in 5:1–3 Paul indirectly continues to deal with the problem of death and emphasises judgment as part of his characterisation of the negative aspect of his pattern of exhortation. Paul employs the day of the Lord motif because of its applicability to community members, since it implies apocalyptic notions of judgment and salvation. The appearance of the political slogan, "peace and security", serves not as some kind of literal indication of those who are to receive judgment, but as an indication that the symbolic day of the Lord is relevant for the social and political spheres of community life.

The *paraenesis* in 5:4–10 is developed primarily through characterisations of insiders and outsiders. Outsiders do not know when the day of the Lord will come, and suffer sudden destruction from which there is no escape (v. 3). For outsiders there is only *orgē* (v. 9). In contrast, insiders are not surprised by the day of the Lord because they are sons of light and sons of the day (v. 5). As such, they are destined to obtain salvation (v. 9), which is defined as living together with the Lord Jesus Christ (v. 10). What is remarkable about this pericope is the subtle way Paul is able to use eschatological motifs to promote a distinction between the two groups. The recurring antitheses and associated exhortations serve to reinforce insider status which has systematic ramifications for his penultimate statement that "whether we are awake or asleep we might live together with him" (vv. 10b, c). The community solidarity signified by the statement that *all* Jesus-followers in Thessalonica are sons of light and sons of the day (v. 5) does not primarily mean that the dead will also be able to live with the Lord Jesus Christ at his *parousia*, although this is a central consolatory message of 4:13–18. Rather, the exhortations in 5:6–8 are addressed to insiders whose destiny is to live with the Lord Jesus (see ἵνα clause in v. 10) such that vigilance and indolence are irrelevant. Consequently, the motivation to respond to Paul's pattern of exhortation stems from the necessity of remaining an insider.

10. Finally, the results of the analysis open the way to a more comprehensive and systematic interpretation of First Thessalonians.[6] With eschatology as a hermeneutical key, it is possible to see how Paul's pervasive references to eschatological motifs throughout the letter are used in his pattern of exhortation. At a more fundamental level, Paul's exhortation arises from his self-presentation as true proclamator of the word of God. This is one reason why there are so many references to the word (of God/the Lord), the gospel (of God/Christ) and, negatively, to the word (of flattery/men). Paul becomes personally involved in the occurrence of proclamation, since he shares not only the gospel but himself, and finds it appropriate to use the relational terms of father/child/son, nurse/child and infant. Paul's mission to non-Jews is legitimated in the Thessalonians' acceptance of the word of God, lest his work be in vain.

Paul's *kērgyma* is essentially eschatological. This is particularly the case for his presentations of pre-Pauline tradition about the death and resurrection of Jesus (1:10; 4:14). In both references, the Thessalonians are given assurance of their eschatological existence. In the first instance, they are described as waiting for God's son from heaven who delivers them (and Paul) from *orgē*. Thus, Paul introduces the eschatological concern of judgment in a positive manner. Later in the letter, he develops the negative connotations of *orgē*, as inevitable retribution for active hostility to God (2:16), and in terms of the day of the Lord (5:1–11). God remains the avenger of transgressions and wrong-doing although the Thessalonians

[6] What follows is a discussion of systematic observations of the text. I proceed with no attempt to provide exhaustive references; the reader is directed to the topical analysis (Chapter 1, §III).

are destined to obtain salvation. In the second instance, they are assured that there is communal identity even in death. Paul explains that those who have died will be brought together with the living. His conclusion, "so we will always be with the Lord" (4:17d), is Paul's consolation in the face of death. The tension between the Thessalonians' previous anthropological identity (as social, political and religious existence) and new theological/christological identity (as eschatological existence) is most keenly felt in that Paul cannot make the problem of death go away. The circumstances of community members dying (whether infant mortality, martyrdom or old age, to cover the extremes), are insignificant beside the fact that death still exists. In the eschatological discourse of First Thessalonians, Paul envisages a transcendent existence, where all community members live with the Lord.

The references to the *parousia* of the Lord provide a means for development of a new community identity, and there is no thought of the individual here. Paul implicitly links the *parousia* of the Lord and the kingdom of God with references to a crown (of boasting) and to glory (2:12, 19–20). Paul's mention of kingdom (see a similar link between kingdom and *parousia* in 1 Cor 15:23–24) is too often overlooked in examinations of First Thessalonians.[7] The expression of joy at the *parousia* of the Lord (2:19; cf. 3:9) is an allusion to the Holy Spirit (1:5, 6) which is given to the community (4:8). Such joy, along with the celebratory language of meeting the Lord (4:17), stands in stark contrast to the Thessalonians' situation.

A communal identity is also encouraged in the association of the *parousia* of the Lord with the motif of sanctification, a motif which Paul develops at some length (4:3–8; 9–12). In particular, the metaphor pairs of day/night, light/darkness, awake/asleep and sobriety/drunkenness, as well as the opposite categories of *orgē* and salvation (5:1–10), serve to accentuate an eschatological community identity. In addition, Paul elsewhere employs an apocalyptic dualism between those pleasing God and doing his will (4:1–3), who have been taught by God (4:9); and those who do not know God (4:5), who are unclean (4:7) and who have no hope (4:13). The motifs of sanctification and *parousia* of the Lord appear even in the *letter-closing* which summarises and concludes the letter as a whole. Weima solves the problematic anthropological reference to the Thessalonians as spirit, soul and body (5:23) by noting that the emphasis is on wholeness (ὁλόκληρος) such that the believer's whole person will be involved in the *parousia* of the Lord, regardless of whether one is dead or alive (1995, 193–194). This is a provocative solution to the tripartite reference although I would emphasise wholeness more in terms of sanctification and blamelessness (5:23) as descriptions of the Thessalonians' new eschatological identity.

It is important to note that Paul's development of an eschatologically identifiable existence for the Thessalonians does not result in a wholesale disintegration

[7] I have sought to correct this oversight among Thessalonian scholars in Luckensmeyer (2007), where I develop a critical definition of the βασιλεία in First Thessalonians and then explore the functions of the motif in the purposes of the letter.

of previous social connections. Enough "damage" has already occurred out of the theological, philosophical, political and ideological differences between the new *ekklēsia* and the citizenship of Thessalonica. Paul seeks to limit further social disintegration with several exhortations regarding the Thessalonians' social standing (4:11–12), and with the expression of a wish prayer that they increase and abound in love to one another and to all men (3:12). This partial reintegration into earthly life appears to have some eschatological significance since Paul envisages a causal link between the Thessalonians' expressions of love, and the establishment of their hearts as unblamable in holiness at the *parousia* of the Lord (3:12–13). However, these observations must be understood in terms of Paul's emphasis on insider/outsider language, which includes descriptions of the Thessalonians as chosen, under the call of God and taught by God (4:9), among others. In contrast, "the rest" (4:13; 5:6) do not know God, disregard God and will be surprised by the day of the Lord.

11. In this monograph, it has been argued that eschatology is the best hermeneutical key to interpret Paul's pattern of exhortation in First Thessalonians. The systematic concern of the letter is to address a community in conflict. Paul's pattern of exhortation has two aspects which are complimentary. First, he provides a way to understand the Thessalonians' current social disintegration. Second, which is in some ways dependent on the first, he provides a means for integration into an eschatologically identifiable existence. Paul effects these two purposes by employing numerous eschatological motifs, which may be regarded as forming an eschatological discourse in the letter. Paul uses these motifs because of their applicability to the Thessalonians' situation. I suggest that this is an area which requires considerably more attention in future scholarly examinations of Paul's letters. Diachronic investigations of eschatological motifs, including the *parousia* of the Lord, the day of the Lord, *orgē*, resurrection and being with the Lord, should be preceded by more thorough synchronic assessments of Paul's letters and of the communities behind those letters. This monograph is an attempt to contribute to scholarly investigations of First Thessalonians only. It now remains to take the results of the analysis, and the concise but comprehensive systematic conclusions above, and apply them to discussions of the eschatology in Paul's other letters, and more broadly still, to the discussions of eschatology as an essential component of the earliest Christian *kērygmata*.

Abbreviations

AASF Annales Academiae Scientiarum Fennicae, Series B

AB Anchor Bible

abbrev. abbreviation(s)

ABD *The Anchor Bible Dictionary*. Ed. by D. N. FREEDMAN et al. 6 vols. New York et al: Doubleday, 1992.

ABRL Anchor Bible Reference Library

ACJD Abhandlungen zum christlich-jüdischen Dialog

ACNT Augsburg Commentaries on the New Testament

add. additions, additional

AGJU Arbeiten zur Geschichte des antiken Judentums und des Urchristentums

AJT *Asia Journal of Theology*

AnBib Analecta biblica

Ang *Angelicum*

ANRW II *Aufstieg und Niedergang der römischen Welt. Geschichte und Kultur Roms im Spiegel der neueren Forschung*. Part 2: *Principat*. Ed. by H. TEMPORINI/W. HAASE. Berlin/New York: W. de Gruyter, 1972–.

ANTC Abingdon New Testament Commentaries

ANTF Arbeiten zur neutestamentlichen Textforschung

Anton *Antonianum*

app. appendix

arr. arranged

ASNU Acta seminarii neotestamentici upsaliensis

ass. assisted, assistance

AsTJ *Asbury Theological Journal*

ATANT Abhandlungen zur Theologie des Alten und Neuen Testaments

ATDan Acta theologica Danica

ATR *Anglican Theological Review*

aug. augmented

AUSS *Andrews University Seminary Studies*

BA *Biblical Archaeologist*

BAGD *A Greek-English Lexicon of the New Testament and Other Early Christian Literature: A Translation and Adaptation of the Fourth Revised and Augmented Edition of WALTER BAUER'S Griechisch-Deutsches Wörterbuch zu den Schriften des Neuen Testaments und der übrigen urchristlichen Literatur.* By W. F. ARNDT/F. W. GINGRICH. 2nd ed. rev. & aug. by F. W. GINGRICH/F. W. DANKER from W. BAUER'S 5th ed. 1958. Chicago/London: University of Chicago Press, 1979.

BASOR *Bulletin of the American Schools of Oriental Research*

BBB Bonner biblische Beiträge

BBET Beiträge zur biblischen Exegese und Theologie

BBR *Bulletin for Biblical Research*

BDAG *A Greek-English Lexicon of the New Testament and Other Early Christian Literature*. 3rd ed. (BDAG) rev. & ed. by F. W. DANKER. Based on W. BAUER'S *Griechisch-deutsches Wörterbuch zu den Schriften des Neuen Testaments und der frühchristlichen Literatur*. 6th ed. Ed. by K. ALAND/B. ALAND, with V. REICHMANN & on previous Eng. eds. by W. F.

	Arndt/W. F. Gingrich/F. W. Danker. Chicago/London: University of Chicago Press, 2000.
BDB	*The Brown-Driver-Briggs Hebrew and English Lexicon: With an Appendix Containing the Biblical Aramaic.* By F. Brown, with the cooperation of S. R. Driver/C. A. Briggs. Based on the lexicon of W. Gesenius, as transl. by E. Robinson, & ed. with constant reference to the thesaurus of Gesenius as compl. by E. Rödiger, & with authorised use of the German ed. of Gesenius' *Handwörterbuch über das Alte Testament.* Peabody, MA: Hendrickson, 1996. Originally publ. by Houghton, Mifflin & Company, 1906.
BDF	*A Greek Grammar of the New Testament and Other Early Christian Literature.* By F. Blass/A. Debrunner. A transl. & rev. of the ninth-tenth German ed. incorporating suppl. notes of A. Debrunner by R. W. Funk. Chicago/London: University of Chicago Press, 1961.
BETL	Bibliotheca ephemeridum theologicarum lovaniensium
BFCT	Beiträge zur Förderung christlicher Theologie
BHS	תורה נביאים וכתובים – *Biblia Hebraica Stuttgartensia.* Quae antea cooperantibus A. Alt/O. Eissfeldt/P. Kahle ediderat R. Kittel. Editio funditus renovata adjuvantibus H. Bardtke/W. Baumgartner/P. A. H. de Boer/O. Eissfeldt/J. Fichtner/G. Gerleman/J. Hempel/F. Horst/A. Jepsen/F. Maass/R. Meyer/G. Quell/Th. H. Robinson/D. W. Thomas cooperantibus H. P. Rüger/J. Ziegler ediderunt K. Elliger/W. Rudolph. Textum Masoreticum curavit H. P. Rüger. Masoram elaboravit G. E. Weil. Stuttgart: Deutsche Bibelgesellschaft, 1966/1977. 4th rev. ed., 1990.
BHT	Beiträge zur historischen Theologie
Bib	*Biblica*
BibInt	*Biblical Interpretation*
BibIntSeries	— Series
bibl.	bibliography
BibLeb	*Bibel und Leben*
BibS(F)	Biblische Studien (Freiburg, 1895–1930)
BJRL	*Bulletin of the John Rylands University Library of Manchester*
BLit	*Bibel und Liturgie*
BN	*Biblische Notizen*
BNTC	Black's New Testament Commentaries
BR	*Biblical Research*
BSac	*Bibliotheca Sacra*
BST	The Bible Speaks Today
BT	*The Bible Translator*
BTB	*Biblical Theology Bulletin*
BU	Biblische Untersuchungen
Budé	Collection Budé
BV	*Biblical Viewpoint*
BZ	*Biblische Zeitschrift*
BZNW	Beihefte zur *ZNW*
CBC	Cambridge Bible Commentary
CBET	Contributions to Biblical Exegesis and Theology
CBQ	*Catholic Biblical Quarterly*
CCWJCW	Cambridge Commentaries on Writings of the Jewish and Christian World, 200 BC to AD 200
cf.	confer
CJT	*Canadian Journal of Theology*
CNS	*Cristianesimo nella storia*
CNT	Commentaire de Nouveau Testament
Comm	*Communio*
comp(s).	compiler(s), compiled
compl.	complete, completed, completely
ConBNT	Coniectanea biblica: New Testament Series

contr. contribution(s)
corr. correction(s)
CP *Classical Philology*
CRBR *Critical Review of Books in Religion*
CRINT Compendia rerum iudaicarum ad Novum Testamentum
CTJ *Calvin Theological Journal*
CTM *Concordia Theological Monthly*
CTSR *The Chicago Theological Seminary Register*
CurBS *Currents in Research: Biblical Studies*
CurTM *Currents in Theology and Mission*
CuW *Christentum und Wissenschaft*
CV *Communio viatorum*
GLB de Gruyter Lehrbuch
DBI *Dictionary of Biblical Interpretation*. Ed. by J. H. HAYES. 2 vols. Nashville: Abingdon, 1999.
diss. dissertation
DLNT *Dictionary of the Later New Testament and Its Development*. Ed. by R. P. MARTIN/P. H. DAVIDS. Downers Grove/Leicester: InterVarsity, 1997.
DNP *Der neue Pauly. Enzyklopädie der Antike*. Ed. by H. CANCIK/N. SCHNEIDER. Stuttgart/Weimar: J. B. Metzler, 1996–.
DNTB *Dictionary of New Testament Background: A Compendium of Contemporary Biblical Scholarship*. Ed. by C. A. EVANS/S. E. PORTER. Project Manager: G. EVANS. Downers Grove/Leicester: InterVarsity, 2000.
DPL *Dictionary of Paul and His Letters*. Ed. by G. F. HAWTHORNE/R. P. MARTIN. Associate ed.: D. G. REID. Downers Grove/Leicester: InterVarsity, 1993.
DTT *Dansk teologisk tidsskrift*
ÉBib. Études bibliques
ECS Early Christian Studies
ed. edition, edited, editor
EDB *Eerdmans Dictionary of the Bible*. Ed. by D. N. FREEDMAN. Associate ed.: A. C. MYERS. Managing ed.: A. B. BECK. Grand Rapids/Cambridge: Eerdmans, 2000.
EDNT *Exegetical Dictionary of the New Testament*. Ed. by H. R. BALZ/G. SCHNEIDER. Vol. 1 [1990] transl. by V. P. HOWARD/J. W. THOMPSON. Vol. 2 [1991] transl. by J. W. THOMPSON/J. W. MEDENDORP. Vol. 3 [1993] transl. by J. W. MEDENDORP/D. W. STOTT. Grand Rapids: Eerdmans, 1990–1993.
EG *Epigrammata Graeca ex lapidibus conlecta*. Ed. by G. KAIBEL. Berolini: G. Reimer, 1878.
e.g. *exempli gratia*
EHPR Études d'histoire et de philosophie religieuses
EHS.T Europäische Hochschulschriften. Reihe 23: Theologie
EKKNT Evangelisch-katholischer Kommentar zum Neuen Testament
EKL *Evangelisches Kirchenlexikon*
Eng. English
enl. enlarged
ErFor Erträge der Forschung
esp. especially
EstBib *Estudios bíblicos*
ET English translation
et al(.) *et alii*
etc. *et cetera*
ETL *Ephemerides theologicae lovanienses*
EThSt Erfurter theologische Studien
ETS Studies Evangelical Theological Society Studies
EvQ *Evangelical Quarterly*
EvT *Evangelische Theologie*

exp. expanded
Exp. *The Expositor*
ExpTim *Expository Times*
F. *Jub.* Fragments of *Jubilees* (Greek)
FAT Forschungen zum Alten Testament
FB Forschung zur Bibel
FBBS Facet Books: Biblical Series
FF Foundations and Facets
FRLANT Forschungen zur Religion und Literatur des Alten und Neuen Testaments
FS Festschrift
FS Andersen (1987) → Conrad/Newing 1987
FS Ashton (1998) → Rowland/Fletcher-Louis 1998
FS Bammel (1991) → Horbury 1991
FS Barr (1994) → Balentine/Barton 1994
FS Barrett (1982) → Hooker/Wilson 1982
FS Beare (1984) → Richardson/Hurd 1984
FS Biser (1998) → Möde/Unger/Woschitz 1998
FS Bornkamm (1980) → Lührmann/Strecker 1980
FS Braun (1973) → Betz/Schottroff 1973
FS Bruce (1980) → Hagner/Harris 1980
FS Bultmann (1964) → Dinkler 1964
FS Catchpole (2000) → Horrell/Tuckett 2000
FS Cullmann (1962) → van Unnik et al. 1962
FS Dahl (1977) → Jervell/Meeks 1977
FS Dodd (1956) → Davies/Daube 1956
FS du Toit (1991) → Roberts 1991
FS Edson (1981) → Dell 1981
FS Ferguson (1998) → Malherbe/Norris/Thompson 1998
FS Fitzmyer (1989) → Horgan/Kobelski 1989
FS Fuchs (1973) → Ebeling/Jüngel/Schunack 1973
FS Fuchs (2002) → Niemand 2002
FS Furnish (1996) → Lovering/Sumney 1996
FS Georgi (1994) → Bormann/Tredici/Standhartinger 1994
FS Gnilka (1989) → Frankemölle/Kertelge 1989
FS Grässer (1997) → Evang/Merklein/Wolter 1997
FS Greeven (1986) → Schrage 1986
FS Gundry (1994) → Schmidt/Silva 1994
FS Haenchen (1964) → Eltester 1964
FS Hahn (1991) → Breytenbach/Paulsen 1991
FS Hartman (1995) → Fornberg/Hellholm 1995
FS Hübner (2000) → Schnelle/Söding 2000
FS Hurd (1993) → McLean 1993
FS Käsemann (1976) → Friedrich/Pöhlmann/Stuhlmacher 1976
FS Keck (1993) → Malherbe/Meeks 1993
FS Kent, Jr. (1991) → Meadors 1991
FS Kertelge (1996) → Kampling/Söding 1996
FS Kittel (1972) → Bloth et al. 1972
FS Klein (1998) → Trowitzsch 1998
FS Knoch (1991) → Degenhardt 1991
FS Knox (1967) → Farmer et al. 1967
FS Koester (1991) → Pearson et al. 1991
FS Kuhn (1999) → Becker/Fenske 1999
FS Kümmel (1985) → Grässer/Merk 1985
FS Lambrecht (2002) → Bieringer/Koperski/Lataire 2002

FS Lattke (2007) → Allen/Franzmann/Strelan 2007
FS Légasse (1996) → Marchadour 1996
FS Lohse (1989) → Aland/Meurer 1989
FS Lührmann (1999) → Maser/Schlarb 1999
FS Malherbe (1990) → Balch/Ferguson/Meeks 1990
FS Manson (1959) → Higgins 1959
FS Martyn (1989) → Marcus/Soards 1989
FS Martyn (1990) → Fortna/Gaventa 1990
FS Meeks (1995) → White/Yarbrough 1995
FS Metzger (1995) → Ehrman/Holmes 1995
FS Michel (1963) → Betz/Hengel/Schmidt 1963
FS Neirynck (1992) → van Segbroeck 1992
FS Pohlschneider (1974) → Delahaye 1974
FS Saunders (1985) → Groh/Jewett 1985
FS Schelkle (1973) → Feld/Nolte 1973
FS Schnackenburg (1989) → Merklein 1989
FS Schreckenberg (1993) → Koch/Lichtenberger 1993
FS Schubert (1966) → Keck/Martyn 1966
FS Schürmann (1977) → Schnackenburg/Ernst/Wanke 1977
FS Schweizer (1983) → Luz/Weder 1983
FS Seitz (1993) → Landau/Schmidt 1993
FS Smith (1975) → Neusner 1975
FS Stanley (1975) → Plevnik 1975
FS Styler (1981) → Horbury/McNeil 1981
FS Tenney (1975) → Hawthorne 1975
FS Thielicke (1968) → Henry et al. 1968
FS Vögtle (1991) → Oberlinner/Fiedler 1991
FS Wedderburn (2002) → Christophersen 2002
FS Williams (1979) → Church/George 1979
FS Woude (1992) → Bremmer/García Martínez 1992
FS Wright (1976) → Cross/Lemke/Miller 1976
GBS Guides to Biblical Scholarship
GGA *Göttingische Gelehrte Anzeigen*
GGBB *Greek Grammar Beyond the Basics: An Exegetical Syntax of the New Testament*. By D. B. Wallace. Grand Rapids: Zondervan, 1996.
GGNT *A Grammar of the Greek New Testament in the Light of Historical Research*. By A. T. Robertson. 4th ed. Nashville: Broadman, 1934.
GL *Geist und Leben*
GLB de Gruyter Lehrbuch
Gn *Gnomon*
GNS Good News Studies
GNTG *A Grammar of New Testament Greek*. By J. H. Moulton. Vol. 1 [1908]: *Prolegomena*. 3rd ed. with corr. & add. by J. H. Moulton. Vol. 2 [1929]: *Accidence and Word-Formation* with an appendix on *Semitisms in the New Testament*. By J. H. Moulton/W. F. Howard. Vol. 3 [1963]: *Syntax*. By N. Turner. Vol. 4 [1976]: *Style*. By N. Turner. Edinburgh: T. & T. Clark, 1908–1976.
GPM *Göttinger Predigtmeditationen*
Greg *Gregorianum*
GS Gedenkschrift
GS Schlatter (1991) → Hengel/Heckel 1991
GS Stuiber (1982) → Klauser/Dassmann/Thraede 1982
GTA Göttinger theologische Arbeiten
GTB Van Gorcum's theologische Bibliotheek
GTJ *Grace Theological Journal*

HBT	*Horizons in Biblical Theology*
HDG	Handbuch der Dogmengeschichte
HDR	Harvard Dissertations in Religion
HerBü	Herder-Bücherei
HeyJ	*Heythrop Journal*
HNT	Handbuch zum Neuen Testament
HO	Handbuch der Orientalistik
HR	*History of Religions*
HrwG	*Handbuch religionswissenschaftlicher Grundbegriffe*. Ed. by H. Cancik/B. Gladigow/M. Laubscher. In collaboration with G. Kehrer/H. G. Kippenberg. Vol. 1 [1988]. Vol. 2 [1990]. Vol. 3 [1993]. Vol. 4 [1998]. Vol. 5 [2001]. Stuttgart et al.: W. Kohlhammer, 1988–2001.
HSCP	*Harvard Studies in Classical Philology*
HTKNT	Herders theologischer Kommentar zum Neuen Testament
HTR	*Harvard Theological Review*
HTS	Harvard Theological Studies
HUCA	*Hebrew Union College Annual*
HUT	Hermeneutische Untersuchungen zur Theologie
IB	*Interpreter's Bible*
IBS	*Irish Biblical Studies*
ICC	International Critical Commentary
IDB	*The Interpreter's Dictionary of the Bible: An Illustrated Encyclopedia Identifying and Explaining all Proper Names and Significant Terms and Subjects in the Holy Scriptures, Including the Apocrypha, with Attention to Archaeological Discoveries and Researches into the Life and Faith of Ancient Times*. Ed. by G. A. Buttrick et al. 4 vols. New York/Nashville: Abingdon, 1962.
IDBSup	*The Interpreter's Dictionary of the Bible: An Illustrated Encyclopedia Identifying and Explaining All Proper Names and Significant Terms and Subjects in the Holy Scriptures, Including the Apocrypha, with Attention to Archaeological Discoveries and Researches into the Life and Faith of Ancient Times*. Ed. by K. Crim et al. Suppl. vol. Nashville: Abingdon, 1976.
i.e.	*id est*
IGUR	*Inscriptiones Graecae urbis Romae*. Curavit L. Moretti. Rome, 1968–
Int	*Interpretation*
intr.	introduction, introduced
JAAR	*Journal of the American Academy of Religion*
JAC	*Jahrbuch für Antike und Christentum*
JAC.E	— Ergänzungsband
JBL	*Journal of Biblical Literature*
JBTh	Jahrbuch für biblische Theologie
JEB	*Jahrbuch des evangelischen Bundes*
JES	*Journal of Ecumenical Studies*
JETS	*Journal of the Evangelical Theological Society*
JHS	*Journal of Hellenic Studies*
JNES	*Journal of Near Eastern Studies*
JPT	*Journal of Pentecostal Theology*
JPTh	*Jahrbücher für protestantische Theologie*
JQRMS	Jewish Quarterly Review Monograph Series
JR	*Journal of Religion*
JSHRZ	Jüdische Schriften aus hellenistisch-römischer Zeit
JSJ	*Journal for the Study of Judaism in the Persian, Hellenistic and Roman Periods*
JSJSup	— Supplement Series
JSNT	*Journal for the Study of the New Testament*
JSNTSup	— Supplement Series

JSOT	*Journal for the Study of the Old Testament*
JSOTSup	— Supplement Series
JSP	*Journal for the Study of the Pseudepigrapha*
JSPSup	— Supplement Series
JTC	*Journal for Theology and the Church*
JTS	*Journal of Theological Studies*
JTSA	*Journal of Theology for Southern Africa*
Kairos	*Kairos. Zeitschrift für Religionswissenschaft und Theologie*
KBANT	Kommentare und Beiträge zum Alten und Neuen Testament
KEK	Kritisch-exegetischer Kommentar über das Neue Testament (Meyer-Kommentar)
KlPauly	*Der kleine Pauly*
KuI	*Kirche und Israel*
LB	*Linguistica Biblica*
LCL	Loeb Classical Library
LD	Lectio divina
LEC	Library of Early Christianity
LS	*Louvain Studies*
LSJ	*A Greek-English Lexicon*. Comp. by H. G. LIDDELL/R. SCOTT. Rev. & aug. throughout by H. S. JONES, with the ass. of R. MCKENZIE, and with the cooperation of many scholars. 9th ed. Oxford: Clarendon, 1940.
LSJSup	*Greek-English Lexicon: Revised Supplement*. Ed. by P. G. W. GLARE with the ass. of A. A. THOMPSON. Oxford: Clarendon, 1996. → LSJ.
LTK	*Lexikon für Theologie und Kirche*
LTP	*Laval théologique et philosophique*
LXX	Septuaginta → RAHLFS 1952 (bibl.); AUCTORITATE ACADEMIAE SCIENTIARUM GOTTINGENESIS eds. 1931–. *Septuaginta: Vetus Testamentum Graecum*. Göttingen: Vandenhoeck & Ruprecht.
MM	*Vocabulary of the Greek Testament*. By J. H. MOULTON/G. MILLIGAN. One-vol. ed. London: Hodder & Stoughton, 1930. Repr. by Hendrickson, 1997.
MNTC	Moffatt New Testament Commentary
MNTS	McMaster New Testament Studies
ms(s).	manuscript(s)
MT	Masoretic Text
MThSt	Marburger theologische Studien
MtR	Matthean Redaction
n(n).	footnote(s), endnote(s)
NA[27]	NESTLE-ALAND: *Novum Testamentum Graece*, post EBERHARD NESTLE et ERWIN NESTLE communiter ediderunt B. ALAND/K. ALAND/J. KARAVIDOPOULOS/C. M. MARTINI/B. M. METZGER. Apparatum criticum novis curis elaboraverunt B. ALAND/K. ALAND una cum Instituto Studiorum Novi Testamenti Monasterii Westphaliae, 27th rev. ed. Stuttgart: Deutsche Bibelgesellschaft, 1993. 5th corrected printing, 1998.
n.b.	*nota bene*
NCB	New Century Bible
n.d.	no date
NEchtB	Neue Echter Bibel
NedTT	*Nederlands Theologisch Tijdschrift*
Neot	*Neotestamentica*
Neth.	Netherlands
NETS	*A New English Translation of the Septuagint and the Other Greek Translations Traditionally Included under That Title*. Ed. by A. PIETERSMA/B. G. WRIGHT. New York/Oxford: Oxford University Press, 2007.
NewDocs	*New Documents Illustrating Early Christianity*. Vols. 1–3 [1981–1983] by G. H. R. HORSLEY. Vol. 4 [1987] by G. H. R. HORSLEY with the collaboration of A. L. CONNOLLY et al. Vol. 5 [1989] by G. H. R. HORSLEY with cumulative indexes to vols. 1–5 newly prepared by

	S. P. Swinn. Vols. 6–7 [1992–1994] by S. R. Llewelyn with the collaboration of R. A. Kearsley. Vol. 8 [1998] by S. R. Llewelyn. Vol. 9 [2002] ed. by S. R. Llewelyn in collaboration with M. Harding et al. Vols. 1–7 publ. at Macquarie University: Ancient History Documentary Research Centre. Vols. 8–9 also publ. at Grand Rapids/Cambridge: Eerdmans, 1981–2002.
NF	Neue Folge
NGS	New Gospel Studies
NHC	Nag Hammadi Codices
NIB	*New Interpreter's Bible*
NIBCNT	New International Biblical Commentary on the New Testament
NICNT	New International Commentary on the New Testament
NIDNTT	*The New International Dictionary of New Testament Theology*. Ed. by C. Brown. Transl., with add. & rev., from the German. Vol. 1 [1975]. Vol. 2 [1976]. Vol. 3 [1978]. Exeter: Paternoster / Grand Rapids: Zondervan, 1975–1978.
NIGTC	New International Greek Testament Commentary
NKZ	*Neue kirchliche Zeitschrift*
NovT	*Novum Testamentum*
NovTSup	— Supplements
n.p.	no place; no publisher; no page
NPNF	Nicene and Post-Nicene Fathers
NT	New Testament → NA^{27}
NTAbh	Neutestamentliche Abhandlungen
NTC	New Testament Commentaries
NTD	Das Neue Testament Deutsch
NTF	Neutestamentliche Forschungen
NTG	New Testament Guides
NTL	New Testament Library
NTS	*New Testament Studies*
NTTS	New Testament Tools and Studies
NZSTh	*Neue Zeitschrift für systematische Theologie und Religionsphilosophie*
OBT	Overtures to Biblical Theology
OJRS	*Ohio Journal of Religious Studies*
Ont.	Ontario
OrChr	*Oriens Christianus*
OT	Old Testament
OTL	Old Testament Library
OTM	Oxford Theological Monographs
OTP	*The Old Testament Pseudepigrapha*. Vol. 1 [1983]: *Apocalyptic Literature and Testaments*. Vol. 2 [1985]: *Expansions of the "Old Testament" and Legends, Wisdom and Philosophical Literature, Prayers, Psalms, and Odes, Fragments of Lost Judeo-Hellenistic Works*. Ed. by J. H. Charlesworth. ABRL. New York et al: Doubleday, 1983–1985. For the Greek texts, see also Denis 1987.
Pa.	Pennsylvania
par.	parallel(s)
pers.	person
pl.	plural
PNTC	The Pillar New Testament Commentary
publ.	published
PVTG	Pseudepigrapha veteris testamenti Graece
QD	Quaestiones disputatae
RAC	*Reallexikon für Antike und Christentum*
RB	*Revue biblique*
rec(s).	recension(s)
ref.	reference, references

RelSRev	*Religious Studies Review*
repr.	reprint, reprinted
republ.	republished
ResQ	*Restoration Quarterly*
rev.	revised, revisers, revision
RevBL	*Review of Biblical Literature*
RevExp	*Review and Expositor*
RevScRel	*Revue des sciences religieuses*
RGG	*(Die) Religion in Geschichte und Gegenwart*
RIBLA	*Revista de interpretación biblica latino-americana*
RNT	Regensburger Neues Testament
RSR	*Recherches de science religieuse*
RThom	*Revue thomiste*
RTR	*Reformed Theological Review*
SacPag	Sacra Pagina
SANT	Studien zum Alten und Neuen Testaments
SBAB	Stuttgarter biblische Aufsatzbände
SBFLA	*Studii biblici Franciscani liber annus*
SBG	Studies in Biblical Greek
SBL	Society of Biblical Literature
SBLDS	— Dissertation Series
SBLMS	— Monograph Series
SBLSBS	— Sources for Biblical Study
SBLSP	— Seminar Papers
SBLSS	— Semeia Studies
SBS	Stuttgarter Bibelstudien
SBT	Studies in Biblical Theology
sc.	scilicet
ScEccl	*Sciences ecclésiastiques*
SD	Studies and Documents
SEÅ	*Svensk exegetisk årsbok*
SFEG	Schriften der Finnischen Exegetischen Gesellschaft
sel.	selected
SIJD	Schriften des Institutum Judaicum Delitzschianum
sing.	singular
SJLA	Studies in Late Judaism in Antiquity
SJT	*Scottish Journal of Theology*
SJTOP	— Occasional Papers
SKKNT	Stuttgarter kleiner Kommentar: Neues Testament
SNT	Studien zum Neuen Testament
SNTSMS	Society for New Testament Studies Monograph Series
SNTU	Studien zum Neuen Testament und seiner Umwelt
SNTU.A	— Serie A (= Aufsätze)
SPAW	Sitzungberichte der preussischen Akademie der Wissenschaften
SPCIC	*Studiorum paulinorum congressus internationalis catholicus*
SPSH	Scholars Press Studies in the Humanities
SR	*Studies in Religion*
SSIA	Skrifter utgivna av svenska institutet i Athen
ST	*Studia Theologica*
STAC	Studien und Texte zu Antike und Christentum
STAEKU	Schriftenreihe des theologischen Ausschusses der evangelischen Kirche der Union
STDJ	Studies on the Texts of the Desert of Judah
STK	*Svensk teologisk kvartalskrift*
StPB	Studia post-biblica

SUNT	Studien zur Umwelt des Neuen Testaments
suppl.	supplement, supplementary
s.v.	sub voce
SVTP	Studia in veteris testamenti pseudepigraphica
SWC	Sammlung wissenschaftlicher Commentare
SwJT	*Southwestern Journal of Theology*
TANZ	Texte und Arbeiten zum neutestamentlichen Zeitalter
TBT	*The Bible Today*
TD	*Theology Digest*
TDNT	*Theological Dictionary of the New Testament*. Vol. 1–4 [1964–1967] ed. by G. Kittel. Vol. 5–9 [1968–1974] ed. by G. Friedrich. Vol. 10 [1976] comp. by R. E. Pitkin. Eng. ed. transl. & ed. by G. W. Bromiley. Grand Rapids: Eerdmans, 1964–1976.
TF	Theologische Forschung
TGl	*Theologie und Glaube*
Them	*Themelios*
ThesSyr	*Thesaurus Syriacus*. Ed. by R. Payne Smith. Hildesheim: Georg Olms, 1999. Originally publ. by Clarendon, 1879–1901.
THKNT	Theologischer Handkommentar zum Neuen Testament
TJ	*Trinity Journal*
TLZ	*Theologische Literaturzeitung*
TQ	*Theologische Quartalschrift*
transl.	translation, translated
TRE	*Theologische Realenzyklopädie*. In Gemeinschaft mit H. R. Balz et al. ed. by (G. Krause &) G. Müller. Berlin/New York: W. de Gruyter, 1977–.
TS	*Theological Studies*
TSAJ	Texte und Studien zum Antiken Judentum
TSK	*Theologische Studien und Kritiken*
TTZ	*Trierer theologische Zeitschrift*
TU	Texte und Untersuchungen
TynBul	*Tyndale Bulletin*
TynNTC	Tyndale New Testament Commentaries
TZ	*Theologische Zeitschrift*
UMI	University Microfilms International
unabr.	unabridged
unch.	unchanged
unpubl.	unpublished
URM	*Ultimate Reality and Meaning*
UTB	Uni-Taschenbücher
VC	*Vigiliae Christianae*
viz.	*videlicet*
vol(s).	volume(s)
VT	*Vetus Testamentum*
VTSup	— Supplements
Vulg.	Vulgate
WBC	Word Biblical Commentary
WdF	Wege der Forschung
WesTJ	*Wesleyan Theological Journal*
WiWei	*Wissenschaft und Weisheit*
WMANT	Wissenschaftliche Monographien zum Alten und Neuen Testament
WPNT	*Word Pictures in the New Testament*. By A. T. Robertson. Vol. 1 [1930]: *The Gospel according to Matthew/The Gospel according to Mark*. Vol. 2 [1930]: *The Gospel according to Luke*. Vol. 3 [1930]: *The Acts of the Apostles*. Vol. 4 [1931]: *The Epistles of Paul*. Vol. 5 [1932]: *The Fourth Gospel/The Epistle to the Hebrews*. Vol. 6 [1933]: *The General Epistles and the Revelation of John*. Grand Rapids: Baker, 1930–1933.

WUNT	Wissenschaftliche Untersuchungen zum Neuen Testament: 1st series (= I); 2nd series (= II).
ZBK	Zürcher Bibelkommentare
ZKT	*Zeitschrift für katholische Theologie*
ZMW	*Zeitschrift für Missionswissenschaft und Religionswissenschaft*
ZNW	*Zeitschrift für die neutestamentliche Wissenschaft*
ZNT	*Zeitschrift für Neues Testament*
ZPE	*Zeitschrift für Papyrologie und Epigraphik*
ZRGG	*Zeitschrift für Religions- und Geistesgeschichte*
ZST	*Zeitschrift für systematische Theologie*
ZTK	*Zeitschrift für Theologie und Kirche*

Bibliography

The bibliography is set out in a continuous A–Z arrangement. This enhances the usefulness of the author-date referencing system because the reader does not have to check multiple lists in order to find a particular reference. Consequently, instead of separating ancient sources and commentaries from the arrangement, a number of abbreviated lists appear for the convenience of the reader. In this way, attention is drawn to the ancient sources and commentaries (on the Thessalonian correspondence and otherwise), used in this book. The full bibliographic data may be found under the respective names and dates below, which are indicated with an "→" (the arrow symbol is used throughout to indicate where to go for a primary bibliographic entry). Abbreviations have been used where possible due to the large number of entries. The abbreviations (see list of abbreviations) follow the conventions set out in *The SBL Handbook of Style* edited by P. H. Alexander et al. 1999, and in the *TRE Abkürzungsverzeichnis* compiled by S. M. Schwertner 1994. Often, multiple entries have the same name and year. In these cases, successive entries are distinguished from the first one with a lower case "a", "b", etc. immediately after the date. Less often is the occurrence of variant spellings of a name (usually associated with the German *Umlaut*). When this occurs, the variant spellings are indicated with an "=" sign. However, attention has been given to reproduce the correct spelling associated with particular articles and monographs. Where a chapter of a monograph with multiple contributors is listed (under the relevant author[s]), that monograph also appears under the editor(s) of the same. Despite possible redundancies, this is done to honour the work of the editor(s). Names beginning with "de", "van" and "von", have all been put in alphabetical order, but with cross-references for alternative placements in the bibliography. For example, "de Jonge" appears under "d" in the bibliography, with a cross reference under "Jonge". Names beginning with "Mc" and "Mac" have been alphabetised according to the "letter-by-letter" rule. For some of the articles from *ABD*, *IB*, *NIDNTT* and *TDNT*, different parts of the article were written by different authors. In these cases, the articles appear in the bibliography under the author(s) who wrote the relevant part(s). The page numbers which appear immediately after the year show the page range of the whole article. An indication of the section(s) written by the author(s), along with the relevant page range for the section(s), appears in square brackets.

I. List of Ancient Sources

Aeschylus
→ Smyth 1922–1926
Apostolic Fathers
→ Lake 1912–1913; Ehrman 2003
Aristotle
Eth. nic. → Rackham 1926
Hist. an. → Peck/Balme 1965–1991
Mund. → Forster/Furley 1955
Part. an. → Peck/Forster 1937
Pol. → Rackham 1932
Babrius
→ Perry 1965
Catullus
→ Cornish 1912
Chrysostom
→ Schaff 1956
Dio Chrysostom
→ Cohoon/Lamar Crosby 1932–1951
Diodorus Siculus
→ Oldfather et al. 1933–1967
Doxographi graeci
→ Diels 1879
Epictetus
→ Oldfather 1925–1928
Epicurus
→ Bailey 1926
Euripides
→ Kovacs 1994–1999
Eusebius
→ Lake/Oulton 1926–1932
Hermes Trismegistus
→ Scott 1968
Hermias Alexandrinus Philosophus
→ Diels 1879
Herodian
→ Whittaker 1969–1970
Herodotus
→ Godley 1920–1925
Hesiod
→ Evelyn-White 1914
Hesychius
→ M. Schmidt 1965
Homer
Iliad → Murray 1999
Isocrates
Panath. → Norlin 1928–1945
Josephus
→ Thackeray et al. 1926–1965
Juvenal
→ Ramsay 1918
Lucian
→ Harmon/Kilburn/MacLeod 1913–1967
Lysias
→ Lamb 1930
Marcus Aurelius Antoninus
→ Haines 1930
Orosius
→ Arnaud-Lindet 1990–1991
Persius
→ Ramsay 1918
Phaedrus
→ Perry 1965
Philo
→ Colson/Whitaker 1929–1962
Philostratus
Vit. Apoll. → Conybeare 1912
Plato
→ Fowler et al. 1914–1935
Pliny the Elder
Nat. → Rackham et al. 1938–1963
Plutarch
Brut. an. → Cherniss/Helmbold 1927–1976
Lives → Perrin 1914–1926
Moralia → Babbitt et al. 1927–1976
Quaest. conv. → Minar/Sandbach/Helmbold 1927–1976
Tu. san. → Babbitt et al. 1927–1976
Sophocles
→ Lloyd-Jones 1994–1996
Strabo
→ Jones 1917–1932
Suetonius
→ Rolfe 1914
Tacitus
→ Jackson 1914–1937
Testaments of the Twelve Patriarchs
→ Charles 1906; 1966; de Jonge 1978; Stone 1969 [*T. Levi*]
Theophilus of Antioch
→ Grant 1970
Thucydides
→ Smith 1919–1923

II. List of Commentaries: First (& Second) Thessalonians

Alford 1958
Auberlen & Riggenbach 1869
Bailey 1955
Best 1972
Bornemann 1894
Bruce 1970; 1982
Calvin → Mackenzie 1961
Collins, R. F. 1990a
Denney 1892
Dibelius 1925
Dobschütz 1909
Dysinger 1944
Eadie 1877
Ellingworth & Nida 1976
Fatum 1994
Findlay 1891; 1904
Frame 1912
Friedrich 1976
Grayston 1967
Green 2002
Haufe 1999
Havener 1983
Hogg & Vine 1929
Holtz 1998 ([1]1986)
Jowett 1859
Laub 1985
Légasse 1999
Lenski 1937
Malherbe 2000
Marshall 1983
Marxsen 1979; 1982
Masson 1957
Milligan 1908
Moffatt 1910
Morris 1959
Müller, P.-G. 2001
Neil 1957
Oepke 1970
Reese 1979
Reinmuth 1998
Richard 1995
Rigaux 1956
Roosen 1971
Ryrie 1959
Saunders 1981
Schlier 1972
Smith 2000
Staab 1965
Stott 1991
Tarazi 1982
Thomas 1978
Trilling 1980
Vawter 1960
Wanamaker 1990
Ward 1973
Williams 1992
Zimmer 1893

III. List of Commentaries: Other

Barrett 1971 (1 Cor); 1994; 1998 (Acts)
Best 1998 (Eph)
Betz 1979 (Gal)
Boring/Berger/Colpe 1995 (various)
Bruce 1988 (Acts)
Byrne 1996 (Rom)
Calvin → Fraser 1960 (1 & 2 Cor)
Conzelmann 1975 (1 Cor); 1987 (Acts)
Cranfield 1979 (Rom 9–16)
Davies & Allison (Matt 8–18)
Dunn 1996 (Acts)
France 2002 (Mark)
Furnish 1984 (2 Cor)
Haenchen 1971 (Acts)
Héring 1962 (1 Cor)
Hollander/de Jonge 1985 (*T. 12 Patr.*)
Horsley 1998 (1 Cor)
Jewett 2007 (Rom)
Käsemann 1980 (Rom)
Luz 2001 (Matt 8–20)
Marshall 1980 (Acts)
Martyn 1997 (Gal)
Munck 1967a (Acts)
Orr & Walther 1976 (1 Cor)
Osiek 1999 (*Shepherd of Hermas*)
Parry 1926 (1 Cor)
Robertson/Plummer 1911 (1 Cor)
Schlier 1977 (Rom)
Schrage 2001 (1 Cor 15–16)
Selwyn 1947 (1 Pet)
Thrall 1965 (1 & 2 Cor); 1994 (2 Cor)

AALEN, Sverre 1951. *Die Begriffe 'Licht' und 'Finsternis' im Alten Testament, im Spätjudentum und im Rabbinismus.* Oslo: Jacob Dybwad.

AARDE, Andries G. van → VAN AARDE, Andries G.

AASGAARD, Reidar 2004. *'My Beloved Brothers and Sisters!': Christian Siblingship in Paul.* JSNTSup 265. London/New York: T&T Clark.

— 2007. "Paul as a Child: Children and Childhood in the Letters of the Apostle." *JBL* 126 (2007) 129–159.

ABRAMOWSKI, Luise 1981. *Drei christologische Untersuchungen.* BZNW 45. Berlin/New York: W. de Gruyter.

ACHTEMEIER, Paul J. ed. 1980. *SBL 1980 Seminar Papers* 19. Chico, CA: Scholars Press.

— 1983. "An Apocalyptic Shift in Early Christian Tradition: Reflections on Some Canonical Evidence." *CBQ* 45 (1983) 231–248.

— 1986. "An Elusive Unity: Paul, Acts, and the Early Church." *CBQ* 48 (1986) 1–26.

— et al. eds. 1996. *The HarperCollins Bible Dictionary.* Rev. & updated ed. San Francisco: HarperSanFrancisco.

ACKROYD, Peter R. 1969. " נצח–εἰς τέλος." *ExpTim* 80 (1969) 126.

ADLER, Ada ed. 1967–1971. *Suidae Lexicon.* 5 vols. Lexicographi Graeci 1. SWC. Stuttgart: B. G. Teubner.

ÅDNA, Jostein/KVALBEIN, Hans eds. 2000. *The Mission of the Early Church to Jews and Gentiles.* WUNT I.127. Tübingen: Mohr Siebeck.

AEJMELAEUS, Lars 1985. *Wachen vor dem Ende. Die traditionsgeschichtlichen Wurzeln von 1. Thess 5:1–11 und Luk 21:34–36.* SFEG 44. Helsinki: Kirjapaino Raamattutalo.

AHN, Joseph Y.-S. 1989. "The Parousia in Paul's Letters to the Thessalonians, the Corinthians, and the Romans, in Relation to Its Old Testament-Judaic Background." PhD diss. Fuller Theological Seminary, 1989. Ann Arbor, MI: UMI, 1989.

AICHELE, George et al. 1995. *The Postmodern Bible.* New Haven/London: Yale University Press.

ALAND, Kurt comp. 1975 [vol. 1]; 1983 [vol. 2]. *Vollständige Konkordanz zum griechischen Neuen Testament. Unter Zugrundelegung aller modernen kritischen Textausgaben und des Textus receptus.* In Verbindung mit H. RIESENFELD/H.-U. ROSENBAUM/CHR. HANNICK. 2 vols. ANTF 4.1, 2 Berlin/New York: W. de Gruyter.

— et al. eds. 1959. *Studia Evangelica.* Vol. 1. TU 73. Berlin: Akademie-Verlag.

— /ALAND, Barbara 1989. *The Text of the New Testament: An Introduction to the Critical Editions and to the Theory and Practice of Modern Textual Criticism.* 2nd rev. & enl. ed. Transl. by E. F. RHODES. Grand Rapids: Eerdmans / Leiden: E. J. Brill.

— /MEURER, Siegfried eds. 1989. *Wissenschaft und Kirche. Festschrift für Eduard Lohse.* Bielefeld: Luther-Verlag.

ALBL, Martin C./EDDY, Paul R./MIRKES, Renée eds. 1993. *Directions in New Testament Methods.* Marquette Studies in Theology 2. Marquette: University Press.

ALETTI, Jean-N. 1996. "L'apôtre Paul et la parousie de Jésus Christ. L'eschatologie paulinienne et ses enjeux." *RSR* 84 (1996) 15–41.

ALEXANDER, Loveday C. A. 1989. "Hellenistic Letter-Forms and the Structure of Philippians." *JSNT*, issue 37 (1989) 87–101.

— 1993. "Chronology of Paul." *DPL* (1993) 115–123.

— 1998. "Fact, Fiction and the Genre of Acts." *NTS* 44 (1998) 380–399.

ALEXANDER, Patrick H. et al. eds. 1999. *The SBL Handbook of Style: For Ancient Near Eastern, Biblical, and Early Christian Studies.* Peabody, MA: Hendrickson.

ALFORD, Henry 1958. *The Greek Testament: With a Critically Revised Text, a Digest of Various Readings, Marginal References to Verbal and Idiomatic Usage, Prolegomena, and a Critical and Exegetical Commentary.* Vol. 3: *Galatians – Philemon.* Rev. by E. F. HARRISON. Chicago: Moody.

ALKIER, Stefan 1997. "Der 1. Thessalonicherbrief als kulturelles Gedächtnis." In: SELLIN/VOUGA (1997) 175–194.

ALLEMAN, Herbert C. ed. 1944. *New Testament Commentary: A General Introduction to and a Commentary on the Books of the New Testament.* Rev. 1 vol. ed. Philadelphia: Fortress.

ALLEN, Pauline/FRANZMANN, Majella/STRELAN, Rick eds. 2007. *"I Sowed Fruits into Hearts" (Odes Sol. 17:13): Festschrift for Professor Michael Lattke.* ECS 12. Sydney: St Pauls.

ALLISON, JR., Dale C. 1982. "The Pauline Epistles and the Synoptic Gospels: The Pattern of the Parallels." *NTS* 28 (1982) 1–32.

ALLO, E. Bernard 1932. "Saint Paul et la 'double résurrection' corporelle." *RB* 41 (1932) 188–209.

ALSOP, John R. ed. 1981. *An Index to the Revised Bauer-Arndt-Gingrich Greek Lexicon.* 2nd ed. Grand Rapids: Zondervan.

ANDERSON, JR., R. Dean 1999. *Ancient Rhetorical Theory and Paul.* Rev. ed. CBET 18. Leuven: Peeters.

— 2000. *Glossary of Greek Rhetorical Terms: Connected to Methods of Argumentation, Figures and Tropes from Anaximenes to Quintilian.* CBET 24. Leuven: Peeters.

ARGYLE, Aubrey W. 1952. "The Influence of the Testaments of the Twelve Patriarchs upon the New Testament." *ExpTim* 63 (1951–1952) 256–258.

ARNAUD-LINDET, Marie-Pierre transl. 1990–1991. *Orose. Histoires (Contre les Païens).* 3 vols. Budé. Paris: Les Belles Lettres.

ARRÓNIZ, José M. 1983. "La parusía y su hermeneútica (1 Tes. 4,13–18)." *Lumen* 32 (1983) 193–213.

ARZT, Peter 1992. *Bedrohtes Christsein. Zu Eigenart und Funktion eschatologisch bedrohlicher Propositionen in den echten Paulusbriefen.* BBET 26. Frankfurt am Main et al.: Peter Lang.

— 1994. "The 'Epistolary Introductory Thanksgiving' in the Papyri and in Paul." *NovT* 36 (1994) 29–46.

ASCOUGH, Richard S. 2000. "The Thessalonian Christian Community as a Professional Voluntary Association." *JBL* 119 (2000) 311–328.

— 2000a. "Macedonia." *EDB* (2000) 841–842.

— 2003. *Paul's Macedonian Associations: The Social Context of Philippians and 1 Thessalonians.* WUNT II.161. Tübingen: Mohr Siebeck.

— 2004. "A Question of Death: Paul's Community-Building Language in 1 Thessalonians 4:13–18." *JBL* 123 (2004) 509–530.

ASHTON, John 2000. *The Religion of Paul the Apostle.* New Haven/London: Yale University Press.

ASKWITH, Edward H. 1911. "The Eschatological Section of 1 Thessalonians." *Exp. 8th Series* 1 (1911) 59–67.

— 1911a. "'I' and 'We' in the Thessalonian Epistles." *Exp. 8th Series* 1 (1911) 149–159.

AUBERLEN, Carl A./RIGGENBACH, Christoph J. 1869. *The Two Epistles of Paul to the Thessalonians.* 4th ed. Transl. with add. by J. LILLIE. New York: Charles Scribner & Co.

AUDET, J. P. 1959. "Literary Forms and Contents of a Normal Εὐχαριστία in the First Century." In: ALAND et al. (1959) 643–662.

AUNE, David E. 1972. *The Cultic Setting of Realized Eschatology in Early Christianity.* NovTSup 28. Leiden: E. J. Brill.

— 1975. "The Significance of the Delay of the Parousia for Early Christianity." In: FS TENNEY (1975) 87–109.

— 1983. *Prophecy in Early Christianity and the Ancient Mediterranean World.* Grand Rapids: Eerdmans.

— 1987. *The New Testament in Its Literary Environment.* LEC 8. Philadelphia: Westminster.

— ed. 1988. *Greco-Roman Literature and the New Testament: Selected Forms and Genres.* SBLSBS 21. Atlanta: Scholars Press.

— 1992. "Eschatology: Early Christian Eschatology." *ABD* 2 (1992) 594–609.

— 1993. "Apocalypticism." *DPL* (1993) 25–35.

AVERY-PECK, Alan J./NEUSNER, Jacob eds. 2000. *Judaism in Late Antiquity. Part Four: Death, Life-After-Death, Resurrection and the World-to-Come in the Judaisms of Antiquity.* HO 49. Leiden et al.: Brill.

BAARDA, Tjitze 1984. "„Maar de toorn is over hen gekommen ...'." In: BAARDA et al. (1984) 15–74.

— 1985. "1 Thess. 2:14–16. Rodrigues in 'Nestle-Aland'." *NedTT* 39 (1985) 186–193.

— 1992. "The Shechem Episode in the Testament of Levi: A Comparison with Other Traditions." In: FS WOUDE (1992) 11–73.

— /KLIJN, Albertus F. J./VAN UNNIK, W. C. eds. 1978. *Miscellanea Neotestamentica.* 2 vols. NovTSup 47. Leiden: E. J. Brill.

— et al. 1984. *Paulus en de andere joden. Exegetische bijdragen en discussie.* Delft: Meinema.

BAASLAND, Ernst 1988. "Die περί-Formel und die Argumentation(ssituation) des Paulus." *ST* 42 (1988) 69–87.

BABBITT, Frank C. et al. transl. 1927–1976. *Plutarch's Moralia*. 16 vols. Vols. 1–5 transl. by F. C. BABBITT. Vol. 6 transl. by W. C. HELMBOLD. Vol. 7 transl. by P. H. DE LACY/B. EINARSON. Vol. 8 transl. by P. A. CLEMENT/H. B. HOFFLEIT. Vol. 9 transl. by E. L. MINAR, JR./F. H. SANDBACH/W. C. HELMBOLD. Vol. 10 transl. by H. N. FOWLER. Vol. 11 transl. by L. PEARSON/F. H. SANDBACH. Vol. 12 transl. by H. CHERNISS/W. C. HELMBOLD. Vol. 13, parts 1–2 transl. by H. CHERNISS. Vol. 14 transl. by B. EINARSON/P. H. DE LACY. Vol. 15 transl. by F. H. SANDBACH. LCL 197, 222, 245, 305, 306, 337, 405, 424, 425, 321, 426, 406, 427, 470, 428, 429. London: William Heinemann / Cambridge: Harvard University Press.

BACON, Benjamin W. 1922. "Wrath 'Unto the Uttermost'." *Exp. 8th Series* 24 (1922) 356–376.

BAHR, Gordon J. 1966. "Paul and Letter Writing in the Fifth [*sic*] Century." *CBQ* 28 (1966) 465–477.

— 1968. "The Subscriptions in the Pauline Letters." *JBL* 87 (1968) 27–41.

BAILEY, Cyril transl. 1926. *Epicurus: The Extant Remains. With Short Critical Apparatus, Translation and Notes*. Oxford: Clarendon.

BAILEY, James L./VANDER BROEK, Lyle D. 1992. *Literary Forms in the New Testament: A Handbook*. Louisville, KY: Westminster/John Knox.

BAILEY, John A. 1979. "Who Wrote II Thessalonians?" *NTS* 25 (1978–1979) 131–145.

BAILEY, John W. 1955. "The First and Second Epistles to the Thessalonians." *IB* 11 (1955) 243–339 [§ Introduction and Exegesis].

BAILEY, Robert E. 1964. "Is 'Sleep' the Proper Biblical Term for the Intermediate State?" *ZNW* 55 (1964) 161–167.

BAIRD, William 1971. "Pauline Eschatology in Hermeneutical Perspective." *NTS* 17 (1970–1971) 314–327.

BALCH, David L./FERGUSON, Everett/MEEKS, Wayne A. eds. 1990. *Greeks, Romans, and Christians: Essays in Honor of Abraham J. Malherbe*. Minneapolis: Fortress.

BALDERMANN, Ingo et al. eds. 1999. *Prophetie und Charisma*. In Verbindung mit P. D. HANSON et al. JBTh 14. Neukirchen-Vluyn: Neukirchener Verlag.

BALTENSWEILER, Heinrich 1963. "Erwägungen zu 1. Thess. 4,3–8." *TZ* 19 (1963) 1–13.

BALZ, Horst R. 1972. "ὕπνος κτλ." *TDNT* 8 (1972) 545–556.

— 1990. "εἴσοδος." *EDNT* 1 (1990) 402.

— 1990a. "ἐκδιώκω." *EDNT* 1 (1990) 408.

— 1990b. "ἅγιος κτλ." *EDNT* 1 (1990) 16–20.

— 1991. "λύπη, λυπέω." *EDNT* 2 (1991) 362–364.

— 1991a. "κέλευσμα." *EDNT* 2 (1991) 280.

— 1991b. "κελεύω." *EDNT* 2 (1991) 280.

— 1991c. "ἔπειτα." *EDNT* 2 (1991) 20.

— /SCHNEIDER, Gerhard eds. 1990–1993. *Exegetical Dictionary of the New Testament*. [see *EDNT* in abbrev.]

BAMMEL, Ernst 1959. "Judenverfolgung und Naherwartung. Zur Eschatologie des Ersten Thessalonicherbriefes." *ZTK* 56 (1959) 294–315. Republ. in: BAMMEL (1997) 237–259.

— 1960. "Ein Beitrag zur paulinischen Staatsanschauung." *TLZ* 85 (1960) 837–840.

— 1981. "Preparation for the Perils of the Last Days: 1 Thessalonians 3:3." In: FS STYLER (1981) 91–100.

— 1984. "Romans 13." In: BAMMEL/MOULE (1984) 365–383.

— 1997. *Judaica et Paulina. Kleine Schriften II*. With an afterword by P. PILHOFER. WUNT I.91. Tübingen: J. C. B. Mohr (Paul Siebeck).

— /MOULE, C. F. D. eds. 1984. *Jesus and the Politics of His Day*. Cambridge et al.: University Press.

BARCLAY, John M. G. 1992. "Thessalonica and Corinth: Social Contrasts in Pauline Christianity." *JSNT*, issue 47 (1992) 49–74. Republ. in: PORTER/EVANS (1997) 267–292.

— 1993. "Conflict in Thessalonica." *CBQ* 55 (1993) 512–530.

— 2000. "'That You May Not Grieve, Like the Rest Who Have No Hope' (1 Thess 4.13): Death and Early Christian Identity." Unpubl. paper. 1–25. Transl. & publ. in: BARCLAY (2000a).

— 2000a. ΘΑΝΑΤΟΣ ΚΑΙ ΠΡΩΤΗ ΧΡΙΣΤΙΑΝΙΚΗ ΤΑΥΤΟΤΗΤΑ. (Ερμηνεία του Α΄ Θεσσα–λονικείς 4:13–5:11). *Deltio biblikōn meletōn* 19 (2000) 26–53.

BARR, James 1961. *The Semantics of Biblical Language*. London: Oxford University Press.

BARRERA, Julio T./MONTANER, Luis V. eds. 1992. *The Madrid Qumran Congress: Proceedings of the International Congress on the Dead Sea Scrolls, Madrid 18–21 March, 1991*. Vol. 1. STDJ 11. Leiden: E. J. Brill / Madrid: Editorial Complutense.

BARRETT, Charles K. 1953. "New Testament Eschatology." *SJT* 6 (1953) 136–155.

— 1971. *A Commentary on the First Epistle to the Corinthians*. 2nd ed. BNTC. London: Adam/Charles Black.

— 1994 [vol. 1]; 1998 [vol. 2]. *The Acts of the Apostles: A Critical and Exegetical Commentary*. Vol. 1: *Preliminary Introduction and Commentary on Acts I–XIV*. Vol. 2: *Introduction and Commentary on Acts XV–XXVIII*. ICC. Edinburgh: T&T Clark.

— 1999. "The Historicity of Acts." *JTS* NS 50 (1999) 515–534.

BARTH, Markus 1968. "Was Paul an Anti-Semite?" *JES* 5 (1968) 78–104.

BARTON, John ed. 1998. *The Cambridge Companion to Biblical Interpretation*. Cambridge: University Press.

— 1998a. "Historical-Critical Approaches." In: BARTON (1998) 9–20.

BARTON, Stephen C. 1998. "Paul and the Limits of Tolerance." In: STANTON/STROUMSA (1998) 121–134.

— 2003. "Paul as Missionary and Pastor." In: DUNN (2003) 34–48.

BASSLER, Jouette M. 1989. "Paul's Theology: Whence and Whither? A Synthesis (of sorts) of the Theology of Philemon, 1 Thessalonians, Philippians, Galatians and 1 Corinthians." In: LULL (1989) 412–423.

— ed. 1991. *Pauline Theology*. Vol. I: *Thessalonians, Philippians, Galatians, Philemon*. Minneapolis: Fortress.

— 1995. "Σκεῦος: A Modest Proposal for Illuminating Paul's Use of Metaphor in 1 Thessalonians 4:4." In: FS MEEKS (1995) 53–66.

BAUCKHAM, Richard 1977. "Synoptic Parousia Parables and the Apocalypse." *NTS* 23 (1976–1977) 162–176.

— 1983. "Synoptic Parousia Parables Again." *NTS* 29 (1983) 129–134.

BAUERNFEIND, Otto 1967. "νήφω, νηφάλιος, ἐκνήφω." *TDNT* 4 (1967) 936–941.

BAUGH, Steven M. 1990. "Phraseology and the Reliability of Acts." *NTS* 36 (1990) 290–294.

BAUMBACH, Günther 1983. "Antijudaismus im Neuen Testament – Fragestellung und Lösungsmöglichkeit. Herrn Professor Kurt Schubert zum 60. Geburtstag." *Kairos* 25 (1983) 68–85.

BAUMERT, Norbert 1990. "Brautwerbung. Das einheitliche Thema von 1 Thess 4,3–8." In: R. F. COLLINS (1990) 316–339.

BAUMGARTEN, Jörg 1975. *Paulus und die Apokalyptik. Die Auslegung apokalyptischer Überlieferungen in den echten Paulusbriefen*. WMANT 44. Neukirchen-Vluyn: Neukirchener Verlag.

— 1993. "καιρός." *EDNT* 2 (1991) 232–235.

BAUR, Ferdinand C. 1875. *Paul the Apostle of Jesus Christ, His Life and Work, His Epistles and His Doctrine: A Contribution to the Critical History of Primitive Christianity*. 2nd ed. 2 vols. Ed. by E. ZELLER. Transl. by A. MENZIES. Vol. 2. London/Edinburgh: Williams & Norgate.

BEALE, G. K. ed. 1994. *The Right Doctrine from the Wrong Texts? Essays on the Use of the Old Testament in the New*. Grand Rapids: Baker.

BEARE, Francis W. 1962a. "Thessalonians, First Letter to the." *IDB* 4 (1962) 621–625.

BEASLEY-MURRAY, George R. 1991. "Resurrection and Parousia of the Son of Man." *TynBul* 42 (1991) 296–309.

BECK, Norman A. 1994. *Mature Christianity in the 21st Century: The Recognition and Repudiation of the Anti-Jewish Polemic of the New Testament*. Exp. & rev. ed. With a prologue & intro. by C. M. LEIGHTON. New York: Crossroad.

BECKER, Jürgen 1970. *Untersuchungen zur Entstehungsgeschichte der Testamente der Zwölf Patriarchen*. AGJU 8. Leiden: E. J. Brill.

— 1970a. "Erwägungen zur apokalyptischen Tradition in der paulinischen Theologie." *EvT* 30 (1970) 593–609.

— 1974. *Die Testamente der zwölf Patriarchen*. JSHRZ 3/I. Gütersloh: Gerd Mohn.

— 1976. *Auferstehung der Toten im Urchristentum*. SBS 82. Stuttgart: Verlag Katholisches Bibelwerk.

— 1980. "Die Frage nach den entschlafenen Christen in 1. Thess 4, 13–18." *JEB* 23 (1980) 45–60.

— 1986. "Die Erwählung der Völker durch das Evangelium. Theologiegeschichtliche Erwägungen zum 1 Thess." In: FS GREEVEN (1986) 82–101.
— 1993. *Paul: Apostle to the Gentiles*. Transl. by O. C. DEAN, JR. Louisville, KY: Westminster/John Knox.
— ed. 1993a. *Christian Beginnings: Word and Community from Jesus to Post-Apostolic Times*. Transl. by A. S. KIDDER/R. KRAUSS. Louisville, KY: Westminster/John Knox.
— 1993b. "Paul and His Churches." In: BECKER (1993a) 132–210.
— 1997. "Endzeitliche Völkermission und antiochenische Christologie." In: FS GRÄSSER (1997) 1–21.
— 1998. "Auferstehung II. Auferstehung Jesu Christ 1. Neues Testament." *RGG* 1 (^{4}1998) 922–924.
— /CONZELMANN, Hans/FRIEDRICH, Gerhard 1976. *Die Briefe an die Galater, Epheser, Philipper, Kolosser, Thessalonicher und Philemon*. 14th new rev. & exp. ed. NTD 8. Göttingen: Vandenhoeck & Ruprecht.
BECKER, Michael/FENSKE, Wolfgang eds. 1999. *Das Ende der Tage und die Gegenwart des Heils. Begegnungen mit dem Neuen Testament und seiner Umwelt. Festschrift für Heinz-Wolfgang Kuhn zum 65. Geburtstag*. AGJU 44. Leiden et al.: Brill.
BEHM, Johannes 1967. "μετανοέω, μετάνοια." *TDNT* 4 (1967) 975–1008 [§ A, C–F: 976–980, 989–1008].
BEKER, J. Christiaan 1982. *Paul's Apocalyptic Gospel: The Coming Triumph of God*. Philadelphia: Fortress.
— 1988. "Paul's Theology: Consistent or Inconsistent?" *NTS* 34 (1988) 364–377.
— 1989. "Paul the Theologian: *Major Motifs in Pauline Theology*." *Int* 43 (1989) 352–365.
— 1990. *The Triumph of God: The Essence of Paul's Thought*. Transl. by L. T. STUCKENBRUCK. Minneapolis: Fortress.
— 1993. "The Promise of Paul's Apocalyptic for Our Times." In: FS KECK (1993) 152–159.
BELL, Richard H. 1994. *Provoked to Jealousy: The Origin and Purpose of the Jealousy Motif in Romans 9–11*. WUNT II.63. Tübingen: J. C. B. Mohr (Paul Siebeck).
BELLEVILLE, Linda L. 1991. *Reflections of Glory: Paul's Polemical Use of the Moses-Doxa Tradition in 2 Corinthians 3.1–18*. JSNTSup 52. Sheffield: JSOT Press.
BEN-CHORIN, Schalom 1980. "Antijüdische Elemente im Neuen Testament." *EvT* 40 (1980) 203–214.
BENDEMANN, Reinhard von → VON BENDEMANN, Reinhard.
BERCOVITZ, J. Peter 1990. "Paul and Thessalonica." *Proceedings: Eastern Great Lakes & Midwest Biblical Societies* 10 (1990) 123–135.
BERGER, Klaus 1974. "Apostelbrief und apostolische Rede/Zum Formular frühchristlicher Briefe." *ZNW* 65 (1974) 190–231.
— /NORD, Christiane 1999. *Das Neue Testament und frühchristliche Schriften. Übersetzt und kommentiert*. Frankfurt am Main/Leipzig: Insel.
BERKEY, Robert F. 1963. "Ἐγγίζειν, φθάνειν, and Realized Eschatology." *JBL* 82 (1963) 177–187.
BERTRAM, Georg 1971. "στρέφω κτλ." *TDNT* 7 (1971) 714–729.
— 1972. "ὕψος κτλ." *TDNT* 8 (1972) 602–620.
— 1974. "ὠδίν, ὠδίνω." *TDNT* 9 (1974) 667–674.
BEST, Ernest 1972. *A Commentary on the First and Second Epistles to the Thessalonians*. BNTC. London: Adam/Charles Black.
— 1998. *A Critical and Exegetical Commentary on Ephesians*. ICC. Edinburgh: T&T Clark.
BETZ, Hans D. 1979. *Galatians: A Commentary on Paul's Letter to the Churches in Galatia*. Hermeneia. Philadelphia: Fortress.
— 1991. "Ἰουδαία." *EDNT* 2 (1991) 191–192.
— 1992. "Paul." *ABD* 5 (1992) 186–201.
— 1998. *Antike und Christentum. Gesammelte Aufsätze IV*. Tübingen: Mohr Siebeck.
— /HENGEL, Martin/SCHMIDT, Peter eds. 1963. *Abraham unser Vater. Juden und Christen im Gespräch über die Bibel. Festschrift für Otto Michel zum 60. Geburtstag*. AGJU 5. Leiden: E. J. Brill.
— /SCHOTTROFF, Luise eds. 1973. *Neues Testament und christliche Existenz. Festschrift für Herbert Braun zum 70. Geburtstag am 4. Mai 1973*. Tübingen: J. C. B. Mohr (Paul Siebeck).
BETZ, Otto 1982. "Entrückung II. Biblische und frühjüdische Zeit." *TRE* 9 (1982) 683–690.
BEYER, Hermann W. et al. 1970. *Die kleineren Briefe des Apostels Paulus*. 12th ed. NTD 8. Göttingen: Vandenhoeck & Ruprecht.

BICKMANN, Jutta 1998. *Kommunikation gegen den Tod. Studien zur paulinischen Briefpragmatik am Beispiel des Ersten Thessalonicherbriefes.* FB 86. Würzburg: Echter.

BIERINGER, Reimund ed. 1996. *The Corinthian Correspondence.* BETL 125. Leuven: University Press.

— /KOPERSKI, Veronica/LATAIRE, Bianca eds. 2002. *Resurrection in the New Testament: Festschrift J. Lambrecht.* BETL 165. Leuven: University Press / Leuven et al.: Peeters.

BINDER, Hermann 1983. "Silvanus. Ein Beitrag zur Theologiegeschichte des Urchristentums." In: ROGGE/SCHILLE (1983) 99–103.

— 1990. "Paulus und die Thessalonicherbriefe." In: R. F. COLLINS (1990) 87–93.

BIRDSALL, J. Neville 1992. "The Recent History of New Testament Textual Criticism (from Westcott and Hort, 1881, to the Present)." *ANRW* II.26.1 (1992) 99–197.

BIZER, Ernst et al. 1967. *Das Kreuz Jesu Christi als Grund des Heils.* STAEKU. Gütersloh: Gerd Mohn.

BJERKELUND, Carl J. 1967. *Parakalô. Form, Funktion und Sinn der parakalô-Sätze in den paulinischen Briefen.* Bibiotheca Theologica Norvegica 1. Oslo et al.: Universitetsforlaget.

BLACK, David A. 1994. *Learn to Read New Testament Greek.* Exp. ed. Nashville: Broadman & Holman.

— 1998. *It's Still Greek to Me: An Easy-to-Understand Guide to Intermediate Greek.* Grand Rapids: Baker.

BLAKE, Buchanan 1925. "The Apocalyptic Setting of the Epistles to the Thessalonians." *The Expositor, 9th Series* 3 (1925) 126–139.

BLANCHETIÈRE, François 1998. "The Threefold Christian Anti-Judaism." In: STANTON/STROUMSA (1998) 185–210.

BLINZLER, Josef 1959. *The Trial of Jesus: The Jewish and Roman Proceedings against Jesus Christ Described and Assessed from the Oldest Accounts.* Transl. by I. MCHUGH/F. MCHUGH. Cork: Mercier.

BLISCHKE, Mareike Verena 2007. *Die Eschatologie in der Sapientia Salomonis.* FAT II.26. Tübingen: Mohr Siebeck.

BLOOMQUIST, L. Gregory 1999. "Methodological Criteria for Apocalyptic Rhetoric: A Suggestion for the Expanded Use of Sociorhetorical Analysis." In: CAREY/BLOOMQUIST (1999) 181–203.

BLOTH, Peter C. et al. eds. 1972. *Mutuum Colloquium. Festgabe aus Pädagogik und Theologie für Helmuth Kittel zum 70. Geburtstag.* Dortmund: W. Cruwell.

BLUMENTHAL, Christian 2005. "Was sagt 1 Thess 1.9b–10 über die Adressaten des 1 Thess? Literarische und historische Erwägungen." *NTS* 51 (2005) 96–105.

BOCCACCINI, Gabriele 1991. *Middle Judaism: Jewish Thought, 300 B.C.E. to 200 C.E.* Foreword by J. H. CHARLESWORTH. Minneapolis: Fortress.

BOCKMUEHL, Markus N. A. 1990. *Revelation and Mystery: In Ancient Judaism and Pauline Christianity.* WUNT II.36. Tübingen: J. C. B. Mohr (Paul Siebeck).

— 1991. "'The Trumpet Shall Sound': *Shofar* Symbolism and Its Reception in Early Christianity." In: FS BAMMEL (1991) 199–225.

— 1998. "Jewish and Christian Public Ethics in the Early Roman Empire." In: STANTON/STROUMSA (1998) 342–355.

BOER, Martinus C. de → DE BOER, Martinus C.

BOERS, Hendrikus 1976. "The Form-Critical Study of Paul's Letters: 1 Thessalonians as a Case Study." *NTS* 22 (1975–1976) 140–158.

BOHLEN, Reinhold 1987. "Die neue Diskussion um die Einheitlichkeit des 1. Thessalonicherbriefes. Eine Kurzinformation für die Verkündingungspraxis." *TTZ* 96 (1987) 313–317.

— 1989. "The Unity of 1 Thessalonians." *Theology Digest* 36 (1989) 132–134.

BOOMERSHINE, Thomas E. 1989. "Epistemology at the Turn of the Ages in Paul, Jesus, and Mark: Rhetoric and Dialectic in Apocalyptic and the New Testament." In: FS MARTYN (1989) 147–167.

BORCHERT, GERALD L. 1993. "Wrath, Destruction." *DPL* (1993) 991–993.

BORGEN, Peder/FUGLSETH, Kåre/SKARSTEN, Roald 2000. *The Philo Index: A Complete Greek Word Index to the Writings of Philo of Alexandria.* Grand Rapids/Cambridge: Eerdmans / Leiden et al.: Brill.

BORING, M. Eugene 1982. *Sayings of the Risen Jesus: Christian Prophecy in the Synoptic Tradition.* SNTSMS 46. Cambridge et al.: University Press.

— 1983. "Christian Prophecy and the Sayings of Jesus: The State of the Question." *NTS* 29 (1983) 104–112.

— 1991. *The Continuing Voice of Jesus: Christian Prophecy and the Gospel Tradition.* Rev. ed. of Boring 1982. Louisville, KY: Westminster/John Knox.

— /Berger, Klaus/Colpe, Carsten eds. 1995. *Hellenistic Commentary to the New Testament.* Nashville: Abingdon.

Bormann, Lukas 2002. "Das 'letzte Gericht' — ein abständiges Mythologumenon?" *ZNT* Heft 9, 5. Jahrgang (2002) 54–59.

— 2003. Review of *Paul between Synagogue and State: Christians, Jews, and Civic Authorities in 1 Thessalonians, Romans, and Philippians*, by M. Tellbe, 2001. *TLZ* 128 (2003) 1293–1294.

— /Tredici, Kelly D./Standhartinger, Angela eds. 1994. *Religious Propaganda and Missionary Competition in the New Testament World: Essays Honoring Dieter Georgi.* NovTSup 74. Leiden et al.: E. J. Brill.

Bornemann, Wilhelm 1894. *Die Thessalonicherbriefe.* 5th ed. KEK 10. Göttingen: Vandenhoeck & Ruprecht.

Bornkamm, Günther 1967. "μυστήριον, μυέω." *TDNT* 4 (1967) 802–828.

— 1971. *Paul.* Transl. by D. M. G. Stalker. New York: Harper & Row.

Börschel, Regina 2001. *Die Konstruktion einer christlichen Identität. Paulus und die Gemeinde von Thessalonich in ihrer hellenistisch-römischen Umwelt.* BBB 128. Berlin/Wien: Philo.

Borse, Udo 1990. "ἄγω." *EDNT* 1 (1990) 24–25.

Bousset, Wilhelm 1970. *Kyrios Christos: A History of the Belief in Christ from the Beginnings of Christianity to Irenaeus.* Transl. by J. E. Steely. Nashville/New York: Abingdon.

Bouttier, Michel 1962. *En Christ. Étude d'exégèse et de théologie pauliniennes.* EHPR 54. Paris: Presses Universitaires de France.

— 1966. *Christianity according to Paul.* Transl. by F. Clarke. SBT 49. London: SCM.

Bovon, François 2001. "A Review of John Dominic Crossan's *The Birth of Christianity.*" *HTR* 94 (2001) 369–374.

Bradley, David G. 1953. "The *Topos* as a Form in the Pauline Paraenesis." *JBL* 72 (1953) 238–246.

Brandenburger, Egon 1984. "Gericht Gottes III. Neues Testament." *TRE* 12 (1984) 469–483.

Brandon, Samuel G. F. 1951. *The Fall of Jerusalem and the Christian Church: A Study of the Effects of the Jewish Overthrow of A.D. 70 on Christianity.* London: SPCK.

Branick, Vincent P. 1985. "Apocalyptic Paul?" *CBQ* 47 (1985) 664–675.

Brant, Jo-Ann A. 1993. "The Place of *Mimēsis* in Paul's Thought." *SR* 22 (1993) 285–300.

Braumann, Georg 1976. "Present, Day, Maranatha, Parousia." *NIDNTT* 2 (1976) 886–935 [§ ἡμέρα cl, ot.1–2, 4, nt; παρουσία: 887–888, 892–895, 898–901].

Braun, Herbert 1953. "Zur nachpaulinischen Herkunft des zweiten Thessalonicherbriefes." *ZNW* 44 (1952–1953) 152–156.

Bremmer, Jan N./García Martínez, Florentino eds. 1992. *Sacred History and Sacred Texts in Early Judaism: A Symposium in Honour of A. S. van der Woude.* CBET 5. Kampen: Kok Pharos.

Breytenbach, Cilliers/Paulsen, Henning eds. 1991. *Anfänge der Christologie. Festschrift für Ferdinand Hahn zum 65. Geburtstag.* Göttingen: Vandenhoeck & Ruprecht.

Bridges, Linda M. 1999. "Terms of Endearment: Paul's Words of Comfort in First Thessalonians." *RevExp* 96 (1999) 211–232.

Bristol, Lyle O. 1944. "Paul's Thessalonian Correspondence." *ExpTim* 55 (1943–1944) 223.

Brocke, Christoph vom → vom Brocke, Christoph.

Broer, Ingo 1983. "'Antisemitismus' und Judenpolemik im Neuen Testament. – Ein Beitrag zum besseren Verständnis von 1Thess 2,14–16." *BN* 20 (1983) 59–91.

— 1990. "„Der ganze Zorn ist schon über sie gekommen". Bemerkungen zur Interpolationshypothese und zur Interpretation von 1 Thes 2,14–16." In: R. F. Collins (1990) 137–159.

— 1990a. "ἀγγέλλω, ἀναγγέλλω, ἀπαγγέλλω." *EDNT* 1 (1990) 12–13.

— 1990b. "ἄγγελος." *EDNT* 1 (1990) 13–16.

— 1991. "Antijudaismus im Neuen Testament? Versuch einer Annäherung anhand von zwei Texten (1 Thess 2,14–16 und Mt 27,24f)." In: FS Vögtle (1991) 321–355.

Brown, Colin 1976. "Present, Day, Maranatha, Parousia." *NIDNTT* 2 (1976) 886–935 [§ ἡμέρα ot.3; μαραναθά 4; The Parousia and Eschatology in the NT: 888–892, 896–898, 901–931].

— 1978. "Resurrection." *NIDNTT* 3 (1978) 259–309 [§ ἀνάστασις CL, OT; The Resurrection in Contemporary Theology: 259–275, 281–305].
BROWN, John P. 1964. "Synoptic Parallels in the Epistles and Form-History." *NTS* 10 (1963–1964) 27–48.
BROWN, Raymond E. 1968. *The Semitic Background of the Term "Mystery" in the New Testament.* FBBS 21. Philadelphia: Fortress.
— 1989. "The Contribution of Historical Biblical Criticism to Ecumenical Church Discussion." In: NEUHAUS (1989) 24–49.
— 1990. "Hermeneutics." In: BROWN/FITZMYER/MURPHY (1990) 1147–1165.
— 1994. *The Death of the Messiah: From Gethsemane to the Grave.* 2 vols. ABRL. New York et al.: Doubleday.
— 1997. *An Introduction to the New Testament.* ABRL. New York et al.: Doubleday.
— /FITZMYER, Joseph A./MURPHY, Roland E. eds. 1990. *The New Jerome Biblical Commentary.* Englewood Cliffs, NJ et al.: Prentice Hall.
BRUCE, Frederick F. 1970. "1 and 2 Thessalonians." In: GUTHRIE et al. (1970) 1154–1165.
— 1977. *Paul: Apostle of the Free Spirit.* Exeter: Paternoster.
— 1979. "St. Paul in Macedonia." *BJRL* 61 (1978–1979) 337–354.
— 1980. "St. Paul in Macedonia: 2. The Thessalonian Correspondence." *BJRL* 62 (1979–1980) 328–345.
— 1982. *1 and 2 Thessalonians.* WBC 45. Waco, TX: Word.
— 1985. "The Acts of the Apostles: Historical Record or Theological Reconstruction?" *ANRW* II.25.3 (1985) 2569–2603.
— 1988. *The Book of the Acts.* NICNT. Grand Rapids: Eerdmans.
— 1992. "Macedonia." *ABD* 4 (1992) 454–457.
— 1993. "Paul in Acts and Letters." *DPL* (1993) 679–692.
BRUNT, John C. 1985. "More on the *Topos* as a New Testament Form." *JBL* 104 (1985) 495–500.
BÜCHSEL, Friedrich 1949. "'In Christus' bei Paulus." *ZNW* 42 (1949) 141–158.
— 1964. "εἴδωλον." *TDNT* 2 (1964) 375–378.
BUCK, Charles/TAYLOR, Greer 1969. *Saint Paul: A Study of the Development of His Thought.* New York: Charles Scribner's Sons.
BUELL, Denise K. 2001. "Rethinking the Relevance of Race for Early Christian Self-Definition." *HTR* 94 (2001) 449–476.
BULTMANN, Rudolf 1952 [vol. 1]; 1955 [vol. 2]. *Theology of the New Testament.* 2 vols. Transl. by K. GROBEL. London: SCM.
— 1955. "History and Eschatology in the New Testament." *NTS* 1 (1954–1955) 5–16.
— 1964. "ἀλήθεια κτλ." *TDNT* 1 (1964) 232–251 [§ C–ἀληθεύω: 238–251].
— 1964a. "ἐλπίς κτλ." *TDNT* 2 (1964) 517–535 [§ A, B, D–προελπίζω: 517–523, 529–535].
— 1964b. "ζάω κτλ." *TDNT* 2 (1964) 832–875 [§ A, B.4, D–ζωοποιέω: 832–843, 849–851, 855–875].
— 1964c. "Ist die Apokalyptik die Mutter der christlichen Theologie? Eine Auseinandersetzung mit Ernst Käsemann." In: FS HAENCHEN (1964) 64–69.
— 1965. "θάνατος κτλ." *TDNT* 3 (1965) 7–25.
— 1965a. "καυχάομαι κτλ." *TDNT* 3 (1965) 645–654.
— 1967. "νεκρός, νεκρόω, νέκρωσις." *TDNT* 4 (1967) 892–895.
— 1967a. "λύπη κτλ." *TDNT* 4 (1967) 313–324.
— 1968. "πιστεύω κτλ." *TDNT* 6 (1968) 174–228 [§ A, C–E; 175–182, 197–228].
— 1980. *Primitive Christianity in Its Contemporary Setting.* Transl. by R. H. FULLER. Philadelphia: Fortress.
— 1984. *New Testament and Mythology: And Other Basic Writings.* Sel., ed. & transl. by S. M. OGDEN. Philadelphia: Fortress.
BURCHARD, Christoph 1985. "Joseph and Aseneth: A New Translation and Introduction." *OTP* 2 (1985) 177–247.
— 2005. "Satzbau und Übersetzung von 1Thess 1,10." *ZNW* 96 (2005) 272–273.
BURKE, Trevor J. 2003. *Family Matters: A Socio-Historical Study of Kinship Metaphors in 1 Thessalonians.* JSNTSup 247. London/New York: T&T Clark.

BURKEEN, W. Howard 1979. "The Parousia of Christ in the Thessalonian Correspondence." PhD diss. University of Aberdeen, 1979.

BURY, Robert G. transl. 1914–1935 → FOWLER et al. 1914–1935.

BUSSMANN, Claus 1975. *Themen der paulinischen Missionspredigt auf dem Hintergrund der spätjüdisch-hellenistischen Missionsliteratur.* 2nd rev. ed. EHS.T 3. Bern: Herbert Lang / Frankfurt am Main: Peter Lang.

BYRNE, Brendan 1996. *Romans.* SacPag 6. Collegeville, MN: Liturgical Press.

BYRON, John 2003. *Slavery Metaphors in Early Judaism and Pauline Christianity: A Traditio-Historical and Exegetical Examination.* WUNT II.162. Tübingen: Mohr Siebeck.

BYRSKOG, Samuel 1996. "Co-Senders, Co-Authors and Paul's Use of the First Person Plural." *ZNW* 87 (1996) 230–250.

CAMPBELL, Donald K. ed. 1982. *Walvoord: A Tribute.* Chicago: Moody.

CAMPENHAUSEN, Hans von → VON CAMPENHAUSEN, Hans.

CANCIK, Hubert 1990. "Eschatologie." *HrwG* 2 (1990) 341–343.

CAREY, Greg 1999. "Introduction: Apocalyptic Discourse, Apocalyptic Rhetoric." In: CAREY/BLOOMQUIST (1999) 1–17.

— /BLOOMQUIST, L. Gregory eds. 1999. *Vision and Persuasion: Rhetorical Dimensions of Apocalyptic Discourse.* St. Louis, MO: Chalice.

CARNLEY, Peter 1987. *The Structure of Resurrection Belief.* Oxford: Clarendon.

CARR, Wesley 1977. "The Rulers of This Age — 1 Corinthians II. 6–8." *NTS* 23 (1976–1977) 20–35.

CARRAS, George P. 1990. "Jewish Ethics and Gentile Converts: Remarks on 1 Thes 4,3–8." In: R. F. COLLINS (1990) 306–315.

CARROLL, Robert P. 1990. "Eschatology." In: COGGINS/HOULDEN (1990) 200–203.

CARSON, Don A. 1993. "An Introduction to the Porter/Fanning Debate." In: PORTER/CARSON (1993) 18–25.

CASEY, Maurice 1982. "Chronology and the Development of Pauline Christology." In: FS BARRETT (1982) 124–134.

CAVALLIN, Hans C. C. 1974. *Life After Death: Paul's Argument for the Resurrection of the Dead in 1 Cor 15. Part 1: An Enquiry into the Jewish Background.* ConBNT 7. Lund: CWK Gleerup.

— 1979. "Leben nach dem Tode im Spätjudentum und im frühen Christentum." *ANRW* II.19.1 (1979) 240–345.

CERFAUX, Lucien 1959. *Christ in the Theology of St. Paul.* Transl. by G. WEBB/A. WALKER. New York: Herder & Herder.

— 1959a. *The Church in the Theology of St. Paul.* Transl. by G. WEBB/A. WALKER. New York: Herder & Herder / Edinburgh/London: Thomas Nelson & Sons.

CHAMPION, Leonard G. 1934. *Benedictions and Doxologies in the Epistles of Paul.* Inaugural-Dissertation zur Erlangung der Doktorwürde der Theologischen Fakultät der Ruprecht-Karls-Universität zu Heidelberg. Oxford: Kemp Hall.

CHAPA, Juan 1990. "Consolatory Patterns? 1 Thes 4,13.18; 5,11." In: R. F. COLLINS (1990) 220–228.

— 1994. "Is First Thessalonians a Letter of Consolation?" *NTS* 40 (1994) 150–160.

CHARLES, Robert H. ed. 1908. *The Testaments of the Twelve Patriarchs: Translated from the Editor's Greek Text.* London: Adam & Charles Black.

— 1963. *Eschatology: The Doctrine of a Future Life in Israel, Judaism and Christianity. A Critical History.* Intro. by G. W. BUCHANAN. New York: Schocken Books.

— 1966. *The Greek Versions of the Testaments of the Twelve Patriarchs: Edited from Nine MSS together with the Variants of the Armenian and Slavonic Versions and Some Hebrew Fragments.* 3rd unch. ed. Oxford: University Press / Darmstadt: Wissenschaftliche Buchgesellschaft.

CHARLESWORTH, James H. ed. 1992. *The Messiah: Developments in Earliest Judaism and Christianity.* With J. BROWNSON et al. The First Princeton Symposium on Judaism and Christian Origins. Minneapolis: Fortress.

CHERNISS, Harold/HELMBOLD, William C. transl. 1927–1976 → BABBITT 1927–1976.

CHRISTOPHERSEN, Alf et al. eds. 2002. *Paul, Luke and the Graeco-Roman World: Essays in Honour of Alexander J. M. Wedderburn.* JSNTSup 217. Sheffield: Academic Press.

CHURCH, F. Forrester/GEORGE, Timothy eds. 1979. *Continuity and Discontinuity in Church History: Essays Presented to George Huntston Williams on the Occasion of his 65th Birthday*. Studies in History of Christian Thought 19. Leiden: E. J. Brill.
CLARK, Kenneth W. 1940. "'Realized Eschatology'." *JBL* 59 (1940) 367–383. Republ. in: CLARK (1980) 48–64.
— 1980. *The Gentile Bias and Other Essays*. Sel. by J. L. SHARPE, III. NovTSup 54. Leiden: E. J. Brill.
CLARKE, Andrew D. 1993. *Secular and Christian Leadership in Corinth: A Socio-Historical and Exegetical Study of 1 Corinthians 1–6*. AGJU 18. Leiden et al.: E. J. Brill.
— 1998. "'Be Imitators of Me': Paul's Model of Leadership." *TynBul* 49 (1998) 329–360.
CLASSEN, C. Joachim 1991. "Paulus und die antike Rhetorik." *ZNW* 82 (1991) 1–33.
— 1992. "St. Paul's Epistles and Ancient Greek and Roman Rhetoric." *Rhetorica* 10 (1992) 319–344.
CLEMEN, Carl 1896. "Paulus und die Gemeinde zu Thessalonike." *NKZ* 7 (1896) 139–164.
COENEN, Lothar 1975. "Death, Kill, Sleep." *NIDNTT* 1 (1975) 429–447 [§ ἀποκτείνω; καθεύδω; νεκρός: 429–430, 441–446].
— 1978. "Resurrection." *NIDNTT* 3 (1978) 259–309 [§ ἀνάστασις CL, NT; ἐγείρω: 259, 275–278, 279–281].
COGGINS, Richard J./HOULDEN, James L. eds. 1990. *A Dictionary of Biblical Interpretation*. London: SCM / Philadelphia: Trinity Press International.
COHOON, James W./CROSBY, H. Lamar transl. 1932–1951. *Dio Chrysostom*. 5 vols. Vols. 1–2 transl. by J. W. COHOON. Vol. 3 transl. by J. W. COHOON/H. L. CROSBY. Vols. 4–5 transl. by H. L. CROSBY. LCL 257, 339, 358, 376, 385. London: William Heinemann / Cambridge: Harvard University Press.
COLLINS, A. Yarbro 1985. "Aristobulus: A New Translation and Introduction." *OTP* 2 (1985) 831–842.
— ed. 1986. *Semeia* 36. *Early Christian Apocalypticism: Genre and Social Setting*. Missoula, MT: Scholars Press.
— 1986a. "Introduction." In: COLLINS, A. Yarbro (1986) 1–11.
— 1988. "Early Christian Apocalyptic Literature." *ANRW* II.25.6 (1988) 4665–4711.
— 1992. "Apocalypses and Apocalypticism: Early Christian." *ABD* 1 (1992) 288–292.
— 1998. "Apokalyptik IV. Neues Testament." *RGG* 1 ([4]1998) 594–595.
— 1999. "Apocalyptic Themes in Biblical Literature." *Int* 53 (1999) 117–130.
COLLINS, John J. 1974. "Apocalyptic Eschatology as the Transcendence of Death." *CBQ* 36 (1974) 21–43. Republ. in: J. J. COLLINS (1997) 75–97.
— ed. 1979. *Semeia* 14. *Apocalypse: The Morphology of a Genre*. Missoula, MT: Scholars Press.
— 1979a. "Introduction: Towards the Morphology of a Genre." *Semeia* 14 (1979) 1–20.
— 1991. "Genre, Ideology and Social Movements in Jewish Apocalypticism." In: J. J. COLLINS/ CHARLESWORTH (1991) 11–32. Republ. in: J. J. COLLINS (1997) 25–38.
— 1992. "Apocalypses and Apocalypticism: Early Jewish Apocalypticism." *ABD* 1 (1992) 282–288.
— 1997. *Seers, Sybils and Sages in Hellenistic-Roman Judaism*. JSJSup 54. Leiden et al.: Brill.
— 1998. *The Apocalyptic Imagination: An Introduction to the Jewish Apocalyptic Literature*. 2nd ed. The Biblical Resource Series. Grand Rapids/Cambridge: Eerdmans.
— ed. 1998a. *The Encyclopedia of Apocalypticism*. Vol. 1: *The Origins of Apocalypticism in Judaism and Christianity*. New York: Continuum.
— 1998b. "Introduction to Volume 1." In: J. J. COLLINS (1998a) xiii–xvii.
— 2000. "The Afterlife in Apocalyptic Literature." In: AVERY-PECK/NEUSNER (2000) 119–139.
— /CHARLESWORTH, James H. eds. 1991. *Mysteries and Revelations: Apocalyptic Studies since the Uppsala Colloquium*. JSPSup 9. Sheffield: JSOT Press.
— /MCGINN, Bernard/STEIN, Stephen J. 1998. "General Introduction." In: J. J. COLLINS (1998a) vii–xi.
COLLINS, Raymond F. 1975. "'The Church of the Thessalonians'." *LS* 5 (1974–1975) 336–349. Republ. in: R. F. COLLINS (1984) 285–298.
— 1977. "The Theology of Paul's First Letter to the Thessalonians." *LS* 6 (1976–1977) 315–337. Republ. in: R. F. COLLINS (1984) 230–252.
— 1979. "The Faith of the Thessalonians." *LS* 7 (1978–1979) 249–269. Republ. in: R. F. COLLINS (1984) 209–229.
— 1979a. "Apropos the Integrity of 1 Thess." *ETL* 65 (1979) 67–106. Republ. in: R. F. COLLINS (1984) 96–135.

— 1980. "1 Thess and the Liturgy of the Early Church." *BTB* 10 (1980) 51–64. Republ. in: R. F. Collins (1984) 136–153.

— 1980a. "Tradition, Redaction, and Exhortation in 1 Thess 4,13–5,11." In: Lambrecht (1980) 325–343. Republ. in: R. F. Collins (1984) 154–172.

— 1980b. "The Growth of Resurrection Faith." *Emmanuel* 86 (1980) 277–282. Republ. in: R. F. Collins (1984) 339–345.

— 1981. "Paul as Seen through His Own Eyes: A Reflection on the First Letter to the Thessalonians." *LS* 8 (1980–1981) 348–381. Republ. in: R. F. Collins (1984) 175–208.

— 1981a. "Paul's First Reflections on Love." *Emmanuel* 87 (1981) 107–113. Republ. in: R. F. Collins (1984) 346–355.

— 1982. "Paul at Prayer." *Emmanuel* 88 (1982) 412–419. Republ. in: R. F. Collins (1984) 356–364.

— 1983. "'... That This Letter Be Read to All the Brethren'." *LS* 9 (1982–1983) 122–127. Republ. in: R. F. Collins (1984) 365–370.

— 1983a. "'This is the Will of God: Your Sanctification.' (1 Thess 4:3)." *LTP* 39 (1983) 27–53. Republ. in: R. F. Collins (1984) 299–325.

— 1983b. "The Unity of Paul's Paraenesis in 1 Thess. 4.3–8. 1 Cor. 7.1–7, A Significant Parallel." *NTS* 29 (1983) 420–429. Republ. in: R. F. Collins (1984) 326–335.

— 1984. *Studies on the First Letter to the Thessalonians*. BETL 66. Leuven: University Press. [collected essays include: R. F. Collins 1975; 1977; 1979; 1979a; 1980; 1980a; 1980b; 1981; 1981a; 1982; 1983; 1983a; 1983b; 1984a; 1984b; 1984c; 1984d]

— 1984a. "Recent Scholarship on Paul's First Letter to the Thessalonians." In: R. F. Collins (1984) 3–75.

— 1984b. "The Text of the Epistles to the Thessalonians in Nestle-Aland[26]." In: R. F. Collins (1984) 79–95.

— 1984c. "Paul's Early Christology." In: R. F. Collins (1984) 253–284.

— 1984d. "The Christian Community: Servant of the Word." In: R. F. Collins (1984) 371–382.

— 1988. "'The Lord Jesus Christ'." *TBT* 26 (1988) 338–343.

— 1988a. *Letters That Paul Did Not Write: The Epistle to the Hebrews and the Pauline Pseudepigrapha*. GNS 28. Wilmington, DE: Michael Glazier.

— ed. 1990. *The Thessalonian Correspondence*. BETL 87. Leuven: University Press.

— 1990a. "The First Letter to the Thessalonians." In: Brown/Fitzmyer/Murphy (1990) 772–779.

— 1990b. "'The Gospel of Our Lord Jesus' (2 Thes 1,8): A Symbolic Shift of Paradigm." In: R. F. Collins (1990) 426–440.

— 1991. "1 Thessalonians." In: Bassler (1991) 273–276.

— 1991a. "God in the First Letter to the Thessalonians: Paul's Earliest Written Appreciation of *ho theos*." *LS* 16 (1991) 137–154.

— 1993. *The Birth of the New Testament: The Origin and Development of the First Christian Generation*. New York: Crossroad.

— 1997. Review of *First and Second Thessalonians*, by E. J. Richard, 1995. *CBQ* 59 (1997) 785–787.

— 1998. "The Function of Paraenesis in 1 Thess 4,1–12; 5,12–22." *ETL* 74 (1998) 398–414.

— 2000. "'I Command That This Letter Be Read': Writing as a Manner of Speaking." In: Donfried/Beutler (2000) 319–339.

— 2002. "What Happened to Jesus' Resurrection from the Dead? A Reflection on Paul and the Pastoral Epistles." In: FS Lambrecht (2002) 423–440.

Colpe, Carsten 1972. "ὁ υἱὸς τοῦ ἀνθρώπου." *TDNT* 8 (1972) 400–477.

— 1996. "Antisemitismus." *DNP* 1 (1996) 790–792.

— et al. 1994. "Jenseitsfahrt I. Himmelfahrt (A. B I/II. IV. C. D I. IV)." *RAC* 17 (1994) 407–466.

Colson, Francis H./Whitaker, George H. transl. 1929–1962. *Philo*. 10 vols. + 2 suppl. vols. LCL 226, 227, 247, 261, 275, 289, 320, 341, 363, 379, 380, 401. London: William Heinemann / Cambridge: Harvard University Press.

Connolly, A. L. 1987. "παρουσία." *NewDocs* 4 (1987) 167–169.

Conrad, Edgar W./Newing, Edward G. eds. 1987. *Perspectives on Language and Text: Essays and Poems in Honor of Francis I. Andersen's Sixtieth Birthday, July 28, 1985*. Winona Lake, IN: Eisenbrauns.

CONYBEARE, Frederick C. transl. 1912. *Philostratus: The Life of Apollonius of Tyana*. 2 Vols. LCL 16, 17. London: William Heinemann / Cambridge: Harvard University Press.
CONZELMANN, Hans 1957. "Auferstehung V. Im NT." *RGG* 1 (^{3}1957) 695–696.
— 1957a. "Auferstehung Christi I. Im NT." *RGG* 1 (^{3}1957) 698–700.
— 1961. "Parusie." *RGG* 5 (^{3}1961) 130–132.
— 1969. *An Outline of the Theology of the New Testament*. Transl. by J. BOWDEN. London: SCM.
— 1971. "σκότος κτλ." *TDNT* 7 (1971) 423–445.
— 1974. "χαίρω κτλ." *TDNT* 9 (1974) 359–415 [§ χαίρω, χαρά, συγχαίρω; χάρις κτλ. A, C–F; χάρισμα; εὐχαριστέω, εὐχαριστία, εὐχάριστος: 359–372, 372–376, 387–402, 402–406, 407–415].
— 1974a. "φῶς κτλ." *TDNT* 9 (1974) 310–358.
— 1975. *1 Corinthians: A Commentary on the First Epistle to the Corinthians*. Ed. by G. W. MACRAE. Transl. by J. W. LEITCH. Bib. & ref. by J. W. DUNKLY. Hermeneia. Philadelphia: Fortress.
— 1987. *Acts of the Apostles: A Commentary on the Acts of the Apostles*. Ed. by E. J. EPP with C. R. MATTHEWS. Transl. by J. LIMBURG/A. T. KRAABEL/D. H. JUEL. Hermeneia. Philadelphia: Fortress.
— 1992. *Gentiles, Jews, Christians: Polemics and Apologetics in the Greco-Roman Era*. Transl. by M. E. BORING. Minneapolis: Fortress.
— et al. 1967. *Zur Bedeutung des Todes Jesu. Exegetische Beiträge*. 2nd ed. STAEKU. Gütersloh: Gerd Mohn.
COOK, John G. 2006. "Pagan Philosophers and 1 Thessalonians." *NTS* 52 (2006) 514–532.
COPPENS, Josef 1975. "Miscellanées bibliques. LXXX. Une diatribe antijuive dans I Thess., II, 13–16." *ETL* 51 (1975) 90–95.
— /DESCAMPS, Albert/MASSAUX, Édouard eds. 1959. *Sacra Pagina: Miscellanea biblica Congressus internationalis catholici de re biblica*. Vol. 2. BETL 12–13. Paris: Gabalda / Gembloux: Duculot.
CORNISH, F. W. transl. 1912. *The Poems of Gaius Valerius Catullus*. LCL 6. London: William Heinemann / New York: Macmillan.
CORRIVEAU, Raymond 1970. *The Liturgy of Life: A Study of the Ethical Thought of St. Paul in His Letters to the Early Christian Communities*. Bruxelles/Paris: Desclée de Brouwer / Montréal: Les Éditions Bellarmin.
COSBY, Michael R. 1994. "Hellenistic Formal Receptions and Paul's Use of ΑΠΑΝΤΗΣΙΣ in 1 Thessalonians 4:17." *BBR* 4 (1994) 15–33.
COURT, John M. 1982. "Paul and the Apocalyptic Pattern." In: FS BARRETT (1982) 57–66.
CRANFIELD, Charles E. B. 1979. *A Critical and Exegetical Commentary on the Epistle to the Romans*. Vol. 2: *Commentary on Romans IX–XVI and Essays*. ICC. Edinburgh: T. & T. Clark.
— 1979. "A Study of 1 Thessalonians 2." *IBS* 1 (1979) 215–226.
— 1982. "Changes of Person and Number in Paul's Epistles." In: FS BARRETT (1982) 280–289.
— 1982a. "Thoughts on New Testament Eschatology." *SJT* 35 (1982) 497–512.
CRAWFORD, Barry S. 1982. "Near Expectation in the Sayings of Jesus." *JBL* 101 (1982) 225–244.
CRIM, Keith et al. eds. 1976. *Interpreter's Dictionary of the Bible*. Suppl. vol. [see *IDBSup* in abbrev.]
CROCKETT, William V. 1991. "Wrath That Endures Forever." *JETS* 34 (1991) 195–202.
CROOK, Zeba A. 1997. "Paul's Riposte and Praise of the Thessalonians." *BTB* 27 (1997) 153–163.
CROSSAN, John D. 1995. *Who Killed Jesus? Exposing the Roots of Anti-Semitism in the Gospel Story of the Death of Jesus*. [San Francisco]: HarperSanFrancisco.
CUKROWSKI, Kenneth L. 2002. Review of *Leadership and Lifestyle: The Portrait of Paul in the Miletus Speech and 1 Thessalonians*, by S. WALTON, 2000. *RelSRev* 28 (2002) 77.
CULLMANN, Oscar 1956. *The Early Church*. Transl. by S. GODMAN/A. J. B. HIGGINS. London: SCM.
— 1956a. "Eschatology and Missions in the New Testament." In: FS DODD (1956) 409–421.
— 1957. *The State in the New Testament*. London: SCM.
— 1963. *The Christology of the New Testament*. 2nd Eng. ed. Transl. by S. C. GUTHRIE/C. A. M. HALL. London: SCM.
— 1965. "Immortality of the Soul or Resurrection of the Dead: The Witness of the New Testament. The Ingersoll Lecture for 1955." In: CULLMANN et al. (1965) 9–53.
— et al. 1965. *Immortality and Resurrection: Four Essays by Oscar Cullmann, Harry A. Wolfson, Werner Jaeger, and Henry J. Cadbury*. Ed. & with an intro. by K. STENDAHL. New York: Macmillan.
CUMING, G. J. 1976. "Service-Endings in the Epistles." *NTS* 22 (1975–1976) 110–113.

CURTIS, Edward M. 1992. "Idol, Idolatry." *ABD* 3 (1992) 376–381.
CUSTER, Stewart 1975. "The Theology of 1 Thessalonians." *BV* 9 (1975) 46–50.

DABELSTEIN, Rolf 1991. "νεκρός." *EDNT* 2 (1991) 459–461.
DAHL, Nils A. 1977. *Studies in Paul: Theology for the Early Christian Mission*. Ass. by P. DONAHUE. Minneapolis: Augsburg.
DANA, Harvey E./MANTEY, Julius R. 1955. *A Manual Grammar of the Greek New Testament*. New York: Macmillan.
DANIEL, Jerry L. 1979. "Anti-Semitism in the Hellenistic-Roman Period." *JBL* 98 (1979) 45–65.
DANKER, Frederick W. rev. & ed. 2000. *A Greek-English Lexicon of the New Testament and Other Early Christian Literature*. [see BDAG in abbrev.]
DAUBE, David 1968. "The Night of Death." *HTR* 61 (1968) 629–632.
DAUTZENBERG, Gerhard 1990. "ἀγών, ἀγωνίζομαι." *EDNT* 1 (1990) 25–27.
— 1997. "Propheten/Prophetie IV. Neues Testament und Alte Kirche." *TRE* 27 (1997) 503–511.
— 1999. "Prophetie bei Paulus." In: BALDERMANN (1999) 55–70.
DAVIES, Alan ed. 1979. *Antisemitism and the Foundations of Christianity*. New York et al.: Paulist.
DAVIES, J. G. 1963. "The Genesis of Belief in an Imminent Parousia." *JTS* NS 14 (1963) 104–107.
DAVIES, Margaret 1990. "Exegesis." In: COGGINS/HOULDEN (1990) 220–222.
DAVIES, William D. 1978. "Paul and the People of Israel." *NTS* 24 (1977–1978) 4–39.
— 1984. *Jewish and Pauline Studies*. London: SPCK.
— /DAUBE, David eds. 1956. *The Background of the New Testament and Its Eschatology: In Honour of Charles Harold Dodd*. Cambridge: University Press.
— /ALLISON, Dale C. 1991. *A Critical and Exegetical Commentary on the Gospel according to Saint Matthew*. Vol. 2: *Commentary on Matthew VIII–XVIII*. ICC. Edinburgh: T&T Clark.
DAVIS, Richard H. 1971. "Remembering and Acting: A Study of the Moral Life in Light of 1 Thessalonians." PhD diss. Yale University, 1971. Ann Arbor, MI: UMI, 1971.
DE BOER, Martinus C. 1988. *The Defeat of Death: Apocalyptic Eschatology in 1 Corinthians 15 and Romans 5*. JSNTSup 22. Sheffield: Academic Press.
— 1989. "Paul and Jewish Apocalyptic Eschatology." In: FS MARTYN (1989) 169–190.
— 2002. "Paul, Theologian of God's Apocalypse." *Int* 56 (2002) 21–33.
DE BOER, Willis P. 1962. *The Imitation of Paul: An Exegetical Study*. Kampen: J. H. Kok.
DE JONGE, Henk J. 1990. "The Original Setting of the Χριστὸς ἀπέθανεν ὑπέρ Formula." In: COLLINS (1990) 229–235.
DE JONGE, Marinus ed. 1975. *Studies on the Testaments of the Twelve Patriarchs: Text and Interpretation*. SVTP 3. Leiden: E. J. Brill.
— 1975a. "Notes on Testament of Levi II–VII." In: DE JONGE (1975) 247–260.
— 1978. *The Testament of the Twelve Patriarchs: A Critical Edition of the Greek Text*. In cooperation with H. W. HOLLANDER/H. J. DE JONGE/TH. KORTEWEG. PVTG 1. Leiden: E. J. Brill.
— 1979. "Some Remarks in Connection with *A Translator's Handbook on Paul's Letters to the Thessalonians*." With a "Comment" by P. ELLINGWORTH/E. A. NIDA. *BT* 30 (1979) 127–135.
— 1988. *Christology in Context: The Earliest Christian Response to Jesus*. Philadelphia: Westminster.
— 1993. "The Transmission of the Testaments of the Twelve Patriarchs by Christians." *VC* 47 (1993) 1–28.
— 1995. "Light on Paul from the *Testaments of the Twelve Patriarchs*?" In: FS MEEKS (1995) 100–115.
DE KRUIJF, Theo C. 1978. "Antisemitismus III. Im Neuen Testament." *TRE* 3 (1978) 122–128.
DE LACEY, Douglas R. 1993. "Gentiles." *DPL* (1993) 335–339.
DE LANGE, Nicholas R. M./THOMA, Clemens 1978. "Antisemitismus I. Begriff/Vorchristlicher Antisemitismus." *TRE* 3 (1978) 113–119.
DE VOS, Craig S. 1999. *Church and Community Conflicts: The Relationships of the Thessalonian, Corinthian and Philippian Churches with Their Wider Civic Communities*. SBLDS 168. Atlanta: Scholars Press.
DEGENHARDT, Johannes J. ed. 1991. *Die Freude an Gott – unsere Kraft. Festschrift für Otto Bernhard Knoch zum 65. Geburtstag*. Stuttgart: Verlag Katholisches Bibelwerk.

DEISSMANN, Adolf 1995. *Light from the Ancient East: The New Testament Illustrated by Recently Discovered Texts of the Graeco-Roman World*. Transl. by L. R. M. STRACHAN. Peabody, MA: Hendrickson. Original ET by George H. Doran Co., New York, 1927.

DELAHAYE, Karl ed. 1974. *Bestellt zum Zeugnis. Festgabe für Bischof Johannes Pohlschneider zur Vollendung des 75. Lebensjahres*. Aachen: Einhard.

DELL, Harry J. ed. 1981. *Ancient Macedonian Studies in Honor of Charles F. Edson*. Institute for Balkan Studies 158. Thessaloniki: Institute for Balkan Studies.

DELLING, Gerhard 1964. "Der Tod Jesu in der Verkündigung des Paulus." FS HAENCHEN (1964) 85–96. Republ. in: HAHN/HOLTZ/WALTER (1970) 336–346.

— 1964a. "ἄρχων." *TDNT* 1 (1964) 488–489.

— 1964b. "ἡμέρα." *TDNT* 2 (1964) 943–953 [§ B–D: 947–953].

— 1965. "καιρός κτλ." *TDNT* 3 (1965) 455–464.

— 1966. "Die Bedeutung der Auferstehung Jesu für den Glauben an Jesus Christus. Ein exegetischer Beitrag." In: MARXSEN et al. (1966) 65–90. Republ. in: HAHN/HOLTZ/WALTER (1970) 347–370.

— 1967. "λαμβάνω κτλ." *TDNT* 4 (1967) 5–15.

— 1967a. "νύξ." *TDNT* 4 (1967) 1123–1126.

— 1968. "πλήρης κτλ." *TDNT* 6 (1968) 283–311.

— 1972. "τέλος κτλ." *TDNT* 8 (1972) 49–87.

— 1974. "χρόνος." *TDNT* 9 (1974) 581–593.

DELOBEL, Joël 1990. "The Fate of the Dead according to 1 Thes 4 and 1 Cor 15." In: R. F. COLLINS (1990) 340–347.

DEMKE, Christoph 1973. "Theologie und Literarkritik im 1. Thessalonicherbrief. Ein Diskussionsbeitrag." In: FS FUCHS (1973) 103–124.

DENAUX, Adelbert 1996. "Theology and Christology in 1 Cor 8,4–6: A Contextual-Redactional Reading." In: BIERINGER (1996) 593–606.

DENIS, Albert-M. 1987. *Concordance grecque des pseudépigraphes d'Ancien Testament. Concordance, corpus des textes, indices*. With the collaboration of Y. JANSSENS. Louvain-la-Neuve: Universitè Catholique de Louvain, Institut Orientaliste.

DENNEY, James 1892. *The Epistles to the Thessalonians*. New York: A. C. Armstrong & Son.

DESILVA, David A. 1996. "'Worthy of His Kingdom': Honor Discourse and Social Engineering in 1 Thessalonians." *JSNT*, issue 64 (1996) 49–79.

DIBELIUS, Martin 1925. *An die Thessalonicher I-II. An die Philipper*. HNT 11. 2nd ed. Tübingen: J. C. B. Mohr (Paul Siebeck).

— 1971. *From Tradition to Gospel*. Transl. by B. L. WOOLF. Library of Theological Translations. Cambridge/London: James Clarke & Co.

DICK, Karl 1900. *Der schriftstellerische Plural bei Paulus*. Halle a. S.: Max Niemeyer.

DICKSON, John P. 2003. *Mission-Commitment in Ancient Judaism and in the Pauline Communities: The Shape, Extent and Background of Early Christian Mission*. WUNT II.159. Tübingen: Mohr Siebeck.

DIELS, Hermann 1879. *Doxographi graeci*. Berlin: G. Reimer [= 4th ed. Berlin: W. de Gruyter, 1965].

DINKLER, Erich ed. 1964. *Zeit und Geschichte. Dankesgabe an Rudolf Bultmann zum 80. Geburtstag*. Tübingen: J. C. B. Mohr (Paul Siebeck).

DOBBS-ALLSOPP, F. W. 1999. "Rethinking Historical Criticism." *BibInt* 7 (1999) 235–271.

DOBSCHÜTZ, Ernst von → VON DOBSCHÜTZ, Ernst.

DODD, Charles H. 1935. *The Parables of the Kingdom*. London: Nisbet & Co.

— 1959. "The Primitive Catechism and the Sayings of Jesus." In: FS MANSON (1959) 106–118. Republ. in: DODD (1968) 11–29.

— 1968. *More New Testament Studies*. Grand Rapids: Eerdmans.

DOIGNON, Jean 1982. "La lecture de *I Thessaloniciens* 4,17 en Occident de Tertullien à Augustin." In: GS STUIBER (1982) 98–106.

DONALDSON, Terence L. 1993. "'Riches for the Gentiles' (Rom 11:12): Israel's Rejection and Paul's Gentile Mission." *JBL* 112 (1993) 81–98.

— 1997. *Paul and the Gentiles: Remapping the Apostle's Convictional World*. Minneapolis: Fortress.

DONFRIED, Karl P. 1976. "Justification and Last Judgment in Paul: For Günther Bornkamm on His 70th Birthday." *ZNW* 67 (1976) 90–110. Republ. in: DONFRIED 2002, 253–278.

— 1984. "Paul and Judaism: I Thessalonians 2:13–16 as a Test Case." *Int* 38 (1984) 242–253. Republ. in: DONFRIED 2002, 195–208.

— 1985. "The Cults of Thessalonica and the Thessalonian Correspondence." *NTS* 31 (1985) 336–356. Republ. in: DONFRIED 2002, 21–48.

— 1987. "The Kingdom of God in Paul." In: WILLIS (1987) 175–190. Republ. in: DONFRIED 2002, 233–252.

— 1989. "The Theology of 1 Thessalonians as a Reflection of Its Purpose." In: HORGAN/KOBELSKI (1989) 243–260. Republ. in: DONFRIED 2002, 119–138.

— 1990. "1 Thessalonians, Acts and the Early Paul." In: R. F. COLLINS (1990) 3–26. Republ. in: DONFRIED 2002, 69–98.

— ed. 1991. *The Romans Debate*. Rev. & exp. ed. Peabody, MA: Hendrickson.

— 1991a. "War Timotheus in Athen? Exegetische Überlegungen zu 1 Thess 3,1–3." In: FS KNOCH (1991) 189–196. Transl., rev. & republ. in: DONFRIED 2002, 209–219.

— 1992. "Chronology: New Testament" *ABD* 1 (1992) 1011–1022. Republ. in: DONFRIED 2002, 99–117.

— 1993. "The Theology of 1 Thessalonians." In: DONFRIED/MARSHALL (1993) 1–79.

— 1993a. "The Theology of 2 Thessalonians." In: DONFRIED/MARSHALL (1993) 81–113.

— 1993b. "2 Thessalonians and the Church of Thessalonica." In: FS HURD (1993) 128–144. Republ. in: DONFRIED (2002) 49–67.

— 1996. "The Assembly of the Thessalonians: Reflections on the Ecclesiology of the Earliest Christian Letter." In: FS KERTELGE (1996) 390–408. Republ. in: DONFRIED 2002, 139–162.

— 1996a. "Thessalonians, the First Letter of Paul to the." ACHTEMEIER et al. (1996) 1140–1142.

— 1996b. "Thessalonians, the Second Letter of Paul to the." ACHTEMEIER et al. (1996) 1142–1143.

— 1996c. "Thessalonica." ACHTEMEIER et al. (1996) 1143.

— 1997. "The Imperial Cults of Thessalonica and Political Conflict in 1 Thessalonians." In: R. A. HORSLEY (1997) 215–223.

— 2000. "The Scope and Nature of the Debate: An Introduction and Some Questions." In: DONFRIED/BEUTLER (2000) 3–27.

— 2000a. "The Epistolary and Rhetorical Context of 1 Thessalonians 2:1–12." In: DONFRIED/BEUTLER (2000) 31–60. Republ. in: DONFRIED 2002, 163–194.

— 2002. *Paul, Thessalonica and Early Christianity*. Grand Rapids/Cambridge: Eerdmans. [collected essays include: DONFRIED 1976; 1984; 1985; 1987; 1989; 1990; 1991a (1st Eng. transl.); 1992; 1993b; 1996; 2000a]

— /BEUTLER, Johannes eds. 2000. *The Thessalonians Debate: Methodological Discord or Methodological Synthesis?* Grand Rapids/Cambridge: Eerdmans.

— /MARSHALL, I. Howard 1993. *The Theology of the Shorter Pauline Letters*. New Testament Theology. Ed. by J. D. G. DUNN. Cambridge et al.: University Press.

DOTY, William G. 1973. *Letters in Primitive Christianity*. GBS. Philadelphia: Fortress.

DOWNING, F. Gerald. 1990. "Historical-Critical Method." In: COGGINS/HOULDEN (1990) 284–285.

DRANE, John W. 1980. Review of *Dating Paul's Life*, by R. JEWETT, 1979. *JSNT*, issue 9 (1980) 70–75.

DUFF, Nancy J. 1989. "The Significance of Pauline Apocalyptic for Theological Ethics." In: FS MARTYN (1989) 279–296.

DUNGAN, David L. 1971. *The Sayings of Jesus in the Churches of Paul: The Use of the Synoptic Tradition in the Regulation of Early Church Life*. Philadelphia: Fortress.

DUNN, James D. G. 1978. "Prophetic 'I'-Sayings and the Jesus Tradition: The Importance of Testing Prophetic Utterances within Early Christianity." *NTS* 24 (1977–1978) 175–198.

— 1984. *Testing the Foundations: Current Trends in New Testament Study. An Inaugural Lecture*. Durham: University of Durham.

— 1990. *Unity and Diversity in the New Testament: An Inquiry into the Character of Earliest Christianity*. 2nd ed. London: SCM / Philadelphia: Trinity Press International.

— ed. 1992. *Jews and Christians: The Parting of the Ways, A.D. 70 to 135. The Second Durham-Tübingen Research Symposium on Earliest Christianity and Judaism (Durham, September, 1989)*. WUNT 66. Tübingen: J. C. B. Mohr (Paul Siebeck).

— 1992a. "The Question of Anti-semitism in the New Testament Writings of the Period." In: Dunn (1992) 179–211.
— 1996. *The Acts of the Apostles*. Narrative Commentaries. Valley Forge: Trinity Press International.
— 1997. "He Will Come Again." *Int* 51 (1997) 42–56.
— 1997a. "Κύριος in Acts." In: Landmesser/Eckstein/Lichtenberger (1997) 363–378.
— 1998. *The Theology of Paul the Apostle*. Grand Rapids/Cambridge: Eerdmans.
— 1998a. "The Pauline Letters." In: Barton (1998) 276–289.
— 1998b. *The Christ and the Spirit: Collected Essays of James D. G. Dunn*. Vol. 1: *Christology*. Grand Rapids/Cambridge: Eerdmans.
— 1999. "Who Did Paul Think He Was? A Study of Jewish-Christian Identity." *NTS* 45 (1999) 174–193.
— ed. 2003. *The Cambridge Companion to St Paul*. Cambridge: University Press.
Dupont, Jacques 1952. *Σὺν Χριστῷ. L'union avec le Christ suivant Saint Paul*. Louvain: E. Nauwelaerts / Paris: Desclée de Brouwer.
Dutch, Robert S. 2005. Review of *Family Matters: A Socio-Historical Study of Kinship Metaphors in 1 Thessalonians*, by T. J. Burke, 2003. *JSNT*, issue 27 (2005) 113.
Dysinger, Holmes 1944. "The First Epistle to the Thessalonians." In: Alleman (1944) 562–570.

Eadie, John 1877. *A Commentary on the Greek Text of the Epistles of Paul to the Thessalonians*. Ed. by W. Young. London: Macmillan.
Ebeling, Gerhard/Jüngel, Eberhard/Schunack, Gerd eds. 1973. *Festschrift für E. Fuchs*. Tübingen: J. C. B. Mohr (Paul Siebeck).
Eckart, Karl-G. 1961. "Der zweite echte Brief des Apostels Paulus an die Thessalonicher. Ernst Fuchs, dem Scheidenden, zum 'Andenken'." *ZTK* 58 (1961) 30–44.
Eckert, Willehad P./Levinson, Nathan P./Stöhr, Martin eds. 1967. *Antijudaismus im Neuen Testament? Exegetische und systematische Beiträge*. ACJD 2. München: Kaiser.
Eckstein, Hans-J. 1987. "'Denn Gottes Zorn wird vom Himmel her offenbar werden'. Exegetische Erwägungen zu Röm 1 18." *ZNW* 78 (1987) 74–89.
Eddy, Paul R. 1993. "Christian and Hellenistic Moral Exhortation: A Literary Comparison Based on 1 Thessalonians 4." In: Albl/Eddy/Mirkes (1993) 45–51.
Edgar, Thomas R. 1979. "The Meaning of 'Sleep' in 1 Thessalonians 5:10." *JETS* 22 (1979) 345–349.
Edson, Charles F. 1940. "Macedonia." *HSCP* 51 (1940) 125–136.
— 1948. "Cults of Thessalonica (Macedonia III)." *HTR* 41 (1948) 153–204.
— 1970. "Early Macedonia." In: Laourdas/Makaronas (1970) 2–44.
Egelkraut, Helmuth 1984. "Die Bedeutung von 1Thess 4,13ff für eine Umschreibung christlicher Zukunftserwartung." In: Maier (1984) 86–97.
Ego, Beate 1996. "Apokalypsen." *DNP* 1 (1996) 851–852.
Ehrman, Bart D. ed. & transl. 2003. *The Apostolic Fathers*. 2 vols. LCL 24–25. Cambridge: Harvard University Press.
Einspahr, Bruce comp. 1976. *Index to Brown, Driver and Briggs Hebrew Lexicon*. Chicago: Moody.
Engberg-Pedersen, Troels ed. 1995. *Paul in His Hellenistic Context*. Minneapolis: Fortress.
— ed. 2001. *Paul Beyond the Judaism/Hellenism Divide*. Louisville, KY: Westminster/John Knox.
Elgvin, Torleif 1997. "'To Master His Own Vessel': 1 Thess 4.4 in Light of New Qumran Evidence." *NTS* 43 (1997) 604–619.
Elias, Jacob W. 1992. "'Jesus Who Delivers Us from the Wrath to Come' (1 Thess 1:10): Apocalyptic and Peace in the Thessalonian Correspondence." In: Lovering (1992) 121–132.
Elliger, Winfried 1978. *Paulus in Griechenland. Philippi, Thessaloniki, Athen, Korinth*. SBS 92/93. Stuttgart: Verlag Katholisches Bibelwerk.
— 1990. "εἰς." *EDNT* 1 (1990) 398–399.
— 1990a. "ἐν." *EDNT* 1 (1990) 447–449.
— 1993. "σύν." *EDNT* 3 (1993) 291–292.
— 2000. "Thessalonike." *LTK* 9 ([3]2000) 1496–1498.
Ellingworth, Paul 1974. "Which Way Are We Going? A Verb of Movement, Especially in 1 Thess. 4:14b." *BT* 25 (1974) 426–431.

— /Nida, Eugene A. 1976. *A Translator's Handbook on Paul's Letters to the Thessalonians*. Helps for Translators 17. London et al.: United Bible Societies.
Ellis, E. Earle 1971. "Paul and His Co-Workers." *NTS* 17 (1970–1971) 437–452.
— 1980. "Dating the New Testament." *NTS* 26 (1979–1980) 487–502.
— 1993. "Coworkers, Paul and His." *DPL* (1993) 183–189.
— 1999. *The Making of the New Testament Documents*. BiblntSeries 39. Leiden et al.: Brill.
— 2000. *Christ and the Future in New Testament History*. NovTSup 97. Leiden et al.: Brill.
— 2000a. "Preformed Traditions and Their Implications for Pauline Christology." In: FS Catchpole (2000) 303–320.
Eltester, Walther ed. 1964. *Apophoreta. Festschrift für Ernst Haenchen zu seinem siebzigsten Geburtstag am 10. Dezember 1964*. BZNW 30. Berlin: A. Töpelmann.
England, Frank 1995. "Afterthought: An Excuse or an Opportunity?" *JTSA* 92 (1995) 56–59.
Epp, Eldon J./Fee, Gordon E. 1993. *Studies in the Theory and Method of New Testament Textual Criticism*. SD 45. Grand Rapids: Eerdmans.
Errington, Robert M. 2002. "Thessalonike (Θεσσαλονίκη) I. Lage, klassische Zeit." *DNP* 12 (2002) 451–453.
Esler, Philip F. ed. 1995. *Modelling Early Christianity: Social-Scientific Studies of the New Testament in Its Context*. London/New York: Routledge.
Evang, Martin/Merklein, Helmut/Wolter, Michael eds. 1997. *Eschatologie und Schöpfung. Festschrift für Erich Gräßer zum siebzigsten Geburtstag*. BZNW 89. Berlin/New York: W. de Gruyter.
Evans, Christopher F. 1970. *Resurrection and the New Testament*. SBT 12. London: SCM.
— 1990. "Resurrection." In: Coggins/Houlden (1990) 586–589.
Evans, Craig A. 1993. "Ascending and Descending with a Shout: Psalm 47.6 and 1 Thessalonians 4.16." In: Evans/Sanders (1993) 238–253.
— /Hagner, Donald A. eds. 1993. *Anti-Semitism and Early Christianity: Issues of Polemic and Faith*. Foreword by J. A. Sanders. Minneapolis: Fortress.
— /Porter, Stanley E. eds. 2000. *Dictionary of New Testament Background*. [see *DNTB* in abbrev.]
— /Sanders, James A. eds. 1993. *Paul and the Scriptures of Israel*. JSNTSup 83. Sheffield: JSOT Press.
Evans, Robert M. 1968. *Eschatology and Ethics: A Study of Thessalonica and Paul's Letters to the Thessalonians*. DTh diss. University of Basel, 1967. Princeton: McMahon, 1968.
Evelyn-White, Hugh G. transl. 1914. *Hesiod: The Homeric Hymns and Homerica*. LCL 57. London: William Heinemann / Cambridge: Harvard University Press.

Fahlbusch, Erwin 1986. "Eschatologie. Begriff und Thematik." *EKL* 1 (1986) 1107–1108.
Fanning, Buist M. 1990. *Verbal Aspect in New Testament Greek*. OTM. Oxford: Clarendon.
— 1993. "Approaches to Verbal Aspect in New Testament Greek: Issues in Definition and Method." In: Porter/Carson (1993) 46–62.
Farmer, William R. ed. 1999. *Anti-Judaism and the Gospels*. Harrisburg, PA: Trinity Press International.
— et al. eds. 1967. *Christian History and Interpretation: Studies Presented to John Knox*. Cambridge: University Press.
Fascher, Erich 1927. "Die Auferstehung Jesu und ihr Verhältnis zur urchristlichen Verkündigung." *ZNW* 26 (1927) 1–26.
Fatum, Lone 1994. "1 Thessalonians." In: Schüssler Fiorenza (1994) 250–262.
— 1997. "Brotherhood in Christ: A Gender Hermeneutical Reading of 1 Thessalonians." In: Moxnes (1997) 183–197.
Faw, Chalmer E. 1952. "On the Writing of First Thessalonians." *JBL* 71 (1952) 217–225.
Fee, Gordon D. 1987. *The First Epistle to the Corinthians*. NICNT. Grand Rapids: Eerdmans.
— 1992. "On Text and Commentary on 1 and 2 Thessalonians." In: Lovering (1992) 165–183.
— 1994. *God's Empowering Presence: The Holy Spirit in the Letters of Paul*. Peabody, MA: Hendrickson.
Feld, Helmut/Nolte, Josef eds. 1973. *Wort Gottes in der Zeit. Festschrift Karl Hermann Schelkle zum 65. Geburtstag dargebracht von Kollegen, Freunden, Schülern*. Düsseldorf: Patmos.
Feldman, Louis H. 1996. *Studies in Hellenistic Judaism*. AGJU 30. Leiden et al.: E. J. Brill.
Fendrich, Herbert 1991. "λοιπός." *EDNT* 2 (1991) 360.

— 1991a. "καταβαίνω." *EDNT* 2 (1991) 254–255.

Ferguson, Everett ed. 1993. *Conversion, Catechumenate, and Baptism in the Early Church*. Studies in Early Christianity 11. New York/London: Garland.

Fergusson, David 1985. "Interpreting the Resurrection." *SJT* 38 (1985) 287–305.

Feuillet, André 1972. "Le 'ravissement' final des justes et la double perspective eschatologique (résurrection glorieuse et vie avec le Christ après la mort) dans la Première Epître aux Thessaloniciens." *RThom* 72 (1974) 533–559.

Fiedler, Peter 1990. "ἁμαρτία κτλ." *EDNT* 1 (1990) 65–69.

Filoramo, Giovanni 1999. "Eschatologie I. Religionswissenschaftlich." *RGG* 2 ([4]1999) 1542–1546.

Findlay, George G. 1891. *The Epistles to the Thessalonians*. Cambridge Bible for Schools and Colleges. Cambridge: University Press.

— 1900. "Recent Criticism of the Epistles to the Thessalonians." *The Expositor, 6th Series* 2 (1900) 251–261.

— 1904. *The Epistles of Paul the Apostle to the Thessalonians*. Cambridge Greek Testament for Schools and Colleges. Cambridge: University Press.

Finegan, J. 1962. "Thessalonica." *IDB* 4 (1962) 629.

Fiore, Benjamin 1992. "Parenesis and Protreptic." *ABD* 5 (1992) 162–165.

Fiorenza, Elisabeth S. → Schüssler Fiorenza, Elisabeth.

Fison, Joseph E. 1954. *The Christian Hope: The Presence and the Parousia*. London et al.: Longmans, Green & Co.

Fitzer, Gottfried 1974. "φθάνω, προφθάνω." *TDNT* 9 (1974) 88–92.

Fitzgerald, John T. 1996. Review of *Neglected Endings: The Significance of the Pauline Letter Closings*, by J. A. D. Weima, 1994. *CBQ* 58 (1996) 781–783.

— 2004. Review of *The Letters to the Thessalonians: A New Translation with Introduction and Commentary*, by A. J. Malherbe, 2000. *RevBL* 6 (2004) 16–18.

Fitzmyer, Joseph A. 1991. "μόνος." *EDNT* 2 (1991) 440–442.

— 1991a. "κύριος, κυριακός." *EDNT* 2 (1991) 328–331.

Flannery, Edward H. 1965. *The Anguish of the Jews: Twenty-Three Centuries of Anti-Semitism*. Quest Books. New York: Macmillan / London: Collier-Macmillan.

— 1973. "Anti-Judaism and Anti-Semitism: A Necessary Distinction." *JES* 10 (1973) 581–588.

Flusser, David 1974. "Ulrich Wilckens und die Juden." *EvT* 34 (1974) 236–243.

Focant, Camille 1990. "Les fils du Jour (1 Thes 5,5)." In: R. F. Collins (1990) 348–355.

Foerster, Werner 1964. "ἁρπάζω, ἁρπαγμός." *TDNT* 1 (1964) 472–474.

— 1964a. "ἀήρ." *TDNT* 1 (1964) 165–166.

— 1964b. "εἰρήνη κτλ." *TDNT* 2 (1964) 400–420. [§ εἰρήνη A, C–F, εἰρηνεύω, εἰρηνικός, εἰρηνοποιός, εἰρηνοποιέω: 400–402, 406–420].

— 1965. "Ἰησοῦς." *TDNT* 3 (1965) 284–293.

— 1965a. "κύριος κτλ." *TDNT* 3 (1965) 1039–1098 [§ A, B, D, κυρία, κυριακός, κυριότης, κυριεύω, κατακυριεύω: 1039–1058, 1081–1098].

— 1971. "σῴζω κτλ." *TDNT* 7 (1971) 965–1024 [§ A, C–G; σωτήρ A, C–G; σωτήριος 1, 3–5: 966–969, 980–1003, 1003–1012, 1013–1021, 1021–1022, 1023–1024].

Förster, Gerhard 1916. "1 Thessalonicher 5,1–10." *ZNW* 17 (1916) 169–177.

Fornberg, Tord/Hellholm, David eds. 1995. *Texts and Contexts: Biblical Texts in Their Textual and Situational Contexts. Essays in Honor of Lars Hartman*. Ass. by C. D. Hellholm. Oslo et al.: Scandinavian University Press.

Forster, Edward S./Furley, David J. transl. 1955. *Aristotle*. Vol. 3: *On Sophistical Refutations, On Coming-to-Be and Passing-Away, On the Cosmos*. LCL 400. London: William Heinemann / Cambridge: Harvard University Press.

Fortna, Robert T./Gaventa, Beverly R. eds. 1990. *The Conversation Continues: Studies in Paul and John in Honor of J. Louis Martyn*. Nashville: Abingdon.

Fossum, Jarl 1992. "Son of God." *ABD* 6 (1992) 128–137.

Fowl, Stephen E. 1993. "Imitation of Paul/of Christ." *DPL* (1993) 428–431.

Fowler, Harold N. et al. transl. 1914–1935. *Plato*. 12 vols. Vols. 1, 4 & 7 transl. by H. N. Fowler. Vols. 2, 3 & 12 transl. by W. R. M. Lamb. Vols. 5 & 6 transl. by P. Shorey. Vol. 8 transl. by H. N.

Fowler/W. R. M. Lamb. Vols. 9–11 transl. by R. G. Bury. LCL 36, 165, 166, 167, 237, 276, 123, 164, 234, 187, 192, 201. London: William Heinemann / Cambridge: Harvard University Press.

Frame, James E. 1912. *A Critical and Exegetical Commentary on the Epistles of St. Paul to the Thessalonians.* ICC. Edinburgh: T. & T. Clark.

France, Richard T. 2002. *The Gospel of Mark: A Commentary on the Greek Text.* NIGTC. Grand Rapids/ Cambridge: Eerdmans / Carlisle: Paternoster.

— /Wenham, David eds. 1981. *Gospel Perspectives: Studies of History and Tradition in the Four Gospels.* 2 vols. Sheffield: JSOT Press.

Frankfurter, David 2001. "Jews or Not? Reconstructing the 'Other' in Rev 2:9 and 3:9." *HTR* 94 (2001) 403–425.

Fransen, P. Iréné 1957. "Der Tag des Herrn. Erster und zweiter Brief an die Thessalonicher." *BLit* 25 (1957) 67–74.

Fraser, J. W. transl. 1960. *The First Epistle of Paul the Apostle to the Corinthians.* Ed. by D. W. Torrance/ T. F. Torrance. Calvin's Commentaries. Edinburgh: Saint Andrew Press.

Freed, Edwin D. 2005. *The Morality of Paul's Converts.* BibleWorld. London/Oakville, CT: Equinox.

Freedman, David N. et al. eds. 1992. *The Anchor Bible Dictionary.* [cf. *ABD* in abbrev.]

— ed. 2000. *Eerdmans Dictionary of the Bible.* Associate ed.: A. C. Myers. Managing ed.: A. B. Beck. Grand Rapids/Cambridge: Eerdmans.

Freudmann, Lillian C. 1994. *Antisemitism in the New Testament.* Lanham, MD et al.: University Press of America.

Friedrich, Gerhard 1965. "Ein Tauflied hellenistischer Judenchristen (1. Thess. 1,9f.)." *TZ* 21 (1965) 502–516. Republ. in: Friedrich (1978) 236–250.

— 1971. "σάλπιγξ, σαλπίζω, σαλπιστής." *TDNT* 7 (1971) 71–88.

— 1973. "1. Thessalonicher 5,1–11, der apologetische Einschub eines Späteren." *ZTK* 70 (1973) 288–315. Republ. in: Friedrich (1978) 251–278.

— 1976. "Der Erste Brief an die Thessalonicher." In: Becker/Conzelmann/Friedrich (1976) 203–251.

— 1978. *Auf das Wort kommt es an. Gesammelte Aufsätze zum 70. Geburtstag. Gerhard Friedrich.* Ed. by J. H. Friedrich. Göttingen: Vandenhoeck & Ruprecht.

Friedrich, Johannes/Pöhlmann, Wolfgang/Stuhlmacher, Peter eds. 1976. *Rechtfertigung. Festschrift für Ernst Käsemann zum 70. Geburtstag.* Tübingen: J. C. B. Mohr (Paul Siebeck) / Göttingen: Vandenhoeck & Ruprecht.

Froitzheim, Franzjosef 1979. *Christologie und Eschatologie bei Paulus.* FB 35. Würzburg: Echter.

Fuchs, Ernst 1964. "Meditation über 1 Thess 1,2–10." *GPM* 18 (1963–1964) 299–303.

— 1965. "Die Zukunft des Glaubens nach 1. Thess 5, 1–11." In: Fuchs (1965a) 334–363.

— 1965a. *Glaube und Erfahrung. Zum christologischen Problem im Neuen Testament.* Tübingen: J. C. B. Mohr (Paul Siebeck).

Fuerbringer, L. 1942. "Leading Thoughts on Eschatology in the Epistles to the Thessalonians." *CTM* 13 (1942) 183–192, 265–273, 321–329, 401–414, 511–518, 591–603, 641–654.

Funk, Robert W. 1966. *Language, Hermeneutic, and Word of God: The Problem of Language in the New Testament and Contemporary Theology.* New York et al.: Harper & Row.

— 1967. "The Apostolic *Parousia*: Form and Significance." In: FS Knox (1967) 249–268. Republ. in: Funk (1982) 81–102.

— 1982. *Parables and Presence: Forms of the New Testament Tradition.* Philadelphia: Fortress.

Furnish, Victor P. 1984. *II Corinthians: Translated with Introduction, Notes, and Commentary.* AB 32a. New York: Doubleday & Company.

Gaebelein, Frank E. et al. eds. 1978. *Ephesians – Philemon.* Expositor's Bible Commentary 11. Grand Rapids: Zondervan.

Gager, John G. 1975. *Kingdom and Community: The Social World of Early Christianity.* Englewood Cliffs, NJ: Prentice-Hall.

— 1983. *The Origins of Anti-Semitism: Attitudes Toward Judaism in Pagan and Christian Antiquity.* New York/Oxford: Oxford University Press.

— 2000. *Reinventing Paul.* Oxford et al.: University Press.

Gamble, jr., Harry 1975. "The Redaction of the Pauline Letters and the Formation of the Pauline Corpus." *JBL* 94 (1975) 403–418.
— 1977. *The Textual History of the Letter to the Romans: A Study in Textual and Literary Criticism*. SD 42. Grand Rapids: Eerdmans.
Gapp, Kenneth S. 1935. "The Universal Famine under Claudius." *HTR* 28 (1935) 258–265.
García-Moreno, Antonio 1981. "La realeza y el señorío de Cristo en Tesalonicenses." *EstB* 39 (1981) 63–82.
Gasque, W. Ward. 1972. "The Historical Value of the Book of Acts: The Perspective of British Scholarship." *TZ* 28 (1972) 177–196.
Gaston, Lloyd 1970. *No Stone on Another: Studies in the Significance of the Fall of Jerusalem in the Synoptic Gospels*. NovTSup 23. Leiden: E. J. Brill.
— 1979. "Paul and the Torah." In: Davies (1979) 48–71.
— 1991. "Israel's Misstep in the Eyes of Paul." In: Donfried (1991) 309–326.
Gaventa, Beverly R. 1986. *From Darkness to Light: Aspects of Conversion in the New Testament*. OBT 20. Philadelphia: Fortress.
— 1992. "Conversion." *ABD* 1 (1992) 1131–1133.
Geiger, Georg 1986. "1 Thess 2,13–16. Der Initiationstext des christlichen Antisemitismus?" *BLit* 59 (1986) 154–160.
Gempf, Conrad 1994. "The Imagery of Birth Pangs in the New Testament." *TynBul* 45 (1994) 119–135.
Georgi, Dieter 1991. *Theocracy in Paul's Praxis and Theology*. Transl. by D. E. Green. Minneapolis: Fortress.
Getty, Mary A. 1988. "Paul and the Salvation of Israel: A Perspective on Romans 9–11." *CBQ* 50 (1988) 456–469.
— 1990. "The Imitation of Paul in the Letters to the Thessalonians." In: R. F. Collins (1990) 277–283.
Gewalt, Dietfried 1982. "1 Thess 4, 15–17; 1 Kor 15, 51 und Mk 9, 1 – Zur Abgrenzung eines 'Herrenwortes'." *LB* 51 (1982) 105–113.
Giblin, Charles H. 1970. *In Hope of God's Glory: Pauline Theological Perspectives*. New York: Herder & Herder.
— 1990. "2 Thessalonians 2 Re-read as Pseudepigraphal: A Revised Reaffirmation of *The Threat to Faith*." In: R. F. Collins (1990) 459–469.
Gibson, Jeffrey B. 2005. "Paul's 'Dying Formula': Prolegomena to an Understanding of Its Import and Significance." 1–38. Cited 22 January 2005. Online: http://www. egroups.com/files/crosstalk2.
Giesen, Heinz 1985. "Naherwartung des Paulus in 1 Thess 4,13–18?" SNTU.A 10 (1985) 123–150.
Gill, David W. J. 1994. "Macedonia." In: Gill/Gempf (1994) 397–417.
— /Gempf, Conrad eds. 1994. *Book of Acts in Its First Century Setting*. Vol. 2: *The Book of Acts in Its Graeco-Roman Setting*. Grand Rapids: Eerdmans.
Gillespie, Thomas W. 1994. *The First Theologians: A Study in Early Christian Prophecy*. Grand Rapids: Eerdmans.
Gilliard, Frank D. 1989. "The Problem of the Antisemitic Comma between 1 Thessalonians 2.14 and 15." *NTS* 35 (1989) 481–502.
— 1994. "Paul and the Killing of the Prophets in 1 Thess. 2:15." *NovT* 36 (1994) 259–270.
Gillman, John 1985. "Signals of Transformation in 1 Thessalonians 4:13–18." *CBQ* 47 (1985) 263–281.
— 1990. "Paul's *εἴσοδος*: The Proclaimed and the Proclaimer (1 Thes 2,8)." In: R. F. Collins (1990) 62–70.
Glare, P. G. W. ed. 1996. *Greek-English Lexicon: Revised Supplement*. [see LSJSup in abbrev.]
Glasson, T. Francis 1947. *The Second Advent: The Origin of the New Testament Doctrine*. 2nd rev. ed. London: Epworth.
— 1981. "What is Apocalyptic?" *NTS* 27 (1981) 98–105.
— 1988. "Theophany and Parousia." *NTS* 34 (1988) 259–270.
Glotz, Gustave 1929. *The Greek City and Its Institutions*. Transl. by N. Mallinson. London: Kegan Paul, Trench, Trubner & Co. / New York: Alfred A. Knopf.

GNILKA, Joachim 1989. "Apokalyptik und Ethik. Die Kategorie der Zukunft als Anweisung für sittliches Handeln." In: FS SCHNACKENBURG (1989) 464–481.

GODLEY, Alfred D. transl. 1920–1925. *Herodotus*. 4 vols. LCL 117, 118, 119, 120. London: William Heinemann / Cambridge: Harvard University Press.

GOETZMANN, Jürgen 1975. "Conversion." *NIDNTT* 1 (1975) 353–362 [§ μετάνοια: 357–359].

GORMAN, Michael J. 2004. *Apostle of the Crucified Lord: A Theological Introduction to Paul and His Letters*. Grand Rapids/Cambridge: Eerdmans.

GOULDER, Michael D. 1974. *Midrash and Lection in Matthew: The Speaker's Lectures in Biblical Studies 1969–71*. London: SPCK.

— 1992. "Silas in Thessalonica." *JSNT*, issue 48 (1992) 87–106.

— 2002. "Psalm 8 and the Son of Man." *NTS* 48 (2002) 18–29.

GRAAFEN, J. 1930. *Die Echtheit des zweiten Briefes an die Thessalonicher*. NTAbh 14; Münster: Aschendorff.

GRANT, Robert M. 1970. *Theophilus of Antioch ad Autolycum: Text and Translation*. Oxford: Clarendon.

GRÄSSER, Erich 1974. "Zum Verständnis der Gottesherrschaft. *Walther Eltester, dem einstigen Lehrer im Marburg, zum 75. Geburtstag.*" *ZNW* 65 (1974) 3–26.

— /MERK, Otto eds. 1985. *Glaube und Eschatologie. Festschrift für Werner Georg Kümmel zum 80. Geburtstag*. Tübingen: J. C. B. Mohr (Paul Siebeck).

GRAYSTON, Kenneth 1967. *The Letters of Paul to the Philippians and to the Thessalonians*. CBC. London: Cambridge University Press.

GREEN, Gene L. 2002. *The Letters to the Thessalonians*. PNTC. Grand Rapids/Cambridge: Eerdmans / Leicester: Apollos.

GREEN, Joel B. ed. 1995. *Hearing the New Testament: Strategies for Interpretation*. Grand Rapids: Eerdmans / Carlisle: Paternoster.

— /MCKNIGHT, Scot eds. 1992. *Dictionary of Jesus and the Gospels*. Downers Grove/Leicester: Inter-Varsity.

GREEN, Michael = GREEN, E. M. B. 1958. "A Note on 1 Thessalonians iv. 15, 17." *ExpTim* 69 (1957–1958) 285–286.

— 1970. *Evangelism in the Early Church*. London: Hodder & Stoughton.

GREGSON, R. 1966. "A Solution to the Problems of the Thessalonian Epistles." *EvQ* 38 (1966) 76–80.

GRESHAKE, Gisbert/KREMER, Jacob 1992. *Resurrectio mortuorum. Zum theologischen Verständnis der leiblichen Auferstehung*. 2nd unch. ed. Darmstadt: Wissenschaftliche Buchgesellschaft.

GRIEB, A. Katherine 1996. Review of *Filling Up the Measure: Polemical Hyperbole in 1 Thessalonians 2.14–16*, by C. J. SCHLUETER, 1994. *JBL* 115 (1996) 766–768.

GRIFFITH-JONES, Robin 1995. Review of *Filling Up the Measure: Polemical Hyperbole in 1 Thessalonians 2.14–16*, by C. J. SCHLUETER, 1994. *JTS* NS 46 (1995) 654–659.

GROH, Dennis E./JEWETT, Robert eds. 1985. *The Living Text: Essays in Honor of Ernest W. Saunders*. Lanham, MD et al.: University Press of America.

GROSSOUW, Willem K. M. 1963. "Die Entwicklung der paulinischen Theologie in ihren Hauptlinien." In: *SPCIC* (1961) = AnBib 17–18, vol. 1. (Rome: Pontifical Biblical Institute, 1963) 79–93.

GRUENWALD, Ithamar 1979. "Jewish Apocalyptic Literature." *ANRW* II.19.1 (1979) 89–118.

GRUNDMANN, Walter 1941. "Die Apostel zwischen Jerusalem und Antiochia." *ZNW* 39 (1941) 110– 137.

— 1964. "δέχομαι κτλ." *TDNT* 2 (1964) 50–59.

— 1964a. "ἁμαρτάνω, ἁμάρτημα, ἁμαρτία." *TDNT* 1 (1964) 267–316 [§ C, E (with G. STÄHLIN), F: 289–293, 296–302, 302–316].

— 1967. "μέμφομαι κτλ." *TDNT* 4 (1967) 571–574.

— 1971. "στέφανος, στεφανόω." *TDNT* 7 (1971) 615–636.

— 1971a. "σύν-μετά κτλ." *TDNT* 7 (1971) 766–797.

— 1974. "χρίω κτλ." *TDNT* 9 (1974) 493–580 [§ A, D–E: 493–496, 527–580].

GUNDRY, Robert H. 1973. *The Church and the Tribulation*. Grand Rapids: Zondervan.

— 1976. *Sōma in Biblical Theology: With Emphasis on Pauline Anthropology*. SNTSMS 29. Cambridge et al.: University Press.

— 1987. "The Hellenization of Dominical Tradition and Christianization of Jewish Tradition in the Eschatology of 1–2 Thessalonians." *NTS* 33 (1987) 161–178.

— 1996. "A Brief Note on 'Hellenistic Formal Receptions and Paul's Use of ΑΠΑΝΤΗΣΙΣ in 1 Thessalonians 4:17'." *BBR* 6 (1996) 39–41.
GUNDRY VOLF, Judith M. 1990. *Paul and Perseverance: Staying in and Falling Away.* WUNT II.37. Tübingen: J. C. B. Mohr (Paul Siebeck).
GUNTERMANN, Friedrich 1932. *Die Eschatologie des hl. Paulus.* NTAbh 13, Heft 4–5. Münster: Aschendorff.
GUTBROD, Walter 1965. "Ἰσραήλ κτλ." *TDNT* 3 (1965) 356–391 [§ C, D: 369–391].
GUTHRIE, Donald et al. eds. 1970. *The New Bible Commentary: Revised.* Completely rev. 3rd ed. London: Inter-Varsity.

HAACK, Ernst 1938. "Eine exegetisch-dogmatische Studie zur Eschatologie über 1 Thessalonicher 4, 13–18." *ZST* 15 (1938) 544–569.
HAACKER, Klaus 1977. "Paulus und das Judentum." *Jud* 33 (1977) 161–177.
— 1988. "Elemente des heidnischen Antijudaismus im Neuen Testament." *EvT* 48 (1988) 404–418.
— 1997. *Paulus. Der Werdegang eines Apostels.* SBS 171. Stuttgart: Verlag Katholisches Bibelwerk.
— 2003. "Paul's Life." In: DUNN (2003) 19–33.
HAAG, Ernst 1995. "Eschatologie B. Thematisch-inhaltlich II. Biblisch: 1. Altes Testament." *LTK* 3 (³1995) 866–868.
HACKENBERG, Wolfgang 1993. "σκότος." *EDNT* 3 (1993) 255–256.
HADORN, Wilhelm 1918. "Die Abfassung der Thessalonicherbriefe auf der dritten Missionsreise und der Kanon des Marcion." *ZNW* 18 (1917–1918) 67–72.
HAENCHEN, Ernst 1971. *The Acts of the Apostles: A Commentary.* Transl. by B. NOBLE/G. SHINN, under the supervision of H. ANDERSON, & with the transl. rev. & brought up to date by R. McL. WILSON. Oxford: Basil Blackwell.
HAGNER, Donald A. 1993. "Paul's Quarrel with Judaism." In: EVANS/HAGNER (1993) 128–150.
— /HARRIS, Murray J. eds. 1980. *Pauline Studies: Essays Presented to F. F. Bruce on his 70th Birthday.* Exeter: Paternoster / Grand Rapids: Eerdmans.
HAHN, Ferdinand 1966. *Christologische Hoheitstitel. Ihre Geschichte im frühen Christentum.* 3rd unch. ed. FRLANT 83. Göttingen: Vandenhoeck & Ruprecht.
— 1969. *The Titles of Jesus in Christology: Their History in Early Christianity.* Transl. by H. KNIGHT/G. OGG. London: Lutterworth.
— 1974. "Die Himmelfahrt Jesu. Ein Gespräch mit Gerhard Lohfink." *Bib* 55 (1974) 418–426.
— 1993. "υἱός." *EDNT* 3 (1993) 381–392.
— 1993a. "Χριστός, χριστός." *EDNT* 3 (1993) 478–486.
— /HOLTZ, Traugott/WALTER, Nikolaus eds. 1970. *Studien zum Neuen Testament und zum hellenistischen Judentum. Gesammelte Aufsätze 1950–1968. Gerhard Delling.* Göttingen: Vandenhoeck & Ruprecht.
HAHN, Hans-Christoph 1975. "Anger, Wrath." *NIDNTT* 1 (1975) 105–113 [§ ὀργή: 107–113].
— 1975a. "Darkness, Night." *NIDNTT* 1 (1975) 420–425.
HAINES, Charles R. transl. 1930. *The Communings with Himself of Marcus Aurelius Antoninus Emperor of Rome: Together with His Speeches and Sayings.* Rev. ed. LCL 58. London: William Heinemann / Cambridge: Harvard University Press.
HAINZ, Josef 1972. *Ekklesia. Strukturen paulinischer Gemeinde-Theologie und Gemeinde-Ordnung.* BU 9. Regensburg: Friedrich Pustet.
— ed. 1976. *Kirche im Werden. Studien zum Thema Amt und Gemeinde im Neuen Testament.* München et al.: Ferdinand Schöningh.
HALL, III, Sidney G. 1993. *Christian Anti-Semitism and Paul's Theology.* Minneapolis: Fortress.
HAMMOND, Nicholas G. L. 1972. *A History of Macedonia.* 3 vols. Oxford: Clarendon.
HANHART, Karel 1969. "Paul's Hope in the Face of Death." *JBL* 88 (1969) 445–457.
HANSE, Hermann 1964. "ἔχω κτλ." *TDNT* 2 (1964) 816–832.
HANSON, Anthony T. 1957. *The Wrath of the Lamb.* London: SPCK.
HANSON, Paul D. 1975. *The Dawn of Apocalyptic.* Philadelphia: Fortress.
— 1976. "Apocalypticism." *IDBSup* (1976) 28–34.
— 1992. "Apocalypses and Apocalypticism: The Genre." *ABD* 1 (1992) 279–280.

— 1992a. "Apocalypses and Apocalypticism: Introductory Overview." *ABD* 1 (1992) 280–282.

HARE, Douglas R. A. 1967. *The Theme of Jewish Persecution of Christians in the Gospel according to St Matthew.* Cambridge: University Press.

HARMON, Austin M./KILBURN, K./MACLEOD, M. D. transl. 1913–1967. *Lucian.* 8 vols. Vols. 1–5 transl. by A. M. HARMON. Vol. 6 transl. by K. KILBURN. Vols. 7–8 transl. by M. D. MACLEOD. LCL 14, 54, 130, 162, 302, 430, 431, 432. London: William Heinemann / Cambridge: Harvard University Press.

HARNACK, Adolf von → VON HARNACK, Adolf.

HARNISCH, Wolfgang 1973. *Eschatologische Existenz. Ein exegetischer Beitrag zum Sachanliegen von 1. Thessalonicher 4,13–5,11.* FRLANT 110. Göttingen: Vandenhoeck & Ruprecht.

HARRINGTON, Daniel J. 2002. "Afterlife Expectations in Pseudo-Philo, 4 Ezra, and 2 Baruch, and Their Implications for the New Testament." FS LAMBRECHT (2002) 21–34.

HARRIS, J. Rendel 1898. "A Study in Letter Writing." *Exp. 5th Series* 8 (1898) 161–180.

HARRIS, R. Laird/ARCHER, Gleason L./WALTKE, Bruce K. eds. 1980. *Theological Wordbook of the Old Testament.* 2 vols. Chicago: Moody.

HARRISON, J. R. 2002. "Paul and the Imperial Gospel at Thessaloniki." *JSNT*, issue 25 (2002) 71–96.

— 2002a. "A Share in All the Sacrifices." *NewDocs* 9 (2002) 1–3.

HARTMAN, Lars 1966. *Prophecy Interpreted: The Formation of Some Jewish Apocalyptic Texts and of the Eschatological Discourse Mark 13 Par.* Transl. by N. TOMKINSON with the ass. of J. GRAY. ConBNT 1. Lund: CWK Gleerup.

HARVEY, Anthony E. 1980. "The Use of Mystery Language in the Bible." *JTS* NS 31 (1980) 320–336.

HARVEY, John D. 1992. "The 'with Christ' Motif in Paul's Thought." *JETS* 35 (1992) 329–340.

— 1998. *Listening to the Text: Oral Patterning in Paul's Letters.* Foreword by R. N. LONGENECKER. ETS Studies 1. Grand Rapids: Baker / Leicester: Apollos.

HASLER, Victor 1990. "εἰρήνη." *EDNT* 1 (1990) 394–397.

— 1993. "φθάνω." *EDNT* 3 (1993) 421–422.

HATCH, Edwin/REDPATH, Henry A. 1954. *A Concordance to the Septuagint and the Other Greek Versions of the Old Testament, including the Apocryphal Books.* 2 vols. Ass. by other scholars. Graz: Akademische Druck & Verlagsanstalt.

HAUCK, Friedrich 1967. "ὑπομένω, ὑπομονή." *TDNT* 4 (1967) 581–588.

HAUFE, Günter 1961. "Entrückung und eschatologische Funktion im Spätjudentum." *ZRGG* 13 (1961) 105–113.

— 1986. "Individuelle Eschatologie des Neuen Testaments." *ZTK* 83 (1986) 436–463.

— 1999. *Der erste Brief des Paulus an die Thessalonicher.* THKNT 12/I. Leipzig: Evangelische Verlagsanstalt.

— 2001. Review of *Vollendung des Auferstehens. Eine exegetische Untersuchung von 1 Kor 15,51–52 und 1 Thess 4,13–18* by S. SCHNEIDER, 2000. *TLZ* 126 (2001) 1159–1161.

HAVENER, Ivan 1981. "The Pre-Pauline Christological Credal Formulae of 1 Thessalonians." In: RICHARDS (1981) 105–128.

— 1983. *First Thessalonians, Philippians, Philemon, Second Thessalonians, Colossians, Ephesians.* Collegeville Bible Commentary 8. Collegeville, MN: Liturgical Press.

HAWTHORNE, Gerald F. ed. 1975. *Current Issues in Biblical and Patristic Interpretation: Studies in Honor of Merrill C. Tenney Presented by His Former Students.* Grand Rapids: Eerdmans.

— /MARTIN, Ralph P. eds. 1993. *Dictionary of Paul and His Letters.* [see *DPL* in abbrev.]

HAYES, D. A. 1911. "A Study of a Pauline Apocalypse: 1 Thess. 4:13–18." *Biblical World* 37 (1911) 163–175.

HAYES, John H. ed. 1999. *Dictionary of Biblical Interpretation.* [see *DBI* in abbrev.]

— /HOLLADAY, Carl R. 1982. *Biblical Exegesis: A Beginner's Handbook.* Atlanta: John Knox.

HAYS, Richard B. 1989. *Echoes of Scripture in the Letters of Paul.* New Haven/London: Yale University Press.

— 1991. "Crucified with Christ: A Synthesis of 1 and 2 Thessalonians, Philemon, Philippians, and Galatians." In: BASSLER (1991) 227–246.

— 2000. "'Why Do You Stand Looking Up Toward Heaven?' New Testament Eschatology at the Turn of the Millennium." *Modern Theology* 16 (2000) 115–135.

HEIL, John P. 2000. "Those Now 'Asleep' (not dead) Must Be 'Awakened' for the Day of the Lord in 1 Thess 5.9–10." *NTS* 46 (2000) 464–471.

HELLHOLM, David ed. 1983. *Apocalypticism in the Mediterranean World and the Near East: Proceedings of the International Colloquium on Apocalypticism, Uppsala, August 12–17, 1979.* Tübingen: J. C. B. Mohr (Paul Siebeck).

— 1998. "Apokalyptik I. Begriffsdefinition als religionsgeschichtliches Problem." *RGG* 1 ([4]1998) 590–591.

HEMBERG, Bengt 1950. *Die Kabiren.* Uppsala: Almquist & Wiksells.

HEMER, Colin J. 1980. "Observations on Pauline Chronology." In: FS BRUCE (1980) 3–18.

HENDRIX, Holland L. 1984. *Thessalonicans Honor Romans.* Cambridge: Harvard University Press.

— 1988. Review of *The Thessalonian Correspondence: Pauline Rhetoric and Millenarian Piety*, by R. JEWETT, 1986. *JBL* 107 (1988) 763–766.

— 1991. "Archaeology and Eschatology at Thessalonica." In: FS KOESTER (1991) 107–118.

— 1992. "Thessalonica." *ABD* 6 (1992) 523–527.

— 1992a. "Benefactor/Patron Networks in the Urban Environment: Evidence from Thessalonica." *Semeia* 56 (1992) 39–58.

HENGEL, Martin 1976. *The Son of God: The Origin of Christology and the History of Jewish-Hellenistic Religion.* Transl. by J. BOWDEN. London: SCM.

— 1980. *Acts and the History of Earliest Christianity.* Transl. by J. BOWDEN. Philadelphia: Fortress.

— 1982. "Erwägungen zum Sprachgebrauch von Χριστός bei Paulus und in der 'vorpaulinischen' Überlieferung." In: FS BARRETT (1982) 135–158. [English Summary, 159.]

— 1991. *The Pre-Christian Paul.* In collaboration with R. DEINES. Transl. by J. BOWDEN. London: SCM / Philadelphia: Trinity Press International.

— 1992. "Christological Titles in Early Christianity." In: CHARLESWORTH (1992) 425–448.

— 1995. *Studies in Early Christology.* Edinburgh: T&T Clark.

— 2002. *Paulus und Jakobus. Kleine Schriften III.* WUNT 141. Tübingen: Mohr Siebeck.

— /BARRETT, Charles K. 1999. *Conflicts and Challenges in Early Christianity.* Ed. by D. A. HAGNER. Harrisburg, PA: Trinity Press International.

— /HECKEL, Ulrich eds. 1991. *Paulus und das antike Judentum. Tübingen-Durham-Symposium im Gedenken an den 50. Todestag Adolf Schlatters (†19. Mai 1938).* WUNT I.58. Tübingen: J. C. B. Mohr (Paul Siebeck).

— /SCHWEMER, Anna M. 1997. *Paul between Damascus and Antioch: The Unknown Years.* Transl. by J. BOWDEN. London: SCM.

HENNEKEN, Bartholomäus 1969. *Verkündigung und Prophetie im 1. Thessalonicherbrief. Ein Beitrag zur Theologie des Wortes Gottes.* SBS 29. Stuttgart: Verlag Katholisches Bibelwerk.

HENRY, Marie L. et al. eds. 1968. *Leben angesichts des Todes. Beiträge zum theologischen Problem des Todes. Helmut Thielicke zum 60. Geburtstag.* Tübingen: J. C. B. Mohr (Paul Siebeck).

HÉRING, Jean 1962. *The First Epistle of Saint Paul to the Corinthians.* Transl. by A. W. HEATHCOTE/P. J. ALLCOCK. London: Epworth.

HERMAN, Zvonimir I. 1980. "Il significato della morte e della risurrezione di Gesù nel contesto escatologico di 1 Ts 4,13–5,11." *Anton* 55 (1980) 327–351.

HERNTRICH, V. 1967. "λεῖμμα κτλ." *TDNT* 4 (1967) 194–214 [§ B: 196–209].

HESTER, James D. 1996. "The Invention of 1 Thessalonians: A Proposal." In: PORTER/OLBRICHT (1996) 251–279.

— 2002. "Apocalyptic Discourse in 1 Thessalonians." In: WATSON (2002) 137–163.

— 2005. Review of *The Thessalonians Debate: Methodological Discord or Methodological Synthesis?*, by K. P. DONFRIED/J. BEUTLER eds., 2000. 1–6. Cited 16 April 2005. Online: http://rhetjournal.net/DebateReview.html.

HIGGINS, Angus J. B. ed. 1959. *New Testament Essays: Studies in Memory of Thomas Walter Manson 1893–1958.* Manchester: University Press.

HILL, David 1979. *New Testament Prophecy.* Marshall's Theological Library. London: Marshall, Morgan & Scott.

HIMMELFARB, Martha 1991. "Revelation and Rapture: The Transformation of the Visionary in the Ascent Apocalypses." In: COLLINS/CHARLESWORTH (1991) 79–90.

HOCK, Ronald F. 1979. "The Workshop as a Social Setting for Paul's Missionary Preaching." *CBQ* 41 (1979) 438–450.
— 1980. *The Social Context of Paul's Ministry: Tentmaking and Apostleship*. Philadelphia: Fortress.
HODGES, Zane C. 1982. "The Rapture in 1 Thessalonians 5:1–11." In: CAMPBELL (1982) 67–79.
HODGSON, JR., Robert 1982. "1 Thess 4:1–12 and the Holiness Tradition (HT)." In: RICHARDS (1982) 199–215.
— 1988. "Gospel and Ethics in First Thessalonians." *TBT* 26 (1988) 344–349.
HOFFMANN, Ernst 1976. "Hope, Expectation." *NIDNTT* 2 (1976) 238–247.
HOFFMANN, Paul 1966. *Die Toten in Christus. Eine religionsgeschichtliche und exegetische Untersuchung zur paulinischen Eschatologie*. NTAbh NF 2. Münster: Aschendorff.
— 1972. *Studien zur Theologie der Logienquelle*. NTAbh NF 8. Münster: Aschendorff.
— 1979. "Auferstehung I. Auferstehung der Toten I/3. Neues Testament." *TRE* 4 (1979) 450–467.
— 1979a. "Auferstehung II. Auferstehung Jesu Christi II/1. Neues Testament." *TRE* 4 (1979) 478–513.
— ed. 1988. *Zur neutestamentlichen Überlieferung von der Auferstehung Jesus*. WdF 522. Darmstadt: Wissenschaftliche Buchgesellschaft.
— 1994. *Studien zur Frühgeschichte der Jesus-Bewegung*. SBAB 17. Stuttgart: Verlag Katholisches Bibelwerk.
HOFIUS, Otfried 1978. "Agrapha." *TRE* 2 (1978) 103–110.
— 1991. "'Unknown Sayings of Jesus'." In: STUHLMACHER (1991) 336–360.
— 2000. "Christus als Schöpfungsmittler und Erlösungsmittler. Das Bekenntnis 1Kor 8,6 im Kontext der paulinischen Theologie." In: FS HÜBNER (2000) 47–58. Republ. in: HOFIUS (2002) 181–192.
— 2002. *Paulusstudien II*. WUNT 143. Tübingen: Mohr Siebeck. [collected essays include: HOFIUS 2000; 2002a]
— 2002a. "'Am dritten Tage auferstanden von den Toten'. Erwägungen zum Passiv ἐγείρεσθαι in christologischen Aussagen des Neuen Testaments." FS LAMBRECHT (2002) 93–106. Republ. in: HOFIUS (2002) 202–214.
HOGG, C. F./VINE, W. E. 1929. *The Epistles of Paul the Apostle to the Thessalonians: With Notes Exegetical and Expository*. 2nd ed. with corr. & add. notes. London/Glasgow: Pickering & Inglis.
HOLLAND, Glenn S. 1988. *The Tradition That You Received from Us: 2 Thessalonians in the Pauline Tradition*. HUT 24. Tübingen: J. C. B. Mohr (Paul Siebeck).
— 1990. "'A Letter Supposedly from Us': A Contribution to the Discussion about the Authorship of 2 Thessalonians." In: R. F. COLLINS (1990) 394–402.
— 1995. Review of *The Theology of the Shorter Pauline Letters*, by K. P. DONFRIED/I. H. MARSHALL, 1993. *CRBR* 8 (1995) 200–203.
HOLLANDER, Harm W./DE JONGE, Marinus 1985. *The Testaments of the Twelve Patriarchs: A Commentary*. SVTP 8. Leiden: E. J. Brill.
HOLLEMAN, Joost 1996. *Resurrection and Parousia: A Traditio-Historical Study of Paul's Eschatology in 1 Corinthians 15*. NovTSup 84. Leiden et al.: E. J. Brill.
HOLMSTRAND, Jonas 1997. *Markers and Meaning in Paul: An Analysis of 1 Thessalonians, Philippians and Galatians*. ConBNT 28. Stockholm: Almquist & Wiksell International.
HOLTZ, Traugott 1977. "‚Euer Glaube an Gott'. *Zu Form und Inhalt von 1 Thess 1,9f.*" In: FS SCHÜRMANN (1977) 459–488.
— 1983. "Traditionen im 1. Thessalonicherbrief." In: FS SCHWEIZER (1983) 55–78.
— 1989. "Das Gericht über die Juden und die Rettung ganz Israels (1 Thess 2, 15f. und Röm 11, 25f.)." In: FS LOHSE (1989) 119–131. Transl. & republ. in: R. F. COLLINS (1990) 284–294.
— 1991. "Paul and the Oral Gospel Tradition." In: WANSBROUGH (1991) 380–393.
— 1998. *Der erste Brief an die Thessalonicher*. EKKNT 13. 3rd ed. [1 1986]. Zürich: Benziger Verlag / Neukirchen-Vluyn: Neukirchener Verlag.
— 2000. "On the Background of 1 Thessalonians 2:1–12." In: DONFRIED/BEUTLER (2000) 69–80.
— 2002. "Thessalonicherbriefe." *TRE* 33 (2002) 412–421.
— 2002a. Review of *The Letters to the Thessalonians: A New Translation with Introduction and Commentary*, by A. J. MALHERBE, 2000. *TLZ* 127 (2002) 176–179.
HOOKER, Morna D. 1971. "Interchange in Christ." *JTS* NS 22 (1971) 349–361.

— 1978. "Interchange and Atonement." *BJRL* 60 (1977–1978) 462–481.
— 1995. *Not Ashamed of the Gospel: New Testament Interpretations of the Death of Christ*. Grand Rapids: Eerdmans. Originally publ. by Paternoster, 1994.
— /Wilson, Stephen G. eds. 1982. *Paul and Paulinism: Essays in Honour of C. K. Barrett*. London: SPCK.
Hoppe, Rudolf 1997. "Der erste Thessalonicherbrief und die antike Rhetorik. Eine Problemskizze." *BZ* 41 (1997) 229–237.
— 1998. "Metaphorik im ersten Thessalonicherbrief. Zur Rede von ‚Amme' und ‚Vater' in 1 Thess 2,7.11." In: FS Biser (1998) 269–281.
— 2000. "The Epistolary and Rhetorical Context of 1 Thessalonians 2:1–12: A Response to Karl P. Donfried." In: Donfried/Beutler (2000) 61–68.
— 2002. "Verkündiger – Botschaft – Gemeinde. Überlegungen zu 1 Thess 2,1–12.13–16." In: FS Fuchs (2002) 325–345.
— 2004. "Parusieglaube zwischen dem ersten Thessalonicherbrief und dem zweiten Petrusbrief — ein unerledigtes Problem." In: Schlosser (2004) 433–450.
— 2004a. "Der Topos der Prophetenverfolgung bei Paulus." *NTS* 50 (2004) 535–549.
— 2006. "La première Épître aux Thessaloniciens dans de cadre de la théologie paulinienne. Réflexions sur la théologie paulinienne de l'élection." *RevScRel* 80 (2006) 67–82.
Horbury, William ed. 1991. *Templum Amicitiae: Essays on the Second Temple Presented to Ernst Bammel*. JSNTSup 48. Sheffield: Academic Press.
— /McNeil, Brian eds. 1981. *Suffering and Martyrdom in the New Testament: Studies Presented to G. M. Styler by the Cambridge New Testament Seminar*. Cambridge et al.: University Press.
Horgan, Maurya P./Kobelski, Paul J. eds. 1989. *To Touch the Text: Biblical and Related Studies in Honor of Joseph A. Fitzmyer*. New York: Crossroad.
Horn, Friedrich W. 2000. "Kyrios und Pneuma bei Paulus." In: FS Hübner (2000) 59–75.
Horrell, David G./Tuckett, Christopher M. eds. 2000. *Christology, Controversy and Community: New Testament Essays in Honour of David R. Catchpole*. Leiden et al.: Brill.
Horsley, Greg H. R. 1981. "The 'Coming' of a Prefect." *NewDocs* 1 (1981) 46.
— 1981a. "An Anxious Letter." *NewDocs* 1 (1981) 58–59.
— 1981b. "θλίψις." *NewDocs* 1 (1981) 84.
— 1981c. "Christian Amulet." *NewDocs* 1 (1981c) 102–103.
— 1982. "Politarchs." *NewDocs* 2 (1982) 34–35.
— 1982a. "A Byzantine Letter Quoting Paul." *NewDocs* 2 (1982) 154–158.
— 1982b. "Five Letters of Sempronius from a Family Archive." *NewDocs* 2 (1982) 63–69.
— 1983b. "Trophimos." *NewDocs* 3 (1983) 91–93.
— 1987. "'Body, Soul and Spirit…'." *NewDocs* 4 (1987) 38–39.
— 1987a. "ἀμέμπτως." *NewDocs* 4 (1987) 141.
— 1994. "The Politarchs." In: Gill/Gempf (1994) 419–431.
— 1994a. "The Politarchs in Macedonia, and Beyond." *Mediterranean Archaeology* 7 (1994) 99–126.
— et al. eds. 1981–2002. *New Documents Illustrating Early Christianity*. [see *NewDocs* in abbrev.]
Horsley, Richard A. ed. 1997. *Paul and Empire: Religion and Power in Roman Imperial Society*. Harrisburg, PA: Trinity Press International.
— 1998. *1 Corinthians*. ANTC. Nashville: Abingdon.
— ed. 2004. *Paul and the Roman Imperial Order*. Harrisburg, PA et al.: Trinity Press International.
Horst, Pieter W. van der → van der Horst, Pieter W.
Howard, Tracy L. 1985. "The Meaning of 'Sleep' in 1 Thessalonians 5:10 – A Reappraisal." *Grace Theological Journal* 6 (1985) 337–348.
— 1988. "The Literary Unity of 1 Thessalonians 4:13–5:11." *GTJ* 9/2 (1988) 163–190.
Hübner, Hans 1990. "εἴδωλον κτλ." *EDNT* 1 (1990) 386–388.
— 1993. "πληρόω, ἀναπληρόω, ἀνταναπληρόω." *EDNT* 3 (1993) 108–110.
— 1993a. "τέλος." *EDNT* 3 (1993) 347–348.
— 1993b. "χρόνος." *EDNT* 3 (1993) 488–489.
— 1993c. *Biblische Theologie des Neuen Testaments*. Vol. 2: *Die Theologie des Paulus und ihre neutestamentliche Wirkungsgeschichte*. Göttingen: Vandenhoeck & Ruprecht.

— 1997. *Vetus Testamentum in Novo*. Vol. 2: *Corpus Paulinum*. Göttingen: Vandenhoeck & Ruprecht.
HUGHES, Frank W. 1989. *Early Christian Rhetoric and 2 Thessalonians*. JSNTSup 30. Sheffield: JSOT Press.
— 1990. "The Rhetoric of 1 Thessalonians." In: R. F. COLLINS (1990) 94–116.
— 1999. "First and Second Letters to the Thessalonians." In: *DBI* 2 (1999) 568–572.
— 2000. "The Rhetoric of Letters." In: DONFRIED/BEUTLER (2000) 194–240. Rev. of HUGHES (1989) 19–50.
— 2000a. "The Social Situations Implied by Rhetoric." In: DONFRIED/BEUTLER (2000) 241–254.
HUGHES, Gerard J. 1988. "Dead Theories, Live Metaphors and the Resurrection." *HeyJ* 29 (1988) 313–328.
HUMPHREYS, Sarah C. 1978. *Anthropology and the Greeks*. International Library of Anthropology. London et al.: Routledge & Kegan Paul.
HUNTER, Archibald M. 1938. "Faith, Hope, Love—A Primitive Christian Triad." *ExpTim* 49 (1937–1938) 428–429.
— 1961. *Paul and His Predecessors*. New rev. ed. London: SCM.
HUNZINGER, Claus-Hunno 1968. "Die Hoffnung angesichts des Todes im Wandel der paulinischen Aussagen." In: FS THIELICKE (1968) 69–88.
HURD, John C. 1967. "Pauline Chronology and Pauline Theology." In: FS KNOX (1967) 225–248. Republ. in: HURD (1998) 9–30.
— 1968. "The Sequence of Paul's Letters." *CJT* 14 (1968) 189–200. Republ. in: HURD (1998) 31–45.
— 1976. "Thessalonians, First Letter to the." *IDBSup* (1976) 900.
— 1976a. "Thessalonians, Second Letter to the." In: CRIM et al. (1976) 900–901.
— 1976b. "Paul the Apostle." *IDBSup* (1976) 648–651.
— 1984. "The Jesus Whom Paul Preaches (Acts 19:13)." In: FS BEARE (1984) 73–89.
— 1986. "Paul ahead of His Time: 1 Thess. 2:13–16." In: RICHARDSON/GRANSKOU (1986) 21–36. Republ. in: HURD (1998) 117–134.
— 1987. *Journal of Biblical Literature: Index 61–100 (1942–1981)*. SBL. Atlanta: Scholars Press.
— 1998. *The Earliest Letters of Paul – and Other Studies*. Studies in the Religion and History of Early Christianity 8. Frankfurt am Main et al.: Peter Lang. [collected essays include: HURD 1967; 1968; 1986]
HURTADO, Larry W. 1993. "Son of God." *DPL* (1993) 900–906.
— 1993a. "Lord." *DPL* (1993) 560–569.
— 1993b. "What Do We Mean by 'First-Century Jewish Monotheism'?" In: LOVERING (1993) 348–368.
— 1998. *One God, One Lord: Early Christian Devotion and Ancient Jewish Monotheism*. 2nd ed. Edinburgh: T&T Clark.
— 2003. "Paul's Christology." In: DUNN (2003) 185–198.
HUTTON, Maurice et al. transl. 1914–1937. *Tacitus*. 5 vols. Vol. 1 transl. by M. HUTTON et al. Vol. 2 transl. by C. H. MOORE. Vol. 3 transl. by C. H. MOORE/J. JACKSON. Vols. 4–5 transl. by J. JACKSON. LCL 35, 111, 249, 312, 322. London: William Heinemann / Cambridge: Harvard University Press.
HYLDAHL, Niels 1980. "Auferstehung Christi – Auferstehung der Toten (1 Thess. 4,13–18)." In: PEDERSEN (1980) 119–135.
— 1986. *Die paulinische Chronologie*. ATDan 19. Leiden: E. J. Brill.

IDINOPULOS, Thomas A./WARD, Roy B. 1977. "Is Christology Inherently Anti-Semitic? A Critical Review of Rosemary Ruether's *Faith and Fratricide*." *JAAR* 45 (1977) 193–214.
ISAAC, E. 1983. "1 (Ethiopic Apocalypse of) Enoch: A New Translation and Introduction." *OTP* 1 (1983) 5–89.
ISAAC, Jules 1964. *The Teaching of Contempt: Christian Roots of Anti-Semitism*. Transl. by H. WEAVER. Biographical intro. by C. H. BISHOP. New York et al.: Holt, Rinehart & Winston.

JACKSON, John 1914–1937 → HUTTON et al. 1914–1937.
JACKSON, Paul N. 1996. *An Investigation of* κοιμάομαι *in the New Testament: The Concept of Eschatological Sleep*. Mellen Biblical Press Series 45. Lewiston, NY et al.: Mellen.

JAQUETTE, James L. 1995. Review of *Filling Up the Measure: Polemical Hyperbole in 1 Thessalonians 2.14–16*, by C. J. SCHLUETER, 1994. *CBQ* 57 (1995) 825–827.
— 1996. "Life and Death, *Adiaphora*, and Paul's Rhetorical Strategies." *NovT* 38 (1996) 30–54.
JEREMIAS, Joachim 1957. "Agrapha." *RGG* 1 (^{3}1957) 177–178.
— 1958. "Chiasmus in den Paulusbriefen." *ZNW* 49 (1958) 145–156.
— 1963. *Unbekannte Jesusworte*. 3rd ed. Gütersloh: Gerd Mohn.
— 1964. *Unknown Sayings of Jesus*. 2nd ed. Transl. by R. H. FULLER. London: SPCK.
JERVIS, L. Ann 1991. *The Purpose of Romans: A Comparative Letter Structure Investigation*. JSNTSup 55. Sheffield: Academic Press.
JEWETT, Robert 1969. "The Form and Function of the Homiletic Benediction." *ATR* 51 (1969) 18–34.
— 1971. *Paul's Anthropological Terms: A Study of Their Use in Conflict Settings*. AGJU 10. Leiden: E. J. Brill.
— 1971a. "The Agitators and the Galatian Congregation." *NTS* 17 (1970–1971) 198–212.
— 1972. "Enthusiastic Radicalism and the Thessalonian Correspondence." In: MCGAUGHY 1 (1972) 181–232.
— 1979. *A Chronology of Paul's Life*. Philadelphia: Fortress.
— 1986. *The Thessalonian Correspondence: Pauline Rhetoric and Millenarian Piety*. FF. Philadelphia: Fortress.
— 1991. "A Matrix of Grace: The Theology of 2 Thessalonians as a Pauline Letter." In: BASSLER (1991) 63–70.
— 1996. Review of *Comfort One Another: Reconstructing the Rhetoric and Audience of 1 Thessalonians*, by A. SMITH, 1995. *CRBR* 9 (1996) 271–273.
— 2007. *Romans: A Commentary*. Ass. by R. KOTANSKY. Hermeneia. Minneapolis: Fortress.
JOHANSON, Bruce C. 1987. *To All the Brethren: A Text-Linguistic and Rhetorical Approach to 1 Thessalonians*. ConBNT 16. Stockholm: Almqvist & Wiksell.
— 1995. "1 Thessalonians 2:15–16: Prophetic Woe-Oracle with ἔφθασεν as Proleptic Aorist." In: FS HARTMAN (1995) 519–534.
JOHNSON, E. Elizabeth 2002. "Apocalyptic Family Values." *Int* 56 (2002) 34–44.
JOHNSON, Luke T. 1989. "The New Testament's Anti-Jewish Slander and the Conventions of Ancient Polemic." *JBL* 108 (1989) 419–441.
JOHNSON, M. D. 1985. "Life of Adam and Eve: A New Translation and Introduction." *OTP* 2 (1985) 249–295.
JOHNSON, Sherman E. 1941. "Notes and Comments." *ATR* 23 (1941) 173–176.
JONES, Horace L. transl. 1917–1932. *The Geography of Strabo*. 8 vols. LCL 49, 50, 182, 196, 211, 223, 241, 267. London: William Heinemann / Cambridge: Harvard University Press.
JONGE, Henk J. de → DE JONGE, Henk J.
JONGE, Marinus de → DE JONGE, Marinus.
JOWETT, Benjamin 1859. *The Epistles of St. Paul to the Thessalonians, Galatians, Romans: With Critical Notes and Dissertations*. 2nd ed. Vol. 1. London: John Murray.
JUDGE, Edwin A. 1971. "The Decrees of Caesar at Thessalonica." *RTR* 30 (1971) 1–7.
— 2002. "Jews, Proselytes and God-fearers Club Together." *NewDocs* 9 (2002) 73–80.
JURGENSEN, Hubert 1992. "Saint Paul et la parousie. 1 Thessaloniciens 4.13–5.11 dans l'exégèse moderne et contemporaine." PhD diss. Université des Sciences Humaines de Strasbourg, 1992.
— 1994. "Awaiting the Return of Christ: A Re-Examination of 1 Thessalonians 4.13–5.11 from a Pentecostal Perspective." *JPT* 4 (1994) 81–113.

KAIBEL, Georg ed. 1878. *Epigrammata Graeca ex lapidibus conlecta*. [see *EG* in abbrev.]
KAMPLING, Rainer 1993. "Eine auslegungsgeschichtliche Skizze zu 1 Thess 2,14–16." In: FS SCHRECKENBERG (1993) 183–213.
— /SÖDING, Thomas eds. 1996. *Ekklesiologie des Neuen Testaments. Für Karl Kertelge*. Freiburg et al.: Herder.
KARRER, Martin 1986. "Eschatologie 2. Im Neuen Testament." *EKL* 1 (1986) 1111–1114.
— 1992. "Parusie." *EKL* 3 (1992) 1059–1061.

— 2002. "Jesus, der Retter (*Sôtêr*). Zur Aufnahme eines hellenistischen Prädikats im Neuen Testament." *ZNW* 93 (2002) 153–176.

KASCH, Wilhelm 1968. "ῥύομαι." *TDNT* 6 (1968) 998–1003.

KÄSEMANN, Ernst 1967. "Die Heilsbedeutung des Todes Jesu nach Paulus." In: CONZELMANN et al. (1967) 11–34.

— 1969. "The Beginnings of Christian Theology." *JTC* 6 (1969) 17–46. Republ. in: KÄSEMANN (1969b) 82–107. Originally in German & publ. in: *ZTK* 57 (1960) 162–185.

— 1969a. "On the Subject of Primitive Christian Apocalyptic." *JTC* 6 (1969) 99–133. Republ. in: Käsemann (1969b) 108–137. Originally in German and publ. in: *ZTK* 59 (1962) 257–284.

— 1969b. *New Testament Questions of Today*. NTL. Transl. by W. J. MONTAGUE. London: SCM.

— 1971. *Perspectives on Paul*. NTL. Transl. by M. KOHL. London: SCM.

— 1980. *Commentary on Romans*. Transl. & ed. by G. W. BROMILEY. Grand Rapids: Eerdmans.

— 1982. *Essays on New Testament Themes*. Transl. by W. J. MONTAGUE. Philadelphia: Fortress.

KASHER, Aryeh 1988. *Jews, Idumaeans, and Ancient Arabs: Relations of the Jews in Eretz-Israel with the Nations of the Frontier and the Desert during the Hellenistic and Roman Era (332 BCE – 70 CE)*. TSAJ 18. Tübingen: J. C. B. Mohr (Paul Siebeck).

— 1990. *Jews and Hellenistic Cities in Eretz-Israel: Relations of the Jews in Eretz-Israel with the Hellenistic Cities during the Second Temple Period (332 BCE – 70 CE)*. TSAJ 21. Tübingen: J. C. B. Mohr (Paul Siebeck).

KAYE, Bruce N. 1975. "Eschatology and Ethics in 1 and 2 Thessalonians." *NovT* 17 (1975) 47–57.

KECK, Leander E./MARTYN, J. Louis eds. 1966. *Studies in Luke-Acts: Essays Presented in Honour of Paul Schubert*. New York: Abingdon.

KEE, Howard C. 1983. "Testaments of the Twelve Patriarchs: A New Translation and Introduction." *OTP* 1 (1983) 775–828.

KEGEL, Günter 1970. *Auferstehung Jesu – Auferstehung der Toten. Eine traditionsgeschichtliche Untersuchung zum Neuen Testament*. Gütersloh: Gerd Mohn.

KEIGHTLEY, Georgia M. 1987. "The Church's Memory of Jesus: A Social Science Analysis of 1 Thessalonians." *BTB* 17 (1987) 149–156.

KEMMLER, Dieter W. 1975. *Faith and Human Reason: A Study of Paul's Method of Preaching as Illustrated by 1–2 Thessalonians and Acts 17, 2–4*. NovTSup 40. Leiden: E. J. Brill.

KENNEDY, George A. 1984. *New Testament Interpretation through Rhetorical Criticism*. Chapel Hill, NC/London: University of North Carolina.

KENNEDY, Harry A. A. 1904. *St Paul's Conceptions of the Last Things*. 2nd ed. Cunningham Lectures 1904. London: Hodder & Stoughton.

KERTELGE, Karl/LOHFINK, Gerhard eds. 1981. *Paulus in den neutestamentlichen Spätschriften. Zur Paulusrezeption im Neuen Testament*. QD 89. Freiburg et al.: Herder.

KHIOK-KHNG, Yeo 1998. "A Political Reading of Paul's Eschatology in I and II Thessalonians." *AJT* 12 (1998) 77–88.

KIEFFER, René 1990. "L'eschatologie en 1 Thessaloniciens dans une perspective rhétorique." In: R. F. COLLINS (1990) 206–219.

KIM, Seyoon 1981. *The Origin of Paul's Gospel*. WUNT II.4. Tübingen: J. C. B. Mohr (Paul Siebeck).

— 1983. *"The 'Son of Man'" as the Son of God*. WUNT I.30. Tübingen: J. C. B. Mohr (Paul Siebeck).

— 1993. "Jesus, Sayings of." *DPL* (1993) 474–492. Republ. in: KIM (2002) 259–292.

— 2002. *Paul and the New Perspective: Second Thoughts on the Origin of Paul's Gospel*. Grand Rapids/Cambridge: Eerdmans.

— 2002a. "The Jesus Tradition in 1 Thess 4.13–5.11." *NTS* 48 (2002) 225–242.

— 2005. "Paul's Entry (εἴσοδος) and the Thessalonians' Faith (1 Thessalonians 1–3)." *NTS* 51 (2005) 519–542.

KITTEL, Gerhard 1964. "ἄγγελος, ἀρχάγγελος, ἰσάγγελος." *TDNT* 1 (1964) 74–87 [§ C, D, ἀρχάγγελος, ἰσάγγελος: 80–87].

— 1967. "λέγω κτλ." *TDNT* 4 (1967) 69–192 [§ D–λογομαξέω, λογομαχία: 100–143].

— /FRIEDRICH, Gerhard eds. 1964–1976. *Theological Dictionary of the New Testament*. [see *TDNT* in abbrev.]

KLASSEN, William 1986. "Anti-Judaism in Early Christianity: The State of the Question." In: RICHARDSON/GRANSKOU (1986) 1–19.

KLAUSER, Theodor/DASSMANN, Ernst/THRAEDE, Klaus eds. 1982. *Jenseitsvorstellungen in Antike und Christentum. Gedenkschrift für Alfred Stuiber.* JAC.E 9. Münster: Aschendorff.

KLEIN, Charlotte 1978. *Anti-Judaism in Christian Theology.* Transl. by E. QUINN. London: SPCK.

KLEIN, Günter 1973. "Apokalyptische Naherwartung bei Paulus." In: FS BRAUN (1973) 241–262.

— 1982. "Eschatologie IV. Neues Testament." *TRE* 10 (1982) 270–299.

KLEIN, William W. 1984. "Paul's Use of *kalein*: A Proposal." *JETS* 27 (1984) 53–64.

KLIJN, Albertus F. J. 1982. "1 Thessalonians 4:13–18 and Its Background in Apocalyptic Literature." In: FS BARRETT (1982) 67–73.

KLOPPENBORG, John S. 1993. "φιλαδελφία, θεοδίδακτος and the Dioscuri: Rhetorical Engagement in 1 Thessalonians 4.9–12." *NTS* 39 (1993) 265–289.

— 2000. *Excavating Q: The History and Setting of the Sayings Gospel.* Edinburgh: T&T Clark.

KNOX, John 1950. *Chapters in a Life of Paul.* Nashville/New York: Abingdon.

— 1966. "Acts and the Pauline Letter Corpus." In: FS SCHUBERT (1966) 279–287.

— 1990. "On the Pauline Chronology: Buck-Taylor-Hurd Revisited." In: FS MARTYN (1990) 258–274.

KOCH, Dietrich-A./LICHTENBERGER, Hermann eds. 1993. *Begegnungen zwischen Christentum und Judentum in Antike und Mittelalter. Festschrift für Heinz Schreckenberg.* In cooperation with K. LEHNARDT/T. LEHNARDT. SIJD 1. Göttingen: Vandenhoeck & Ruprecht.

KOCH, Klaus 1970. *Ratlos vor der Apokalyptik. Eine Streitschrift über ein vernachlässigtes Gebiet der Bibelwissenschaft und die schädlichen Auswirkungen auf Theologie und Philosophie.* Gütersloh: Gerd Mohn.

— 1986. "Apokalyptik 3. A. im Neuen Testament." *EKL* 1 (1986) 196–199.

KOENIG, John 1979. *Jews and Christians in Dialogue: New Testament Foundations.* Philadelphia: Westminster.

KOPERSKI, Veronica 2002. "Resurrection Terminology in Paul." In: FS LAMBRECHT (2002) 265–281.

KÖSTER = KOESTER, Helmut 1979. "I Thessalonians—Experiment in Christian Writing." In: FS WILLIAMS (1979) 33–44.

— 1980. "Apostel und Gemeinde in den Briefen an die Thessalonicher." In: FS BORNKAMM (1980) 287–298.

— 1982 [vol. 2]; 1995 [vol. 1]. *Introduction to the New Testament.* Vol. 1: *History, Culture, and Religion of the Hellenistic Age.* 2nd ed. New York: W. de Gruyter. Vol. 2: *History and Literature of Early Christianity.* Transl. by H. KÖSTER. FF. Philadelphia: Fortress / Berlin/New York: W. de Gruyter.

— 1985. "The Text of 1 Thessalonians." In: FS SAUNDERS (1985) 219–227.

— 1990. "From Paul's Eschatology to the Apocalyptic Schemata of 2 Thessalonians." In: R. F. COLLINS (1990) 441–458.

— 1994. "Archäologie und Paulus in Thessalonike." In: FS GEORGI (1994) 393–404.

— 1997. "Imperial Ideology and Paul's Eschatology in 1 Thessalonians." In: R. A. HORSLEY (1997) 158–166.

KONRADT, Matthias 2001. "Εἰδέναι ἕκαστον ὑμῶν τὸ ἑαυτοῦ σκεῦος κτᾶσθαι…: Zu Paulus' sexualethischer Weisung in 1Thess 4,4f." *ZNW* 92 (2001) 128–135.

— 2003. *Gericht und Gemeinde. Eine Studie zur Bedeutung und Funktion von Gerichtsaussagen im Rahmen der paulinischen Ekklesiologie und Ethik im 1 Thess und 1 Kor.* BZNW 117. Berlin/New York: W. de Gruyter.

KOUKOULI-CHRYSANTHAKI, Chaïdo 1981. "Politarchs in a New Inscription from Amphipolis." In: FS EDSON (1981) 229–241.

KOVACS, David ed. & transl. 1994–2002. *Euripides.* 5 vols. LCL 12, 484, 9, 10, 11. Cambridge/London: Harvard University Press.

KRAFT, Robert A. 1975. "The Multiform Jewish Heritage of Early Christianity." In: FS SMITH 4 (1975) 174–199.

KRÄMER, Helmut 1991. "μυστήριον." *EDNT* 2 (1991) 446–449.

KRAMER, Werner 1966. *Christ, Lord, Son of God.* SBT 50. Transl. by B. HARDY. Naperville, IL: Alec R. Allenson.

KREITZER, Larry J. 1987. *Jesus and God in Paul's Eschatology.* JSNTSup 19. Sheffield: JSOT Press.

— 1993. "Eschatology." *DPL* (1993) 253–269.

— 1993a. "Resurrection." *DPL* (1993) 805–812.

KREMER, Jacob 1974. "Was heisst Parusie und Parusieerwartung heute? Überlegungen zu den Parusieaussagen von 1 Thess." In: FS POHLSCHNEIDER (1974) 251–268.

— 1990. "ἐγείρω." *EDNT* 1 (1990) 372–376.

— 1990a. "ἀνάστασις κτλ." *EDNT* 1 (1990) 88–92.

— 1991. "θλῖψις, θλίβω." *EDNT* 2 (1991) 151–153.

— 1992. "Auferstehung der Toten in bibeltheologischer Sicht." In: GRESHAKE/KREMER (1992) 5–161.

— 1993. "Auferstehung Christi I. Im Neuen Testament." *LTK* 1 (³1993) 1177–1182.

— 1993a. "Auferstehung der Toten, Auferstehung des Fleisches IV. Im Neuen Testament." *LTK* 1 (³1993) 1195–1198.

— 1993b. "πάθημα." *EDNT* 3 (1993) 1–2.

— 1993c. "πάσχω." *EDNT* 3 (1993) 51–52.

KRENTZ, Edgar M. 1987. "Evangelism and Spirit: 1 Thessalonians 1." *CurTM* 14 (1987) 22–30.

— 1988. "Roman Hellenism and Paul's Gospel." *TBT* 26 (1988) 328–337.

— 1990. "Traditions Held Fast: Theology and Fidelity in 2 Thessalonians." In: R. F. COLLINS (1990) 505–515.

— 1992. "First and Second Epistles to the Thessalonians." *ABD* 6 (1992) 515–523.

— 2000. "1 Thessalonians: Rhetorical Flourishes and Formal Constraints." In: DONFRIED/BEUTLER (2000) 287–318.

— 2004. Review of *The Letters to the Thessalonians: A New Translation with Introduction and Commentary*, by A. J. MALHERBE, 2000. *RevBL* 6 (2004) 21–27.

KRÖTKE, Wolf 1997. "Die christologische Bedeutung der Auferstehung Jesu Christi von den Toten." *EvT* 57 (1997) 209–225.

KRUIJF, Theo C. de → DE KRUIJF, Theo C.

KUCK, David W. 1992. *Judgment and Community Conflict: Paul's Use of Apocalyptic Judgment Language in 1 Corinthians 3:5–4:5*. NovTSup 66. Leiden et al.: E. J. Brill.

KUDLIEN, Fridolf 1975. "Thessalonike." *KlPauly* 5 (1975) 761–763.

KUHLI, Horst 1991. "Ἰουδαῖος." *EDNT* 2 (1991) 193–197.

KUHN, Heinz-W. 1992. "Die Bedeutung der Qumrantexte für das Verständnis des Ersten Thessalonicherbriefes. Vorstellung des Münchener Projekts: Qumran und das Neue Testament." In: BARRERA/MONTANER (1992) 339–353.

KÜMMEL, Werner G. 1961. *Promise and Fulfilment: The Eschatological Message of Jesus*. 2nd ed. Transl. by D. M. BARTON. SBT 23. London: SCM.

— 1962. "Das literarische und geschichtliche Problem des Ersten Thessalonicherbriefes." In: FS CULLMANN (1962) 213–227. Republ. in: KÜMMEL (1965) 406–416.

— 1965. *Heilsgeschehen und Geschichte. Gesammelte Aufsätze 1933–1964*. Ed. by E. GRÄSSER/O. MERK/A. FRITZ. MThSt 3. Marburg: N. G. Elwert.

— 1975. *Introduction to the New Testament*. Rev. ed. Transl. by H. C. KEE. London: SCM.

KUSS, Otto 1971. *Paulus. Die Rolle des Apostels in der theologischen Entwicklung der Urkirche*. Auslegung und Verkündigung 3. Regensburg: Friedrich Pustet.

KVALBEIN, Hans 2000. "Has Matthew Abandoned the Jews? A Contribution to a Disputed Issue in Recent Scholarship" In: ÅDNA/KVALBEIN (2000) 45–62.

LABAHN, Antje/LABAHN, Michael 2000. "Jesus als Sohn Gottes bei Paulus. Eine soteriologische Grundkonstante der paulinischen Christologie." In: FS HÜBNER (2000) 97–120.

LACEY, Douglas R. de → DE LACEY, Douglas R.

LAKE, Kirsopp transl. 1912–1913. *Apostolic Fathers*. 2 vols. LCL 24, 25. Cambridge: Harvard University Press / London: William Heinemann.

— /OULTON, John E. L. transl. 1926–1932. *Eusebius: The Ecclesiastical History*. 2 vols. LCL 153, 265. Cambridge: Harvard University Press / London: William Heinemann.

LAMB, Walter R. M. transl. 1930. *Lysias: With an English Translation*. LCL 244. Cambridge: Harvard University Press / London: William Heinemann.

LAMBRECHT, Jan ed. 1980. *L'Apocalypse johannique et l'apocalyptique dans le Nouveau Testament*. BETL 53. Gembloux: Duculot / Leuven: University Press.

— 1990. "Thanksgiving in 1 Thessalonians 1–3." In: R. F. COLLINS (1990) 183–205. Republ. in: LAMBRECHT (1994) 319–341. "Slightly revised" & republ. in: DONFRIED/BEUTLER (2000) 135–162.

— 1990a. "'De Heer tegemoet' (1 Tess. 4,17). De Schrift over het leven na de dood." In: LAMBRECHT/KENIS (1990) 87–125. Transl. & republ. as: "To Meet the Lord: Scripture about Life after Death." In: LAMBRECHT (1994) 411–441.

— 1991. "A Call to Witness by All: Evangelisation in 1 Thessalonians." In: FS DU TOIT (1991) 321–343. Republ. in: LAMBRECHT (1994) 343–361.

— 1994. *Pauline Studies: Collected Essays*. BETL 115. Leuven: University Press/Peeters. [collected essays include: LAMBRECHT 1990; 1990a; 1991]

— 2000. "A Structural Analysis of 1 Thessalonians 4–5." In: DONFRIED/BEUTLER (2000) 163–178.

— 2004. Review of *The Letters to the Thessalonians: A New Translation with Introduction and Commentary*, by A. J. MALHERBE, 2000. *RevBL* 6 (2004) 18–21.

— /KENIS, L. eds. 1990. *Leven over de dood heen. Verslagboek van een interdisciplinair Leuvens Colloquium*. Leuven-Amersfoort: Acco.

LAMP, Jeffrey S. 2003. "Is Paul Anti-Jewish? *Testament of Levi* 6 in the Interpretation of 1 Thessalonians 2:13–16." *CBQ* 65 (2003) 408–427.

LANDAU, Rudolf/SCHMIDT, Günter R. eds. 1993. *'Daß allen Menschen geholfen werde …'. Theologische und anthropologische Beiträge für Manfred Seitz zum 65. Geburtstag*. Stuttgart: Calwer.

LANDMESSER, Christof/ECKSTEIN, Hans-J./LICHTENBERGER, Hermann eds. 1997. *Jesus Christus als die Mitte der Schrift. Studien zur Hermeneutik des Evangeliums*. Berlin/New York: W. de Gruyter.

LANGE, Nicholas R. M. de → DE LANGE, Nicholas R. M.

LANGEVIN, Paul-É. 1965. "Le Seigneur Jésus selon un texte prépaulinien, 1 Th 1, 9–10." *ScEccl* 17 (1965) 263–282. Republ. in: LANGEVIN (1967) 43–58.

— 1965a. "Le Seigneur Jésus selon un texte prépaulinien, 1 Th 1, 9–10 (Suite)." *ScEccl* 17 (1965) 473–512. Republ. in: LANGEVIN (1967) 58–106.

— 1967. *Jésus Seigneur et l'eschatologie. Exégèse de textes prépauliniens*. Studia 21. Bruges/Paris: Desclée de Brouwer.

— 1990. "L'intervention de Dieu selon 1 Thes 5,23–24." In: R. F. COLLINS (1990) 236–256.

LANGKAMMER, Hugolinus 1993. "πρῶτον." *EDNT* 3 (1993) 187–188.

LAOURDAS, Basil/MAKARONAS, Ch. eds. 1970. *Ancient Macedonia: Papers Read at the First International Symposium Held in Thessaloniki, 26–29 August 1968*. Institute for Balkan Studies 122. Thessaloniki: Institute for Balkan Studies.

— eds. 1977. *Ancient Macedonia II: Papers Read at the Second International Symposium Held in Thessaloniki, 19–24 August 1973*. Institute for Balkan Studies 155. Thessaloniki: Institute for Balkan Studies.

LARSSON, Edvin 1985. "Heil und Erlösung III. Neues Testament." *TRE* 14 (1985) 616–622.

— 1991. "μιμέομαι, μιμητής." *EDNT* 2 (1991) 428–430.

LATTIMORE, Richmond 1962. *Themes in Greek and Latin Epitaphs*. Illinois Studies in Language & Literature 28. Urbana: University of Illinois Press.

LATTKE, Michael 1985. "Heiligkeit III. Neues Testament." *TRE* 14 (1985) 703–708.

— 1987. "Holiness and Sanctification in the New Testament." In: FS ANDERSEN (1987) 351–357.

— 1990. "ἀπαντάω, ἀπάντησις." *EDNT* 1 (1990) 114–115.

LAUB, Franz 1973. *Eschatologische Verkündigung und Lebensgestaltung nach Paulus. Eine Untersuchung zum Wirken des Apostels beim Aufbau der Gemeinde in Thessalonike*. BU 10. Regensburg: Friedrich Pustet.

— 1976. "Paulus als Gemeindegründer (1 Thess)." In: HAINZ (1976) 17–38.

— 1985. *1. und 2. Thessalonicherbrief*. NEchtB 13. Würzburg: Echter.

— 1990. "Paulinische Autorität in nachpaulinischer Zeit (2 Thes)." In: R. F. COLLINS (1990) 403–417.

LAUBACH, Fritz 1975. "Conversion, Penitence, Repentance, Proselyte." *NIDNTT* 1 (1975) 353–362 [§ ἐπιστρέφω; μεταμέλομαι: 354–357].

LAUTENSCHLAGER, Markus 1990. "εἴτε γρηγορῶμεν εἴτε καθεύδωμεν. Zum Verhältnis von Heiligung und Heil in 1Thess 5,10." *ZNW* 81 (1990) 39–59.

LEANEY, Alfred R. C. 1984. *The Jewish and Christian World, 200 BC to AD 200*. CCWJCW 7. Cambridge et al.: University Press.

LEE, Robert/LEE, Carolyn 1975. "An Analysis of the Larger Semantic Units of 1 Thessalonians." *Notes on Translation* 56 (1975) 28–42.

LÉGASSE, Simon 1991. "ἐπιστρέφω, ἐπιστροφή." *EDNT* 2 (1991) 40–41.

— 1991a. "κωλύω." *EDNT* 2 (1991) 332–333.

— 1999. *Les Épîtres de Paul aux Thessaloniciens*. LD Commentaires 7. Paris: Les Éditions du Cerf.

LEHNERT, Volker A. 2002. "Wenn der liebe Gott ›böse‹ wird — Überlegungen zum Zorn Gottes im Neuen Testament." *ZNT* Heft 9, 5. Jahrgang (2002) 15–25.

LENSKI, Richard C. H. 1937. *The Interpretation of St. Paul's Epistles to the Colossians, to the Thessalonians, to Timothy, to Titus and to Philemon*. Minneapolis: Augsburg.

LEVENSON, Jon D. 1993. *The Hebrew Bible, the Old Testament, and Historical Criticism: Jews and Christians in Biblical Studies*. Louisville, KY: Westminster/John Knox.

LEWIS, Clive S. 1975. *Fern-seed and Elephants: And other Essays on Christianity*. Ed. by W. HOOPER. London: HarperCollins.

LICHTENBERGER, Hermann 1993. "ῥύομαι." *EDNT* 3 (1993) 214–215.

— 1993a. "σάλπιγξ." *EDNT* 3 (1993) 225–226.

LIDDELL, Henry G./SCOTT, Robert comps 1940. *A Greek-English Lexicon*. [see LSJ in abbrev.]

LIETAERT Peerbolte/JAN, Bert 2005. Review of *Paul, Thessalonica and Early Christianity*, by K. P. DONFRIED, 2002. *RevBL* 7 (2005) 400–404.

LIEU, Judith M. 1986. "'Grace to You and Peace': The Apostolic Greeting." *BJRL* 68 (1985–1986) 161–178.

LINCOLN, Andrew T. 1981. *Paradise Now and Not Yet: Studies in the Role of the Heavenly Dimension in Paul's Thought with Special Reference to His Eschatology*. SNTSMS 43. Cambridge et al.: University Press.

LINDARS, Barnabas 1985. "The Sound of the Trumpet: Paul and Eschatology." *BJRL* 67 (1984–1985) 766–782.

LINDEMANN, Andreas 1977. "Zum Abfassungszweck des Zweiten Thessalonicherbriefes." *ZNW* 68 (1977) 35–47. Republ. in: LINDEMANN (1999a) 228–240.

— 1991. "Paulus und die korinthische Eschatologie. Zur These von einer 'Entwicklung' im paulinischen Denken." *NTS* 37 (1991) 373–399. Republ. in: LINDEMANN (1999a) 64–90.

— 1995. "Der jüdische Jesus als der Christus der Kirche. Historische Beobachtungen am Neuen Testament." *EvT* 55 (1995) 28–49.

— 1997. "Die Auferstehung der Toten. Adam und Christus nach 1.Kor 15." In: FS GRÄSSER (1997) 155–167.

— 1998. "Paulus als Zeuge der Auferstehung Jesu Christi." In: FS KLEIN (1998) 55–64. Republ. in: LINDEMANN (1999a) 27–36.

— 1999. "Eschatologie III. Neues Testament." *RGG* 2 (^{4}1999) 1553–1560.

— 1999a. *Paulus, Apostel und Lehrer der Kirche. Studien zu Paulus und zum frühen Paulusverständnis*. Tübingen: Mohr Siebeck. [collected essays include: LINDEMANN 1977; 1991; 1998]

LINSS, Wilhelm C. 1992. Review of *The Thessalonian Correspondence: Pauline Rhetoric and Millenarian Piety*, by R. JEWETT, 1986. *CurTM* 19 (1992) 135–136.

LLEWELYN, S. R. 1992. "Ammonios to Apollonios (*P. Oxy.* XLII 3057): The Earliest Christian Letter on Papyrus?" *NewDocs* 6 (1992) 169–177.

— 1994. "Letters in the Early Church." *NewDocs* 7 (1994) 48–57.

— 2002. "The King as 'Living Image' of Zeus." *NewDocs* 9 (2002) 36–38.

— 2002a. "Escaping the Birth of a Daughter." *NewDocs* 9 (2002) 57–58.

— et al. eds. 2002. *A Review of the Greek Inscriptions and Papyri: Published in 1986–87*. [see *NewDocs* in abbrev.]

LLOYD-JONES, Hugh ed. & transl. 1994–1996. *Sophocles*. 3 vols. LCL 20, 21, 483. Cambridge/London: Harvard University Press.

LOADER, William 2004. Review of *Gericht und Gemeinde. Eine Studie zur Bedeutung und Funktion von Gerichtsaussagen im Rahmen der paulinischen Ekklesiologie und Ethik im 1 Thess und 1 Kor*, by M. KONRADT, 2003. *Bib* 85 (2004) 435–438.

LOFTHOUSE, W. F. 1955. "'I' and 'We' in the Pauline Letters." *BT* 6 (1955) 72–80. Originally publ. in: *ExpTim* 64 (1952–1953) 241–245.

LOHFINK, Gerhard 1971. *Die Himmelfahrt Jesu. Untersuchungen zu den Himmelfahrts- und Erhöhungstexten bei Lukas.* SANT 26. München: Kösel.

LOHMEYER, Ernst 1927. "Probleme paulinischer Theologie." *ZNW* 26 (1927) 158–173.

LÖHR, Gebhard 1980. "1 Thess 4 15–17: Das 'Herrenwort'." *ZNW* 71 (1980) 269–273.

LOHSE, Eduard 1987. "Jesu Worte im Zeugnis seiner Gemeinde." *TLZ* 112 (1987) 705–716. Republ. in: LOHSE (2000) 23–38.

— 1996. "Changes of Thought in Pauline Theology? Some Reflections on Paul's Ethical Teaching in the Context of His Theology." In: FS FURNISH (1996) 146–160. Republ. in: LOHSE (2000) 75–88.

— 1998. "Die Wahrheit der Osterbotschaft." *CV* 40 (1998) 5–15. Republ. in: LOHSE (2000) 232–240.

— 2000. *Das Neue Testament als Urkunde des Evangeliums. Exegetische Studien zur Theologie des Neuen Testaments III.* FRLANT 192. Göttingen: Vandenhoeck & Ruprecht. [collected essays include: LOHSE 1987; 1996; 1998; 2000a]

— 2000a. "Das Neue Testament – Urkunde des Evangeliums." In: LOHSE (2000) 11–22.

LONA, Horacio E. 1986. "Eschatologie im Neuen Testament." In: *HDG* IV, 7a (1986) 44–83.

LONGENECKER, Richard N. 1974. "Ancient Amanuenses and the Pauline Epistles." In: LONGENECKER/TENNEY (1974) 281–297.

— 1985. "The Nature of Paul's Early Eschatology." *NTS* 31 (1985) 85–95.

— ed. 1996. *Patterns of Discipleship in the New Testament.* MNTS. Grand Rapids/Cambridge: Eerdmans.

— /TENNEY, Merrill C. eds. 1974. *New Dimensions in New Testament Study.* Grand Rapids: Zondervan.

LÖNING, Karl 1993. "The Circle of Stephen and Its Mission." In: BECKER (1993a) 103–131.

LOVERING, JR., Eugene H. ed. 1992. *SBL Seminar Papers, 1992.* SBLSP 31. Atlanta: Scholars Press.

— ed. 1993. *SBL Seminar Papers, 1993.* SBLSP 32. Atlanta: Scholars Press.

— /SUMNEY, Jerry L. eds. 1996. *Theology and Ethics in Paul and His Interpreters: Essays in Honor of Victor Paul Furnish.* Nashville: Abingdon.

LÖVESTAM, Evald 1963. *Spiritual Wakefulness in the New Testament.* Transl. by W. F. SALISBURY. Lund: CWK Gleerup.

LOWE, John 1941. "An Examination of Attempts to Detect Developments in St. Paul's Theology: A Paper Read to the Oxford Society of Historical Theology on 9 May 1940." *JTS* 42 (1941) 129–142.

LOWE, Malcolm 1976. "Who Were the Ἰουδαῖοι?" *NovT* 18 (1976) 101–130.

LUBAHN, Erich 1984. "Hermeneutischer Ansatz für Eschatologie, mit beispielhafter Anwendung auf 2. Thessalonicher 2." In: MAIER (1984) 114–123.

LUCCHESI, Enzo 1977. "Précédents non bibliques à l'expression néo-testamentaire. 'Les temps et les moments'." *JTS* NS 28 (1977) 537–540.

LUCKENSMEYER, David 2005. "Eschatology in First Thessalonians: A Key to Understanding an Early Christian Letter." PhD diss. University of Queensland, 2005.

— 2007. "Βασιλεία in First Thessalonians (2:12)." In: FS LATTKE (2007) 137–155.

LÜDEMANN = LUEDEMANN, Gerd 1980. "The Hope of the Early Paul: From the Foundation-Preaching at Thessalonika to I Cor. 15:51–57." *Perspectives in Religious Studies* 7 (1980) 195–201.

— 1980a. *Paulus, der Heidenapostel.* Vol. 1: *Studien zur Chronologie.* FRLANT 123. Göttingen: Vandenhoeck & Ruprecht. Transl. by F. STANLEY JONES & republ. as: *Paul, Apostle to the Gentiles: Studies in Chronology.* Philadelphia: Fortress, 1984.

— 1989. *Early Christianity according to the Traditions of Acts: A Commentary.* Transl. by J. BOWDEN. London: SCM.

— 1993. "Paul, Christ and the Problem of Death." In: FS HURD (1993) 26–43.

— 1994. *The Resurrection of Jesus: History, Experience, Theology.* Transl. by J. BOWDEN. London: SCM.

LÜHRMANN, Dieter 1990. "The Beginnings of the Church at Thessalonica." In: FS MALHERBE (1990) 237–249.

— 1998. "Agrapha." *RGG* 1 ([4]1998) 190–191.

— /STRECKER, Georg eds. 1980. *Kirche. Festschrift für Günther Bornkamm zum 75. Geburtstag.* Tübingen: J. C. B. Mohr (Paul Siebeck).

LULL, David J. ed. 1989. *SBL Seminar Papers, 1989.* SBLSP 28. Atlanta: Scholars Press.

— 1991. "Salvation History: Theology in 1 Thessalonians, Philemon, Philippians, and Galatians. A Response to N. T. Wright, R. B. Hays, and R. Scroggs." In: BASSLER (1991) 247–265.

LUST, Johan/EYNIKEL, Erik/HAUSPIE, Katrin comps 2003. *Greek-English Lexicon of the Septuagint.* Rev. ed. Stuttgart: Deutsche Bibelgesellschaft.

LÜTGERT, Wilhelm E. 1909. *Die Vollkommenen im Philipperbrief und die Enthusiasten in Thessalonich.* BFCT 6. Gütersloh: Bertelsmann.

LUZ, Ulrich 1968. *Das Geschichtsverständnis des Paulus.* BET 49. München: Kaiser.

— 1981. "Eschatologie und Friedenshandeln bei Paulus." In: LUZ et al. (1981) 153–193.

— 2001. *Matthew 8–20.* Transl. by J. E. CROUCH. Ed. by H. KOESTER. Vol. 2. Hermeneia. Minneapolis: Fortress.

— et al. 1981. *Eschatologie und Friedenshandeln. Exegetische Beiträge zur Frage christlicher Friedensverantwortung.* SBS 101. Stuttgart: Verlag Katholisches Bibelwerk.

— /WEDER, Hans eds. 1983. *Die Mitte des Neuen Testaments. Einheit und Vielfalt neutestamentlicher Theologie. Festschrift für Eduard Schweizer zum siebzigsten Geburtstag.* Göttingen: Vandenhoeck & Ruprecht.

LYONS, George 1985. *Pauline Autobiography: Toward a New Understanding.* SBLDS 73. Atlanta: Scholars Press.

— 1995. "Modeling the Holiness Ethos: A Study Based on First Thessalonians." *WesTJ* 30 (1995) 187–211.

MACGREGOR, George H. C. 1961. "The Concept of the Wrath of God in the New Testament." *NTS* 7 (1960–1961) 101–109.

MACKENZIE, Ross transl. 1961. *The Epistles of Paul the Apostle to the Romans and to the Thessalonians.* Ed. by D. W. TORRANCE/T. F. TORRANCE. Calvin's Commentaries. Edinburgh: Saint Andrew Press.

MACKINTOSH, H. R. 1914. "Studies in Christian Eschatology." *The Expositor, 8th Series* 7 (1914) 111–126, 213–223, 298–315, 427–440, 538–552.

MACMULLEN, Ramsay 1974. *Roman Social Relations: 50 B.C. to A.D. 284.* New Haven/London: Yale University Press.

— 1984. *Christianizing the Roman Empire: (A.D. 100–400).* New Haven: Yale University Press.

— 1993. "Two Types of Conversion to Early Christianity." In: FERGUSON (1993) 26–44.

MAGNIEN, P. M. 1907. "La Résurrection des Morts: D'après la première épître aux Thessaloniciens. Étude exégétique sur I Th. IV, 13 – V, 3." *RB* 4 (1907) 349–382.

MAIER, Gerhard ed. 1984. *Zukunftserwartung in biblischer Sicht. Beiträge zur Eschatologie.* Wuppertal: R. Brockhaus / Giessen/Basel: Brunnen.

MAILE, John F. 1993. "Exaltation and Enthronement." *DPL* (1993) 275–278.

MALBON, Elizabeth S. 1983. "'No Need to Have Any One Write'? A Structural Exegesis of 1 Thessalonians." *Semeia* 26 (1983) 57–83.

MALHERBE, Abraham J. 1958. "Christology in Luke-Acts (2)." *ResQ* 2 (1958) 115–127.

— 1970. "'Gentle as a Nurse': The Cynic Background to I Thess ii." *NovT* 12 (1970) 203–217. Republ. in: MALHERBE (1989) 35–48.

— 1977. "Ancient Epistolary Theorists." *OJRS* 5 (1977) 3–77. Republ. with minor changes as: MALHERBE (1988).

— 1983. "Exhortation in First Thessalonians." *NovT* 25 (1983) 238–256. Republ. in: MALHERBE (1989) 49–66.

— 1983a. *Social Aspects of Early Christianity.* 2nd enl. ed. Philadelphia: Fortress.

— 1985. "Paul: Hellenistic Philosopher or Christian Pastor?" *American Theological Library Association: Proceedings* 39 (1985) 86–98. Republ. in: *ATR* 68 (1986) 3–13; MALHERBE (1989) 67–77.

— 1986. *Moral Exhortation: A Greco-Roman Sourcebook.* LEC 4. Philadelphia: Westminster.

— 1987. *Paul and the Thessalonians: The Philosophic Tradition of Pastoral Care.* Philadelphia: Fortress.

— 1988. *Ancient Epistolary Theorists.* SBLSBS 19. Atlanta: Scholars Press.

— 1989. *Paul and the Popular Philosophers.* Minneapolis: Fortress. [collected essays include: MALHERBE 1970; 1983; 1985]

— 1990. "Did the Thessalonians Write to Paul?" In: FS MARTYN (1990) 246–257.

— 1990a. "'Pastoral Care' in the Thessalonian Church." *NTS* 36 (1990) 375–391.

— 1992. "Hellenistic Moralists and the New Testament." *ANRW* II.26.1 (1992) 267–333.
— 1995. "God's New Family in Thessalonica." In: FS MEEKS (1995) 116–125.
— 1998. "Conversion to Paul's Gospel." In: FS FERGUSON (1998) 230–244.
— 1999. "Anti-Epicurean Rhetoric in 1 Thessalonians." In: FS LÜHRMANN (1999) 136–142.
— 2000. *The Letters to the Thessalonians: A New Translation with Introduction and Commentary.* AB 32B. Philadelphia: Fortress.
— /MEEKS, Wayne A. eds. 1993. *The Future of Christology: Essays in Honor of Leander E. Keck.* Minneapolis: Fortress.
— /NORRIS, Frederick W./THOMPSON, James W. eds. 1998. *The Early Church in Its Context: Essays in Honor of Everett Ferguson.* NovTSup 90. Leiden et al.: Brill.
MANSON, Thomas W. 1953. "St. Paul in Greece: The Letters to the Thessalonians." *BJRL* 35 (1952–1953) 428–447.
MANUS, Chris U. 1990. "Luke's Account of Paul in Thessalonica (Acts 17,1–9)." In: R. F. COLLINS (1990) 27–38.
MARCUS, Joel/SOARDS, Marion L. eds. 1989. *Apocalyptic and the New Testament: Essays in Honor of J. Louis Martyn.* JSNTSup 24. Sheffield: Academic Press.
MARCUS, Ralph transl. 1926–1965 → THACKERAY et al. 1926–1965.
MARROW, Stanley B. 1986. *Paul: His Letters and His Theology. An Introduction to Paul's Epistles.* New York/Mahwah, NJ: Paulist.
MARSHALL, I. Howard ed. 1979. *New Testament Interpretation: Essays on Principles and Methods.* Rev. ed. Exeter: Paternoster.
— 1979a. "Historical Criticism." In: MARSHALL (1979) 126–138.
— 1980. *The Acts of the Apostles: An Introduction and Commentary.* TynNTC. Leicester: Inter-Varsity / Grand Rapids: Eerdmans.
— 1980a. Review of *Der erste Brief an die Thessalonicher*, by W. MARXSEN, 1979. *JSNT*, issue 9 (1980) 75–76.
— 1982. "Pauline Theology in the Thessalonian Correspondence." In: FS BARRETT (1982) 173–183.
— 1983. *1 and 2 Thessalonians: Based on the Revised Standard Version.* NCB Commentary. Grand Rapids: Eerdmans / London: Marshall Morgan & Scott.
— 1990. "Election and Calling to Salvation in 1 and 2 Thessalonians." In: R. F. COLLINS (1990) 259–276.
MARTIN, Dale B. 1990. *Slavery as Salvation: The Metaphor of Slavery in Pauline Christianity.* New Haven/London: Yale University Press.
MARTIN, Ralph P. 1979. "Approaches to New Testament Study." In: MARSHALL (1979) 220–251.
— /DAVIDS, Peter H. eds. 1997. *Dictionary of the Later New Testament and Its Development.* [see *DLNT* in abbrev.]
MARTYN, J. Louis 1997. *Galatians: A New Translation with Introduction and Commentary.* AB 33A. New York et al.: Doubleday.
MARXSEN, Willi 1969. "Auslegung von 1Thess 4,13–18." *ZTK* 66 (1969) 22–37.
— 1970. *The Resurrection of Jesus of Nazareth.* Transl. by M. KOHL. Philadelphia: Fortress.
— 1972. "Unterwegs. Gedanken zum 1. Thessalonicherbrief." In: FS KITTEL (1972) 241–245.
— 1979. *Der erste Brief an die Thessalonicher.* ZBK 11.1. Zürich: Theologischer Verlag.
— 1982. *Der zweite Brief an die Thessalonicher.* ZBK 11.2. Zürich: Theologischer Verlag.
— 1990. *Jesus and Easter: Did God Raise the Historical Jesus from the Dead?* Transl. by V. P. FURNISH. Nashville: Abingdon.
— et al. 1966. *Die Bedeutung der Auferstehungsbotschaft für den Glauben an Jesus Christus.* 2nd ed. STAEKU. Gütersloh: Gerd Mohn.
MÄRZ, Claus-P. 1992. "Das Gleichnis vom Dieb. Überlegungen zur Verbindung von Lk 12,39 par Mt 24,43 und 1 Thess 5,2.4." In: FS NEIRYNCK (1992) 633–648.
MASER, Stefan/SCHLARB, Egbert eds. 1999. *Text und Geschichte. Facetten theologischen Arbeitens aus dem Freundes- und Schülerkreis. Dieter Lührmann zum 60. Geburtstag.* Marburg: N. G. Elwert.
MASON, John P. 1993. *The Resurrection according to Paul.* Lewiston, NY: Mellen.
MASSON, Charles 1957. *Les deux Épîtres de Saint Paul aux Thessaloniciens.* CNT 11. Neuchâtel: Delachaux & Niestlé.

MATLOCK, R. Barry 1996. *Unveiling the Apocalyptic Paul: Paul's Interpreters and the Rhetoric of Criticism*. JSNTSup 127. Sheffield: Academic Press.
MAURER, Christian 1971. "σκεῦος." *TDNT* 7 (1971) 358–367.
— 1972. "τίθημι κτλ." *TDNT* 8 (1972) 152–168.
— 1974. "φυλή." *TDNT* 9 (1974) 245–250.
MAXWELL, Donald M. 1968. *The Significance of the Parousia in the Theology of Paul: A Study in Pauline Eschatology*. PhD diss. Drew University, 1968. Ann Arbor, Mich.: UMI, 1968.
MAY, John 1981. "'Making Sense of Death' in Christianity and Buddhism: Towards a 'Pragmasemantic' Analysis of 1 Thess 4:13–5:11 and Sutta-Nipāta III, 8 ('The Dart Sutta')." *ZMW* 65 (1981) 51–69.
MAYER, Bernhard 1974. *Unter Gottes Heilsratschluß. Prädestinationsaussagen bei Paulus*. FB 15. Würzburg: Echter.
— 1990. "ἐλπίς κτλ." *EDNT* 1 (1990) 437–441.
MAYER, Roland 1976. "Israel, Jew, Hebrew, Jacob, Judah." *NIDNTT* 2 (1976) 304–323 [§ Ἰσραήλ: 304–316].
MAYHUE, Richard L. 1991. "The Apostle's Watchword: Day of the Lord." In: FS KENT, JR. (1991) 239–263.
MCALPINE, Thomas H. 1987. *Sleep, Divine and Human, in the Old Testament*. JSOTSup 38. Sheffield: Academic Press.
MCDONALD, Lee M. 1994. Review of *The Birth of the New Testament: The Origin and Development of the First Christian Generation*, by R. F. COLLINS, 1993. *CRBR* 7 (1994) 165–168.
— /PORTER, Stanley E. 2000. *Early Christianity and Its Sacred Literature*. Peabody, MA: Hendrickson.
MCGAUGHY, Lane C. ed. 1972. *SBL Seminar Papers, 1972*. 2 vols. n.p.
MCGEHEE, Michael 1989. "A Rejoinder to Two Recent Studies Dealing with 1 Thess 4:4." *CBQ* 51 (1989) 82–89.
MCKNIGHT, Scot 1996. Review of *Anti-Judaism and Early Christian Identity: A Critique of the Scholarly Consensus*, by M. S. TAYLOR, 1995. *CRBR* 9 (1996) 286–289.
MCLAREN, James S. 1998. *Turbulent Times? Josephus and Scholarship on Judaea in the First Century* CE. JSPSup 29. Sheffield: Academic Press.
MCLEAN, Bradley H. ed. 1993. *Origins and Method: Towards a New Understanding of Judaism and Christianity. Essays in Honour of John C. Hurd*. JSNTSup 86. Sheffield: Academic Press.
MCNICOL, Allan J. 1996. *Jesus' Directions for the Future: A Source and Redaction-History Study of the Use of the Eschatological Traditions in Paul and in the Synoptic Accounts of Jesus' Last Eschatological Discourse*. NGS 9. Macon, GA: Mercer University Press.
MEADORS, Gary T. ed. 1991. *New Testament Essays in Honor of Homer A. Kent, Jr.* Winona Lake, IN: BMH Books.
MEAGHER, John C. 1979. "As the Twig Was Bent: Antisemitism in Greco-Roman and Earliest Christian Times." In: DAVIES (1979) 1–26.
MEARNS, Christopher L. 1981. "Early Eschatological Development in Paul: The Evidence of I and II Thessalonians." *NTS* 27 (1981) 137–157.
— 1984. "Early Eschatological Development in Paul: The Evidence of 1 Corinthians." *JSNT*, issue 22 (1984) 19–35.
MEEKS, Wayne A. 1983. *The First Urban Christians: The Social World of the Apostle Paul*. New Haven: Yale University Press.
— 1983a. "Social Functions of Apocalyptic Language in Pauline Christianity." In: HELLHOLM (1983) 687–705.
— 1985. "Breaking Away: Three New Testament Pictures of Christianity's Separation from the Jewish Communities." In: NEUSNER/FRERICHS (1985) 93–115.
MERK, Otto 1968. *Handeln aus Glauben. Die Motivierungen der paulinischen Ethik*. Marburger Theologische Studien 5. Marburg: N. G. Elwert.
— 1985. "Zu Rudolf Bultmanns Auslegung des 1. Thessalonicherbriefes." In: FS KÜMMEL (1985) 189–198. Republ. in: MERK (1998a) 350–359.
— 1989. "Nachahmung Christi. Zu ethischen Perspektiven in der paulinischen Theologie." In: FS SCHNACKENBURG (1989) 172–206. Republ. in: MERK (1998a) 302–336.

— 1990. "ἄρχων." *EDNT* 1 (1990) 167–168.

— 1991. "Zur Christologie im Ersten Thessalonicherbrief." In: FS HAHN (1991) 97–110. Republ. in: MERK (1998a) 360–373.

— 1993. "Miteinander. Zur Sorge um den Menschen im Ersten Thessalonicherbrief." In: FS SEITZ (1993) 125–133. Republ. in: MERK (1998a) 374–382.

— 1996. "Thessalonicherbriefe." *EKL* 4 (1996) 871–872.

— 1997. "1.Thessalonicher 4,13–18 im Lichte des gegenwärtigen Forschungsstandes." In: FS GRÄSSER (1997) 213–230. Republ. in: MERK (1998a) 404–421.

— 1998. "1 Thessalonicher 2,1–12. Ein exegetisch-theologischer Überblick. Traugott Holtz zum 65. Geburtstag am 9. Juli 1996 in dankbarer Verbundenheit zugeeignet." In: MERK (1998a) 383–403. Transl. & republ. in: DONFRIED/BEUTLER (2000) 89–113.

— 1998a. *Wissenschaftsgeschichte und Exegese. Gesammelte Aufsätze zum 65. Geburtstag.* Ed. by R. GEBAUER/M. KARRER/M. MEISER. *BZNW* 95. Berlin/New York: W. de Gruyter. [collected essays include: MERK 1985; 1989; 1991; 1993; 1997; 1998]

MERKLEIN, Helmut ed. 1989. *Neues Testament und Ethik. Für Rudolf Schnackenburg.* Freiburg et al.: Herder.

— 1990. "ἀήρ." *EDNT* 1 (1990) 34.

— 1992. "Der Theologe als Prophet. Zur Funktion prophetischen Redens im theologischen Diskurs des Paulus." *NTS* 38 (1992) 402–429.

— 1995. "Eschatologie B. Thematisch-inhaltlich II. Biblisch: 2. Neues Testament." *LTK* 3 (^{3}1995) 868–872.

METZGER, Bruce M. 1983. "The Fourth Book of Ezra: With the Four Additional Chapters. A New Translation and Introduction." *OTP* 1 (1983) 517–559.

— 1994. *A Textual Commentary on the Greek New Testament: A Companion Volume to the United Bible Societies' Greek New Testament (Fourth Revised Edition).* 2nd ed. Stuttgart: Deutsche Bibelgesellschaft.

MEYER, Ben F. 1986. "Did Paul's View of the Resurrection of the Dead Undergo Development?" *TS* 47 (1986) 363–387.

— 1987. "Paul and the Resurrection of the Dead." *TS* 48 (1987) 157–158.

MICHAELIS, Wilhelm 1967. "εἴσοδος, ἔξοδος, διέξοδος." *TDNT* 5 (1967) 103–109.

— 1967a. "μιμέομαι, μιμητής, συμμιμητής." *TDNT* 4 (1967) 659–674.

— 1967b. "πάσχω κτλ." *TDNT* 5 (1967) 904–939.

— 1968. "πρῶτος κτλ." *TDNT* 6 (1968) 865–882.

MICHAELS, J. Ramsey 1994. "Everything that Rises Must Converge: Paul's Word from the Lord." In: FS GUNDRY (1994) 182–195.

MICHEL, Otto 1936. "Zur Lehre vom Todesschlaf." *ZNW* 35 (1936) 285–290.

— 1967. "Fragen zu 1 Thessalonicher 2, 14–16. Antijüdische Polemik bei Paulus." In: ECKERT/LEVINSON/STÖHR (1967) 50–59.

— 1967a. "οἶκος κτλ." *TDNT* 5 (1967) 119–159.

MILLER, Gene 1972. "Ἀρχόντων τοῦ αἰῶνος τούτου — A New Look at 1 Corinthians 2:6–8." *JBL* 91 (1972) 522–528.

MILLIGAN, George 1908. *St. Paul's Epistles to the Thessalonians: The Greek Text with Introduction and Notes.* London: Macmillan.

MILLS, Watson E. 1993. *An Index to Periodic Literature on the Apostle Paul.* NTTS 16. Leiden/New York: E. J. Brill.

— comp. 2000. *1 & 2 Thessalonians.* Bibliographies for Biblical Research: New Testament Series 13. Lewiston, NY et al.: Mellen.

— /MILLS, Joyce H. comps 1994. *Novum Testamentum: An Index to Novum Testamentum Volumes 1–35.* Vol. 36a. Leiden et al.: E. J. Brill.

MINAR, JR., Edwin L./SANDBACH, Francis H./HELMBOLD, William C. transl. 1927–1976 → BABBITT et al. 1927–1976.

MINEAR, Paul S. 1954. *Christian Hope and the Second Coming.* Philadelphia: Westminster.

MITCHELL, Alan C. 2005. Review article of *From Hope to Despair in Thessalonica: Situating 1 and 2 Thessalonians*, by C. R. NICHOLL, 2004. *JR* 85 (2005) 654–656.

MITCHELL, Margaret M. 1992. "New Testament Envoys in the Context of Greco-Roman Diplomatic and Epistolary Conventions: The Example of Timothy and Titus." *JBL* 111 (1992) 641–662.
— 2003. "1 and 2 Thessalonians." In: DUNN (2003) 51–63.
— 2004. Review article of *The Letters to the Thessalonians: A New Translation with Introduction and Commentary*, by A. J. MALHERBE, 2000. *RevBL* 6 (2004) 36–48.
— 2005. "Thessalonicherbriefe." *RGG* 8 ([4]2005) 360–362.
MÖDE, Erwin/UNGER, Felix/WOSCHITZ, Karl. M. eds. 1998. *An-Denken. Festgabe für Eugen Biser.* Europäsche Akademie der Wissenschaften und Künste. Graz: Verlag Styria.
MOFFATT, James 1901. *The Historical New Testament: Being the Literature of the New Testament Arranged in the Order of Its Literary Growth and According to the Dates of the Documents. A New Translation Edited with Prolegomena, Historical Tables, Critical Notes, and an Appendix.* 2nd rev. ed. Edinburgh: T. & T. Clark.
— 1910. *The First and Second Epistles of Paul the Apostle to the Thessalonians.* The Expositor's Greek Testament 4. London: Hodder & Stoughton.
MOLITOR, Joseph 1971; 1972 [*Fortsetzung*]. "Die syrische Übersetzung des 1. und 2. Thessalonicherbriefes. Ins Lateinische übertragen und mit der altarmenischen Version verglichen." *OrChr* 55 (1971) 166–181 & *OrChr* 56 (1972) 150–163.
MOLTMANN, Jürgen 1968. "Resurrection as Hope." *HTR* 61 (1968) 129–147.
MOORE, Arthur L. 1966. *The Parousia in the New Testament.* NovTSup 13. Leiden: E. J. Brill.
MORETTI, Luigi curavit 1968–. *Inscriptiones Graecae urbis Romae.* [see *IGUR* in abbrev.]
MORGAN GILLMAN, Florence 1990. "Jason of Thessalonica." In: R. F. COLLINS (1990) 39–49.
MORRIS, Leon 1959. *The First and Second Epistles to the Thessalonians: The English Text with Introduction, Exposition and Notes.* NICNT. Grand Rapids: Eerdmans.
— 1993. "Salvation." *DPL* (1993) 858–862.
— 1993a. "Sin, Guilt." *DPL* (1993) 877–881.
MOULE, Charles F. D. 1959. *An Idiom Book of New Testament Greek.* 2nd ed. Cambridge: University Press.
— 1964. "The Influence of Circumstances on the Use of Eschatological Terms." *JTS* NS 15 (1964) 1–15.
— ed. 1968. *The Significance of the Message of the Resurrection for Faith in Jesus Christ.* SBT 8. London: SCM.
MOULTON, James H. 1908–1976. *Grammar of New Testament Greek.* [see *GNTG* in abbrev.]
MOUNT, Christopher 2002. *Pauline Christianity: Luke-Acts and the Legacy of Paul.* NovTSup 104. Leiden et al.: Brill.
— 2002a. Review of *Leadership and Lifestyle: The Portrait of Paul in the Miletus Speech and 1 Thessalonians*, by S. WALTON, 2000. *JR* 82 (2002) 100–101.
MOXNES, Halvor ed. 1997. *Constructing Early Christian Families: Family as Social Reality and Metaphor.* London/New York: Routledge.
MÜLLER, Hans-P. 1999. "Eschatologie II. Altes Testament." *RGG* 2 ([4]1999) 1546–1553.
MÜLLER, Karlheinz 1993. "Apokalyptik II. A. im NT." *LTK* 1 ([3]1993) 817.
MÜLLER, Markus 1997. *Vom Schluß zum Ganzen. Zur Bedeutung des paulinischen Briefkorpusabschlusses.* FRLANT 172. Göttingen: Vandenhoeck & Ruprecht.
MÜLLER, Paul-G. 1991. "νύξ." *EDNT* 2 (1991) 481–483.
— 2001. *Der Erste und Zweite Brief an die Thessalonicher.* RNT. Regensburg: Friedrich Pustet.
MÜLLER, Peter 1988. *Anfänge der Paulusschule. Dargestellt am zweiten Thessalonicherbrief und am Kolosserbrief.* ATANT 74. Zürich: Theologischer Verlag.
MÜLLER, Ulrich B. 1975. *Prophetie und Predigt im Neuen Testament. Formgeschichtliche Untersuchungen zur urchristlichen Prophetie.* SNT 10. Gütersloh: Gerd Mohn.
— 1993. "Apocalyptic Currents." In: BECKER (1993a) 281–329.
— 2001. "Parusie und Menschensohn." *ZNW* 92 (2001) 1–19.
MULLINS, Terence Y. 1962. "Petition as a Literary Form." *NovT* 5 (1962) 46–54.
— 1965. "Disclosure: A Literary Form in the New Testament." *NovT* 7 (1964–1965) 44–50.
— 1968. "Greeting as a New Testament Form." *JBL* 87 (1968) 418–426.
— 1972. "Formulas in New Testament Epistles." *JBL* 91 (1972) 380–390.

— 1973. "Visit Talk in New Testament Letters." *CBQ* 35 (1973) 350–358.
— 1977. "Benediction as a NT Form." *AUSS* 15 (1977) 59–64.
— 1980. "Topos as a New Testament Form." *JBL* 99 (1980) 541–547.
MÜNCHOW, Christoph 1981. *Ethik und Eschatologie. Ein Beitrag zum Verständnis der frühjüdischen Apokalyptik mit einem Ausblick auf das Neue Testament.* Göttingen: Vandenhoeck & Ruprecht.
MUNCK, Johannes 1959. *Paul and the Salvation of Mankind.* 1st Engl. ed. Richmond: John Knox.
— 1963. "I Thess. I. 9–10 and the Missionary Preaching of Paul: Textual Exegesis and Hermeneutical Reflections." *NTS* 9 (1962–1963) 95–110.
— 1967. *Christ and Israel: An Interpretation of Romans 9–11.* Transl. by I. NIXON. Foreword by K. STENDAHL. Philadelphia: Fortress.
— 1967a. *The Acts of the Apostles: Introduction, Translation, and Notes.* Rev. by W. F. ALBRIGHT/C. S. MANN. AB 31. Garden City: Doubleday.
MUNDLE, Wilhelm 1975. "Come." *NIDNTT* 1 (1975) 319–327 [§ ἔρχομαι; καταντάω: 320–324, 324–325].
— 1976. "Present, Day, Maranatha, Parousia." *NIDNTT* 2 (1976) 886–935 [§ μαραναθά 1–3: 895–896].
— 1976a. "Image, Idol, Imprint, Example." *NIDNTT* 2 (1976) 284–293 [§ εἴδωλον: 284–286].
MUNRO, Winsome 1983. *Authority in Paul and Peter: The Identification of a Pastoral Stratum in the Pauline Corpus and 1 Peter.* SNTSMS 45. Cambridge et al.: University Press.
MURPHY-O'CONNOR, Jerome 1982. "Pauline Missions before the Jerusalem Conference." *RB* 89 (1982) 71–91.
— 1985. "Bulletin: Pauline Studies." *RB* 92 (1985) 456–464.
— 1988. "Bulletin: Pauline Letters." *RB* 95 (1988) 311–314.
— 1993. "Paul and Gallio." *JBL* 112 (1993) 315–317.
— 1995. *Paul the Letter-Writer: His World, His Options, His Skills.* GNS 41. Collegeville, MN: Liturgical Press.
— 1996. *Paul: A Critical Life.* Oxford: Clarendon.
— 2003. "Bulletin: Thessalonica." *RB* 110 (2003) 133–134.
MURRAY, A. T. transl. 1999. *Homer Iliad.* 2 vols. LCL 170, 171. 2nd ed. rev. by W. F. WYATT. Cambridge/London: Harvard University Press.
MURRAY, Robert 1982. "Jews, Hebrews and Christians: Some Needed Distinctions." *NovT* 24 (1982) 194–208.
MUSSNER, Franz 1984. *Tractate on the Jews: The Significance of Judaism for Christian Faith.* Transl. & with an intro. by L. SWIDLER. Philadelphia: Fortress / London: SPCK.
— 1991. *Dieses Geschlecht wird nicht vergehen. Judentum und Kirche.* Freiburg et al.: Herder.

NATIONS, Archie L. 1983. "Historical Criticism and the Current Methodological Crisis." *SJT* 36 (1983) 59–71.
NEBE, Gottfried 1983. *'Hoffnung' bei Paulus. Elpis und ihre Synonyme im Zusammenhang der Eschatologie.* SUNT 16. Göttingen: Vandenhoeck & Ruprecht.
NEIL, William 1957. *St. Paul's Epistles to the Thessalonians: Introduction and Commentary.* Torch Bible Commentaries. London: SCM.
NEIRYNCK, Frans 1986. "Paul and the Sayings of Jesus." In: VANHOYE (1986) 265–321.
NEPPER-CHRISTENSEN, Poul 1965. "Das verborgene Herrnwort. Eine Untersuchung über 1. Thess. 4,13–18." *ST* 19 (1965) 136–154.
NEUGEBAUER, Fritz 1958. "Das paulinische 'in Christo'." *NTS* 4 (1957–1958) 124–138.
— 1961. *In Christus. Eine Untersuchung zum paulinischen Glaubensverständnis.* Göttingen: Vandenhoeck & Ruprecht.
NEUHAUS, Richard J. ed. 1989. *Biblical Interpretation in Crisis: The Ratzinger Conference on Bible and Church.* Grand Rapids: Eerdmans.
NEUMANN, Kenneth J. 1993. "Major Variations in Pauline and Other Epistles in Light of Genre and the Pauline Letter Form." In: FS HURD (1993) 199–209.
NEUSNER, Jacob ed. 1975. *Christianity, Judaism and Other Greco-Roman Cults: Studies for Morton Smith at Sixty.* Part 1: *New Testament.* Part 2: *Early Christianity.* Part 3: *Judaism before 70.* Part 4: *Judaism after 70, Other Greco-Roman Cults, Bibliography.* SJLA 12. Leiden: E. J. Brill.

— /Frerichs, Ernest S. eds. 1985. *"To See Ourselves as Others See Us": Christians, Jews, "Others" in Late Antiquity*. Literary ed. C. McCracken-Flesher. SPSH. Chico, CA: Scholars Press.

Newsom, Carol A. 1992. "Angels." *ABD* 1 (1992) 248–255 [§ Old Testament: 248–253].

Neyrey, Jerome H. 1980. "Eschatology in 1 Thessalonians: The Theological Factor in 1:9–10; 2:4–5; 3:11–13; 4:6 and 4:13–18." In: Achtemeier (1980) 219–231.

Nicholl, Colin R. 2004. *From Hope to Despair in Thessalonica: Situating 1 and 2 Thessalonians*. Cambridge: University Press.

Nickelsburg, George W. E. 1972. *Resurrection, Immortality, and Eternal Life in Intertestamental Judaism*. HTS 26. Cambridge: Harvard University Press.

— 1992. "Resurrection." *ABD* 5 (1992) 680–691 [§ Early Judaism and Christianity: 684–691].

— 1992a. "Son of Man." *ABD* 6 (1992) 137–150.

— 1992b. "Eschatology: Early Jewish Literature." *ABD* 2 (1992) 579–594.

— 2000. "Judgment, Life-after-Death, and Resurrection in the Apocrypha and the Non-Apocalyptic Pseudepigrapha." In: Avery-Peck/Neusner (2000) 141–162.

Nicklas, Tobias 2005. Review of *Gericht und Gemeinde. Eine Studie zur Bedeutung und Funktion von Gerichtsaussagen im Rahmen der paulinischen Ekklesiologie und Ethik im 1 Thess und 1 Kor*, by M. Konradt, 2003. *RevBL* 7 (2005) 388–392.

Niemand, Christoph ed. 2002. *Forschungen zum Neuen Testament und seiner Umwelt. Festschrift für Albert Fuchs*. Frankfurt am Main et al.: Peter Lang.

Nigdelis, Pantelis M. 1994. "Synagoge(n) und Gemeinde der Juden in Thessaloniki. Fragen Aufgrund einer neuen jüdischen Grabinschrift der Kaiserzeit." *ZPE* 102 (1994) 297–306.

Nilsson, Martin P. 1951. *Cults, Myths, Oracles, and Politics in Ancient Greece: With Two Appendices: The Ionian Phylae, The Phratries*. SSIA 8. Lund: CWK Gleerup.

Nock, Arthur D. 1928. "Early Gentile Christianity and Its Hellenistic Background." In: Rawlinson (1928) 51–156. Republ. in: Stewart (1972) 49–133.

— 1933. *Conversion: The Old and the New in Religion from Alexander the Great to Augustine of Hippo*. Oxford: Clarendon.

— 1961. "'Son of God' in Pauline and Hellenistic Thought." *Gn* 33 (1961) 581–590. Republ. in: Stewart (1972) 928–939.

Norlin, George transl. 1928–1945 → Norlin/Van Hook 1928–1945.

— /Van Hook, Larue transl. 1928–1945. *Isocrates*. 3 vols. Vols. 1–2 transl. by G. Norlin. Vol. 3 transl. by L. Van Hook. LCL 209, 229, 373. London: William Heinemann / Cambridge: Harvard University Press.

Nützel, Johannes M. 1990. "γρηγορέω." *EDNT* 1 (1990) 264–265.

Oakes, Peter 2002. Review of *Thessaloniki – Stadt des Kassander und Gemeinde des Paulus. Eine frühe christliche Gemeinde in ihrer heidnischen Umwelt*, by C. vom Brocke, 2001. *JTS* NS 53 (2002) 244–247.

— 2005. "Re-mapping the Universe: Paul and the Emperor in 1 Thessalonians and Philippians." *JSNT*, issue 27 (2005) 301–322.

— 2005a. Review of *From Hope to Despair in Thessalonica: Situating 1 and 2 Thessalonians*, by C. R. Nicholl, 2004. *JSNT*, issue 27 (2005) 113–114.

Oberlinner, Lorenz/Fiedler, Peter eds. 1991. *Salz der Erde – Licht der Welt. Exegetische Studien zum Matthäusevangelium. Festschrift für Anton Vögtle zum 80. Geburtstag*. Stuttgart: Verlag Katholisches Bibelwerk.

O'Brien, Peter T. 1975. "Thanksgiving and the Gospel in Paul." *NTS* 21 (1974–1975) 144–155.

— 1977. *Introductory Thanksgivings in the Letters of Paul*. NovTSup 49. Leiden: E. J. Brill.

— 1980. "Thanksgiving within the Structure of Pauline Theology." In: FS Bruce (1980) 50–66.

— 1993. "Mystery." *DPL* (1993) 621–623.

O'Collins, Gerald G. 1973. *The Resurrection of Jesus Christ*. Valley Forge, PA: Judson. Also publ. as: *The Easter Jesus*. London: Darton, Longman & Todd, 1973.

— 1992. "Salvation." *ABD* 5 (1992) 907–914.

— 1995. *Christology: A Biblical, Historical, and Systematic Study of Jesus*. Oxford et al.: University Press.

O'Donnell, Matthew B. 1999. "Some New Testament Words for Resurrection and the Company They Keep." In: Porter/Hayes/Tombs (1999) 136–163.
Oepke, Albrecht 1964. "γρηγορέω." *TDNT* 2 (1964) 338–339.
— 1964a. "ἀνίστημι κτλ." *TDNT* 1 (1964) 368–372.
— 1964b. "ἐγείρω." *TDNT* 2 (1964) 333–337.
— 1964c. "διώκω." *TDNT* 1 (1964) 229–230.
— 1964d. "διά." *TDNT* 2 (1964) 65–70.
— 1964e. "ἐν." *TDNT* 2 (1964) 537–543.
— 1964f. "δύω κτλ." *TDNT* 2 (1964) 318–321.
— 1965. "καθεύδω." *TDNT* 3 (1965) 431–437.
— 1965a. "κενός κτλ." *TDNT* 3 (1965) 659–662.
— 1967. "παρουσία, πάρειμι." *TDNT* 5 (1967) 858–871.
— 1967a. "νεφέλη, νέφος." *TDNT* 4 (1967) 902–910.
— 1970. "Die Briefe an die Thessalonicher." In: Beyer et al. (1970) 157–179.
Okeke, G. E. 1981. "I Thessalonians 2. 13–16: The Fate of the Unbelieving Jews." *NTS* 27 (1981) 127–136.
Okorie, A. M. 1994. "The Pauline Work Ethic in I and II Thessalonians." *Bulletin for Biblical Studies* 24 (1994) 55–64.
Olbricht, Thomas H. 1990. "An Aristotelian Rhetorical Analysis of 1 Thessalonians." In: FS Malherbe (1990) 216–236.
Oldfather, Charles H. et al. transl. 1933–1967. *Diodorus Siculus: Library of History.* 12 vols. Vols. 1–6 transl. by C. H. Oldfather. Vol. 7 transl. by C. L. Sherman. Vol. 8 transl. by C. B. Welles. Vols. 9–10 transl. by R. M. Geer. Vols. 11–12 transl. by F. R. Walton. LCL 279, 303, 340, 375, 384, 399, 389, 422, 377, 390, 409, 423. London: William Heinemann / Cambridge: Harvard University Press.
Oldfather, William A. transl. 1925–1928. *Epictetus: The Discourses as Reported by Arrian, the Manual, and Fragments.* 2 vols. LCL 131, 218. London: William Heinemann / Cambridge: Harvard University Press.
Orchard, J. Bernard 1938. "Thessalonians and the Synoptic Gospels." *Bib* 19 (1938) 19–42.
Oropeza, B. J. 2000. *Paul and Apostasy: Eschatology, Perseverance, and Falling Away in the Corinthian Congregation.* WUNT II.115. Tübingen: Mohr Siebeck.
Orr, William F./Walther, James A. 1976. *I Corinthians: A New Translation. Introduction, with a Study of the Life of Paul, Notes, and Commentary.* AB 32. Garden City: Doubleday.
Osborne, Robert E. 1965. "St. Paul's Silent Years." *JBL* 84 (1965) 59–65.
Osiek, Carolyn 1999. *Shepherd of Hermas: A Commentary.* Ed. by H. Koester. Hermeneia. Minneapolis: Fortress.
Otto, Randall E. 1997. "The Meeting in the Air (1 Thess 4:17)." *HBT* 19 (1997) 192–212.
Owen, H. P. 1959. "The Parousia of Christ in the Synoptic Gospels." *SJT* 12 (1959) 171–192.
— 1962. "Eschatology and Ethics in the New Testament." *SJT* 15 (1962) 369–382.

Paddison, Angus 2005. *Theological Hermeneutics and 1 Thessalonians.* SNTSMS 133. Cambridge: University Press.
Palmer, Darryl W. 1981. "Thanksgiving, Self-Defence, and Exhortation in 1 Thessalonians 1–3." *Colloquium* 14 (1981) 23–31.
Parkes, James W. 1974. *The Conflict of the Church and the Synagogue: A Study in the Origins of Antisemitism.* New York: Hermon. Originally publ. by Soncino, 1934.
Parry, R. St. John ed. 1926. *The First Epistle of Paul the Apostle to the Corinthians: With Introduction and Notes.* 2nd ed. Cambridge Greek Testament for Schools and Colleges. Cambridge: University Press.
Patte, Daniel 1983. *Paul's Faith and the Power of the Gospel: A Structural Introduction to the Pauline Letters.* Philadelphia: Fortress.
— 1983a. "Method for a Structural Exegesis of Didactic Discourses: Analysis of 1 Thessalonians." *Semeia* 26 (1983) 85–136.
— 1988. "Anti-Semitism in the New Testament: Confronting the Dark Side of Paul's and Matthew's Teaching." *CTSR* 78 (1988) 31–52.

PATTERSON, Stephen J. 1991. "Paul and the Jesus Tradition: It is Time for Another Look." *HTR* 84 (1991) 23–41.

PAULSEN, Henning 1990. "ἐνδύω." *EDNT* 1 (1990) 451–452.

PAX, Elpidius 1963. "Parusie I. Schrift und Judentum." *LTK* 8 (^{2}1963) 120–123.

— 1971. "Beobachtungen zur Konvertitensprache im ersten Thessalonicherbrief." *SBFLA* 21 (1971) 220–262.

— 1972. "Konvertitenprobleme im ersten Thessalonicherbrief." *BibLeb* 13 (1972) 24–37.

PAYNE, Philip B. 1994. "The Fallacy of Equating Meaning with the Human Author's Intention." In: BEALE (1994) 70–81.

PEARSON, Birger A. 1971. "1 Thessalonians 2:13–16: A Deutero-Pauline Interpolation." *HTR* 64 (1971) 79–94. Republ. with minor changes in: PEARSON (1997) 58–74.

— 1997. *The Emergence of the Christian Religion: Essays on Early Christianity.* Harrisburg, PA: Trinity Press International.

— et al. eds. 1991. *The Future of Early Christianity: Essays in Honor of Helmut Koester.* Minneapolis: Fortress.

PECK, Arthur L./BALME, David M. transl. 1965–1991. *Aristotle.* Vols. 9–11: *History of Animals.* Vols. 9–10 transl. by A. L. PECK. Vol. 11 transl. by D. M. BALME. LCL 437, 438, 439. London: William Heinemann / Cambridge: Harvard University Press.

— /FORSTER, Edward S. transl. 1937. *Aristotle.* Vol. 12: *Parts of Animals, Movements of Animals, Progression of Animals.* Foreword by F. H. A. MARSHALL. LCL 323. London: William Heinemann / Cambridge: Harvard University Press.

PEDERSEN, Sigfred ed. 1980. *Die Paulinische [sic] Literatur und Theologie. Anlässlich der 50. jährigen Gründungs-Feier der Universität von Aarhus.* Teologiske Studier 7. Århus: Forlaget Aros / Göttingen: Vandenhoeck & Ruprecht.

PELSER, Gert M. M. 1998. "Could the 'Formulas' *Dying* and *Rising with Christ* Be Expressions of Pauline Mysticism?" *Neot* 32 (1998) 115–134.

PERKINS, Pheme 1989. "1 Thessalonians and Hellenistic Religious Practices." In: FS FITZMYER (1989) 325–334.

PERRIN, Bernadotte transl. 1914–1926. *Plutarch's Lives.* 11 vols. Vol. 11 contains: *Index to All the Lives,* by J. W. COHOON (pp. 321–492). LCL 46, 47, 65, 80, 87, 98, 99, 100, 101, 102, 103. London: William Heinemann / Cambridge: Harvard University Press.

PERRY, Ben E. transl. 1965. *Babrius and Phaedrus.* LCL 436. London: William Heinemann / Cambridge: Harvard University Press.

PESCH, Rudolf 1984. *Die Entdeckung des ältesten Paulus-Briefes. Paulus – neu gesehen: Die Briefe an die Gemeinde der Thessalonicher.* HerBü 1167. Freiburg et al.: Herder.

— 1988. "Zur Entstehung des Glaubens an die Auferstehung Jesu." In: HOFFMANN (1988) 228–255.

PESCH, Wilhelm 1991. "ὀργή." *EDNT* 2 (1991) 529–530.

PETERSEN, David L. 1992. "Eschatology: Early Jewish Literature." *ABD* 2 (1992) 575–579.

PETERSON, Erik 1926. *ΕΙΣ ΘΕΟΣ. Epigraphische, formgeschichtliche und religionsgeschichtliche Untersuchungen.* FRLANT 24. Göttingen: Vandenhoeck & Ruprecht.

— 1930. "Die Einholung des Kyrios." *ZST* 7 (1929–1930) 682–702.

— 1964. "ἀπάντησις." *TDNT* 1 (1964) 380–381.

PETTERSON, Anthony 2000. "Antecedents of the Christian Hope of Resurrection, Part 2: Intertestamental Literature." *RTR* 59 (2000) 53–64.

PFITZNER, Victor C. 1967. *Paul and the Agon Motif: Traditional Athletic Imagery in the Pauline Literature.* NovTSup 16. Leiden: E. J. Brill.

PLEVNIK, Joseph ed. 1975. *Word and Spirit: Essays in Honor of David Michael Stanley on his 60th Birthday.* Toronto: Regis College.

— 1975a. "The Parousia as Implication of Christ's Resurrection: An Exegesis of 1 Thes 4,13–18." In: FS STANLEY (1975) 199–277.

— 1979. "1 Thess 5,1–11: Its Authenticity, Intention and Message." *Bib* 60 (1979) 71–90.

— 1984. "The Taking Up of the Faithful and the Resurrection of the Dead in 1 Thessalonians 4:13–18." *CBQ* 46 (1984) 274–283.

— 1989. "The Ultimate Reality in 1 Thessalonians." *URM* 12 (1989) 256–271.

— 1989a. "The Center of Pauline Theology." *CBQ* 51 (1989) 461–478.
— 1990. "Pauline Presuppositions." In: R. F. COLLINS (1990) 50–61.
— 1997. *Paul and the Parousia: An Exegetical and Theological Investigation.* Peabody, MA: Hendrickson.
— 1999. "1 Thessalonians 4,17: The Bringing in of the Lord or the Bringing in of the Faithful?" *Bib* 80 (1999) 537–546.
— 2000. "The Destination of the Apostle and of the Faithful: Second Corinthians 4:13b–14 and First Thessalonians 4:14." *CBQ* 62 (2000) 83–95.
POBEE, John S. 1985. *Persecution and Martyrdom in the Theology of Paul.* JSNTSup 6. Sheffield: JSOT Press.
POLIAKOV, Léon 1966. *The History of Anti-Semitism.* 4 vols. Vol. 1: *From the Time of Christ to the Court Jews.* Transl. by R. HOWARD. London: Elek Books.
POPKES, Wiard 2002. "Zum Thema ›Anti-imperiale Deutung neutestamentlicher Schriften‹." *TLZ* 127 (2002) 850–862.
PORTER, Stanley E. 1989. *Verbal Aspect in the Greek of the New Testament, with Reference to Tense and Mood.* SBG 1. New York et al.: Peter Lang.
— 1993. "In Defence of Verbal Aspect." In: PORTER/CARSON (1993) 26–45.
— 1993a. "Holiness, Sanctification." *DPL* (1993) 397–402.
— 1994. *Idioms of the Greek New Testament.* 2nd ed. Biblical Languages: Greek 2. Sheffield: Academic Press.
— 1999. "Developments in German and French Thessalonians Research: A Survey and Critique." *CurBS* 7 (1999) 309–334.
— 1999a. "Resurrection, the Greeks and the New Testament." In: PORTER/HAYES/TOMBS (1999) 52–81.
— ed. 2002. *Handbook to Exegesis of the New Testament.* Boston/Leiden: Brill Academic Publishers.
— 2002a. "Exegesis of the Pauline Letters, including the Deutero-Pauline Letters." In: STANLEY (2002) 503–553.
— /CARSON, Don A. eds. 1993. *Biblical Greek Language and Linguistics: Open Questions in Current Research.* JSNTSup 80. Sheffield: Academic Press.
— /EVANS, Craig A. eds. 1997. *New Testament Interpretation and Methods: A Sheffield Reader.* Biblical Seminar 45. Sheffield: Academic Press.
— /HAYES, Michael A./TOMBS, David eds. 1999. *Resurrection.* JSNTSup 186. Sheffield: Academic Press.
— /OLBRICHT, Thomas H. eds. 1996. *Rhetoric, Scripture and Theology: Essays from the 1994 Pretoria Conference.* JSNTSup 131. Sheffield: Academic Press.
— /REED, Jeffrey T. 1998. "Philippians as a Macro-Chiasm and Its Exegetical Significance." *NTS* 44 (1998) 213–231.
PREISKER, Herbert 1965. "κλέπτω, κλέπτης." *TDNT* 3 (1965) 754–756.
— 1967. "μέθη κτλ." *TDNT* 4 (1967) 545–548.
PRENDERGAST, Terrence 1992. "Hope (NT)." *ABD* 3 (1992) 282–285.
PREUSS, Horst D. 1986. "Eschatologie 1. Im Alten Testament." *EKL* 1 (1986) 1109–1111.
PRICKETT, Stephen/BARNES, Robert 1991. *The Bible.* Landmarks of World Literature. Cambridge et al.: University Press.
PROCKSCH, Otto 1964. "ἅγιος κτλ." *TDNT* 1 (1964) 88–115 [§ A–C, E–ἁγιωσύνη: 88–97, 100–115].
PRYOR, J. W. 2002. "Awaiting the Trumpet of God." *NewDocs* 9 (2002) 102–105.

RACKHAM, Harris transl. 1926. *Aristotle.* Vol. 19: *The Nicomachean Ethics.* LCL 73. London: William Heinemann / Cambridge: Harvard University Press.
— 1932. *Aristotle.* Vol. 21: *Politics.* LCL 264. London: William Heinemann / Cambridge: Harvard University Press.
— et al. transl. 1938–1963. *Pliny: Natural History.* 10 vols. Vols. 1–5, 9 transl. by H. RACKHAM. Vols. 6, 8 transl. by W. H. S. JONES. Vol. 7 transl. by W. H. S. JONES/A. C. ANDREWS. Vol. 10 transl. by D. E. EICHHOLZ. LCL 330, 352, 353, 370, 371, 392, 393, 418, 394, 419. London: William Heinemann/ Cambridge: Harvard University Press.

RAD, Gerhard von → VON RAD, Gerhard.
RADL, Walter 1981. *Ankunft des Herrn. Zur Bedeutung und Funktion der Parusieaussagen bei Paulus.* BBET 15. Frankfurt am Main et al.: Peter Lang.
— 1993. "σῴζω." *EDNT* 3 (1993) 319–321.
— 1993a. "παρουσία." *EDNT* 3 (1993) 43–44.
— 1993b. "ὠδίν, ὠδίνω." *EDNT* 3 (1993) 506.
— 1998. "Parusie I. Biblisch-theologisch." *LTK* 7 (³1998) 1402–1404.
RÄISÄNEN, Heikki 1995. "Die 'Hellenisten' der Urgemeinde." *ANRW* II.26.2 (1995) 1468–1514.
— 2002. "Did Paul Expect an Earthly Kingdom?" In: FS WEDDERBURN (2002) 2–20.
RAMSAY, George G. transl. 1918. *Juvenal and Persius.* LCL 91. London: William Heinemann / Cambridge: Harvard University Press.
RAWLINSON, Alfred E. J. ed. 1928. *Essays on the Trinity and the Incarnation.* London et al.: Longmans, Green & Co.
REED, Jeffrey T. 1996. "Are Paul's Thanksgivings 'Epistolary'?" *JSNT*, issue 61 (1996) 87–99.
REESE, James M. 1979. *1 and 2 Thessalonians.* New Testament Message 16. Wilmington, DE: Michael Glazier.
— 1980. "A Linguistic Approach to Paul's Exhortation in 1 Thess 4:13–5:11." In: ACHTEMEIER (1980) 209–218.
REFSHAUGE, Ebba 1971. "Literærkritiske overvejelser. Til de to Thessalonikerbreve." *DTT* 34 (1971) 1–19.
REICKE, Bo I. 1988. "Paulus über den Tag des Herrn. Homiletisch orientierte Auslegung von I Thess 5,1–11." *TZ* 44 (1988) 91–96.
REID, Daniel G. 1993. "Angels, Archangels." *DPL* (1993) 20–23.
REINBOLD, Wolfang 1994. *Der älteste Bericht über den Tod Jesu. Literarische Analyse und historische Kritik der Passionsdarstellungen der Evangelien.* BZNW 69. Berlin/New York: W. de Gruyter.
REINMUTH, Eckart 1998. "Der erste Brief an die Thessalonicher. Übersetzt und erklärt." In: WALTER/REINMUTH/LAMPE (1998) 103–156.
RENGSTORF, Karl H. 1964. "δοῦλος κτλ." *TDNT* 2 (1964) 261–280.
REUMANN, John 1987. "The Theologies of 1 Thessalonians and Philippians: Contents, Comparison, and Composite." In: RICHARDS (1987) 521–536.
— 1992. "After Historical Criticism, What? Trends in Biblical Interpretation and Ecumenical, Interfaith Dialogues." *JES* 29 (1992) 55–86.
RHOADS, David M. 1976. *Israel in Revolution: 6–74 C.E. A Political History Based on the Writings of Josephus.* Philadelphia: Fortress.
RICHARD, Earl J. 1988. *Jesus: One and Many. The Christological Concept of New Testament Authors.* Wilmington, DE: Michael Glazier.
— 1990. "Contemporary Research on 1 (& 2) Thessalonians." *BTB* 20 (1990) 107–115.
— 1991. "Early Pauline Thought: An Analysis of 1 Thessalonians." In: BASSLER (1991) 39–51.
— 1995. *1 and 2 Thessalonians.* SacPag 11. Collegeville, MN: Liturgical Press.
RICHARDS, E. Randolph 1991. *The Secretary in the Letters of Paul.* WUNT II.42. Tübingen: J. C. B. Mohr (Paul Siebeck).
— 1999. "Ministering in a Tough Place: Paul's Pattern in Thessalonica." *SwJT* 42 (1999) 17–38.
RICHARDS, Kent H. ed. 1981. *SBL Seminar Papers, 1981.* SBLSP 20. Chico, CA: Scholars Press.
— ed. 1982. *SBL Seminar Papers, 1982.* SBLSP 21. Chico, CA: Scholars Press.
— ed. 1983. *SBL Seminar Papers, 1983.* SBLSP 22. Chico, CA: Scholars Press.
— ed. 1987. *SBL Seminar Papers, 1987.* SBLSP 26. Atlanta: Scholars Press.
RICHARDSON, Peter 1969. *Israel in the Apostolic Church.* SNTSMS 10. Cambridge: University Press.
— 1980. "'I Say, Not the Lord': Personal Opinion, Apostolic Authority and the Development of Early Christian Halakah." *TynBul* 31 (1980) 65–86.
— 1997. Review of *Paul: A Critical Life*, by J. MURPHY-O'CONNOR, 1996. *RB* 104 (1997) 592–598.
— /GRANSKOU, David eds. 1986. *Anti-Judaism in Early Christianity.* I. *Paul and the Gospels.* Studies in Christianity and Judaism 2. Waterloo, Ont.: Wilfrid Laurier University Press.
— /HURD, John C. eds. 1984. *From Jesus to Paul: Studies in Honour of Francis Wright Beare.* Waterloo, Ont.: Wilfrid Laurier University Press.

RIESNER, Rainer 1998. *Paul's Early Period: Chronology, Mission Strategy, Theology*. Transl. by D. SCOTT. Grand Rapids: Eerdmans.
RIGAUX, Béda 1956. *Saint Paul. Les epîtres aux Thessaloniciens*. ÉBib. Paris: Gabalda.
— 1959. "Vocabulaire chrétien antérieur à la première épître aux Thessaloniciens." In: COPPENS/DESCAMPS/MASSAUX (1959) 380–389.
— 1965. "Thessalonicherbriefe." *LTK* 10 ([2]1965) 105–108.
— 1968. *The Letters of St. Paul: Modern Studies*. Transl. by S. YONICK. Chicago: Franciscan Herald Press.
— 1972. "Evangelium im ersten Thessalonicherbrief." *WiWei* 35 (1972) 1–12.
— 1975. "Tradition et rédaction dans 1 Th. V.1–10." *NTS* 21 (1974–1975) 318–340.
RIGGANS, Walter 1995. "The Parousia: Getting Our Terms Right." *Them* 21 (1995) 14–16.
RILEY, Gregory J. 1995. *Resurrection Reconsidered: Thomas and John in Controversy*. Minneapolis: Fortress.
RITT, Hubert 1993. "φῶς." *EDNT* 3 (1993) 447–448.
ROBERTS, John H. 1986. "Pauline Transitions to the Letter Body." In: VANHOYE (1986) 93–99.
— 1986a. "The Eschatological Transitions to the Pauline Letter Body." *Neot* 20 (1986) 29–35.
— et al. eds. 1991. *Teologie in Konteks. Opgedra aan A. B. du Toit*. Pretoria: Orion.
ROBERTSON, Archibald T. 1934. *A Grammar of the Greek New Testament*. [see *GGNT* in abbrev.]
— /PLUMMER, Alfred 1911. *A Critical and Exegetical Commentary on the First Epistle of St Paul to the Corinthians*. ICC. Edinburgh: T. & T. Clark.
ROBINSON, James M. director 1977. *The Nag Hammadi Library in English*. Transl. by members of the Coptic Gnostic Library Project of the Institute for Antiquity and Christianity. San Francisco et al.: Harper & Row.
— /KOESTER, Helmut 1971. *Trajectories through Early Christianity*. Philadelphia: Fortress.
ROBINSON, John A. T. 1957. *Jesus and His Coming: The Emergence of a Doctrine*. London: SCM.
— 1976. *Redating the New Testament*. London: SCM.
ROETZEL, Calvin J. 1972. *Judgement in the Community: A Study of the Relationship between Eschatology and Ecclesiology in Paul*. Leiden: E. J. Brill.
— 1972a. "I Thess. 5:12–28: A Case Study." In: MCGAUGHY (1972, vol. 2) 367–383.
— 1989. Review of *Paul and the Thessalonians: The Philosophic Tradition of Pastoral Care*, by A. J. MALHERBE, 1987. *JBL* 108 (1989) 357–359.
— 1991. *The Letters of Paul: Conversations in Context*. 3rd ed. Louisville, KY: Westminster/John Knox.
ROGGE, Joachim/SCHILLE, Gottfried eds. 1983. *Theologische Versuche XIII*. Berlin: Evangelische Verlagsanstalt.
ROLFE, John C. transl. 1914. *Suetonius: The Lives of the Caesars*. 2 vols. Intr. by K. R. BRADLEY. LCL 31, 38. London: William Heinemann / Cambridge: Harvard University Press.
ROLLINS, Wayne G. 1971. "The New Testament and Apocalyptic." *NTS* 17 (1970–1971) 454–476.
ROOSE, Hanna 2005. "Polyvalenz durch Intertextualität im Spiegel der aktuellen Forschung zu den Thessalonicherbriefen." *NTS* 51 (2005) 250–269.
ROOSEN, Antoon 1971. *De Brieven van Paulus aan de Tessalonicenzen*. Het Nieuwe Testament. Rome: Roermond.
RÖSCH, Konstantin 1918. "‚Wir Lebenden, wir Übrigbleibenden? in 1. Thess. 4, 15. 17." *TGl* 10 (1918) 492–495.
ROSNER, Brian 2003. "Paul's Ethics." In: DUNN (2003) 212–223.
ROSS, J. M. 1975. "1 Thessalonians 3.13." *BT* 26 (1975) 444.
ROWLAND, Christopher 1982. *The Open Heaven: A Study of Apocalyptic in Judaism and Early Christianity*. London: SPCK.
— 1990. "Parousia." In: COGGINS/HOULDEN (1990) 512–515.
— 1990a. "Apocalyptic." In: COGGINS/HOULDEN (1990) 34–36.
— 1992. "Parousia." *ABD* 5 (1992) 166–170.
— /FLETCHER-LOUIS, Crispin H. T. eds. 1998. *Understanding, Studying and Reading: New Testament Essays in Honour of John Ashton*. JSNTSup 153. Sheffield: Academic Press.
RUETHER, Rosemary R. 1974. *Faith and Fratricide: The Theological Roots of Anti-Semitism*. New York: Seabury.

— 1979. "The *Faith and Fratricide* Discussion: Old Problems and New Dimensions." In: Davies (1979) 230–256.

Ryrie, Charles C. 1959. *First & Second Thessalonians*. Everyman's Bible Commentary. Chicago: Moody.

Sabourin, Leopold 1974. "The Biblical Cloud: Terminology and Traditions." *BTB* 4 (1974) 290–311.

Sand, Alexander 1972. "Zur Frage nach dem 'Sitz im Leben' der apokalyptischen Texte des Neuen Testaments." *NTS* 18 (1971–1972) 167–177.

Sanders, Edward P. 1977. *Paul and Palestinian Judaism: A Comparison of Patterns of Religion*. Philadelphia: Fortress.

— 1985. *Paul, the Law, and the Jewish People*. London: SCM.

— 1985a. *Jesus and Judaism*. London: SCM.

— 1991. *Paul*. Oxford/New York: Oxford University Press.

— 1999. "Reflections on Anti-Judaism in the New Testament and in Christianity." In: Farmer (1999) 265–286.

Sanders, Jack T. 1962. "The Transition from Opening Epistolary Thanksgiving to Body in the Letters of the Pauline Corpus." *JBL* 81 (1962) 348–362.

— 1996. "The First Decades of Jewish-Christian Relations: The Evidence of the New Testament (Gospels and Acts)." *ANRW* II.26.3 (1996) 1937–1978.

Sandmel, Samuel 1962. "Parallelomania." *JBL* 81 (1962) 1–13.

— 1978. *Anti-Semitism in the New Testament?* Philadelphia: Fortress.

Sandnes, Karl O. 1991. *Paul – One of the Prophets? A Contribution to the Apostle's Self-Understanding*. WUNT II.43. Tübingen: J. C. B. Mohr (Paul Siebeck).

Sass, Gerhard 1941. "Zur Bedeutung von δοῦλος bei Paulus." *ZNW* 24 (1941) 24–32.

Saunders, Ernest W. 1981. *1 Thessalonians, 2 Thessalonians, Philippians, Philemon*. Knox Preaching Guides. Atlanta: John Knox.

Sauter, Gerhard 1988. "The Concept and Task of Eschatology – Theological and Philosophical Reflections." *SJT* 41 (1988) 499–515.

Schade, Hans-H. 1984. *Apokalyptische Christologie bei Paulus. Studien zum Zusammenhang von Christologie und Eschatologie in den Paulusbriefen*. 2nd rev. ed. GTA 18. Göttingen: Vandenhoeck & Ruprecht.

Schäfer, Peter 1997. *Judeophobia: Attitudes toward the Jews in the Ancient World*. Cambridge/London: Harvard University Press.

Schaff, Philip ed. 1956. John Chrysostom: *Homilies on Galatians, Ephesians, Philippians, Colossians, Thessalonians, Timothy, Titus, and Philemon*. NPNF 13. Grand Rapids: Eerdmans.

Schaller, Berndt 1998. "Antisemitismus/Antijudaismus." *RGG* 1 (⁴1998) 556–574.

Schenk, Wolfgang 1978. "Auferweckung der Toten oder Gericht nach den Werken. Tradition und Redaktion in Mattäus xxv 1–13." *NovT* 20 (1978) 278–299.

— 1993. "πῶς." *EDNT* 3 (1993) 202–203.

Schenke, Hans-M. 1991. "Four Problems in the Life of Paul Reconsidered." In: FS Koester (1991) 319–328.

— /Fischer, Karl M. 1978. *Einleitung in die Schriften des Neuen Testaments*. Vol. 1: *Die Briefe des Paulus und Schriften des Paulinismus*. Unter Mitarbeit von H.-G. Bethge/G. Schenke. 2 vols. Gütersloh: Gerd Mohn.

Schippers, Reinier 1966. "The Pre-Synoptic Tradition in 1 Thessalonians II 13–16." *NovT* 8 (1966) 223–234.

Schlier, Heinrich 1962. "Auslegung des 1. Thessalonicherbriefes (1,1–10)." *BibLeb* 3 (1962) 16–25.

— 1962a. "Auslegung des 1. Thessalonicherbriefes (2,1–16)." *BibLeb* 3 (1962) 89–97.

— 1962b. "Auslegung des 1. Thessalonicherbriefes (2,17–3,13)." *BibLeb* 3 (1962) 174–184.

— 1962c. "Auslegung des 1. Thessalonicherbriefes (4,1–12)." *BibLeb* 3 (1962) 240–249.

— 1963. "Auslegung des 1. Thessalonicherbriefes (4,13–5,11)." *BibLeb* 4 (1963) 19–30.

— 1963a. "Auslegung des 1. Thessalonicherbriefes (5,12–28)." *BibLeb* 4 (1963) 96–103.

— 1964. "ἐλεύθερος κτλ." *TDNT* 2 (1964) 487–502.

— 1965. "θλίβω, θλῖψις." *TDNT* 3 (1965) 139–148.

— 1971. *Das Ende der Zeit. Exegetische Aufsätze und Vorträge III.* Freiburg et al.: Herder.
— 1972. *Der Apostel und seine Gemeinde. Auslegung des ersten Briefes an die Thessalonicher.* 2nd ed. Freiburg et al.: Herder.
— 1977. *Der Römerbrief.* HTKNT. Freiburg et al.: Herder.
SCHLOSSER, J. ed. 2004. *The Catholic Epistles and the Tradition.* BETL 176. Leuven: Peeters.
SCHLUETER, Carol J. 1994. *Filling Up the Measure: Polemical Hyperbole in 1 Thessalonians 2.14–16.* JSNTSup 98. Sheffield: JSOT Press.
SCHMID, Josef 1957. "Agrapha." *LTK* 1 (²1957) 206.
SCHMID, Lothar 1965. "κέλευσμα." *TDNT* 3 (1965) 656–659.
SCHMIDT, Daryl D. 1983. "1 Thess 2:13–16: Linguistic Evidence for an Interpolation." *JBL* 102 (1983) 269–279.
— 1983a. "The Authenticity of 2 Thessalonians: Linguistic Arguments." In: RICHARDS (1983) 289–296.
— 1990. Review of *To All the Brethren: A Text-Linguistic and Rhetorical Approach to 1 Thessalonians,* by B. C. JOHANSON, 1987. *CRBR* 3 (1990) 208–211.
— 1990a. "The Syntactical Style of 2 Thessalonians: How Pauline Is It?" In: R. F. COLLINS (1990) 383–393.
— 1993. "Verbal Aspect in Greek: Two Approaches." In: PORTER/CARSON (1993) 63–73.
SCHMIDT, Karl L. 1965. "καλέω κτλ." *TDNT* 3 (1965) 487–536.
SCHMIDT, Mauricius rev. 1965. *Hesychii Alexandrini Lexicon. post Ioannem Albertum.* 5 vols. Repr. of the edition Halle 1858–1868. Amsterdam: Adolf M. Hakkert.
SCHMIDT, Thomas E./SILVA, Moisés eds. 1994. *To Tell the Mystery: Essays on New Testament Eschatology in Honor of Robert H. Gundry.* JSNTSup 100. Sheffield: JSOT Press.
SCHMITHALS, Walter 1960. "Zur Abfassung und ältesten Sammlung der paulinischen Hauptbriefe." *ZNW* 51 (1960) 225–245.
— 1964. "Die Thessalonicherbriefe als Briefkompositionen." In: FS BULTMANN (1964) 295–315.
— 1965. *Paulus und die Gnostiker. Untersuchungen zu den kleinen Paulusbriefen.* TF 35. Hamburg-Bergstedt: Herbert Reich, Evangelischer Verlag.
— 1975. "Death, Kill, Sleep." *NIDNTT* 1 (1975) 429–447 [§ θάνατος: 430–441].
— 1984. *Die Briefe des Paulus in ihrer ursprünglichen Form.* Zürcher Werkkommentare zur Bibel. Zürich: Theologischer Verlag.
— 1988. "1. Thessalonicher 4,13–14." *GPM* 77 (1988) 194–198.
SCHMITT, Armin 1976. *Entrückung – Aufnahme – Himmelfahrt. Untersuchungen zu einem Vorstellungsbereich im Alten Testament.* 2nd ed. FB 10. Stuttgart: Verlag Katholisches Bibelwerk.
SCHMITT, Joseph 1957. "Auferstehung Christi I. Die neutestamentlichen Auferstehungsberichte." *LTK* 1 (²1957) 1028–1031.
— 1957a. "Auferstehung Christi II. Das apostolische Auferstehungskerygma." *LTK* 1 (²1957) 1032–1035.
SCHMITZ, Otto 1967. "παρακαλέω, παράκλησις." *TDNT* 5 (1967) 773–799 [§ A, B, E (with G. STÄHLIN), F; 774–779, 790–793, 793–799].
SCHNACKENBURG, Rudolf/ERNST, Josef/WANKE, Joachim eds. 1977. *Die Kirche des Anfangs. Festschrift für Heinz Schürmann zum 65. Geburtstag.* ETS 38. Leipzig: St. Benno-Verlag.
SCHNEIDER, Gerhard 1969. "Urchristliche Gottesverkündigung in hellenistischer Umwelt." *BZ* 13 (1969) 59–75.
— 1991. "Ἰησοῦς." *EDNT* 2 (1991) 180–184.
— 1991a. "ὁποῖος." *EDNT* 2 (1991) 524.
— 1993. "Σιλᾶς, Σιλουανός." *EDNT* 3 (1993) 243–244.
SCHNEIDER, Johannes 1964. "βαίνω κτλ." *TDNT* 1 (1964) 518–523.
— 1967. "ὀλεθρεύω κτλ." *TDNT* 5 (1967) 167–171.
SCHNEIDER, Sebastian 2000. *Vollendung des Auferstehens. Eine exegetische Untersuchung von 1 Kor 15,51–52 und 1 Thess 4,13–18.* FB 97. Würzburg: Echter.
SCHNEIDERS, Sandra M. 1990. "Hermeneutics." In: BROWN/FITZMYER/MURPHY (1990) 1146–1165.
SCHNELLE, Udo 1986. "Der Erste Thessalonicherbrief und die Entstehung der paulinischen Anthropologie." *NTS* 32 (1986) 207–224.

— 1990. "Die Ethik des 1. Thessalonicherbriefes." In: R. F. COLLINS (1990) 295–305.
— 1994. *Einleitung in das Neue Testament.* Göttingen: Vandenhoeck & Ruprecht.
— 2000. "Heilsgegenwart. Christologische Hoheitstitel bei Paulus." In: FS HÜBNER (2000) 178–193.
— 2000a. Review of *Kommunikation gegen den Tod. Studien zur paulinischen Briefpragmatik am Beispiel des Ersten Thessalonicherbriefes*, by J. BICKMANN, 1998. *TLZ* 125 (2000) 65–66.
— 2001. "Transformation und Partizipation als Grundgedanken paulinischer Theologie." *NTS* 47 (2001) 58–75.
— 2003. *Paulus. Leben und Denken.* GLB. Berlin/New York: W. de Gruyter.
— /SÖDING, Thomas eds. 2000. *Paulinische Christologie. Exegetische Beiträge. Hans Hübner zum 70. Geburtstag.* In Verbindung mit M. LABAHN. Göttingen: Vandenhoeck & Ruprecht.
SCHNIDER, Franz/STENGER, Werner 1987. *Studien zum neutestamentlichen Briefformular.* NTTS 11. Leiden et al.: E. J. Brill.
SCHNIEWIND, Julius 1964. "ἀγγελία κτλ." *TDNT* 1 (1964) 56–73.
SCHOENBORN, Ulrich 1991. "οὐρανός." *EDNT* 2 (1991) 543–547.
SCHOEPS, Hans J. 1950. *Aus frühchristlicher Zeit. Religionsgeschichtliche Untersuchungen.* Tübingen: J. C. B. Mohr (Paul Siebeck).
SCHOONHEIM, Pieter L. 1978. "Probleme und Impulse der neutestamentlichen Apokalyptik." In: BAARDA/KLIJN/VAN UNNIK (1978, vol. 1) 129–145.
SCHOON-JANSSEN, Johannes 1991. *Umstrittene "Apologien" in den Paulusbriefen. Studien zur rhetorischen Situation des 1. Thessalonicherbriefes, des Galaterbriefes und des Philipperbriefes.* GTA 45. Göttingen: Vandenhoeck & Ruprecht.
— 2000. "On the Use of Elements of Ancient Epistolography in 1 Thessalonians." In: DONFRIED/BEUTLER (2000) 179–193.
SCHORCH, Stefan 2000. *Euphemismen in der Hebräischen Bibel.* Orientalia Biblica et Christiana 12. Wiesbaden: Harrassowitz.
SCHOTTROFF, Luise 1991. "ζῶ, ζωή." *EDNT* 2 (1991) 105–109.
SCHRAGE, Wolfgang 1967. "Das Verständnis des Todes Jesu Christi im Neuen Testament." In: BIZER et al. (1967) 49–89.
— ed. 1986. *Studien zum Text und zur Ethik des Neuen Testaments. Festschrift zum 80. Geburtstag von Heinrich Greeven.* BZNW 47. Berlin/New York: W. de Gruyter.
— 1986a. "Heil und Heilung im Neuen Testament. Ernst Käsemann zum 80. Geburtstag am 12.7.1986." *EvT* 46 (1986) 197–214.
— 1997. "Der gekreuzigte und auferweckte Herr. Zur *theologia crucis* und *theologia resurrectionis* bei Paulus." *ZTK* 94 (1997) 25–38.
— 2001. *Der erste Brief an die Korinther.* Vol. 4: *1Kor 15,1–16,24.* EKKNT 7.4. Düsseldorf: Benziger Verlag / Neukirchen-Vluyn: Neukirchener Verlag.
— 2001a. "Unterwegs zur Einzigkeit und Einheit Gottes. Zum 'Monotheismus' des Paulus und seiner alttestamentlich-jüdischen Tradition." *EvT* 61 (2001) 190–203.
— 2001b. Review of *Der erste Brief des Paulus an die Thessalonicher* by G. HAUFE, 1999. *TLZ* 126 (2001) 1152–1153.
SCHREIBER, Stefan 2007. "Eine neue Jenseitshoffnung in Thessaloniki und ihre Probleme (1 Thess 4,13–18)." *Bib* 88 (2007) 326–350.
SCHRENK, Gottlob 1964. "βιάζομαι, βιαστής." *TDNT* 1 (1964) 609–614.
— 1965. "θέλω, θέλημα, θέλησις." *TDNT* 3 (1965) 44–62.
— 1967. "λεῖμμα." *TDNT* 4 (1967) 194–214 [§ A, C: 194–196, 209–214].
SCHRÖTER, Jens 2004. "Anfänge der Jesusüberlieferung. Überlieferungsgeschichtliche Beobachtungen zu einem Bereich urchristlicher Theologiegeschichte." *NTS* 50 (2004) 53–76.
SCHUBERT, Paul 1939. *Form and Function of the Pauline Thanksgivings.* BZNW 20. Berlin: A. Töpelmann.
SCHULZ, Siegfried 1985. "Der frühe und der späte Paulus. Überlegungen zur Entwicklung seiner Theologie und Ethik." *TZ* 41 (1985) 228–236.
SCHÜSSLER FIORENZA, Elisabeth 1976. "Eschatology of the NT." *IDBSup* (1976) 271–277.
— 1983. "The Phenomenon of Early Christian Apocalyptic: Some Reflections on Method." In: HELLHOLM (1983) 295–316.

— ed. 1994. *Searching the Scriptures*. Vol. 2: *A Feminist Commentary*. With the ass. of A. Brock/S. Matthews. New York: Crossroad.

Schwank, Benedikt 1971. "Der sogenannte Brief an Gallio und die Datierung des 1 Thess." *BZ* 15 (1971) 265–266.

Schwartz, Daniel R. 1990. *Agrippa I: The Last King of Judea*. TSAJ 23. Tübingen: J. C. B. Mohr (Paul Siebeck).

Schweitzer, Albert 1953. *The Mysticism of Paul the Apostle*. 2nd ed. Transl. by W. Montgomery. London: A. & C. Black.

Schweizer, Eduard 1953. "Miszelle. Zur Trichotomie von 1. Thess. 5,23 und der Unterscheidung des πνευματικόν vom ψυχικόν in 1. Kor. 2,14; 15,44; Jak. 3,15; Jud. 19." *TZ* 9 (1953) 76–77.

— 1968. "Dying and Rising with Christ." *NTS* 14 (1967–1968) 1–14.

— 1972. "υἱός, υἱοθεσία." *TDNT* 8 (1972) 334–399 [§ C.I.1.b–C.I.3, D; υἱοθεσία 2, 3: 354–357, 363–392, 399].

— 1982. "Paul's Christology and Gnosticism." In: FS Barrett (1982) 115–123.

Schwertner, Siegfried M. comp. 1994. *Theologische Realenzyklopädie. Abkürzungsverzeichnis*. 2nd ed. Berlin/New York: W. de Gruyter.

Scott, jr., J. Julius 1972. "Paul and Late-Jewish Eschatology — A Case Study, I Thessalonians 4:13–18 and II Thessalonians 2:1–12." *JETS* 15 (1972) 133–143.

Scott, James M. 1993. "Paul's Use of Deuteronomic Tradition." *JBL* 112 (1993) 645–665.

Scott, Robert 1909. *The Pauline Epistles: A Critical Study*. The Literature of the New Testament. Edinburgh: T. & T. Clark.

Scott, Robert B. Y. 1959. "'Behold, He Cometh with Clouds'." *NTS* 5 (1958–1959) 127–132.

Scott, Walter ed. & transl. 1968. *Hermetica: The Ancient Greek and Latin Writings Which Contain Religious or Philosophic Teachings Ascribed to Hermes Trismegistus*. Vol. 1: *Introduction, Texts and Translation*. London: Dawsons of Pall Mall.

Scroggs, Robin 1991. "Salvation History: The Theological Structure of Paul's Thought (1 Thessalonians, Philippians, and Galatians)." In: Bassler (1991) 212–226.

Segal, Alan F. 1980. "Heavenly Ascent in Hellenistic Judaism, Early Christianity and Their Environment." *ANRW* II.23.2 (1980) 1333–1394.

— 1992. "Conversion and Messianism: Outline for a New Approach." In: Charlesworth (1992) 296–340.

— 1998. "Paul's Thinking about Resurrection in Its Jewish Context." *NTS* 44 (1998) 400–419.

Segbroeck, Frans van → van Segbroeck, Frans.

Seifrid, Mark A. 1993. "In Christ." *DPL* (1993) 433–436.

— 1998. Review of *Neglected Endings: The Significance of the Pauline Letter Closings*, by J. A. D. Weima, 1994. *JETS* 41 (1998) 491–492.

Selby, Gary S. 1999. "'Blameless at His Coming': The Discursive Construction of Eschatological Reality in 1 Thessalonians." *Rhetorica* 17 (1999) 385–410.

Sellin, Gerhard 1983. "'Die Auferstehung ist schon geschehen'. Zur Spiritualisierung apokalyptischer Terminologie im Neuen Testament." *NovT* 25 (1983) 220–237.

— 1986. *Der Streit um die Auferstehung der Toten. Eine religionsgeschichtliche und exegetische Untersuchung von 1 Korinther 15*. FRLANT 138. Göttingen: Vandenhoeck & Ruprecht.

— 1998. "Auferstehung I. Auferstehung der Toten 4. Neues Testament." *RGG* 1 ([4]1998) 916–917.

— /Vouga, François eds. 1997. *Logos und Buchstabe. Mündlichkeit und Schriftlichkeit im Judentum und Christentum der Antike*. In cooperation with S. Alkier/A. Cornils/K. Heinemann. TANZ 20. Tübingen/Basel: Francke.

Selwyn, Edward G. 1947. *The First Epistle of St. Peter: The Greek Text with Introduction, Notes and Essays*. 2nd ed. London et al.: Macmillan.

Semmelroth, Otto 1957. "'Erbauet einer den anderen' (1 Thess 5,11). Zur Wiedereroberung eines christlichen Begriffes." *GL* 30 (1957) 262–271.

Setzer, Claudia J. 1994. *Jewish Responses to Early Christians: History and Polemics, 30–150 c.e.* Minneapolis: Fortress.

Sevenster, Jan N. 1975. *The Roots of Pagan Anti-Semitism in the Ancient World*. NovTSup 41. Leiden: E. J. Brill.

SHIRES, Henry M. 1966. *The Eschatology of Paul in the Light of Modern Scholarship*. Philadelphia: Westminster.

SHUTT, Rowland J. H. 1985. "Letter of Aristeas: A New Translation and Introduction." *OTP* 2 (1985) 7–34.

SIBER, Peter 1971. *Mit Christus leben. Eine Studie zur paulinischen Auferstehungshoffnung*. ATANT 61. Zürich: Theologischer Verlag.

SIGEL, Dorothea 1998. "Eschatologie." *DNP* 4 (1998) 123–128.

SIKER, Jeffrey S. 1994. Review of *Christian Anti-Semitism and Paul's Theology*, by S. G. HALL, III, 1993. *CRBR* 7 (1994) 194–196.

SILVA, Moisés 1993. "A Response to Fanning and Porter on Verbal Aspect." In: PORTER/CARSON (1993) 74–82.

SIMPSON, JR., John W. 1988. "The Future of Non-Christian Jews: 1 Thessalonians 2:15–16 and Romans 9–11." PhD diss. Fuller Theological Seminary, 1988. Ann Arbor, MI: UMI, 1988.

— 1990. "The Problems Posed by 1 Thessalonians 2:15–16 and a Solution." *HBT* 12 (1990) 42–72.

— 1993. "Thessalonians, Letter to the." *DPL* (1993) 932–939.

— 1998. "Shaped by the Stories: Narrative in 1 Thessalonians." *AsTJ* 53 (1998) 15–25.

SIMUNDSON, Daniel J. 1992. "Suffering." *ABD* 6 (1992) 219–225.

SLEEPER, C. Freeman 1999. "Christ's Coming and Christian Living." *Int* 53 (1999) 131–142.

SLINGERLAND, Dixon 1990. "Acts 18:1–17 and Luedemann's Pauline Chronology." *JBL* 109 (1990) 686–690.

— 1991. "Acts 18:1–18, the Gallio Inscription, and Absolute Pauline Chronology." *JBL* 110 (1991) 439–449.

SMALLEY, Stephen S. 1964. "The Delay of the Parousia." *JBL* 83 (1964) 41–54.

— 1964a. "The Theatre of Parousia." *SJT* 17 (1964) 406–413.

SMALLWOOD, E. Mary 1981. *The Jews under Roman Rule: From Pompey to Diocletian. A Study in Political Relations*. Corrected ed. SJLA 20. Leiden: E. J. Brill.

SMEND, Rudolf 1982. "Eschatologie II. Altes Testament." *TRE* 10 (1982) 256–264.

SMITH, Abraham 1995. *Comfort one Another: Reconstructing the Rhetoric and Audience of 1 Thessalonians*. Literary Currents in Biblical Interpretation. Louisville, KY: Westminster/John Knox.

— 2000. "The First Letter to the Thessalonians: Introduction, Commentary, and Reflections." *NIB* 11 (2000) 671–737.

— 2004. "'Unmasking the Powers': Toward a Postcolonial Analysis of 1 Thessalonians." In: R. A. HORSLEY (2004) 47–66.

SMITH, Charles F. transl. 1919–1923. *Thucydides*. 4 vols. LCL 108, 109, 110, 169. London: William Heinemann / Cambridge: Harvard University Press.

SMITH, Morton 1983. "On the History of ΑΠΟΚΑΛΥΠΤΩ and ΑΠΟΚΑΛΥΨΙΣ." In: HELLHOLM (1983) 9–19.

SMITMANS, Adolf 1973. "Das Gleichnis vom Dieb." In: FS SCHELKLE (1973) 43–68.

SMYTH, Herbert W. 1916. *A Greek Grammar for Schools and Colleges*. Greek Series for Colleges and Schools. New York et al.: American Book Company.

— transl. 1922–1926. *Aeschylus*. 2 vols. Appendix ed. by H. LLOYD-JONES. LCL 145, 146. London: William Heinemann / Cambridge: Harvard University Press.

SMYTH, Kevin 1963. "Heavenly Man and Son of Man in St Paul." In: *SPCIC* (1961) = AnBib 17–18. Vol. 1. Rome: Pontifical Biblical Institute (1963) 219–230.

SNYDER, Graydon F. 1972. "A Summary of Faith in an Epistolary Context: 1 Thess. 1:9,10." In: MCGAUGHY (1972, vol. 2) 355–365.

— 1972a. "Apocalyptic and Didactic Elements in 1 Thessalonians." In: MCGAUGHY (1972, vol. 1) 233–244.

— 1975. "Sayings on the Delay of the End." *BR* 20 (1975) 19–35.

SÖDING, Thomas 1991. "Der Erste Thessalonicherbrief und die frühe paulinische Evangeliumsverkündigung. Zur Frage einer Entwicklung der paulinischen Theologie." *BZ* 35 (1991) 180–203.

— 1992. *Die Trias Glaube, Hoffnung, Liebe bei Paulus. Eine exegetische Studie*. SBS 150. Stuttgart: Verlag Katholisches Bibelwerk.

— 1995. "Eschatologie A. Wissenschaftstheoretisch I. Biblisch." *LTK* 3 ([3]1995) 859.

— 2000. "Thessalonicherbriefe." *LTK* 9 ([3]2000) 1494–1496.

Spörlein, Bernhard 1971. *Die Leugnung der Auferstehung. Eine historisch-kritische Untersuchung zu 1 Kor 15*. BU 7. Regensburg: Friedrich Pustet.

Staab, Karl 1965. "An die Thessalonicher I." In: Staab/Freundorfer (1965) 11–46.

— /Freundorfer, Joseph 1965. *Die Thessalonicherbriefe. Die Gefangenschaftsbriefe. Die Pastoralbriefe.* RNT 7. 4th ed. Regensburg: Friedrich Pustet.

Stacy, R. Wayne 1999. "Introduction to the Thessalonian Correspondences." *RevExp* 96 (1999) 175–194.

Stählin, Gustav 1962. "Zum Gebrauch von Beteuerungsformeln im Neuen Testament." *NovT* 5 (1962) 115–143.

— 1967. "ὀργή κτλ." *TDNT* 5 (1967) 382–447 [§ E: 419–447].

Stanley, Christopher D. 2002. "Who's Afraid of a Thief in the Night?" *NTS* 48 (2002) 468–486.

Stanley, David M. 1959. "'Become Imitators of Me': The Pauline Conception of Apostolic Tradition." *Bib* 40 (1959) 859–877.

— 1961. *Christ's Resurrection in Pauline Soteriology*. AnBib 13. Rome: Pontifical Biblical Institute.

— 1984. "Imitation in Paul's Letters: Its Significance for His Relationship to Jesus and to His Own Christian Foundations." In: FS Beare (1984) 127–141.

Stanton, Graham N. 2003. "Paul's Gospel." In: Dunn (2003) 173–184.

— /Stroumsa, Guy G. eds. 1998. *Tolerance and Intolerance in Early Judaism and Christianity*. Cambridge: University Press.

Stauffer, Ethelbert 1964a. "ἐγώ." *TDNT* 2 (1964) 343–362.

Steck, Odil H. 1967. *Israel und das gewaltsame Geschick der Propheten. Untersuchungen zur Überlieferung des deuteronomistischen Geschichtsbildes im Alten Testament, Spätjudentum und Urchristentum.* WMANT 23. Neukirchen-Vluyn: Neukirchener Verlag.

Steck, R. 1883. "Das Herrnwort 1. Thess. 4, 15." *JPTh* 13 (1883) 509–524.

Stegemann, Ekkehard W. 1990. "Zur antijüdischen Polemik in 1Thess 2,14–16." *KuI* 5 (1990) 54–64.

Steimle, Christopher 2007. *Religion im römischen Thessaloniki. Sakraltopographie, Kult und Gesellschaft.* STAC. Tübingen: Mohr Siebeck.

Stempvoort, P. A. van → van Stempvoort, P. A.

Stendahl, Krister 1976. *Paul Among Jews and Gentiles*. Philadelphia: Fortress.

— 1995. *Final Account, Paul's Letter to the Romans*. Minneapolis: Fortress.

Stenger, Werner 1993. *Introduction to New Testament Exegesis*. Transl. by D W. Stott. Grand Rapids: Eerdmans.

Stewart, Zeph sel. & ed. 1972. *Arthur Darby Nock: Essays on Religion and the Ancient World*. 2 vols. With an intr., bibl. & indexes by Z. Stewart. Oxford: Clarendon. [collected essays include: Nock 1928; 1961]

Still, Todd D. 1999. *Conflict at Thessalonica: A Pauline Church and Its Neighbours*. JSNTSup 183. Sheffield: Academic Press.

— 1999a. "Eschatology in the Thessalonian Letters." *RevExp* 96 (1999) 195–210.

— 1999b. "Paul's Thessalonian Mission." *SwJT* 42 (1999) 4–16.

Stolina, Ralf 2002. "Tod und Heil. Zur Heilsbedeutung des Todes Jesu." *NZSTh* 44 (2002) 89–106.

Stone, Michael E. 1969. *The Testament of Levi: A First Study of the Armenian MSS of the Testaments of the XII Patriarchs in the Convent of St. James, Jerusalem. With Text, Critical Apparatus, Notes and Translation*. Jerusalem: St. James.

— ed. 1984. *The Literature of the Jewish People in the Period of the Second Temple and the Talmud*. Vol. 2: *Jewish Writings of the Second Temple Period: Apocrypha, Pseudepigrapha, Qumran Sectarian Writings, Philo, Josephus.* CRINT. Assen: Van Gorcum / Philadelphia: Fortress.

— 1984a. "Apocalyptic Literature." In: Stone (1984) 383–441.

Stott, John R. W. 1991. *The Message of the New Testament: Preparing for the Coming King*. BST. Leicester: InterVarsity.

Stowers, Stanley K. 1986. *Letter Writing in Greco-Roman Antiquity*. LEC 5. Philadelphia: Westminster.

— 1995. "Greeks Who Sacrifice and Those Who Do Not: Toward an Anthropology of Greek Religion." In: FS Meeks (1995) 293–333.

STRATHMANN, Hermann 1967. "μαρτυς κτλ." *TDNT* 4 (1967) 474–514.

STRELAN, Rick 2004. *Strange Acts: Studies in the Cultural World of the Acts of the Apostles*. BZNW 126. Berlin/New York: W. de Gruyter.

STROBEL, August 1961. *Untersuchungen zum eschatologischen Verzögerungsproblem*. NovTSup 2. Leiden/Köln: E. J. Brill.

— 1978. "Apokalyptik/Apokalypsen IV. Neues Testament." *TRE* 3 (1978) 251–257.

— 1990. "ἀνάγκη." *EDNT* 1 (1990) 77–79.

STROKER, William D. 1992. "Agrapha." *ABD* 1 (1992) 92–95.

STUHLMACHER, Peter 1967. "Erwägungen zum Problem von Gegenwart und Zukunft in der paulinischen Eschatologie." *ZTK* 64 (1967) 423–450.

— 1968. *Das paulinische Evangelium. I. Vorgeschichte*. Göttingen: Vandenhoeck & Ruprecht.

— ed. 1991. *The Gospel and the Gospels*. Grand Rapids: Eerdmans.

— 2000. "Eschatology and Hope in Paul." Transl. by D. C. MOHRMAN. *EvQ* 72 (2000) 315–333.

STUHLMANN, Rainer 1983. *Das eschatologische Maß im Neuen Testament*. FRLANT 132. Göttingen: Vandenhoeck & Ruprecht.

STURM, Richard E. 1989. "Defining the Word 'Apocalyptic': A Problem in Biblical Criticism." In: FS MARTYN (1989) 17–48.

SUGGS, M. Jack. 1960. "Concerning the Date of Paul's Macedonian Ministry." *NovT* 4 (1960) 60–68.

SUHL, Alfred 1975. *Paulus und seine Briefe. Ein Beitrag zur paulinischen Chronologie*. SNTU 11. Gütersloh: Gerd Mohn.

— 1992. "Der Beginn der selbständigen Mission des Paulus. Ein Beitrag zur Geschichte des Urchristentums." *NTS* 38 (1992) 430–447.

— 1995. "Paulinische Chronologie im Streit der Meinungen." *ANRW* II.26.2 (1995) 939–1188.

SULLIVAN, Clayton 1988. *Rethinking Realized Eschatology*. Macon, GA: Mercer University Press.

SUMNEY, Jerry L. 1990. "The Bearing of a Pauline Rhetorical Pattern on the Integrity of 2Thessalonians." *ZNW* 81 (1990) 192–204.

— 1996. Review of *Neglected Endings: The Significance of the Pauline Letter Closings*, by J. A. D. WEIMA, 1994. *JBL* 115 (1996) 557–559.

TANNEHILL, Robert C. 1967. *Dying and Rising with Christ: A Study in Pauline Theology*. BZNW 32. Berlin: A. Töpelmann.

TARAZI, Paul N. 1982. *1 Thessalonians: A Commentary*. Orthodox Biblical Studies. Crestwood, NY: St. Vladimir's Seminary Press.

TAYLOR, Miriam S. 1995. *Anti-Judaism and Early Christian Identity: A Critique of the Scholarly Consensus*. StPB 46. Leiden et al.: E. J. Brill.

TAYLOR, Nicholas H. 1995. "The Social Nature of Conversion in the Early Christian World." In: ESLER (1995) 128–136.

TEICHMANN, Ernst 1896. *Die paulinischen Vorstellungen von Auferstehung und Gericht und ihre Beziehung zur jüdischen Apokalyptik*. Freiburg i. B.: J. C. B. Mohr.

TELLBE, Mikael 2001. *Paul between Synagogue and State: Christians, Jews, and Civic Authorities in 1 Thessalonians, Romans, and Philippians*. ConBNT 34. Stockholm: Almquist & Wiksell International.

THACKERAY, Henry St. J. et al. transl. 1926–1965. *Josephus*. 9 vols. Vols. 1–4 transl. by H. ST. J. THACKERAY. Vol. 5 transl. by H. ST. J. THACKERAY/R. MARCUS. Vols. 6–7 transl. by R. MARCUS. Vol. 8 transl. by R. MARCUS/A. WIKGREN. Vol. 9 transl. by L. H. GOLDMAN. LCL 186, 203, 210, 242, 281, 326, 365, 410, 433. London: William Heinemann / Cambridge: Harvard University Press.

THEISSEN, Gerd 1991. "Judentum und Christentum bei Paulus. Sozialgeschichtliche Überlegungen zu einem beginnenden Schisma. H. Thyen zum 60. Geburtstag am 21.4.1987." In: GS SCHLATTER (1991) 331–359.

— 1999. "Vom Davidssohn zum Weltherrscher. Pagane und jüdische Endzeiterwartungen im Spiegel des Matthäusevangeliums." In: FS KUHN (1999) 145–164.

THEOBALD, Michael 1991. "'Prophetenworte verachtet nicht!' (1 Thess 5, 20). Paulinische Perspektiven gegen eine institutionelle Versuchung." *TQ* 171 (1991) 30–47.

Thieme, Karl 1963. "Die Struktur des ersten Thessalonicher-Briefes." In: FS Michel (1963) 450–458.

Thiselton, Anthony C. 1979. "Semantics and New Testament Interpretation." In: Marshall (1979) 75–104.

— 1995. "New Testament Interpretation in Historical Perspective." In: Green (1995) 10–36.

Thom, Johan C. 2004. Review of *The Letters to the Thessalonians: A New Translation with Introduction and Commentary*, by A. J. Malherbe, 2000. *RevBL* 6 (2004) 33–36.

Thomas, Robert L. 1978. "1 Thessalonians." In: Gaebelein (1978) 227–298.

Thompson, Edward 1945. "The Sequence of the Two Epistles to the Thessalonians." *ExpTim* 56 (1944–1945) 306–307.

Thompson, James W. 2002. Review of *Vollendung des Auferstehens. Eine exegetische Untersuchung von 1 Kor 15,51–52 und 1 Thess 4,13–18*, by S. Schneider, 2000. *RelSRev* 28 (2002) 78.

Thompson, Leonard L. 1996. "Social Location of Early Christian Apocalyptic." *ANRW* II.26.3 (1996) 2615–2656.

Thompson, Michael B. 1991. *Clothed with Christ: The Example and Teaching of Jesus in Romans 12.1–15.13*. JSNTSup 59. Sheffield: JSOT Press.

— 1993. "Teaching/Paraenesis." *DPL* (1993) 922–923.

Thrall, Margaret E. 1965. *The First and Second Letters of Paul to the Corinthians*. CBC. Cambridge: University Press.

— 1994. *The Second Epistle to the Corinthians: A Critical and Exegetical Commentary*. Vol. 1: *Introduction and Commentary on II Corinthians I–VII*. ICC. Edinburgh: T&T Clark.

— 2002. "Paul's Understanding of Continuity between the Present Life and the Life of the Resurrection." FS Lambrecht (2002) 283–300.

Thurston, Robert W. 1974. "The Relationship between the Epistles to the Thessalonians." *ExpTim* 85 (1973–1974) 52–56.

Tomson, Peter J. 2001. *"If This Be From Heaven…": Jesus and the New Testament Authors in Their Relationship to Judaism*. The Biblical Seminar 76. Sheffield: Academic Press.

Torm, Frederik 1934. "Der Pluralis οὐρανοί." *ZNW* 33 (1934) 48–50.

Traub, Helmut 1967. "οὐρανός κτλ." *TDNT* 5 (1967) 497–543 [§ A, C–E; οὐράνιος, ἐπουράνιος, οὐρανόθεν: 497–502, 509–543].

Travis, Stephen H. 1992. "Wrath of God." *ABD* 6 (1992) 989–998 [§ New Testament: 996–998].

Trebilco, Paul 1993. "Itineraries, Travel Plans, Journeys, Apostolic Parousia." *DPL* (1993) 446–456.

Trilling, Wolfgang 1972. *Untersuchungen zum zweiten Thessalonicherbrief*. ETS 27. Leipzig: St. Benno-Verlag.

— 1980. *Der zweite Brief an die Thessalonicher*. EKKNT 14. Neukirchen-Vluyn: Neukirchener Verlag.

— 1981. "Literarische Paulusimitation im 2. Thessalonicherbrief." In: Kertelge/Lohfink (1981) 146–156.

— 1987. "Die beiden Briefe des Apostels Paulus an die Thessalonicher. Eine Forschungsübersicht." *ANRW* II.25.4 (1987) 3365–3403.

— 1990. "ἁρπάζω." *EDNT* 1 (1990) 156–157.

— 1991. "ἡμέρα." *EDNT* 2 (1991) 119–121.

Trocmé, Etienne 1985. "The Jews as Seen by Paul and Luke." In: Neusner/Frerichs (1985) 145– 161.

Trowitzsch, Michael ed. 1998. *Paulus, Apostel Jesu Christi. Festschrift für Günter Klein zum 70. Geburtstag*. Tübingen: Mohr Siebeck.

Trudinger, Paul 1995. "The Priority of *2 Thessalonians* Revisited: Some Fresh Evidence." *DRev* 113 (1995) 31–35.

Tuckett, Christopher M. 1990. "Synoptic Tradition in 1 Thessalonians?" In: R. F. Collins (1990) 160–182.

Turner, Nigel 1965. *Grammatical Insights into the New Testament*. Edinburgh: T. & T. Clark.

Turner, Seth 2003. "The Interim, Earthly Messianic Kingdom in Paul." *JSNT*, issue 25 (2003) 323–342.

Uffenheimer, Benjamin 1982. "Eschatologie III. Judentum." *TRE* 10 (1982) 264–270.

Ulonska, Herbert 1987. "Christen und Heiden. Die paulinische Paränese in I Thess 4,3–8." *TZ* 43 (1987) 210–218.

UNNIK, Willem C. van → VAN UNNIK, Willem C.

UPRICHARD, Robert E. H. 1976. "An Examination of the Early Date Hypothesis for the Writing of 1 Thessalonians, with Particular Reference to Development in Paul's Theology." PhD diss. Queens' University, 1976.

— 1979. "Exposition of 1 Thessalonians 4.13–18." *IBS* 1 (1979) 150–156.

— 1981. "The Person and Work of Christ in 1 Thessalonians." *EvQ* 53 (1981) 108–114.

VAN AARDE, Andries G. 1990. "The Struggle against Heresy in the Thessalonian Correspondence and the Origin of the Apostolic Tradition." In: R. F. COLLINS (1990) 418–425.

VAN DER HORST, Pieter W. 1991. *Ancient Jewish Epitaphs: An Introductory Survey of a Millennium of Jewish Funerary Epigraphy (300 BCE – 700 CE).* CBET 2. Kampen: Kok Pharos.

— 2000. "'Only Then Will All Israel Be Saved': A Short Note on the Meaning of καὶ οὕτως in Romans 11:26." *JBL* 119 (2000) 521–525.

VAN DER WATT, Jan G. 1990. "The Use of ζάω in 1 Thessalonians: A Comparison with ζάω/ζωή in the Gospel of John." In: R. F. COLLINS (1990) 356–369.

VAN SEGBROECK, Frans ed. 1992. *The Four Gospels: Festschrift Franz Neirynck.* 3 vols. BETL 100. Leuven: University Press/Peeters.

VAN STEMPVOORT, P. A. 1961. "Eine stilistische Lösung einer alten Schwierigkeit in 1. Thess. V. 23." *NTS* 7 (1960–1961) 262–265.

VAN UNNIK, Willem C. et al. eds. 1962. *Neotestamentica et Patristica. Eine Freundesgabe, Herrn Professor Dr. Oscar Cullmann zu seinem 60. Geburtstag überreicht.* NovTSup 6. Leiden: E. J. Brill.

VANDERKAM, James C. 1998. "Apocalyptic Literature." In: BARTON (1998) 305–322.

VANHOYE, Albert ed. 1986. *L'Apôtre Paul. Personnalité, style et conception du ministère.* BETL 73. Leuven: University Press.

— 1990. "La composition de 1 Thessaloniciens." In: R. F. COLLINS (1990) 73–86.

VAWTER, Bruce 1960. *Introduction to the Pauline Epistles: I Thessalonians, II Thessalonians. Introduction and Commentary.* New Testament Reading Guide 6. Collegeville, MN: Liturgical Press.

— 1963. "'And He Shall Come Again with Glory': Paul and Christian Apocalyptic." In: *SPCIC* (1961) = AnBib 17–18. Vol. 1. Rome: Pontifical Biblical Institute, 1963. 143–150.

VENA, Osvaldo D. 2001. *The Parousia and Its Rereadings: The Development of the Eschatological Consciousness in the Writings of the New Testament.* SBLit 27. New York et al.: Peter Lang.

VERBURG, Winfried 1996. *Endzeit und Entschlafene. Syntaktisch-sigmatische, semantische und pragmatische Analyse von 1 Kor 15.* FB 78. Würzburg: Echter.

VERHOEF, Eduard 1995. "Die Bedeutung des Artikels τῶν in 1Thess 2,15." *BN* 80 (1995) 41–46.

— 1997. "The Relation between 1 Thessalonians and 2 Thessalonians and the Inauthenticity of 2 Thessalonians." *Hervormde Teologiese Studies* 53 (1997) 163–171.

VERMES, Geza 1995. *The Dead Sea Scrolls in English.* 4th ed. London et al.: Penguin Books.

VICKERS, Michael J. 1970. "Towards Reconstruction of the Town Planning of Roman Thessaloniki." In: LAOURDAS/MAKARONAS (1970) 239–251.

— 1972. "Hellenistic Thessaloniki." *JHS* 92 (1972) 156–170.

— 1981. "Therme and Thessaloniki." In: FS EDSON (1981) 327–333.

VIELHAUER, Philipp 1975. *Geschichte der urchristlichen Literatur. Einleitung in das Neue Testament, die Apokryphen und die Apostolischen Väter.* GLB. Berlin/New York: W. de Gruyter.

VINCE, James H. et al. transl. 1926–1949. *Demosthenes.* 7 vols. Vols. 1, 3 transl. by J. H. VINCE. Vol. 2 transl. by J. H. VINCE/C. A. VINCE. Vols. 4–6 transl. by A. T. MURRAY. Vol. 7 transl. by N. W. DEWITT/N. J. DEWITT. LCL 238, 155, 299, 318, 346, 351, 374. London: William Heinemann / Cambridge: Harvard University Press.

VÖGTLE, Anton 1976. "Röm 13,11–14 und die ‚Nah'-Erwartung." In: FS KÄSEMANN (1976) 557–573.

— 1994. *Die ‚Gretchenfrage' des Menschensohnproblems. Bilanz und Perspektive.* QD 152. Freiburg et al.: Herder.

VOLF, Judith M. Gundry → GUNDRY VOLF, Judith M.

VOLK, Otto 1965. "Thessalonike." *LTK* 10 (²1965) 108–111.

VÖLKEL, Martin 1991. "καθεύδω." *EDNT* 2 (1991) 221–222.

— 1991a. "κοιμάομαι." *EDNT* 2 (1991) 301–302.

VOLLENWEIDER, Samuel 2003. "Paulus." *RGG* 6 ([4]2003) 1035–1065.

VOM BROCKE, Christoph 2001. *Thessaloniki – Stadt des Kassander und Gemeinde des Paulus. Eine frühe christliche Gemeinde in ihrer heidnischen Umwelt.* WUNT II.125. Tübingen: Mohr Siebeck.

VON BENDEMANN, Reinhard 2000. "›Frühpaulinisch‹ und/oder ›spätpaulinisch‹? Erwägungen zu der These einer Entwicklung der paulinischen Theologie am Beispiel des Gesetzesverständnisses." *EvT* 60 (2000) 210–229.

VON CAMPENHAUSEN, Hans 1968. *Tradition and Life in the Church: Essays and Lectures in Church History.* Transl. by A. V. LITTLEDALE. Philadelphia: Fortress / London: William Collins Sons & Co.

VON DOBSCHÜTZ, Ernst 1909. *Die Thessalonicher-Briefe.* Ed. by F. HAHN. KEK 10. 7th ed. Göttingen: Vandenhoeck & Ruprecht.

VON HARNACK, Adolf 1904 [vol. 1]; 1905 [vol. 2]. *The Expansions of Christianity in the First Three Centuries.* 2 vols. Transl. & ed. by J. MOFFATT. Theological Translation Library 19–20. London: Williams & Norgate / New York: G. P. Putnam's Sons.

— 1908. "Das Problem des zweiten Thessalonicherbriefes." In: *SPAW* 31 (1910) 560–578.

VON RAD, Gerhard 1965. *Old Testament Theology.* Vol. II: *The Theology of Israel's Prophetic Traditions.* Transl. by D. M. G. STALKER. Edinburgh: Oliver & Boyd.

VOS, Craig S. de → DE VOS, Craig S.

VOS, Geerhardus 1953. *The Pauline Eschatology.* Grand Rapids: Eerdmans.

VOS, Johan S. 1984. "Antijudaismus/Antisemitismus im Theologischen Wörterbuch zum Neuen Testament." *NTT* 38 (1984) 89–110.

VOS, Johannes S. 1973. *Traditionsgeschichtliche Untersuchungen zur Paulinischen Pneumatologie.* GTB 47. Assen: Van Gorcum.

WALKER, JR., William O. 1985. "Acts and the Pauline Corpus Reconsidered." *JSNT*, issue 24 (1985) 3–23.

— 1987. "The Burden of Proof in Identifying Interpolations in the Pauline Letters." *NTS* 33 (1987) 610–618.

— 1988. "Text-Critical Evidence for Interpolations in the Letters of Paul." *CBQ* 50 (1988) 622–631.

WALLACE, Daniel B. 1990. "A Textual Problem in 1 Thessalonians 1:10: Ἐκ τῆς Ὀργῆς vs. Ἀπὸ τῆς Ὀργῆς." *BSac* 147 (1990) 470–479.

— 1996. *Greek Grammar Beyond the Basics.* [see *GGBB* in abbrev.]

WALTER, Nikolaus 1985. "Paulus und die urchristliche Jesustradition." *NTS* 31 (1985) 498–522. Transl. & republ. in: WEDDERBURN (1989) 51–80.

— 1998. "Leibliche Auferstehung? Zur Frage der Hellenisierung der Auferweckungshoffnung bei Paulus." In: FS KLEIN (1998) 109–127.

— /REINMUTH, Eckart/LAMPE, Peter 1998. *Die Briefe an die Philipper, Thessalonicher und an Philemon. Übersetzt und erklärt.* 18th ed. NTD 8. Göttingen: Vandenhoeck & Ruprecht.

WALTON, Steve 1995. "What Has Aristotle to Do with Paul? Rhetorical Criticism and 1 Thessalonians." *TynBul* 46 (1995) 229–250.

— 2000. *Leadership and Lifestyle: The Portrait of Paul in the Miletus Speech and 1 Thessalonians.* SNTSMS 108. Cambridge: University Press.

WANAMAKER, Charles A. 1987. "Apocalypticism at Thessalonica." *Neot* 21 (1987) 1–10.

— 1990. *The Epistles to the Thessalonians: A Commentary on the Greek Text.* NIGTC. Grand Rapids: Eerdmans / Exeter: Paternoster.

— 1995. "'Like a Father Treats His Own Children': Paul and the Conversion of the Thessalonians." *JTSA* 92 (1995) 46–55.

— 2000. "Epistolary vs. Rhetorical Analysis: Is a Synthesis Possible?" In: DONFRIED/BEUTLER (2000) 255–286.

— 2004. Review of *The Letters to the Thessalonians: A New Translation with Introduction and Commentary*, by A. J. MALHERBE, 2000. *RevBL* 6 (2004) 27–33.

WANSBROUGH, Henry ed. 1991. *Jesus and the Oral Gospel Tradition.* JSNTSup 64. Sheffield: JSOT Press.

WARD, Ronald A. 1973. *Commentary on 1 & 2 Thessalonians.* Waco, TX: Word.

WARE, James 1992. "The Thessalonians as a Missionary Congregation: 1 Thessalonians 1,5–8." *ZNW* 83 (1992) 126–131.

WARE, Phil 1979. "The Coming of the Lord: Eschatology and 1 Thessalonians." *ResQ* 22 (1979) 109–120.

WATERMAN, G. Henry 1975. "The Sources of Paul's Teaching on the 2nd Coming of Christ in 1 and 2 Thessalonians." *JETS* 18 (1975) 105–113.

WATSON, Duane F. 1992. "Angels." *ABD* 1 (1992) 248–255 [§ New Testament: 253–255].

— 1999. "Paul's Appropriation of Apocalyptic Discourse: The Rhetorical Strategy of 1 Thessalonians." In: CAREY/BLOOMQUIST (1999) 61–80.

— ed. 2002. *The Intertexture of Apocalyptic Discourse in the New Testament*. SBLSymS 14. Atlanta: Society of Biblical Literature.

WATT, Jan G. van der → VAN DER WATT, Jan G.

WEATHERLY, Jon A. 1991. "The Authenticity of 1 Thessalonians 2.13–16: Additional Evidence." *JSNT*, issue 42 (1991) 79–98.

WEBB, Robert L. 1990. "'Apocalyptic': Observations on a Slippery Term." *JNES* 49 (1990) 115–126.

WEDDERBURN, Alexander J. M. 1985. "Some Observations on Paul's Use of the Phrases 'in Christ' and 'with Christ'." *JSNT*, issue 25 (1985) 83–97.

— 1986. "Paul's Use of the Phrases 'in Christ' and 'with Christ'." In: VANHOYE (1986) 362.

— ed. 1989. *Paul and Jesus: Collected Essays*. JSNTSup 37. Sheffield: JSOT Press.

WEDER, Hans 1986. "Hoffnung II. Neues Testament." *TRE* 15 (1986) 484–491.

WEIMA, Jeffrey A. D. 1994. *Neglected Endings: The Significance of the Pauline Letter Closings*. JSNTSup 101. Sheffield: Academic Press.

— 1995. "The Pauline Letter Closings: Analysis and Hermeneutical Significance." *BBR* 5 (1995) 177–197.

— 1996. "'How You Must Walk to Please God': Holiness and Discipleship in 1 Thessalonians." In: LONGENECKER (1996) 98–119.

— 1997. "An Apology for the Apologetic Function of 1 Thessalonians 2:1–12." *JSNT*, issue 68 (1997) 73–99.

— 1997a. "What Does Aristotle Have to Do with Paul? An Evaluation of Rhetorical Criticism." *CTJ* 32 (1997) 458–468.

— 1997b. Review of *First and Second Thessalonians*, by E. J. RICHARD, 1995. *JBL* 116 (1997) 761–763.

— 1997c. Review of *Comfort One Another: Reconstructing the Rhetoric and Audience of 1 Thessalonians*, by A. SMITH, 1995. *JETS* 40 (1997) 482–483.

— 1999. Review of *Vom Schluß zum Ganzen. Zur Bedeutung des paulinischen Briefkorpusabschlusses*, by M. MÜLLER, 1997. *RevBL* 1 (1999) 347–351.

— 2000. "The Function of 1 Thessalonians 2:1–12 and the Use of Rhetorical Criticism: A Response to Otto Merk." In: DONFRIED/BEUTLER (2000) 114–131.

— 2000a. "'But We Became Infants Among You': The Case for νήπιοι in 1 Thess 2.7." *NTS* 46 (2000) 547–564.

— /PORTER, Stanley E. 1998. *An Annotated Bibliography of 1 and 2 Thessalonians*. NTTS 26. Leiden et al.: Brill.

WEISER, Alfons 1990. "δουλεύω κτλ." *EDNT* 1 (1990) 349–352.

WEISS, Johannes 1959 [vol. 1]; 1970 [vol. 2]. *Earliest Christianity: A History of the Period A. D. 30–150*. 2 vols. Transl. & ed. by F. C. GRANT. Vol. 2 compl. by R. KNOPF. New York: Harper / Gloucester: Peter Smith.

WENGST, Klaus 1972. *Christologische Formeln und Lieder des Urchristentums*. SNT 7. Gütersloh: Gerd Mohn.

— 1972a. "Der Apostel und die Tradition. Zur theologischen Bedeutung urchristlicher Formeln bei Paulus." *ZTK* 69 (1972) 145–162.

— 1987. *Pax Romana and the Peace of Jesus Christ*. Philadelphia: Fortress.

WENHAM, David 1981. "Paul and the Synoptic Apocalypse." In: FRANCE/WENHAM (1981, vol. 2) 345–375.

— 1984. *The Rediscovery of Jesus' Eschatological Discourse*. Sheffield: JSOT Press.

— 1988. "The Paulinism of Acts Again: Two Historical Clues in 1 Thessalonians." *Them* 13 (1988) 53–55.

— 1995. *Paul: Follower of Jesus or Founder of Christianity?* Grand Rapids/Cambridge: Eerdmans.

WENK, Matthias 2000. "Conversion and Initiation: A Pentecostal View of Biblical and Patristic Perspectives." *JPT* 17 (2000) 56–80.
WEST, J. C. 1914. "The Order of 1 and 2 Thessalonians." *JTS* 15 (1914) 66–74.
WHITE, John L. 1971. "Introductory Formulae in the Body of the Pauline Letter." *JBL* 90 (1971) 91–97.
— 1972. *The Form and Function of the Body of the Greek Letter: A Study of the Letter-Body in the Non-Literary Papyri and in Paul the Apostle.* SBLDS 2. Missoula, MT: Scholars Press.
— 1982. "The Ancient Epistolography Group in Retrospect." *Semeia* 22 (1982) 1–14.
— 1982a. "The Greek Documentary Letter Tradition Third Century B.C.E. to Third Century C.E." *Semeia* 22 (1982) 89–106.
— 1983. "Saint Paul and the Apostolic Letter Tradition." *CBQ* 45 (1983) 433–444.
— 1984. "New Testament Epistolary Literature in the Framework of Ancient Epistolography." *ANRW* II.25.2 (1984) 1730–1756.
— 1986. *Light from Ancient Letters.* FF. Philadelphia: Fortress.
— 1988. "Ancient Greek Letters." In: AUNE (1988) 85–105.
— 1993. "Apostolic Mission and Apostolic Message: Congruence in Paul's Epistolary Rhetoric, Structure and Imagery." In: FS HURD (1993) 145–161.
— 1999. *The Apostle of God: Paul and the Promise of Abraham.* Peabody, MA: Hendrickson.
WHITE, L. Michael/YARBROUGH, O. Larry eds. 1995. *The Social World of the First Christians: Essays in Honor of Wayne A. Meeks.* Minneapolis: Fortress.
WHITELEY, Denys E. H. 1974. *The Theology of St. Paul.* 2nd ed. Oxford: Basil Blackwell.
WHITTAKER, C. R. transl. 1969–1970. *Herodian.* 2 vols. LCL 454, 455. London: William Heinemann / Cambridge: Harvard University Press.
WHITTAKER, Molly 1984. *Jews and Christians: Graeco-Roman Views.* CCWJCW 6. Cambridge et al.: University Press.
WHITTON, J. 1982. "A Neglected Meaning for *Skeuos* in 1 Thessalonians 4.4." *NTS* 28 (1982) 142–143.
WICK, Peter 1994. "Ist I Thess 2,13–16 antijüdisch? Der rhetorische Gesamtzusammenhang des Briefes als Interpretationshilfe für eine einzelne Perikope." *TZ* 50 (1994) 9–23.
WIEFEL, Wolfgang 1974. "Die Hauptrichtung des Wandels im eschatologischen Denken des Paulus." *TZ* 30 (1974) 65–81.
WILCKE, Hans-A. 1967. *Das Problem eines messianischen Zwischenreichs bei Paulus.* Zürich/Stuttgart: Zwingli.
WILCKENS, Ulrich 1961. *Die Missionsreden der Apostelgeschichte. Form- und traditions-geschichtliche Untersuchungen.* WMANT 5. Neukirchen-Vluyn: Neukirchener Verlag.
— 1966. "Die Überlieferungsgeschichte der Auferstehung Jesu." In: MARXSEN et al. (1966) 41–63. Transl. & republ. in: MOULE (1968) 51–76.
— 1974. "Das Neue Testament und die Juden. Antwort an David Flusser." *EvT* 34 (1974) 602–611.
— 1988. "Der Ursprung der Überlieferung der Erscheinungen des Auferstandenen. Zur traditionsgeschichtlichen Analyse von 1.Kor. 15,1–11 " In: HOFFMANN (1988) 139–193.
WILES, Gordon P. 1974. *Paul's Intercessory Prayers: The Significance of the Intercessory Prayer Passages in the Letters of St Paul.* Cambridge: University Press.
WILKINS, Michael J. 1997. "Teaching, Paraenesis." *DLNT* (1997) 1156–1159.
WILLIAMS, David J. 1992. *1 and 2 Thessalonians.* NIBCNT. Peabody, MA: Hendrickson.
— 1999. *Paul's Metaphors: Their Context and Character.* Peabody, MA: Hendrickson.
WILLIAMS, Trevor 1998. "The Trouble with the Resurrection." In: FS ASHTON (1998) 219–235.
WILLIS, Wendell L. ed. 1987. *The Kingdom of God in 20th-Century Interpretation.* Peabody, MA: Hendrickson.
WILSON, Jack H. 1968. "The Corinthians Who Say There Is No Resurrection of the Dead." *ZNW* 59 (1968) 90–107.
WIMMER, Anselm 1955. "Trostworte des Apostels Paulus an Hinterbliebene in Thessalonich (1 Th 4,13–17)." *Bib* 36 (1955) 273–286.
WINTER, Bruce W. 1993. "The Entries and Ethics of Orators and Paul (1 Thessalonians 2:1–12)." *TynBul* 44 (1993) 55–74.
— 1993a. *The Book of Acts in Its Ancient Literary Setting.* Vol. 1: *Book of Acts in Its First Century Setting.* Grand Rapids: Eerdmans.

WISSMANN, Hans 1982. "Eschatologie I. Religionsgeschichtlich." *TRE* 10 (1982) 254–256.

WITHERINGTON, III, Ben 1992. *Jesus, Paul, and the End of the World: A Comparative Study in New Testament Eschatology*. Downers Grove: InterVarsity.

— 1994. *Paul's Narrative Thought World: The Tapestry of Tragedy and Triumph*. Louisville, KY: Westminster/John Knox.

— 2006. *1 and 2 Thessalonians: A Socio-Rhetorical Commentary*. Grand Rapids/Cambridge: Eerdmans.

WITMER, Stephen E. 2006. "θεοδίδακτοι in 1 Thessalonians 4.9: A Pauline Neologism." *NTS* 52 (2006) 239–250.

WITT, Rex E. 1977. "The Kabeiroi in Ancient Macedonia." In: LAOURDAS/MAKARONAS (1977) 67–80.

WOLTER, Michael 1980. "Bekehrung I. Alte Kirche und Mittelalter 1.2.2. Zur jüdischen Bekehrungsterminologie." *TRE* 5 (1980) 442–443.

— 2005. "Apokalyptik als Redeform im Neuen Testament." *NTS* 51 (2005) 171–191.

WORTHAM, Robert A. 1995. "The Problem of Anti-Judaism in 1 Thess 2:14–16 and Related Pauline Texts." *BTB* 25 (1995) 37–44.

WREDE, William 1903. *Die Echtheit des zweiten Thessalonicherbriefs*. TU NF 9.2. Leipzig: J. C. Hinrichs.

WRIGHT, Nicholas T. 1991. "Putting Paul Together Again: Toward a Synthesis of Pauline Theology (1 and 2 Thessalonians, Philippians, and Philemon)." In: BASSLER (1991) 183–211.

WUELLNER, Wilhelm 1990. "The Argumentative Structure of 1 Thessalonians as Paradoxical Encomium." In: R. F. COLLINS (1990) 117–136.

YARBRO COLLINS, Adela → COLLINS, A. Yarbro.

YARBROUGH, Robert W. 1999. "Sexual Gratification in 1 Thess 4:1–8." *TJ* 20 (1999) 215–232.

YODER-NEUFELD, Thomas R. 1997. *'Put on the Armour of God': The Divine Warrior from Isaiah to Ephesians*. JSNTSup 140. Sheffield: Academic Press.

ZIMMER, Friedrich 1893. *Der Text der Thessalonicherbriefe. Samt textkritischem Apparat und Kommentar*. Quedlinburg: Chr. Friedr. Viewegs.

ZIMMERLI, Walther 1967. "παῖς θεοῦ." *TDNT* 5 (1967) 654–717 [§ A, B: 656–677].

ZUMSTEIN, Jean 1998. "Bekehrung/Konversion." *RGG* 1 ([4]1998) 1228–1241.

ZÜRNER, Bernhard 1996. *Paulus ohne Gott. Eine charakterologische Untersuchung*. Bonn: Bouvier.

ZWIEP, Arie W. 1997. *The Ascension of the Messiah in Lukan Christology*. NovTSup 87. Leiden et al.: Brill.

Indices

The indices have been prepared in an exhaustive manner for the convenience of the reader. The arrangement is straightforward (see Table of Contents) and hopefully user-friendly. Attention is drawn to the use of the em rule (—) to distinguish between primary and secondary entries. In particular, for Greek and Latin Words (§III), the em rule is used to arrange words or phrases under a head term, while for Subjects and Names (§IV), it is used to show different types of relationships between entries. Thus, the em rule is used to list a genitive of qualification as in "agent — of God", an adjectival qualification as in "age — new", and to show compound relationships as in "Adam — -typology" and "chiasm — macro-". Finally, cross-references are denoted with an arrow (→).

I. Ancient Authors and Texts

a. Old Testament (including Septuagint)

b. Apocrypha and Pseudepigrapha of the Old Testament

c. Other Jewish Authors and Texts in Antiquity

d. New Testament

Second Thessalonians (2 Thess)

First Timothy (1 Tim)

e. Early Christian Literature outside the New Testament

f. Other Greek and Latin Authors and Texts in Antiquity

II. Modern Authors, Editors and Translators

III. Aramaic, Hebrew, Greek and Latin Words

a. Aramaic Words

b. Hebrew Words

c. Greek Words

d. Latin Words

IV. Subjects and Names